PRAISE FOR ARUNDHATI ROY

"The world has never had to face such global confusion. Only in facing it can we make sense of what we have to do. And this is precisely what Arundhati Roy does. She makes sense of what we have to do. Thereby offering an example. An example of what? Of being fully alive in our world, such as it is, and of getting close to and listening to those for whom this world has become intolerable."

—JOHN BERGER

"Arundhati Roy is one of the most confident and original thinkers of our time."

—NAOMI KLEIN

"Arundhati Roy calls for 'factual precision' alongside of the 'real precision of poetry.' Remarkably, she combines those achievements to a degree that few can hope to approach."

—NOAM CHOMSKY

"Arundhati Roy combines her brilliant style as a novelist with her powerful commitment to social justice in producing these eloquent, penetrating essays."

—HOWARD ZINN

"Arundhati Roy is one of the few great revolutionary intellectuals in our time . . . courageous, visionary, and erudite."

—CORNEL WEST

"Arundhati Roy is incandescent in her brilliance and her fearlessness. And in these extraordinary essays—which are clarions for justice, for witness, for a true humanity—Roy is at her absolute best."

—JUNOT DÍAZ

MY SEDITIOUS HEART

COLLECTED NONFICTION

ARUNDHATI ROY

MY
SEDITIOUS
HEART

COLLECTED NONFICTION

HAMISH HAMILTON

an imprint of Penguin Canada, a division of Penguin Random House Canada Limited

Canada • USA • UK • Ireland • Australia • New Zealand •
India • South Africa • China

Published in Hamish Hamilton hardcover by Penguin Canada, 2019
Simultaneously published in the United States by Haymarket Books

www.penguinrandomhouse.ca

LIBRARY AND ARCHIVES CANADA CATALOGUING IN PUBLICATION

Title: My seditious heart / Arundhati Roy
Other titles: Essays. Selections
Names: Roy, Arundhati, author.
Identifiers: Canadiana (print) 20190044632 | Canadiana
(ebook) 2019004540X | ISBN 9780735238299
(hardcover) | ISBN 9780735238305 (PDF)
Classification: LCC PR9499.3.R59 A6 2019 | DDC 824/.92—dc23

Printed and bound in the United States of America

10 9 8 7 6 5 4 3 2 1

Penguin
Random House
HAMISH HAMILTON CANADA

CONTENTS

MAP OF INDIA

Map not to scale

For
Vinod Mehta
I had no idea how much I would
miss you—

FOREWORD

IN THE WINTER of 1961 the tribespeople of Kothie, a small hamlet in the western state of Gujarat, were chased off their ancestral lands as though they were intruders. Kothie quickly turned into Kevadiya Colony, a grim concrete homestead for the government engineers and bureaucrats who would, over the next few decades, build the gigantic 138.68-meter-high Sardar Sarovar Dam. It was one of four mega dams—and thousands of smaller dams—that were part of the Narmada Valley Development Project, planned on the Narmada and her forty-one tributaries. The people of Kothie joined the hundreds of thousands of others whose lands and homes would be submerged—farmers, farmworkers, and fisherfolk in the plains, ancient indigenous tribespeople in the hills—to fight against what they saw as wanton destruction. Destruction, not just of themselves and their communities, but of soil, water, forests, fish, and wildlife—a whole ecosystem, an entire riparian civilization. The material welfare of human beings was never their only concern.

Under the banner of the Narmada Bachao Andolan (Save the Narmada Movement), they did everything that was humanly and legally possible under the Indian Constitution to stop the dams.

They were beaten, jailed, abused, and called "antinational" foreign agents who wanted to sabotage India's "development." They fought the Sardar Sarovar as it went up, meter by meter, for decades. They went on hunger strike, they went to court, they marched on Delhi, they sat in protest as the rising waters of the reservoir swallowed their fields and entered their homes. Still, they lost. The government reneged on every promise it had made to them. On September 17, 2017, the prime minister of India, Narendra Modi, inaugurated the Sardar Sarovar Dam. It was his birthday present to himself on the day he turned sixty-seven.

Even as they went down fighting, the people of the Narmada taught the world some profound lessons—about ecology, equity, sustainability, and democracy. They taught me that we must make ourselves visible, even when we lose, *whatever* it is that we lose—land, livelihood, or a worldview. And that we must make it impossible for those in power to pretend that they do not know the costs and consequences of what they do. They also taught me the limitations of constitutional methods of resistance. "The Greater Common Good," the second essay in this collection, is about the historic struggle in the Narmada valley. Although I wrote it almost twenty years ago, in 1999, it is still, in some ways, the bedrock on which much of my thinking rests. Today, even the harshest critics of the Narmada Bachao Andolan have had to admit that the movement was right about almost everything it said. But it's too late. For decades, the Sardar Sarovar sponged up almost all of Gujarat's irrigation budget. It hasn't delivered anything like what the planners and politicians promised it would. Nor have its benefits, such as they are, gone to the farmers in whose name it was built. Now it straddles the river it murdered, like a beast brooding over a kill that it cannot eat. A monument to human folly.

One would have thought that this would be lesson enough.

Almost exactly a year after he inaugurated the dam, on October 31, 2018, the prime minister traveled to Kevadiya

Colony again, this time to inaugurate the world's tallest statue. The Statue of Unity is a 182-meter-tall bronze likeness of Sardar Vallabhbhai Patel, a popularly revered freedom fighter and India's first deputy prime minister, after whom the Sardar Sarovar Dam was named. Sardar Patel was, by all accounts, a man who lived simply. But there's nothing simple about the $430-million-dollar statue that has been built in his memory. It towers out of a 12-square-kilometer artificial lake and is made of 200,000 cubic tons of cement concrete and 25,000 tons of reinforced steel, all of it plated with 1,700 tons of bronze.[1] Indian expertise proved unequal to a task on such a scale, so the statue was forged in a Chinese foundry and erected by Chinese workers under Chinese supervision. So much for nationalism. The Statue of Unity is nearly four times as tall as the Statue of Liberty, and more than six times higher than the Christ the Redeemer statue in Rio de Janeiro. On a clear day, it is visible from a distance of 7 kilometers. The whole of the village of Kothie, had it still existed, could have been accommodated in its big toe. Kothie's former residents and their comrades-in-arms are probably meant to feel like dirt in the statue's toenails. As are the writers who write about them.

Four hundred kilometers south of the Statue of Unity, on Altamount Road, in the city of Bombay, home to the largest slums in Asia, is modern India's other great monument, Antilla, the most expensive private home ever built. It has twenty-seven floors, three helipads, nine lifts, hanging gardens, and six floors of private parking. It's home to Mukesh Ambani, India's richest man and the CEO of India's richest corporation, Reliance Industries Limited (RIL), with a market capitalization of $47 billion. Mukesh Ambani's personal wealth is estimated to be $20 billion. His global business interests include petrochemicals, oil, natural gas, fresh food retail, and a TV consortium that runs twenty-seven news channels in almost every regional language. Reliance Jio Infocomm Limited is the largest telecommunications network in India, with a subscriber base of 250 million people.

Jio Institute, a state-of-the-art private university that Reliance *plans* to start but does not actually *exist* yet, has already made it to the government's list of the six "Institutions of Eminence." Such is the craven desire to please Mukesh Ambani, the real ruler of India. In December 2018, all of Bollywood's A-list superstars danced like chorus extras at his daughter's $100-million-dollar wedding. Beyoncé performed. Hillary Clinton arrived to pay her respects. The country must have suffered a temporary shortage of flowers and jewelry.

❖

I find myself thinking of the essays in this book as pieces of laundry—poor people's washing—strung out across the landscape between these two monuments, interrupting the good news bulletins and spoiling the view.

They were written over a period of twenty years during which India was changing faster than ever before. The opening of the Indian markets to international finance had created a new middle class—a market of millions—and had investors falling over themselves to find a foothold. The international media, for the most part, was at pains to portray the world's favorite new finance destination in the best possible light. But the news was certainly not all good. India's fleet of brand new billionaires and its new consumers was being created at an immense cost to its environment and to an even larger underclass. Backstage, away from the razzle-dazzle, labor laws were dismantled, trade unions disbanded. The state was withdrawing from its responsibilities to provide food, education, and health care. Public assets were turned over to private corporations, massive infrastructure and mining projects were pushing hundreds of thousands of rural people off their lands into cities that didn't want them. The poor were in free fall.

At the very same time that it unlocked the protected market, the Congress government of the day (which calls itself liberal and secular on its CV), with an eye to the "Hindu vote," opened another lock, too. The lock on an old sixteenth-century mosque. The Babri Masjid in Ayodhya had been sealed by the courts in 1949 following a dispute between Hindus and Muslims, who both laid claim to the land—Muslims asserting it was a historical place of worship, Hindus that it was the birthplace of Lord Ram. Opening the Babri Masjid, purportedly to allow Hindus to worship at the site, changed India forever. The Congress was swept aside. Leaders of the Hindu nationalist Bharatiya Janata Party (BJP) traveled the length and breadth of the country orchestrating a storm of religious frenzy. On December 6, 1992, they, along with members of the Vishwa Hindu Parishad, gathered in Ayodhya and, while a shocked country and a spineless Congress prime minister watched, exhorted a mob of 150,000 "volunteers" to storm the structure and bring down the Babri Masjid.

The demolition of the mosque and the simultaneous opening of the markets was the beginning of a complicated waltz between corporate globalization and medieval religious fundamentalism. It was obvious quite early on that, far from being antagonistic forces that represented Old and New India, they were actually lovers performing an elaborate ritual of seduction and coquetry that could sometimes be misread as hostility.

For me, personally it was a time of odd disquiet. As I watched the great drama unfold, my own fortunes seemed to have been touched by magic. My first novel, *The God of Small Things*, had won a big international prize. I was a front-runner in the lineup of people who were chosen to personify the confident, new, market-friendly India that was finally taking its place at the high table. It was flattering in a way, but deeply disturbing, too. As I watched people being pushed into penury, my book was selling millions of copies. My bank account was burgeoning. Money on that scale confused me. What did it really mean to be a writer in times such as these?

As I thought about this, almost without meaning to, I began to write a long, bewildering, episodic, astonishingly violent story about the courting ritual of these unusual lovers and the trail of destruction they were leaving in their wake. And of the remarkable people who had risen to resist them.

The backlash to almost every one of the essays when I first published them—in the form of police cases, legal notices, court appearances, and even a short jail sentence—was often so wearying that I would resolve never to write another. But equally, almost every one of them—each a broken promise to myself—took me on journeys deeper and deeper into worlds that enriched my understanding, and complicated my view, of the times we live in. They opened doors for me to secret places where few are trusted, led me into the very heart of insurrections, into places of pain, rage, and ferocious irreverence. On these journeys, I found my dearest friends and my truest loves. These are my real royalties, my greatest reward.

Although writers usually walk alone, most of what I wrote rose from the heart of a crowd. It was never meant as neutral commentary, pretending to be observations of a bystander. It was just another stream that flowed into the quick, immense, rushing currents that I was writing about. My contribution to our collective refusal to obediently fade away.

When my publishers suggested that the essays be compiled into a single volume, we thought long and hard about how best to do this. Should they be arranged thematically? Could we come up with some workable "subject headings"? We tried, but soon realized it wasn't possible, because even though most of the essays are about specific subjects or specific events—nuclear weapons, dams, privatization, caste, class, war, imperialism, colonialism, capitalism, militarism, terrorist strikes, government-backed massacres, and the rise of Hindu nationalism—they are also about how each of these connect to each other, feed off one another. We decided that it would be best to arrange the essays chronologically, in the order in which they first appeared. I have not updated any of them, but the resolute (and probably rare) reader who reads them in sequence will find they more or less update each other. Since each appeared as a stand-alone piece, sometimes separated by months and even years, I often had to restate facts or retell parts of stories. Forgive me for leaving the repetitions in.

What I wish I could have done for the readers of this book is to recreate the prevailing atmosphere in which I published each essay. They were written when a certain political space closed down, when a false consensus was being broadcast, when I could no longer endure the relentless propaganda and the sheer vicious bullying of vulnerable people by an increasingly corporatized media and its increasingly privatized commentators. Most often I wrote because it became easier to do that than to put up with the angry, persistent hum of my own silence. I also wrote to reclaim language. Because it was distressing to see words being deployed to mean the opposite of what they really meant. ("Deepening democracy" meant destroying it. "A level playing field" actually meant a very steep slope, the "free market" a rigged market. "Empowering women" meant undermining them in every possible way.)

I wrote because I saw that what I needed to do would challenge my abilities as a writer. I had in the past written screenplays and a novel. I had written about love and loss, about childhood, caste, violence, and families—the eternal preoccupations of writers and poets. Could I write equally compellingly about *irrigation*? About the salinization of soil? About drainage? Dams? Crop patterns? About the per unit cost of electricity? About the law? About things that affect ordinary people's lives? Could I turn these topics into literature? I tried.

My unfaltering partners in this endeavor were N. Ram, then editor of *Frontline*, and the late Vinod Mehta, editor of *Outlook*, two of the best mass market news magazines in India at the time. Almost every essay in this book has been published by one or both of them. Regardless of what I wrote, and its content or length, Mehta never blinked. Not when I was cutting and blunt about an incumbent prime minister; not even when I expressed a proscribed opinion about that most contentious subject of all: India's military occupation of Kashmir. Toward the end of his career as the editor, he dedicated an entire issue of *Outlook* to "Walking with the Comrades," my account of the weeks I spent with Maoist guerrillas in the forests of Bastar. Our unspoken pact was that he would publish everything I wrote, and that I would never complain about the insults—pages and pages of them—that he published with glee in the letters section in the weeks that followed (the early avatar of trolling). Sometimes, the insults would appear before I wrote. In anticipation of what I *might* write. I learned to wear them as a badge of honor.

The first essay in this book, "The End of Imagination," was a response to the series of nuclear tests conducted in 1998 by the coalition government led by the BJP. The tests, the manner in which they were announced, and the enthusiasm with which they were celebrated—including by academics, editors, artists, liberals, and secular nationalists—ushered in a dangerous new public discourse of aggressive majoritarian nationalism—officially sanctioned now, by the government itself. My horror about nuclear war between India and Pakistan becoming a real possibility was matched by my sorrow over what this ugly new language would do to our imaginations, to our idea of ourselves. Looking back now, I see that the nuclear tests magnified every crack and fissure of an already fractured and divided polity. The danger of an all-out nuclear war that jeopardises the planet cannot be minimized. Almost exactly twenty years after the nuclear tests, In February 2019, after a tragic suicide bomb attack in Kashmir, India and Pakistan became the first two nuclear powers in history to bomb each other.

The September 11, 2001, attacks and the US-led "War on Terror" came as a gift to fascists all over the world. The rising tide of Hindu nationalism (Hindutva) was quick to harness the headwind of international Islamophobia that followed in its wake. Just a few weeks after 9/11, the BJP suddenly removed its sitting chief minister and installed an unelected political novice in his place. His name was Narendra Modi. He had for years been an activist of the Rashtriya Swayamsevak Sangh (RSS), the Hindu nationalist cultural guild that has long demanded the dissolution of the Indian Constitution and the declaration of India as a Hindu Nation. Four months into Modi's tenure as chief minister, in February 2002, following the mysterious burning of a railway coach in which fifty-nine Hindu pilgrims were burned to death, Gujarat witnessed a pogrom against Muslims in which 2,000 people were publicly slaughtered by Hindu vigilante mobs. Following the massacre, Modi announced state elections, which he won. He remained the chief minister of Gujarat for the next twelve years. At a formal meeting of Indian industrialists that took place in Gujarat soon after the pogrom, several major corporate heads, including Mukesh Ambani, enthusiastically endorsed Modi as a future prime ministerial candidate. In 2014, after an opulent election campaign, the like of which India had never seen, and another orchestrated massacre in Muzaffarnagar, UP, the RSS's main man became prime minister of India, with a huge majority in parliament.

The RSS, Hindutva's mothership, was founded in 1924. It is the most powerful organization in India today. It has thousands of local branches and hundreds of thousands of dedicated "volunteers" all over the country. Its people are now in place in almost every institution in the country. It has penetrated the army, intelligence services, courts, high schools, universities, banks. The institutions that make up what Turks call the "deep state" are either entirely under its control or heavily influenced by it. India has become a country in which writers and intellectuals are assassinated in cold blood, and lynch mobs that regularly beat Muslims to death roam through cities and villages, assured of impunity. RSS ideology—a peculiarly Indian brand of fascism—has transcended election cycles and will continue to be an existential threat to the fabric of the country, regardless of which political party is in power.

Writing about the coalescing of neoliberalism and Hindu nationalism in India was to run one kind of gauntlet. Writing about

US imperialism in the immediate aftermath of the September 11 attacks and the US invasions of Iraq and Afghanistan was a quite different enterprise. When I published "The Algebra of Infinite Justice," "War Is Peace," and "The Ordinary Person's Guide to Empire," I fully expected a good number of the million copies of *The God of Small Things* that had sold in the United States to end up in bonfires on the streets. I had followed what happened to people like Susan Sontag—and indeed almost anybody else who expressed a point of view that was different from an establishment one. Yes, I did receive one copy of my book, returned with a message of quivering outrage. But there were no bonfires. When I traveled to the United States to speak at the Lensic Theater in New Mexico on the first anniversary of 9/11 ("Come September") and at the Riverside Church soon after the invasion of Iraq ("Instant-Mix Imperial Democracy (Buy One, Get One Free)"), I was at first terrified and later thrilled by the large crowds that showed up. They didn't represent mainstream opinion. Of course not. But they existed. They came, despite the malignant atmosphere of aggressive nationalism we all had to contend with during those days. (Who can forget the George W. Bushism that ruled the day: "If you're not with us, you are with the terrorists.") It was a good lesson in seditious thinking. I learned never to lazily conflate countries, their government's policies, and the people who live in them. I learned to think from first principles—ones that predate the existence of the nation-state.

The longest section of this book, "The Doctor and the Saint," is about the debate between Dr. B. R. Ambedkar and Mohandas Gandhi, India's two most iconic figures. It was first published as an introduction to an annotated edition of *Annihilation of Caste*, Ambedkar's searing and legendary 1936 text. Caste, that ancient iron grid of institutionalized inequality, continues to be the engine that runs modern India, and the Ambedkar-Gandhi debate is among the most contentious subjects of the day. As Dalit movements gather momentum, Ambedkar, more than anybody else, living or dead, occupies center stage in contemporary

Indian politics. He ought to be read, heard, and studied in all his complexity. As for the words and deeds of Gandhi, especially on caste, class, race, and gender—they could do with some serious scrutiny. "The Doctor and the Saint" is probably the closest thing to a densely footnoted academic text as I will ever write.

The last two essays in this collection, "The Great Indian Rape Trick" (Parts I and II), are actually the earliest essays I published. I wrote them in 1994, years before *The God of Small Things* was published. We decided to put them in the appendix because they are a little different from the rest of the essays thematically. They're about the celebrated film *Bandit Queen*, which claims to be the true story of Phoolan Devi, whose gang ruled the Chambal valley for years and was never caught. Phoolan Devi eventually surrendered voluntarily and served time in prison. The film incensed me because it took the story of a most extraordinary woman and portrayed her as someone who had no volition, someone whose life had been entirely shaped by men and what they had done to her. Outfitted in a noisy, rustling costume of faux feminist concern, it turned India's most famous bandit into history's most famous victim of rape.

I saw *Bandit Queen* at a premier screening to which Phoolan Devi had not been invited. "She's too much trouble," one of the film's producers said to me when I asked. I went to see her after reading the next morning's papers, which reported that she was upset with the filmmakers, that she had not given them permission to show her being raped, and that the explicit rape scenes, screened to jeering male audiences, made her feel she had been raped all over again. In her prison diaries, which the film claimed to be based on, she had alluded to rape only very elliptically. It made me wonder: Should anyone have the right to restage the rape of a living woman without her consent?

When the real Phoolan Devi spoke up, it was extraordinary how the very same people who celebrated the film were willing to turn on her, dismissing her as an avaricious and immoral extortionist. Why should she be trusted? Was she not, after all, a bandit, a woman of loose morals—and "low-caste," too? Twenty-five years have gone by since I wrote these essays. Not one iota of my anger has diminished.

On July 25, 2001, masked gunmen assassinated Phoolan Devi outside her house in Delhi. It is not my case that she was killed because of the film. But she was killed the way I worried she would be. As I wrote then, "[T]he film seriously jeopardizes Phoolan Devi's life. It passes judgments that ought to be passed in Courts of Law. Not in Cinema Halls. The threads that connect Truth to Half-Truths to Lies could very quickly tighten into a noose around Phoolan Devi's neck. Or put a bullet through her head. Or a knife in her back."

Yes, #SheToo.

❖

This book of broken promises goes to press around the time that an era we think we understand is coming to a close. Capitalism's gratuitous wars and sanctioned greed have jeopardized the life of the planet and filled it with refugees. It has done more damage to the earth in the last one hundred or so years than countless millennia that went before. In the last thirty years, the scale of damage has accelerated exponentially. The World Wildlife Fund reports that the population of vertebrates—mammals, birds, fish, amphibians, and reptiles—has declined by 60 percent in the last forty years. We have sentenced ourselves to an era of sudden catastrophes—wild fires and strange storms, earthquakes and flash floods. To guide us through it all, we have the steady hand of new imperialists in China, white supremacists in the White House, and benevolent neo-Nazis on the streets of Europe.

In India, Hindu fascists are marching to demand a grand temple where the mosque they demolished once stood. Farmers deep in debt are marching for their very survival. The unemployed are marching for jobs.

More temples? Easy. But more jobs?

As we know, the age of Artificial Intelligence is upon us. Human labor will soon become largely redundant. Humans will consume. But many will not be required to participate in (or be remunerated for) economic activity.

So, the question before us is, who—or *what*—will rule the world? And what will become of so many surplus people? The next thirty years will be unlike anything that we as a species have ever encountered. To prepare us for what's coming, to give us tools with which to think about the unthinkable, old ideas—whether they come from the left, the right, or from the spectrum somewhere in between—will not do.

We will need algorithms that show us how to snatch the scepters from our slow, stupid, maddened kings.

Until then, beloved reader, I leave you with. . . . my seditious heart.

Arundhati Roy
December 2018

THE END OF
IMAGINATION

"THE DESERT SHOOK," the government of India informed us (its people).

"The whole mountain turned white," the government of Pakistan replied.

By afternoon the wind had fallen silent over Pokhran. At 3:45 p.m., the timer detonated the three devices. Around 200 to 300 meters deep in the earth, the heat generated was equivalent to a million degrees centigrade—as hot as temperatures on the sun. Instantly, rocks weighing around a thousand tons, a mini-mountain underground, vaporized . . . shock waves from the blast began to lift a mound of earth the size of a football field by several meters. One scientist on seeing it said, "I can now believe stories of Lord Krishna lifting a hill" (*India Today*).

May 1998. It'll go down in history books, provided of course we have history books to go down in. Provided, of course, we have a future. There's nothing new or original left to be said about nuclear weapons. There can be nothing more humiliating

First published in *Outlook* and *Frontline*, July 27, 1998.

for a writer of fiction to have to do than restate a case that has, over the years, already been made by other people in other parts of the world, and made passionately, eloquently, and knowledgeably.

I am prepared to grovel. To humiliate myself abjectly, because, in the circumstances, silence would be indefensible. So those of you who are willing: let's pick our parts, put on these discarded costumes, and speak our secondhand lines in this sad secondhand play. But let's not forget that the stakes we're playing for are huge. Our fatigue and our shame could mean the end of us. The end of our children and our children's children. Of everything we love. We have to reach within ourselves and find the strength to think. To fight.

Once again we are pitifully behind the times—not just scientifically and technologically (ignore the hollow claims), but more pertinently in our ability to grasp the true nature of nuclear weapons. Our Comprehension of the Horror Department is hopelessly obsolete. Here we are, all of us in India and in Pakistan, discussing the finer points of politics, and foreign policy, behaving for all the world as though our governments have just devised a newer, bigger bomb, a sort of immense hand grenade with which they will annihilate the enemy (each other) and protect us from all harm. How desperately we want to believe that. What wonderful, willing, well-behaved, gullible subjects we have turned out to be. The rest of humanity (yes, yes, I know, I *know*, but let's ignore them for the moment. They forfeited their votes a long time ago), the rest of the rest of humanity may not forgive us, but then the rest of the rest of humanity, depending on who fashions its views, may not know what a tired, dejected, heartbroken people we are. Perhaps it doesn't realize how urgently we need a miracle. How deeply we yearn for magic.

If only, if *only*, nuclear war was just another kind of war. If only it was about the usual things—nations and territories, gods and histories. If only those of us who dread it are just worthless moral cowards who are not prepared to die in defense of our beliefs. If only nuclear war was the kind of war in which

2

countries battle countries and men battle men. But it isn't. If there is a nuclear war, our foes will not be China or America or even each other. Our foe will be the earth herself. The very elements—the sky, the air, the land, the wind and water—will all turn against us. Their wrath will be terrible.

Our cities and forests, our fields and villages will burn for days. Rivers will turn to poison. The air will become fire. The wind will spread the flames. When everything there is to burn has burned and the fires die, smoke will rise and shut out the sun. The earth will be enveloped in darkness. There will be no day. Only interminable night. Temperatures will drop to far below freezing and nuclear winter will set in. Water will turn into toxic ice. Radioactive fallout will seep through the earth and contaminate groundwater. Most living things, animal and vegetable, fish and fowl, will die. Only rats and cockroaches will breed and multiply and compete with foraging, relict humans for what little food there is.

What shall we do then, those of us who are still alive? Burned and blind and bald and ill, carrying the cancerous carcasses of our children in our arms, where shall we go? What shall we eat? What shall we drink? What shall we breathe?

The head of the Health, Environment, and Safety Group of the Bhabha Atomic Research Center in Bombay has a plan. He declared in an interview (*Pioneer*, April 24, 1998) that India could survive nuclear war. His advice is that if there is a nuclear war, we take the same safety measures as the ones that scientists have recommended in the event of accidents at nuclear plants.

Take iodine pills, he suggests. And other steps such as remaining indoors, consuming only stored water and food and avoiding milk. Infants should be given powdered milk. "People in the danger zone should immediately go to the ground floor and if possible to the basement."

What do you do with these levels of lunacy? What do you do if you're trapped in an asylum and the doctors are all dangerously deranged?

Ignore it, it's just a novelist's naiveté, they'll tell you, Doomsday Prophet hyperbole. It'll never come to that. There will *be* no war. Nuclear weapons are about peace, not war. "Deterrence" is the buzzword of the people who like to think of themselves as hawks. (Nice birds, those. Cool. Stylish. Predatory. Pity there won't be many of them around after the war. "Extinction" is a word we must try and get used to.) Deterrence is an old thesis that has been resurrected and is being recycled with added local flavor. The Theory of Deterrence cornered the credit for having prevented the Cold War from turning into a Third World War. The only immutable fact about the Third World War is that if there's going to be one, it will be fought after the Second World War. In other words, there's no fixed schedule. In other words, we still have time. And perhaps the pun (the Third World War) is prescient. True, the Cold War is over, but let's not be hoodwinked by the ten-year lull in nuclear posturing. It was just a cruel joke. It was only in remission. It wasn't cured. It proves no theories. After all, what is ten years in the history of the world? Here it is again, the disease. More widespread and less amenable to any sort of treatment than ever. No, the Theory of Deterrence has some fundamental flaws.

Flaw Number One is that it presumes a complete, sophisticated understanding of the psychology of your enemy. It assumes that what deters you (the fear of annihilation) will deter them. What about those who are *not* deterred by that? The suicide-bomber psyche—the "We'll take you with us" school—is that an outlandish thought? How did Rajiv Gandhi die?

In any case who's the "you" and who's the "enemy"? Both are only governments. Governments change. They wear masks within masks. They molt and reinvent themselves all the time. The one we have at the moment, for instance, does not even have enough seats to last a full term in office, but demands that we trust it to do pirouettes and party tricks with nuclear bombs even as it scrabbles around for a foothold to maintain a simple majority in Parliament.

Flaw Number Two is that deterrence is premised on fear. But fear is premised on knowledge. On an understanding of the true extent and scale of the devastation that nuclear war will wreak. It is not some inherent, mystical attribute of nuclear bombs that they automatically inspire thoughts of peace. On the contrary, it is the endless, tireless, confrontational work of people who have had the courage to openly denounce them, the marches, the demonstrations, the films, the outrage—*that* is what has averted, or perhaps only postponed, nuclear war. Deterrence will not and cannot work given the levels of ignorance and illiteracy that hang over our two countries like dense, impenetrable veils. (Witness the Vishwa Hindu Parishad—VHP—wanting to distribute radioactive sand from the Pokhran desert as prasad all across India. A cancer yatra?) The Theory of Deterrence is nothing but a perilous joke in a world where iodine pills are prescribed as a prophylactic for nuclear irradiation.

India and Pakistan have nuclear bombs now and feel entirely justified in having them. Soon others will, too. Israel, Iran, Iraq, Saudi Arabia, Norway, Nepal (I'm trying to be eclectic here), Denmark, Germany, Bhutan, Mexico, Lebanon, Sri Lanka, Burma, Bosnia, Singapore, North Korea, Sweden, South Korea, Vietnam, Cuba, Afghanistan, Uzbekistan . . . and why not? Every country in the world has a special case to make. Everybody has borders and beliefs. And when all our larders are bursting with shiny bombs and our bellies are empty (deterrence is an exorbitant beast), we can trade bombs for food. And when nuclear technology goes on the market, when it gets truly competitive and prices fall, not just governments, but anybody who can afford it can have their own private arsenal—businessmen, terrorists, perhaps even the occasional rich writer (like myself). Our planet will bristle with beautiful missiles. There will be a new world order. The dictatorship of the pro-nuke elite. We can get our kicks by threatening each other. It'll be like bungee jumping when you can't rely on the bungee cord, or playing Russian roulette all day long. An additional perk will be the thrill of Not Knowing What to Believe. We can be victims of the predatory imagination of every green card–seeking charlatan who surfaces in the West with concocted stories of imminent missile attacks. We can delight at the prospect of being held to ransom by every petty troublemaker and rumormonger, the more the merrier if truth be told, anything for an excuse to make more bombs. So you see, even without a war, we have a lot to look forward to.

But let us pause to give credit where it's due. Whom must we thank for all this?

The Men who made it happen. The Masters of the Universe. Ladies and gentlemen, the United States of America! Come on up here, folks, stand up and take a bow. Thank you for doing this to the world. Thank you for making a difference. Thank you for showing us the way. Thank you for altering the very meaning of life.

From now on it is not dying we must fear, but living.

It is such supreme folly to believe that nuclear weapons are deadly only if they're used. The fact that they exist at all, their very presence in our lives, will wreak more havoc than we can begin to fathom. Nuclear weapons pervade our thinking. Control our behavior. Administer our societies. Inform our dreams. They bury themselves like meat hooks deep in the base of our brains. They are purveyors of madness. They are the ultimate colonizer. Whiter than any white man that ever lived. The very heart of whiteness.

All I can say to every man, woman, and sentient child here in India, and over there, just a little ways away in Pakistan, is: take it personally. Whoever you are—Hindu, Muslim, urban, agrarian—it doesn't matter. The only good thing about nuclear war is that it is the single most egalitarian idea that man has ever had. On the day of reckoning, you will not be asked to present your credentials. The devastation will be undiscriminating. The bomb isn't in your backyard. It's in your body. And mine. *Nobody*, no nation, no government, no man, no god, has the right to put it there. We're radioactive already, and the war hasn't even begun. So stand up and say something. Never mind if it's been said before. Speak up on your own behalf. Take it very personally.

THE BOMB AND I

In early May (before the bomb), I left home for three weeks. I thought I would return. I had every intention of returning. Of course, things haven't worked out quite the way I had planned.

While I was away, I met a friend of mine whom I have always loved for, among other things, her ability to combine deep affection with a frankness that borders on savagery.

"I've been thinking about you," she said, "about *The God of Small Things*—what's in it, what's over it, under it, around it, above it . . ."

She fell silent for a while. I was uneasy and not at all sure that I wanted to hear the rest of what she had to say. She, however, was sure that she was going to say it. "In this last year—less than a year actually—you've had too much of everything—fame, money, prizes, adulation, criticism, condemnation, ridicule, love, hate, anger, envy, generosity—everything. In some ways it's a perfect story. Perfectly baroque in its excess. The trouble is that it has, or can have, only one perfect ending." Her eyes were on me, bright with a slanting, probing brilliance. She knew that I knew what she was going to say. She was insane.

She was going to say that nothing that happened to me in the future could ever match the buzz of this. That the whole of the rest of my life was going to be vaguely unsatisfying. And, therefore, the only perfect ending to the story would be death. *My* death.

The thought had occurred to me, too. Of course it had. The fact that all this, this global dazzle—these lights in my eyes, the applause, the flowers, the photographers, the journalists feigning a deep interest in my life (yet struggling to get a single fact straight), the men in suits fawning over me, the shiny hotel bathrooms with endless towels—none of it was likely to happen again. Would I miss it? Had I grown to need it? Was I a fame junkie? Would I have withdrawal symptoms?

The more I thought about it, the clearer it became to me that if fame was going to be my permanent condition it would kill me. Club me to death with its good manners and hygiene. I'll admit that I've enjoyed my own five minutes of it immensely, but primarily *because* it was just five minutes. Because I knew (or thought I knew) that I could go home when I was bored and giggle about it. Grow old and irresponsible. Eat mangoes in the moonlight. Maybe write a couple of failed books—worstsellers—to see what it felt like. For a whole year I've cartwheeled across the world, anchored always to thoughts of home and the life I would go back to. Contrary to all the enquiries and predictions about my impending emigration, that was the well I dipped into. That was my sustenance. My strength.

I told my friend there was no such thing as a perfect story. I said in any case hers was an external view of things, this assumption that the trajectory of a person's happiness, or let's say fulfillment, had peaked (and now must trough) because she had accidentally stumbled upon "success." It was premised on the unimaginative belief that wealth and fame were the mandatory stuff of everybody's dreams.

You've lived too long in New York, I told her. There are other worlds. Other kinds of dreams. Dreams in which failure is feasible. Honorable. Sometimes even worth striving for. Worlds in which recognition is not the only barometer of brilliance or human worth. There are plenty of warriors whom I know and love, people far more valuable than myself, who go to war each day, knowing in advance that they will fail. True, they are less "successful" in the most vulgar sense of the word, but by no means less fulfilled.

The only dream worth having, I told her, is to dream that you will live while you're alive and die only when you're dead. (Prescience? Perhaps.)

"Which means exactly what?" (Arched eyebrows, a annoyed.)

I tried to explain, but didn't do a very good job of it. Sometimes I need to write to think. So I wrote it down for her on a paper napkin. This is what I wrote: *To love. To be loved. To never forget your own insignificance. To never get used to the unspeakable violence and the vulgar disparity of life around you. To seek joy in the saddest places. To pursue beauty to its lair. To never simplify what is complicated or complicate what is simple. To respect strength, never power. Above all, to watch. To try and understand. To never look away. And never, never to forget.*

I've known her for many years, this friend of mine. She's an architect, too.

She looked dubious, somewhat unconvinced by my paper-napkin speech. I could tell that structurally, just in terms of the sleek, narrative symmetry of things, and because she loved me, her thrill at my "success" was so keen, so generous, that it weighed in evenly with her (anticipated) horror at the idea of my death. I understood that it was nothing personal. Just a design thing.

Anyhow, two weeks after that conversation, I returned to India. To what I think/thought of as home. Something had died, but it wasn't me. It was infinitely more precious. It was a world that has been ailing for a while, and has finally breathed its last. It's been cremated now. The air is thick with ugliness and there's the unmistakable stench of fascism on the breeze.

Day after day, in newspaper editorials, on the radio, on TV chat shows, on MTV for heaven's sake, people whose instincts one thought one could trust—writers, painters, journalists—make the crossing. The chill seeps into my bones as it becomes painfully apparent from the lessons of everyday life that what you read in history books is true. That fascism is indeed as much about people as about governments. That it begins at home. In drawing rooms. In bedrooms. In beds. "Explosion of Self-Esteem," "Road to Resurgence," "A Moment of Pride," these were headlines in the papers in the days following the nuclear tests. "We have proved that we are not eunuchs any more," said Mr. Thackeray of the Shiv Sena. (Whoever said we were? True, a good number of us are women, but that, as far as I know, isn't the same thing.) Reading the papers, it was often hard to tell when people were referring to Viagra (which was competing for second place on the front pages) and when they were talking about the bomb—"We have superior strength and potency." (This was our minister for defense after Pakistan completed its tests.)

"These are not just nuclear tests, they are nationalism tests," we were repeatedly told.

This has been hammered home, over and over again. The bomb is India. India is the bomb. Not just India, Hindu India. Therefore, be warned, any criticism of it is not just antinational, but anti-Hindu. (Of course, in Pakistan the bomb is Islamic. Other than that, politically, the same physics applies.) This is one of the unexpected perks of having a nuclear bomb. Not only can the government use it to threaten the enemy, they can use it to declare war on their own people. Us.

In 1975, one year after India first dipped her toe into the nuclear sea, Mrs. Gandhi declared the Emergency. What will 1999 bring? There's talk of cells being set up to monitor antinational activity. Talk of amending cable laws to ban networks "harming national culture" (*Indian Express*, July 3). Of churches being struck off the list of religious places because "wine is served" (announced and retracted, *Indian Express*, July 3; *Times of India*, July 4). Artists, writers, actors, and singers are being harassed, threatened (and are succumbing to the threats). Not just by goon squads, but by instruments of the government. And in courts of law. There are letters and articles circulating on the Net—creative interpretations of Nostradamus's predictions claiming that a mighty, all-conquering Hindu nation is about to emerge—a resurgent India that will "burst forth upon its former oppressors and destroy them completely." That "the beginning of the terrible revenge (that will wipe out all Moslems) will be in the seventh month of 1999." This may well be the work of some lone nut, or a bunch of arcane god-squadders. The trouble is that having a nuclear bomb makes thoughts like these seem feasible. It *creates* thoughts like these. It bestows on people these utterly misplaced, utterly deadly notions of their own power. It's happening. It's all happening. I wish I could say "slowly but surely"—but I can't. Things are moving at a pretty fair clip.

Why does it all seem so familiar? Is it because, even as you watch, reality dissolves and seamlessly rushes forward into the silent, black-and-white images from old films—scenes of people being hounded out of their lives, rounded up and herded into camps? Of massacre, of mayhem, of endless columns of broken people making their way to nowhere? Why is there no sound track? Why is the hall so quiet? Have I been seeing too many films? Am I mad? Or am I right? Could those images be the inevitable culmination of what we have set into motion? Could our future be rushing forward into our past? I think so. Unless, of course, nuclear war settles it once and for all.

When I told my friends that I was writing this piece, they cautioned me. "Go ahead," they said, "but first make sure you're not vulnerable. Make sure your papers are in order. Make sure your taxes are paid."

My papers are in order. My taxes are paid. But how can one *not* be vulnerable in a climate like this? Everyone is vulnerable. Accidents happen. There's safety only in acquiescence. As I write, I am filled with foreboding. In this country, I have truly known what it means for a writer to feel loved (and, to some degree, hated too). Last year I was one of the items being paraded in the media's end-of-the-year National Pride Parade. Among the others, much to my mortification, were a bomb maker and an international beauty queen. Each time a beaming person stopped me on the street and said, "You have made India proud" (referring to the prize I won, not the book I wrote), I felt a little uneasy. It frightened me then and it terrifies me now, because I know how easily that swell, that tide of emotion, can turn against me. Perhaps the time for that has come. I'm going to step out from under the tiny twinkling lights and say what's on my mind.

It's this:

If protesting against having a nuclear bomb implanted in my brain is anti-Hindu and antinational, then I secede. I hereby declare myself an independent, mobile republic. I am a citizen of the earth. I own no territory. I have no flag. I'm female, but have nothing against eunuchs. My policies are simple. I'm willing to sign any nuclear nonproliferation treaty or nuclear test-ban treaty that's going. Immigrants are welcome. You can help me design our flag.

My world has died. And I write to mourn its passing.

Admittedly it was a flawed world. An unviable world. A scarred and wounded world. It was a world that I myself have criticized unsparingly, but only because I loved it. It didn't deserve to die. It didn't deserve to be dismembered. Forgive me, I realize that sentimentality is uncool—but what shall I do with my desolation?

I loved it simply because it offered humanity a choice. It was a rock out at sea. It was a stubborn chink of light that insisted that there was a different way of living. It was a functioning possibility. A real option. All that's gone now. India's nuclear tests, the manner in which they were conducted, the euphoria with which they have been greeted (by us) is indefensible. To me, it signifies dreadful things. The end of imagination. The end of freedom actually, because, after all, that's what freedom is. Choice.

On August 15 last year we celebrated the fiftieth anniversary of India's independence. In May we can mark our first anniversary in nuclear bondage.

Why did they do it?

Political expediency is the obvious, cynical answer, except that it only raises another, more basic question: Why should it have been politically expedient?

The three Official Reasons given are: China, Pakistan, and Exposing Western Hypocrisy.

Taken at face value, and examined individually, they're somewhat baffling. I'm not for a moment suggesting that these are not real issues. Merely that they aren't new. The only new thing on the old horizon is the Indian government. In his appallingly cavalier letter to the president of the United States (why bother to write at all if you're going to write like this?) our prime minister says India's decision to go ahead with the nuclear tests was due to a "deteriorating security environment." He goes on to mention the war with China in 1962 and the "three aggressions we have suffered in the last fifty years from Pakistan. And for the last ten years we have been the victim of unremitting terrorism and militancy sponsored by it . . . especially in Jammu and Kashmir."

The war with China is thirty-five years old. Unless there's some vital state secret that we don't know about, it certainly seemed as though matters had improved slightly between us. Just a few days before the nuclear tests, general Fu Quanyou, chief of general staff of the Chinese People's Liberation Army, was the guest of our chief of army staff. We heard no words of war.

The most recent war with Pakistan was fought twenty-seven years ago. Admittedly, Kashmir continues to be a deeply troubled region and no doubt Pakistan is gleefully fanning the flames. But surely there must be flames to fan in the first place? Surely the kindling is crackling and ready to burn? Can the Indian state with even a modicum of honesty absolve itself completely of having a hand in Kashmir's troubles? Kashmir, and for that matter, Assam, Tripura, Nagaland—virtually the whole of the Northeast—Jharkhand, Uttarakhand, and all the trouble that's still to come—these are symptoms of a deeper malaise. It cannot and will not be solved by pointing nuclear missiles at Pakistan.

Even Pakistan can't be solved by pointing nuclear missiles at Pakistan. Though we are separate countries, we share skies, we share winds, we share water. Where radioactive fallout will land on any given day depends on the direction of the wind and rain. Lahore and Amritsar are thirty miles apart. If we bomb Lahore, Punjab will burn. If we bomb Karachi, then Gujarat and Rajasthan, perhaps even Bombay, will burn. Any nuclear war with Pakistan will be a war against ourselves.

As for the third Official Reason: exposing Western Hypocrisy—how much more exposed can they be? Which decent human being on earth harbors any illusions about it? These are people whose histories are spongy with the blood of others. Colonialism, apartheid, slavery, ethnic cleansing, germ warfare, chemical weapons—they virtually invented it all. They have plundered nations, snuffed out civilizations, exterminated entire populations. They stand on the world's stage stark naked but entirely unembarrassed, because they know that they have more money, more food, and bigger bombs than anybody else. They know they can wipe us out in the course of an ordinary working day. Personally, I'd say it is more arrogance than hypocrisy.

We have less money, less food, and smaller bombs. However, we have, or had, all kinds of other wealth. Delightful, unquantifiable. What we've done with it is the opposite of what we think we've done. We've pawned it all. We've traded it in. For what? In order to enter into a contract with the very people we claim to despise. In the larger scheme of things, we've agreed to play their game and play it their way. We've accepted their terms and conditions unquestioningly. The Comprehensive Test Ban Treaty ain't nothin' compared to this.

All in all, I think it is fair to say that *we're* the hypocrites. We're the ones who've abandoned what was arguably a moral position, i.e.: *we have the technology, we can make bombs if we want to, but we won't. We don't believe in them.*

We're the ones who have now set up this craven clamoring to be admitted into the club of superpowers. (If we are, we will no doubt gladly slam the door after us, and say to hell with principles about fighting Discriminatory World Orders.) For India to demand the status of a superpower is as ridiculous as demanding to play in the World Cup finals simply because we have a ball. Never mind that we haven't qualified, or that we don't play much soccer and haven't got a team.

Since we've chosen to enter the arena, it might be an idea to begin by learning the rules of the game. Rule number one is Acknowledge the Masters. Who are the best players? The ones with more money, more food, more bombs.

Rule number two is Locate Yourself in Relation to Them, i.e.: make an honest assessment of your position and abilities. The honest assessment of ourselves (in quantifiable terms) reads as follows:

We are a nation of nearly a billion people. In development terms we rank No. 138 out of the 175 countries listed in the United Nations Development Program's Human Development Index. More than four hundred million of our people are illiterate and live in absolute poverty, over six hundred million lack even basic sanitation, and over two hundred million have no safe drinking water.

So the three Official Reasons, taken individually, don't hold much water. However, if you link them, a kind of twisted logic reveals itself. It has more to do with us than them.

The key words in our prime minister's letter to the president of the United States were "suffered" and "victim." That's the substance of it. That's our meat and drink. We *need* to feel like victims. We need to feel beleaguered. We need enemies. We have so little sense of ourselves as a nation and therefore constantly cast about for targets to define ourselves against. Prevalent political wisdom suggests that to prevent the state from crumbling, we need a national cause, and other than our currency (and, of course, poverty, illiteracy, and elections), we have none. This is the heart of the matter. This is the road that has led us to the bomb. This search for selfhood. If we are looking for a way out, we need some honest answers to some uncomfortable questions. Once again, it isn't as though these questions haven't been asked before. It's just that we prefer to mumble the answers and hope that no one's heard.

Is there such a thing as an Indian identity?

Do we really need one?

Who is an authentic Indian and who isn't?

Is India Indian?

Does it matter?

Whether or not there has ever been a single civilization that could call itself "Indian Civilization," whether or not India was, is, or ever will become a cohesive cultural entity, depends on whether you dwell on the differences or the similarities in the cultures of the people who have inhabited the subcontinent for centuries. India, as a modern nation-state, was marked out with precise geographical boundaries, in their precise geographical way, by a British Act of Parliament in 1899. Our country, as we know it, was forged on the anvil of the British Empire for the entirely unsentimental reasons of commerce and administration. But even as she was born, she began her struggle against her creators. So is India Indian? It's a tough question. Let's just say that we're an ancient people learning to live in a recent nation.

What is true is that India is an artificial state—a state that was created by a government, not a people. A state created from the top down, not the bottom up. The majority of India's citizens will not (to this day) be able to identify her boundaries on a map, or say which language is spoken where or which god is worshiped in what region. Most are too poor and too uneducated to have even an elementary idea of the extent and complexity of their own country. The impoverished, illiterate agrarian majority have no stake in the state. And indeed, why should they, how can they, when they don't even know what the state is? To them, India is, at best, a noisy slogan that comes around during the elections. Or a montage of people on government TV programs wearing regional costumes and saying "*Mera Bharat Mahaan*" (My India Is Great).

The people who have a vital stake (or, more to the point, a business interest) in India's having a single, lucid, cohesive national identity are the politicians who constitute our national political parties. The reason isn't far to seek, it's simply because their struggle, their career goal, is—and must necessarily be—to *become* that identity. To be identified with that identity. If there isn't one, they have to manufacture one and persuade people to vote for it. It isn't their fault. It comes with the territory. It is inherent in the nature of our system of centralized government. A congenital defect in our particular brand of democracy. The greater the numbers of illiterate people, the poorer the country and the more morally bankrupt the politicians, the cruder the ideas of what that identity should be. In a situation like this, illiteracy is not just sad, it's downright dangerous. However, to be fair, cobbling together a viable predigested "National identity" for India would be a formidable challenge even for the wise and the visionary. Every single Indian citizen could, if he or she wants to, claim to belong to some minority or the other. The fissures, if you look for them, run vertically, horizontally, and are layered, whorled, circular, spiral, inside out, and outside in. Fires when they're lit race along any one of these schisms, and in the process, release tremendous bursts of political energy. Not unlike what happens when you split an atom.

It is this energy that Gandhi sought to harness when he rubbed the magic lamp and invited Ram and Rahim to partake of human politics and India's war of independence against the British. It was a sophisticated, magnificent, imaginative struggle, but its objective was simple and lucid, the target highly visible, easy to identify and succulent with political sin. In the circumstances, the energy found an easy focus. The trouble is that the circumstances are entirely changed now, but the genie is out of its lamp, and won't go back in. (It *could* be sent back, but nobody wants it to go, it's proved itself too useful.) Yes, it won us freedom. But it also won us the carnage of Partition. And now, in the hands of lesser statesmen, it has won us the Hindu Nuclear Bomb.

To be fair to Gandhi and to other leaders of the National Movement, they did not have the benefit of hindsight, and could not possibly have known what the eventual, long-term consequences of their strategy would be. They could not have predicted how quickly the situation would career out of control. They could not have foreseen what would happen when they passed their flaming torches into the hands of their successors, or how venal those hands could be.

It was Indira Gandhi who started the real slide. It is she who made the genie a permanent State Guest. She injected the venom into our political veins. She invented our particularly vile local brand of political expediency. She showed us how to conjure enemies out of thin air, to fire at phantoms that she had carefully fashioned for that very purpose. It was she who discovered the benefits of never burying the dead, but preserving their putrid carcasses and trundling them out to worry old wounds when it suited her. Between herself and her sons she managed to bring the country to its knees. Our new government has just kicked us over and arranged our heads on the chopping block.

The Bharatiya Janata Party (BJP) is, in some senses, a specter that Indira Gandhi and the Congress created. Or, if you want to be less harsh, a specter that fed and reared itself in the political spaces and communal suspicion that the Congress nourished and cultivated. It has put a new complexion on the politics of governance. While Mrs. Gandhi played hidden games with politicians and their parties, she reserved a shrill convent-school rhetoric, replete with tired platitudes, to address the general public. The BJP, on the other hand, has chosen to light its fires directly on the streets and in the homes and hearts of people. It is prepared to do by day what the Congress would do only by night. To legitimize what was previously considered unacceptable (but done anyway). There is perhaps a fragile case to be made here in favor of hypocrisy. Could the hypocrisy of the Congress Party, the fact that it conducts its wretched affairs surreptitiously instead of openly, could that possibly mean there is a tiny glimmer of guilt somewhere? Some small fragment of remembered decency?

Actually, no.

No.

What am I doing? Why am I foraging for scraps of hope?

The way it has worked—in the case of the demolition of the Babri Masjid as well as in the making of the nuclear bomb—is that the Congress sowed the seeds, tended the crop, then the BJP stepped in and reaped the hideous harvest. They waltz together, locked in each other's arms. They're inseparable, despite their professed differences. Between them they have brought us here, to this dreadful, dreadful place.

The jeering, hooting young men who battered down the Babri Masjid are the same ones whose pictures appeared in the papers in the days that followed the nuclear tests. They were on the streets, celebrating India's nuclear bomb and simultaneously "condemning Western Culture" by emptying crates of Coke and Pepsi into public drains. I'm a little baffled by their logic: Coke is Western Culture, but the nuclear bomb is an old Indian tradition?

Yes, I've heard—the bomb is in the Vedas. It might be, but if you look hard enough, you'll find Coke in the Vedas, too. That's the great thing about all religious texts. You can find anything you want in them—as long as you know what you're looking for.

But returning to the subject of the non-Vedic 1990s: We storm the heart of whiteness, we embrace the most diabolical creation of Western science and call it our own. But we protest against their music, their food, their clothes, their cinema, and their literature. That's not hypocrisy. That's humor.

It's funny enough to make a skull smile.

We're back on the old ship. The SS *Authenticity & Indianness.*

If there is going to be a pro-authenticity/antinational drive, perhaps the government ought to get its history straight and its facts right. If they're going to do it, they may as well do it properly.

First of all, the original inhabitants of this land were not Hindu. Ancient though it is, there were human beings on earth before there was Hinduism. India's Adivasis have a greater claim to being indigenous to this land than anybody else, and how are they treated by the state and its minions? Oppressed, cheated, robbed of their lands, shunted around like surplus goods. Perhaps the place to start would be to restore to them the dignity that was once theirs. Perhaps the government could make a public undertaking that more dams like the Sardar Sarovar on the Narmada will not be built, that more people will not be displaced.

But, of course, that would be inconceivable, wouldn't it? Why? Because it's impractical. Because Adivasis don't really matter. Their histories, their customs, their deities are dispensable. They must learn to sacrifice these things for the greater good of the nation (that has snatched from them everything they ever had).

Okay, so that's out.

For the rest, I could compile a practical list of things to ban and buildings to break. It'll need some research, but off the top of my head, here are a few suggestions.

They could begin by banning a number of ingredients from our cuisine: chilies (Mexico), tomatoes (Peru), potatoes (Bolivia), coffee (Morocco), tea, white sugar, cinnamon (China) . . . they could then move into recipes. Tea with milk and sugar, for instance (Britain).

Smoking will be out of the question. Tobacco came from North America.

Cricket, English, and Democracy should be forbidden. Either kabaddi or kho-kho could replace cricket. I don't want to start a riot, so I hesitate to suggest a replacement for English (Italian . . . ? It has found its way to us via a kinder route: marriage, not imperialism). We have already discussed (earlier in this essay) the emerging, apparently acceptable alternative to democracy.

All hospitals in which Western medicine is practiced or prescribed should be shut down. All national newspapers discontinued. The railways dismantled. Airports closed. And what about our newest toy—the mobile phone? Can we live without it, or shall I suggest that they make an exception there? They could put it down in the column marked "universal." (Only essential commodities will be included here. No music, art, or literature.)

Needless to say, sending your children to college in the US and rushing there yourself to have your prostate operated upon will be a cognizable offense.

The building demolition drive could begin with the Rashtrapati Bhavan and gradually spread from cities to the countryside, culminating in the destruction of all monuments (mosques, churches, temples) that were built on what was once Adivasi or forest land.

It will be a long, long list. It would take years of work. I couldn't use a computer because that wouldn't be very authentic of me, would it?

I don't mean to be facetious, merely to point out that this is surely the shortcut to hell. There's no such thing as an Authentic India or a Real Indian. There is no Divine Committee that has the right to sanction one single, authorized version of what India is or should be. There is no one religion or language or caste or region or person or story or book that can claim to be its sole representative. There are, and can only be, visions of India, various ways of seeing it—honest, dishonest, wonderful, absurd, modern, traditional, male, female. They can be argued over, criticized, praised, scorned, but not banned or broken. Not hunted down.

Railing against the past will not heal us. History has *happened*. It's over and done with. All we can do is to change its course by encouraging what we love instead of destroying what we don't. There is beauty yet in this brutal, damaged world of ours. Hidden, fierce, immense. Beauty that is uniquely ours and beauty that we have received with grace from others, enhanced, reinvented, and made our own. We have to seek it out, nurture it, love it. Making bombs will only destroy us. It doesn't *matter* whether or not we use them. They will destroy us either way.

India's nuclear bomb is the final act of betrayal by a ruling class that has failed its people.

However many garlands we heap on our scientists, however many medals we pin to their chests, the truth is that it's far easier to make a bomb than to educate four hundred million people.

According to opinion polls, we're expected to believe that there's a national consensus on the issue. It's official now. Everybody loves the bomb. (Therefore the bomb is good.)

Is it possible for a man who cannot write his own name to understand even the basic, elementary facts about the nature of nuclear weapons? Has anybody told him that nuclear war has nothing at all to do with his received notions of war? Nothing to do with honor, nothing to do with pride? Has anybody bothered to explain to him about thermal blasts, radioactive fallout, and the nuclear winter? Are there even words in his language to describe the concepts of enriched uranium, fissile material, and critical mass? Or has his language itself become obsolete? Is he trapped in a time capsule, watching the world pass him by, unable to understand or communicate with it because his language never took into account the horrors that the human race would dream up? Does he not matter at all, this man? Shall we just treat him like some kind of a cretin? If he asks any questions, ply him with iodine pills and parables about how Lord Krishna lifted a hill or how the destruction of Lanka by Hanuman was unavoidable in order to preserve Sita's virtue and Ram's reputation? Use his own beautiful stories as weapons against him? Shall we release him from his capsule only during elections, and once he's voted, shake him by the hand, flatter him with some bullshit about the Wisdom of the Common Man, and send him right back in?

I'm not talking about one man, of course, I'm talking about millions and millions of people who live in this country. This is their land, too, you know. They have the right to make an informed decision about its fate, and, as far as I can tell, nobody has informed them about anything. The tragedy is that nobody could, even if they wanted to. Truly, literally, there's no language to do it in. This is the real horror of India. The orbits of the powerful and the powerless spinning further and further apart from each other, never intersecting, sharing nothing. Not a language. Not even a country.

Who the hell conducted those opinion polls? Who the hell is the prime minister to decide whose finger will be on the nuclear button that could turn everything we love—our earth, our skies, our mountains, our plains, our rivers, our cities and villages—to ash in an instant? Who the hell is he to reassure us that there will be no accidents? How does he know? Why should we trust him? What has he ever done to make us trust him? What have any of them ever done to make us trust them?

The nuclear bomb is the most antidemocratic, antinational, antihuman, outright evil thing that man has ever made.

If you are religious, then remember that this bomb is Man's challenge to God.

It's worded quite simply: we have the power to destroy everything that You have created.

If you're not (religious), then look at it this way. This world of ours is four thousand six hundred million years old.

It could end in an afternoon.

"Nuclear weapons pervade our thinking. Control our behavior. Administer our societies. Inform our dreams. They bury themselves like meat hooks deep in the base of our brains. They are purveyors of madness. They are the ultimate colonizer. Whiter than any white man that ever lived. The very heart of whiteness."

THE GREATER
COMMON GOOD

If you are to suffer, you should suffer in the interest of the country . . .
—Jawaharlal Nehru, speaking to villagers who were to be displaced by the Hirakud dam, 1948[1]

I STOOD ON a hill and laughed out loud.

I had crossed the Narmada by boat from Jalsindhi and climbed the headland on the opposite bank, from where I could see, ranged across the crowns of low bald hills, the Adivasi hamlets of Sikka, Surung, Neemgavan, and Domkhedi. I could see their airy, fragile homes. I could see their fields and the forests behind them. I could see little children with littler goats scuttling across the landscape like motorized peanuts. I knew I was looking at a civilization older than Hinduism, slated—*sanctioned* (by the highest court in the

---

First published in *Outlook* and *Frontline*, June 4, 1999.

land)—to be drowned this monsoon [1999], when the waters of the Sardar Sarovar reservoir will rise to submerge it.

Why did I laugh?

Because I suddenly remembered the tender concern with which the Supreme Court judges in Delhi (before vacating the legal stay on further construction of the Sardar Sarovar Dam) had inquired whether Adivasi children in the resettlement colonies would have children's parks to play in. The lawyers representing the government had hastened to assure them that indeed they would, and what's more, that there were seesaws and slides and swings in every park. I looked up at the endless sky and down at the river rushing past, and for a brief, brief moment the absurdity of it all reversed my rage and I laughed. I meant no disrespect.

Let me say at the outset that I'm not a city-basher. I've done my time in a village. I've had firsthand experience of the isolation, the inequity, and the potential savagery of it. I'm not an anti-development junkie, nor a proselytizer for the eternal upholding of custom and tradition. What I *am*, however, is curious. Curiosity took me to the Narmada valley. Instinct told me that this was the big one. The one in which the battle lines were clearly drawn, the warring armies massed along them. The one in which it would be possible to wade through the congealed morass of hope, anger, information, disinformation, political artifice, engineering ambition, disingenuous socialism, radical activism, bureaucratic subterfuge, misinformed emotionalism, and, of course, the pervasive, invariably dubious, politics of International Aid.

Instinct led me to set aside Joyce and Nabokov, to postpone reading Don DeLillo's big book and substitute for it reports on drainage and irrigation, with journals and books and documentary films about dams and why they're built and what they do.

My first tentative questions revealed that few people know what is really going on in the Narmada valley. Those who know, know a lot. Most know nothing at all. And yet almost everyone has a passionate opinion. Nobody's neutral. I realized very quickly that I was straying into mined territory.

In India over the last ten years, the fight against the Sardar Sarovar Dam has come to represent far more than the fight for one river. This has been its strength as well as its weakness. Some years ago it became a debate that captured the popular imagination. That's what raised the stakes and changed the complexion of the battle. From being a fight over the fate of a river valley, it began to raise doubts about an entire political system. What is at issue now is the very nature of our democracy. Who owns this land? Who owns its rivers? Its forests? Its fish? These are huge questions. They are being taken hugely seriously by the state. They are being answered in one voice by every institution at its command—the army, the police, the bureaucracy, the courts. And not just answered, but answered unambiguously, in bitter, brutal ways.

For the people of the valley, the fact that the stakes were raised to this degree has meant that their most effective weapon—*specific* facts about *specific* issues in this *specific* valley—has been blunted by the debate on the big issues. The basic premise of the argument has been inflated until it has burst into bits that have, over time, bobbed away. Occasionally, a disconnected piece of the puzzle floats by—an emotionally charged account of the government's callous treatment of displaced people; an outburst at how the Narmada Bachao Andolan (NBA), "a handful of activists," is holding the nation to ransom; a legal correspondent reporting on the progress of the NBA's writ petition in the Supreme Court.

Though there has been a fair amount of writing on the subject, most of it is for a "special interest" readership. News reports tend to be about isolated aspects of the project. Government documents are classified as secret. I think it's fair to say that public perception of the issue is pretty crude and is divided crudely, into two categories.

On the one hand, it is seen as a war between modern, rational, progressive forces of "Development" versus a sort of neo-Luddite impulse—an irrational, emotional "antidevelopment" resistance, fueled by an arcadian, preindustrial dream.

On the other, as a Nehru v. Gandhi contest. This lifts the whole sorry business out of the bog of deceit, lies, false promises, and increasingly successful propaganda (which is what it's *really* about) and confers on it a false legitimacy. It makes out that both sides have the Greater Good of the Nation in mind—but merely disagree about the means by which to achieve it.

Both interpretations put a tired spin on the dispute. Both stir up emotions that cloud the particular facts of this particular story. Both are indications of how urgently we need new heroes—new *kinds* of heroes—and how we've overused our old ones (like we overbowl our bowlers).

The Nehru v. Gandhi argument pushes this very contemporary issue back into an old bottle. Nehru and Gandhi were generous men. Their paradigms for development are based on assumptions of inherent morality. Nehru's on the paternal, protective morality of the Soviet-style centralized State. Gandhi's on the nurturing, maternal morality of romanticized village republics. Both would probably work, if only we were better human beings. If we all wore homespun khadi and suppressed our base urges. Fifty years down the line, it's safe to say that we haven't made the grade. We haven't even come close. We need an updated insurance plan against our own basic natures.

It's possible that as a nation we've exhausted our quota of heroes for this century, but while we wait for shiny new ones to come along, we have to limit the damage. We have to support our small heroes. (Of these we have many. Many.) We have to fight specific wars in specific ways. Who knows, perhaps that's what the twenty-first century has in store for us. The dismantling of the Big. Big bombs, big dams, big ideologies, big contradictions, big countries, big wars, big heroes, big mistakes. Perhaps it will be the Century of the Small. Perhaps right now, this very minute, there's a small god up in heaven readying herself for us. Could it be? Could *it possibly* be? It sounds finger-licking good to me.

I was drawn to the valley because I sensed that the fight for the Narmada had entered a newer, sadder phase. I went because writers are drawn to stories the way vultures are drawn to kills. My motive was not compassion. It was sheer greed. I was right. I found a story there.

And what a story it is . . .

People say that the Sardar Sarovar dam is an expensive project. But it is bringing drinking water to millions. This is our lifeline. Can you put a price on this? Does the air we breathe have a price? We will live. We will drink. We will bring glory to the state of Gujarat.
—Urmilaben Patel, wife of Gujarat Chief Minister
Chimanbhai Patel, speaking at a public rally in Delhi in 1993

We will request you to move from your houses after the dam comes up. If you move, it will be good. Otherwise we shall release the waters and drown you all.
—Morarji Desai, speaking at a public meeting in the
submergence zone of the Pong Dam in 1961[2]

Why didn't they just poison us? Then we wouldn't have to live in this shithole and the government could have survived alone with its precious dam all to itself.
—Ram Bai, whose village was submerged when the Bargi Dam
was built on the Narmada; she now lives in a slum in Jabalpur[3]

In the fifty years since Independence, after Nehru's famous "Dams Are the Temples of Modern India" speech (one that he grew to regret in his own lifetime),[4] his foot soldiers threw themselves into the business of building dams with unnatural fervor. Dam building grew to be equated with nation-building. Their enthusiasm alone should have been reason enough to make one suspicious. Not only did they build new dams and new irrigation systems, they took control of small traditional systems that had been managed by village communities for thousands of years, and allowed them to atrophy.[5] To compensate the loss, the government built more and more dams. Big ones, little ones, tall ones, short ones. The result of its exertions is that India now boasts of being the world's third largest dam builder. According to the Central Water Commission, we have 3,600 dams that qualify as Big Dams, 3,300 of them built after Independence. One thousand more are under construction.[6] Yet one-fifth of our population—two hundred million people—does not have safe drinking water, and two-thirds—six hundred million—lack basic sanitation.[7]

Big Dams started well but have ended badly. There was a time when everybody loved them, everybody had them—the Communists, capitalists, Christians, Muslims, Hindus, Buddhists. There was a time when Big Dams moved men to poetry. Not any longer. All over the world there is a movement growing against Big Dams.

In the first world they're being decommissioned, blown up.[8] The fact that they do more harm than good is no longer just conjecture. Big Dams are obsolete. They're uncool. They're undemocratic. They're a government's way of accumulating authority (deciding who will get how much water and who will grow what where). They're a guaranteed way of taking a farmer's wisdom away from him. They're a brazen means of taking water, land, and irrigation away from the poor and gifting it to the rich. Their reservoirs displace huge populations of people, leaving them homeless and destitute.

Ecologically, too, they're in the doghouse.[9] They lay the earth to waste. They cause floods, waterlogging, salinity; they spread disease. There is mounting evidence that links Big Dams to earthquakes.

Big Dams haven't really lived up to their role as the monuments of Modern Civilization, emblems of Man's ascendancy over Nature. Monuments are supposed to be timeless, but dams have an all too finite lifetime. They last only as long as it takes Nature to fill them with silt.[10] It's common knowledge now that Big Dams do the opposite of what their Publicity People say they do—the Local Pain for National Gain myth has been blown wide open.

For all these reasons, the dam-building industry in the first world is in trouble and out of work. So it's exported to the third world in the name of Development Aid, along with their other waste, like old weapons, superannuated aircraft carriers, and banned pesticides.[11]

On the one hand the Indian government, *every* Indian government, rails self-righteously against the first world, and on the other, it actually *pays* to receive their gift-wrapped garbage. Aid is just another praetorian business enterprise. Like colonialism was. It has destroyed most of Africa. Bangladesh is reeling from its ministrations. We *know* all this, in numbing detail. Yet in India our leaders welcome it with slavish smiles (and make nuclear bombs to shore up their flagging self-esteem).

Over the last fifty years, India has spent Rs 87,000 crore[12] on the irrigation sector alone.[13] Yet there are more drought-prone areas and more flood-prone areas today than there were in 1947. Despite the disturbing evidence of irrigation disasters, dam-induced floods, and rapid disenchantment with the Green Revolution[14] (declining yields, degraded land), the government has not commissioned a post-project evaluation of a *single one* of its 3,600 dams to gauge whether or not it has achieved what it set out to achieve, whether or not the (always phenomenal) costs were justified, or even what the costs actually were.

The government of India has detailed figures for how many million tons of food grain or edible oils the country produces and how much more we produce now than we did in 1947. It can tell you how much bauxite is mined in a year or what the total surface area of the national highways adds up to. It's possible to access minute-by-minute information about the stock exchange or the value of the rupee in the world market. We know how many cricket matches we've lost on a Friday in Sharjah. It's not hard to find out how many graduates India produces, or how many men had vasectomies in any given year. But the government of India does not have a figure for the number of people who have been displaced by dams or sacrificed in other ways at the altars of "national progress." Isn't this *astounding*? How can you measure progress if you don't know what it costs and who has paid for it? How can the "market" put a price on things—food, clothes, electricity, running water—when it doesn't take into account the *real* cost of production?

According to a detailed study of fifty-four Big Dams done by the Indian Institute of Public Administration,[15] the *average* number of people displaced by a Big Dam in India is 44,182. Admittedly, 54 dams out of 3,300 is not a big enough sample. But since it's all we have, let's try and do some rough arithmetic. A first draft.

To err on the side of caution, let's halve the number of people. Or let's err on the side of *abundant* caution and take an average of just 10,000 people per Big Dam. It's an improbably low figure, I know, but . . . never mind. Whip out your calculators. 3,300 × 10,000 = 33,000,000.

That's what it works out to. Thirty-three *million* people. Displaced by Big Dams *alone* in the last fifty years. What about those who have been displaced by the thousands of other Development projects? In a private lecture, N. C. Saxena, secretary to the Planning Commission, said he thought the number was in the region of fifty million (of whom forty million were displaced by dams).[16] We daren't say so, because it isn't official. It isn't official because we daren't say so. You have to murmur it, for fear of being accused of hyperbole. You have to whisper it to yourself, because it really does sound unbelievable. It *can't be*, I've been telling myself. I must have muddled the zeroes. *It can't be true*. I barely have the courage to say it aloud. To run the risk of sounding like a sixties hippie dropping acid ("It's the System, man!"), or a paranoid schizophrenic with a persecution complex. But it *is* the System, man. What else can it be?

Fifty million people.

Go on, government, quibble. Bargain. Beat it down. Say *something*.

I feel like someone who's just stumbled on a mass grave.

Fifty million is more than the population of Gujarat. Almost three times the population of Australia. More than three times the number of refugees that Partition created in India. Ten times the number of Palestinian refugees. The Western world today is convulsed over the future of one million people who have fled from Kosovo.

A huge percentage of the displaced are Adivasis (57.6 percent in the case of the Sardar Sarovar Dam).[17] Include Dalits and the figure becomes obscene. According to the Commissioner for Scheduled Castes and Tribes, it's about 60 percent.[18] If you consider that Adivasis account for only 8 percent, and Dalits another 15 percent, of India's population, it opens up a whole other dimension to the story. The ethnic "otherness" of their victims takes some of the pressure off the nation-builders. It's like having an expense account. Someone else pays the bills. People from another country. Another world. India's poorest people are subsidizing the lifestyles of her richest.

Did I hear someone say something about the world's biggest democracy?

What has happened to all these millions of people? Where are they now? How do they earn a living? Nobody really knows. (Recently the *Indian Express* had an account of how Adivasis displaced from the Nagarjunasagar Dam Project are selling their babies to foreign adoption agencies.[19] The government intervened and put the babies in two public hospitals, where six infants died of neglect.) When it comes to rehabilitation, the government's priorities are clear. India does not *have* a national rehabilitation policy. According to the Land Acquisition Act of 1894 (amended in 1984) the government is not legally bound to provide a displaced person anything but a cash compensation. Imagine that. A cash compensation, to be paid by an Indian government official to an illiterate male Adivasi (the women get nothing) in a land where even the postman demands a tip for a delivery! Most Adivasis have no formal title to their land and

therefore cannot claim compensation anyway. Most Adivasis—
or let's say most small farmers—have as much use for money as
a Supreme Court judge has for a bag of fertilizer.

The millions of displaced people don't exist anymore. When
history is written, they won't be in it. Not even as statistics. Some
of them have subsequently been displaced three and four times—a
dam, an artillery-proof range, another dam, a uranium mine, a
power project. Once they start rolling, there's no resting place. The
great majority is eventually absorbed into slums on the periphery
of our great cities, where it coalesces into an immense pool of cheap
construction labor (that builds more projects that displace more
people). True, they're not being annihilated or taken to gas chambers, but I can warrant that the quality of their accommodation is
worse than in any concentration camp of the Third Reich. They're
not captive, but they redefine the meaning of liberty.

And still the nightmare doesn't end. They continue to be
uprooted even from their hellish hovels by government bulldozers that fan out on cleanup missions whenever elections are
comfortingly far away and the urban rich get twitchy about
hygiene. In cities like Delhi, they run the risk of being shot by
the police for shitting in public places—like three slum dwellers
were not more than two years ago.

In the French-Canadian wars of the 1770s, Lord Amherst exterminated most of Canada's Native Indians by offering them blankets
infested with the smallpox virus. Two centuries on, we of the Real
India have found less obvious ways of achieving similar ends.

The millions of displaced people in India are nothing but
refugees of an unacknowledged war. And we, like the citizens
of White America and French Canada and Hitler's Germany, are
condoning it by looking away. Why? Because we're told that it's
being done for the sake of the Greater Common Good. That it's
being done in the name of Progress, in the name of the National
Interest (which, of course, is paramount). Therefore gladly,
unquestioningly, almost gratefully, we believe what we're told.
We believe what it benefits us to believe.

Allow me to shake your faith. Put your hand in mine and let me lead you through the maze. Do this because it's important that you understand. If you find reason to disagree, by all means take the other side. But please don't ignore it, don't look away. It isn't an easy tale to tell. It's full of numbers and explanations. Numbers used to make my eyes glaze over. Not anymore. Not since I began to follow the direction in which they point.

Trust me. There's a story here.

It's true that India has progressed. It's true that in 1947, when colonialism formally ended, India was food deficient. In 1950 we produced 51 million tons of food grain. Today we produce close to 200 million tons.[20]

It's true that in 1995 the state granaries were overflowing with 30 million tons of unsold grain. It's also true that at the same time, 40 percent of India's population—more than 350 million people—were living below the poverty line.[21] That's more than the country's population in 1947.

Indians are too poor to buy the food their country produces. Indians are being forced to grow the kinds of food they can't afford to eat themselves. Look at what happened in Kalahandi District in western Orissa, best known for its starvation deaths. In the drought of 1996, people died of starvation (sixteen according to the state, over one hundred according to the press).[22] Yet that same year rice production in Kalahandi was higher than the national average! Rice was exported from Kalahandi District to the center.

Certainly India has progressed, but most of its people haven't. Our leaders say that we must have nuclear missiles to protect us from the threat of China and Pakistan. But who will protect us from ourselves?

What kind of country is this? Who owns it? Who runs it? What's going on?

It's time to spill a few state secrets. To puncture the myth about the inefficient, bumbling, corrupt, but ultimately genial, essentially democratic Indian State. Carelessness cannot account for fifty million disappeared people. Nor can Karma. Let's not delude ourselves. There is method here, precise, relentless, and 100 percent man-made.

The Indian State is not a state that has failed. It is a state that has succeeded impressively in what it set out to do. It has been ruthlessly efficient in the way it has appropriated India's resources—its land, its water, its forests, its fish, its meat, its eggs, its air—and redistributed them to a favored few (in return, no doubt, for a few favors). It is superbly accomplished in the art of protecting its cadres of paid-up elite, consummate in its methods of pulverizing those who inconvenience its intentions. But its finest feat of all is the way it achieves all this and emerges smelling sweet. The way it manages to keep its secrets, to contain information—that vitally concerns the daily lives of one billion people—in government files, accessible only to the keepers of the flame: ministers, bureaucrats, state engineers, defense strategists. Of course we make it easy for them, we its beneficiaries. We take care not to dig too deep. We don't really *want* to know the grisly details.

Thanks to us, Independence came (and went), elections come and go, but there has been no shuffling of the deck. On the contrary, the old order has been consecrated, the rift fortified. We, the rulers, won't pause to look up from our groaning table. We don't seem to know that the resources we're feasting on are finite and rapidly depleting. There's cash in the bank, but soon there'll be nothing left to buy with it. The food's running out in the kitchen. And the servants haven't eaten yet. Actually, the servants stopped eating a long time ago.

India lives in her villages, we're told, in every other sanctimonious public speech. That's bullshit. It's just another fig leaf from the government's bulging wardrobe. India doesn't live in her villages. India *dies* in her villages. India gets kicked around in her villages. India lives in her cities. India's villages live only to serve her cities. Her villagers are her citizens' vassals and for that reason must be controlled and kept alive, but only just.

This impression we have of an overstretched State, struggling to cope with the sheer weight and scale of its problems, is a dangerous one. The fact is that it's *creating* the problems. It's a giant poverty-producing machine, masterful in its methods of pitting the poor against the very poor, of flinging crumbs to the wretched so that they dissipate their energies fighting each other, while peace (and advertising) reigns in the Master's Lodgings.

Until this process is recognized for what it is, until it is addressed and attacked, elections—however fiercely they're contested—will continue to be mock battles that serve only to further entrench unspeakable inequity. Democracy (our version of it) will continue to be the benevolent mask behind which a pestilence flourishes unchallenged. On a scale that will make old wars and past misfortunes look like controlled laboratory experiments. Already fifty million people have been fed into the Development mill and have emerged as air conditioners and popcorn and rayon suits—*subsidized* air conditioners and popcorn and rayon suits. If we must have these nice things—and they *are* nice—at least we should be made to pay for them.

There's a hole in the flag that needs mending.

It's a sad thing to have to say, but as long as we have faith, we have no hope. To hope, we have to *break* the faith. We have to fight specific wars in specific ways and we have to fight to win. Listen, then, to the story of the Narmada valley. Understand it. And, if you wish, enlist. Who knows, it may lead to magic.

The Narmada wells up on the plateau of Amarkantak in the Shahdol District of Madhya Pradesh, then winds its way through 1,300 kilometers of beautiful, broad-leaved forest and perhaps the most fertile agricultural land in India. Twenty-five million people live in the river valley, linked to the ecosystem and to each other by an ancient intricate web of interdependence (and, no doubt, exploitation).

Though the Narmada has been targeted for "water resource development" for more than fifty years now, the reason it has, until recently, evaded being captured and dismembered is that it flows through three states—Madhya Pradesh, Maharashtra, and Gujarat.

Ninety percent of the river flows through Madhya Pradesh; it merely skirts the northern border of Maharashtra, then flows through Gujarat for about 180 kilometers before emptying into the Arabian Sea at Bharuch.

As early as 1946, plans had been afoot to dam the river at Gora in Gujarat. In 1961 Nehru laid the foundation stone for a 49.8-meter-high dam—the midget progenitor of the Sardar Sarovar.

Around the same time, the Survey of India drew up new topographical maps of the river basin. The dam planners in Gujarat studied the new maps and decided that it would be more profitable to build a much bigger dam. But this meant hammering out an agreement with neighboring states.

For years the three states bickered and balked but failed to agree on a water-sharing formula. Eventually, in 1969, the central government set up the Narmada Water Disputes Tribunal. It took the tribunal another ten years to announce its award.

The people whose lives were going to be devastated were neither informed nor consulted nor heard.

To apportion shares in the waters, the first, most basic thing the tribunal had to do was to find out how much water there was in the river. Usually this can only be reliably estimated if there is at least forty years of recorded data on the volume of actual flow in the river. Since this was not available, they decided to extrapolate from rainfall data. They arrived at a figure of 27.22 million acre feet (MAF).[23]

This figure is the statistical bedrock of the Narmada Valley Projects. We are still living with its legacy. It more or less determines the overall design of the projects—the height, location, and number of dams. By inference, it determines the cost of the projects, how much area will be submerged, how many people will be displaced, and what the benefits will be.

In 1992 actual observed flow data for the Narmada—which was now available for forty-five years (from 1948 to 1992)—showed that the yield from the river was only 22.69 MAF—18 percent less![24] The Central Water Commission admits that there is less water in the Narmada than had previously been assumed.[25] The government of India says: "It may be noted that clause II [of the decision of the tribunal] relating to determination of dependable flow as 28 MAF is nonreviewable"![26]

Never mind the data—the Narmada is legally bound by human decree to produce as much water as the government of India commands.

Its proponents boast that the Narmada Valley Projects are the most ambitious river valley development scheme ever conceived in human history. They plan to build 3,200 dams that will reconstitute the Narmada and her forty-one tributaries into a series of step reservoirs—an immense staircase of amenable water. Of these, 30 will be major dams, 135 medium, and the rest small. Two of the major dams will be multipurpose megadams. The Sardar Sarovar in Gujarat and the Narmada Sagar in Madhya Pradesh will, between them, hold more water than any other reservoir on the Indian subcontinent.

Whichever way you look at it, the Narmada Valley Development Projects are Big. They will alter the ecology of the entire river basin of one of India's biggest rivers. For better or for worse, they will affect the lives of twenty-five million people who live in the valley. They will submerge and destroy 4,000 square kilometers of natural deciduous forest.[27] Yet even before the Ministry of Environment cleared the projects, the World Bank offered to finance the linchpin of the project—the Sardar Sarovar Dam, whose reservoir displaces people in Madhya Pradesh and Maharashtra but whose benefits go to Gujarat. The Bank was ready with its checkbook *before* any costs were computed, *before* any studies had been done, *before* anybody had any idea of what the human cost or the environmental impact of the dam would be!

The $450 million loan for the Sardar Sarovar Projects was sanctioned and in place in 1985. The Ministry of Environment clearance for the project came only in 1987! Talk about enthusiasm. It fairly borders on evangelism. Can anybody care so much?

Why were they so keen?

Between 1947 and 1994 the World Bank's management had submitted six thousand projects to the executive board. The board hadn't turned down a single one. *Not a single one.* Terms like "moving money" and "meeting loan targets" suddenly begin to make sense.

India is in a situation today where it pays back more money to the Bank in interest and repayment installments than it receives from it. We are forced to incur new debts in order to be able to repay our old ones. According to the World Bank Annual Report, last year (1998), after the arithmetic, India paid the Bank $478 million more than it borrowed. Over the last five years (1993 to 1998) India paid the Bank $1.475 billion more than it received.[28]

The relationship between us is exactly like the relationship between a landless laborer steeped in debt and the village money-lender—it is an affectionate relationship, the poor man loves his moneylender because he's always there when he's needed. It's not for nothing that we call the world a global village. The only difference between the landless laborer and the government of India is that one uses the money to survive; the other just funnels it into the private coffers of its officers and agents, pushing the country into an economic bondage that it may never overcome.

The international dam industry is worth $20 billion a year.[29] If you follow the trails of Big Dams the world over, wherever you go—China, Japan, Malaysia, Thailand, Brazil, Guatemala—you'll rub up against the same story, encounter the same actors: the Iron Triangle (dam jargon for the nexus comprising politicians, bureaucrats, and dam-construction companies), the racketeers who call themselves International Environmental Consultants (who are usually directly employed by dam builders or their subsidiaries), and, more often than not, the friendly neighborhood World Bank. You'll grow to recognize the same inflated rhetoric, the same noble "Peoples' Dam" slogans, the same swift, brutal repression that follows the first sign of civil insubordination. (Of late, especially after its experience in the Narmada valley, the Bank is more cautious about choosing the countries in which it finances projects that involve mass displacement. At present China is its most favored client. It's the great irony of our times—American citizens protest the massacre in Tiananmen Square, but the Bank has used their money to fund studies for the Three Gorges dam in China, which is going to displace 1.3 million people. The Bank is today the biggest foreign financier of large dams in China.)[30]

It's a skillful circus, and the acrobats know each other well. Occasionally, they'll swap parts—a bureaucrat will join the Bank, a banker will surface as a project consultant. At the end of play, a huge percentage of what's called "Development Aid" is rechanneled back to the countries it came from, masquerading as equipment cost or consultants' fees or salaries to the agencies' own staff. Often aid is openly "tied" (as in the case of the Japanese loan for the Sardar Sarovar Dam—to a contract for purchasing turbines from the Sumitomo Corporation).[31] Sometimes the connections are more murky. In 1993 Britain financed the Pergau Dam in Malaysia with a subsidized loan of £234 million, despite an Overseas Development Administration report that said that the dam would be a "bad buy" for Malaysia. It later emerged that the loan was offered to "encourage" Malaysia to sign a £1.3 *billion* contract to buy British arms.[32]

In 1994 British consultants earned $2.5 billion on overseas contracts.[33] The second biggest sector of the market after Project Management was writing what are called EIAs (Environmental Impact Assessments). In the Development racket, the rules are pretty simple. If you get invited by a government to write an EIA for a big dam project and you point out a problem (say, you quibble about the amount of water available in a river, or, God forbid, you suggest that the human costs are perhaps too high), then you're history. You're an OOWC. An Out-of-Work Consultant. And oops! There goes your Range Rover. There goes your holiday in Tuscany. There goes your children's private boarding school. There's good money in poverty. Plus perks.

In keeping with Big Dam tradition, concurrent with the construction of the 138.68-meter-high Sardar Sarovar Dam began the elaborate government pantomime of conducting studies to estimate the actual project costs and the impact it would have on people and the environment. The World Bank participated wholeheartedly in the charade—occasionally it beetled its brows and raised feeble requests for more information on issues like the resettlement and rehabilitation of what it calls PAPs—Project-Affected Persons. (They help, these acronyms; they manage to mutate muscle and blood into cold statistics. PAPs soon cease to be people.)

The merest crumbs of information satisfied the Bank, and it proceeded with the project. The implicit, unwritten, but fairly obvious understanding between the concerned agencies was that whatever the costs—economic, environmental, or human—the project would go ahead. They would justify it as they went along. They knew full well that eventually, in a courtroom or to a committee, no argument works as well as a Fait Accompli.

Milord, the country is losing two crore a day due to the delay.

The government refers to the Sardar Sarovar Projects as the "most studied project in India," yet the game goes something like this: when the Tribunal first announced its award and the Gujarat government announced its plan of how it was going to use its share of water, *there was no mention of drinking water for villages in Kutch and Saurashtra*, the arid areas of Gujarat. When the project ran into political trouble, the government suddenly discovered the emotive power of thirst. Suddenly, quenching the thirst of parched throats in Kutch and Saurashtra became the whole *point* of the Sardar Sarovar Projects. (Never mind that water from two rivers—the Sabarmati and the Mahi, both of which are *miles* closer to Kutch and Saurashtra than the Narmada—have been dammed and diverted to Ahmedabad, Mehsana, and Kheda. Neither Kutch nor Saurashtra has seen a drop of it.) Officially, the number of people who will be provided drinking water by the Sardar Sarovar canal fluctuates from 28 million (1983) to 32.5 million (1989)—nice touch, the decimal point!—to 40 million (1992) and down to 25 million (1993).[34]

In 1979 the number of villages that would receive drinking water was zero. In the early 1980s it was 4,719. In 1990 it was 7,234. In 1991 it was 8,215.[35] When pressed, the government admitted that the figures for 1991 included 236 *uninhabited* villages![36]

Every aspect of the project is approached in this almost playful manner, as if it's a family board game. Even when it concerns the lives and futures of vast numbers of people.

In 1979 the number of families that would be displaced by the Sardar Sarovar reservoir was estimated to be a little over 6,000. In 1987 it grew to 12,000. In 1991 it surged to 27,000. In 1992 the government acknowledged that 40,000 families would be affected. Today, the official figure hovers between 40,000 and 41,500.[37] (Of course even this is an absurd figure, because the reservoir isn't the *only* thing that displaces people. According to the NBA the actual figure is about 85,000 families—that's *half a million* people.)

The estimated cost of the project bounced up from under Rs 5,000 crore[38] to Rs 20,000 crore (officially). The NBA says that it will cost Rs 44,000 crore.[39]

The government claims the Sardar Sarovar Projects will produce 1,450 megawatts of power.[40] The thing about multipurpose dams like the Sardar Sarovar is that their "purposes" (irrigation, power production, and flood control) conflict with one another. Irrigation uses up the water you need to produce power. Flood control requires you to keep the reservoir empty during the monsoon months to deal with an anticipated surfeit of water. And if there's no surfeit, you're left with an empty dam. And this defeats the purpose of irrigation, which is to *store* the monsoon water. It's like the conundrum of trying to ford a river with a fox, a chicken, and a bag of grain. The result of these mutually conflicting aims, studies say, is that when the Sardar Sarovar Projects are completed and the scheme is fully functional, it will end up producing only 3 percent of the power that its planners say it will. About 50 megawatts. And if you take into account the power needed to pump water through its vast network of canals, the Sardar Sarovar Projects will end up *consuming* more electricity than they produce![41]

In an old war, everybody has an ax to grind. So how do you pick your way through these claims and counterclaims? How do you decide whose estimate is more reliable? One way is to take a look at the track record of Indian dams.

The Bargi Dam near Jabalpur was the first dam on the Narmada to be completed (in 1990). It cost ten times more than was budgeted and submerged three times more land than the engineers said it would. About seventy thousand people from 101 villages were supposed to be displaced, but when they filled the reservoir (without warning anybody), 162 villages were submerged. Some of the resettlement sites built by the government were submerged as well. People were flushed out like rats from the land they had lived on for centuries. They salvaged what they could and watched their houses being washed away. One hundred fourteen thousand people were displaced.[42] There was no rehabilitation policy. Some were given meager cash compensation. Many got absolutely nothing. A few were moved to government rehabilitation sites. The site at Gorakhpur is, according to government publicity, an "ideal village." Between 1990 and 1992, five people died of starvation there. The rest either returned to live illegally in the forests near the reservoir or moved to slums in Jabalpur.

The Bargi dam irrigates only as much land as it submerged in the first place—*and only 5 percent of the area that its planners claimed it would irrigate.*[43] Even that is waterlogged.

Time and again, it's the same story. The Andhra Pradesh Irrigation II scheme claimed it would displace 63,000 people. When completed, it displaced 150,000 people.[44] The Gujarat Medium Irrigation II scheme displaced 140,000 people instead of 63,600.[45] The revised estimate of the number of people to be displaced by the Upper Krishna irrigation project in Karnataka is 240,000, against its initial claims of displacing only 20,000.[46]

These are World Bank figures. Not the NBA's. Imagine what this does to our conservative estimate of thirty-three million.

Construction work on the Sardar Sarovar Dam site, which had continued sporadically since 1961, began in earnest in 1988. At the time, nobody, not the government, nor the World Bank, was aware that a woman called Medha Patkar had been wandering through the villages slated to be submerged, asking people whether they had any idea of the plans that the government had in store for them. When she arrived in the valley all those years ago, opposing the construction of the dam was the furthest thing from her mind. Her chief concern was that displaced villagers should be resettled in an equitable, humane way. It gradually became clear to her that the government's intentions toward them were far from honorable. By 1986 word had spread, and each state had a people's organization that questioned the promises about resettlement and rehabilitation that were being bandied about by government officials. It was only some years later that the full extent of the horror—the impact that the dams would have, both on the people who were to be displaced and the people who were supposed to benefit—began to surface. The Narmada Valley Development Projects came to be known as India's Greatest Planned Environmental Disaster. The various people's organizations massed into a single organization, and the Narmada Bachao Andolan—the extraordinary NBA—was born.

In 1988 the NBA formally called for all work on the Narmada Valley Development Projects to be stopped. People declared that they would drown if they had to but would not move from their homes. Within two years the struggle had burgeoned and had support from other resistance movements. In September 1989, more than fifty thousand people gathered in the valley from all over India to pledge to fight "destructive development." The dam site and its adjacent areas, already under the Indian Official Secrets Act, were clamped under Section 144, which prohibits the gathering of groups of more than five people. The whole area was turned into a police camp. Despite the barricades, one year later, on September 28, 1990, thousands of villagers made their way on foot and by boat to a little town called Badwani, in Madhya Pradesh, to reiterate their pledge to drown rather than agree to move from their homes.

News of the people's opposition to the projects spread to other countries. The Japanese arm of Friends of the Earth mounted a campaign in Japan that succeeded in getting the government of Japan to withdraw its ¥27 billion loan to finance the Sardar Sarovar Projects. (The contract for the turbines still holds.) Once the Japanese withdrew, international pressure from various environmental activist groups who supported the struggle began to mount on the World Bank.

This, of course, led to an escalation of repression in the valley. Government policy, described by a particularly articulate minister, was to "flood the valley with khaki."

On Christmas Day 1990, six thousand men and women walked more than a hundred kilometers, carrying their provisions and their bedding, accompanying a seven-member sacrificial squad that had resolved to lay down its lives for the river. They were stopped at Ferkuwa on the Gujarat border by battalions of armed police and crowds of people from the city of Baroda, many of whom were hired, some of whom perhaps genuinely believed that the Sardar Sarovar was "Gujarat's lifeline." It was a telling confrontation. Middle-class urban India versus a rural, predominantly Adivasi army. The marching people demanded they be allowed to cross the border and walk to the dam site. The police refused them passage. To stress their commitment to nonviolence, each villager had his or her hands bound together. One by one, they defied the battalions of police. They were beaten, arrested, and dragged into waiting trucks in which they were driven off and dumped some miles away, in the wilderness. They just walked back and began all over again.

The faceoff continued for almost two weeks. Finally, on January 7, 1991, the seven members of the sacrificial squad announced that they were going on an indefinite hunger strike.

Tension rose to dangerous levels. The Indian and international press, TV camera crews, and documentary filmmakers were present in force. Reports appeared in the papers almost every day. Environmental activists stepped up the pressure in Washington. Eventually, acutely embarrassed by the glare of unfavorable media, the World Bank announced that it would commission an independent review of the Sardar Sarovar Projects—unprecedented in the history of Bank behavior. When the news reached the valley, it was received with distrust and uncertainty. The people had no reason to trust the World Bank. But still, it was a victory of sorts. The villagers, understandably upset by the frightening deterioration in the condition of their comrades, who had not eaten for twenty-two days, pleaded with them to call off the fast. On January 28 the fast at Ferkuwa was called off and the brave, ragged army returned to their homes shouting *"Hamara gaon mein hamara raj!"* (Our rule in our villages!).

There has been no army quite like this one anywhere else in the world. In other countries—China (Chairman Mao got a Big Dam for his seventy-seventh birthday), Malaysia, Guatemala, Paraguay—every sign of revolt has been snuffed out almost before it began. Here in India, it goes on and on. Of course, the state would like to take credit for this, too. It would like us to be grateful to it for not crushing the movement completely, for *allowing* it to exist. After all, what *is* all this, if not a sign of a healthy, functioning democracy in which the state has to intervene when its people have differences of opinion?

I suppose that's one way of looking at it. (Is this my cue to cringe and say "Thank you, thank you, for allowing me to write the things I write"?)

We don't need to be grateful to the state for permitting us to protest. We can thank ourselves for that. It is we who have insisted on these rights. It is we who have refused to surrender them. If we have anything to be truly proud of as a people, it is this.

The struggle in the Narmada valley lives, *despite* the state.

The Indian State makes war in devious ways. Apart from its apparent benevolence, its other big weapon is its ability to wait. To roll with the punches. To wear out the opposition. The state never tires, never ages, never needs a rest. It runs an endless relay.

But fighting people tire. They fall ill, they grow old. Even the young age prematurely. For twenty years now, since the Tribunal's award, the ragged army in the valley has lived with the fear of eviction. For twenty years, in most areas there has been no sign of "development"—no roads, no schools, no wells, no medical help. For twenty years, it has borne the stigma "slated for submergence"—so it's isolated from the rest of society (no marriage proposals, no land transactions). They're a bit like the Hibakusha in Japan (the victims and their descendants of the bombing in Hiroshima and Nagasaki). The "fruits of modern development," when they finally came, brought only horror. Roads brought surveyors. Surveyors brought trucks. Trucks brought policemen. Policemen brought bullets and beatings and rape and arrest, and in one case murder. The only genuine "fruit" of modern development that reached them, reached them inadvertently—the right to raise their voices, the right to be heard. But they have fought for twenty years now. How much longer will they last?

The struggle in the valley is tiring. It's no longer as fashionable as it used to be. The international camera crews and the radical reporters have moved (like the World Bank) to newer pastures. The documentary films have been screened and appreciated. Everybody's sympathy is all used up. But the dam goes on. It's getting higher and higher . . .

Now, more than ever before, the ragged army needs reinforcements. If we let it die, if we allow the struggle to be crushed, if we allow the people to be brutalized, we will lose the most precious thing we have: our spirit, or what's left of it.

"India will go on," they'll tell you, the sage philosophers who don't want to be troubled by piddling current affairs. As though "India" is somehow more valuable than her people.

Old Nazis probably soothe themselves in similar ways.

It's too late, some people say. Too much time and money has gone into the project to revoke it now.

So far, the Sardar Sarovar reservoir has submerged only a fourth of the area that it will when (if) the dam reaches its full height. If we stop it now, we would save 325,000 people from certain destitution. As for the economics of it—it's true that the government has already spent Rs 7,500 crore ($1.5 billion), but continuing with the project would mean throwing good money after bad. We would save something like Rs 35,000 crore ($7 billion) of public money, probably enough to fund local water-harvesting projects in every village in all of Gujarat. What could possibly be a more worthwhile war?

The war for the Narmada valley is not just some exotic tribal war, or a remote rural war or even an exclusively Indian war. It's a war for the rivers and the mountains and the forests of the world. All sorts of warriors from all over the world, anyone who wishes to enlist, will be honored and welcomed. Every kind of warrior will be needed. Doctors, lawyers, teachers, judges, journalists, students, sportsmen, painters, actors, singers, lovers . . . The borders are open, folks! Come on in.

Anyway, back to the story.

In June 1991 the World Bank appointed Bradford Morse, a former head of the United Nations Development Program, as chairman of the Independent Review. His brief was to make a thorough assessment of the Sardar Sarovar Projects. He was guaranteed free access to all secret World Bank documents relating to the projects.

Morse and his team arrived in India in September 1991. The NBA, convinced that this was yet another setup, at first refused to meet them. The Gujarat government welcomed the team with a red carpet (and a nod and a wink) as covert allies.

A year later, in June 1992, the historic Independent Review (known also as the Morse Report) was published.

The Independent Review unpeels the project delicately, layer by layer, like an onion. Nothing was too big and nothing too small for the members of the Morse Committee to inquire into. They met ministers and bureaucrats, they met NGOs working in the area, went from village to village, from resettlement site to resettlement site. They visited the good ones. The bad ones. The temporary ones, the permanent ones. They spoke to hundreds of people. They traveled extensively in the submergence area and the command area. They went to Kutch and other drought-hit areas in Gujarat. They commissioned their own studies. They examined every aspect of the project: hydrology and water management, the upstream environment, sedimentation, catchment-area treatment, the downstream environment, the anticipation of likely problems in the command area—water logging, salinity, drainage, health, the impact on wildlife.

What the Independent Review reveals, in temperate, measured tones (which I admire but cannot achieve), is scandalous. It is the most balanced, unbiased, yet damning indictment of the relationship between the Indian State and the World Bank. Without appearing to, perhaps even without intending to, the report cuts through to the cozy core, to the space where they live together and love each other (somewhere between what they say and what they do).

The core recommendation of the 357-page Independent Review was unequivocal and wholly unexpected:

We think the Sardar Sarovar Projects as they stand are flawed, that resettlement and rehabilitation of all those displaced by the Projects is not possible under prevailing circumstances, and that environmental impacts of the Projects have not been properly considered or adequately addressed. Moreover we believe that the Bank shares responsibility with the borrower for the situation that has developed. . . . It seems clear that engineering and economic imperatives have driven the Projects to the exclusion of human and environmental concerns. . . . India and the states involved . . . have spent a great deal of money. No one wants to see this money wasted. But we caution that it may be more wasteful to proceed without full

*knowledge of the human and environmental costs. . . . As a result,
we think that the wisest course would be for the Bank to step back
from the Projects and consider them afresh.*[47]

Four committed, knowledgeable, truly independent men—
they do a lot to make up for the faith eroded by hundreds of
other venal ones who are paid to do similar jobs.

The World Bank, however, was still not prepared to give up. It
continued to fund the project. Two months after the Independent
Review, it sent out the Pamela Cox Committee, which did exactly
what the Morse Review had cautioned against ("it would be irresponsible for us to patch together a series of recommendations on
implementation when the flaws in the Projects are as obvious as
they seem to us")[48] and suggested a sort of patchwork remedy to
try and salvage the operation. In October 1992, on the recommendation of the Pamela Cox Committee, the Bank asked the Indian
government to meet some minimum primary conditions within a
period of six months.[49] Even that much the government couldn't
do. Finally, on March 30, 1993, the World Bank pulled out of the
Sardar Sarovar Projects. (Actually, technically, on March 29, one
day *before* the deadline, the government of India asked the World
Bank to withdraw.)[50] Details. Details.

No one has ever managed to make the World Bank step back
from a project before. Least of all a ragtag army of the poorest
people in one of the world's poorest countries. A group of people
whom Lewis Preston, then president of the Bank, never managed
to fit into his busy schedule when he visited India.[51] Sacking the
Bank was and is a huge moral victory for the people in the valley.

The euphoria didn't last. The government of Gujarat announced that it was going to raise the $200 million shortfall on
its own and push ahead with the project.

During the period of the Independent Review and after it was
published, confrontation between people and the authorities continued unabated in the valley—humiliation, arrests, baton charges.
Indefinite fasts terminated by temporary promises and permanent

betrayals. People who had agreed to leave the valley and be resettled had begun returning to their villages from their resettlement sites. In Manibeli, a village in Maharashtra and one of the nerve centers of the resistance, hundreds of villagers participated in a Monsoon Satyagraha. In 1993, families in Manibeli remained in their homes as the waters rose. They clung to wooden posts with their children in their arms and refused to move. Eventually, policemen prized them loose and dragged them away. The NBA declared that if the government did not agree to review the project, on August 6, 1993, a band of activists would drown themselves in the rising waters of the reservoir. On August 5 the Union government constituted yet another committee called the Five Member Group (FMG) to review the Sardar Sarovar Projects.

The government of Gujarat refused it entry into Gujarat.[52]

The FMG report[53] (a "desk report") was submitted the following year. It tacitly endorsed the grave concerns of the Independent Review. But it made no difference. Nothing changed. This is another of the state's tested strategies. It kills you with committees.

In February 1994 the government of Gujarat ordered the permanent closure of the sluice gates of the dam.

In May 1994 the NBA filed a writ petition in the Supreme Court questioning the whole basis of the Sardar Sarovar Dam and seeking a stay on its construction.[54]

During the monsoon of that year, when the level in the reservoir rose and water smashed down on the other side of the dam, 65,000 cubic meters of concrete and 35,000 cubic meters of rock were torn out of a stilling basin, leaving a crater 65 meters wide. The riverbed powerhouse was flooded. The damage was kept secret for months.[55] Reports started appearing about it in the press only in January 1995.

In early 1995, on the grounds that the rehabilitation of displaced people had not been adequate, the Supreme Court ordered work on the dam to be suspended until further notice.[56] The height of the dam was 80 meters above mean sea level.

Meanwhile, work had begun on two more dams in Madhya Pradesh—the massive Narmada Sagar (without which the Sardar Sarovar loses 17 to 30 percent of its efficiency)[57] and the Maheshwar Dam. The Maheshwar Dam is next in line, upstream from the Sardar Sarovar. The government of Madhya Pradesh has signed a power purchase contract with a private company—S. Kumars, one of India's leading textile magnates.

Tension in the Sardar Sarovar area abated temporarily, and the battle moved upstream, to Maheshwar, in the fertile plains of Nimad.

The case pending in the Supreme Court led to a palpable easing of repression in the valley. Construction work had stopped on the dam, but the rehabilitation charade continued. Forests (slated for submergence) continued to be cut and carted away in trucks, forcing people who depended on them for a livelihood to move out.

Even though the dam is nowhere near its eventual projected height, its impact on the environment and the people living along the river is already severe.

Around the dam site and the nearby villages, the number of cases of malaria has increased sixfold.[58]

Several kilometers upstream from the Sardar Sarovar dam, huge deposits of silt, hip deep and over 200 meters wide, have cut off access to the river. Women carrying water pots now have to walk miles, literally *miles*, to find a negotiable entry point. Cows and goats get stranded in the mud and die. The little single-log boats that the Adivasis use have become unsafe on the irrational circular currents caused by the barricade downstream.

Farther upstream, where the silt deposits have not yet become a problem, there's another tragedy. Landless people (predominantly Adivasis and Dalits) have traditionally cultivated rice, melons, cucumbers, and gourds on the rich, shallow silt banks the river leaves when it recedes in the dry months. Every now and then, the engineers manning the Bargi Dam (way upstream, near Jabalpur) release water from the reservoir without warning. Downstream, the water level in the river suddenly rises. Hundreds of families have had their crops washed away several times, leaving them with no livelihood.

Suddenly they can't trust their river anymore. It's like a loved one who has developed symptoms of psychosis. Anyone who has loved a river can tell you that the loss of a river is a terrible, aching thing. But I'll be rapped on the knuckles if I continue in this vein. When we're discussing the Greater Common Good there's no place for sentiment. One must stick to facts. Forgive me for letting my heart wander.

The state governments of Madhya Pradesh and Maharashtra continue to be completely cavalier in their dealings with displaced people. The government of Gujarat has a rehabilitation policy (on paper) that makes the other two states look medieval. It boasts of having the best rehabilitation package in the world.[59] The program offers land for land to displaced people from Maharashtra and Madhya Pradesh and recognizes the claims of "encroachers" (usually Adivasis with no papers). The deception, however, lies in its definition of who qualifies as "Project Affected."

In point of fact, the government of Gujarat hasn't even managed to rehabilitate people from its own 19 villages slated for submergence, let alone the rest of the 226 villages in the other two states. The inhabitants of these 19 villages have been scattered to 175 separate rehabilitation sites. Social links have been smashed, communities broken up.

In practice, the resettlement story (with a few "ideal village" exceptions) continues to be one of callousness and broken promises. Some people have been given land, others haven't. Some have land that is stony and uncultivable. Some have land that is irredeemably waterlogged. Some have been driven out by landowners who had sold their land to the government but hadn't been paid.[60]

Some who were resettled on the periphery of other villages have been robbed, beaten, and chased away by their host villagers.

There have been instances when displaced people from two different dam projects have been allotted contiguous lands. In one case, displaced people from *three* dams—the Ukai Dam, the Sardar Sarovar Dam, and the Karjan Dam—were resettled in the *same* area.[61] In addition to fighting among themselves for resources—water, grazing land, jobs—they had to fight a group of landless laborers who had been sharecropping the land for absentee landlords who had subsequently sold it to the government.

There's another category of displaced people—people whose lands have been acquired by the government for resettlement sites. There's a pecking order even among the wretched—Sardar Sarovar "oustees" are more glamorous than other "oustees" because they're occasionally in the news and have a case in court. (In other development projects where there's no press, no NBA, no court case, there are no records. The displaced leave no trail at all.)

In several resettlement sites, people have been dumped in rows of corrugated tin sheds that are furnaces in summer and fridges in winter. Some of them are located in dry riverbeds that during the monsoon turn into fast-flowing drifts. I've been to some of these "sites." I've seen film footage[62] of others: shivering children, perched like birds on the edges of cots, while swirling waters enter their tin homes. Frightened, fevered eyes watch pots and pans carried through the doorway by the current, floating out into the flooded fields, thin fathers swimming after them to retrieve what they can.

When the waters recede they leave ruin. Malaria, diarrhea, sick cattle stranded in the slush. The ancient teak beams dismantled from their previous homes, carefully stacked away like postponed dreams, now spongy, rotten, and unusable.

Forty households were moved from Manibeli to a resettlement site in Gujarat. In the first year, thirty-eight children died.[63] In today's paper (*Indian Express*, April 26, 1999) there's a report about nine deaths in a single rehabilitation site in Gujarat. In the course of a single week. That's 1.2875 PAPs a day, if you're counting.

Many of those who have been resettled are people who have lived all their lives deep in the forest with virtually no contact with money and the modern world. Suddenly they find themselves left with the option of starving to death or walking several kilometers to the nearest town, sitting in the marketplace (both men and women), offering themselves as wage laborers like goods on sale.

Instead of a forest from which they gathered everything they needed—food, fuel, fodder, rope, gum, tobacco, tooth powder, medicinal herbs, housing materials—they earn between ten and twenty rupees (twenty to forty cents) a day with which to feed and keep their families. Instead of a river, they have a hand pump. In their old villages they had no money, but they were insured. If the rains failed, they had the forests to turn to. The river to fish in. Their livestock was their fixed deposit. Without all this, they're a heartbeat away from destitution.

In Vadaj, a resettlement site I visited near Baroda, the man who was talking to me rocked his sick baby in his arms, clumps of flies gathered on its sleeping eyelids. Children collected around us, taking care not to burn their bare skin on the scorching tin walls of the shed they call a home. The man's mind was far away from the troubles of his sick baby. He was making me a list of the fruits he used to pick in the forest. He counted forty-eight kinds. He told me that he didn't think he or his children would ever be able to afford to eat any fruit again. Not unless he stole it. I asked him what was wrong with his baby. He said it would be better for the baby to die than live like this. I asked what the baby's mother thought about that. She didn't reply. She just stared.

For the people who've been resettled, everything has to be relearned. Every little thing, every big thing: from shitting and pissing (where d'you do it when there's no jungle to hide you?) to buying a bus ticket, to learning a new language, to understanding money. And worst of all, learning to be supplicants. Learning to take orders. Learning to have masters. Learning to answer only when you're addressed.

In addition to all this, they have to learn how to make written representations (in triplicate) to the Grievance Redressal Committee or the Sardar Sarovar Narmada Nigam for any particular problems they might have. Recently 3,000 people came to Delhi to protest their situation—traveling overnight by train, living on the blazing streets.[64] The president wouldn't meet them because he had an eye infection. Maneka Gandhi, the Minister for Social Justice and Empowerment, wouldn't meet them but asked for a written representation (*Dear Maneka, Please don't build the dam, Love, The People*). When the representation was handed to her, she scolded the little delegation for not having written it in English.

From being self-sufficient and free to being impoverished and yoked to the whims of a world you know nothing, *nothing* about—what d'you suppose it must feel like? Would you like to trade your beach house in Goa for a hovel in Paharganj? No? Not even for the sake of the nation?

Truly, it is just not possible for a state administration, *any* state administration, to carry out the rehabilitation of a people as fragile as this, on such an immense scale. It's like using a pair of hedge clippers to trim an infant's fingernails. You can't do it without clipping its fingers off.

Land for land sounds like a reasonable swap, but how do you implement it? How do you uproot 200,000 people (the official blinkered estimate)—of whom 117,000 are Adivasi—and relocate them in a humane fashion? How do you keep their communities intact in a country where every inch of land is fought over, where almost all litigation pending in courts has to do with land disputes?

Where is all this fine, unoccupied, but arable land that is waiting to receive these intact communities?

The simple answer is that there isn't any. Not even for the "officially" displaced of this one dam.

What about the rest of the 3,199 dams?

What about the remaining thousands of PAPs earmarked for annihilation? Shall we just put the Star of David on their doors and get it over with?

The reservoir of the Maheshwar Dam will wholly or partially submerge sixty villages in the Nimad plains of Madhya Pradesh. A significant section of the population in these villages—roughly a third—are Kevats and Kahars, ancient communities of ferrymen, fisherfolk, sand quarriers, and cultivators of the riverbank when the waters recede in the dry season. Most of them own no land, but the river sustains them and means more to them than to anyone else. When the dam is built, thousands of Kevats and Kahars will lose their only source of livelihood. Yet simply because they are landless, they do not qualify as project affected and will not be eligible for rehabilitation.

Jalud is the first of sixty villages that will be submerged by the reservoir of the Maheshwar Dam. Jalud is not an Adivasi village and is therefore riven with the shameful caste divisions that are the scourge of every ordinary Hindu village. A majority of the landowning farmers (the ones who qualify as PAPs) are Rajputs. They farm some of the most fertile soil in India. Their houses are piled with sacks of wheat and lentils and rice. They boast so much about the things they grow on their land that if it weren't so tragic, it could get on your nerves. Their houses have already begun to crack with the impact of the dynamiting on the dam site.

Twelve families who had small holdings in the vicinity of the dam site had their land acquired. They told me how, when they objected, cement was poured into their water pipes, their standing crops were bulldozed, and the police occupied the land by force. All twelve families are now landless and work as wage laborers.

The area that the Rajputs of Jalud are going to be moved to is a few kilometers inland, away from the river, adjoining a predominantly Dalit and Adivasi precinct in a village called Samraj. I saw the huge tract of land that had been marked off for them. It was a hard, stony hillock with stubbly grass and scrub, on which truckloads of silt were being unloaded and spread out in a thin layer to make it look like rich black humus.

The story goes like this: on behalf of the S. Kumars (textile tycoons turned nation-builders) the district magistrate acquired the hillock, which was actually village common grazing land that belonged to the people of Samraj. In addition to this, the land of eighty-four Dalit and Adivasi villagers was acquired. No compensation was paid.

The villagers, whose main source of income was their livestock, had to sell their goats and buffalo because they no longer had anywhere to graze them. Their only remaining source of income lies (lay) on the banks of a small lake on the edge of the village. In summer, when the water level recedes, it leaves a shallow ring of rich silt on which the villagers grow (grew) rice and melons and cucumber.

The S. Kumars have excavated this silt to cosmetically cover the stony grazing ground (which the Rajputs of Jalud don't want). The banks of the lake are now steep and uncultivable.

The already impoverished people of Samraj have been left to starve, while this photo opportunity is being readied for German and Swiss funders, Indian courts, and anybody else who cares to pass that way.

This is how India works. This is the genesis of the Maheshwar Dam. The story of the first village. What will happen to the other fifty-nine? May bad luck pursue this dam. May bulldozers turn upon the textile tycoons.

Nothing can justify this kind of behavior.

In circumstances like these, to even entertain a debate about rehabilitation is to take the first step toward setting aside the principles of justice. Resettling two hundred thousand people in order to take (or pretend to take) drinking water to forty million—there's something very wrong with the *scale* of operations here. This is fascist math. It strangles stories. Bludgeons detail. And manages to blind perfectly reasonable people with its spurious, shining vision.

When I arrived on the banks of the Narmada in late March 1999, it was a month after the Supreme Court had suddenly vacated the stay on construction work of the Sardar Sarovar Dam. I had read pretty much everything I could lay my hands on (all those "secret" government documents). I had a clear idea of the lay of the land—of what had happened where and when and to whom. The story played itself out before my eyes like a tragic film whose actors I'd already met. Had I not known its history, nothing would have made sense. Because in the valley there are stories within stories, and it's easy to lose the clarity of rage in the sludge of other people's sorrow.

I ended my journey in Kevadia Colony, where it all began.

Thirty-eight years ago, this is where the government of Gujarat decided to locate the infrastructure it would need for starting work on the dam: guesthouses, office blocks, accommodation for engineers and their staff, roads leading to the dam site, warehouses for construction material.

It is located on the cusp of what is now the Sardar Sarovar reservoir and the Wonder Canal, Gujarat's "lifeline," that is going to quench the thirst of millions.

Nobody knows this, but Kevadia Colony is the key to the world. Go there, and secrets will be revealed to you.

In the winter of 1961, a government officer arrived in a village called Kothie and told the villagers that some of their land would be needed to construct a helipad because someone terribly important was going to come visiting. In a few days a bulldozer arrived and flattened standing crops. The villagers were made to sign papers and were paid a sum of money, which they assumed was payment for their destroyed crops. When the helipad was ready, a helicopter landed on it, and out came Prime Minister Nehru. Most of the villagers couldn't see him because he was surrounded by policemen. Nehru made a speech. Then he pressed a button and there was an explosion on the other side of the river. After the explosion he flew away.[65] That was the genesis of what was to become the Sardar Sarovar dam.

Could Nehru have known when he pressed that button that he had unleashed an incubus?

After Nehru left, the government of Gujarat arrived in strength. It acquired 1,600 acres of land from 950 families from six villages.[66] The people were Tadvi Adivasis who, because of their proximity to the city of Baroda, were not entirely unversed in the ways of a market economy. They were sent notices and told that they would be paid cash compensation and given jobs on the dam site. Then the nightmare began.

Trucks and bulldozers rolled in. Forests were felled, standing crops destroyed. Everything turned into a whirl of jeeps and engineers and cement and steel. Mohan Bai Tadvi watched eight acres of his land with standing crops of sorghum, lentils, and cotton being leveled. Overnight he became a landless laborer. *Three years later* he received his cash compensation of Rs 250 (five dollars) an acre in three separate installments.

Dersukh Bhai Vesa Bhai's father was given Rs 3,500 (seventy dollars) for his house and five acres of land with its standing crops and all the trees on it. He remembers walking all the way to Rajpipla (the district headquarters) as a little boy, holding his father's hand.

He remembers how terrified they were when they were called in to the Tehsildar's office. They were made to surrender their compensation notices and sign a receipt. They were illiterate, so they didn't know how much the receipt was made out for.

Everybody had to go to Rajpipla, but they were always summoned on different days, one by one. So they couldn't exchange information or compare stories.

Gradually, out of the dust and bulldozers, an offensive, diffuse configuration emerged. Kevadia Colony. Row upon row of ugly cement flats, offices, guesthouses, roads. All the graceless infrastructure of Big Dam construction. The villagers' houses were dismantled and the villagers moved to the periphery of the colony where they remain today, squatters on their own land. Those that caused trouble were intimidated by the police and the construction company. The villagers told me that in the contractor's headquarters they have a "lockup" like a police lockup, where recalcitrant villagers are incarcerated and beaten.

The people who were evicted to build Kevadia Colony do not qualify as "Project Affected" in Gujarat's rehabilitation package.

Some of them work as servants in the officers' bungalows and waiters in the guesthouse built on the land where their own houses once stood. Can there be anything more poignant?

Those who had some land left tried to cultivate it, but Kevadia municipality introduced a scheme in which they brought in pigs to eat uncollected refuse on the streets. The pigs stray into the villagers' fields and destroy their crops.

In 1992, thirty years later, each family has been offered a sum of Rs 12,000 ($180) per acre, up to a maximum of Rs 36,000 ($540), *provided* they agree to leave their homes and go away! Yet 40 percent of the land that was acquired is lying unused. The government refuses to return it. Eleven acres acquired from Deviben, who is a widow now, has been given over to the Swami Narayan Trust (a big religious sect). On a small portion of it, the trust runs a little school. The rest it cultivates, while Deviben watches through the barbed-wire fence. On two hundred acres acquired in the village of Gora, villagers were evicted and blocks of flats were built. They lay empty for years. Eventually, the government rented them for a nominal fee to Jai Prakash Associates, the dam contractors, who, the villagers say, sublet them privately for Rs 32,000 ($650) a month. (Jai Prakash Associates, the biggest dam contractors in the country, the *real* nation-builders, owns the Siddharth Continental and the Vasant Continental Hotels in Delhi.)

On an area of about thirty acres, there is an absurd cement Public Works Department replica of the ancient Shoolpaneshwar temple that was submerged in the reservoir. The same political formation that plunged a whole nation into a bloody, medieval nightmare because it insisted on destroying an old mosque to dig up a nonexistent temple thinks nothing of submerging a hallowed pilgrimage route and hundreds of temples that have been worshiped in for centuries.

It thinks nothing of destroying the sacred hills and groves, the places of worship, the ancient homes of the gods and demons of the Adivasis.

It thinks nothing of submerging a valley that has yielded

fossils, microliths, and rock paintings, the only valley in India, according to archaeologists, that contains an uninterrupted record of human occupation from the Old Stone Age.

What can one say?

In Kevadia Colony, the most barbaric joke of all is the wildlife museum. The Shoolpaneshwar Sanctuary Interpretation Center gives you quick, comprehensive evidence of the government's sincere commitment to conservation.

The Sardar Sarovar reservoir, when the dam reaches its full height, is going to submerge about 13,000 hectares of prime forest land. (In anticipation of submergence, the forest began to be felled many greedy years ago.) Between the Narmada Sagar Dam and the Sardar Sarovar Dam, 50,000 hectares of old-growth, broad-leaved forest will be submerged. Madhya Pradesh has the highest rate of forest-cover loss in the whole of India. This is partly responsible for the reduced flow in the Narmada and the increase in siltation. Have engineers made the connection between forest, rivers, and rain? Unlikely. It isn't part of their brief. Environmentalists and conservationists were quite rightly alarmed at the extent of loss of biodiversity and wildlife habitat that the submergence would cause. To mitigate this loss, the government decided to expand the Shoolpaneshwar Wildlife Sanctuary near the dam, south of the river. There is a harebrained scheme that envisages drowning animals from the submerged forests swimming their way to "wildlife corridors" that will be created for them, and setting up home in the New! Improved! Shoolpaneshwar Sanctuary.

Presumably wildlife and biodiversity can be protected and maintained only if human activity is restricted and traditional rights to use forest resources curtailed. Forty thousand Adivasis from 101 villages within the boundaries of the Shoolpaneshwar Sanctuary depend on the forest for a livelihood. They will be "persuaded" to leave.

They are not included in the definition of "Project Affected."

Where will they go? I imagine you know by now.

Whatever their troubles in the real world, in the Shoolpaneshwar Sanctuary Interpretation Center (where an old stuffed leopard and a moldy sloth bear have to make do with a shared corner) the Adivasis have a whole room to themselves. On the walls there are clumsy wooden carvings, government-approved Adivasi art, with signs that say TRIBAL ART. In the center there is a life-sized thatched hut with the door open. The pot's on the fire, the dog is asleep on the floor, and all's well with the world. Outside, to welcome you, are Mr. and Mrs. Adivasi. A lumpy papier-mâché couple, smiling.

Smiling. They're not even permitted the grace of rage. That's what I can't get over.

Oh, but have I got it wrong? What if they're smiling with national pride? Brimming with the joy of having sacrificed their lives to bring drinking water to thirsty millions in Gujarat?

For twenty years now, the people of Gujarat have waited for the water they believe the Wonder Canal will bring them. For years the government of Gujarat has invested 85 percent of the state's irrigation budget into the Sardar Sarovar Projects. Every smaller, quicker, local, more feasible scheme has been set aside for the sake of this. Election after election has been contested and won on the "water ticket." Everyone's hopes are pinned to the Wonder Canal. Will she fulfill Gujarat's dreams?

From the Sardar Sarovar Dam, the Narmada flows through 180 kilometers of rich lowland into the Arabian Sea in Bharuch. What the Wonder Canal does, more or less, is to reroute most of the river, bending it almost 90 degrees northward. It's a pretty drastic thing to do to a river. The Narmada estuary in Bharuch is one of the last-known breeding places of the hilsa, probably the hottest contender for India's favorite fish.

The Stanley Dam wiped out hilsa from the Cauvery River in South India, and Pakistan's Ghulam Mohammed Dam destroyed its spawning area on the Indus. Hilsa, like the salmon, is an anadromous fish—born in freshwater, migrating to the ocean as a smolt, and returning to the river to spawn. The drastic reduction in water flow, the change in the chemistry of the water because of all the sediment trapped *behind* the dam, will radically alter the ecology of the estuary and modify the delicate balance of freshwater and seawater, which is bound to affect the spawning. At present, the Narmada estuary produces 13,000 metric tons of hilsa and freshwater prawn (which also breeds in brackish water). Ten thousand fisher families depend on it for a living.[67]

The Morse Committee was appalled to discover that no studies had been done of the downstream environment[68]—no documentation of the riverine ecosystem, its seasonal changes, its biological species, or the pattern of how its resources are used. The dam builders had no idea what the impact of the dam would be on the people and the environment downstream, let alone any ideas on what steps to take to mitigate it.

The government simply says that it will alleviate the loss of hilsa fisheries by stocking the reservoir with hatchery-bred fish. (Who'll control the reservoir? Who'll grant the commercial fishing to its favorite paying customers?) The only hitch is that, so far, scientists have not managed to breed hilsa artificially. The rearing of hilsa depends on getting spawn from wild adults, which will in all likelihood be eliminated by the dam. Dams have either eliminated or endangered one-fifth of the world's freshwater fish.[69]

So! Quiz question—where will the 40,000 fisherfolk go? E-mail your answers to The Government That Cares dot com.

At the risk of losing readers—I've been warned several times, "How can you write about *irrigation?* Who the *hell* is interested?"—let me tell you what the Wonder Canal is and what she's meant to achieve. *Be* interested, if you want to snatch your future back from the sweaty palms of the Iron Triangle.

Most rivers in India are monsoon-fed. Eighty to eighty-five percent of the flow takes place during the rainy months—usually between June and September. The purpose of a dam, an irrigation dam, is to store monsoon water in its reservoir and then use it judiciously for the rest of the year, distributing it across dry land through a system of canals. The area of land irrigated by the canal network is called the "command area."

How will the command area, accustomed only to seasonal irrigation, its entire ecology designed for that single pulse of monsoon rain, react to being irrigated the whole year round? Perennial irrigation does to soil roughly what anabolic steroids do to the human body. Steroids can turn an ordinary athlete into an Olympic medal–winner; perennial irrigation can convert soil that produced only a single crop a year into soil that yields *several* crops a year. Land on which farmers traditionally grew crops that don't need a great deal of water (maize, millet, barley, and a whole range of pulses) suddenly yield water-guzzling cash crops—cotton, rice, soybeans, and the biggest guzzler of all (like those finned fifties cars), sugarcane. This completely alters traditional crop patterns in the command area. People stop growing things that they can afford to *eat* and start growing things that they can only afford to *sell*. By linking themselves to the "market" they lose control over their lives.

Ecologically too this is a poisonous payoff. Even if the markets hold out, the soil doesn't. Over time it becomes too poor to support the extra demands made on it. Gradually, in the way a steroid-using athlete becomes an invalid, the soil becomes depleted and degraded, and agricultural yields begin to decrease.[70]

In India, land irrigated by well water is today almost twice as productive as land irrigated by canals.[71] Certain kinds of soil are less suitable for perennial irrigation than others. Perennial canal irrigation raises the level of the water table. As the water moves up through the soil, it absorbs salts. Saline water is drawn to the surface by capillary action, and the land becomes waterlogged. The "logged" water (to coin a phrase) is then breathed into the atmosphere by plants, causing an even greater concentration of salts in the soil. When the concentration of salts in the soil reaches 1 percent, that soil becomes toxic to plant life. This is what's called salinization.

A study[72] by the Center for Resource and Environmental Studies at the Australian National University says that one-fifth of the world's irrigated land is salt affected.

By the mid-1980s, 25 million of the 37 million hectares under irrigation in Pakistan were estimated to be either salinized or waterlogged or both.[73] In India the estimates vary between 6 and 10 million hectares.[74] According to "secret" government studies,[75] more than 52 percent of the Sardar Sarovar command area is prone to waterlogging and salinization.

And that's not the end of the bad news.

The 460-kilometer-long, concrete-lined Sardar Sarovar Wonder Canal and its 75,000-kilometer network of branch canals and sub-branch canals is designed to irrigate a total of 2 million hectares of land spread over twelve districts. The districts of Kutch and Saurashtra (the billboards of Gujarat's thirst campaign) are at the very tail end of this network.

The system of canals superimposes an arbitrary concrete grid on the existing pattern of natural drainage in the command area. It's a little like reorganizing the pattern of reticulate veins on the surface of a leaf. When a canal cuts across the path of a natural drain, it blocks the flow of the natural, seasonal water and leads to waterlogging. The engineering solution to this is to map the pattern of natural drainage in the area and replace it with an alternate artificial drainage system that is built in conjunction with the canals. The problem, as you can imagine, is that doing this is enormously expensive. The cost of drainage is not included as part of the Sardar Sarovar Projects. It usually isn't, in most irrigation projects.

David Hopper, the World Bank's vice president for South Asia, has admitted[76] that the Bank does not usually include the cost of drainage in its irrigation projects in South Asia because irrigation projects *with* adequate drainage are just too expensive. *It costs five times as much to provide adequate drainage as it does to irrigate the same amount of land.* It makes the cost of a complete project appear unviable.

The Bank's solution to the problem is to put in the irrigation system and wait—for salinity and waterlogging to set in. When all the money's spent and the land is devastated and the people are in despair, who should pop by? Why, the friendly neighborhood banker! And what's that bulge in his pocket? Could it be a loan for a drainage project?

In Pakistan, the World Bank financed the Tarbela (1977) and Mangla dam (1967) projects on the Indus. The command areas are waterlogged.[77] Now the Bank has given Pakistan a $785 million loan for a drainage project. In India, in Punjab and in Haryana, it's doing the same.

Irrigation without drainage is like having a system of arteries and no veins. Pretty damn pointless.

Since the World Bank stepped back from the Sardar Sarovar Projects, it's a little unclear where the money for the drainage is going to come from. This hasn't deterred the government from going ahead with the canal work. The result is that even before the dam is ready, before the Wonder Canal has been commissioned, before a single drop of irrigation water has been delivered, waterlogging has set in. Among the worst-affected areas are the resettlement colonies.

There is a difference between the planners of the Sardar Sarovar irrigation scheme and the planners of previous projects. At least they acknowledge that water-logging and salinization are *real* problems and need to be addressed.

Their solutions, however, are corny enough to send a Hoolock gibbon to a hooting hospital.

They plan to have a series of electronic groundwater sensors placed in every 100 square kilometers of the command area. (That works out to about 1,800 ground sensors.) These will be linked to a central computer that will analyze the data and send out commands to the canal heads to stop water flowing into areas that show signs of waterlogging. A network of "Only irrigation," "Only drainage," and "Irrigation cum drainage" tube-wells will be sunk, and electronically synchronized by the central computer. The saline water will be pumped out, mixed with mathematically computed quantities of freshwater, and then recirculated into a network of surface and subsurface drains (for which more land will be acquired).[78]

To achieve the irrigation efficiency that they claim they'll achieve, according to a study done by Dr. Rahul Ram for Kalpavriksh,[79] 82 percent of the water that goes into the Wonder Canal network will have to be pumped out again!

They've never implemented an electronic irrigation scheme before, not even as a pilot project. It hasn't occurred to them to experiment with some already degraded land, just to see if it works. No, they'll use our money to install it over the whole of the 2 million hectares and *then* see if it works.

What if it doesn't? If it doesn't, it won't matter to the planners. They'll still draw the same salaries. They'll still get their pensions and their bonuses and whatever else you get when you retire from a career of inflicting mayhem on a people.

How can it possibly work? It's like sending in a rocket scientist to milk a troublesome cow. How can they manage a gigantic electronic irrigation system when they can't even line the walls of the canals without having them collapse and cause untold damage to crops and people?

When they can't even prevent the Big Dam itself from breaking off in bits when it rains?

To quote from one of their own studies: "The design, the implementation and management of the integration of groundwater and surface water in the above circumstance is complex."[80]

Agreed. To say the least.

Their recommendation of how to deal with the complexity: "It will only be possible to implement such a system if all groundwater and surface water supplies are managed by a single authority."[81]

Aha!

It's beginning to make sense now. Who will own the water? The Single Authority.

Who will sell the water? The Single Authority.

Who will profit from the sales? The Single Authority.

The Single Authority has a scheme whereby it will sell water by the liter, not to individuals but to farmers' cooperatives (which don't exist just yet, but no doubt the Single Authority can create cooperatives and force farmers to cooperate).

Computer water, unlike ordinary river water, is expensive. Only those who can afford it will get it. Gradually, small farmers will get edged out by big farmers, and the whole cycle of uprootment will begin all over again.

The Single Authority, because it owns the computer water, will also decide who will grow what. It says that farmers getting computer water will not be allowed to grow sugarcane because they'll use up the share of the thirsty millions who live at the tail end of the canal. But the Single Authority has *already* given licenses to ten large sugar mills right near the head of the canal.[82] The chief promoter of one of them is Sanat Mehta, who was chairman of the Sardar Sarovar Narmada Nigam for several years. The chief promoter of another sugar mill was Chimanbhai Patel, former chief minister of Gujarat. He (along with his wife) was the most vocal, ardent proponent of the Sardar Sarovar Dam. When he died, his ashes were scattered over the dam site.

In Maharashtra, thanks to a different branch of the Single Authority, the politically powerful sugar lobby that occupies one-tenth of the state's irrigated land uses *half* the state's irrigation water.

In addition to the sugar growers, the Single Authority has recently announced a scheme[83] that envisages a series of five-star hotels, golf courses, and water parks that will come up along the Wonder Canal. What earthly reason could possibly justify this?

The Single Authority says it's the only way to raise money to complete the project!

I really worry about those millions of good people in Kutch and Saurashtra.

Will the water *ever* reach them?

First of all, we know that there's a lot less water in the river than the Single Authority claims there is.

Second of all, in the absence of the Narmada Sagar Dam, the irrigation benefits of the Sardar Sarovar drop by a further 17 to 30 percent.

Third of all, the irrigation efficiency of the Wonder Canal (the actual amount of water delivered by the system) has been arbitrarily fixed at 60 percent. The *highest* irrigation efficiency in India, taking into account system leaks and surface evaporation, is 35 percent.[84] This means it's likely that only half of the command area will be irrigated.

Which half? The first half.

Fourth, to get to Kutch and Saurashtra, the Wonder Canal has to negotiate its way past the ten sugar mills, the golf courses, the five-star hotels, the water parks, and the cash-crop-growing, politically powerful, Patel-rich districts of Baroda, Kheda, Ahmedabad, Gandhinagar, and Mehsana. (Already, in complete contravention of its own directives, the Single Authority has allotted the city of Baroda a sizable quantity of water.[85] When Baroda gets it, can Ahmedabad be left behind? The political clout of powerful urban centers in Gujarat will ensure that they secure their share.)

Fifth, even in the (100 percent) unlikely event that water gets there, it has to be piped and distributed to those eight thousand waiting villages.

It's worth knowing that of the one billion people in the world who have no access to safe drinking water, 855 million live in rural areas.[86] This is because the cost of installing an energy-intensive network of thousands of kilometers of pipelines, aqueducts, pumps, and treatment plants that would be needed to provide drinking water to scattered rural populations is prohibitive. *Nobody* builds Big Dams to provide drinking water to rural people. Nobody can *afford* to.

When the Morse Committee first arrived in Gujarat, it was impressed by the Gujarat government's commitment to taking drinking water to such distant rural districts.[87] The members of the committee asked to see the detailed drinking-water plans. There weren't any. (There still aren't any.)

They asked if any costs had been worked out. "A few thousand crores" was the breezy answer.[88] A billion dollars is an expert's calculated guess. It's not included as part of the project cost. So where is the money going to come from?

Never mind. Jus' askin'.

It's interesting that the Farakka Barrage that diverts water from the Ganga to Calcutta Port has reduced the drinking water availability for forty million people who live downstream in Bangladesh.[89]

At times there's something so precise and mathematically chilling about nationalism.

Build a dam to take water *away* from forty million people. Build a dam to pretend to *bring* water to forty million people.

Who are these gods that govern us? Is there no limit to their powers?

The last person I met in the valley was Bhaiji Bhai. He is a Tadvi Adivasi from Undava, one of the first villages where the government began to acquire land for the Wonder Canal and its 75,000-kilometer network. Bhaiji Bhai lost seventeen of his nineteen acres to the Wonder Canal. It crashes through his land, 700 feet wide including its walkways and steep, sloping embankments, like a velodrome for giant bicyclists.

The canal network affects more than 200,000 families. People have lost wells and trees, people have had their houses separated from their farms by the canal, forcing them to walk 2 or 3 kilometers to the nearest bridge and then 2 or 3 kilometers back along the other side. Twenty-three thousand families, let's say 100,000 people, will be, like Bhaiji Bhai, seriously affected. They don't count as "Project Affected" and are not entitled to rehabilitation.

Like his neighbors in Kevadia Colony, Bhaiji Bhai became a pauper overnight.

Bhaiji Bhai and his people, forced to smile for photographs on government calendars. Bhaiji Bhai and his people, denied the grace of rage. Bhaiji Bhai and his people, squashed like bugs by this country they're supposed to call their own.

It was late evening when I arrived at his house. We sat down on the floor and drank oversweet tea in the dying light. As he spoke, a memory stirred in me, a sense of déjà vu. I couldn't imagine why. I knew I hadn't met him before. Then I realized what it was. I didn't recognize him, but I remembered his story. I'd seen him in an old documentary film, shot more than ten years ago in the valley. He was frailer now, his beard softened with age. But his story hadn't aged. It was still young and full of passion. It broke my heart, the patience with which he told it. I could tell he had told it over and over and over again, hoping, praying, that one day, one of the strangers passing through Undava would turn out to be Good Luck. Or God.

Bhaiji Bhai, Bhaiji Bhai, when will you get angry? When will you stop waiting? When will you say "That's enough!" and reach for your weapons, whatever they may be? When will you show us the whole of your resonant, terrifying, invincible strength? When will you break the faith? *Will* you break the faith? Or will you let it break you?

To slow a beast, you break its limbs. To slow a nation, you break its people. You rob them of volition. You demonstrate your absolute command over their destiny. You make it clear that ultimately it falls to you to decide who lives, who dies, who prospers, who doesn't. To exhibit your capability you show off all that you can do, and how easily you can do it. How easily you could press a button and annihilate the earth. How you can start a war or sue for peace. How you can snatch a river away from one and gift it to another. How you can green a desert, or fell a forest and plant one somewhere else. You use caprice to fracture a people's faith in ancient things—earth, forest, water, air.

Once that's done, what do they have left? Only you. They will turn to you because you're all they have. They will love you even while they despise you. They will trust you even though they know you well. They will vote for you even as you squeeze the very breath from their bodies. They will drink what you give them to drink. They will breathe what you give them to breathe. They will live where you dump their belongings. They have to. What else can they do? There's no higher court of redress. You are their mother and their father. You are the judge and the jury. You are the World. You are God.

Power is fortified not just by what it destroys but also by what it creates. Not just by what it takes but also by what it gives. And powerlessness reaffirmed not just by the helplessness of those who have lost but also by the gratitude of those who have (or *think* they have) gained.

This cold contemporary cast of power is couched between the lines of noble-sounding clauses in democratic-sounding constitutions. It's wielded by the elected representatives of an ostensibly free people. Yet no monarch, no despot, no dictator in any other century in the history of human civilization has had access to weapons like these.

Day by day, river by river, forest by forest, mountain by mountain, missile by missile, bomb by bomb—almost without our knowing it—we are being broken.

Big Dams are to a nation's "development" what nuclear bombs are to its military arsenal. They're both weapons of mass destruction. They're both weapons governments use to control their own people. Both twentieth-century emblems that mark a point in time when human intelligence has outstripped its own instinct for survival. They're both malignant indications of a civilization turning upon itself. They represent the severing of the link, not just the link—the *understanding*—between human beings and the planet they live on. They scramble the intelligence that connects eggs to hens, milk to cows, food to forests, water to rivers, air to life, and the earth to human existence.

Can we unscramble it?

Maybe. Inch by inch. Bomb by bomb. Dam by dam. Maybe by fighting specific wars in specific ways. We could begin in the Narmada valley.

This July will bring the last monsoon of the twentieth century. The ragged army in the Narmada valley has declared that it will not move when the waters of the Sardar Sarovar reservoir rise to claim its lands and homes. Whether you love the dam or hate it, whether you want it or you don't, it is in the fitness of things that you understand the price that's being paid for it. That you have the courage to watch while the dues are cleared and the books are squared.

Our dues. Our books. Not theirs.

Be there.

POWER POLITICS:
THE REINCARNATION
OF RUMPELSTILTSKIN

Remember him? The gnome who could turn straw into gold? Well, he's back now, but you wouldn't recognize him. To begin with, he's not an individual gnome anymore. I'm not sure how best to describe him. Let's just say he's metamorphosed into an accretion, a cabal, an assemblage, a malevolent, incorporeal, transnational multi-gnome. Rumpelstiltskin is a notion (gnotion), a piece of deviant, insidious white logic that will eventually self-annihilate. But for now, he's more than okay. He's cock of the walk. King of All That Really Counts (Cash). He's decimated the competition, killed all the other kings, the other kinds of kings. He's persuaded us that he's all we have left. Our only salvation.

What kind of potentate is Rumpelstiltskin? Powerful, pitiless, and armed to the teeth. He's a kind of king the world has never known before. His realm is raw capital, his conquests emerging markets, his prayers profits, his borders limitless, his weapons

---

First published in *Outlook*, November 27, 2000.

nuclear. To even try and imagine him, to hold the whole of him in your field of vision, is to situate yourself at the very edge of sanity, to offer yourself up for ridicule. King Rumpel reveals only part of himself at a time. He has a bank account heart. He has television eyes and a newspaper nose in which you see only what he wants you to see and read only what he wants you to read. (See what I mean about the edge of sanity?) There's more: a Surround Sound stereo mouth that amplifies his voice and filters out the sound of the rest of the world, so that you can't hear it even when it's shouting (or starving, or dying), and King Rumpel is only whispering, rolling his *r*'s in his North American way.

Listen carefully. This is most of the rest of his story. (It hasn't ended yet, but it will. It must.) It ranges across seas and continents, sometimes majestic and universal, sometimes confining and local. Now and then I'll peg it down with disparate bits of history and geography that could mar the gentle art of storytelling. So please bear with me.

In March this year (AD 2000), the president of the United States (H.E., the most exalted plenipotentiary of Rumpeldom) visited India. He brought his own bed, the feather pillow he hugs at night, and a merry band of businessmen. He was courted and fawned over by the genuflecting representatives of this ancient civilization with a fervor that can only be described as indecent. Whole cities were superficially spruced up. The poor were herded away, hidden from the presidential gaze. Streets were soaped and scrubbed and festooned with balloons and welcome banners. In Delhi's dirty sky, vindicated nuclear hawks banked and whistled: *Dekho ji dekho!* (Look, sir! Look!) Bill is here because we have the Bomb.

Those Indian citizens with even a modicum of self-respect were so ashamed they stayed in bed for days. Some of us had puzzled furrows on our brows. Since everybody behaved like a craven, happy slave when Master visited, we wondered why we hadn't gone the whole distance. Why hadn't we just crawled under Master's nuclear umbrella in the first place? Then we could spend our pocket money on other things (instead of bombs) and still be all safe and slavey. No?

Just before The Visit, the Government of India lifted import restrictions on fourteen hundred commodities, including milk, grain, sugar, and cotton (even though there was a glut of sugar and cotton in the market, even though 42 million tons of grain were rotting in government storehouses). During The Visit, contracts worth about three (some say four) billion US dollars were signed.[1]

For reasons of my own, I was particularly interested in a Memorandum of Intent signed by the Ogden Energy Group, a company that specializes in operating garbage incinerators in the United States, and S. Kumars, an Indian textile company that manufactures what it calls "suiting blends."[2]

Now what might garbage incineration and suiting blends possibly have in common? Suit-incineration? Guess again. Garbage-blends? Nope. A big hydroelectric dam on the River Narmada in central India. Neither Ogden nor S. Kumars has ever built or operated a large dam before.

The 400-megawatt Shri Maheshwar Hydel Project being promoted by S. Kumars is part of the Narmada Valley Development Project, which boasts of being the most ambitious river valley project in the world. It envisages building 3,200 dams (30 big dams, 135 medium dams, and the rest small) that will reconstitute the Narmada and her forty-one tributaries into a series of step reservoirs. It will alter the ecology of an entire river basin, affect the lives of about twenty-five million people who live in the valley, and submerge 4,000 square kilometers of old-growth deciduous forest and hundreds of temples, as well as archaeological sites dating back to the Lower Paleolithic Age.[3]

The dams that have been built on the river so far are all government projects. The Maheshwar Dam is slated to be India's first major private hydel power project.

What is interesting about this is not only that it's part of the most bitterly opposed river valley project in India, but also that it is a strand in the skein of a mammoth global enterprise. Understanding what is happening in Maheshwar, decoding the nature of the deals that are being struck between two of the world's great democracies, will go a long way toward gaining a rudimentary grasp of what is being done to us, while we, poor fools, stand by and clap and cheer and hasten things along. (When I say "us," I mean people, human beings. Not countries, not governments.)

Personally, I took the first step toward arriving at this understanding when, over a few days in March this year (AD 2000), I lived through a writer's bad dream. I witnessed the ritualistic slaughter of language as I know and understand it. Let me explain.

On the very days that President Clinton was in India, in faraway Holland the World Water Forum was convened.[4] Four thousand five hundred bankers, businessmen, government ministers, policy writers, engineers, economists—and, in order to pretend that the "other side" was also represented, a handful of activists, indigenous dance troupes, impoverished street theater groups, and half a dozen young girls dressed as inflatable silver faucets—gathered at The Hague to discuss the future of the world's water. Every speech was generously peppered with phrases like "women's empowerment," "people's participation," and "deepening democracy." Yet it turned out that the whole purpose of the forum was to press for the privatization of the world's water. There was pious talk of having access to drinking water declared a Basic Human Right. How would this be implemented, you might ask. Simple. By putting a market value on water. By selling it at its "true price." (It's common knowledge that water is becoming a scarce resource. One billion people in the world have no access to safe drinking water.)[5] The "market" decrees that the scarcer something is, the more expensive it becomes. But there is a difference between valuing water and putting a market value on water. No one values water more than a village woman who has to walk miles to fetch it. No one values it less than urban folk who pay for it to flow endlessly at the turn of a tap.

So the talk of connecting human rights to a "true price" was more than a little baffling. At first I didn't quite get their drift. Did they believe in human rights for the rich, that only the rich are human, or that all humans are rich? But I see it now. A shiny, climate-controlled human rights supermarket with a clearance sale on Christmas Day.

One marrowy American panelist put it rather nicely: "God gave us the rivers," he drawled, "but he didn't put in the delivery systems. That's why we need private enterprise." No doubt with a little Structural Adjustment to the rest of the things God gave us, we could all live in a simpler world. (If all the seas were one sea, what a big sea it would be . . . Evian could own the water, Rand the earth, Enron the air. Old Rumpelstiltskin could be the handsomely paid supreme CEO.)

When all the rivers and valleys and forests and hills of the world have been priced, packaged, bar-coded, and stacked in the local supermarket, when all the hay and coal and earth and wood and water have been turned to gold, what then shall we do with all the gold? Make nuclear bombs to obliterate what's left of the ravaged landscapes and the notional nations in our ruined world?

As a writer, one spends a lifetime journeying into the heart of language, trying to minimize, if not eliminate, the distance between language and thought. "Language is the skin on my thought," I remember saying to someone who once asked what language meant to me. At The Hague I stumbled on a denomination, a sub-world, whose life's endeavor was entirely the opposite of mine. For them the whole purpose of language is to mask intent. They earn their abundant livings by converting bar graphs that plot their companies' profits into consummately written, politically exemplary, socially just policy documents that are impossible to implement and designed to remain forever on paper, secret even (especially) from the people they're written for. They breed and prosper in the space that lies between what they say and what they sell. What they're lobbying for is not simply the privatization of natural resources and essential infrastructure, but the privatization of policy making itself. Dam builders want to control public water policies. Power utility companies want to draft power policies, and financial institutions want to supervise government disinvestment.

Let's begin at the beginning. What does privatization really mean? Essentially, it is the transfer of productive public assets from the state to private companies. Productive assets include natural resources. Earth, forest, water, air. These are assets that the state holds in trust for the people it represents. In a country like India, 70 percent of the population lives in rural areas.[6] That's seven hundred million people. Their lives depend directly on access to natural resources. To snatch these away and sell them as stock to private companies is a process of barbaric dispossession on a scale that has no parallel in history.

What happens when you "privatize" something as essential to human survival as water? What happens when you commodify water and say that only those who can come up with the cash to pay the "market price" can have it?

In 1999, the government of Bolivia privatized the public water supply system in the city of Cochabamba and signed a forty-year lease with a consortium headed by Bechtel, a giant US engineering firm. The first thing Bechtel did was to raise the price of water. Hundreds of thousands of people simply couldn't afford it anymore. Citizens came out on the streets to protest. A transport strike brought the entire city to a standstill. Hugo Banzer, the former Bolivian dictator (then the president), ordered the police to confront the crowds. One person was killed, and many more were injured. The protest continued because people had no options—what's the option to thirst? In April 2000, Banzer declared martial law. The protest continued. Eventually Bechtel was forced to flee its offices. Many people expect Bechtel will try to extort a $12 million exit payment from the Bolivian government for loss of future profits.[7]

Cochabamba has a population of six hundred thousand people. Think of what would happen in an Indian city. Even a small one.

Rumpelstiltskin thinks big. Today he's stalking mega-game: dams, mines, armaments, power plants, public water supply, telecommunications, the management and dissemination of knowledge, biodiversity, seeds (he wants to own life and the very process of reproduction), and the industrial infrastructure that supports all this. His minions arrive in third world countries masquerading as missionaries come to redeem the wretched. They have a completely different dossier in their briefcases. To understand what they're really saying (selling), you have to teach yourself to unscramble their vernacular.

Recently Jack Welch, the CEO of General Electric (GE), was on TV in India. "I beg and pray to the Indian government to improve infrastructure," he said, and added touchingly, "Don't do it for GE's sake, do it for yourselves." He went on to say that privatizing the power sector was the only way to bring India's one billion people into the digital network. "You can talk about information and intellectual capital, but without the power to drive it, you will miss the next revolution."[8]

What he meant, of course, was "You are a market of one billion customers. If you don't buy our equipment, *we* will miss the next revolution."

Will someone please tell Jack Welch that of his one billion "customers," three hundred million are illiterate and live without even one square meal a day, and two hundred million have no access to safe drinking water?[9] Being brought into the "digital framework" is hardly what's uppermost on their minds.

The story behind the story is as follows: There are four corporations that dominate the production of power-generation equipment in the world. GE is one of them. Together, each year they manufacture (and therefore need to sell) equipment that can generate at least 20,000 megawatts of power.[10] For a variety of reasons, there is little (read: almost zero) additional demand for power equipment in the first world. This leaves these mammoth multinationals with a redundant capacity that they desperately need to offload. India and China are their big target markets because, between these two countries, the demand for power-generating equipment is 10,000 megawatts per year.[11]

The first world needs to sell, the third world needs to buy—it ought to be a reasonable business proposition. But it isn't. For many years, India has been more or less self-sufficient in power equipment. The Indian public sector company Bharat Heavy Electricals (BHEL) manufactured and even exported world-class power equipment. All that's changed now. Over the years, our own government has starved it of orders, cut off funds for research and development, and more or less edged it out of a dignified existence. Today BHEL is no more than a sweatshop. It is being forced into "joint ventures" (one with GE and one with Siemens) in which its only role is to provide cheap, unskilled labor while they—Siemens and GE—provide the equipment and the technology.[12]

Why? Why does more expensive imported equipment suit our bureaucrats and politicians better? We all know why. Because graft is factored into the deal. Buying equipment from your local store is just not the same thing. It's not surprising that almost half the officials named in the major corruption scandal that came to be known as the Jain Hawala case were officials from the power sector involved with the selection and purchase of power equipment.[13]

The privatization of power (felicitous phrase!) is at the top of the Indian government's agenda. The United States is the single largest foreign investor in the power sector (which, to some extent, explains The Visit).[14] The argument being advanced (both by the government and by the private sector) in favor of privatization is that over the last fifty years the government has bungled its brief. It has failed to deliver. The State Electricity Boards (SEBs) are insolvent. Inefficiency, corruption, theft, and heavy subsidies have run them into the ground.

In the push for privatization, the customary depiction of the corrupt, oily third world government official selling his country's interests for personal profit fits perfectly into the scheme of things. The private sector bristles accusingly. The government coyly acknowledges the accusation and pleads its inability to reform itself. In fact, it goes out of its way to exaggerate its own inefficiencies. This is meant to come across as refreshing candor.

In a speech he made just before he died, Minister for Power P. R. Kumaramangalam said that the overall figure of loss and deficit in the power sector was 7.86 billion US dollars. He went on to say that India's transmission and distribution (T&D) losses are between 35 and 40 percent. Of the remaining 60 percent, according to the minister, billing is restricted to only 40 percent. His conclusion: that only about a quarter of the electricity that is produced in India is metered.[15] Official sources say that this is a somewhat exaggerated account. The situation is bad enough. It doesn't need to be exaggerated. According to figures put out by the Power Ministry, the national average T&D losses are 23 percent. In 1947 they were 14.39 percent. Even without the minister's hyperbole, this puts India in the same league as countries with the worst T&D losses in the world, like the Dominican Republic, Myanmar, and Bangladesh.[16]

The solution to this malaise, we discover, is not to improve our housekeeping skills, not to try and minimize our losses, not to force the state to be more accountable, but to permit it to abdicate its responsibility altogether and privatize the power sector. Then magic will happen. Economic viability and Swiss-style efficiency will kick in like clockwork.

But there's a subplot missing in this narrative. Over the years, the SEBs have been bankrupted by massive power thefts. Who's stealing the power? Some of it no doubt is stolen by the poor—slum dwellers, people who live in unauthorized colonies on the fringes of big cities. But they don't have the electrical gadgetry to consume the quantum of electricity we're talking about. The big stuff, the megawatt thievery, is orchestrated by the industrial sector in connivance with politicians and government officers.

Consider as an example the state of Madhya Pradesh, in which the Maheshwar Dam is being built. Seven years ago it was a power surplus state. Today it finds itself in an intriguing situation. Industrial demand has declined by 30 percent. Power production has increased from 3,813 megawatts to 4,025 megawatts. And the State Electricity Board is showing a loss of $255 million. An inspection drive solved the puzzle. It found that 70 percent of the industrialists in the state steal electricity![17] The theft adds up to a loss of nearly $106 million. That's 41 percent of the total deficit. Madhya Pradesh is by no means an unusual example. States like Orissa, Andhra Pradesh, and Delhi have T&D losses of between 30 and 50 percent (way over the national average), which indicates massive power theft.[18]

No one talks very much about this. It's so much nicer to blame the poor. The average economist, planner, or drawing-room intellectual will tell you that the SEBs have gone belly up for two reasons: (a) because "political compulsions" ensure that domestic power tariffs are kept unviably low, and (b) because subsidies given to the farm sector result in enormous hidden losses.

The first step that a "reformed" privatized power sector is expected to take is to cut agricultural subsidies and put a "realistic" tariff (market value) on power.

What are political compulsions? Why are they considered such a bad thing? Basically, it seems to me, *political compulsions* is a phrase that describes the fancy footwork that governments have to perform in order to strike a balance between redeeming a sinking economy and serving an impoverished electorate. Striking a balance between what the market demands and what people can afford is—or certainly ought to be—the primary, fundamental responsibility of any democratic government. Privatization seeks to disengage politics from the market. To do that would be to blunt the very last weapon that India's poor still have—their vote. Once that's gone, elections will become even more of a charade than they already are, and democracy will just become the name of a new rock band. The poor will be absent from the negotiating table. They will simply cease to matter.

But the cry has already gone up. The demand to cut subsidies has almost become a blood sport. It's a small world. Bolivia is only a short walk down the road from here.

When it recommends privatizing the power sector, does the government mean that it is going to permit just anybody who wishes to generate power to come in and compete in a free market? Of course not. There's nothing free about the market in the power sector. Reforming the power sector in India means that the concerned state government underwrites preposterously one-sided Power Purchase Agreements with select companies, preferably huge multinationals. Essentially, it is the transfer of assets and infrastructure from bribe taker to bribe giver, which involves more bribery than ever. Once the agreements are signed, the companies are free to produce power at exorbitant rates that no one can afford. Not even, ironically enough, the Indian industrialists who have been rooting for them all along. They, poor chaps, end up like vultures on a carcass that get chased off by a visiting hyena.

The fishbowl of the drive to privatize power, its truly star turn, is the story of Enron, the Houston-based natural gas company.[19] The Enron project was the first private power project in India. The Power Purchase Agreement between Enron and the Congress Party–ruled State Government of Maharashtra for a 695-megawatt power plant was signed in 1993. The opposition parties, the Hindu nationalist Bharatiya Janata Party (BJP) and the Shiv Sena, set up a howl of *swadeshi* (nationalist) protest and filed legal proceedings against Enron and the state government. They alleged malfeasance and corruption at the highest level. A year later, when state elections were announced, it was the only campaign issue of the BJP–Shiv Sena alliance.

In February 1995, this alliance won the elections. True to their word, they "scrapped" the project. In a savage, fiery statement, the opposition leader L. K. Advani attacked the phenomenon he called "loot-through-liberalization."[20] He more or less directly accused the Congress Party government of having taken a $13 million bribe from Enron. Enron had made no secret of the fact that, in order to secure the deal, it had paid out millions of dollars to "educate" the politicians and bureaucrats involved in the deal.[21]

Following the annulment of the contract, the US government began to pressure the Maharashtra government. US ambassador Frank Wisner made several statements deploring the cancelation. (Soon after he completed his term as ambassador, he joined Enron as a director.)[22] In November 1995, the BJP–Shiv Sena government in Maharashtra announced a "renegotiation" committee. In May 1996, a minority federal government headed by the BJP was sworn in at New Delhi. It lasted for exactly thirteen days and then resigned before facing a vote of no confidence in Parliament. On its last day in office, even as the motion of no confidence was in progress, the cabinet met for a hurried "lunch" and reratified the national government's counter-guarantee (which had become void because of the earlier "canceled" contract with Enron). In August 1996, the government of Maharashtra signed a fresh contract with Enron on terms that would astound the most hardboiled cynic.[23]

The impugned contract had involved annual payments to Enron of $430 million for Phase I (695 megawatts) of the project, with Phase II (2,015 megawatts) being optional. The "renegotiated" Power Purchase Agreement makes Phase II of the project mandatory and legally binds the Maharashtra State Electricity Board (MSEB) to pay Enron a sum of $30 billion! It constitutes the largest contract ever signed in the history of India.

In India, experts who have studied the project have called it the most massive fraud in the country's history. The project's gross profits work out to between $12 and $14 billion. The official return on equity is more than 30 percent.[24] That's almost double what Indian law and statutes permit in power projects. In effect, for an increase in installed capacity of 18 percent, the MSEB has to set aside 70 percent of its revenue to be able to pay Enron. There is, of course, no record of what mathematical formula was used to "reeducate" the new government. Nor any trace of how much trickled up or down or sideways and to whom.

But there's more: in one of the most extraordinary decisions in its not entirely pristine history, in May 1997 the Supreme Court of India refused to entertain an appeal against Enron.[25]

Today, four years later, everything that critics of the project predicted has come true with an eerie vengeance. The power that the Enron plant produces is twice as expensive as that of its nearest competitor and seven times as expensive as the cheapest electricity available in Maharashtra.[26] In May 2000, the Maharashtra Electricity Regulatory Committee (MERC) ruled that temporarily, until as long as was absolutely necessary, no power should be bought from Enron.[27] It was based on a calculation that it would be cheaper to just pay Enron the mandatory fixed charges for the maintenance and administration of the plant that they are contractually obliged to pay than to actually buy any of its exorbitant power. The fixed charges alone work out to around $220 million a year for Phase I of the project. Phase II will be nearly twice the size.

Two hundred and twenty million dollars a year for the next twenty years.

Meanwhile, industrialists in Maharashtra have begun to generate their own power at a much cheaper rate, with private generators. The demand for power from the industrial sector has begun to decline rapidly. The SEB, strapped for cash, with Enron hanging like an albatross around its neck, will now have no choice but to make private generators illegal. That's the only way that industrialists can be coerced into buying Enron's exorbitantly priced electricity.

According to the MSEB's calculations, from January 2002 onward, even if it were to buy 90 percent of Enron's output, its losses will amount to $1.2 billion a year.

That's more than 60 percent of India's annual rural development budget.[28]

In contravention of the MERC ruling, the MSEB is cutting back production from its own cheaper plants in order to buy electricity from Enron. Hundreds of small industrial units have closed down because they cannot afford such expensive electricity.

In January 2001, the Maharashtra government (the Congress Party is back in power with a new chief minister) announced that it did not have the money to pay Enron's bills. On January 31, only five days after the earthquake in the neighboring state of Gujarat, at a time when the country was still reeling from the disaster, the newspapers announced that Enron had decided to invoke the counter-guarantee and that if the government did not come up with the cash, it would have to auction the government properties named as collateral security in the contract.[29]

At the time that this book [*Power Politics*] is going to press, Enron and the government of Maharashtra are locked in a legal battle in the High Court of the State of Maharashtra. But Enron has friends in high places.[30] It was one of the biggest corporate contributors to president George W. Bush's election campaign. President Bush has helped Enron with its global business from as far back as 1998. So the old circus has started up all over again. The former US ambassador (Richard Celeste this time) publicly chastised the Maharashtra chief minister for reneging on payments.[31] US government officials have warned India about vitiating the "investment climate" and running the risk of frightening away future investors. In other words: Allow us to rob you blind, or else we'll go away.

The pressure is on for re-re-negotiation. Who knows, perhaps Phase III is on the anvil.

In business circles, the Enron contract is called "the sweetheart deal." A euphemism for rape without redress. There are plenty of Enron clones in the pipeline. Indian citizens have a lot to look forward to.

Here's to the "free" market.

Having said all this, there's no doubt that there *is* a power-shortage crisis in India. But there's another, more serious crisis on hand.

Planners in India boast that India consumes twenty times more electricity today than it did fifty years ago. They use it as an index of progress. They omit to mention that 70 percent of rural households still have no electricity.[32] In the poorest states, Bihar, Uttar Pradesh, and Orissa, more than 85 percent of the poorest people, mostly Dalit and Adivasi households, have no electricity. What a shameful, shocking record for the world's biggest democracy.

Unless this crisis is acknowledged and honestly addressed, generating "lots and lots of power" (as Mr. Welch put it) will only mean that it will be siphoned off by the rich with their endless appetites. It will require a very imaginative, very radical form of "structural adjustment" to right this.

"Privatization" is presented as being the only alternative to an inefficient, corrupt state. In fact, it's not a choice at all. It's only made to look like one. Essentially, privatization is a mutually profitable business contract between the private (preferably foreign) company or financial institution and the ruling elite of the third world. (One of the fallouts is that even corruption becomes an elitist affair. Your average small-fry government official is in grave danger of losing his or her bit on the side.)

India's politicians have virtually mortgaged their country to the World Bank. Today, India pays back more money in interest and repayment installments than it receives. It is forced to incur new debts in order to repay old ones.[33] In other words, it's exporting capital. Of late, however, institutions like the World Bank and the International Monetary Fund, which have bled the third world all these years, look like benevolent saints compared to the new mutants in the market. These are known as ECAs—export credit agencies. If the World Bank is a colonizing army hamstrung by red tape and bureaucracy, the ECAs are freewheeling, marauding mercenaries.

Basically, ECAs insure private companies operating in foreign countries against commercial and political risks. The device is called an export credit guarantee. It's quite simple, really. No first world private company wants to export capital or goods or services to a politically and/or economically unstable country without insuring itself against unforeseen contingencies. So the private company covers itself with an export credit guarantee. The ECA, in turn, has an agreement with the government of its own country. The government of its own country has an agreement with the government of the importing country. The upshot of this fine imbrication is that if a situation does arise in which the ECA has to pay its client, its own government pays the ECA and recovers its money by adding it to the bilateral debt owed by the importing country. (So the real guarantors are actually, once again, the poorest people in the poorest countries.) Complicated, but cool. And foolproof.

The quadrangular private company–ECA–government–government formation neatly circumvents political accountability. Though they're all actually business associates, flak from noisy, tiresome nongovernmental organizations and activist groups can be diverted and funneled to the ECA, where, like noxious industrial effluent, it lies in cooling ponds before being disposed of. The attraction of the ECAs (for both governments and private companies) is that they are secretive and don't bother with tedious details like human rights violations and environmental guidelines. (The rare ones that do, like the US Export-Import Bank, are under pressure to change.) It short-circuits lumbering World Bank–style bureaucracy. It makes projects like Big Dams (which involve the displacement and impoverishment of large numbers of people, which in turn is politically risky) that much easier to finance. With an ECA guarantee, "developers" can go ahead and dig and quarry and mine and dam the hell out of people's lives without having to even address, never mind answer, embarrassing questions.

Now, coming back to Maheshwar . . .

In order to place India's first private Big Dam in perspective, I need to briefly set out the short, vulgar history of Big Dams in India in general and on the Narmada in particular.

The international dam industry alone is worth $32 to $46 billion a year.[34] In the first world, dams are being decommissioned, blown up. That leaves us with another industry threatened with redundancy desperately in search of dumping grounds. Fortunately (for the industry) most third world countries, India especially, are deeply committed to Big Dams.

India has the third largest number of Big Dams in the world. Three thousand six hundred Indian dams qualify as Big Dams under the ICOLD (International Commission on Large Dams) definition. Six hundred and ninety-five more are under construction. This means that 40 percent of all the Big Dams being built in the world are being built in India.[35] For reasons more cynical than honorable, politicians and planners have successfully portrayed Big Dams to an unquestioning public as symbols of nationalism—huge, wet cement flags. Jawaharlal Nehru's famous speech about Big Dams being "the temples of modern India" has made its way into primary school textbooks in every Indian language.[36] Every schoolchild is taught that Big Dams will deliver the people of India from hunger and poverty.

Will they? Have they?

To merely ask these questions is to invite accusations of sedition, of being antinational, of being a spy, and, most ludicrous of all, of receiving "foreign funds." The distinguished home minister, Mr. Advani, while speaking at the inauguration of construction at the Sardar Sarovar dam site on October 31, 2000, said that the three greatest achievements of his government were the nuclear tests in 1998, the war with Pakistan in 1999, and the Supreme Court verdict in favor of the construction of the Sardar Sarovar dam in 2000. He called it a victory for "developmental nationalism" (a twisted variation of cultural nationalism). For the home minister to call a Supreme Court verdict a victory for his government doesn't say much for the Supreme Court.

I have no quarrel with Mr. Advani clubbing together nuclear bombs, Big Dams, and wars. However, calling them "achievements" is sinister. Mr. Advani then went on to make farcical allegations about how those of us who were against the dam were "working at the behest of . . . outsiders" and "those who do not wish to see India becoming strong in security and socio-economic development."[37] Unfortunately, this is not imbecilic paranoia. It's a deliberate, dangerous attempt to suppress outrageous facts by whipping up mindless mob frenzy. He did it in the run-up to the destruction of the Babri Masjid. He's doing it again. He has given notice that he will stop at nothing. Those who come in his way will be dealt with by any methods he deems necessary.

Nevertheless, there is too much at stake to remain silent. After all, we don't want to be like good middle-class Germans in the 1930s, who drove their children to piano classes and never noticed the concentration camps springing up around them—or do we?

There are questions that must be asked. And answered. There is space here for no more than a brief summary of the costs and benefits of Big Dams. A brief summary is all we need.

Ninety percent of the Big Dams in India are irrigation dams.[38] They are the key, according to planners, to India's "food security."

So how much food do Big Dams produce?

The extraordinary thing is that there is no official government figure for this.

The India Country Study section in the World Commission on Dams Report was prepared by a team of experts—the former secretary of Water Resources, the former director of the Madras Institute of Development Studies, a former secretary of the Central Water Commission, and two members of the faculty of the Indian Institute of Public Administration.[39] One of the chapters in the study deduces that the contribution of large dams to India's food grain produce is less than 10 percent.[40] *Less than 10 percent!*

Ten percent of the total produce currently works out to 20 million tons. This year, more than double that amount is rotting in government storehouses while at the same time 350 million Indian citizens live below the poverty line.[41] The Ministry of Food and Civil Supplies says that 10 percent of India's total food grain produce every year is spoiled or eaten by rats.[42] India must be the only country in the world that builds dams, uproots millions of people, and submerges thousands of acres of forest in order to feed rats.

It's hard to believe that things can go so grievously, so perilously wrong. But they have. It's understandable that those who are responsible find it hard to own up to their mistakes, because Big Dams did not start out as a cynical enterprise. They began as a dream. They have ended as grisly nightmare. It's time to wake up.

So much for the benefits of India's Big Dams. Let's take a look at the costs. How many people have been displaced by Big Dams?

Once again, there is no official record.

In fact, there's no record at all. This is unpardonable on the part of the Indian state. And unpardonable on the part of planners, economists, funding agencies, and the rest of the urban intellectual community who are so quick to rise up in defense of Big Dams.

Last year, just in order to do a sanity check, I extrapolated an average from a study of fifty-four dams done by the Indian Institute of Public Administration. After quartering the average they arrived at, my very conservative estimate of the number of people displaced by Big Dams in India over the last fifty years was thirty-three million people. This was jeered at by some economists and planners as being a preposterously exaggerated figure. India's secretary for rural development put the figure at forty million.

Today, a chapter in the India Country Study says the figure could be as high as fifty-six million people.[43]

That's almost twice the population of Canada. More than three times the population of Australia.

Think about it: fifty-six million people displaced by Big Dams in the last fifty years. And India still does not have a national rehabilitation policy.

When the history of India's miraculous leap to the forefront of the Information Revolution is written, let it be said that fifty-six million Indians (and their children and their children's children) paid for it with everything they ever had. Their homes, their lands, their languages, their histories.

You can see them from your car window when you drive home every night. Try not to look away. Try to meet their eyes. Fifty-six million displaced, impoverished, pulverized people. Almost half of them are Dalit and Adivasi.[44] (There is devastating meaning couched in this figure.)

There's a saying in the villages of the Narmada valley: "You can wake someone who's sleeping. But you can't wake someone who's pretending to be asleep." When it comes to the politics of forced, involuntary displacement, there's a deafening silence in this country. People's eyes glaze over. They behave as though it's just a blip in the democratic process.

The nicer ones say, "Oh, but it's such a pity. People must be resettled." (Where? I want to scream. Where's the land? Has someone invented a Land-Manufacturing Machine?)

The nasties say, "Someone has to pay the price for National Development."

The point is that fifty-six million is more than a blip, folks. It's civil war.

Quite apart from the human costs of Big Dams, there are the staggering environmental costs. More than 3 million acres of submerged forest, ravaged ecosystems, destroyed rivers, defunct, silted-up reservoirs, endangered wildlife, disappearing biodiversity, and 24 million acres of agricultural land that is now waterlogged and saline. Today there are more drought-prone and flood-prone areas in India than there were in 1947. Not a single river in the plains has potable water. Remember, two hundred million Indians have no access to safe drinking water.[45]

Planners, when confronted with past mistakes, say sagely, "Yes, it's true that mistakes have been made. But we're on a learning curve." The lives and livelihoods of fifty-six million people and all this environmental mayhem serve only to extend the majestic arc of their learning curve.

Will they ever get off the curve and actually *learn*?

The evidence against Big Dams is mounting alarmingly. None of it appears on the balance sheet. There *is* no balance sheet. There has not been an official audit, a comprehensive post-project evaluation, of a single Big Dam in India to see whether or not it has achieved what it set out to achieve.

This is what is hardest to believe. That the Indian government's unshakable faith in Big Dams is based on nothing. No studies. No system of checks and balances. Nothing at all. And of course, those of us who question it are spies.

Is it unreasonable to call for a moratorium on the construction of Big Dams until past mistakes have been rectified and the millions of uprooted people have been truly recompensed and rehabilitated? It is the only way an industry that has so far been based on lies and false promises can redeem itself.

Of the series of thirty Big Dams proposed on the main stem of the Narmada River, four are megadams. Of these, only one—the Bargi dam—has been completed. Three are under construction.

The Bargi dam was completed in 1990. It cost ten times more than was budgeted and submerged three times more land than engineers said it would.[46] To save the cost and effort of doing a detailed survey, in order to mark the Full Reservoir Level, the government closed the sluice gates one monsoon and filled the reservoir without warning. Water entered villagers' homes at night. They had to take their children, their cattle, their pots and pans, and flee up the hillside. The Narmada Control Authority had estimated that 70,000 people from 101 villages would be displaced. Instead, when they filled the reservoir, 114,000 people from 162 villages were displaced. In addition, twenty-six government "resettlement colonies" (which consisted of house plots but no agricultural land) were submerged.[47] Eventually there was no rehabilitation. Some "oustees" got a meager cash compensation. Most got nothing. Some died of starvation. Others moved to slums in Jabalpur, where they now work as rickshaw pullers and construction labor.

Today, ten years after it was completed, the Bargi Dam irrigates only as much land as it submerged. Only 5 percent of the land its planners claimed it would irrigate. The government says it has no money to make the canals. Yet work has begun downstream, on the mammoth Narmada Sagar Dam, which will submerge 251 villages, on the Maheshwar Dam, and, of course, on the most controversial dam in history, the Sardar Sarovar.[48]

The Sardar Sarovar dam is currently 90 meters high. Its final projected height is 138 meters. It is located in Gujarat, but most of the villages that will be submerged by its gigantic reservoir are in Maharashtra and Madhya Pradesh. The Sardar Sarovar Dam has become the showcase of India's Violation of Human Rights Initiative. It has ripped away the genial mask of Dams-as-Development and revealed its brutish innards.

I have written about Sardar Sarovar extensively in a previous essay ("The Greater Common Good"), so I'll be brief. The Sardar Sarovar dam will displace close to half a million people. More than half of them do not officially qualify as "project affected" and are not entitled to rehabilitation. It will submerge thirty-two thousand acres of deciduous forest.[49]

In 1985, before a single study had been done, before anyone had any idea what the human cost or environmental impact of the dam would be, the World Bank sanctioned a $450 million loan for the dam. The Ministry of Environment's conditional clearance (without any studies being done) came in 1987! At no point in the decision-making process were the people to be affected consulted or even informed about the project. In 1993, after a spectacular struggle by the NBA, the people of the valley forced the Bank to withdraw from the project.[50] The Gujarat government decided to go ahead with the project.

In 1994 the NBA filed a petition in the Supreme Court. For six years, the court put a legal injunction on further construction of the dam. On October 18, 2000, in a shocking 2–1 majority judgment, the Supreme Court lifted the injunction.[51] After having seen fit to hold up the construction for six years, the court chastised (using unseemly, insulting language) the people of the Narmada valley for approaching it too late and said that on these grounds alone their petition should be dismissed. It permitted construction to continue according to the guidelines laid down by the Narmada Water Disputes Tribunal.

It did this despite the fact that it was aware that the tribunal guidelines have been consistently violated for thirteen years. Despite the fact that none of the conditions of the environment ministry's clearance have been met. Despite the fact that thirteen years have passed and the government hasn't even produced a resettlement plan. Despite the fact that not a single village has been resettled according to the directives of the tribunal. Despite the fact that the Madhya Pradesh government has stated on oath that it has no land on which to resettle "oustees" (80 percent of them live in Madhya Pradesh).[52] Despite the fact that since construction began, the Madhya Pradesh government has not given a single acre of agricultural land to displaced families. Despite the fact that the court was fully aware that even families displaced by the dam at its current height have not been rehabilitated.

In other words, the Supreme Court has actually ordered and sanctioned the violation of the Narmada Water Disputes Tribunal Award.

"But this is the problem with the government," Mr. and Mrs. Well-Meaning say. "It's so inefficient. These things wouldn't happen with a private company. Things like resettlement and rehabilitation of poor people will be so much better managed."

The Maheshwar experience teaches you otherwise.

In a private project, the only things that are better managed are the corruption, the lies, and the swiftness and brutality of repression. And, of course, the escalating costs.

In 1994, the project cost of the Maheshwar Dam was estimated at $99 million. In 1996, following the contract with S. Kumars, it rose to $333 million. Today it stands at $467 million.[53] Initially, 80 percent of this money was to be raised from foreign investors. There has been a procession of them—Pacgen of the United States and Bayernwerk, VEW, Siemens, and the HypoVereinsbank of Germany. And now, the latest in the line of ardent suitors, Ogden of the United States.

According to the NBA's calculations, the cost of the electricity at the factory gate will be 13.9 cents per kilowatt hour, which is twenty-six times more expensive than existing hydel power in the state, five and a half times more expensive than thermal power, and four times more expensive than power from the central grid. (It's worth mentioning here that Madhya Pradesh today generates 1,500 megawatts more power than it can transmit and distribute.)

Though the installed capacity of the Maheshwar project is supposed to be 400 megawatts, studies using twenty-eight years of actual river flow data show that 80 percent of the electricity will be generated only during the monsoon months, when the river is full. What this means is that most of the supply will be generated when it's least needed.[54]

S. Kumars has no worries on this count. They have Enron as a precedent. They have an escrow clause in their contract, which guarantees them first call on government funds. This means that however much (or however little) electricity they produce, whether anybody buys it or not, for the next thirty-five years they are guaranteed a minimum payment from the government of approximately $127 million a year. This money will be paid to them even before employees of the bankrupt State Electricity Board get their salaries.

What did S. Kumars do to deserve this largesse? It isn't hard to guess.

So who's actually paying for this dam that nobody needs?

According to government surveys, the reservoir of the Maheshwar Dam will submerge sixty-one villages. Thirteen will be wholly submerged; the rest will lose their farmlands.[55] As usual, none of the villagers were informed about the dam or their impending eviction. (Of course, if they go to court now they'll be told it's too late, since construction has already begun.)

The first surveys were done under a ruse that a railway line was being constructed. It was only in 1997, when blasting began at the dam site, that realization dawned on people and the NBA became active in Maheshwar. The agency in charge of the survey is the same one that was in charge of the surveys for the Bargi reservoir. We know what happened there.

People in the submergence zone of the Maheshwar Dam say that the surveys are completely wrong. Some villages marked for submergence are at a higher level than villages that are not counted as project affected. Since the Maheshwar Dam is located in the broad plains of Nimad, even a small miscalculation in the surveys will lead to huge discrepancies between what is marked for submergence and what is actually submerged. The consequences of these errors will be far worse than what happened at Bargi.

There are other egregious assumptions in the "survey." Annexure Six of the resettlement plan states that there are 176 trees and thirty-eight wells in all the affected sixty-one villages combined. The villagers point out that in just a single village—Pathrad—there are forty wells and more than 4,000 trees.

As with trees and wells, so with people.

There is no accurate estimate of how many people will be affected by the dam. Even the project authorities admit that new surveys must be done. So far they've managed to survey only one out of the sixty-one villages. The number of affected households rose from 190 (in the preliminary survey) to 300 (in the new one).

In circumstances such as these, it's impossible for even the NBA to have an accurate idea of the number of project-affected people. Their rough guess is about fifty thousand. More than half of them are Dalits, Kevats, and Kahars—ancient communities of ferrymen, fisherfolk, sand quarriers, and cultivators of the

remember thinking: "This is my land, this is the dream to which the whole of me belongs, this is worth more to me than anything else in the world." We were not just fighting against a dam. We were fighting for a philosophy. For a worldview.

We walked in utter silence. Not a throat was cleared. Not a *beedi* lit. We arrived at the dam site at dawn. Though the police were expecting us, they didn't know exactly where we would come from. We captured the dam site. People were beaten, humiliated, and arrested.

I was arrested and pushed into a private car that belonged to S. Kumars. I remember feeling a hot stab of shame—as quick and sharp as my earlier sense of pride. This was my land, too. My feudal land. Where even the police have been privatized. (On the way to the police station, they complained that S. Kumars had given them nothing to eat all day.) That evening there were so many arrests, the jail could not contain the people. The administration broke down and abandoned the jail. The people locked themselves in and demanded answers to their questions. So far, none have been forthcoming.

A Dutch documentary filmmaker recently asked me a very simple question: What can India teach the world?

A documentary filmmaker needs to see to understand. I thought of three places I could take him to.

First, to a "Call Center College" in Gurgaon, on the outskirts of Delhi. I thought it would be interesting for a filmmaker to see how easily an ancient civilization can be made to abase itself completely. In a Call Center College, hundreds of young English-speaking Indians are being groomed to staff the back-room operations of giant transnational companies.[64] They are trained to answer telephone queries from the United States and the United Kingdom (on subjects ranging from a credit card inquiry to advice about a malfunctioning washing machine or the availability of cinema tickets). On no account must the caller know that his or her inquiry is being attended to by an Indian sitting at a desk on the outskirts of Delhi. The Call Center

Colleges train their students to speak in American and British accents. They have to read foreign papers so they can chitchat about the news or the weather. On duty they have to change their given names. Sushma becomes Susie, Govind becomes Jerry, Advani becomes Andy. (Hi! I'm Andy. Gee, hot day, innit? Shoot, how can I help ya?) Actually it's worse: Sushma becomes Mary. Govind becomes David. Perhaps Advani becomes Ulysses.

Call center workers are paid one-tenth of the salaries of their counterparts abroad. From all accounts, call centers are billed to become a multibillion-dollar industry.[65] Recently the giant Tata industrial group announced its plans to redeploy twenty thousand of its retrenched workers in call centers after a brief "period of training" for the business, such as "picking up [the] American accent and slang."[66] The news report said that the older employees may find it difficult to work at night, a requirement for US-based companies, given the time difference between India and the United States.

The second place I thought I'd take the filmmaker was another kind of training center, a Rashtriya Swayamsevak Sangh (RSS) *shakha*, where the terrible backlash to this enforced abasement is being nurtured and groomed. Where ordinary people march around in khaki shorts and learn that amassing nuclear weapons, religious bigotry, misogyny, homophobia, book burning, and outright hatred are the ways in which to retrieve a nation's lost dignity. Here he might see for himself how the two arms of government work in synergy. How they have evolved and pretty near perfected an extraordinary pincer action—while one arm is busy selling the nation off in chunks, the other, to divert attention, is orchestrating a baying, howling, deranged chorus of cultural nationalism. It would be fascinating to actually see how the inexorable ruthlessness of one process results in the naked, vulgar terrorism perpetrated by the other. They're Siamese twins—Advani and Andy. They share organs. They have the ability to say two entirely contradictory things simultaneously, to hold all positions at all times. There's no separating them.

The third place I thought I'd take him was the Narmada valley. To witness the ferocious, magical, magnificent, tenacious, and above all nonviolent resistance that has grown on the banks of that beautiful river.

What is happening to our world is almost too colossal for human comprehension to contain. But it is a terrible, terrible thing. To contemplate its girth and circumference, to attempt to define it, to try and fight it all at once, is impossible. The only way to combat it is by fighting specific wars in specific ways. A good place to begin would be the Narmada valley.

The borders are open. Come on in. Let's bury Rumpelstiltskin.

THE LADIES HAVE
FEELINGS, SO . . .
SHALL WE LEAVE IT
TO THE EXPERTS?

INDIA LIVES IN several centuries at the same time. Somehow we manage to progress and regress simultaneously. As a nation we age by pushing outward from the middle—adding a few centuries on to either end of our extraordinary CV. We greaten like the maturing head of a hammerhead shark with eyes looking in diametrically opposite directions. I have no doubt that even here in North America you have heard that Germany is considering changing its immigration laws in order to import Indian software engineers.[1] I have even less doubt that you've heard of the Naga Sadhu at the Kumbh Mela who towed the district commissioner's car with his penis while the commissioner sat in it solemnly with his wife and children.[2]

As Indian citizens we subsist on a regular diet of caste

Based on a talk given as the Third Annual Eqbal Ahmad Lecture, February 15, 2001, at Hampshire College, Amherst, Massachusetts.

massacres and nuclear tests, mosque breaking and fashion shows, church burnings and expanding cell phone networks, bonded labor and the digital revolution, female infanticide and the Nasdaq crash, husbands who continue to burn their wives for dowry and our delectable stockpile of Miss Worlds. I don't mean to put a simplistic value judgment on this peculiar form of "progress" by suggesting that Modern is Good and Traditional is Bad—or vice versa. What's hard to reconcile oneself to, both personally and politically, is the schizophrenic nature of it. That applies not just to the ancient/modern conundrum, but to the utter illogic of what appears to be the current national enterprise. In the lane behind my house, every night I walk past road gangs of emaciated laborers digging a trench to lay fiber-optic cables to speed up our digital revolution. In the bitter winter cold, they work by the light of a few candles.

It's as though the people of India have been rounded up and loaded onto two convoys of trucks (a huge big one and a tiny little one) that have set off resolutely in opposite directions. The tiny convoy is on its way to a glittering destination somewhere near the top of the world. The other convoy just melts into the darkness and disappears. A cursory survey that tallies the caste, class, and religion of who gets to be on which convoy would make a good Lazy Person's Concise Guide to the History of India. For some of us, life in India is like being suspended between two of the trucks, one in each convoy, and being neatly dismembered as they move apart, not bodily, but emotionally and intellectually.

Of *course* India is a microcosm of the world. Of *course* versions of what happens there happen everywhere. Of *course*, if you're willing to look, the parallels are easy to find. The difference in India is only in the scale, the magnitude, and the sheer proximity of the disparity. In India your face is slammed right up against it. To address it, to deal with it, to not deal with it, to try and understand it, to insist on not understanding it, to simply survive it—on a daily, hourly basis—is a fine art in itself. Either an art or a form of insular, inward-looking insanity. Or both.

To be a writer—a supposedly "famous" writer—in a country where 300 million people are illiterate is a dubious honor.[3] To be a writer in a country that gave the world Mahatma Gandhi, that invented the concept of nonviolent resistance, and then, half a century later, followed that up with nuclear tests, is a ferocious burden. (Though no more ferocious a burden, it has to be said, than being a writer in a country that has enough nuclear weapons to destroy the earth several times over.) To be a writer in a country where something akin to an undeclared civil war is being waged on its subjects in the name of "development" is an onerous responsibility. When it comes to writers and writing, I use words like *onerous* and *responsibility* with a heavy heart and not a small degree of sadness.

This is what I'm here to talk to you, to think aloud with you, about. What is the role of writers and artists in society? Do they have a definable role? Can it be fixed, described, characterized in any definite way? Should it be?

Personally, I can think of few things more terrifying than if writers and artists were charged with an immutable charter of duties and responsibilities that they had to live and work by. Imagine if there was this little black book—a sort of Approved Guide to Good Writing—that said: All writers shall be politically conscious and sexually moral, or: All writers should believe in God, globalization, and the joys of family life . . .

Rule One for a writer, as far as I'm concerned, is There Are No Rules. And Rule Two (since Rule One was made to be broken) is There Are No Excuses for Bad Art. Painters, writers, singers, actors, dancers, filmmakers, musicians are meant to fly, to push at the frontiers, to worry the edges of the human imagination, to conjure beauty from the most unexpected things, to find magic in places where others never thought to look. If you limit the trajectory of their flight, if you weight their wings with society's existing notions of morality and responsibility, if you truss them up with preconceived values, you subvert their endeavor.

A good or great writer may refuse to accept any responsibility or morality that society wishes to impose on her. Yet the best and greatest of them know that if they abuse this hard-won freedom, it can only lead to bad art. There is an intricate web of morality, rigor, and responsibility that art, that writing itself, imposes on a writer. It's singular, it's individual, but nevertheless it's there. At its best, it's an exquisite bond between the artist and the medium. At its acceptable end, it's a sort of sensible cooperation. At its worst, it's a relationship of disrespect and exploitation.

The absence of external rules complicates things. There's a very thin line that separates the strong, true, bright bird of the imagination from the synthetic, noisy bauble. Where is that line? How do you recognize it? How do you know you've crossed it? At the risk of sounding esoteric and arcane, I'm tempted to say that you just know. The fact is that nobody—no reader, no reviewer, agent, publisher, colleague, friend, or enemy—can tell for sure. A writer just has to ask herself that question and answer it as honestly as possible. The thing about this "line" is that once you learn to recognize it, once you see it, it's impossible to ignore. You have no choice but to live with it, to follow it through. You have to bear with all its complexities, contradictions, and demands. And that's not always easy. It doesn't always lead to compliments and standing ovations. It can lead you to the strangest, wildest places. In the midst of a bloody military coup, for instance, you could find yourself fascinated by the mating rituals of a purple sunbird, or the secret life of captive goldfish, or an old aunt's descent into madness. And nobody can say that there isn't truth and art and beauty in that. Or, on the contrary, in the midst of putative peace, you could, like me, be unfortunate enough to stumble on a silent war. The trouble is that once you see it, you can't unsee it. And once you've seen it, keeping quiet, saying nothing, becomes as political an act as speaking out. There's no innocence. Either way, you're accountable.

Today, perhaps more so than in any other era in history, the writer's right to free speech is guarded and defended by the civil societies and state establishments of the most powerful countries in the world. Any overt attempt to silence or muffle a voice is met with furious opposition. The writer is embraced and protected. This is a wonderful thing. The writer, the actor, the musician, the filmmaker—they have become radiant jewels in the crown of modern civilization. The artist, I imagine, is finally as free as he or she will ever be. Never before have so many writers had their books published. (And now, of course, we have the Internet.) Never before have we been more commercially viable. We live and prosper in the heart of the marketplace. True, for every so-called success there are hundreds who "fail." True, there are myriad art forms, both folk and classical, myriad languages, myriad cultural and artistic traditions that are being crushed and cast aside in the stampede to the big bumper sale in Wonderland. Still, there have never been more writers, singers, actors, or painters who have become influential, wealthy superstars. And they, the successful ones, spawn a million imitators, they become the torchbearers, their work becomes the benchmark for what art is, or ought to be.

Nowadays in India the scene is almost farcical. Following the recent commercial success of some Indian authors, Western publishers are desperately prospecting for the next big Indo-Anglian work of fiction. They're doing everything short of interviewing English-speaking Indians for the post of "writer." Ambitious middle-class parents who, a few years ago, would only settle for a future in Engineering, Medicine, or Management for their children, now hopefully send them to creative writing schools. People like myself are constantly petitioned by computer companies, watch manufacturers, even media magnates to endorse their products. A boutique owner in Bombay once asked me if he could "display" my book *The God of Small Things* (as if it were an accessory, a bracelet or a pair of earrings) while he filmed me shopping for clothes! Jhumpa Lahiri, the American writer of Indian origin who won the Pulitzer Prize, came to India recently to have a traditional Bengali wedding. The wedding was reported on the front page of national newspapers.

Now where does all this lead us? Is it just harmless nonsense that's best ignored? How does all this ardent wooing affect our art? What kind of lenses does it put in our spectacles? How far does it remove us from the world around us?

There is very real danger that this neoteric seduction can shut us up far more effectively than violence and repression ever could. We have free speech. Maybe. But do we have Really Free Speech? If what we have to say doesn't "sell," will we still say it? Can we? Or is everybody looking for Things That Sell to say? Could writers end up playing the role of palace entertainers? Or the subtle twenty-first-century version of court eunuchs attending to the pleasures of our incumbent CEOs? You know—naughty, but nice. Risqué perhaps, but not risky.

It has been nearly four years now since my first, and so far only, novel, *The God of Small Things*, was published. In the early days, I used to be described—introduced—as the author of an almost freakishly "successful" (if I may use so vulgar a term) first book. Nowadays I'm introduced as something of a freak myself. I am, apparently, what is known in twenty-first-century vernacular as a "writer-activist." (Like a sofa-bed.)

Why am I called a "writer-activist" and why—even when it's used approvingly, admiringly—does that term make me flinch? I'm called a writer-activist because after writing *The God of Small Things* I wrote three political essays: "The End of Imagination," about India's nuclear tests, "The Greater Common Good," about Big Dams and the "development" debate, and "Power Politics: The Reincarnation of Rumpelstiltskin," about the privatization and corporatization of essential infrastructure like water and electricity. Apart from the building of the temple in Ayodhya, these currently also happen to be the top priorities of the Indian government.[4]

Now, I've been wondering why it should be that the person who wrote *The God of Small Things* is called a writer, and the person who wrote the political essays is called an activist. True, *The God of Small Things* is a work of fiction, but it's no less political than any of my essays. True, the essays are works of nonfiction, but since when did writers forgo the right to write nonfiction?

My thesis—my humble theory, as we say in India—is that I've been saddled with this double-barreled appellation, this awful professional label, not because my work is political but because in my essays, which are about very contentious issues, I take sides. I take a position. I have a point of view. What's worse, I make it clear that I think it's right and moral to take that position, and what's even worse, I use everything in my power to flagrantly solicit support for that position. Now, for a writer of the twenty-first century, that's considered a pretty uncool, unsophisticated thing to do. It skates uncomfortably close to the territory occupied by political party ideologues—a breed of people that the world has learned (quite rightly) to mistrust. I'm aware of this. I'm all for being circumspect. I'm all for discretion, prudence, tentativeness, subtlety, ambiguity, complexity. I love the unanswered question, the unresolved story, the unclimbed mountain, the tender shard of an incomplete dream. Most of the time.

But is it mandatory for a writer to be ambiguous about everything? Isn't it true that there have been fearful episodes in human history when prudence and discretion would have just been euphemisms for pusillanimity? When caution was actually cowardice? When sophistication was disguised decadence? When circumspection was really a kind of espousal?

Isn't it true, or at least theoretically possible, that there are times in the life of a people or a nation when the political climate demands that we—even the most sophisticated of us—overtly take sides? I believe that such times are upon us. And I believe that in the coming years intellectuals and artists in India will be called upon to take sides.

And this time, unlike the struggle for Independence, we won't have the luxury of fighting a colonizing "enemy." We'll be fighting ourselves.

We will be forced to ask ourselves some very uncomfortable questions about our values and traditions, our vision for the future, our responsibilities as citizens, the legitimacy of our "democratic institutions," the role of the state, the police, the army, the judiciary, and the intellectual community.

Fifty years after Independence, India is still struggling with the legacy of colonialism, still flinching from the "cultural insult." As citizens we're still caught up in the business of "disproving" the white world's definition of us. Intellectually and emotionally, we have just begun to grapple with communal and caste politics that threaten to tear our society apart. But in the meanwhile, something new looms on our horizon.

It's not war, it's not genocide, it's not ethnic cleansing, it's not a famine or an epidemic. On the face of it, it's just ordinary, day-to-day business. It lacks the drama, the large-format, epic magnificence, of war or genocide or famine. It's dull in comparison. It makes bad TV. It has to do with boring things like jobs, money, water supply, electricity, irrigation. But it also has to do with a process of barbaric dispossession on a scale that has few parallels in history. You may have guessed by now that I'm talking about the modern version of globalization.

What is globalization? Who is it for? What is it going to do to a country like India, in which social inequality has been institutionalized in the caste system for centuries? A country in which seven hundred million people live in rural areas.[1] In which 80 percent of the landholdings are small farms. In which three hundred million people are illiterate.

Is the corporatization and globalization of agriculture, water supply, electricity, and essential commodities going to pull India out of the stagnant morass of poverty, illiteracy, and religious bigotry? Is the dismantling and auctioning off of elaborate public sector infrastructure, developed with public money over the last fifty years, really the way forward? Is globalization going to close the gap between the privileged and the underprivileged, between the upper castes and the lower castes, between the educated and the illiterate? Or is it going to give those who already have a centuries-old head start a friendly helping hand?

Is globalization about "eradication of world poverty," or is it a mutant variety of colonialism, remote controlled and digitally operated? These are huge, contentious questions. The answers vary depending on whether they come from the villages and fields of rural India, from the slums and shantytowns of urban India, from the living rooms of the burgeoning middle class, or from the boardrooms of the big business houses.

Today India produces more milk, more sugar, more food grain than ever before. This year government warehouses are overflowing with 42 million tons of food grain.[6] That's almost a quarter of the total annual food grain produce. Farmers with too much grain on their hands were driven to despair. In regions that wielded enough political clout, the government went on a buying spree, purchasing more grain than it could possibly store or use. While the grain rots in government warehouses, 350 million Indian citizens live below the poverty line and do not have the means to eat a square meal a day.[7] And yet in March 2000, just before President Clinton's visit to India, the Indian government lifted import restrictions on 1,400 commodities, including milk, grain, sugar, cotton, tea, coffee, and palm oil.[8] This despite the fact that there was a glut of these products in the market.

From April 1—April Fool's Day—2001, according to the terms of its agreement with the World Trade Organization (WTO), the Indian government will have to drop its quantitative import restrictions. The Indian market is already flooded with cheap imports. Though India is technically free to export its agricultural produce, in practice most of it cannot be exported because it doesn't meet the first world's "environmental standards." (You don't eat bruised mangoes, or bananas with mosquito bites, or rice with a few weevils in it. Whereas we don't mind the odd mosquito and the occasional weevil.)

Developed countries like the United States, whose hugely subsidized farm industry engages only 2 to 3 percent of its total population, are using the WTO to pressure countries like

India to drop agricultural subsidies in order to make the market "competitive." Huge, mechanized corporate enterprises working thousands of acres of farmland want to compete with impoverished subsistence farmers who own a couple of acres of land.

In effect, India's rural economy, which supports seven hundred million people, is being garroted. Farmers who produce too much are in distress, farmers who produce too little are in distress, and landless agricultural laborers are out of work as big estates and farms lay off their workers. They're all flocking to the cities in search of employment.

"Trade Not Aid" is the rallying cry of the headmen of the new Global Village headquartered in the shining offices of the WTO. Our British colonizers stepped onto our shores a few centuries ago disguised as traders. We all remember the East India Company. This time around, the colonizer doesn't even need a token white presence in the colonies. The CEOs and their men don't need to go to the trouble of tramping through the tropics, risking malaria, diarrhea, sunstroke, and an early death. They don't have to maintain an army or a police force, or worry about insurrections and mutinies. They can have their colonies and an easy conscience. "Creating a good investment climate" is the new euphemism for third world repression. Besides, the responsibility for implementation rests with the local administration.

In India, in order to clear the way for "development projects," the government is in the process of amending the present Land Acquisition Act (which, ironically, was drafted by the British in the nineteenth century) and making it more draconian than it already is.[9] State governments are preparing to ratify "anti-terrorist" laws so that those who oppose development projects (in Madhya Pradesh, for example) will be counted as terrorists. They can be held without trial for three years. They can have their lands and cattle seized.

Recently, globalization has come in for some criticism. The protests in Seattle and Prague will go down in history. Each time the WTO or the World Economic Forum wants to have a meeting, ministers have to barricade themselves with thousands of heavily armed police. Still, all its admirers, from Bill Clinton, Kofi Annan, and A. B. Vajpayee (the Indian prime minister) to the cheering brokers in the stalls, continue to say the same lofty things. If we have the right institutions of governance in place—effective courts, good laws, honest politicians, participatory democracy, a transparent administration that respects human rights and gives people a say in decisions that affect their lives—then the globalization project will work for the poor as well. They call this "globalization with a human face."

The point is, if all this were in place, almost *anything* would succeed: socialism, capitalism, you name it. Everything works in Paradise, a Communist State as well as a Military Dictatorship. But in an imperfect world, is it globalization that's going to bring us all this bounty? Is that what's happening in India now that it's on the fast track to the free market? Does any one thing on that lofty list apply to life in India today?

Are state institutions transparent? Have people had a say, have they even been informed—let alone consulted—about decisions that vitally affect their lives? And are Mr. Clinton (or now Mr. Bush) and Prime Minister Vajpayee doing everything in their power to see that the "right institutions of governance" are in place? Or are they involved in exactly the opposite enterprise? Do they mean something else altogether when they talk of the "right institutions of governance"?

On October 18, 2000, in one of the most extraordinary legal decisions in post-Independence India, the Supreme Court permitted the construction of the Sardar Sarovar Dam on the Narmada River to proceed.[10] The court did this despite indisputable evidence placed before it that the Sardar Sarovar Projects did not have the mandatory environmental clearance from the central government. Despite the fact that no comprehensive studies have ever been done on the social and ecological impact of the dam. Despite the fact that in the last fifteen years not one single village has been resettled according to the project's own guidelines, and that there was no possibility of rehabilitating the four hundred thousand people who would be displaced by the project.[11] In effect, the Supreme Court has virtually endorsed the violation of human rights to life and livelihood.

Big Dams in India have displaced not hundreds, not thousands, but millions—more than thirty million people in the last fifty years.[12] Almost half of them are Dalit and Adivasi, the poorest of the poor.[13] Yet India is the only country in the world that refused permission to the World Commission on Dams to hold a public hearing. The government in Gujarat, the state in which the Sardar Sarovar Dam is being built, threatened members of the commission with arrest.[14] The World Commission on Dams report was released by Nelson Mandela in November 2000.[15] In February 2001, the Indian government formally rejected the report. Does this sound like a transparent, accountable, participatory democracy?

Recently the Supreme Court ordered the closure of seventy-seven thousand "polluting and nonconforming" industrial units in Delhi. The order could put five hundred thousand people out of work. What are these "industrial units"? Who are these people? They're the millions who have migrated from their villages, some voluntarily, others involuntarily, in search of work. They're the people who aren't supposed to exist, the "noncitizens" who survive in the folds and wrinkles, the cracks and fissures, of the "official" city. They exist just outside the net of the "official" urban infrastructure.

Close to 40 percent of Delhi's population of twelve million—about five million people—live in slums and unauthorized colonies.[16] Most of them are not serviced by municipal services—no electricity, no water, no sewage systems. About fifty thousand people are homeless and sleep on the streets. The "noncitizens" are employed in what economists rather stuffily call the "informal sector," the fragile but vibrant parallel economy. That both shocks and delights the imagination. They work as hawkers, rickshaw pullers, garbage recyclers, car battery rechargers, street tailors, transistor knob makers, buttonhole stitchers, paper bag makers, dyers, printers, barbers. These are the "industrial units" that have been targeted as nonconforming by the Supreme Court. (Fortunately, I haven't heard *that* knock on my door yet, though I'm as nonconforming a unit as the rest of them.)

The trains that leave Delhi these days carry thousands of people who simply cannot survive in the city. They're returning to the villages they fled in the first place. Millions of others, because they're "illegal," have become easy meat for the rapacious, bribe-seeking police and predatory government officials. They haven't yet been driven out of the city but now must live in perpetual fear and anticipation of that happening.

In India the times are full of talk of the "free market," reforms, deregulation, and the dismantling of the "license raj"—all in the name of encouraging entrepreneurship and discouraging corruption. Yet when the state, supported by the judiciary, curbs freedom and obliterates a flourishing market, when it breaks the backs of numerous imaginative, resourceful, small-scale entrepreneurs and delivers millions of others as fodder to the doorstep of the corruption industry, few comment on the irony.

No doubt it's true that the informal sector is polluting and, according to a colonial understanding of urban land use, "nonconforming." But then we don't live in a clean, perfect world. What about the fact that 67 percent of Delhi's pollution comes from motor vehicles?[17] Is it conceivable that the Supreme Court will come up with an act that bans private cars? The courts and the government have shown no great enthusiasm for closing down big factories run by major industrialists that have polluted rivers, denuded forests, depleted and poisoned groundwater, and destroyed the livelihoods of hundreds of thousands of people who depend on these resources for a living. The Grasim factory in Kerala, the Orient Paper Mill in Madhya Pradesh, the "sunrise belt" industries in Gujarat. The uranium mines in Jadugoda, the aluminum plants in Orissa. And hundreds of others.

This is our in-house version of first world bullying in the global warming debate: i.e., we pollute, you pay.

In circumstances like these, the term *writer-activist* as a professional description of what I do makes me flinch doubly. First, because it is strategically positioned to diminish both writers and activists. It seeks to reduce the scope, the range, the sweep of what a writer is and can be. It suggests somehow that the writer by definition is too effete a being to come up with the clarity, the explicitness, the reasoning, the passion, the grit, the audacity, and, if necessary, the vulgarity to publicly take a political position. And, conversely, it suggests that the activist occupies the coarser, cruder end of the intellectual spectrum. That the activist is by profession a "position-taker" and therefore lacks complexity and intellectual sophistication, and is instead fueled by a crude, simple-minded, one-sided understanding of things. But the more fundamental problem I have with the term is that professionalizing the whole business of protest, putting a label on it, has the effect of containing the problem and suggesting that it's up to the professionals—activists and writer-activists— to deal with.

The fact is that what's happening in India today is not a *problem*, and the issues that some of us are raising are not *causes*. They are huge political and social upheavals that are convulsing the nation. One is not involved by virtue of being a writer or activist. One is involved because one is a human being. Writing about it just happens to be the most effective thing I can do. I think it's vital to deprofessionalize the public debate on matters that vitally affect the lives of ordinary people. It's time to snatch our futures back from the "experts." Time to ask, in ordinary language, the public question and to demand, in ordinary language, the public answer.

Frankly, however trenchantly, however angrily, however combatively one puts forward one's case, at the end of the day I'm only a citizen, one of many, who is demanding public information, asking for a public explanation. I have no ax to grind. I have no professional stakes to protect. I'm prepared to be persuaded. I'm prepared to change my mind. But instead of an argument, or an explanation, or a disputing of facts, one gets insults, invective, legal threats, and the Expert's Anthem: "You're too emotional. You don't understand, and it's too complicated to explain." The subtext, of course, is: Don't worry your little head about it. Go and play with your toys. Leave the real world to us.

It's the old Brahminical instinct. Colonize knowledge, build four walls around it, and use it to your advantage. The Manusmriti, the Vedic Hindu code of conduct, says that if a Dalit overhears a *shloka* or any part of a sacred text, he must have molten lead poured into his ear. It isn't a coincidence that while India is poised to take its place at the forefront of the Information Revolution, three hundred million of its citizens are illiterate. (It would be interesting, as an exercise, to find out how many "experts"—scholars, professionals, consultants—in India are actually Brahmins and upper castes.)

If you're one of the lucky people with a berth booked on the small convoy, then Leaving it to the Experts is, or can be, a mutually beneficial proposition for both the expert and yourself. It's a convenient way of shrugging off your own role in the circuitry. And it creates a huge professional market for all kinds of "expertise." There's a whole ugly universe waiting to be explored there. This is not at all to suggest that all consultants are racketeers or that expertise is unnecessary, but you've heard the saying—there's a lot of money in poverty. There are plenty of ethical questions to be asked of those who make a professional living off their expertise in poverty and despair.

For instance, at what point does a scholar stop being a scholar and become a parasite who feeds off despair and dispossession? Does the source of your funding compromise your scholarship? We know, after all, that World Bank studies are among the most quoted studies in the world. Is the World Bank a dispassionate observer of the global situation? Are the studies it funds entirely devoid of self-interest?

Take, for example, the international dam industry. It's worth US $32 billion to $46 billion a year.[18] It's bursting with experts and consultants. Given the number of studies, reports, books, PhDs, grants, loans, consultancies, EIAs, it's odd, wouldn't you say, that there is no really reliable estimate of how many people have been displaced by Big Dams in India? That there is no estimate for exactly what the contribution of Big Dams has been to overall food production in India? That there hasn't been an official audit, a comprehensive, honest, thoughtful, post-project evaluation of a single Big Dam to see whether or not it has achieved what it set out to achieve? Whether or not the costs were justified, or even what the costs actually were?

What *are* the experts up to?

If you manage to ignore the invective, shut out the din of the Expert's Anthem, and keep your eye on the ball, you'll find that a lot of dubious politics lurks inside the stables of "expertise." Probe further, and it all precipitates in a bilious rush of abuse, intimidation, and blind anger. The intellectual equivalent of a police baton charge. The advantage of provoking this kind of unconstrained, spontaneous rage is that it allows you to get a good look at the instincts of some of these normally cautious, supposedly "neutral" people, the pillars of democracy—judges, planners, academics. It becomes very clear that it's not really a question of experts versus laypersons or of knowledge versus ignorance. It's the pitting of one value system against another, one kind of political instinct against another. It's interesting to watch so many supposedly "rational" people turn into irrational, instinctive political beings. To see how they find reasons to support their views, and how, if those reasons are argued away, they continue to cling to their views anyway. Perhaps for this alone, provocation is important. In a crisis, it helps to clarify who's on which side.

A wonderful illustration of this is the Supreme Court's reaction to my essay "The Greater Common Good," which was published in May 1999. In July and August of that year, the monsoon waters rose in the Narmada and submerged villages. While villagers stood in their homes for days together in chest-deep water to protest against the dam, while their crops were submerged, and while the NBA—Narmada Bachao Andolan, the people's movement in the Narmada valley—pointed out (citing specific instances) that government officials had committed perjury by signing false affidavits claiming that resettlement had been carried out when it hadn't, the three-judge bench in the Supreme Court met over three sessions. The only subject they discussed was whether or not the dignity of the court had been undermined. To assist them in their deliberations, they appointed what is called an *amicus curiae* (friend of the court) to advise them about whether or not they should initiate criminal proceedings against the NBA and me for contempt of court. The thing to keep in mind is that while the NBA was the petitioner, I was (and hopefully still am) an independent citizen. I wasn't present in court, but I was told that the three-judge bench ranted and raved and referred to me as "that woman." (I began to think of myself as the hooker who won the Booker.)

On October 15, 1999, they issued an elaborate order.[16] Here's an extract:

> *Judicial process and institution cannot be permitted to be scan-dalised or subjected to contumacious violation in such a blatant manner in which it has been done by her [Arundhati Roy] . . . vicious stultification and vulgar debunking cannot be permitted to pollute the stream of justice . . . we are unhappy at the way in which the leaders of NBA and Ms. Arundhati Roy have attempted to undermine the dignity of the Court. We expected better behaviour from them . . . After giving this matter thoughtful consideration . . . we are not inclined to initiate contempt proceedings against the petitioners, its leaders or Arundhati Roy . . . after the 22nd of July 1999 . . . nothing has come to our notice which may show that Ms. Arundhati Roy has continued with the objectionable*

writings insofar as the judiciary is concerned. She may have by now realised her mistake . . .

What's dissent without a few good insults?

Anyway, eventually, as you can see, they let me off. And I continued with my Objectionable Writings. I hope in the course of this lecture I've managed to inspire at least some of the students in this audience to embark on careers as Vicious Stultificators and Vulgar Debunkers. We could do with a few more of those.

On the whole, in India, the prognosis is—to put it mildly—Not Good. And yet one cannot help but marvel at the fantastic range and depth and wisdom of the hundreds of people's resistance movements all over the country. They're being beaten down, but they simply refuse to lie down and die.

Their political ideologies and battle strategies span the range. We have the maverick Malayali professor who petitions the president every day against the communalization of history texts; Sunderlal Bahugana, who risks his life on indefinite hunger strikes protesting the Tehri Dam; the Adivasis in Jadugoda protesting uranium mining on their lands; the Koel Karo Sanghathan resisting a megadam project in Jharkhand; the awe-inspiring Chattisgarh Mukti Morcha; the relentlessly dogged Mazdoor Kisan Shakti Sangathan; the Beej Bachao Andolan in Tehri-Garhwal fighting to save biodiversity of seeds; and of course, the Narmada Bachao Andolan, the people's movement in the Narmada valley.

India's redemption lies in the inherent anarchy and factiousness of its people, and in the legendary inefficiency of the Indian State. Even our heel-clicking, boot-stamping Hindu fascists are undisciplined to the point of being chaotic. They can't bring themselves to agree with each other for more than five minutes at a time. Corporatizing India is like trying to impose an iron grid on a heaving ocean and forcing it to behave.

My guess is that India will not behave. It cannot. It's too old and too clever to be made to jump through the hoops all over again. It's too diverse, too grand, too feral, and—eventually, I hope—too democratic to be lobotomized into believing in one single idea, which is, ultimately, what globalization really is: Life Is Profit.

What is happening to the world lies, at the moment, just outside the realm of common human understanding. It is the writers, the poets, the artists, the singers, the filmmakers who can make the connections, who can find ways of bringing it into the realm of common understanding. Who can translate cash-flow charts and scintillating boardroom speeches into real stories about real people with real lives. Stories about what it's like to lose your home, your land, your job, your dignity, your past, and your future to an invisible force. To someone or something you can't see. You can't hate. You can't even imagine.

It's a new space that's been offered to us today. A new kind of challenge. It offers opportunities for a new kind of art. An art which can make the impalpable palpable, make the intangible tangible, and the invisible visible. An art which can draw out the incorporeal adversary and make it real. Bring it to book.

Cynics say that real life is a choice between the failed revolution and the shabby deal. I don't know—maybe they're right. But even they should know that there's no limit to just how shabby that shabby deal can be. What we need to search for and find, what we need to hone and perfect into a magnificent, shining thing, is a new kind of politics. Not the politics of governance, but the politics of resistance. The politics of opposition. The politics of forcing accountability. The politics of slowing things down. The politics of joining hands across the world and preventing certain destruction. In the present circumstances, I'd say that the only thing worth globalizing is dissent. It's India's best export.

"*Bhaiji Bhai, Bhaiji Bhai, when will you get angry? When will you stop waiting? When will you say 'That's enough!' and reach for your weapons, whatever they may be? When will you show us the whole of your resonant, terrifying, invincible strength? When will you break the faith? Will you break the faith? Or will you let it break you?*"

THE ALGEBRA OF INFINITE JUSTICE

IN THE AFTERMATH of the unconscionable September 11 suicide attacks on the Pentagon and the World Trade Center, an American newscaster said: "Good and Evil rarely manifest themselves as clearly as they did last Tuesday. People who we don't know massacred people who we do. And they did so with contemptuous glee." Then he broke down and wept.[1]

Here's the rub: America is at war against people it doesn't know (because they don't appear much on TV). Before it has properly identified or even begun to comprehend the nature of its enemy, the US government has, in a rush of publicity and embarrassing rhetoric, cobbled together an "International Coalition Against Terror," mobilized its army, its air force, its navy, and its media, and committed them to battle.

The trouble is that once America goes off to war, it can't very well return without having fought one. If it doesn't find its enemy, for the sake of the enraged folks back home it will have to

First published in the *Guardian*, September 29, 2001, and *Outlook*, October 8, 2001.

manufacture one. Once war begins, it will develop a momentum, a logic, and a justification of its own, and we'll lose sight of why it's being fought in the first place.

What we're witnessing here is the spectacle of the world's most powerful country reaching reflexively, angrily, for an old instinct to fight a new kind of war. Suddenly, when it comes to defending itself, America's streamlined warships, its cruise missiles, and its F-16 jets look like obsolete, lumbering things. As deterrence, its arsenal of nuclear bombs is no longer worth its weight in scrap. Box cutters, penknives, and cold anger are the weapons with which the wars of the new century will be waged. Anger is the lock pick. It slips through customs unnoticed. Doesn't show up in baggage checks.

Who is America fighting? On September 20, the FBI said that it had doubts about the identities of some of the hijackers. On the same day, President George Bush said he knew exactly who the terrorists were and which governments were supporting them.[2] It sounds as though the president knows something that the FBI and the American public don't.

In his September 20 address to the US Congress, president George Bush called the enemies of America "enemies of freedom." "Americans are asking, 'Why do they hate us?'" he said. "They hate our freedoms—our freedom of religion, our freedom of speech, our freedom to vote and assemble and disagree with each other."[3] People are being asked to make two leaps of faith here. First, to assume that The Enemy is who the US government says it is, even though it has no substantial evidence to support that claim. And second, to assume that The Enemy's motives are what the US government says they are, and there's nothing to support that either.

For strategic, military, and economic reasons, it is vital for the US government to persuade the American public that America's commitment to freedom and democracy and the American Way of Life are under attack. In the current atmosphere of grief, outrage, and anger, it's an easy notion to peddle. However, if that were true, it's reasonable to wonder why the symbols of America's economic and military dominance—the World Trade Center and the Pentagon—were chosen as the targets of the attacks. Why not the Statue of Liberty? Could it be that the stygian anger that led to the attacks has its taproot not in American freedom and democracy, but in the US government's record of commitment to and support for exactly the opposite things—military and economic terrorism, insurgency, military dictatorship, religious bigotry, and unimaginable genocide (outside America)?

It must be hard for ordinary Americans so recently bereaved to look up at the world with their eyes full of tears and encounter what might appear to them to be indifference. It isn't indifference. It's just augury. An absence of surprise. The tired wisdom of knowing that what goes around eventually comes around. American people ought to know that it is not them but their government's policies that are so hated. All of us have been moved by the courage and grace shown by America's firefighters, rescue workers, and ordinary office-goers in the days that followed the attacks. American people can't possibly doubt that they themselves, their extraordinary musicians, their writers, their actors, their spectacular athletes, and their cinema, are universally welcomed.

America's grief at what happened has been immense and immensely public. It would be grotesque to expect it to calibrate or modulate its anguish. However, it will be a pity if, instead of using this as an opportunity to try and understand why September 11 happened, Americans use it as an opportunity to usurp the whole world's sorrow to mourn and avenge only their own. Because then it falls to the rest of us to ask the hard questions and say the harsh things. And for our pains, for our bad timing, we will be disliked, ignored, and perhaps eventually silenced.

The world will probably never know what motivated those particular hijackers who flew planes into those particular American buildings. They were not glory boys. They left no suicide notes, no political messages. No organization has claimed credit for the attacks. All we know is that their belief in what they were doing outstripped the natural human instinct for survival or any desire to be remembered. It's almost as though they could not scale down the enormity of their rage to anything smaller than their deeds. And what they did has blown a hole in the world as we knew it.

In the absence of information, politicians, political commentators, and writers (like myself) will invest the act with their own politics, with their own interpretations. This speculation, this analysis of the political climate in which the attacks took place, can only be a good thing.

But war is looming large. Whatever remains to be said must be said quickly.

Before America places itself at the helm of the International Coalition Against Terror, before it invites (and coerces) countries to actively participate in its almost godlike mission—called Operation Infinite Justice until it was pointed out that this could be seen as an insult to Muslims, who believe that only Allah can mete out infinite justice, and was renamed Operation Enduring Freedom—it would help if some small clarifications are made. For example, Infinite Justice / Enduring Freedom for whom?

Is this America's "War on Terror" in America or against terror in general? What exactly is being avenged here? Is it the tragic loss of almost seven thousand lives, the gutting of 15 million square feet of office space in Manhattan, the destruction of a section of the Pentagon, the loss of several hundreds of thousands of jobs, the potential bankruptcy of some airline companies, and the crash of the New York Stock Exchange?[4] Or is it more than that?

In 1996, Madeleine Albright, then the US ambassador to the United Nations, was asked on national television what she felt about the fact that five hundred thousand Iraqi children had died as a result of US-led economic sanctions. She replied that it was "a very hard choice" but that, all things considered, "we think the price is worth it."[5] Albright never lost her job for saying this. She continued to travel the world representing the views and aspirations of the US government. More pertinently, the sanctions against Iraq remain in place. Children continue to die.

So here we have it. The equivocating distinction between civilization and savagery, between the "massacre of innocent people," or, if you like, "a clash of civilizations," and "collateral damage." The sophistry and fastidious algebra of Infinite Justice. How many dead Iraqis will it take to make the world a better place? How many dead Afghans for every dead American? How many dead children for every dead man? How many dead mujahideen for each dead investment banker?

As we watch, mesmerized, Operation Enduring Freedom unfolds on television monitors across the world. A coalition of the world's superpowers is closing in on Afghanistan, one of the poorest, most ravaged, war-torn countries in the world, whose ruling Taliban government is sheltering Osama bin Laden, the man being held responsible for the September 11 attacks. The only thing in Afghanistan that could possibly count as collateral value is its citizenry. (Among them, half a million maimed orphans.[6] There are accounts of hobbling stampedes that occur when artificial limbs are airdropped into remote, inaccessible villages.)

Afghanistan's economy is in a shambles. In fact, the problem for an invading army is that Afghanistan has no conventional coordinates or signposts to plot on a map—no military bases, no industrial complexes, no water treatment plants. Farms have been turned into mass graves. The countryside is littered with land mines—10 million is the most recent estimate.[7] The American army would first have to clear the mines and build roads in order to take its soldiers in.

Fearing an attack from America, one million citizens have fled from their homes and arrived at the border between Pakistan and Afghanistan. The United Nations estimates that there are 7.5 million Afghan citizens who will need emergency aid.[8] As

supplies run out—food and aid agencies have been evacuated—
the BBC reports that one of the worst humanitarian disasters of
recent times has begun to unfold.[9] Witness the Infinite Justice of
the new century. Civilians starving to death while they're waiting
to be killed.

In America there has been rough talk of "bombing Afghanistan
back to the Stone Age."[10] Someone please break the news that
Afghanistan is already there. And if it's any consolation, America
played no small part in helping it on its way. The American
people may be a little fuzzy about where exactly Afghanistan is
(we hear reports that there's a run on maps of the country), but
the US government and Afghanistan are old friends.[11]

In 1979, after the Soviet invasion of Afghanistan, the CIA
and Pakistan's ISI (Inter-Services Intelligence) launched the
CIA's largest covert operation since the Vietnam War.[12] Their
purpose was to harness the energy of Afghan resistance to the
Soviets and expand it into a holy war, an Islamic jihad, which
would turn Muslim countries within the Soviet Union against
the Communist regime and eventually destabilize it. When it
began, it was meant to be the Soviet Union's Vietnam. It turned
out to be much more than that. Over the years, through the ISI,
the CIA funded and recruited tens of thousands of radical mujahideen from forty Islamic countries as soldiers for America's
proxy war.[13] The rank and file of the mujahideen were unaware
that their jihad was actually being fought on behalf of Uncle
Sam. (The irony is that America was equally unaware that it was
financing a future war against itself.)

In 1989, after being bloodied by ten years of relentless conflict,
the Russians withdrew, leaving behind a civilization reduced to
rubble. Civil war in Afghanistan raged on. The jihad spread to
Chechnya, Kosovo, and eventually Kashmir. The CIA continued
to pour in money and military equipment, but the overheads had
become immense, and more money was needed. The mujahideen
ordered farmers to plant opium as a "revolutionary tax."[14]
Under the protection of the ISI, hundreds of heroin-processing

laboratories were set up across Afghanistan. Within two years of the CIA's arrival, the Pakistan–Afghanistan borderland had become the biggest producer of heroin in the world, and the single biggest source on American streets. The annual profits, said to be between one hundred and two hundred billion dollars, were plowed back into training and arming militants.[15]

In 1996 the Taliban—then a marginal sect of dangerous hard-line fundamentalists—fought its way to power in Afghanistan. It was funded by the ISI, that old cohort of the CIA, and supported by many political parties in Pakistan.[16] The Taliban unleashed a regime of terror. Its first victims were its own people, particularly women. It closed down girls' schools, dismissed women from government jobs, and enforced Sharia laws under which women deemed to be "immoral" are stoned to death and widows guilty of being adulterous are buried alive.[17] Given the Taliban government's human rights track record, it seems unlikely that it will in any way be intimidated or swerved from its purpose by the prospect of war or the threat to the lives of its civilians.

After all that has happened, can there be anything more ironic than Russia and America joining hands to re-destroy Afghanistan? The question is, can you destroy destruction? Dropping more bombs on Afghanistan will only shuffle the rubble, scramble some old graves, and disturb the dead.

The desolate landscape of Afghanistan was the burial ground of Soviet Communism and the springboard of a unipolar world dominated by America. It made the space for neoliberal capitalism and corporate globalization, again dominated by America. And now Afghanistan is poised to become the graveyard for the unlikely soldiers who fought and won this war for America.

And what of America's trusted ally? Pakistan, too, has suffered enormously. The US government has not been shy to support military dictators who have blocked the idea of democracy from taking root in the country. Before the CIA arrived, there was a small rural market for opium in Pakistan. Between 1979 and 1985, the number of heroin addicts grew from next to nothing to a massive number.[18] Even before September 11, there were millions of Afghan refugees living in tented camps along the border.

Pakistan's economy is crumbling.[19] Sectarian violence, globalization's Structural Adjustment Programs, and drug lords are tearing the country to pieces. Set up to fight the Soviets, the terrorist training centers and madrassas, sown like dragon's teeth across the country, produced fundamentalists with tremendous popular appeal within Pakistan itself. The Taliban, which the Pakistan government has supported, funded, and propped up for years, has material and strategic alliances with Pakistan's own political parties.[20] Now the US government is asking (asking?) Pakistan to garrote the pet it has hand-reared in its backyard for so many years. President Pervez Musharraf, having pledged his support to the US, could well find he has something resembling civil war on his hands.[21]

India, thanks in part to its geography and in part to the vision of its former leaders, has so far been fortunate enough to be left out of this Great Game. Had it been drawn in, it's more than likely that our democracy, such as it is, would not have survived. Today, as some of us watch in horror, the Indian government is furiously gyrating its hips, begging the US to set up its base in India rather than Pakistan.[22]

Having had this ringside view of Pakistan's sordid fate, it isn't just odd, it's unthinkable, that India should want to do this. Any third world country with a fragile economy and a complex social base should know by now that to invite a superpower such as America in (whether it says it's staying or just passing through) would be like inviting a brick to drop through your windshield.

In the media blitz that followed September 11, mainstream television stations largely ignored the story of America's involvement with Afghanistan. So to those unfamiliar with the story, the coverage of the attacks could have been moving, disturbing, and, perhaps to cynics, self-indulgent. However, to those of us who are familiar with Afghanistan's recent history, American TV coverage and the rhetoric of the International Coalition Against

Terror is just plain insulting. America's "free press," like its "free market," has a lot to account for.

Operation Enduring Freedom is ostensibly being fought to uphold the American Way of Life. It'll probably end up undermining it completely. It will spawn more anger and more terror across the world. For ordinary people in America, it will mean lives lived in a climate of sickening uncertainty: Will my child be safe in school? Will there be nerve gas in the subway? A bomb in the cinema hall? Will my love come home tonight? There have been warnings about the possibility of biological warfare—smallpox, bubonic plague, anthrax—the deadly payload of an innocuous crop duster.[23] Being picked off a few at a time may end up being worse than being annihilated all at once by a nuclear bomb.

The US government, and no doubt governments all over the world, will use the climate of war as an excuse to curtail civil liberties, deny free speech, lay off workers, harass ethnic and religious minorities, cut back on public spending, and divert huge amounts of money to the defense industry.

To what purpose? President George Bush can no more "rid the world of evildoers" than he can stock it with saints.[24] It's absurd for the US government to even toy with the notion that it can stamp out terrorism with more violence and oppression. Terrorism is the symptom, not the disease. Terrorism has no country. It's transnational, as global an enterprise as Coke or Pepsi or Nike. At the first sign of trouble, terrorists can pull up stakes and move their "factories" from country to country in search of a better deal. Just like the multinationals.

Terrorism as a phenomenon may never go away. But if it is to be contained, the first step is for America to at least acknowledge that it shares the planet with other nations, with other human beings who, even if they are not on TV, have loves and griefs and stories and songs and sorrows and, for heaven's sake, rights. Instead, when Donald Rumsfeld, the US defense secretary, was asked what he would call a victory in America's new war, he said that if he could convince the world that Americans must be allowed to continue with their way of life, he would consider it a victory.[25]

The September 11 attacks were a monstrous calling card from a world gone horribly wrong. The message may have been written by bin Laden (who knows?) and delivered by his couriers, but it could well have been signed by the ghosts of the victims of America's old wars.

The millions killed in Korea, Vietnam, and Cambodia, the seventeen thousand killed when Israel—backed by the United States—invaded Lebanon in 1982, the tens of thousands of Iraqis killed in Operation Desert Storm, the thousands of Palestinians who have died fighting Israel's occupation of the West Bank. And the millions who died, in Yugoslavia, Somalia, Haiti, Chile, Nicaragua, El Salvador, the Dominican Republic, Panama, at the hands of all the terrorists, dictators, and genocidists whom the American government supported, trained, bankrolled, and supplied with arms.[26] And this is far from being a comprehensive list.

For a country involved in so much warfare and conflict, the American people have been extremely fortunate. The strikes on September 11 were only the second on American soil in more than a century. The first was Pearl Harbor. The reprisal for this took a long route but ended with Hiroshima and Nagasaki. This time the world waits with bated breath for the horrors to come.

Someone recently said that if Osama bin Laden didn't exist, America would have had to invent him.[27] But in a way, America did invent him. He was among the jihadists who moved to Afghanistan after 1979, when the CIA commenced its operations there. Bin Laden has the distinction of being created by the CIA and wanted by the FBI. In the course of a fortnight he has been promoted from Suspect to Prime Suspect, and then, despite the lack of any real evidence, straight up the charts to being "wanted dead or alive."

From all accounts, it will be impossible to produce evidence (of the sort that would stand up to scrutiny in a court of law) to link bin Laden to the September 11 attacks.[28] So far, it appears that the most incriminating piece of evidence against him is the fact that he has not condemned them. From what is known about the location of bin Laden and the living conditions where he operates, it's entirely possible that he did not personally plan and carry out the attacks—that he is the inspirational figure, "the CEO of the holding company."[29]

The Taliban's response to US demands for the extradition of bin Laden has been uncharacteristically reasonable: produce the evidence, then we'll hand him over. President Bush's response is that the demand is "nonnegotiable."[30]

(While talks are on for the extradition of CEOs—can India put in a side request for the extradition of Warren Anderson of the USA? He was the chairman of Union Carbide, responsible for the 1984 Bhopal gas leak, which killed sixteen thousand people.[31] We have collated the necessary evidence. It's all in the files. Could we have him, please?)

But who is Osama bin Laden really?

Let me rephrase that. What is Osama bin Laden?

He's America's family secret. He is the American president's dark doppelganger. The savage twin of all that purports to be beautiful and civilized. He has been sculpted from the spare rib of a world laid to waste by America's foreign policy: its gunboat diplomacy, its nuclear arsenal, its vulgarly stated policy of "full spectrum dominance," its chilling disregard for non-American lives, its barbarous military interventions, its support for despotic and dictatorial regimes, its merciless economic agenda that has munched through the economies of poor countries like a cloud of locusts.[32] Its marauding multinationals, which are taking over the air we breathe, the ground we stand on, the water we drink, the thoughts we think.

Now that the family secret has been spilled, the twins are blurring into one another and gradually becoming interchangeable. Their guns, bombs, money, and drugs have been going around in the loop for a while. (The Stinger missiles that will greet US helicopters were supplied by the CIA. The heroin used by America's drug addicts comes from Afghanistan. The Bush administration recently gave Afghanistan a $43 million subsidy to its "war on drugs.")[33]

Now they've even begun to borrow each other's rhetoric. Each refers to the other as "the head of the snake." Both invoke God and use the loose millenarian currency of Good and Evil as their terms of reference. Both are engaged in unequivocal political crimes.

Both are dangerously armed—one with the nuclear arsenal of the obscenely powerful, the other with the incandescent, destructive power of the utterly hopeless.

The fireball and the ice pick. The bludgeon and the ax. The important thing to keep in mind is that neither is an acceptable alternative to the other.

President Bush's ultimatum to the people of the world— "either you are with us or you are with the terrorists"[34]—is a piece of presumptuous arrogance.

It's not a choice that people want to, need to, or should have to make.

WAR IS PEACE

AS DARKNESS DEEPENED over Afghanistan on Sunday, October 7, 2001, the US government, backed by the International Coalition Against Terror (the new, amenable surrogate for the United Nations), launched air strikes against Afghanistan. TV channels lingered on computer-animated images of cruise missiles, stealth bombers, Tomahawks, "bunker-busting" missiles, and Mark 82 high drag bombs.[1] All over the world, little boys watched goggle-eyed and stopped clamoring for new video games.

The UN, reduced now to an ineffective acronym, wasn't even asked to mandate the air strikes. (As Madeleine Albright once said, "We will behave multilaterally when we can and unilaterally when we must.")[2]

The "evidence" against the terrorists was shared among friends in the International Coalition. After conferring, they announced that it didn't matter whether or not the "evidence" would stand up in a court of law.[3] Thus in an instant were centuries of jurisprudence carelessly trashed.

First published in *Outlook*, October 29, 2001.

Nothing can excuse or justify an act of terrorism, whether it is committed by religious fundamentalists, private militias, people's resistance movements—or whether it's dressed up as a war of retribution by a recognized government. The bombing of Afghanistan is not revenge for New York and Washington. It is yet another act of terror against the people of the world. Each innocent person that is killed must be added to, not set off against, the grisly toll of civilians who died in New York and Washington.

People rarely win wars; governments rarely lose them. People get killed. Governments molt and regroup, hydra-headed. They first use flags to shrink-wrap people's minds and smother real thought, and then as ceremonial shrouds to bury the willing dead. On both sides, in Afghanistan as well as America, civilians are now hostage to the actions of their own governments. Unknowingly, ordinary people in both countries share a common bond—they have to live with the phenomenon of blind, unpredictable terror. Each batch of bombs that is dropped on Afghanistan is matched by a corresponding escalation of mass hysteria in America about anthrax, more hijackings, and other terrorist acts.

There is no easy way out of the spiraling morass of terror and brutality that confronts the world today. It is time now for the human race to hold still, to delve into its wells of collective wisdom, both ancient and modern. What happened on September 11 changed the world forever. Freedom, progress, wealth, technology, war—these words have taken on new meaning. Governments have to acknowledge this transformation and approach their new tasks with a modicum of honesty and humility. Unfortunately, up to now, there has been no sign of any introspection from the leaders of the International Coalition. Or the Taliban.

When he announced the air strikes, president George Bush said, "We're a peaceful nation."[4] America's favorite ambassador, Tony Blair (who also holds the portfolio of prime minister of the UK), echoed him: "We're a peaceful people."

So now we know. Pigs are horses. Girls are boys. War is peace.

Speaking at the FBI's headquarters a few days later, President Bush said, "This is the calling of the United States of America, the most free nation in the world, a nation built on fundamental values; that rejects hate, rejects violence, rejects murderers, rejects evil. And we will not tire."[5]

Here is a list of the countries that America has been at war with—and bombed—since World War II: China (1945–46, 1950–53), Korea (1950–53), Guatemala (1954, 1967–69), Indonesia (1958), Cuba (1959–60), the Belgian Congo (1964), Peru (1965), Laos (1964–73), Vietnam (1961–73), Cambodia (1969–70), Grenada (1983), Libya (1986), El Salvador (1980s), Nicaragua (1980s), Panama (1989), Iraq (1991–2001), Bosnia (1995), Sudan (1998), Yugoslavia (1999). And now Afghanistan.

Certainly it does not tire—this, the Most Free Nation in the world. What freedoms does it uphold? Within its borders, the freedoms of speech, religion, thought; of artistic expression, food habits, sexual preferences (well, to some extent), and many other exemplary, wonderful things. Outside its borders, the freedom to dominate, humiliate, and subjugate—usually in the service of America's real religion, the "free market." So when the US government christens a war Operation Infinite Justice, or Operation Enduring Freedom, we in the third world feel more than a tremor of fear. Because we know that Infinite Justice for some means Infinite Injustice for others. And Enduring Freedom for some means Enduring Subjugation for others.

The International Coalition Against Terror is largely a cabal of the richest countries in the world. Between them, they manufacture and sell almost all of the world's weapons. They possess the largest stockpile of weapons of mass destruction—chemical, biological, and nuclear. They have fought the most wars, account for most of the genocide, subjection, ethnic cleansing, and human rights violations in modern history, and have sponsored, armed, and financed untold numbers of dictators and despots. Between them, they have worshiped, almost deified, the cult of violence and war. For all its appalling sins, the Taliban just isn't in the same league.

The Taliban was compounded in the crumbling crucible of rubble, heroin, and land mines in the backwash of the Cold War. Its oldest leaders are in their early forties. Many of them are disfigured and handicapped, missing an eye, an arm, or a leg. They grew up in a society scarred and devastated by war. Between the Soviet Union and America, over twenty years, about $45 billion worth of arms and ammunition was poured into Afghanistan.[6]

The latest weaponry was the only shard of modernity to intrude upon a thoroughly medieval society. Young boys—many of them orphans—who grew up in those times had guns for toys, never knew the security and comfort of family life, never experienced the company of women. Now, as adults and rulers, the Taliban beat, stone, rape, and brutalize women. They don't seem to know what else to do with them. Years of war has stripped them of gentleness, inured them to kindness and human compassion. They dance to the percussive rhythms of bombs raining down around them. Now they've turned their monstrosity on their own people.

With all due respect to President Bush, the people of the world do not have to choose between the Taliban and the US government. All the beauty of human civilization—our art, our music, our literature—lies beyond these two fundamentalist ideological poles. There is as little chance that the people of the world can all become middle-class consumers as there is that they will all embrace any one particular religion.

The issue is not about Good versus Evil or Islam versus Christianity as much as it is about space. About how to accommodate diversity, how to contain the impulse toward hegemony—every kind of hegemony: economic, military, linguistic, religious, and cultural. Any ecologist will tell you how dangerous and fragile a monoculture is. A hegemonic world is like having a government without a healthy opposition. It becomes a kind of dictatorship. It's like putting a plastic bag over the world and preventing it from breathing. Eventually, it will be torn open.

One and a half million Afghan people lost their lives in the twenty years of conflict that preceded this new war.[7]

Afghanistan was reduced to rubble, and now the rubble is being pounded into finer dust. By the second day of the air strikes, US pilots were returning to their bases without dropping their assigned payload of bombs.[8]

As one senior official put it, Afghanistan is "not a target-rich environment."[9] At a press briefing at the Pentagon, US defense secretary Donald Rumsfeld was asked if America had run out of targets. "First we're going to re-hit targets," he said, "and second, we're not running out of targets, Afghanistan is . . ." This was greeted with gales of laughter in the briefing room.[10]

By the third day of the strikes, the US Defense Department boasted that it had "achieved air supremacy over Afghanistan."[11] (Did it mean that it had destroyed both, or maybe all sixteen, of Afghanistan's planes?)

On the ground in Afghanistan, the Northern Alliance—the Taliban's old enemy, and therefore the International Coalition's newest friend—is making headway in its push to capture Kabul. (For the archives, let it be said that the Northern Alliance's track record is not very different from the Taliban's. But for now, because it's inconvenient, that little detail is being glossed over.)[12]

The visible, moderate, "acceptable" leader of the Alliance, Ahmed Shah Massoud, was killed in a suicide-bomb attack early in September 2001.[13] The rest of the Northern Alliance is a brittle confederation of brutal warlords, ex-Communists, and unbending clerics. It is a disparate group divided along ethnic lines, some of whom have tasted power in Afghanistan in the past.

Until the US air strikes, the Northern Alliance controlled about 5 percent of the geographical area of Afghanistan. Now, with the International Coalition's help and "air cover," it is poised to topple the Taliban.[14] Meanwhile, Taliban soldiers, sensing imminent defeat, have begun to defect to the Alliance. So the fighting forces are busy switching sides and changing uniforms. But in an enterprise as cynical as this one, it seems to matter hardly at all. Love is hate, north is south, peace is war.

Among the global powers, there is talk of "putting in a representative government." Or, on the other hand, of "restoring" the kingdom to Afghanistan's eighty-six-year-old former king, Muhammad Zahir Shah, who has lived in exile in Rome since 1973.[15] That's the way the game goes—support Saddam Hussein, then "take him out"; finance the mujahideen, then bomb them to smithereens; put in Zahir Shah and see if he's going to be a good boy. (Is it possible to "put in" a representative government? Can you place an order for democracy—with extra cheese and jalapeño peppers?)

Reports have begun to trickle in about civilian casualties, about cities emptying out as Afghan civilians flock to the borders, which have been closed.[16] Main arterial roads have been blown up or sealed off. Those who have experience of working in Afghanistan say that by early November, food convoys will not be able to reach the millions of Afghans (7.5 million according to the UN) who run the very real risk of starving to death during the course of this winter.[17] They say that in the days that are left before winter sets in, there can be either a war or an attempt to reach food to the hungry. Not both.

As a gesture of humanitarian support, the US government airdropped thirty-seven thousand packets of emergency rations into Afghanistan. It says it plans to drop more than five hundred thousand packets. That will still only add up to a single meal for half a million people out of the several million in dire need of food. Aid workers have condemned this as a cynical, dangerous public relations exercise. They say that airdropping food packets is worse than futile. First, because the food will never get to those who really need it. More dangerously, because those who run out to retrieve the packets risk being blown up by land mines.[18] A tragic alms race.

Nevertheless, the food packets had a photo-op all to themselves. Their contents were listed in major newspapers. They were vegetarian, we're told, as per Muslim Dietary Law (!). Each yellow packet, decorated with the American flag, contained rice, peanut butter, bean salad, strawberry jam, crackers, raisins, flat bread, an apple fruit bar, seasoning, matches, a set of plastic cutlery, a napkin, and illustrated user instructions.[19]

After three years of unremitting drought, an airdropped airline meal in Jalalabad! The level of cultural ineptitude, the failure to understand what months of relentless hunger and grinding poverty really mean, the US government's attempt to use even this abject misery to boost its self-image, beggars description.

Reverse the scenario for a moment. Imagine if the Taliban government were to bomb New York City, saying all the while that its real target was the US government and its policies. And suppose, during breaks between the bombing, the Taliban dropped a few thousand packets containing nan and kabobs impaled on an Afghan flag. Would the good people of New York ever find it in themselves to forgive the Afghan government? Even if they were hungry, even if they needed the food, even if they ate it, how would they ever forget the insult, the condescension? Rudy Giuliani, Mayor of New York City, returned a gift of $10 million from a Saudi prince because it came with a few words of friendly advice about American policy in the Middle East.[20] Is pride a luxury that only the rich are entitled to?

Far from stamping it out, igniting this kind of rage is what creates terrorism. Hate and retribution don't go back into the box once you've let them out. For every "terrorist" or his "supporter" who is killed, hundreds of innocent people are being killed, too. And for every hundred innocent people killed, there is a good chance that several future terrorists will be created.

Where will it all lead?

Setting aside the rhetoric for a moment, consider the fact that the world has not yet found an acceptable definition of what "terrorism" is. One country's terrorist is too often another's freedom fighter. At the heart of the matter lies the world's deep-seated ambivalence toward violence. Once violence is accepted as a legitimate political instrument, then the morality and political acceptability of terrorists (insurgents or freedom fighters) become contentious, bumpy terrain.

The US government itself has funded, armed, and sheltered plenty of rebels and insurgents around the world. The CIA and Pakistan's ISI trained and armed the mujahideen who, in the 1980s, were seen as terrorists by the government in Soviet-occupied Afghanistan, while President Reagan praised them as freedom fighters.[21]

Today, Pakistan—America's ally in this new war—sponsors insurgents who cross the border into Kashmir in India. Pakistan lauds them as freedom fighters, India calls them terrorists. India, for its part, denounces countries that sponsor and abet terrorism, but the Indian Army has in the past trained separatist Tamil rebels asking for a homeland in Sri Lanka—the LTTE, responsible for countless acts of bloody terrorism.

(Just as the CIA abandoned the mujahideen after they had served its purpose, India abruptly turned its back on the LTTE for a host of political reasons. It was an enraged LTTE suicide bomber who assassinated former Indian prime minister Rajiv Gandhi in 1991.)

It is important for governments and politicians to understand that manipulating these huge, raging human feelings for their own narrow purposes may yield instant results, but eventually and inexorably, they have disastrous consequences. Igniting and exploiting religious sentiments for reasons of political expediency is the most dangerous legacy that governments or politicians can bequeath to any people—including their own. People who live in societies ravaged by religious or communal bigotry know that every religious text, from the Bible to the Bhagavad Gita, can be mined and misinterpreted to justify anything from nuclear war to genocide to corporate globalization.

This is not to suggest that the terrorists who perpetrated the outrage on September 11 should not be hunted down and brought to book. They must be. But is war the best way to track them down? Will burning the haystack find you the needle? Or will it escalate the anger and make the world a living hell for all of us?

At the end of the day, how many people can you spy on, how many bank accounts can you freeze, how many conversations can you eavesdrop on, how many emails can you intercept, how many letters can you open, how many phones can you tap? Even before September 11, the CIA had accumulated more information than is humanly possible to process. (Sometimes too much data can actually hinder intelligence—small wonder the US spy satellites completely missed the preparation that preceded India's nuclear tests in 1998.)

The sheer scale of the surveillance will become a logistical, ethical, and civil rights nightmare. It will drive everybody clean crazy. And freedom—that precious, precious thing—will be the first casualty. It's already hurt and hemorrhaging dangerously.

Governments across the world are cynically using the prevailing paranoia to promote their own interests. All kinds of unpredictable political forces are being unleashed. In India, for instance, members of the All India People's Resistance Forum who were distributing antiwar and anti-US pamphlets in Delhi have been jailed. Even the printer of the leaflets was arrested.[22] The right-wing government (while it shelters Hindu extremist groups like the Vishwa Hindu Parishad and the Bajrang Dal) has banned the Students' Islamic Movement of India and is trying to revive an antiterrorist act that had been withdrawn after the Human Rights Commission reported that it had been more abused than used.[23] Millions of Indian citizens are Muslim. Can anything be gained by alienating them?

Every day that the war goes on, raging emotions are being let loose into the world. The international press has little or no independent access to the war zone. In any case, the mainstream media, particularly in the United States, has more or less rolled over, allowing itself to be tickled on the stomach with press handouts from military men and government officials. Afghan radio stations have been destroyed by the bombing. The Taliban has always been deeply suspicious of the press. In the propaganda war, there is no accurate estimate of how many people have been killed, or how much destruction has taken place. In the absence of reliable information, wild rumors spread.

Put your ear to the ground in this part of the world, and you can hear the thrumming, the deadly drumbeat of burgeoning anger. Please. Please, stop the war now. Enough people have died. The smart missiles are just not smart enough. They're blowing up whole warehouses of suppressed fury.

President George Bush recently boasted, "When I take action, I'm not going to fire a two million dollar missile at a ten dollar empty tent and hit a camel in the butt. It's going to be decisive."[24] President Bush should know that there are no targets in Afghanistan that will give his missiles their money's worth. Perhaps, if only to balance his books, he should develop some cheaper missiles to use on cheaper targets and cheaper lives in the poor countries of the world. But then, that may not make good business sense to the International Coalition's weapons manufacturers.

It wouldn't make any sense at all, for example, to the Carlyle Group—described by the *Industry Standard* as "one of the world's largest private investment funds," with $13 billion under management.[25] Carlyle invests in the defense sector and makes its money from military conflicts and weapons spending.

Carlyle is run by men with impeccable credentials. Former US defense secretary Frank Carlucci is its chairman and managing director (he was a college roommate of Donald Rumsfeld's). Carlyle's other partners include former US secretary of state James A. Baker III, George Soros, and Fred Malek (George Bush Sr.'s campaign manager).

An American paper—the *Baltimore Chronicle and Sentinel*— says that former president Bush is reported to be seeking investments for the Carlyle Group from Asian markets. He is reportedly paid not inconsiderable sums of money to make "presentations" to potential government clients.[26]

Ho Hum. As the tired saying goes, it's all in the family.

Then there's that other branch of traditional family business—oil. Remember, president George Bush (Jr.) and vice president Dick Cheney both made their fortunes working in the US oil industry.

Turkmenistan, which borders the Northwest of Afghanistan, holds the world's third-largest gas reserves and an estimated 6 billion barrels of oil reserves. Enough, experts say, to meet American energy needs for the next thirty years (or a developing country's energy requirements for a couple of centuries).[27]

America has always viewed oil as a security consideration and protected it by any means it deems necessary. Few of us doubt that its military presence in the Gulf has little to do with its concern for human rights and almost entirely to do with its strategic interest in oil.

Oil and gas from the Caspian region currently move northward to European markets. Geographically and politically, Iran and Russia are major impediments to American interests.

In 1998 Dick Cheney—then CEO of Halliburton, a major player in the oil industry—said, "I can't think of a time when we've had a region emerge as suddenly to become as strategically significant as the Caspian. It's almost as if the opportunities have arisen overnight."[28] True enough.

For some years now, an American oil giant called Unocal has been negotiating with the Taliban for permission to construct an oil pipeline through Afghanistan to Pakistan and out to the Arabian Sea. From here, Unocal hopes to access the lucrative "emerging markets" in South and Southeast Asia. In December 1997 a delegation of Taliban mullahs traveled to America and even met US State Department officials and Unocal executives in Houston.[29]

At that time the Taliban's taste for public executions and its treatment of Afghan women were not made out to be the crimes against humanity that they are now. Over the next six months, pressure from hundreds of outraged American feminist groups was brought to bear on the Clinton administration. Fortunately, they managed to scuttle the deal. And now comes the US oil industry's big chance.

In America, the arms industry, the oil industry, the major media networks, and, indeed, US foreign policy are all controlled by the same business combines. Therefore, it would be foolish to expect this talk of guns and oil and defense deals to get any real play in the media.

In any case, to a distraught, confused people whose pride has just been wounded, whose loved ones have been tragically killed, whose anger is fresh and sharp, the inanities about the "clash of civilizations" and the "good versus evil" home in unerringly. They are cynically doled out by government spokesmen like a daily dose of vitamins or antidepressants. Regular medication ensures that mainland America continues to remain the enigma it has always been—a curiously insular people administered by a pathologically meddlesome, promiscuous government.

And what of the rest of us, the numb recipients of this onslaught of what we know to be preposterous propaganda? The daily consumers of the lies and brutality smeared in peanut butter and strawberry jam being airdropped into our minds just like those yellow food packets. Shall we look away and eat because we're hungry, or shall we stare unblinking at the grim theater unfolding in Afghanistan until we retch collectively and say, in one voice, that we have had enough?

As the first year of the new millennium rushes to a close, one wonders: Have we forfeited our right to dream? Will we ever be able to reimagine beauty? Will it be possible ever again to watch the slow, amazed blink of a newborn gecko in the sun, or whisper back to the marmot who has just whispered in one's ear, without thinking of the World Trade Center and Afghanistan?

ON CITIZENS' RIGHTS
TO EXPRESS DISSENT

In February 2001, a criminal petition filed by five advocates was listed before the Supreme Court of India. The petition accused Medha Patkar (leader of the Narmada Bachao Andolan), Prashant Bhushan (legal counsel for the NBA), and Arundhati Roy of committing criminal contempt of court by organizing and participating in a demonstration outside the gates of the Supreme Court to protest the court judgment on the Sardar Sarovar Dam on the Narmada River. Based on the petition, the Supreme Court sent notices to the three accused, ordering them to appear personally in court on April 23, 2001.

The case is still pending in court. The maximum punishment for committing contempt of court in India is six months' imprisonment.

Arundhati Roy did not have a lawyer at her trial. Reproduced here is the text of her affidavit in reply to the criminal charges.

IN THE SUPREME COURT OF INDIA
ORIGINAL JURISDICTION

Legal affidavit filed in New Delhi, April 16, 2001.

CONTEMPT PETITION (CR) NO: 2/2001
IN THE MATTER OF:
J. R. PARASHAR & OTHERS
VERSUS
PRASHANT BHUSHAN & OTHERS
AFFIDAVIT IN REPLY FILED BY RESPONDENT NO: 3

The gravamen of the charges in the petition against me are contained in the FIR [First Information Report] that the petitioners say they lodged in the Tilak Marg police station on the 14th of December 2000. The FIR is annexed to the main petition and is reproduced verbatim below.

First Information Report dated December 14, 2000

I, Jagdish Prasar, with colleagues Shri Umed Singh and Rajender were going out from Supreme Court at 7.00 p.m and saw that Gate No. C was closed.

We came out from the Supreme Court premises from other path and inquired why the gate is close. The were [we were] surrounded by Prasant Bhusan, Medha Patekar and Arundhanti Roy alongwith their companion and they told Supreme Court your father's property. On this we told them they could not sit on Dharna by closing the gate. The proper place of Dharna is Parliament. In the mean time Prastant Bhusan said, "You Jagdish Prasar are the tout of judiciary." Again medha said *"sale ko jaan se maar do"* [kill him]. Arundhanti Roy commanded the crow [crowd] that Supreme Court of India is the thief and all these are this touts. Kill them, Prasant Bhushan "pulled" by having "caught" my "haired [*sic*] and said that if you would be seen in the Supreme Court again he would get them killed." But they were shouting inspite of the presence of S.H.O and ACP Bhaskar [of] Tilak Marg [Police Station]. We ran away with great with great hardship otherwise their goonda might have done some mischief because of their drunken state. Therefore, it is requested to you that proper action may be taken after registering our complaint in order to save on our lives and property. We complainants will be highly obliged.

Sd. Complainants.

The main petition is as shoddily drafted as the FIR. The lies, the looseness, the ludicrousness of the charges displays more contempt for the Apex Court than any of the offenses allegedly committed by Prashant Bhushan, Medha Patkar, and myself. Its contents are patently false and malicious. The police station in Tilak Marg, where the FIR was lodged, has not registered a case. No policeman ever contacted me, there was no police investigation, no attempt to verify the charges, to find out whether the people named in the petition were present at the *dharna*, and whether indeed the incident described in the FIR (on which the entire contempt petition is based) occurred at all.

Under the circumstances, it is distressing that the Supreme Court has thought it fit to entertain this petition and issue notice directing me and the other respondents to appear personally in court on the 23rd of April 2001, and to "continue to attend the Court on all the days thereafter to which the case against you stands and until final orders are passed on the charges against you. WHEREIN FAIL NOT."

For the ordinary working citizen, these enforced court appearances mean that in effect, the punishment for the uncommitted crime has already begun.

The facts relating to the petition are as follows:

Contrary to everything the petition says, insinuates, and implies—I am not a leader of the Narmada Bachao Andolan. I am a writer, an independent citizen with independent views who supports and admires the cause of the Andolan. I was not a petitioner in the Public Interest Litigation petition in the case of the Sardar Sarovar Project. I am not an "interested party." Prashant Bhushan is not my lawyer and has never represented me.

Furthermore in all humility I aver that I do not know who the petitioners are. That I never tried to murder anybody, or incite anybody to murder anybody, in broad daylight outside the gates of the Supreme Court in full view of the Delhi police. That I did not raise any slogans against the court. That I did not see Prashant Bhushan "pulled" anyone by having "caught" their "haired" [sic] and said that "if you would be seen in the Supreme Court again he would get them killed." That I did not see Medha Patkar, leader of India's most prominent nonviolent resistance movement, metamorphose into a mediocre film actor and say, "*Sale ko jaan se maar do*" (Kill the bastard). That I did not notice the presence of any "*goondas*" in a "drunken state." And finally, that my name is spelled wrong.

On the morning of the 13th of December 2000, I learned that people from the Narmada valley had gathered outside the gates of the Supreme Court. When I arrived at the Supreme Court at about 11:30 a.m., gate No. C was already closed. Four to five hundred people were standing outside. Most of them were Adivasi people who, as a consequence of the recent Supreme Court judgment that allowed the construction of the Sardar Sarovar Dam to proceed, will lose their lands and homes this monsoon to the rising waters of the reservoir. They have not been rehabilitated. In a few months they will be destitute and have nowhere to go. These people had traveled all the way from the Narmada valley to personally convey their despair and anguish to the court. To tell the court that, in contravention of its order, no land has been offered to them for rehabilitation and that the reality of the situation in the Narmada valley is very different from the one portrayed in the Supreme Court judgment. They asked the registrar of the court for a meeting with the chief justice.

A number of representatives of peoples' movements in Delhi, and other supporters of the Andolan like myself, were also there to express their solidarity. I would like to stress that I did not see Prashant Bhushan, the main accused in the petition, at the *dharna*. Medha Patkar, who was there, asked me to speak to the people for five minutes.

My exact words were: "*Mujhe paanch minute bhi nahi chahiye aapke saamne apni baat rakhne ke liye. Mein aapke saath hoon*" (I do not even need five minutes to tell you why I'm here. I'm here because I support you). This is easy to verify as there were several film and television crews shooting the event. The villagers had cloth labels hung around their necks that said, "Project-Affected at 90 Meters" (the current height of the dam). As time went by and it became clear that the request for a meeting with the chief justice was not going to be granted, people grew disheartened. Several people (who I don't know or recognize) made speeches critical of the court, its inaccessibility to common people, and its process. Others spoke about corruption in the judiciary, about the judges and how far removed they are from ground realities. I admit that I made absolutely no attempt to intervene. I am not a policeman or a public official. As a writer I am deeply interested in people's perceptions of the functioning of one of the most important institutions in this country.

However, I would like to clarify that I have never, either in my writing or in any public forum, cast aspersions on the character or integrity of the judges. I believe that the reflexive instinct of the powerful to protect the powerful is sufficient explanation for the kind of iniquitous judgment as in the case of the Sardar Sarovar Project. I did not raise slogans against the court. I did not, as the petition claims, say, "Supreme Court *bika hua hai*" (The Supreme Court has sold out). I certainly did not "command the crow that Supreme Court of India is the thief and all these are this touts." (Perhaps the petitioners meant "crowd"?) I went to the *dharna* because I have been deeply distressed and angered by the Supreme Court's majority—and therefore operative—verdict on the Sardar Sarovar Project. The verdict allowed the project to proceed even though the court was well aware that the Narmada Water Disputes Tribunal had been consistently violated for thirteen years. That not a single village had been resettled according to the directives of the tribunal, and that the Madhya Pradesh government (which is responsible for 80 percent of the oustees) had given a written affidavit in court stating that it has no land to resettle them. In effect, the Supreme Court ordered the violation of the fundamental rights to life and livelihood of hundreds of thousands of Indian citizens, most of them Dalit and Adivasi.

As a consequence of the Supreme Court judgment, it is these unfortunate citizens who stand to lose their homes, their livelihoods, their gods and their histories. When they came calling on the Supreme Court on the morning of December 13, 2000, they were asking the court to restore their dignity. To accuse them of lowering the dignity of the court suggests that the dignity of the court and the dignity of Indian citizens are incompatible, oppositional, adversarial things. That the dignity of one can only exist at the cost of the other. If this is so, it is a sad and shameful proposition. In his Republic Day speech, president K. R. Narayanan called upon the nation, and specifically the judiciary, to take special care of these fragile communities. He said, "The developmental path we have adopted is hurting them, the marginalized, the Scheduled Castes and Scheduled Tribes, and threatening their very existence."

I believe that the people of the Narmada valley have the constitutional right to protest peacefully against what they consider an unjust and unfair judgment. As for myself, I have every right to participate in any peaceful protest meeting that I choose to. Even outside the gates of the Supreme Court. As a writer I am fully entitled to put forward my views, my reasons and arguments for why I believe that the judgment in the Sardar Sarovar case is flawed and unjust and violates the human rights of Indian citizens. I have the right to use all my skills and abilities, such as they are, and all the facts and figures at my disposal, to persuade people to my point of view.

The petition is a pathetic attempt to target what the petitioners perceive to be the three main fronts of the resistance movement in the Narmada valley. The activist Medha Patkar, leader of the Narmada Bachao Andolan and representative of the people in the valley; the lawyer, Prashant Bhushan, legal counsel for the Narmada Bachao Andolan; and the writer (me), who is seen as one of those who carries the voice of the Andolan to the world outside. It is significant that this is the third time that I, as a writer, have had to face legal harassment connected with my writing.

In July 1999, the three-judge bench in the Supreme Court hearing the public interest petition on the Sardar Sarovar Project took offense at my essay "The Greater Common Good," published in *Outlook* and *Frontline* magazines. While the waters rose in the Narmada, while villagers stood in their homes in chest-deep water for days on end, protesting the court's interim order, the Supreme Court held three hearings in which the main topic they discussed was whether or not the dignity of the court had been violated by my essay. On the 15th of October 1999, without giving me an opportunity to be heard, the court passed an insulting order. Here is an extract:

> *Judicial process and institution cannot be permitted to be scandalised or subjected to contumacious violation in such a blatant manner in which it has been done by her [Arundhati Roy] . . . vicious stultification and vulgar debunking cannot be permitted to pollute the stream of justice . . . we are unhappy at the way in which the leaders of NBA and Ms. Arundhati Roy have attempted to undermine the dignity of the Court. We expected better behaviour from them . . .*

The order contained a veiled warning to me not to continue with my "objectionable writings."

In 1997, a criminal case for Corrupting Public Morality was filed against me in a district magistrate's court in Kerala for my book *The God of Small Things*. It has been pending for the last four years. I have had to hire criminal lawyers, draft affidavits, and travel all the way to Kerala to appear in court.

And now I have to defend myself on this third, ludicrous charge.

As a writer I wish to state as emphatically as I can that this is a dangerous trend. If the court uses the Contempt of Court law, and allows citizens to abuse its process to intimidate and harass writers, it will have the chilling effect of interfering with a writer's imagination and the creative act itself. This fear of harassment will create a situation in which even before a writer puts pen to paper, she will have to anticipate what the court might think of her work. It will induce a sort of enforced, fearful self-censorship. It would be bad for law, worse for literature, and sad for the world of art and beauty.

I have written and published several essays and articles on the Narmada issue and the Supreme Court judgment. None of them was intended to show contempt to the court. However, I have every right to disagree with the court's views on the subject and to express my disagreement in any publication or forum that I choose to. Regardless of everything the operative Supreme Court judgment on the Sardar Sarovar says, I continue to be opposed to Big Dams. I continue to believe that they are economically unviable, ecologically destructive, and deeply undemocratic. I continue to believe that the judgment disregarded the evidence placed before the court. I continue to write what I believe. Not to do so would undermine the dignity of writers, their art, their very purpose. I need hardly add that I also believe that those who hold the opposite point of view to mine, those who wish to disagree with my views, criticize them, or denounce them, have the same rights to free speech and expression as I do.

I left the *dharna* at about 6 p.m. Until then, contrary to the lurid scenario described in the petitioners' FIR, I can state on oath that no blood was spilled, no mob was drunk, no hair was pulled, no murder attempted. A little *khichdi* was cooked and consumed. No litter was left. There were over a hundred police constables and some senior police officers present. Though I would very much like to, I cannot say in good conscience that I have never set eyes on the petitioners because I don't know who they are or what they look like. They could have been any one of the hundreds of people who were milling around on that day.

But whoever they are, and whatever their motives, for the petitioners to attempt to misuse the Contempt of Court Act and the good offices of the Supreme Court to stifle criticism and stamp out dissent strikes at the very roots of the notion of democracy.

In recent months this court has issued judgments on several major public issues. For instance, the closure of polluting industries in Delhi, the conversion of public transport buses from diesel to CNG [compressed natural gas], and the judgment permitting the construction of the Sardar Sarovar Dam to proceed. All of these have had far-reaching and often unanticipated impacts. They have materially affected, for better or for worse, the lives and livelihoods of millions of Indian citizens. Whatever the justice or injustice of these judgments, whatever their finer legal points, for the court to become intolerant of criticism or expressions of dissent would mark the beginning of the end of democracy.

An "activist" judiciary that intervenes in public matters to provide a corrective to a corrupt, dysfunctional executive surely has to be more, not less accountable. To a society that is already convulsed by political bankruptcy, economic distress, and religious and cultural intolerance, any form of judicial intolerance will come as a crippling blow. If the judiciary removes itself from public scrutiny and accountability, and severs its links with the society that it was set up to serve in the first place, it would mean that yet another pillar of Indian democracy will crumble. A judicial dictatorship is as fearsome a prospect as a military dictatorship or any other form of totalitarian rule.

The Tehelka tapes broadcast recently on a national television network show the repulsive sight of the presidents of the Bhartiya Janata Party and the Samata Party (both part of the ruling coalition) accepting bribes from spurious arms dealers.[1] Though this ought to have been considered *prima facie* evidence of corruption, the Delhi High Court declined to entertain a petition seeking an enquiry into the defense deals that were referred to in the tapes. The bench took strong exception to the petitioner approaching the court without substantial evidence and even warned the petitioner's counsel that if he failed to substantiate its allegations, the court would impose costs on the petitioner.

On the grounds that judges of the Supreme Court were too busy, the chief justice of India refused to allow a sitting judge to head the judicial enquiry into the Tehelka scandal, even though it involves matters of national security and corruption in the highest places.[2]

Yet, when it comes to an absurd, despicable, entirely unsubstantiated petition in which all the three respondents happen to be people who have publicly—though in markedly different ways—questioned the policies of the government and severely criticized a recent judgment of the Supreme Court, the court displays a disturbing willingness to issue notice.

It indicates a disquieting inclination on the part of the court to silence criticism and muzzle dissent, to harass and intimidate those who disagree with it. By entertaining a petition based on an FIR that even a local police station does not see fit to act upon, the Supreme Court is doing its own reputation and credibility considerable harm.

In conclusion, I wish to reaffirm that as a writer I have the right to state my opinions and beliefs. As a free citizen of India, I have the right to be part of any peaceful *dharna*, demonstration, or protest march. I have the right to criticize any judgment of any court that I believe to be unjust. I have the right to make common cause with those I agree with. I hope that each time I exercise these rights I will not be dragged to court on false charges and forced to explain my actions.

The petitioners have committed civil and criminal defamation. They ought to be investigated and prosecuted for perjury. They ought to be made to pay damages for the time they have wasted of this Apex Court by filing these false charges. Above all they ought to be made to apologize to all those citizens who are patiently awaiting the attention of the Supreme Court in more important matters.

POSTSCRIPT: In the trial that followed, the Supreme Court asked Arundhati Roy to apologize for this affidavit. When she refused she was convicted for Contempt of Court and sentenced to one day in prison. She served the sentence in Delhi's Tihar Jail.

DEMOCRACY:
WHO IS SHE WHEN
SHE'S AT HOME?

LAST NIGHT A friend from Baroda called. Weeping. It took her fifteen minutes to tell me what the matter was. It wasn't very complicated. Only that a friend of hers, Sayeeda, had been caught by a mob. Only that her stomach had been ripped open and stuffed with burning rags. Only that after she died someone carved "OM" on her forehead.[1]

Precisely which Hindu scripture preaches this?

Our prime minister, A. B. Vajpayee, justified this as part of the retaliation by outraged Hindus against Muslim "terrorists" who burned alive fifty-eight Hindu passengers on the Sabarmati Express in Godhra.[2] Each of those who died that hideous death was someone's brother, someone's mother, someone's child. Of course they were.

Which particular verse in the Koran required that they be roasted alive?

The more the two sides try and call attention to their religious

First published in *Outlook* on May 6, 2002.

differences by slaughtering each other, the less there is to distinguish them from one another. They worship at the same altar. They're both apostles of the same murderous god, whoever he is. In an atmosphere so vitiated, for anybody, and in particular the prime minister, to arbitrarily decree exactly where the cycle started is malevolent and irresponsible.

Right now we're sipping from a poisoned chalice—a flawed democracy laced with religious fascism. Pure arsenic.

What shall we do? What *can* we do?

We have a ruling party that's hemorrhaging. Its rhetoric against terrorism, the passing of the Prevention of Terrorism Act, the saber-rattling against Pakistan (with the underlying nuclear threat), the massing of almost a million soldiers on the border on hair-trigger alert, and, most dangerous of all, the attempt to communalize and falsify school history textbooks—none of this has prevented it from being humiliated in election after election.[3] Even its old party trick—the revival of the plans to replace the destroyed mosque in Ayodhya with the Ram Mandir (a Hindu Temple to Lord Ram)—didn't quite work out.[4] Desperate now, it has turned for succor to the state of Gujarat.

Gujarat, the only major state in India to have a Bharatiya Janata Party (BJP) government, has for some years been the petri dish in which Hindu fascism has been fomenting an elaborate political experiment. In March 2002, the initial results were put on public display.

Within hours of the Godhra outrage, a meticulously planned pogrom was unleashed against the Muslim community. It was led from the front by the Hindu nationalist Vishwa Hindu Parishad (VHP) and the Bajrang Dal. Officially, the number of dead is eight hundred. Independent reports put the figure as high as two thousand.[5] More than 150,000 people, driven from their homes, now live in refugee camps.[6] Women were stripped, gang-raped; parents were bludgeoned to death in front of their children.[7] Two hundred forty *dargahs* and one hundred eighty *masjids* were destroyed. In Ahmedabad, the tomb of Wali Gujarati, the founder of the modern Urdu poem, was demolished and paved over in the course of a night.[8] The tomb of the musician Ustad Faiyaz Ali Khan was desecrated and wreathed in burning tires.[9] Arsonists burned and looted shops, homes, hotels, textile mills, buses, and private cars. Tens of thousands have lost their jobs.[10]

A mob surrounded the house of former Congress MP Ehsan Jaffri. His phone calls to the director general of police, the police commissioner, the chief secretary, the additional chief secretary (home) were ignored. The mobile police vans around his house did not intervene. The mob dragged Ehsan Jaffri out of his house, and dismembered him.[11] Of course it's only a coincidence that Jaffri was a trenchant critic of Gujarat's chief minister, Narendra Modi, during his campaign for the Rajkot Assembly by-election in February.

Across Gujarat, thousands of people made up the mobs. They were armed with petrol bombs, guns, knives, swords, and tridents.[12] Apart from the VHP and Bajrang Dal's usual lumpen constituency, there were Dalits and Adivasis who were brought in buses and trucks. Middle-class people participated in the looting. (On one memorable occasion a family arrived in a Mitsubishi Lancer.)[13] There was a deliberate, systematic attempt to destroy the economic base of the Muslim community. The leaders of the mob had computer-generated cadastral lists marking out Muslim homes, shops, businesses, and even partnerships. They had mobile phones to coordinate the action. They had trucks loaded with thousands of gas cylinders, hoarded weeks in advance, which they used to blow up Muslim commercial establishments. They had not just police protection and police connivance but also covering fire.[14]

While Gujarat burned, our prime minister was on MTV promoting his new poems.[15] (Reports say cassettes have sold a hundred thousand copies.) It took him more than a month—and two vacations in the hills—to make it to Gujarat.[16] When he did, shadowed by the chilling Modi, he gave a speech at the Shah Alam refugee camp.[17] His mouth moved, he tried to express concern, but no real sound emerged except the mocking of the wind whistling through a burned, bloodied, broken world. Next we knew, he was bobbing around in a golf cart, striking business deals in Singapore.[18]

The killers still stalk Gujarat's streets. For weeks the lynch mob was the arbiter of the routine affairs of daily life: who can live where, who can say what, who can meet whom, and where and when. Its mandate expanded from religious affairs to property disputes, family altercations, the planning and allocation of water resources . . . (which is why Medha Patkar of the Narmada Bachao Andolan was assaulted).[19] Muslim businesses have been shut down. Muslim people are not served in restaurants. Muslim children are not welcome in schools. Muslim students are too terrified to sit for their exams.[20] Muslim parents live in dread that their infants might forget what they've been told and give themselves away by saying "Ammi!" or "Abba!" in public and invite sudden and violent death.

Notice has been given: *this is just the beginning.*

Is this the Hindu Rashtra, the Nation that we've all been asked to look forward to? Once the Muslims have been "shown their place," will milk and Coca-Cola flow across the land? Once the Ram Mandir is built, will there be a shirt on every back and a roti in every belly?[21] Will every tear be wiped from every eye? Can we expect an anniversary celebration next year? Or will there be someone else to hate by then? Alphabetically: Adivasis, Buddhists, Christians, Dalits, Parsis, Sikhs? Those who wear jeans or speak English or those who have thick lips or curly hair? We won't have to wait long. It's started already. Will the established rituals continue? Will people be beheaded, dismembered, and urinated upon? Will fetuses be ripped from their mothers' wombs and slaughtered? (What kind of depraved vision can even *imagine* India without the range and beauty and spectacular anarchy of all these cultures? India would become a tomb and smell like a crematorium.)

No matter who they were, or how they were killed, each person who died in Gujarat in the weeks gone by deserves to be

mourned. There have been hundreds of outraged letters to journals and newspapers asking why the "pseudo-secularists" do not
condemn the burning of the Sabarmati Express in Godhra with
the same degree of outrage with which they condemn the killings
in the rest of Gujarat. What they don't seem to understand is
that there *is* a fundamental difference between a pogrom such
as the one taking place in Gujarat now and the burning of the
Sabarmati Express in Godhra. We still don't know who exactly
was responsible for the carnage in Godhra.[22]

Whoever did it—whatever their political or religious persuasion—committed a terrible crime. But every independent report
says the pogrom against the Muslim community in Gujarat—billed
by the government as a spontaneous "reaction"—has at best been
conducted under the benign gaze of the state and, at worst, with
active state collusion.[23] Either way, the state is criminally culpable.
And the state acts in the name of its citizens. So, as a citizen, I am
forced to acknowledge that I am somehow made complicit in the
Gujarat pogrom. It is this that outrages me. And it is this that puts
a completely different complexion on the two massacres.

After the Gujarat massacres, at its convention in Bangalore,
the Rashtriya Swayamsevak Sangh (RSS), the moral and cultural
guild of the BJP, of which the prime minister, the home minister,
and chief minister Modi himself are all members, called upon
Muslims to earn the "good will" of the majority community.[24]

At the meeting of the national executive of the BJP in Goa,
Narendra Modi was greeted as a hero. His smirking offer to resign
from the chief minister's post was unanimously turned down.[25]
In a recent public speech he compared the events of the last few
weeks in Gujarat to Gandhi's Dandi March—both, according to
him, significant moments in the Struggle for Freedom.

While the parallels between contemporary India and pre-war
Germany are chilling, they're not surprising. (The founders of
the RSS have, in their writings, been frank in their admiration for
Hitler and his methods.)[26] One difference is that here in India we
don't have a Hitler. We have, instead, a traveling extravaganza,

a mobile symphonic orchestra. The hydra-headed, many-armed Sangh Parivar—the "joint family" of Hindu political and cultural organizations—with the BJP, the RSS, the VHP, and the Bajrang Dal, each playing a different instrument. Its utter genius lies in its apparent ability to be all things to all people at all times.

The Parivar has an appropriate head for every occasion. An old versifier with rhetoric for every season. A rabble-rousing hardliner, Lal Krishna Advani, for Home Affairs; a suave one, Jaswant Singh, for Foreign Affairs; a smooth English-speaking lawyer, Arun Jaitley, to handle TV debates; a cold-blooded creature, Narendra Modi, for a chief minister; and the Bajrang Dal and the VHP, grassroots workers in charge of the physical labor that goes into the business of genocide. Finally, this many-headed extravaganza has a lizard's tail which drops off when it's in trouble and grows back again: a specious socialist dressed up as defense minister, whom it sends on its damage-limitation missions—wars, cyclones, genocides. They trust him to press the right buttons, hit the right note.

The Sangh Parivar speaks in as many tongues as a whole corsage of tridents. It can say several contradictory things simultaneously. While one of its heads (the VHP) exhorts millions of its cadres to prepare for the Final Solution, its titular head (the prime minister) assures the nation that all citizens, regardless of their religion, will be treated equally. It can ban books and films and burn paintings for "insulting Indian culture." Simultaneously, it can mortgage the equivalent of 60 percent of the entire country's rural development budget as profit to Enron.[27] It contains within itself the full spectrum of political opinion, so what would normally be a public fight between two adversarial political parties is now just a family matter. However acrimonious the quarrel, it's *always* conducted in public, always resolved amicably, and the audience always goes away satisfied it's got value for its money—anger, action, revenge, intrigue, remorse, poetry, and plenty of gore. It's our own vernacular version of Full Spectrum Dominance.[28]

But when the chips are down, *really* down, the squabbling heads quiet, and it becomes chillingly apparent that underneath all the clamor and the noise, a single heart beats. And an unforgiving mind with saffron-saturated tunnel vision works overtime.

There have been pogroms in India before, every kind of pogrom—directed at particular castes, tribes, religious faiths. In 1984, following the assassination of Indira Gandhi, the Congress Party presided over the massacre of three thousand Sikhs in Delhi, every bit as macabre as the one in Gujarat.[29] At the time Rajiv Gandhi, never known for an elegant turn of phrase, said, "When a large tree falls, the earth shakes."[30] In 1985 the Congress swept the polls. On a *sympathy* wave! Eighteen years have gone by, and almost no one has been punished.

Take any politically volatile issue—the nuclear tests, the Babri Masjid, the Tehelka scam, the stirring of the communal cauldron for electoral advantage—and you'll see the Congress Party has been there before. In every case, the Congress sowed the seed and the BJP has swept in to reap the hideous harvest. So in the event that we're called upon to vote, *is* there a difference between the two? The answer is a faltering but distinct yes. Here's why: It's true that the Congress Party has sinned, and grievously, and for decades together. But it has done by night what the BJP does by day. It has done covertly, stealthily, hypocritically, shamefacedly what the BJP does with pride. And this is an important difference.

Whipping up communal hatred is part of the mandate of the Sangh Parivar. It has been planned for *years*. It has been injecting a slow-release poison directly into civil society's bloodstream. Hundreds of RSS shakhas and Saraswati shishu mandirs across the country have been indoctrinating thousands of children and young people, stunting their minds with religious hatred and falsified history, including unfactual or wildly exaggerated accounts of the rape and pillaging of Hindu women and Hindu temples by Muslim rulers in the precolonial period. They're no different from, and no less dangerous than, the madrassas all over Pakistan and Afghanistan that spawned the Taliban. In states like Gujarat, the police, the administration, and the political cadres at every level have been systematically penetrated.[31] The whole enterprise has huge popular appeal, which it would be foolish to underestimate or misunderstand. It has a formidable religious, ideological, political, and administrative underpinning. This kind of power, this kind of reach, can only be achieved with state backing.

Some madrassas, the Muslim equivalent of hothouses cultivating religious hatred, try and make up in frenzy and foreign funding what they lack in state support. They provide the perfect foil for Hindu communalists to dance their dance of mass paranoia and hatred. (In fact, they serve that purpose so perfectly they might just as well be working as a team.)

Under this relentless pressure, what will most likely happen is that the majority of the Muslim community will resign itself to living in ghettos as second-class citizens, in constant fear, with no civil rights and no recourse to justice. What will daily life be like for them? Any little thing, an altercation in a cinema queue or a fracas at a traffic light, could turn lethal. So they will learn to keep very quiet, to accept their lot, to creep around the edges of the society in which they live. Their fear will transmit itself to other minorities. Many, particularly the young, will probably turn to militancy. They will do terrible things. Civil society will be called upon to condemn them. Then President Bush's canon will come back to us: "Either you are with us or you are with the terrorists."[32]

Those words hang frozen in time like icicles. For years to come, butchers and genocidists will fit their grisly mouths around them ("lip-sync," filmmakers call it) in order to justify their butchery.

Bal Thackeray of the Shiv Sena, who has lately been feeling a little upstaged by Modi, has the lasting solution. He's called for civil war. Isn't that just perfect? Then Pakistan won't need to bomb us, we can bomb ourselves. Let's turn all of India into

Kashmir. Or Bosnia. Or Palestine. Or Rwanda. Let's all suffer forever. Let's buy expensive guns and explosives to kill each other with. Let the British arms dealers and the American weapons manufacturers grow fat on our spilled blood.[33] We could ask the Carlyle Group—of which the Bush and bin Laden families were both shareholders—for a bulk discount.[34] Maybe if things go really well, we'll become like Afghanistan. (And look at the publicity they've gone and got themselves.) When all our farmlands are mined, our buildings destroyed, our infrastructure reduced to rubble, our children physically maimed and mentally wrecked, when we've nearly wiped ourselves out with self-manufactured hatred, maybe we can appeal to the Americans to help us out. Airdropped airline meals, anyone?

How close we have come to self-destruction! Another step and we'll be in free fall. And yet the government presses on. At the Goa meeting of the BJP's national executive, the prime minister of secular, democratic India, A. B. Vajpayee, made history. He became the first Indian prime minister to cross the threshold and publicly unveil an unconscionable bigotry against Muslims, which even George Bush and Donald Rumsfeld would be embarrassed to own up to. "Wherever Muslims are," he said, "they do not want to live peacefully."[35]

Shame on him. But if only it were just him: in the immediate aftermath of the Gujarat holocaust, confident of the success of its "experiment," the BJP wants a snap poll. "The *gentlest* of people," my friend from Baroda said to me, "the *gentlest* of people, in the gentlest of voices, says 'Modi is our hero.'"

Some of us nurtured the naive hope that the magnitude of the horror of the last few weeks would make the secular parties, however self-serving, unite in sheer outrage. On its own, the BJP does not have the mandate of the people of India. It does not have the mandate to push through the Hindutva project. We hoped that the twenty-two allies that make up the BJP-led coalition would withdraw their support. We thought, quite stupidly, that they would see that there could be no bigger test of their moral fiber, of their commitment to their avowed principles of secularism.

It's a sign of the times that not a single one of the BJP's allies has withdrawn support. In every shifty eye you see that faraway look of someone doing mental math to calculate which constituencies and portfolios they'll retain and which ones they'll lose if they pull out. Deepak Parekh is one of the only CEOs of India's corporate community to condemn what happened.[36] Farooq Abdullah, chief minister of Jammu and Kashmir and the only prominent Muslim politician left in India, is currying favor with the government by supporting Modi because he nurses the dim hope that he might become vice president of India very soon.[37] And worst of all, Mayawati, leader of the Bahujan Samaj Party (BSP), the People's Socialist Party, the great hope of the lower castes, has forged an alliance with the BJP in Uttar Pradesh.[38]

The Congress and the left parties have launched a public agitation asking for Modi's resignation.[39] *Resignation?* Have we lost all sense of proportion? Criminals are not meant to *resign*. They're meant to be charged, tried, and convicted. As those who burned the train in Godhra should be. As the mobs and those members of the police force and the administration who planned and participated in the pogrom in the rest of Gujarat should be. As those responsible for raising the pitch of the frenzy to boiling point must be. The Supreme Court has the option of acting against Modi and the Bajrang Dal and the VHP. There are hundreds of testimonies. There are masses of evidence.

But in India if you are a butcher or a genocidist who happens to be a politician, you have every reason to be optimistic. No one even *expects* politicians to be prosecuted. To demand that Modi and his henchmen be arraigned and put away would make other politicians vulnerable to their own unsavory pasts. So instead they disrupt Parliament, shout a lot. Eventually, those in power set up commissions of inquiry, ignore the findings, and between themselves makes sure the juggernaut chugs on.

Already the issue has begun to morph. Should elections be allowed or not? Should the Election Commission decide that? Or the Supreme Court? Either way, whether elections are held or deferred, by allowing Modi to walk free, by allowing him to continue with his career as a politician, the fundamental, governing principles of democracy are not just being subverted but deliberately sabotaged. This kind of democracy is the *problem*, not the solution. Our society's greatest strength is being turned into her deadliest enemy. What's the point of us all going on about "deepening democracy," when it's being bent and twisted into something unrecognizable?

What if the BJP *does* win the elections? After all, George Bush had a 60 percent rating in his War on Terror, and Ariel Sharon has an even stronger mandate for his bestial invasion of Palestine.[40] Does that make everything all right? Why not dispense with the legal system, the constitution, the press—the whole shebang—morality *itself*, why not chuck it and put everything up for a vote? Genocides can become the subject of opinion polls, and massacres can have marketing campaigns.

Fascism's firm footprint has appeared in India. Let's mark the date: Spring 2002. While we can thank the American president and the Coalition Against Terror for creating a congenial international atmosphere for fascism's ghastly debut, we cannot credit them for the years it has been brewing in our public and private lives.

It breezed in after the Pokhran nuclear tests in 1998.[41] From then onward, the massed energy of bloodthirsty patriotism became openly acceptable political currency. The "weapons of peace" trapped India and Pakistan in a spiral of brinkmanship—threat and counterthreat, taunt and countertaunt.[42] And now, one war and hundreds of dead later,[43] more than a million soldiers from both armies are massed at the border, eyeball to eyeball, locked in a pointless nuclear standoff. The escalating belligerence against Pakistan has ricocheted off the border and entered our own body politic, like a sharp blade slicing through the vestiges of communal harmony and tolerance between the Hindu and Muslim communities. In no time at all, the god-squadders from hell have colonized the public imagination. And we allowed them in. Each time the hostility between India and Pakistan is cranked up, within India there's a corresponding increase in the hostility toward the Muslims. With each battle cry against Pakistan, we inflict a wound on ourselves, on our way of life, on our spectacularly diverse and ancient civilization, on everything that makes India different from Pakistan. Increasingly, Indian nationalism has come to mean Hindu nationalism, which defines itself not through a respect or regard for itself but through a hatred of the Other. And the Other, for the moment, is not just Pakistan, it's Muslims. It's disturbing to see how neatly nationalism dovetails into fascism. While we must not allow the fascists to define what the nation is, or who it belongs to, it's worth keeping in mind that nationalism—in all its many avatars: communist, capitalist, and fascist—has been at the root of almost all the genocide of the twentieth century. On the issue of nationalism, it's wise to proceed with caution.

Can we not find it in ourselves to belong to an ancient civilization instead of to just a recent nation? To love a *land* instead of just patrolling a territory? The Sangh Parivar understands nothing of what civilization means. It seeks to limit, reduce, define, dismember, and desecrate the memory of what we were, our understanding of what we are, and our dreams of who we want to be. What kind of India do they want? A limbless, headless, soulless torso, left bleeding under the butcher's cleaver with a flag driven deep into her mutilated heart? Can we let that happen? Have we let it happen?

The incipient, creeping fascism of the past few years has been groomed by many of our "democratic" institutions. Everyone has flirted with it—Parliament, the press, the police, the administration, the public. Even "secularists" have been guilty of helping to create the right climate. Each time you defend the right of an institution, *any* institution (including the Supreme Court), to exercise unfettered, unaccountable powers that must never be challenged, you move toward fascism. To be fair, perhaps not everyone recognized the early signs for what they were.

The national press has been startlingly courageous in its denunciation of the events of the last few weeks. Many of the BJP's fellow travelers, who have journeyed with it to the brink, are now looking down the abyss into the hell that was once Gujarat and turning away in genuine dismay. But how hard and for how long will they fight? This is not going to be like a publicity campaign for an upcoming cricket season. And there will not always be spectacular carnage to report on. Fascism is also about the slow, steady infiltration of all the instruments of state power. It's about the slow erosion of civil liberties, about unspectacular day-to-day injustices. Fighting it means fighting to win back the minds and hearts of people. Fighting it does not mean asking for RSS shakhas and the madrassas that are overtly communal to be banned, it means working toward the day when they're voluntarily abandoned as bad ideas. It means keeping an eagle eye on public institutions and demanding accountability. It means putting your ear to the ground and listening to the whispering of the truly powerless. It means giving a forum to the myriad voices from the hundreds of resistance movements across the country which are speaking about *real* things—about bonded labor, marital rape, sexual preferences, women's wages, uranium dumping, unsustainable mining, weavers' woes, farmers' suicides. It means fighting displacement and dispossession and the relentless, everyday violence of abject poverty. Fighting it also means not allowing your newspaper columns and prime-time TV spots to be hijacked by their spurious passions and their staged theatrics, which are designed to divert attention from everything else.

While most people in India have been horrified by what happened in Gujarat, many thousands of the indoctrinated are preparing to journey deeper into the heart of the horror. Look around you and you'll see in little parks, in empty lots, in village commons, the RSS is marching, hoisting its saffron flag. Suddenly they're everywhere, grown men in khaki shorts marching, marching, marching. To *where*? For *what*? Their disregard for history shields them from the knowledge that fascism will thrive for a short while and then self-annihilate because of its inherent stupidity. But unfortunately, like the radioactive fallout of a nuclear strike, it has a half-life that will cripple generations to come.

These levels of rage and hatred cannot be contained, cannot be expected to subside, with public censure and denunciation. Hymns of brotherhood and love are great, but not enough.

Historically, fascist movements have been fueled by feelings of national disillusionment. Fascism has come to India after the dreams that fueled the Freedom Struggle have been frittered away like so much loose change.

Independence itself came to us as what Gandhi famously called a "wooden loaf "—a notional freedom tainted by the blood of the thousands who died during Partition.[44] For more than half a century now, the hatred and mutual distrust has been exacerbated, toyed with, and never allowed to heal by politicians, led from the front by Indira Gandhi. Every political party has tilled the marrow of our secular parliamentary democracy, mining it for electoral advantage. Like termites excavating a mound, they've made tunnels and underground passages, undermining the meaning of "secular," until it has become just an empty shell that's about to implode. Their tilling has weakened the foundations of the structure that connects the constitution, Parliament, and the courts of law—the configuration of checks and balances that forms the backbone of a parliamentary democracy. Under the circumstances, it's futile to go on blaming politicians and demanding from them a morality of which they're incapable. There's something pitiable about a people that constantly bemoans its leaders. If they've let us down, it's only because we've allowed them to. It could be argued that civil society has failed its leaders as much as leaders have failed civil society. We have to accept that there is a dangerous, systemic flaw in our parliamentary democracy that politicians *will* exploit. And that's what results in the kind of conflagration that we have witnessed in Gujarat. There's fire in the ducts. We have to address this issue and come up with a *systemic* solution.

But politicians' exploitation of communal divides is by no means the only reason that fascism has arrived on our shores.

Over the past fifty years, ordinary citizens' modest hopes for lives of dignity, security, and relief from abject poverty have been systematically snuffed out. Every "democratic" institution in this country has shown itself to be unaccountable, inaccessible to the ordinary citizen, and either unwilling or incapable of acting in the interests of genuine social justice. *Every* strategy for real social change—land reform, education, public health, the equitable distribution of natural resources, the implementation of positive discrimination—has been cleverly, cunningly, and consistently scuttled and rendered ineffectual by those castes and that class of people which have a stranglehold on the political process. And now corporate globalization is being relentlessly and arbitrarily imposed on an essentially feudal society, tearing through its complex, tiered social fabric, ripping it apart culturally and economically.

There is very real grievance here. And the fascists didn't create it. But they have seized upon it, upturned it, and forged from it a hideous, bogus sense of pride. They have mobilized human beings using the lowest common denominator—religion. People who have lost control over their lives, people who have been uprooted from their homes and communities, who have lost their culture and their language, are being made to feel proud of *something*. Not something they have striven for and achieved, not something they can count as a personal accomplishment, but something they just happen to be. Or, more accurately, something they happen *not* to be. And the falseness, the emptiness, of that pride is fueling a gladiatorial anger that is then directed toward a simulated target that has been wheeled into the amphitheater.

How else can you explain the project of trying to disenfranchise, drive out, or exterminate the second-poorest community in this country, using as your foot soldiers the very poorest (Dalits and Adivasis)? How else can you explain why Dalits in Gujarat, who have been despised, oppressed, and treated worse than refuse by the upper castes for thousands of years, have joined hands with their oppressors to turn on those who are only marginally less unfortunate than they themselves? Are they just wage slaves, mercenaries for hire? Is it all right to patronize them and absolve them of responsibility for their own actions? Or am I being obtuse? Perhaps it's common practice for the unfortunate to vent their rage and hatred on the *next* most unfortunate, because their *real* adversaries are inaccessible, seemingly invincible, and completely out of range. Because their own leaders have cut loose and are feasting at the high table, leaving them to wander rudderless in the wilderness, spouting nonsense about returning to the Hindu fold. (The first step, presumably, toward founding a global Hindu empire, as realistic a goal as fascism's previously failed projects—the restoration of Roman glory, the purification of the German race, or the establishment of an Islamic sultanate.)

One hundred thirty million Muslims live in India.[45] Hindu fascists regard them as legitimate prey. Do people like Modi and Bal Thackeray think that the world will stand by and watch while they're liquidated in a "civil war"? Press reports say that the European Union and several other countries have condemned what happened in Gujarat and likened it to Nazi rule.[46] The Indian government's portentous response is that foreigners should not use the Indian media to comment on what is an "internal matter" (like the chilling goings-on in Kashmir?).[47] What next? Censorship? Closing down the Internet? Blocking international calls? Killing the wrong "terrorists" and fudging the DNA samples? There is no terrorism like state terrorism.

But who will take them on? Their fascist cant can perhaps be dented by some blood and thunder from the Opposition. So far only Laloo Yadav, head of the Rashtriya Janata Dal (RJD), the

National People's Party, in Bihar, has shown himself to be truly passionate: "*Kaun mai ka lal kehtha hai ki yeh Hindu Rashtra hai? Usko yahan bhej do, chhaahti phad doonga!*" (Which mother's son says this is a Hindu Nation? Send him here, I'll tear his chest open!)[48]

Unfortunately, there's no quick fix. Fascism itself can only be turned away if all those who are outraged by it show a commitment to social justice that equals the intensity of their indignation.

Are we ready to get off our starting blocks? Are we ready, many millions of us, to rally, not just on the streets but at work and in schools and in our homes, in every decision we take, and every choice we make?

Or not just yet . . . ?

If not, then years from now, when the rest of the world has shunned us (as it should), we too will learn, like the ordinary citizens of Hitler's Germany, to recognize revulsion in the gaze of our fellow human beings. We too will find ourselves unable to look our own children in the eye, for the shame of what we did and didn't do. For the shame of what we allowed to happen.

This is *us*. In *India*. Heaven help us make it through the night.

WAR TALK:
SUMMER GAMES WITH
NUCLEAR BOMBS

WHEN INDIA AND Pakistan conducted their nuclear tests in 1998, even those of us who condemned them balked at the hypocrisy of Western nuclear powers. Implicit in their denunciation of the tests was the notion that Blacks cannot be trusted with the Bomb. Now we are presented with the spectacle of our governments competing to confirm that belief.

As diplomats' families and tourists disappear from the sub-continent, Western journalists arrive in Delhi in droves. Many call me. "Why haven't you left the city?" they ask. "Isn't nuclear war a real possibility? Isn't Delhi a prime target?"

If nuclear weapons exist, then nuclear war is a real possibility. And Delhi is a prime target. It is.

But where shall we go? Is it possible to go out and buy another life because this one's not panning out?

If I go away, and everything and everyone—every friend,

First appeared in *Frontline* (India) 19, no. 12 (June 8–21, 2002).

every tree, every home, every dog, squirrel, and bird that I have known and loved—is incinerated, how shall I live on? Whom shall I love? And who will love me back? Which society will welcome me and allow me to be the hooligan that I am here, at home?

So we're all staying. We huddle together. We realize how much we love each other. And we think, what a shame it would be to die now. Life's normal only because the macabre has become normal. While we wait for rain, for football, for justice, the old generals and eager boy-anchors on TV talk of first-strike and second-strike capabilities as though they're discussing a family board game.

My friends and I discuss *Prophecy*, the documentary about the bombing of Hiroshima and Nagasaki.[1] The fireball. The dead bodies choking the river. The living stripped of skin and hair. The singed, bald children, still alive, their clothes burned into their bodies. The thick, black, toxic water. The scorched, burning air. The cancers, implanted genetically, a malignant letter to the unborn. We remember especially the man who just melted into the steps of a building. We imagine ourselves like that. As stains on staircases. I imagine future generations of hushed schoolchildren pointing at my stain . . . That was a writer. Not she or he. *That.*

I'm sorry if my thoughts are stray and disconnected, not always worthy. Often ridiculous.

I think of a little mixed-breed dog I know. Each of his toes is a different color. Will he become a radioactive stain on a staircase too? My husband's writing a book on trees. He has a section on how figs are pollinated. Each fig only by its own specialized fig wasp. There are nearly a thousand different species of fig wasps, each a precise, exquisite synchrony, the product of millions of years of evolution.

All the fig wasps will be nuked. Zzzz. Ash. And my husband. And his book.

A dear friend, who's an activist in the anti-dam movement in the Narmada valley, is on indefinite hunger strike. Today is the fourteenth day of her fast. She and the others fasting with her are weakening quickly. They're protesting because the Madhya Pradesh government is bulldozing schools, clear-felling forests, uprooting hand pumps, forcing people from their villages to make way for the Maan Dam. The people have nowhere to go. And so the hunger strike.[2]

What an act of faith and hope! How brave it is to believe that in today's world, reasoned, nonviolent protest will register, will matter. But will it? To governments that are comfortable with the notion of a wasted world, what's a wasted valley?

The threshold of horror has been ratcheted up so high that nothing short of genocide or the prospect of nuclear war merits mention. Peaceful resistance is treated with contempt. Terrorism's the real thing. The underlying principle of the war on terror, the very notion that war is an acceptable solution to terrorism, has ensured that terrorists in the subcontinent now have the power to trigger a nuclear war.

Displacement, dispossession, starvation, poverty, disease— these are now just the funnies, the comic-strip items. Our home minister says that Nobel laureate Amartya Sen has it all wrong— the key to India's development is not education and health but defense (and don't forget the kickbacks, O Best Beloved).[3]

Perhaps what he really meant was that war is the key to distracting the world's attention from fascism and genocide. To avoid dealing with any single issue of real governance that urgently needs to be addressed.

For the governments of India and Pakistan, Kashmir is not a *problem*, it's their perennial and spectacularly successful *solution*. Kashmir is the rabbit they pull out of their hats every time they need a rabbit. Unfortunately, it's a radioactive rabbit now, and it's careening out of control.

No doubt there is Pakistan-sponsored cross-border terrorism in Kashmir. But there are other kinds of terror in the valley. There's the inchoate nexus between jihadist militants, ex-militants, foreign mercenaries, local mercenaries, underworld mafiosi, security forces, arms dealers, and criminalized politicians and officials on both sides of the border. There are also rigged elections, daily humiliation, "disappearances," and staged "encounters."[4]

And now the cry has gone up in the heartland: India is a Hindu country. Muslims can be murdered under the benign gaze of the state. Mass murderers will not be brought to justice. Indeed, they will stand for elections. Is India to be a Hindu nation in the heartland and a secular one around the edges?

Meanwhile the International Coalition Against Terror makes war and preaches restraint. While India and Pakistan bay for each other's blood, the coalition is quietly laying gas pipelines, selling us weapons, and pushing through their business deals. (Buy now, pay later.) Britain, for example, is busy arming both sides.[5] Tony Blair's "peace" mission a few months ago was actually a business trip to discuss a billion-pound deal (and don't forget the kickbacks, O Best Beloved) to sell sixty-six Hawk fighter-bombers to India.[6] Roughly, for the price of a *single* Hawk bomber, the government could provide 1.5 million people with clean drinking water for life.[7]

"Why isn't there a peace movement?" Western journalists ask me ingenuously. How can there be a peace movement when, for most people in India, peace means a daily battle: for food, for water, for shelter, for dignity? War, on the other hand, is something professional soldiers fight far away on the border. And nuclear war—well, that's completely outside the realm of most people's comprehension. No one knows what a nuclear bomb is. No one cares to explain. As the home minister said, education is not a pressing priority.

The last question every visiting journalist always asks me is: Are you writing another book? That question mocks me. Another book? Right *now*? This talk of nuclear war displays such contempt for music, art, literature, and everything else that defines civilization. So what kind of book should I write?

It's not just the one million soldiers on the border who are living on hair-trigger alert. It's all of us. That's what nuclear bombs do. Whether they're used or not, they violate everything that is humane. They alter the meaning of life itself.

Why do we tolerate them? Why do we tolerate the men who use nuclear weapons to blackmail the entire human race?

AHIMSA:
(NONVIOLENT
RESISTANCE)

WHILE THE REST of us are mesmerized by talk of war and terrorism and wars against terror, in the state of Madhya Pradesh in central India, a little life raft has set sail into the wind. On a pavement in Bhopal, in an area called Tin Shed, a small group of people has embarked on a journey of faith and hope. There's nothing new in what they're doing. What's new is the climate in which they're doing it.

Today is the twenty-ninth day of the indefinite hunger strike by four activists of the Narmada Bachao Andolan (NBA), the Save the Narmada Movement.[1] They have fasted two days longer than Gandhi did on any of his fasts during the freedom struggle. Their demands are more modest than his ever were. They are protesting against the Madhya Pradesh government's forcible eviction of more than one thousand

---

First published in the *Hindustan Times* (India), June 12, 2002. This version is based on the version published in the *Christian Science Monitor* on July 5, 2002, as "Listen to the Nonviolent Poor: Allow for Peaceful Change, before Violent Change Becomes Inevitable."

Adivasi (indigenous) families to make way for the Maan Dam. All they're asking is that the government of Madhya Pradesh implement its own policy of providing land to those being displaced by the Maan Dam.

There's no controversy here. The dam has been built. The displaced people must be resettled before the reservoir fills up in the monsoon and submerges their villages. The four activists on fast are Vinod Patwa, who was one of the 114,000 people displaced in 1990 by the Bargi Dam (which now, twelve years later, irrigates less land than it submerged); Mangat Verma, who will be displaced by the Maheshwar Dam if it is ever completed; Chittaroopa Palit, who has worked with the NBA for almost fifteen years; and twenty-two-year-old Ram Kunwar, the youngest and frailest of the activists. Hers is the first village that will be submerged when the waters rise in the Maan reservoir. In the weeks since she began her fast, Ram Kunwar has lost twenty pounds—almost one-fourth of her original body weight.

Unlike the other large dams such as the Sardar Sarovar, Maheshwar, and Indira Sagar, where the resettlement of hundreds of thousands of displaced people is simply not possible (except on paper, in court documents), in the case of Maan the total number of displaced people is about six thousand. People have even identified land that is available and could be bought and allotted to them by the government. And yet the government refuses.

Instead it's busy distributing paltry cash compensation, which is illegal and violates its own policy. It says quite openly that if it were to give in to the demands of the Maan "oustees" (that is, if it implemented its own policy), it would set a precedent for the hundreds of thousands of people, most of them Dalits (Untouchables) and Adivasis, who are slated to be submerged (without rehabilitation) by the twenty-nine other big dams planned in the Narmada valley. And the state government's commitment to these projects remains absolute, regardless of the social and environmental costs.

As Vinod, Mangat, Chittaroopa, and Ram Kunwar gradually weaken, as their systems close down and the risk of irreversible organ failure and sudden death sets in, no government official has bothered to even pay them a visit.

Let me tell you a secret—it's not all unwavering resolve and steely determination on the burning pavement under the pitiless sun at Tin Shed. The jokes about slimming and weight loss are becoming a little poignant now. There are tears of anger and frustration. There is trepidation and real fear. But underneath all that, there's pure grit.

What will happen to them? Will they just go down in the ledgers as "the price of progress"? That phrase cleverly frames the whole argument as one between those who are pro-development versus those who are anti-development—and suggests the inevitability of the choice you have to make: pro-development, what else? It slyly suggests that movements like the NBA are antiquated and absurdly anti-electricity or anti-irrigation. This of course is nonsense.

The NBA believes that big dams are obsolete. It believes there are more democratic, more local, more economically viable and environmentally sustainable ways of generating electricity and managing water systems. It is demanding *more* modernity, not less. It is demanding *more* democracy, not less. And look at what's happening instead.

Even at the height of the war rhetoric, even as India and Pakistan threatened each other with nuclear annihilation, the question of reneging on the Indus Waters Treaty between the two countries did not arise. Yet in Madhya Pradesh, the police and administration entered Adivasi villages with bulldozers. They sealed hand pumps, demolished school buildings, and clear-felled trees in order to force people from their homes. They *sealed* hand pumps. And so the indefinite hunger strike.

Any government's condemnation of terrorism is only credible if it shows itself to be responsive to persistent, reasonable, closely argued, nonviolent dissent. And yet what's happening is just the opposite. The world over, nonviolent resistance movements are being crushed and broken. If we do not respect and honor them, by default we privilege those who turn to violent means.

Across the world, when governments and the media lavish all their time, attention, funds, research, space, sophistication, and seriousness on war talk and terrorism, then the message that goes out is disturbing and dangerous: if you seek to air and redress a public grievance, violence is more effective than nonviolence. Unfortunately, if peaceful change is not given a chance, then violent change becomes inevitable. That violence will be (and already is) random, ugly, and unpredictable. What's happening in Kashmir, the northeastern states of India, and Andhra Pradesh is all part of this process.

Right now the NBA is not just fighting big dams. It's fighting for the survival of India's greatest gift to the world: nonviolent resistance. You could call it the Ahimsa Bachao Andolan (*ahimsa* means "nonviolent resistance"), or the Save Nonviolence Movement.

Over the years our government has shown nothing but contempt for the people of the Narmada valley. Contempt for their argument. Contempt for their movement.

In the twenty-first century the connection between religious fundamentalism, nuclear nationalism, and the pauperization of whole populations because of corporate globalization is becoming impossible to ignore. While the Madhya Pradesh government has categorically said it has no land for the rehabilitation of displaced people, reports say that it is preparing the ground (pardon the pun) to make huge tracts of land available for corporate agriculture. This in turn will set off another cycle of displacement and impoverishment.

Can we prevail on Digvijay Singh—the secular "green" chief minister of Madhya Pradesh—to substitute some of his public relations with a *real* change in policy? If he did, he would go down in history as a man of vision and true political courage.

If the Congress Party wishes to be taken seriously as an alternative to the destructive right-wing religious fundamentalists who have brought us to the threshold of ruin, it will have to do more than condemn communalism and participate in empty nationalist rhetoric. It will have to do some real work and some real listening to the people it claims to represent.

As for the rest of us, concerned citizens, peace activists, and the like—it's not enough to sing songs about giving peace a chance. Doing everything we can to support movements like the Narmada Bachao Andolan is *how* we give peace a chance. *This* is the real war on terror.

Go to Bhopal. Just ask for Tin Shed.[2]

COME SEPTEMBER

WRITERS IMAGINE THAT they cull stories from the world. I'm beginning to believe that vanity makes them think so. That it's actually the other way around. Stories cull writers from the world. Stories reveal themselves to us. The public narrative, the private narrative—they colonize us. They commission us. They insist on being told. Fiction and nonfiction are only different techniques of storytelling. For reasons I do not fully understand, fiction dances out of me. Nonfiction is wrenched out by the aching, broken world I wake up to every morning.

The theme of much of what I write, fiction as well as nonfiction, is the relationship between power and powerlessness and the endless, circular conflict they're engaged in. John Berger, that most wonderful writer, once wrote: "Never again will a single story be told as though it's the only one."[1]

There can never be a single story. There are only ways of seeing. So when I tell a story, I tell it not as an ideologue who wants to pit one absolutist ideology against another but as a storyteller who wants to share her way of seeing. Though it

First presented as a lecture in Santa Fe, New Mexico, at the Lensic Performing Arts Center, September 18, 2002. Sponsored by Lannan Foundation: www.lannan.org.

might appear otherwise, my writing is not really about nations and histories, it's about power. About the paranoia and ruthlessness of power. About the physics of power. I believe that the accumulation of vast unfettered power by a state or a country, a corporation or an institution—or even an individual, a spouse, friend, or sibling—regardless of ideology, results in excesses such as the ones I will recount here.

Living as I do, as millions of us do, in the shadow of the nuclear holocaust that the governments of India and Pakistan keep promising their brainwashed citizenry, and in the global neighborhood of the war on terror (what President Bush rather biblically calls "the task that does not end"), I find myself thinking a great deal about the relationship between citizens and the state.[2]

In India, those of us who have expressed views on nuclear bombs, Big Dams, corporate globalization, and the rising threat of communal Hindu fascism—views that are at variance with the Indian government's—are branded "antinational." While this accusation does not fill me with indignation, it's not an accurate description of what I do or how I think. An antinational is a person who is against her own nation and, by inference, is pro some other one. But it isn't necessary to be antinational to be deeply suspicious of all nationalism, to be antinational*ism*. Nationalism of one kind or another was the cause of most of the genocide of the twentieth century. Flags are bits of colored cloth that governments use first to shrink-wrap people's minds and then as ceremonial shrouds to bury the dead. When independent, thinking people (and here I do not include the corporate media) begin to rally under flags, when writers, painters, musicians, filmmakers suspend their judgment and blindly yoke their art to the service of the nation, it's time for all of us to sit up and worry. In India we saw it happen soon after the nuclear tests in 1998 and during the Kargil War against Pakistan in 1999.

In the US we saw it during the Gulf War and we see it now, during the war on terror. That blizzard of made-in-China American flags.[3]

Recently those who have criticized the actions of the US government (myself included) have been called "anti-American." Anti-Americanism is in the process of being consecrated into an ideology.

The term *anti-American* is usually used by the American establishment to discredit and—not falsely, but shall we say inaccurately—define its critics. Once someone is branded anti-American, the chances are that he or she will be judged before they're heard and the argument will be lost in the welter of bruised national pride.

What does the term *anti-American mean*? Does it mean you're anti-jazz? Or that you're opposed to free speech? That you don't delight in Toni Morrison or John Updike? That you have a quarrel with giant sequoias? Does it mean you don't admire the hundreds of thousands of American citizens who marched against nuclear weapons, or the thousands of war resisters who forced their government to withdraw from Vietnam? Does it mean that you hate all Americans?

This sly conflation of America's culture, music, literature, the breathtaking physical beauty of the land, the ordinary pleasures of ordinary people, with criticism of the US government's foreign policy (about which, thanks to America's "free press," sadly, most Americans know very little) is a deliberate and extremely effective strategy. It's like a retreating army taking cover in a heavily populated city, hoping that the prospect of hitting civilian targets will deter enemy fire.

There are many Americans who would be mortified to be associated with their government's policies. The most scholarly, scathing, incisive, hilarious critiques of the hypocrisy and the contradictions in US government policy come from American citizens. When the rest of the world wants to know what the US government is up to, we turn to Noam Chomsky, Edward Said, Howard Zinn, Ed Herman, Amy Goodman, Michael Albert, Chalmers Johnson, William Blum, and Anthony Arnove to tell us what's really going on.

Similarly, in India, not hundreds but millions of us would be ashamed and offended if we were in any way implicated with the present Indian government's fascist policies, which, apart from the perpetration of state terrorism in the valley of Kashmir (in the name of fighting terrorism), have also turned a blind eye to the recent state-supervised pogrom against Muslims in Gujarat.[4] It would be absurd to think that those who criticize the Indian government are "anti-Indian"—although the government itself never hesitates to take that line. It is dangerous to cede to the Indian government or the American government, or *anyone* for that matter, the right to define what "India" or "America" is or ought to be.

To call someone anti-American, indeed, to *be* anti-American (or for that matter anti-Indian, or anti-Timbuktuan), is not just racist, it's a failure of the imagination. An inability to see the world in terms other than those that the establishment has set out for you: If you're not a Bushie, you're a Taliban. If you don't love us, you hate us. If you're not Good, you're Evil. If you're not with us, you're with the terrorists.

Last year, like many others, I too made the mistake of scoffing at this post–September 11 rhetoric, dismissing it as foolish and arrogant. I've realized that it's not foolish at all. It's actually a canny recruitment drive for a misconceived, dangerous war. Every day I'm taken aback at how many people believe that opposing the war in Afghanistan amounts to supporting terrorism or voting for the Taliban. Now that the initial aim of the war—capturing Osama bin Laden (dead or alive)—seems to have run into bad weather, the goalposts have been moved.[5] It's being made out that the whole point of the war was to topple the Taliban regime and liberate Afghan women from their burqas. We're being asked to believe that the US marines are actually on a feminist mission. (If so, will their next stop be America's military ally Saudi Arabia?) Think of it this way: In India there are some pretty reprehensible social practices, against "Untouchables," against Christians and Muslims, against women. Pakistan and Bangladesh have even worse ways of dealing with minority communities and women. Should they be bombed? Should Delhi, Islamabad, and Dhaka be destroyed? Is it possible to bomb bigotry out of India? Can we bomb our way to a feminist paradise? Is that how women won the vote in the United States? Or how slavery was abolished? Can we win redress for the genocide of the millions of Native Americans, upon whose corpses the United States was founded, by bombing Santa Fe?

None of us need anniversaries to remind us of what we cannot forget. So it is no more than coincidence that I happen to be here, on American soil, in September—this month of dreadful anniversaries. Uppermost on everybody's mind of course, particularly here in America, is the horror of what has come to be known as "9/11." Three thousand civilians lost their lives in that lethal terrorist strike.[6] The grief is still deep. The rage still sharp. The tears have not dried. And a strange, deadly war is raging around the world. Yet each person who has lost a loved one surely knows secretly, deeply, that no war, no act of revenge, no daisy-cutters dropped on someone else's loved ones or someone else's children will blunt the edges of their pain or bring their own loved ones back. War cannot avenge those who have died. War is only a brutal desecration of their memory.

To fuel yet another war—this time against Iraq—by cynically manipulating people's grief, by packaging it for TV specials sponsored by corporations selling detergent or running shoes, is to cheapen and devalue grief, to drain it of meaning. What we are seeing now is a vulgar display of the *business* of grief, the commerce of grief, the pillaging of even the most private human feelings for political purpose. It is a terrible, violent thing for a state to do to its people.

It's not a clever enough subject to speak of from a public platform, but what I would really love to talk to you about is loss. Loss and losing. Grief, failure, brokenness, numbness, uncertainty, fear, the death of feeling, the death of dreaming. The absolute, relentless, endless, habitual unfairness of the world. What does loss mean to individuals? What does it mean to whole cultures, whole peoples who have learned to live with it as a constant companion?

Since it is September 11 that we're talking about, perhaps it's in the fitness of things that we remember what that date means, not only to those who lost their loved ones in America last year but to those in other parts of the world to whom that date has long held significance. This historical dredging is not offered as an accusation or a provocation. But just to share the grief of history. To thin the mist a little. To say to the citizens of America, in the gentlest, most human way: Welcome to the World.

Twenty-nine years ago, in Chile, on the eleventh of September 1973, General Pinochet overthrew the democratically elected government of Salvador Allende in a CIA-backed coup. "I don't see why we need to stand by and watch a country go Communist due to the irresponsibility of its own people," said Henry Kissinger, Nobel Peace laureate, then President Nixon's national security adviser.[7]

After the coup President Allende was found dead inside the presidential palace. Whether he was killed or whether he killed himself, we'll never know. In the regime of terror that ensued, thousands of people were killed. Many more simply "disappeared." Firing squads conducted public executions. Concentration camps and torture chambers were opened across the country. The dead were buried in mine shafts and unmarked graves. For more than sixteen years, the people of Chile lived in dread of the midnight knock, of routine disappearances, of sudden arrest and torture.[8]

In 2000, following the 1998 arrest of General Pinochet in Britain, thousands of secret documents were declassified by the US government.[9] They contain unequivocal evidence of the CIA's involvement in the coup as well as the fact that the US government had detailed information about the situation in Chile during General Pinochet's reign. Yet Kissinger assured the general of his support: "In the United States, as you know, we are sympathetic with what you are trying to do," he said. "We wish your government well."[10]

Those of us who have only ever known life in a democracy, however flawed, would find it hard to imagine what living in a dictatorship and enduring the absolute loss of freedom really means. It isn't just those who Pinochet murdered, but the lives he stole from the living that must be accounted for, too.

Sadly, Chile was not the only country in South America to be singled out for the US government's attentions. Guatemala, Costa Rica, Ecuador, Brazil, Peru, the Dominican Republic, Bolivia, Nicaragua, Honduras, Panama, El Salvador, Peru, Mexico, and Colombia—they've all been the playground for covert—and overt—operations by the CIA.[11] Hundreds of thousands of Latin Americans have been killed, tortured, or have simply disappeared under the despotic regimes and tin-pot dictators, drug runners, and arms dealers that were propped up in their countries. (Many of them learned their craft in the infamous US government–funded School of the Americas in Fort Benning, Georgia, which has produced sixty thousand graduates.)[12] If this were not humiliation enough, the people of South America have had to bear the cross of being branded as a people who are incapable of democracy—as if coups and massacres are somehow encrypted in their genes.

This list does not of course include countries in Africa or Asia that suffered US military interventions—Somalia, Vietnam, Korea, Indonesia, Laos, and Cambodia.[13] For how many Septembers for decades together have millions of Asian people been bombed, burned, and slaughtered? How many Septembers have gone by since August 1945, when hundreds of thousands of ordinary Japanese people were obliterated by the nuclear strikes in Hiroshima and Nagasaki? For how many Septembers have the thousands who had the misfortune of surviving those strikes endured the living hell that was visited on them, their unborn children, their children's children, on the earth, the sky, the wind, the water, and all the creatures that swim and walk and crawl and fly? Not far from here, in Albuquerque, is the National Atomic Museum, where Fat Man and Little Boy (the affectionate nicknames for the bombs that were dropped on Hiroshima and Nagasaki) were available as souvenir earrings. Funky young people wore them. A massacre dangling in each ear. But I am straying from my theme. It's September that we're talking about, not August.

September 11 has a tragic resonance in the Middle East, too. On the eleventh of September 1922, ignoring Arab outrage, the British government proclaimed a mandate in Palestine, a follow-up to the 1917 Balfour Declaration, which imperial Britain issued, with its army massed outside the gates of the city of Gaza.[14] The Balfour Declaration promised European Zionists "a national home for Jewish people."[15] (At the time, the empire on which the sun never set was free to snatch and bequeath national homes like the school bully distributes marbles.) Two years after the declaration, Lord Arthur James Balfour, the British foreign secretary, said, "In Palestine we do not propose even to go through the form of consulting the wishes of the present inhabitants of the country. . . . Zionism, be it right or wrong, good or bad, is rooted in age-long tradition, in present needs, in future hopes, of far profounder import than the desires and prejudices of the 700,000 Arabs who now inhabit that ancient land."[16]

How carelessly imperial power decreed whose needs were profound and whose were not. How carelessly it vivisected ancient civilizations. Palestine and Kashmir are imperial Britain's festering, blood-drenched gifts to the modern world. Both are fault lines in the raging international conflicts of today.

In 1937 Winston Churchill said of the Palestinians:

> *I do not agree that the dog in a manger has the final right to the manger, even though he may have lain there for a very long time. I do not admit that right. I do not admit, for instance, that a great wrong has been done to the Red Indians of America, or the black people of Australia. I do not admit that a wrong has been done to these people by the fact that a stronger race, a higher grade race, a more worldly-wise race, to put it that way, has come in and taken their place.*[17]

That set the trend for the Israeli state's attitude toward Palestinians. In 1969 Israeli prime minister Golda Meir said, "Palestinians do not exist." Her successor, prime minister Levi Eshkol, said, "Where are Palestinians? When I came here [to Palestine] there were 250,000 non-Jews, mainly Arabs and Bedouins. It was desert, more than underdeveloped. Nothing." Prime minister Menachem Begin called Palestinians "two-legged beasts." Prime minister Yitzhak Shamir called them "'grasshoppers' who could be crushed."[18] This is the language of heads of state, not the words of ordinary people. In 1947 the UN formally partitioned Palestine and allotted 55 percent of Palestine's land to the Zionists. Within a year they had captured more than 76 percent.[19] On May 14, 1948, the State of Israel was declared. Minutes after the declaration, the United States recognized Israel. The West Bank was annexed by Jordan. The Gaza Strip came under the military control of Egypt.[20] Formally, Palestine ceased to exist except in the minds and hearts of the hundreds of thousands of Palestinian people who became refugees.

In the summer of 1967, Israel occupied the West Bank and the Gaza Strip. Settlers were offered state subsidies and development aid to move into the occupied territories. Almost every day more Palestinian families are forced off their lands and driven into refugee camps. Palestinians who continue to live in Israel do not have the same rights as Israelis and live as second-class citizens in their former homeland.[21]

Over the decades there have been uprisings, wars, intifadas. Thousands have lost their lives.[22] Accords and treaties have been signed. Ceasefires declared and violated. But the bloodshed doesn't end. Palestine still remains illegally occupied. Its people live in inhuman conditions, in virtual Bantustans, where they are subjected to collective punishments and twenty-four-hour curfews, where they are humiliated and brutalized on a daily basis. They never know when their homes will be demolished, when their children will be shot, when their precious trees will be cut, when their roads will be closed, when they will be allowed to walk down to the market to buy food and medicine. And when they will not. They live with no semblance of dignity. With not much hope in sight. They have no control over their lands, their security, their movement, their communication, their water supply. So when accords are signed and words like *autonomy* and even *statehood* are bandied about, it's always worth asking: What sort of autonomy? What sort of state? What sort of rights will its citizens have?

Young Palestinians who cannot contain their anger turn themselves into human bombs and haunt Israel's streets and public places, blowing themselves up, killing ordinary people, injecting terror into daily life, and eventually hardening both societies' suspicion and mutual hatred of each other. Each bombing invites merciless reprisals and even more hardship on Palestinian people. But then suicide bombing is an act of individual despair, not a revolutionary tactic. Although Palestinian attacks strike terror into Israeli civilians, they provide the perfect cover for the Israeli government's daily incursions into Palestinian territory, the perfect excuse for old-fashioned nineteenth-century colonialism, dressed up as a new-fashioned twenty-first-century war.

Israel's staunchest political and military ally is and always has been the US government. The US government has blocked, along with Israel, almost every UN resolution that sought a peaceful, equitable solution to the conflict.[23] It has supported almost every war that Israel has fought. When Israel attacks Palestine, it is American missiles that smash through Palestinian homes. And every year Israel receives several billion dollars from the United States.[24]

What lessons should we draw from this tragic conflict? Is it really impossible for Jewish people who suffered so cruelly themselves—more cruelly perhaps than any other people in history—to understand the vulnerability and the yearning of those whom they have displaced? Does extreme suffering always kindle cruelty? What hope does this leave the human race with? What will happen to the Palestinian people in the event of a victory? When a nation without a state eventually proclaims a state, what kind of state will it be? What horrors will be perpetrated under its flag? Is it a separate state that we should be fighting for, or the rights to a life of liberty and dignity for everyone regardless of their ethnicity or religion?

Palestine was once a secular bulwark in the Middle East. But now the weak, undemocratic, by all accounts corrupt, but avowedly nonsectarian Palestinian Liberation Organization (PLO) is losing ground to Hamas, which espouses an overtly sectarian ideology and fights in the name of Islam. To quote from its manifesto: "We will be its soldiers and the firewood of its fire, which will burn the enemies."[25]

The world is called upon to condemn suicide bombers. But can we ignore the long road they have journeyed on before they arrived at this destination? September 11, 1922, to September 11, 2002—eighty years is a long, long time to have been waging war. Is there some advice the world can give the people of Palestine? Some scrap of hope we can hold out? Should they just settle for the crumbs that are thrown their way and behave like the grasshoppers or two-legged beasts they've been described as? Should they just take Golda Meir's suggestion and make a real effort to not exist?

In another part of the Middle East, September 11 strikes a more recent chord. It was on the eleventh of September 1990 that George W. Bush Sr., then president of the United States, made a speech to a joint session of Congress announcing his government's decision to go to war against Iraq.[26]

The US government says that Saddam Hussein is a war criminal, a cruel military despot who has committed genocide against his own people. That's a fairly accurate description of the man. In 1988 he razed hundreds of villages in northern Iraq and used chemical weapons and machine guns to kill thousands of Kurdish people. Today we know that that same year the US government provided him with $500 million in subsidies to buy American agricultural products. The next year, after he had successfully completed his genocidal campaign, the US government doubled its subsidy to $1 billion.[27] It also provided him with high-quality germ seed for anthrax, as well as helicopters and dual-use material that could be used to manufacture chemical and biological weapons.[28]

So it turns out that while Saddam Hussein was carrying out his worst atrocities, the US and the UK governments were his close allies. Even today the government of Turkey, which has one of the most appalling human rights records in the world, is one of the US government's closest allies. The fact that the Turkish government has oppressed and murdered Kurdish people for years has not prevented the US government from plying Turkey with weapons and development aid.[29] Clearly it was not concern for the Kurdish people that provoked President Bush's speech to Congress.

What changed? In August 1990, Saddam Hussein invaded Kuwait. His sin was not so much that he had committed an act of war but that he acted independently, without orders from his masters. This display of independence was enough to upset the power equation in the Gulf. So it was decided that Saddam Hussein should be exterminated, like a pet that has outlived its owner's affection.

The first Allied attack on Iraq took place in January 1991. The world watched the prime-time war as it was played out on TV. (In India those days, you had to go to a five-star hotel lobby to watch CNN.) Tens of thousands of people were killed in a month of devastating bombing.[30] What many do not know is that the war did not end then. The initial fury simmered down into the longest sustained air attack on a country since the Vietnam War. Over the last decade, American and British forces have fired thousands of missiles and bombs on Iraq. Iraq's fields and farmlands have been shelled with three hundred tons of depleted uranium.[31] In their bombing sorties, the Allies targeted and destroyed water treatment plants, aware of the fact that they could not be repaired without foreign assistance.[32] In southern

Iraq there has been a fourfold increase in cancer among children. In the decade of economic sanctions that followed the war, Iraqi civilians have been denied food, medicine, hospital equipment, ambulances, clean water—the basic essentials.[33]

About half a million Iraqi children have died as a result of the sanctions. Of them, Madeleine Albright, then US ambassador to the United Nations, famously said, "I think this is a very hard choice, but the price—we think the price is worth it."[34] "Moral equivalence" was the term that was used to denounce those who criticized the war on Afghanistan. Madeleine Albright cannot be accused of moral equivalence. What she said was just straightforward algebra.

A decade of bombing has not managed to dislodge Saddam Hussein, the "Beast of Baghdad." Now, almost twelve years on, president George Bush Jr. has ratcheted up the rhetoric once again. He's proposing an all-out war whose goal is nothing short of a "regime change." The *New York Times* says that the Bush administration is "following a meticulously planned strategy to persuade the public, the Congress and the allies of the need to confront the threat of Saddam Hussein." Andrew Card, the White House Chief of Staff, described how the administration was stepping up its war plans for the fall: "From a marketing point of view," he said, "you don't introduce new products in August."[35] This time the catchphrase for Washington's "new product" is not the plight of Kuwaiti people but the assertion that Iraq has weapons of mass destruction. Forget "the feckless moralising of 'peace' lobbies," wrote Richard Perle, chairman of the Defense Policy Board; the United States will "act alone if necessary" and use a "pre-emptive strike" if it determines it's in US interests.[36]

Weapons inspectors have conflicting reports about the status of Iraq's "weapons of mass destruction," and many have said clearly that its arsenal has been dismantled and that it does not have the capacity to build one.[37] However, there is no confusion over the extent and range of America's arsenal of nuclear and chemical weapons. Would the US government welcome weapons inspectors? Would the UK? Or Israel?

What if Iraq *does* have a nuclear weapon, does that justify a preemptive US strike? The United States has the largest arsenal of nuclear weapons in the world. It's the only country in the world to have actually used them on civilian populations. If the United States is justified in launching a preemptive attack on Iraq, why then any nuclear power is justified in carrying out a preemptive attack on any other. India could attack Pakistan, or the other way around. If the US government develops a distaste for the Indian prime minister, can it just "take him out" with a preemptive strike?

Recently the United States played an important part in forcing India and Pakistan back from the brink of war. Is it so hard for it to take its own advice? Who is guilty of feckless moralizing? Of preaching peace while it wages war? The United States, which George Bush calls "a peaceful nation," has been at war with one country or another every year for the last fifty years.[38]

Wars are never fought for altruistic reasons. They're usually fought for hegemony, for business. And then of course, there's the business of war. Protecting its control of the world's oil is fundamental to US foreign policy. The US government's recent military interventions in the Balkans and Central Asia have to do with oil. Hamid Karzai, the puppet president of Afghanistan installed by the United States, is said to be a former employee of Unocal, the American-based oil company.[39] The US government's paranoid patrolling of the Middle East is because it has two-thirds of the world's oil reserves.[40] Oil keeps America's engines purring sweetly. Oil keeps the free market rolling. Whoever controls the world's oil controls the world's markets.

And how do you control the oil? Nobody puts it more elegantly than the *New York Times* columnist Thomas Friedman. In an article called "Craziness Pays," he says, "[T]he U.S. has to make clear to Iraq and U.S. allies that . . . America will use force, without negotiation, hesitation, or UN approval."[41] His advice was well taken. In the wars against Iraq and Afghanistan, as well as in the almost daily humiliation the US government heaps on the UN. In his book on globalization, *The Lexus and the Olive Tree,* Friedman says, "The hidden hand of the market will never work without a hidden fist. McDonald's cannot flourish without McDonnell Douglas. . . . And the hidden fist that keeps the world safe for Silicon Valley's technologies to flourish is called the U.S. Army, Air Force, Navy, and Marine Corps."[42]

Perhaps this was written in a moment of vulnerability, but it's certainly the most succinct, accurate description of the project of corporate globalization that I have read.

After September 11, 2001, and the war on terror, the hidden hand and fist have had their cover blown, and we have a clear view now of America's other weapon—the free market—bearing down on the developing world, with a clenched unsmiling smile. The Task That Does Not End is America's perfect war, the perfect vehicle for the endless expansion of American imperialism. In Urdu, the word for profit is *fayda. Al-Qaeda* means The Word, The Word of God, The Law. So in India some of us call the war on terror *Al-Qaeda versus Al Fayda*—The Word versus The Profit (no pun intended). For the moment it looks as though *Al Fayda* will carry the day. But then you never know . . . In the last ten years of unbridled corporate globalization, the world's total income has increased by an average of 2.5 percent a year. And yet the number of the poor in the world has increased by 100 million. Of the top hundred biggest economies, fifty-one are corporations, not countries. The top 1 percent of the world has the same combined income as the bottom 57 percent, and the disparity is growing.[43] Now, under the spreading canopy of the war on terror, this process is being hustled along. The men in suits are in an unseemly hurry. While bombs rain down on us and cruise missiles skid across the skies, while nuclear weapons are stockpiled to make the world a safer place, contracts are being signed, patents are being registered, oil pipelines are being laid, natural resources are being plundered, water is being privatized, and democracies are being undermined.

In a country like India, the "structural adjustment" end of the corporate globalization project is ripping through people's lives. "Development" projects, massive privatization, and labor "reforms" are pushing people off their lands and out of their jobs, resulting in a kind of barbaric dispossession that has few parallels in history. Across the world as the free market brazenly protects Western markets and forces developing countries to lift their trade barriers, the poor are getting poorer and the rich richer. Civil unrest has begun to erupt in the global village. In countries like Argentina, Brazil, Mexico, Bolivia, and India, the resistance movements against corporate globalization are growing. To contain them, governments are tightening their control. Protesters are being labeled "terrorists" and then being dealt with as such. But civil unrest does not only mean marches and demonstrations and protests against globalization. Unfortunately, it also means a desperate downward spiral into crime and chaos and all kinds of despair and disillusionment, which, as we know from history (and from what we see unspooling before our eyes), gradually becomes a fertile breeding ground for terrible things—cultural nationalism, religious bigotry, fascism, and of course terrorism.

All these march arm in arm with corporate globalization.

There is a notion gaining credence that the free market breaks down national barriers and that corporate globalization's ultimate destination is a hippie paradise where the heart is the only passport and we all live together happily inside a John Lennon song (*Imagine there's no countries . . .*). This is a canard.

What the free market undermines is not national sovereignty but *democracy*. As the disparity between the rich and poor grows, the hidden fist has its work cut out for it. Multinational corporations on the prowl for sweetheart deals that yield enormous profits cannot push through those deals and administer those projects in developing countries without the active connivance of state machinery—the police, the courts, sometimes even the army. Today corporate globalization needs an international confederation of loyal, corrupt, authoritarian governments in poorer countries to push through unpopular reforms and quell the mutinies. It needs a press that pretends to be free. It needs courts that pretend to dispense justice. It needs nuclear bombs, standing armies, sterner immigration laws, and watchful coastal patrols to make sure that it's only money, goods, patents, and services that are globalized—not the free movement of people, not a respect for human rights, not international treaties on racial discrimination, or chemical and nuclear weapons, or greenhouse gas emissions, climate change, or, god forbid, justice.[44] It's as though even a *gesture* toward international accountability would wreck the whole enterprise.

Close to one year after the war on terror was officially flagged off in the ruins of Afghanistan, freedoms are being curtailed in country after country in the name of protecting freedom, civil liberties are being suspended in the name of protecting democracy.[45] All kinds of dissent is being defined as "terrorism." All kinds of laws are being passed to deal with it. Osama bin Laden seems to have vanished into thin air. Mullah Omar is said to have made his escape on a motorbike.[46] (They could have sent Tin-Tin after him.) The Taliban may have disappeared, but their spirit, and their system of summary justice, is surfacing in the unlikeliest of places. In India, in Pakistan, in Nigeria, in America, in all the Central Asian republics run by all manner of despots, and of course in Afghanistan under the US-backed Northern Alliance.[47]

Meanwhile down at the mall there's a midseason sale. Everything's discounted—oceans, rivers, oil, gene pools, fig wasps, flowers, childhoods, aluminum factories, phone companies, wisdom, wilderness, civil rights, ecosystems, air—all 4.6 billion years of evolution. It's packed, sealed, tagged, valued, and available off the rack (no returns). As for justice—I'm told it's on offer, too. You can get the best that money can buy.

Donald Rumsfeld said that his mission in the war on terror

was to persuade the world that Americans must be allowed to continue their way of life.[48] When the maddened king stamps his foot, slaves tremble in their quarters. So, standing here today, it's hard for me to say this, but The American Way of Life is simply not sustainable. Because it doesn't acknowledge that there is a world beyond America.

Fortunately, power has a shelf life. When the time comes, maybe this mighty empire will, like others before it, overreach itself and implode from within. It looks as though structural cracks have already appeared. As the war on terror casts its net wider and wider, America's corporate heart is hemorrhaging. For all the endless empty chatter about democracy, today the world is run by three of the most secretive institutions in the world: the International Monetary Fund, the World Bank, and the World Trade Organization, all three of which, in turn, are dominated by the United States. Their decisions are made in secret. The people who head them are appointed behind closed doors. Nobody really knows anything about them, their politics, their beliefs, their intentions. Nobody elected them. Nobody said they could make decisions on our behalf. A world run by a handful of greedy bankers and CEOs whom nobody elected can't possibly last.

Soviet-style communism failed, not because it was intrinsically evil, but because it was flawed. It allowed too few people to usurp too much power. Twenty-first-century market capitalism, American style, will fail for the same reasons. Both are edifices constructed by human intelligence, undone by human nature.

The time has come, the Walrus said. Perhaps things will get worse and then better. Perhaps there's a small god up in heaven readying herself for us. Another world is not only possible, she's on her way. Maybe many of us won't be here to greet her, but on a quiet day, if I listen very carefully, I can hear her breathing.

"Our strategy should be not only to confront empire but to lay siege to it. To deprive it of oxygen. To shame it. To mock it. With our art, our music, our literature, our stubbornness, our joy, our brilliance, our sheer relentlessness—and our ability to tell our own stories."

THE LONELINESS
OF NOAM CHOMSKY

*I will never apologize for the United States of America—I
don't care what the facts are.*
—President George Bush Sr.[1]

SITTING IN MY home in New Delhi, watching an American
TV news channel promote itself ("We report. You decide"), I
imagine Noam Chomsky's amused, chipped-tooth smile.

Everybody knows that authoritarian regimes, regardless of
their ideology, use the mass media for propaganda. But what
about democratically elected regimes in the "free world"?

Today, thanks to Noam Chomsky and his fellow media
analysts, it is almost axiomatic for thousands, possibly millions,
of us that public opinion in "free market" democracies is

Written as an introduction to the new edition of Noam Chomsky's *For Reasons
of State* (New York: New Press, 2003).

manufactured just like any other mass market product—soap, switches, or sliced bread.[2] We know that while, legally and constitutionally, speech may be free, the space in which that freedom can be exercised has been snatched from us and auctioned to the highest bidders. Neoliberal capitalism isn't just about the accumulation of capital (for some). It's also about the accumulation of power (for some), the accumulation of freedom (for some). Conversely, for the rest of the world, the people who are excluded from neoliberalism's governing body, it's about the *erosion* of capital, the *erosion* of power, the *erosion* of freedom. In the "free" market, free speech has become a commodity like everything else—justice, human rights, drinking water, clean air. It's available only to those who can afford it. And naturally, those who can afford it use free speech to manufacture the kind of product, confect the kind of public opinion, that best suits their purpose. (News they can use.) Exactly how they do this has been the subject of much of Noam Chomsky's political writing. Prime minister Silvio Berlusconi, for instance, has a controlling interest in major Italian newspapers, magazines, television channels, and publishing houses. "The prime minister in effect controls about 90 percent of Italian TV viewership," reports the *Financial Times*.[3] What price free speech? Free speech for *whom*? Admittedly, Berlusconi is an extreme example. In other democracies—the United States in particular—media barons, powerful corporate lobbies, and government officials are imbricated in a more elaborate but less obvious manner. (George Bush Jr.'s connections to the oil lobby, to the arms industry, and to Enron, and Enron's infiltration of US government institutions and the mass media—all this is public knowledge now.)

After the September 11, 2001, terrorist strikes in New York and Washington, the mainstream media's blatant performance as the US government's mouthpiece, its display of vengeful patriotism, its willingness to publish Pentagon press handouts as news, and its explicit censorship of dissenting opinion became the butt of some pretty black humor in the rest of the world.

Then the New York Stock Exchange crashed, bankrupt airline companies appealed to the government for financial bail-outs, and there was talk of circumventing patent laws in order to manufacture generic drugs to fight the anthrax scare (*much more important and urgent of course than the production of generics to fight AIDS in Africa*).[4] Suddenly, it began to seem as though the twin myths of free speech and the free market might come crashing down alongside the Twin Towers of the World Trade Center.

But of course that never happened. The myths live on.

There is, however, a brighter side to the amount of energy and money that the establishment pours into the business of "managing" public opinion. It suggests a very real *fear* of public opinion. It suggests a persistent and valid worry that if people were to discover (and fully comprehend) the real nature of the things that are done in their name, they might *act* upon that knowledge. Powerful people know that ordinary people are not always reflexively ruthless and selfish. (When ordinary people weigh costs and benefits, something like an uneasy conscience could easily tip the scales.) For this reason, they must be guarded against reality, reared in a controlled climate, in an altered reality, like broiler chickens or pigs in a pen.

Those of us who have managed to escape this fate and are scratching about in the backyard no longer believe everything we read in the papers and watch on TV. We put our ears to the ground and look for other ways of making sense of the world. We search for the untold story, the mentioned-in-passing military coup, the unreported genocide, the civil war in an African country written up in a one-column-inch story next to a full-page advertisement for lace underwear.

We don't always remember, and many don't even know, that this way of thinking, this easy acuity, this instinctive mistrust of the mass media, would at best be a political hunch and at worst a loose accusation if it were not for the relentless and unswerving media analysis of one of the world's greatest minds. And this is only *one* of the ways in which Noam Chomsky has radically altered our understanding of the society in which we live. Or should I say, our understanding of the elaborate rules of the lunatic asylum in which we are all voluntary inmates?

Speaking about the September 11 attacks in New York and Washington, president George W. Bush called the enemies of the United States "enemies of freedom." "Americans are asking, why do they hate us?" he said. "They hate our freedoms, our freedom of religion, our freedom of speech, our freedom to vote and assemble and disagree with each other."[5]

If people in the United States want a real answer to that question (as opposed to the ones in the *Idiot's Guide to Anti-Americanism*, that is: "Because they're jealous of us," "Because they hate freedom," "Because they're losers," "Because we're good and they're evil"), I'd say, read Chomsky. Read Chomsky on US military interventions in Indochina, Latin America, Iraq, Bosnia, the former Yugoslavia, Afghanistan, and the Middle East. If ordinary people in the United States read Chomsky, perhaps their questions would be framed a little differently. Perhaps it would be "Why don't they hate us more than they do?" or "Isn't it surprising that September 11 didn't happen earlier?"

Unfortunately, in these nationalistic times, words like *us* and *them* are used loosely. The line between citizens and the state is being deliberately and successfully blurred, not just by governments but also by terrorists. The underlying logic of terrorist attacks, as well as "retaliatory" wars against governments that "support terrorism," is the same: both punish citizens for the actions of their governments.

(A brief digression: I realize that for Noam Chomsky, a US citizen, to criticize his own government is better manners than for someone like myself, an Indian citizen, to criticize the US government. I'm no patriot and am fully aware that venality, brutality, and hypocrisy are imprinted on the leaden soul of every state. But when a country ceases to be merely a country and becomes an empire, then the scale of operations changes dramatically. So may I clarify that I speak as a subject of the US empire? I speak as a slave who presumes to criticize her king.)

If I were asked to choose *one* of Noam Chomsky's major contributions to the world, it would be the fact that he has unmasked the ugly, manipulative, ruthless universe that exists behind that beautiful, sunny word *freedom*. He has done this rationally and empirically. The mass of evidence he has marshaled to construct his case is formidable. Terrifying, actually. The starting premise of Chomsky's method is not ideological, but it *is* intensely political. He embarks on his course of inquiry with an anarchist's instinctive mistrust of power. He takes us on a tour through the bog of the US establishment and leads us through the dizzying maze of corridors that connects the government, big business, and the business of managing public opinion.

Chomsky shows us how phrases like *free speech*, *the free market*, and *the free world* have little, if anything, to do with freedom. He shows us that among the myriad freedoms claimed by the US government are the freedom to murder, annihilate, and dominate other people. The freedom to finance and sponsor despots and dictators across the world. The freedom to train, arm, and shelter terrorists. The freedom to topple democratically elected governments. The freedom to amass and use weapons of mass destruction—chemical, biological, and nuclear. The freedom to go to war against any country whose government it disagrees with. And, most terrible of all, the freedom to commit these crimes against humanity in the name of "justice," in the name of "righteousness," in the name of "freedom."

Attorney general John Ashcroft has declared that US freedoms are "not the grant of any government or document, but . . . our endowment from God."[6] So, basically, we're confronted with a country armed with a mandate from heaven. Perhaps this explains why the US government refuses to judge itself by the same moral standards by which it judges others. (Any attempt to do this is shouted down as "moral equivalence.") Its technique is to position itself as the well-intentioned giant whose good deeds are confounded in strange countries by their scheming natives, whose markets it's trying to free, whose societies it's trying to modernize, whose women it's trying to liberate, whose souls it's trying to save.

Perhaps this belief in its own divinity also explains why the US government has conferred upon itself the right and freedom to murder and exterminate people "for their own good."

When he announced the US air strikes against Afghanistan, President Bush Jr. said, "We're a peaceful nation."[7] He went on to say, "This is the calling of the United States of America, the most free nation in the world, a nation built on fundamental values, that rejects hate, rejects violence, rejects murderers, rejects evil. And we will not tire."[8]

The US empire rests on a grisly foundation: the massacre of millions of indigenous people, the stealing of their lands, and following this, the kidnapping and enslavement of millions of Black people from Africa to work that land. Thousands died on the seas while they were being shipped like caged cattle between continents.[9] "Stolen from Africa, brought to America"—Bob Marley's "Buffalo Soldier" contains a whole universe of unspeakable sadness.[10] It tells of the loss of dignity, the loss of wilderness, the loss of freedom, the shattered pride of a people. Genocide and slavery provide the social and economic underpinning of the nation whose fundamental values reject hate, murderers, and evil.

Here is Chomsky, writing in the essay "The Manufacture of Consent," on the founding of the United States of America:

> *During the Thanksgiving holiday a few weeks ago, I took a walk with some friends and family in a national park. We came across a gravestone, which had on it the following inscription: "Here lies an Indian woman, a Wampanoag, whose family and tribe gave of themselves and their land that this great nation might be born and grow."*
>
> *Of course, it is not quite accurate to say that the indigenous population gave of themselves and their land for that noble*

purpose. Rather, they were slaughtered, decimated, and dispersed in the course of one of the greatest exercises in genocide in human history . . . which we celebrate each October when we honor Columbus—a notable mass murderer himself—on Columbus Day.

Hundreds of American citizens, well-meaning and decent people, troop by that gravestone regularly and read it, apparently without reaction; except, perhaps, a feeling of satisfaction that at last we are giving some due recognition to the sacrifices of the native peoples. . . . They might react differently if they were to visit Auschwitz or Dachau and find a gravestone reading: "Here lies a woman, a Jew, whose family and people gave of themselves and their possessions that this great nation might grow and prosper."[11]

How has the United States survived its terrible past and emerged smelling so sweet? Not by owning up to it, not by making reparations, not by apologizing to Black Americans or Native Americans, and certainly not by changing its ways (it *exports* its cruelties now). Like most other countries, the United States has rewritten its history. But what sets the United States apart from other countries, and puts it way ahead in the race, is that it has enlisted the services of the most powerful, most successful publicity firm in the world: Hollywood.

In the best-selling version of popular myth as history, US "goodness" peaked during World War II (aka America's War Against Fascism). Lost in the din of trumpet sound and angel song is the fact that when fascism was in full stride in Europe, the US government actually looked away. When Hitler was carrying out his genocidal pogrom against Jews, US officials refused entry to Jewish refugees fleeing Germany. The United States entered the war only *after* the Japanese bombed Pearl Harbor. Drowned out by the noisy hosannas is its most barbaric act, in fact the single most savage act the world has ever witnessed: the dropping of the atomic bomb on civilian populations in Hiroshima and Nagasaki. The war was nearly over. The hundreds of thousands of Japanese people who were killed, the countless others who were crippled by cancers for generations to come, were not a threat to world peace. They were *civilians*. Just as the victims of the World Trade Center and Pentagon bombings were civilians. Just as the hundreds of thousands of people who died in Iraq because of the US-led sanctions were civilians. The bombing of Hiroshima and Nagasaki was a cold, calculated experiment carried out to demonstrate America's power. At the time, President Truman described it as "the greatest thing in history."[12]

The Second World War, we're told, was a "war for peace." The atomic bomb was a "weapon of peace."

We're invited to believe that nuclear deterrence prevented World War III. (That was before President George Bush Jr. came up with the "preemptive strike doctrine.")[13] *Was* there an outbreak of peace after the Second World War? Certainly there was (relative) peace in Europe and America—but does that count as world peace? Not unless savage proxy wars fought in lands where the colored races live (chinks, niggers, dinks, wogs, gooks) don't count as wars at all.

Since the Second World War, the United States has been at war with or has attacked, among other countries, Korea, Guatemala, Cuba, Laos, Vietnam, Cambodia, Grenada, Libya, El Salvador, Nicaragua, Panama, Iraq, Somalia, Sudan, Yugoslavia, and Afghanistan. This list should also include the US government's covert operations in Africa, Asia, and Latin America, the coups it has engineered, and the dictators it has armed and supported. It should include Israel's US-backed war on Lebanon, in which thousands were killed. It should include the key role America has played in the conflict in the Middle East, in which thousands have died fighting Israel's illegal occupation of Palestinian territory. It should include America's role in the civil war in Afghanistan in the 1980s, in which more than one million people were killed.[14] It should include the embargos and sanctions that have led directly and indirectly to the death of hundreds of thousands of people, most visibly in Iraq.[15] Put it all together, and it sounds very much as though there has been a World War III, and that the US government was (or is) one of its chief protagonists.

Most of the essays in Chomsky's *For Reasons of State* are about US aggression in South Vietnam, North Vietnam, Laos, and Cambodia. It was a war that lasted more than twelve years. Fifty-eight thousand Americans and approximately two million Vietnamese, Cambodians, and Laotians lost their lives.[16] The US deployed half a million ground troops, dropped more than six million tons of bombs.[17] And yet, though you wouldn't believe it if you watched most Hollywood movies, America lost the war.

The war began in South Vietnam and then spread to North Vietnam, Laos, and Cambodia. After putting in place a client regime in Saigon, the US government invited itself in to fight a communist insurgency—Vietcong guerrillas who had infiltrated rural regions of South Vietnam where villagers were sheltering them. This was exactly the model that Russia replicated when, in 1979, it invited itself into Afghanistan. Nobody in the "free world" is in any doubt about the fact that Russia invaded Afghanistan. After glasnost, even a Soviet foreign minister called the Soviet invasion of Afghanistan "illegal and immoral."[18] But there has been no such introspection in the United States. In 1984, in a stunning revelation, Chomsky wrote:

> *For the past twenty-two years, I have been searching to find some reference in mainstream journalism or scholarship to an American invasion of South Vietnam in 1962 (or ever), or an American attack against South Vietnam, or American aggression in Indochina—without success. There is no such event in history. Rather, there is an American defense of South Vietnam against terrorists supported from the outside (namely from Vietnam).[19]*

There is no such event in history!

In 1962 the US Air Force began to bomb rural South Vietnam, where 80 percent of the population lived. The bombing lasted for more than a decade. Thousands of people were killed. The idea was to bomb on a scale colossal enough to induce panic migration from villages into cities, where people could be held in refugee camps. Samuel Huntington referred to this as a process of "urbanization."[20] (I learned about urbanization when I was in architecture school in India. Somehow I don't remember aerial bombing being part of the syllabus.) Huntington—famous today for his essay "The Clash of Civilizations?"—was at the time chairman of the Council on Vietnamese Studies of the Southeast Asia Development Advisory Group. Chomsky quotes him describing the Vietcong as "a powerful force which cannot be dislodged from its constituency so long as the constituency continues to exist."[21] Huntington went on to advise "direct application of mechanical and conventional power"—in other words, to crush a people's war, eliminate the people.[22] (Or, perhaps, to update the thesis—in order to prevent a clash of civilizations, annihilate a civilization.)

Here's one observer from the time on the limitations of America's mechanical power: "The problem is that American machines are not equal to the task of killing communist soldiers except as part of a scorched-earth policy that destroys everything else as well."[23] That problem has been solved now. Not with less destructive bombs but with more imaginative language. There's a more elegant way of saying "that destroys everything else as well." The phrase is "collateral damage."

And here's a firsthand account of what America's "machines" (Huntington called them "modernizing instruments" and staff officers in the Pentagon called them "bomb-o-grams") can do.[24] This is T. D. Allman flying over the Plain of Jars in Laos:

> Even if the war in Laos ended tomorrow, the restoration of its ecological balance might take several years. The reconstruction of the Plain's totally destroyed towns and villages might take just as long. Even if this was done, the Plain might long prove perilous to human habitation because of the hundreds of thousands of unexploded bombs, mines and booby traps.
>
> A recent flight around the Plain of Jars revealed what less than

three years of intensive American bombing can do to a rural area, even after its civilian population has been evacuated. In large areas, the primary tropical colour—bright green—has been replaced by an abstract pattern of black, and bright metallic colours. Much of the remaining foliage is stunted, dulled by defoliants.

Today, black is the dominant colour of the northern and eastern reaches of the Plain. Napalm is dropped regularly to burn off the grass and undergrowth that covers the Plains and fills its many narrow ravines. The fires seem to burn constantly, creating rectangles of black. During the flight, plumes of smoke could be seen rising from freshly bombed areas.

The main routes, coming into the Plain from communist-held territory, are bombed mercilessly, apparently on a non-stop basis. There, and along the rim of the Plain, the dominant colour is yellow. All vegetation has been destroyed. The craters are countless. . . . The area has been bombed so repeatedly that the land resembles the pocked, churned desert in storm-hit areas of the North African desert.

Further to the southeast, Xieng Khouangville—once the most populous town in communist Laos—lies empty, destroyed. To the north of the Plain, the little resort of Khang Khay also has been destroyed.

Around the landing field at the base of King Kong, the main colours are yellow (from upturned soil) and black (from napalm), relieved by patches of bright red and blue: parachutes used to drop supplies.

. . . The last local inhabitants were being carted into air transports. Abandoned vegetable gardens that would never be harvested grew near abandoned houses with plates still on the tables and calendars on the walls.[25]

(Never counted in the "costs" of war are the dead birds, the charred animals, the murdered fish, incinerated insects, poisoned water sources, destroyed vegetation. Rarely mentioned is the arrogance of the human race toward other living things with which it shares this planet. All these are forgotten in the fight for markets and ideologies. This arrogance will probably be the ultimate undoing of the human species.)

The centerpiece of *For Reasons of State* is an essay called "The Mentality of the Backroom Boys," in which Chomsky offers an extraordinarily supple, exhaustive analysis of the Pentagon Papers, which he says "provide documentary evidence of a conspiracy to use force in international affairs in violation of law."[26] Here, too, Chomsky makes note of the fact that while the bombing of North Vietnam is discussed at some length in the Pentagon Papers, the invasion of South Vietnam barely merits a mention.[27]

The Pentagon Papers are mesmerizing, not as documentation of the history of the US war in Indochina but as insight into the minds of the men who planned and executed it. It's fascinating to be privy to the ideas that were being tossed around, the suggestions that were made, the proposals that were put forward. In a section called "The Asian Mind—the American Mind," Chomsky examines the discussion of the mentality of the enemy that "stoically accept[s] the destruction of wealth and the loss of lives," whereas "we want life, happiness, wealth, power," and for us "death and suffering are irrational choices when alternatives exist."[28] So we learn that the Asian poor, presumably because they cannot comprehend the meaning of happiness, wealth, and power, invite America to carry this "strategic logic to its conclusion, which is genocide." But then "we" balk because "genocide is a terrible burden to bear."[29] (Eventually, of course, "we" went ahead and committed genocide anyway, and then pretended that it never really happened.)

Of course the Pentagon Papers contain some moderate proposals, as well.

Strikes at population targets (per se) are likely not only to create a counterproductive wave of revulsion abroad and at home but also to greatly increase the risk of enlarging the war with China and the Soviet Union. Destruction of locks and dams, however—if handled right—might offer promise. It should be studied. Such destruction does not kill or drown people. By shallow-flooding the rice, it leads after time to widespread starvation (more than a million?) unless food is provided—which we could offer to do "at the conference table."[30]

Layer by layer, Chomsky strips down the process of decision making by US government officials, to reveal at its core the pitiless heart of the American war machine, completely insulated from the realities of war, blinded by ideology, and willing to annihilate millions of human beings, civilians, soldiers, women, children, villages, whole cities, whole ecosystems—with scientifically honed methods of brutality.

Here's an American pilot talking about the joys of napalm:

We sure are pleased with those backroom boys at Dow. The original product wasn't so hot—if the gooks were quick they could scrape it off. So the boys started adding polystyrene—now it sticks like shit to a blanket. But then if the gooks jumped under water it stopped burning, so they started adding Willie Peter [white phosphorous] so's to make it burn better. It'll even burn under water now. And just one drop is enough, it'll keep on burning right down to the bone so they die anyway from phosphorous poisoning.[31]

So the lucky gooks were annihilated for their own good. Better Dead than Red.

Thanks to the seductive charms of Hollywood and the irresistible appeal of America's mass media, all these years later, the world views the war as an *American* story. Indochina provided the lush tropical backdrop against which the United States played out its fantasies of violence, tested its latest technology, furthered its ideology, examined its conscience, agonized over its moral dilemmas, and dealt with its guilt (or pretended to). The Vietnamese, the Cambodians, and the Laotians were only script props. Nameless, faceless, slit-eyed humanoids. They were just the people who died. Gooks.

The only real lesson the US government learned from its invasion of Indochina is how to go to war without committing American troops and risking American lives. So now we have wars waged with long-range cruise missiles, Black Hawks, "bunker busters." Wars in which the "Allies" lose more journalists than soldiers.

As a child growing up in the state of Kerala, in South India— where the first democratically elected communist government in the world came to power in 1959, the year I was born—I worried terribly about being a gook. Kerala was only a few thousand miles west of Vietnam. We had jungles and rivers and rice fields, and communists, too. I kept imagining my mother, my brother, and myself being blown out of the bushes by a grenade, or mowed down, like the gooks in the movies, by an American marine with muscled arms and chewing gum and a loud background score. In my dreams, I was the burning girl in the famous photograph taken on the road from Trang Bang.

As someone who grew up on the cusp of both American and Soviet propaganda (which more or less neutralized each other), when I first read Noam Chomsky, it occurred to me that his marshaling of evidence, the volume of it, the relentlessness of it, was a little—how shall I put it?—insane. Even a quarter of the evidence he had compiled would have been enough to convince me. I used to wonder why he needed to do so much *work*. But now I understand that the magnitude and intensity of Chomsky's work is a barometer of the magnitude, scope, and relentlessness of the propaganda machine that he's up against. He's like the wood borer who lives inside the third rack of my bookshelf. Day and night, I hear his jaws crunching through the wood, grinding it to a fine dust. It's as though he disagrees with the literature and wants to destroy the very structure on which it rests. I call him Chompsky.

Being an American working in America, writing to convince Americans of his point of view must really be like having to tunnel through hard wood. Chomsky is one of a small band of individuals fighting a whole industry. And that makes him not only brilliant, but heroic.

Some years ago, in a poignant interview with James Peck, Chomsky spoke about his memory of the day Hiroshima was bombed. He was sixteen years old:

> *I remember that I literally couldn't talk to anybody. There was nobody. I just walked off by myself. I was at a summer camp at the time, and I walked off into the woods and stayed alone for a couple of hours when I heard about it. I could never talk to anyone about it and never understood anyone's reaction. I felt completely isolated.*[32]

That isolation produced one of the greatest, most radical public thinkers of our time.

When the sun sets on the American empire, as it will, as it must, Noam Chomsky's work will survive. It will point a cool, incriminating finger at a merciless, Machiavellian empire as cruel, self-righteous, and hypocritical as the ones it has replaced. (The only difference is that it is armed with technology that can visit the kind of devastation on the world that history has never known and the human race cannot begin to imagine.)

As a could've been gook, and who knows, perhaps a potential gook, hardly a day goes by when I don't find myself thinking—for one reason or another—"Chomsky Zindabad."

CONFRONTING
EMPIRE

I'VE BEEN ASKED to speak about "how to confront empire." It's a huge question, and I have no easy answers.

When we speak of confronting empire, we need to identify what empire means. Does it mean the US government (and its European satellites), the World Bank, the International Monetary Fund, the World Trade Organization (WTO), and multinational corporations? Or is it something more than that?

In many countries, empire has sprouted other subsidiary heads, some dangerous byproducts—nationalism, religious bigotry, fascism, and, of course, terrorism. All these march arm in arm with the project of corporate globalization.

Let me illustrate what I mean. India—the world's biggest democracy—is currently at the forefront of the corporate globalization project. Its "market" of one billion people is being pried open by the WTO. Corporatization and privatization are being welcomed by the government and the Indian elite.

First presented at the closing rally of the World Social Forum in Porto Alegre, Brazil, January 27, 2003.

It is not a coincidence that the prime minister, the home minister, the disinvestment minister—the men who signed the deal with Enron in India, the men who are selling the country's infrastructure to corporate multinationals, the men who want to privatize water, electricity, oil, coal, steel, health, education, and telecommunication—are all members or admirers of the Rashtriya Swayamsevak Sangh (RSS), a right-wing, ultra-nationalist Hindu guild which has openly admired Hitler and his methods.

The dismantling of democracy is proceeding with the speed and efficiency of a Structural Adjustment Program. While the project of corporate globalization rips through people's lives in India, massive privatization and labor "reforms" are pushing people off their land and out of their jobs. Hundreds of impoverished farmers are committing suicide by consuming pesticide.[1]

Reports of starvation deaths are coming in from all over the country.[2]

While the elite journeys to its imaginary destination somewhere near the top of the world, the dispossessed are spiraling downward into crime and chaos. This climate of frustration and national disillusionment is the perfect breeding ground, history tells us, for fascism.

The two arms of the Indian government have evolved the perfect pincer action. While one arm is busy selling India off in chunks, the other, to divert attention, is orchestrating a howling, baying chorus of Hindu nationalism and religious fascism. It is conducting nuclear tests, rewriting history books, burning churches, and demolishing mosques. Censorship, surveillance, the suspension of civil liberties and human rights, the questioning of who is an Indian citizen and who is not, particularly with regard to religious minorities, are all becoming common practice now.

Last March, in the state of Gujarat, two thousand Muslims were butchered in a state-sponsored pogrom. Muslim women were specially targeted. They were stripped, and gang-raped, before being burned alive. Arsonists burned and looted shops, homes, textile mills, and mosques.³

More than a hundred fifty thousand Muslims have been driven from their homes. The economic base of the Muslim community has been devastated.

While Gujarat burned, the Indian Prime Minister was on MTV promoting his new poems. In December 2002, the government that orchestrated the killing was voted back into office with a comfortable majority.⁴ Nobody has been punished for the genocide. Narendra Modi, architect of the pogrom, proud member of the RSS, has embarked on his second term as the chief minister of Gujarat. If he were Saddam Hussein, of course each atrocity would have been on CNN. But since he's not—and since the Indian "market" is open to global investors—the massacre is not even an embarrassing inconvenience.

There are more than one hundred million Muslims in India. A time bomb is ticking in our ancient land.

All this to say that it is a myth that the free market breaks down national barriers. The free market does not threaten national sovereignty, it undermines democracy.

As the disparity between the rich and the poor grows, the fight to corner resources is intensifying. To push through their "sweetheart deals," to corporatize the crops we grow, the water we drink, the air we breathe, and the dreams we dream, corporate globalization needs an international confederation of loyal, corrupt, authoritarian governments in poorer countries to push through unpopular reforms and quell the mutinies.

Corporate globalization—or shall we call it by its name?—Imperialism—needs a press that pretends to be free. It needs courts that pretend to dispense justice.

Meanwhile, the countries of the North harden their borders and stockpile weapons of mass destruction. After all, they have to make sure that it's only money, goods, patents, and services that are globalized. Not the free movement of people. Not a respect for human rights. Not international treaties on racial discrimination or chemical and nuclear weapons or greenhouse gas emissions or climate change or—god forbid—justice.

So this—*all* this—is empire. This loyal confederation, this obscene accumulation of power, this greatly increased distance between those who make the decisions and those who have to suffer them.

Our fight, our goal, our vision of another world must be to eliminate that distance.

So how do we resist empire?

The good news is that we're not doing too badly. There have been major victories. Here in Latin America you have had so many—in Bolivia, you have Cochabamba.[5] In Peru, there was the uprising in Arequipa.[6] In Venezuela, President Hugo Chavez is holding on, despite the US government's best efforts.[7]

And the world's gaze is on the people of Argentina, who are trying to refashion a country from the ashes of the havoc wrought by the IMF.[8]

In India the movement against corporate globalization is gathering momentum and is poised to become the only real political force to counter religious fascism.

As for corporate globalization's glittering ambassadors— Enron, Bechtel, WorldCom, Arthur Andersen—where were they last year, and where are they now?

And of course here in Brazil we must ask: Who was the president last year, and who is it now?

Still, many of us have dark moments of hopelessness and despair. We know that under the spreading canopy of the war on terror, the men in suits are hard at work.

While bombs rain down on us and cruise missiles skid across the skies, we know that contracts are being signed, patents are being registered, oil pipelines are being laid, natural resources are being plundered, water is being privatized, and George Bush is planning to go to war against Iraq.

If we look at this conflict as a straightforward eyeball-to-eyeball confrontation between empire and those of us who are resisting it, it might seem that we are losing.

But there is another way of looking at it. We, all of us gathered here, have, each in our own way, laid siege to empire.

We may not have stopped it in its tracks—yet—but we have stripped it down. We have made it drop its mask. We have forced it into the open. It now stands before us on the world's stage in all its brutish, iniquitous nakedness.

Empire may well go to war, but it's out in the open now—too ugly to behold its own reflection. Too ugly even to rally its own people. It won't be long before the majority of American people become our allies.

In Washington, a quarter of a million people marched against the war on Iraq.[9] Each month, the protest is gathering momentum.

Before September 11, 2001, America had a secret history. Secret especially from its own people. But now America's secrets are history, and its history is public knowledge. It's street talk.

Today, we know that every argument that is being used to escalate the war against Iraq is a lie. The most ludicrous of them being the US government's deep commitment to bring democracy to Iraq.

Killing people to save them from dictatorship or ideological corruption is, of course, an old US government sport. Here in Latin America, you know that better than most.

Nobody doubts that Saddam Hussein is a ruthless dictator, a murderer (whose worst excesses were supported by the governments of the United States and Great Britain). There's no doubt that Iraqis would be better off without him.

But, then, the whole world would be better off without a certain Mr. Bush. In fact, he is far more dangerous than Saddam Hussein.

So should we bomb Bush out of the White House?

It's more than clear that Bush is determined to go to war against Iraq, *regardless* of the facts—and regardless of international public opinion.

In its recruitment drive for allies, the United States is prepared to *invent* facts.

The charade with weapons inspectors is the US government's offensive, insulting concession to some twisted form of international etiquette. It's like leaving the "doggie door" open for last-minute "allies" or maybe the United Nations to crawl through.

But for all intents and purposes, the new war against Iraq has begun.

What can we do?

We can hone our memory, we can learn from our history. We can continue to build public opinion until it becomes a deafening roar.

We can turn the war on Iraq into a fishbowl of the US government's excesses.

We can expose George Bush and Tony Blair—and their allies—for the cowardly baby killers, water poisoners, and pusillanimous long-distance bombers that they are.

We can reinvent civil disobedience in a million different ways. In other words, we can come up with a million ways of becoming a collective pain in the ass.

When George Bush says "You're either with us, or you are with the terrorists," we can say "No thank you." We can let him know that the people of the world do not need to choose between a Malevolent Mickey Mouse and the Mad Mullahs.

Our strategy should be not only to confront empire but to lay siege to it. To deprive it of oxygen. To shame it. To mock it. With our art, our music, our literature, our stubbornness, our joy, our brilliance, our sheer relentlessness—and our ability to tell our own stories. Stories that are different from the ones we're being brainwashed to believe.

The corporate revolution will collapse if we refuse to buy what they are selling—their ideas, their version of history, their wars, their weapons, their notion of inevitability.

Remember this: We be many and they be few. They need us more than we need them.

PEACE IS WAR:
THE COLLATERAL
DAMAGE OF
BREAKING NEWS

THERE'S BEEN A delicious debate in the Indian press of late. A prominent English daily announced that it would sell space on page 3 (its gossip section) to anyone who was willing to pay to be featured. (The inference is that the rest of the news in the paper is in some way unsponsored, unsullied, "pure news.") The announcement provoked a series of responses—most of them outraged that the proud tradition of impartial journalism could sink to such depths. Personally, I was delighted. For a major mainstream newspaper to introduce the *notion* of "paid-for" news is a giant step forward in the project of educating a largely credulous public about how the mass media operates. Once the

This is the text of a speech first delivered March 7, 2003, at the Center for the Study of Developing Societies (CSDS), New Delhi, at a workshop organized by Sarai: The New Media Initiative, CSDS, and the Waag Society in Delhi. It was first published in the *Sarai Reader 4: Crisis/Media* (New Delhi: Sarai, 2004). See http://www.sarai.net for additional information on Sarai.

idea of "paid-for" news has been mooted, once it's been ushered through the portals of popular imagination, it won't be hard for people to work out that if gossip columns in newspapers can be auctioned, why not the rest of the column space? After all, in this age of the "market" when everything's up for sale—rivers, forests, freedom, democracy, and justice—what's special about news? Sponsored News—what a delectable idea! "This report is brought to you by . . ." There could be a state-regulated sliding scale for rates (headlines, page 1, page 2, sports section, and so on). Or, on second thought, we could leave that to be regulated by the "free market"—as it is now. Why change a winning formula?

The debate about whether mass-circulation newspapers and commercial TV channels are finely plotted ideological conspiracies or apolitical, benign anarchies that bumble along as best they can is an old one and needs no elaboration. After the September 11 attack on the World Trade Center, the US mainstream media's blatant performance as the government's mouthpiece was the butt of some pretty black humor in the rest of the world. It brought the myth of the free press in America crashing down. But before we gloat, the Indian mass media behaved no differently during the Pokhran nuclear tests and the Kargil War. There was no bumbling and very little was benign in the shameful coverage of the December 13 attack on the Indian Parliament and the trial of S. A. R. Geelani, who has been sentenced to death after having been the subject of a media trial fueled by a campaign of nationalist hysteria and outright lies. On a more everyday basis: Would anybody who depends on the Indian mass media for information know that eighty thousand people have been killed in Kashmir since 1989, most of them Muslim, most of them by Indian security forces?[1] Most Indians would be outraged if it were suggested to them that the killings and "disappearances" in the Kashmir valley put India on a par with any banana republic.

Modern democracies have been around long enough for neoliberal capitalists to learn how to subvert them. They have mastered the technique of infiltrating the instruments of democracy—the "independent" judiciary, the "free" press, the parliament—and molding them to their purpose. The project of corporate globalization has cracked the code. Free elections, a free press, and an independent judiciary mean little when the free market has reduced them to commodities available on sale to the highest bidder.

To control a democracy, it is becoming more and more vital to control the media. The principal media outlets in America are owned by six major companies.[2] The six largest cable companies have 80 percent of cable television subscribers.[3] Even Internet websites are being colonized by giant media corporations.[4]

It's a mistake to think that the corporate media supports the neoliberal project. It *is* the neoliberal project. It is the nexus, the confluence, the convergence, the union, the chosen medium of those who have power and money. As the project of corporate globalization increases the disparity between the rich and the poor, as the world grows more and more restive, corporations on the prowl for sweetheart deals need repressive governments to quell the mutinies in the servants' quarters. And governments, of course, need corporations. This mutual dependence spawns a sort of corporate nationalism, or, more accurately, a corporate/ nationalism—if you can imagine such a thing. Corporate/nationalism has become the unwavering anthem of the mass media.

One of our main tasks is to expose the complex mess of cables that connect power to money to the supposedly "neutral" free press.

In the last couple of years, New Media has embarked on just such an enterprise. It has descended on Old Media like an annoying swarm of bees buzzing around an old buffalo, going where it goes, stopping where it stops, commenting on and critiquing its every move. New Media has managed not to transform but to create the possibility of transforming conventional mass media from the sophisticated propaganda machine into a vast CD-ROM. Picture it: The old buffalo is the text, the bees are the hyperlinks that deconstruct it. Click a bee, get the inside story.

Basically, for the lucky few who have access to the Internet, the mass media has been contextualized and shown up for what it really is—an elaborate boardroom bulletin that reports and analyzes the concerns of powerful people. For the bees it's a phenomenal achievement. For the buffalo, obviously, it's not much fun.

For the bees (the nice, lefty ones) it's a significant victory but by no means a conquest. Because it's still the annoyed buffalo stumbling across the plains, lurching from crisis to crisis, from war to war, who sets the pace. It's still the buffalo that decides which particular crisis will be the main course on the menu and what's for dessert. So here we are today, the buffalo and the bees—on the verge of a war that could redraw the political map of the world and alter the course of history. As the United States gears up to attack Iraq, the US government's lies are being amplified, its reheated doctrine of preemptive strike talked up, its war machine deployed. There is still no sign of Iraq's so-called arsenal of weapons of mass destruction.

Even before the next phase of the war—the American occupation of Iraq—has begun (the war itself is thirteen years old), thanks to the busy bees the extent and scale, the speed and strength of the mobilization against the war has been unprecedented in history. On February 15, 2003, in an extraordinary display of public morality, millions of people took to the streets in hundreds of cities across the world to protest against the invasion of Iraq.[5] If the US government and its allies choose to ignore this and continue with their plans to invade and occupy Iraq, it could bring about a serious predicament in the modern world's understanding of democracy.

But then again, maybe we'll get used to it. Governments have learned to wait out crises—because they know that crises by definition must be short-lived. They know that a crisis-driven media simply cannot afford to hang about in the same place for too long. It must be off for its next appointment with the next crisis. Like business houses need a cash turnover, the media needs a crisis turnover. Whole countries become old news. They cease to exist. And the darkness becomes deeper than it was before the light was shined on them. We saw that in Afghanistan when the Soviets withdrew. We are being given a repeat performance now.

And eventually, when the buffalo stumbles away, the bees go, too.

Crisis reportage in the twenty-first century has evolved into an independent discipline—almost a science. The money, the technology, and the orchestrated mass hysteria that go into crisis reporting have a curious effect. It isolates the crisis, unmoors it from the particularities of the history, the geography, and the culture that produced it. Eventually it floats free like a hot-air balloon, carrying its cargo of international gadflies—specialists, analysts, foreign correspondents, and crisis photographers with their enormous telephoto lenses.

Somewhere mid-journey and without prior notice, the gad-flies auto-eject and parachute down to the site of the next crisis, leaving the crestfallen, abandoned balloon drifting aimlessly in the sky, pathetically masquerading as a current event, hoping it will at least make history.

There are few things sadder than a consumed, spent crisis. (For field research, look up Kabul, Afghanistan, AD 2002, and Gujarat, India, AD 2003.)

Crisis reportage has left us with a double-edged legacy. While governments hone the art of crisis management (the art of waiting out a crisis), resistance movements are increasingly being ensnared in a sort of vortex of crisis production. They have to find ways of precipitating crises, of manufacturing them in easily consumable, spectator-friendly formats. We have entered the era of crisis as a consumer item, crisis as spectacle, as theater. It's not new, but it's evolving, morphing, taking on new aspects. Flying planes into buildings is its most modern, most extreme form.

The disturbing thing nowadays is that Crisis as Spectacle has cut loose from its origins in genuine, long-term civil disobedience and is gradually becoming an instrument of resistance that is more symbolic than real. Also, it has begun to stray into other territory. Right now, it's blurring the lines that separate resistance movements from campaigns by political parties. I'm thinking here of L. K. Advani's *Rath Yatra*, which eventually led to the demolition of the Babri Masjid, and of the *kar seva* campaign for the construction of the Ram Temple at Ayodhya, which is brought to a boil by the Sangh Parivar each time elections come around.[6]

Both resistance movements and political election campaigns are in search of spectacle—though, of course, the kind of spectacle they choose differs vastly.

On the occasions when symbolic political theater shades into action that actually breaks the law, then it is the response of the State which usually provides the clarity to differentiate between a campaign by a political party and an action by a people's resistance movement. For instance, the police never opened fire on the rampaging mob that demolished the Babri Masjid, or those who participated in the genocidal campaign by the Congress Party against Sikhs in Delhi in 1984, or the Shiv Sena's massacre of Muslims in Bombay in 1993, or the Bajrang Dal's genocide against Muslims in Gujarat in 2002.[7] Neither the police, nor the courts, nor the government has taken serious action against anybody who participated in this violence.

Yet recently the police have repeatedly opened fire on unarmed people, including women and children, who have protested against the violation of their rights to life and livelihood by the government's "development projects."[8]

In this era of crisis reportage, if you don't have a crisis to call your own, you're not in the news. And if you're not in the news, you don't exist. It's as though the virtual world constructed in the media has become more real than the real world.

Every self-respecting people's movement, every "issue," needs to have its own hot-air balloon in the sky advertising its brand and purpose. For this reason, starvation deaths are more effective advertisements for drought and skewed food distribution than cases of severe malnutrition—which don't quite make the cut. Standing in the rising water of a reservoir for days on end watching your home and belongings float away to protest against a big dam used to be an effective strategy but isn't anymore. People resisting dams are expected to either conjure new tricks or give up the struggle. In the despair created by the Indian Supreme Court's appalling judgment on the Sardar Sarovar Dam, senior activists of the Narmada Bachao Andolan (NBA) began once again to talk of *jal samarpan*—drowning themselves in the rising waters.[9] They were mocked for not really meaning what they said.

Crisis as a blood sport.

The Indian state and the mass media have shown themselves to be benignly tolerant of the phenomenon of Resistance as a Symbolic Spectacle. (It actually helps them to hold down the country's reputation as the world's biggest democracy.) But whenever civil resistance has shown the slightest signs of metamorphosing from symbolic acts (dharnas, demonstrations, hunger strikes) into anything remotely resembling genuine civil disobedience—blockading villages, occupying forest land—the State has cracked down mercilessly.

In April 2001 the police opened fire on a peaceful meeting of the Adivasi Mukti Sangathan in Mehndi Kheda, Madhya Pradesh. On February 2, 2001, police fired on a peaceful protest of Munda Adivasis in Jharkhand, who were part of the protest against the Koel Karo hydroelectric, killing eight people and wounding twelve. On April 7, 2000, Gujarat police attacked a peaceful demonstration by the Kinara Bachao Sangharsh Samiti (the Save the Coast Action Committee) against the consortium of Natelco and Unocal who were trying to do a survey for a proposed private port.[10] Lieutenant Colonel Pratap Save, one of the main activists, was beaten to death.[11] In Orissa, three Adivasis were killed for protesting a bauxite mining project in December 2000.[12] In Chilika, police fired on fisherfolk demanding the restoration of their fishing rights. Four people were killed.[13]

The instances of repression go on and on—Jambudweep, Kashipur, Maikanj. The most recent, of course, is the incident in the Muthanga in Wyanad, Kerala. In February 2003, four thousand displaced Adivasis, including women and children, occupied a small part of a wildlife sanctuary, demanding that they be given the land the government had promised them the previous year. The deadline had come and gone, and there had been no sign that the government had any intention of keeping its word. As the tension built up over the days, the Kerala police surrounded the protesters and opened fire, killing one person and severely injuring several others.[14]

Interestingly, when it comes to the poor, and in particular Dalit and Adivasi communities, they get killed for encroaching on forest land (Muthanga), as well as when they're trying to protect forest land from dams, mining operations, steel plants (Koel Karo, Nagarnar).[15]

In almost every instance of police firing, the state's strategy is to say the firing was provoked by an act of violence. Those who have been fired upon are immediately called militant (PWG, MCC, ISI, LTTE) agents.[16] In Muthanga, the police and the government claimed that the Adivasis had staged an armed insurrection and attempted to set up a parallel government. The speaker of the Kerala assembly said that they should have been "suppressed or shot."[17]

At the scene of the firing, the police had put together an "ammunition display." It consisted of some stones, a couple of sickles and axes, bows and arrows, and a few kitchen knives. One of the major weapons used in the uprising was a polythene bag full of bees.[18] (Imagine the young man collecting bees in the forest to protect himself and his little family against the Kerala police. What a delightful parallel government his would be!)

According to the State, when victims refuse to be victims, they become terrorists and are dealt with as such. They're either killed or arrested under POTA (Prevention of Terrorism Act). In states like Orissa, Bihar, and Jharkhand, which are rich in mineral resources and therefore vulnerable to ruthless corporations on the hunt, hundreds of villagers, including minors, have been arrested under POTA and are being held in jail without trial. Some states have special police battalions for "antidevelopment" activity. This is quite apart from the other use that POTA is being put to—terrorizing Muslims, particularly in states like Jammu and Kashmir and Gujarat. The space for genuine nonviolent civil disobedience is atrophying. In the era of corporate globalization, poverty is a crime, and protesting against further impoverishment is terrorism. In the era of the war on terror, poverty is being slyly conflated with terrorism.

Calling anyone who protests against the violation of their human and constitutional rights a terrorist can end up becoming a self-fulfilling accusation. When every avenue of nonviolent dissent is closed down, should we really be surprised that the forests are filling up with extremists, insurgents, and militants? Vast parts of the country are already more or less beyond the control of the Indian state—Kashmir, the Northeast, large parts of Madhya Pradesh, Chhattisgarh, and Jharkhand.

It is utterly urgent for resistance movements and those of us who support them to reclaim the space for civil disobedience. To do this we will have to liberate ourselves from being manipulated, perverted, and headed off in the wrong direction by the desire to feed the media's endless appetite for theater. Because that saps energy and imagination.

There are signs that the battle has been joined. At a massive rally on February 27, 2003, the Nimad Malwa Kisan Mazdoor Sangathan (Nimad Malwa Farmers and Workers' Organization), in its protest against the privatization of power, declared that farmers and agricultural workers would not pay their electricity bills.[19] The Madhya Pradesh government has not yet responded. It'll be interesting to see what happens.

We have to find a way of forcing the real issues back into the news. For example, the real issue in the Narmada valley is not whether people will drown themselves or not. The NBA's strategies, its successes and failures, are an issue, but a separate issue from the problem of Big Dams.

The real issue is that the privatization of essential infrastructure is essentially undemocratic. The real issue is the towering mass of incriminating evidence against Big Dams. The real issue is the fact that over the last fifty years in India alone Big Dams have displaced more than thirty-three million people.[20] The real issue is the fact that Big Dams are obsolete. They're ecologically destructive, economically unviable, and politically undemocratic. The real issue is the fact that the Supreme Court of India ordered the construction of the Sardar Sarovar Dam to proceed even though it is aware that it violates the fundamental rights to life and livelihood of the citizens of India.[21]

Unfortunately, the mass media, through a combination of ignorance and design, has framed the whole argument as one between those who are prodevelopment and those who are antidevelopment. It slyly suggests that the NBA is antielectricity and anti-irrigation. And, of course, anti-Gujarat. This is complete nonsense. The NBA believes that Big Dams are obsolete. They're not just bad for displaced people, they're bad for Gujarat, too. They're too expensive, the water will not go where it's supposed to, and eventually the area that is supposed to "benefit" will pay a heavy price. Like what is happening in the command area of India's favorite dam—the Bhakra Nangal.[22] The NBA believes that there are more local, more democratic, ecologically sustainable, economically viable ways of generating electricity and managing water systems. It is demanding more modernity, not less. More democracy, not less.

After the Supreme Court delivered what is generally considered to be a knockout blow to the most spectacular resistance movement in India, the vultures are back, circling over the kill. The World Bank's new *Water Resources Sector Strategy* clarifies that the World Bank will return to its policy of funding Big Dams.[23] Meanwhile the Indian government, directed by the venerable Supreme Court, has trundled out an ancient, harebrained, Stalinist scheme of linking India's rivers. The order was given based on no real information or research—just on the whim of an aging judge.[24] The river-linking project makes Big Dams look like enlightenment itself. It will become to the development debate what the Ram Mandir in Ayodhya is to the communal debate—a venal campaign gimmick that can be rolled out just before every election. It is destructive even if it is never realized. It will be used to block every other more local, more effective, more democratic irrigation project. It will be used to siphon off enormous sums of public money.

Linking India's rivers would lead to massive social upheavals and ecological devastation. Any modern ecologist who hears about this plan bursts out laughing. Yet leading papers and journals like *India Today* and *Indian Express* carry laudatory pieces full of absurd information.

Coming back to the tyranny of crisis reportage: one way to cut loose is to understand that for most people in the world, peace is war—a daily battle against hunger, thirst, and the violation of their dignity. Wars are often the end result of a flawed peace, a putative peace. And it is the flaws, the systemic flaws in what is normally *considered* to be "peace," that we ought to be writing about. We have to—at least some of us have to—become peace correspondents instead of war correspondents. We have to lose our terror of the mundane. We have to use our skills and imagination and our art to re-create the rhythms of the endless crisis of normality, and in doing so, expose the policies and processes that make ordinary things—food, water, shelter, and dignity—such a distant dream for ordinary people.

Most important of all, we have to turn our skills toward understanding and exposing the instruments of the state. In India, for instance, the institution that is least scrutinized and least accountable makes every major political, cultural, and executive decision today. The Indian Supreme Court is one of the most powerful courts in the world. It decides whether dams should be built or not, whether slums should be cleared, whether industry should be removed from urban areas. It makes decisions on issues like privatization and disinvestment. On the content of school textbooks. It micromanages our lives. Its orders affect the lives of millions of people. Whether you agree with the Supreme Court's decisions—all of them, some of them, none of them—or not, as an institution the Supreme Court has to be accountable. In a democracy, you have checks and balances, not hierarchies. And yet because of the Contempt of Court law, we cannot criticize the Supreme Court or call it to account. How can you have an undemocratic institution in a democratic society? It will automatically become a floor trap that accumulates authority, that confers supreme powers on itself. And that's exactly what has happened. We live in a judicial dictatorship. And we don't seem to have even begun to realize it.

The only way to make democracy real is to begin a process of constant questioning, permanent provocation, and continuous public conversation between citizens and the state. That conversation is quite different from the conversation between political parties. (Representing the views of rival political parties is what the mass media thinks of as "balanced" reporting.) Patrolling the borders of our liberty is the only way we can guard against the snatching away of our freedoms. All over the world today, freedoms are being curbed in the name of protecting freedom. Once freedoms are surrendered by civil society, they cannot be retrieved without a struggle. It is so much easier to relinquish them than to recover them.

It is important to remember that our freedoms, such as they are, were never given to us by any government; they have been wrested by us. If we do not use them, if we do not test them from time to time, they atrophy. If we do not guard them constantly, they will be taken away from us. If we do not demand more and more, we will be left with less and less.

Understanding these things and then using them as tools to interrogate what we consider "normalcy" is a way of subverting the tyranny of crisis reportage.

Finally, there's another worrying kind of collateral damage caused by crisis reportage. Crisis reportage flips history over, turns it belly up. It tells stories back to front. So we begin with the news of a crisis and end (if we're lucky) with an account of the events that led to it. For example, we enter the history of Afghanistan through the debris of the World Trade Center in New York, the history of Iraq through Operation Desert Storm. We enter the story of the Adivasi struggle for justice in Kerala through the news of police firing on those who dared to encroach on a wildlife sanctuary. So crisis reportage forces us to view a complex evolving historical process through the distorting prism of a single current event.

Crises polarize people. They hustle us into making uninformed choices: "You're either with us or with the terrorists." "You're either pro-privatization or pro-state." "If you're not pro-Bush, you're pro–Saddam Hussein." "If you're not good, you're evil."

These are spurious choices. They're not the only ones available to us. But in a crisis, we become like goalkeepers in a penalty shootout of a soccer match. We imagine that we have to commit ourselves to one side or another. We have nothing to go on but instinct and social conditioning. And once we're committed, it's hard to realign ourselves. In this process, those who ought to be natural allies become enemies.

For example, when the police fired on the Adivasis who "encroached" on the wildlife sanctuary in Muthanga, Kerala, environmentalists did not come to their defense because they were outraged that the Adivasis had dared to encroach on a wildlife sanctuary. In actual fact the "sanctuary" was a eucalyptus plantation.[25] Years ago, old-growth forest had been clear-felled by the government to plant eucalyptus for the Birla's Grasim Rayon Factory, set up in 1958. A huge mass of incriminating data accuses the factory of devastating the bamboo forests in the region, polluting the Chaliyar River, emitting toxins into the air, and causing a great deal of suffering to a great number of people.[26] In the name of employing three thousand people, it destroyed the livelihood of what has been estimated to be about three hundred thousand bamboo workers, sand miners, and fisherfolk. The state government did nothing to control the pollution or the destruction of forests and rivers. There were no police firing at the owners or managers of Grasim. But then, they had not committed the crime of being poor, being Adivasi, or being on the brink of starvation. When the natural resources (bamboo, eucalyptus, pulp) ran out, the factory closed down. The workers were abandoned.[27]

Crisis reportage elides these facts and forces people to make uninformed choices.

The real crisis—the dispossession, the disempowerment, the daily violation of the democratic rights and the dignity of not thousands but millions of people, which has been set into motion not by accident but by deliberate design—does not fit into the predetermined format of crisis reporting.

Fifteen years ago, the corrupt, centralized Indian state was too grand, too top-heavy, and too far away for its poor to have access to it—to its institutions of education, of health, of water supply, and of electricity. Even its sewage system was inaccessible, too good for most. Today, the project of corporate globalization has increased the distance between those who make the decisions and those who must suffer them even more. For the poor, the uneducated, the displaced and dispossessed, that distance puts justice out of reach.

So the unrelenting daily grind of injustice goes unreported, and the silent, unformatted battle spreads subcutaneously through our society, ushering us toward a future that doesn't bear thinking about.

But we continue sailing on our *Titanic* as it tilts slowly into the darkened sea. The deckhands panic. Those with cheaper tickets have begun to be washed away. But in the banquet halls, the music plays on. The only signs of trouble are slightly slanting waiters, the kabobs and canapés sliding to one side of their silver trays, the somewhat exaggerated sloshing of the wine in the crystal wineglasses. The rich are comforted by the knowledge that the lifeboats on the deck are reserved for club-class passengers. The tragedy is that they are probably right.

AN ORDINARY
PERSON'S GUIDE
TO EMPIRE

MESOPOTAMIA. BABYLON. THE Tigris and Euphrates. How many children in how many classrooms, over how many centuries, have hang-glided through the past, transported on the wings of these words?

And now the bombs are falling, incinerating, and humiliating that ancient civilization.

On the steel torsos of their missiles, adolescent American soldiers scrawl colorful messages in childish handwriting: "For Saddam, from the Fat Boy Posse."[1] A building goes down. A marketplace. A home. A girl who loves a boy. A child who only ever wanted to play with his older brother's marbles.

On March 21, the day after American and British troops began their illegal invasion and occupation of Iraq, an "embedded" CNN correspondent interviewed an American soldier. "I wanna

---

The original version of this essay was first published in the *Guardian* (London), April 2, 2003.

get in there and get my nose dirty," Private AJ said. "I wanna take revenge for 9/11."[2]

To be fair to the correspondent, even though he was "embedded," he did sort of weakly suggest that so far there was no real evidence that linked the Iraqi government to the September 11 attacks. Private AJ stuck his teenage tongue out all the way down to the end of his chin. "Yeah, well, that stuff's way over my head," he said.[3]

According to a *New York Times* / CBS News survey, 42 percent of the American public believes that Saddam Hussein is directly responsible for the September 11 attacks on the World Trade Center and the Pentagon.[4] And an ABC News poll says that 55 percent of Americans believe that Saddam Hussein directly supports Al-Qaeda.[5] What percentage of America's armed forces believes these fabrications is anybody's guess.

It is unlikely that British and American troops fighting in Iraq are aware that their governments supported Saddam Hussein both politically and financially through his worst excesses.

But why should poor AJ and his fellow soldiers be burdened with these details? It doesn't matter anymore, does it? Hundreds of thousands of men, tanks, ships, choppers, bombs, ammunition, gas masks, high-protein food, whole aircrafts ferrying toilet paper, insect repellent, vitamins, and bottled mineral water are on the move. The phenomenal logistics of Operation Iraqi Freedom make it a universe unto itself. It doesn't need to justify its existence any more. It exists. It *is*.

President George W. Bush, commander in chief of the US Army, Navy, Air Force, and Marines, has issued clear instructions: "Iraq. Will. Be. Liberated."[6] (Perhaps he means that even if Iraqi people's bodies are killed, their souls will be liberated.) American and British citizens owe it to the Supreme Commander to forsake thought and rally behind their troops. Their countries are at war.

And what a war it is.

After using the "good offices" of UN diplomacy (economic sanctions and weapons inspections) to ensure that Iraq was brought to its knees, its people starved, half a million of its children killed, its infrastructure severely damaged, after making sure that most of its weapons have been destroyed, in an act of cowardice that must surely be unrivaled in history, the "Allies" / "Coalition of the Willing" (better known as the Coalition of the Bullied and Bought) sent in an invading army!

Operation Iraqi Freedom? I don't think so. It's more like Operation Let's Run a Race, but First Let Me Break Your Knees.

So far the Iraqi Army, with its hungry, ill-equipped soldiers, its old guns and aging tanks, has somehow managed to temporarily confound and occasionally even outmaneuver the "Allies." Faced with the richest, best-equipped, most powerful armed forces the world has ever seen, Iraq has shown spectacular courage and has even managed to put up what actually amounts to a defense. A defense which the Bush/Blair Pair have immediately denounced as deceitful and cowardly. (But then deceit is an old tradition with us natives. When we're invaded/colonized/occupied and stripped of all dignity, we turn to guile and opportunism.)

Even allowing for the fact that Iraq and the "Allies" are at war, the extent to which the "Allies" and their media cohorts are prepared to go is astounding to the point of being counterproductive to their own objectives.

When Saddam Hussein appeared on national TV to address the Iraqi people following the failure of the most elaborate assassination attempt in history—Operation Decapitation—we had Geoff Hoon, British defense secretary, deriding him for not having the courage to stand up and be killed, calling him a coward who hides in trenches.[7] We then had a flurry of coalition speculation: Was it really Saddam Hussein, was it his double? Or was it Osama with a shave? Was it prerecorded? Was it a speech? Was it black magic? Will it turn into a pumpkin if we really, really want it to?

After dropping not hundreds but thousands of bombs on Baghdad, when a marketplace was mistakenly blown up and civilians killed, a US Army spokesman implied that the Iraqis were blowing themselves up! "They're also using very old stocks . . . and those stocks are not reliable, and [their] missiles are going up and coming down."[8]

If so, may we ask how this squares with the accusation that the Iraqi regime is a paid-up member of the Axis of Evil and a threat to world peace?

When the Arab TV station Al-Jazeera shows civilian casualties, it's denounced as "emotive" Arab propaganda aimed at orchestrating hostility toward the "Allies," as though Iraqis are dying only in order to make the "Allies" look bad. Even French television has come in for some stick for similar reasons. But the awed, breathless footage of aircraft carriers, stealth bombers, and cruise missiles arcing across the desert sky on American and British TV is described as the "terrible beauty" of war.[9]

When invading American soldiers (from the army "that's only here to help") are taken prisoner and shown on Iraqi TV, George Bush says it violates the Geneva Convention and exposes "the Iraqi regime and the evil at its heart."[10] But it is entirely acceptable for US television stations to show the hundreds of prisoners being held by the US government in Guantánamo Bay, kneeling on the ground with their hands tied behind their backs, blinded with opaque goggles and with earphones clamped on their ears, to ensure complete visual and aural deprivation.[11] When questioned about the treatment of prisoners in Guantánamo Bay, US government officials don't deny that they're being ill-treated. They deny that they're prisoners of war! They call them "unlawful combatants,"[12] implying that their ill-treatment is legitimate! (So what's the party line on the massacre of prisoners in Mazar-e-Sharif, Afghanistan?[13] Forgive and forget? And what of the prisoner tortured to death by the Special Forces at the Bagram Air Force Base? Doctors have formally called it homicide.[14])

When the "Allies" bombed the Iraqi television station (also, incidentally, a contravention of the Geneva Convention), there was vulgar jubilation in the American media. In fact, Fox TV had been lobbying for the attack for a while.[15] It was seen as a righteous blow against Arab propaganda. But mainstream American and British TV continue to advertise themselves as "balanced" when their propaganda has achieved hallucinatory levels.

Why should propaganda be the exclusive preserve of the Western media? Just because they do it better?

Western journalists "embedded" with troops are given the status of heroes reporting from the front lines of war. Non-"embedded" journalists (like the BBC's Rageh Omaar, reporting from besieged and bombed Baghdad, witnessing, and clearly affected by, the sight of bodies of burned children and wounded people)[16] are undermined even before they begin their reportage: "We have to tell you that he is being monitored by the Iraqi authorities."

Increasingly, on British and American TV, Iraqi soldiers are being referred to as "militia" (i.e., rabble). One BBC correspondent portentously referred to them as "quasi-terrorists." Iraqi defense is "resistance" or, worse still, "pockets of resistance," Iraqi military strategy is deceit. (The US government bugging the phone lines of UN Security Council delegates, reported by the London *Observer*, is hardheaded pragmatism.)[17] Clearly for the "Allies" the only morally acceptable strategy the Iraqi Army can pursue is to march out into the desert and be bombed by B-52s or be mowed down by machine-gun fire. Anything short of that is cheating.

And now we have the siege of Basra. About a million and a half people, 40 percent of them children.[18] Without clean water, and with very little food. We're still waiting for the legendary Shia "uprising," for the happy hordes to stream out of the city and rain roses and hosannas on the "liberating" army. Where are the hordes? Don't they know that television productions work to tight schedules? (It may well be that if the Saddam Hussein regime falls there will be dancing on the streets the world over.)

After days of enforcing hunger and thirst on the citizens of Basra, the "Allies" have brought in a few trucks of food and water and positioned them tantalizingly on the outskirts of the city. Desperate people flock to the trucks and fight each other for food. (The water, we hear, is being sold.[19] To revitalize the dying economy, you understand.) On top of the trucks, desperate photographers fought each other to get pictures of desperate people fighting each other for food. Those pictures will go out through photo agencies to newspapers and glossy magazines that pay extremely well. Their message: The messiahs are at hand, distributing fishes and loaves.

As of July 2002, the delivery of $5.4 billion worth of supplies to Iraq was blocked by the Bush/Blair Pair.[20] It didn't really make the news. But now, under the loving caress of live TV, 230 tons of humanitarian aid—a minuscule fraction of what's actually needed (call it a script prop)—arrived on a British ship, the *Sir Galahad*.[21] Its arrival in the port of Umm Qasr merited a whole day of live TV broadcasts. Barf bag, anyone?

Nick Guttmann, head of emergencies for Christian Aid, writing for the *Independent on Sunday*, said that it would take thirty-two *Sir Galahad*s a day to match the amount of food Iraq was receiving before the bombing began.[22]

We oughtn't to be surprised, though. It's old tactics. They've been at it for years. Remember this moderate proposal by John McNaughton from the Pentagon Papers published during the Vietnam War.

Strikes at population targets (per se) are likely not only to create a counterproductive wave of revulsion abroad and at home, but greatly to increase the risk of enlarging the war with China or the Soviet Union. Destruction of locks and dams, however—if handled right—might . . . offer promise. Such destruction does not kill or drown people. By shallow-flooding the rice, it leads after time to widespread starvation (more than a million?) unless food is provided—which we could offer to do "at the conference table."[23]

Times haven't changed very much. The technique has evolved into a doctrine. It's called "Winning Hearts and Minds."

So here's the moral math as it stands: Two hundred thousand Iraqis estimated to have been killed in the first Gulf War.[24] Hundreds of thousands dead because of the economic sanctions. (At least that lot has been saved from Saddam Hussein.) More being killed every day. Tens of thousands of US soldiers who fought the 1991 war officially declared "disabled" by a disease called Gulf War Syndrome, believed to be caused in part by exposure to depleted uranium.[25] It hasn't stopped the "Allies" from continuing to use depleted uranium.[26]

And now this talk of bringing the United Nations back into the picture.

But that old UN girl—it turns out that she just ain't what she was cracked up to be. She's been demoted (although she retains her high salary). Now she's the world's janitor. She's the Filipina cleaning lady, the Indian *jamadarni*, the mail-order bride from Thailand, the Mexican household help, the Jamaican au pair. She's employed to clean other people's shit. She's used and abused at will.

Despite Tony Blair's earnest submissions, and all his fawning, George Bush has made it clear that the United Nations will play no independent part in the administration of postwar Iraq. The United States will decide who gets those juicy "reconstruction" contracts.[27] But Bush has appealed to the international community not to "politicize" the issue of humanitarian aid. On March 28, 2003, after Bush called for the immediate resumption of the UN's Oil for Food program, the UN Security Council voted unanimously for the resolution.[28] This means that everybody agrees that Iraqi money (from the sale of Iraqi oil) should be used to feed Iraqi people who are starving because of US-led sanctions and the illegal US-led war.

Contracts for the "reconstruction" of Iraq, we're told, in discussions on the business news, could jump-start the world economy. It's funny how the interests of American corporations are so often, so successfully, and so deliberately confused with the interests of the world economy. While the American people will end up paying for the war, oil companies, weapons manufacturers, arms dealers, and corporations involved in "reconstruction" work will make direct gains from the war. Many of them are old friends and former employers of the Bush/Cheney/Rumsfeld/Rice cabal. Bush has already asked Congress for $75 billion.[29] Contracts for "reconstruction" are already being negotiated. The news doesn't hit the stands because much of the US corporate media is owned and managed by the same interests.

Operation Iraqi Freedom, Tony Blair assures us, is about returning Iraqi oil to the Iraqi people. That is, returning Iraqi oil to the Iraqi people via corporate multinationals. Like Shell, like Chevron, like Halliburton. Or are we missing the plot here? Perhaps Halliburton is actually an Iraqi company? Perhaps US vice president Dick Cheney (who was a former director of Halliburton) is a closet Iraqi?

As the rift between Europe and America deepens, there are signs that the world could be entering a new era of economic boycotts. CNN reported that Americans are emptying French wine into gutters, chanting, "We don't need your stinking wine."[30] We've heard about the re-baptism of french fries. Freedom fries, they're called now.[31] There's news trickling in about Americans boycotting German goods.[32] The thing is that if the fallout of the war takes this turn, it is the United States who will suffer the most. Its homeland may be defended by border patrols and nuclear weapons, but its economy is strung out across the globe. Its economic outposts are exposed and vulnerable to attack in every direction. Already the Internet is buzzing with elaborate lists of American and British government products and companies that should be boycotted. These lists are being honed and refined by activists across the world. They could become a practical guide that directs and channels the amorphous but growing fury in the world. Suddenly, the "inevitability" of the project of corporate globalization is beginning to seem more than a little evitable.

It's become clear that the war on terror is not really about terror, and the War on Iraq not only about oil. It's about a superpower's self-destructive impulse toward supremacy, stranglehold, global hegemony. The argument is being made that the people of Argentina and Iraq have both been decimated by the same process. Only the weapons used against them differ: In the one case it's an IMF checkbook. In the other, the cruise missiles.

Finally, there's the matter of Saddam Hussein's arsenal of Weapons of Mass Destruction. (Oops, nearly forgot about those!)

In the fog of war one thing's for sure: if the Saddam Hussein regime indeed has weapons of mass destruction, it is showing an astonishing degree of responsibility and restraint in the teeth of extreme provocation. Under similar circumstances (say, if Iraqi troops were bombing New York and laying siege to Washington, DC) could we expect the same of the Bush regime? Would it keep its thousands of nuclear warheads in their wrapping paper? What about its chemical and biological weapons? Its stocks of anthrax, smallpox, and nerve gas? Would it?

Excuse me while I laugh.

In the fog of war we're forced to speculate: Either Saddam Hussein is an extremely responsible tyrant. Or—he simply does not possess Weapons of Mass Destruction. Either way, regardless of what happens next, Iraq comes out of the argument smelling sweeter than the US government.

So here's Iraq—rogue state, grave threat to world peace, paid-up member of the Axis of Evil. Here's Iraq, invaded, bombed, besieged, bullied, its sovereignty shat upon, its children killed by cancers, its people blown up on the streets. And here's all of us watching CNN–BBC, BBC–CNN late into the night. Here's all of us, enduring the horror of the war, enduring the horror of the propaganda, and enduring the slaughter of language as we know and understand it. Freedom now means mass murder (or, in the United States, fried potatoes). When someone says "humanitarian aid" we automatically go looking for induced starvation. "Embedded," I have to admit, is a great find. It's what it sounds like. And what about "arsenal of tactics"? Nice!

In most parts of the world, the invasion of Iraq is being seen as a racist war. The real danger of a racist war unleashed by racist regimes is that it engenders racism in everybody—perpetrators, victims, spectators. It sets the parameters for the debate, it lays out a grid for a particular way of thinking. There is a tidal wave of hatred for the United States rising from the ancient heart of the world. In Africa, Latin America, Asia, Europe, Australia. I encounter it every day. Sometimes it comes from the most unlikely sources. Bankers, businessmen, yuppie students, who bring to it all the crassness of their conservative, illiberal politics. That absurd inability to separate governments from people: America is a nation of morons, a nation of murderers, they say (with the same carelessness with which they say "All Muslims are terrorists"). Even in the grotesque universe of racist insult, the British make their entry as add-ons. Arse-lickers, they're called.

Suddenly, I, who have been vilified for being "anti-American" and "anti-West," find myself in the extraordinary position of defending the people of America. And Britain.

Those who descend so easily into the pit of racist abuse would do well to remember the hundreds of thousands of American and British citizens who protested against their country's stockpile of nuclear weapons. And the thousands of American war resisters who forced their government to withdraw from Vietnam. They should know that the most scholarly, scathing, hilarious critiques of the US government and the "American Way of Life" come from American citizens. And that the funniest, most bitter condemnation of their prime minister comes from the British media. Finally, they should remember that right now, hundreds of thousands of British and American citizens are on the streets protesting the war. The Coalition of the Bullied and Bought consists of governments, not people. More than a third of America's citizens have survived the relentless propaganda they've been subjected to, and many thousands are actively fighting their own government. In the ultra-patriotic climate that prevails in the United States, that's as brave as any Iraqi fighting for his or her homeland.

While the "Allies" wait in the desert for an uprising of Shia Muslims on the streets of Basra, the real uprising is taking place in hundreds of cities across the world. It has been the most spectacular display of public morality ever seen.

Most courageous of all are the hundreds of thousands of American people on the streets of America's great cities— Washington, New York, Chicago, San Francisco. The fact is that the only institution in the world today that is more powerful than the American government is American civil society. American citizens have a huge responsibility riding on their shoulders. How can we not salute and support those who not only acknowledge but act upon that responsibility? They are our allies, our friends.

At the end of it all, it remains to be said that dictators like Saddam Hussein, and all the other despots in the Middle East, in the Central Asian republics, in Africa, and Latin America, many of them installed, supported, and financed by the US government, are a menace to their own people. Other than strengthening the hand of civil society (instead of weakening it, as has been done in the case of Iraq), there is no easy, pristine way of dealing with them. (It's odd how those who dismiss the peace movement as utopian don't hesitate to proffer the most absurdly dreamy reasons for going to war: to stamp out terrorism, install democracy, eliminate fascism, and, most entertainingly, to "rid the world of evildoers.")[33]

Regardless of what the propaganda machine tells us, these tin-pot dictators are not the greatest threat to the world. The real and pressing danger, the greatest threat of all, is the locomotive force that drives the political and economic engine of the US government, currently piloted by George Bush. Bush-bashing is fun, because he makes such an easy, sumptuous target. It's true that he is a dangerous, almost suicidal pilot, but the machine he handles is far more dangerous than the man himself.

Despite the pall of gloom that hangs over us today, I'd like to file a cautious plea for hope: In time of war, one wants one's weakest enemy at the helm of his forces. And president George

W. Bush is certainly that. Any other even averagely intelligent US president would have probably done the very same things but would have managed to smoke up the glass and confuse the opposition. Perhaps even carry the United Nations with him. George Bush's tactless imprudence and his brazen belief that he can run the world with his riot squad has done the opposite. He has achieved what writers, activists, and scholars have striven to achieve for decades. He has exposed the ducts. He has placed on full public view the working parts, the nuts and bolts, of the apocalyptic apparatus of the American empire.

Now that the blueprint, The Ordinary Person's Guide to Empire, has been put into mass circulation, it could be disabled quicker than the pundits predicted.

Bring on the spanners.

INSTANT-MIX
IMPERIAL DEMOCRACY:
(BUY ONE, GET
ONE FREE)

IN THESE TIMES when we have to race to keep abreast of the speed at which our freedoms are being snatched from us, and when few can afford the luxury of retreating from the streets for a while in order to return with an exquisite, fully formed political thesis replete with footnotes and references, what profound gift can I offer you tonight?

As we lurch from crisis to crisis, beamed directly into our brains by satellite TV, we have to think on our feet. On the move. We enter histories through the rubble of war. Ruined cities, parched fields, shrinking forests, and dying rivers are our archives. Craters left by daisy cutters, our libraries.

So what can I offer you tonight? Some uncomfortable thoughts

This talk was first delivered May 13, 2003, at the Riverside Church, New York City, and broadcast live on Pacifica Radio. The lecture, sponsored by Lannan Foundation and the Center for Economic and Social Rights, was delivered as an acceptance speech for the 2002 Lannan Prize for Cultural Freedom.

about money, war, empire, racism, and democracy. Some worries that flit around my brain like a family of persistent moths that keep me awake at night.

Some of you will think it bad manners for a person like me, officially entered in the Big Book of Modern Nations as an "Indian citizen," to come here and criticize the US government. Speaking for myself, I'm no flag-waver, no patriot, and am fully aware that venality, brutality, and hypocrisy are imprinted on the leaden soul of every state. But when a country ceases to be merely a country and becomes an empire, then the scale of operations changes dramatically. So may I clarify that tonight I speak as a subject of the American empire? I speak as a slave who presumes to criticize her king.

Since lectures must be called something, mine tonight is called Instant-Mix Imperial Democracy (Buy One, Get One Free).

Way back in 1988, on July 3, the USS *Vincennes*, a missile cruiser stationed in the Persian Gulf, accidentally shot down an Iranian airliner and killed 290 civilian passengers.[1] George Bush the First, who was at the time on his presidential campaign, was asked to comment on the incident. He said quite subtly, "I will never apologize for the United States. I don't care what the facts are."[2]

I don't care what the facts are. What a perfect maxim for the New American Empire. Perhaps a slight variation on the theme would be more apposite: the facts can be whatever we want them to be.

When the United States invaded Iraq, a *New York Times* / CBS News survey estimated that 42 percent of the American public believed that Saddam Hussein was directly responsible for the September 11 attacks on the World Trade Center and the Pentagon.[3] And an ABC News poll said that 55 percent of Americans believed that Saddam Hussein directly supported Al-Qaeda.[4] None of this opinion is based on evidence (because there isn't any). All of it is based on insinuation, auto-suggestion, and outright lies circulated by the US corporate media, otherwise known as the "free press," that hollow pillar on which contemporary American democracy rests.

Public support in the United States for the war against Iraq was founded on a multitiered edifice of falsehood and deceit, coordinated by the US government and faithfully amplified by the corporate media.

Apart from the invented links between Iraq and Al-Qaeda, we had the manufactured frenzy about Iraq's Weapons of Mass Destruction. George Bush the Lesser went to the extent of saying it would be "suicide" for the United States not to attack Iraq.[5] We once again witnessed the paranoia that a starved, bombed, besieged country was about to annihilate almighty America. (Iraq was only the latest in a succession of countries—earlier there was Cuba, Nicaragua, Libya, Grenada, Panama.) But this time it wasn't just your ordinary brand of friendly neighborhood frenzy. It was frenzy with a purpose. It ushered in an old doctrine in a new bottle: the doctrine of preemptive strike, aka The United States Can Do Whatever the Hell It Wants, And That's Official.

The war against Iraq has been fought and won, and no Weapons of Mass Destruction have been found. Not even a little one. Perhaps they'll have to be planted before they're discovered. And then the more troublesome amongst us will need an explanation for why Saddam Hussein didn't use them when his country was being invaded.

Of course, there'll be no answers. True believers will make do with those fuzzy TV reports about the discovery of a few barrels of banned chemicals in an old shed. There seems to be no consensus yet about whether they're really chemicals, whether they're actually banned, and whether the vessels they're contained in can technically be called barrels. (There were unconfirmed rumors that a teaspoonful of potassium permanganate and an old harmonica were found there, too.)

Meanwhile, in passing, an ancient civilization has been casually decimated by a very recent, casually brutal nation.

Then there are those who say, so what if Iraq had no chemical and nuclear weapons? So what if there is no Al-Qaeda connection? So what if Osama bin Laden hates Saddam Hussein as much as he hates the United States? Bush the Lesser has said Saddam Hussein was a "Homicidal Dictator."[6] And so, the reasoning goes, Iraq needed a "regime change."

Never mind that forty years ago, the CIA, under president John F. Kennedy, orchestrated a regime change in Baghdad. In 1963, after a successful coup, the Ba'ath Party came to power in Iraq. Using lists provided by the CIA, the new Ba'ath regime systematically eliminated hundreds of doctors, teachers, lawyers, and political figures known to be leftists.[7] An entire intellectual community was slaughtered. (The same technique was used to massacre hundreds of thousands of people in Indonesia and East Timor.)[8] The young Saddam Hussein was said to have had a hand in supervising the bloodbath. In 1979, after factional infighting within the Ba'ath Party, Saddam Hussein became the president of Iraq. In April 1980, while Hussein was massacring Shias, US national security adviser Zbigniew Brzezinski declared, "We see no fundamental incompatibility of interests between the United States and Iraq."[9] Washington and London overtly and covertly supported Saddam Hussein. They financed him, equipped him, armed him, and provided him with dual-use materials to manufacture weapons of mass destruction.[10] They supported his worst excesses financially, materially, and morally. They supported the eight-year war against Iran and the 1988 gassing of Kurdish people in Halabja, crimes which fourteen years later were reheated and served up as reasons to justify invading Iraq.[11] After the first Gulf War, the "Allies" fomented an uprising of Shias in Basra and then looked away while Saddam Hussein crushed the revolt and slaughtered thousands in an act of vengeful reprisal.[12]

The point is, if Saddam Hussein was evil enough to merit the most elaborate, openly declared assassination attempt in history (the opening move of Operation Shock and Awe), then surely those who supported him ought at least to be tried for war crimes? Why aren't the faces of US and UK government officials on the infamous pack of cards of wanted men and women?

Because when it comes to Empire, facts don't matter.

Yes, but all that's in the past, we're told. Saddam Hussein is a monster who must be stopped now. And only the United States can stop him. It's an effective technique, this use of the urgent morality of the present to obscure the diabolical sins of the past and the malevolent plans for the future. Indonesia, Panama, Nicaragua, Iraq, Afghanistan—the list goes on and on. Right now there are brutal regimes being groomed for the future—Egypt, Saudi Arabia, Turkey, Pakistan, the Central Asian republics.

US attorney general John Ashcroft recently declared that US freedoms are "not the grant of any government or document, but . . . our endowment from God."[13] (Why bother with the United Nations when God himself is on hand?)

So here we are, the people of the world, confronted with an empire armed with a mandate from heaven (and, as added insurance, the most formidable arsenal of weapons of mass destruction in history). Here we are, confronted with an empire that has conferred upon itself the right to go to war at will and the right to deliver people from corrupting ideologies, from religious fundamentalists, dictators, sexism, and poverty, by the age-old, tried-and-tested practice of extermination. Empire is on the move, and democracy is its sly new war cry. Democracy, home-delivered to your doorstep by daisy cutters. Death is a small price for people to pay for the privilege of sampling this new product: Instant-Mix Imperial Democracy (bring to a boil, add oil, then bomb).

But then perhaps chinks, negroes, dinks, gooks, and wogs don't really qualify as real people. Perhaps our deaths don't qualify as real deaths. Our histories don't qualify as history. They never have.

Speaking of history, in these past months, while the world watched, the US invasion and occupation of Iraq was broadcast on live TV. Like Osama bin Laden and the Taliban in

Afghanistan, the regime of Saddam Hussein simply disappeared. This was followed by what analysts called a "power vacuum."[14] Cities that had been under siege, without food, water, or electricity for days, cities that had been bombed relentlessly, people who had been starved and systematically impoverished by the UN sanctions regime for more than a decade, were suddenly left with no semblance of urban administration. A seven-thousand-year-old civilization slid into anarchy. On live TV.

Vandals plundered shops, offices, hotels, and hospitals. American and British soldiers stood by and watched.[15] They said they had no orders to act. In effect, they had orders to kill people but not to protect them. Their priorities were clear. The safety and security of Iraqi people was not their business. The security of whatever little remained of Iraq's infrastructure was not their business. But the security and safety of Iraq's oil fields were. Of course they were. The oil fields were "secured" almost before the invasion began.[16]

On CNN and the BBC the scenes of the rampage were played and replayed. TV commentators, army and government spokespersons, portrayed it as a "liberated people" venting their rage at a despotic regime. US defense secretary Donald Rumsfeld said: "It's untidy. . . . Freedom's untidy. And free people are free to make mistakes and commit crimes and do bad things."[17] Did anybody know that Donald Rumsfeld was an anarchist? I wonder—did he hold the same view during the riots in Los Angeles following the beating of Rodney King? Would he care to share his thesis about the Untidiness of Freedom with the two million people being held in US prisons right now?[18] (The world's "freest" country has one of the highest numbers of prisoners per capita in the world.)[19] Would he discuss its merits with young African American men, 28 percent of whom will spend some part of their adult lives in jail?[20] Could he explain why he serves under a president who oversaw 152 executions when he was governor of Texas?[21]

Before the war on Iraq began, the Office of Reconstruction and Humanitarian Assistance (ORHA) sent the Pentagon a list of sixteen crucial sites to protect. The National Museum was second on that list.[22] Yet the museum was not just looted, it was desecrated. It was a repository of an ancient cultural heritage. Iraq as we know it today was part of the river valley of Mesopotamia. The civilization that grew along the banks of the Tigris and the Euphrates produced the world's first writing, first calendar, first library, first city, and, yes, the world's first democracy. King Hammurabi of Babylon was the first to codify laws governing the social life of citizens.[23] It was a code in which abandoned women, prostitutes, slaves, and even animals had rights. The Hammurabi Code is acknowledged not just as the birth of legality but the beginning of an understanding of the concept of social justice. The US government could not have chosen a more inappropriate land in which to stage its illegal war and display its grotesque disregard for justice.

At a Pentagon briefing during the days of looting, Secretary Rumsfeld, Prince of Darkness, turned on his media cohorts who had served him so loyally through the war. "The images you are seeing on television, you are seeing over and over and over, and it's the same picture, of some person walking out of some building with a vase. And you see it twenty times. And you think, 'My goodness, were there that many vases? Is it possible that there were that many vases in the whole country?'"[24]

Laughter rippled through the press room. Would it be all right for the poor of Harlem to loot the Metropolitan Museum? Would it be greeted with similar mirth?

The last building on the ORHA list of sixteen sites to be protected was the Ministry of Oil.[25] It was the only one that was given adequate protection.[26] Perhaps the occupying army thought that in Muslim countries lists are read upside down?

Television tells us that Iraq has been "liberated" and that Afghanistan is well on its way to becoming a paradise for women—thanks to Bush and Blair, the twenty-first century's leading feminists. In reality, Iraq's infrastructure has been destroyed. Its people brought to the brink of starvation. Its food stocks depleted. And its cities devastated by a complete administrative breakdown. Iraq is being ushered in the direction of a civil war between Shias and Sunnis. Meanwhile, Afghanistan has lapsed back into the pre-Taliban era of anarchy, and its territory has been carved up into fiefdoms by hostile warlords.[27]

Undaunted by all this, on May 2, 2003, Bush the Lesser launched his 2004 campaign hoping to be finally elected US president. In what probably constitutes the shortest flight in history, a military jet landed on an aircraft carrier, the USS *Abraham Lincoln*, which was so close to shore that, according to the Associated Press, administration officials "acknowledged positioning the massive ship to provide the best TV angle for Bush's speech, with the vast sea as his background instead of the very visible San Diego coastline."[28] President Bush, who never served his term in the military,[29] emerged from the cockpit in fancy dress—a US military bomber jacket, combat boots, flying goggles, helmet. Waving to his cheering troops, he officially proclaimed victory over Iraq. He was careful to say that it was just "one victory in a war on terror . . . [which] still goes on."[30]

It was important to avoid making a straightforward victory announcement, because under the Geneva Convention a victorious army is bound by the legal obligations of an occupying force, a responsibility that the Bush administration does not want to burden itself with.[31] Also, closer to the 2004 elections, in order to woo wavering voters, another victory in the war on terror might become necessary. Syria is being fattened for the kill.

It was Hermann Goering, that old Nazi, who said, "People can always be brought to the bidding of the leaders. . . . All you have to do is tell them they're being attacked and denounce the pacifists for a lack of patriotism and exposing the country to danger. It works the same way in any country."[32]

He's right. It's dead easy. That's what the Bush regime banks on. The distinction between election campaigns and war, between democracy and oligarchy, seems to be closing fast.

The only caveat in these campaign wars is that US lives must not be lost. It shakes voter confidence. But the problem of US soldiers being killed in combat has been licked. More or less.

At a media briefing before Operation Shock and Awe was unleashed, general Tommy Franks announced, "This campaign will be like no other in history."[33] Maybe he's right.

I'm no military historian, but when was the last time a war was fought like this?

As soon as the war began, the governments of France, Germany, and Russia, which refused to allow a final resolution legitimizing the war to be passed in the UN Security Council, fell over each other to say how much they wanted the United States to win. President Jacques Chirac offered French airspace to the Anglo-American air force.[34] US military bases in Germany were open for business.[35] German foreign minister Joschka Fischer publicly hoped that Saddam Hussein's regime would "collapse as soon as possible."[36] Vladimir Putin publicly hoped for the same.[37] These are governments that colluded in the enforced disarming of Iraq before their dastardly rush to take the side of those who attacked it. Apart from hoping to share the spoils, they hoped empire would honor their pre-war oil contracts with Iraq. Only the very naive could expect old Imperialists to behave otherwise.

Leaving aside the cheap thrills and the lofty moral speeches made in the UN during the run-up to the war, eventually, at the moment of crisis, the unity of Western governments—despite the opposition from the majority of their people—was overwhelming.

When the Turkish government temporarily bowed to the views of 90 percent of its population and turned down the US government's offer of billions of dollars of blood money for the use of Turkish soil, it was accused of lacking "democratic credentials."[38] According to a Gallup International poll, in no European country was support for a war carried out "unilaterally by America and its allies" higher than 11 percent.[39] But the governments of England, Italy, Spain, Hungary, and other countries of Eastern Europe were praised for disregarding the views of the majority of their people and supporting the illegal invasion. That, presumably, was fully in keeping with democratic principles. What's it called? New Democracy? (Like Britain's New Labour?)

In stark contrast to the venality displayed by their governments, on February 15, 2003, weeks before the invasion, in the most spectacular display of public morality the world has ever seen, more than ten million people marched against the war on five continents.[40] Many of you, I'm sure, were among them. They—we—were disregarded with utter disdain. When asked to react to the antiwar demonstrations, President Bush said, "It's like deciding, well, I'm going to decide policy based upon a focus group. The role of a leader is to decide policy based upon the security, in this case, the security of the people."[41]

Democracy, the modern world's holy cow, is in crisis. And the crisis is a profound one. Every kind of outrage is being committed in the name of democracy. It has become little more than a hollow word, a pretty shell, emptied of all content or meaning. It can be whatever you want it to be. Democracy is the Free World's whore, willing to dress up, dress down, willing to satisfy a whole range of tastes, available to be used and abused at will.

Until quite recently, right up to the 1980s, democracy did seem as though it might actually succeed in delivering a degree of real social justice.

But modern democracies have been around for long enough for neoliberal capitalists to learn how to subvert them. They have mastered the technique of infiltrating the instruments of democracy—the "independent" judiciary, the "free" press, the parliament—and molding them to their purpose. The project of corporate globalization has cracked the code. Free elections, a free press, and an independent judiciary mean little when the free market has reduced them to commodities on sale to the highest bidder.

To fully comprehend the extent to which democracy is under siege, it might be an idea to look at what goes on in some of our contemporary democracies. The world's largest: India (which I have written about at some length and, therefore, will not speak about tonight). The world's most interesting: South Africa. The world's most powerful: the United States of America. And, most instructive of all, the plans that are being made to usher in the world's newest: Iraq.

In South Africa, after three hundred years of brutal domination of the Black majority by a white minority through colonialism and apartheid, a nonracial, multiparty democracy came to power in 1994. It was a phenomenal achievement. Within two years of coming to power, the African National Congress had genuflected with no caveats to the Market God. Its massive program of structural adjustment, privatization, and liberalization has only increased the hideous disparities between the rich and the poor. Official unemployment among Blacks has increased from 40 percent to 50 percent since the end of apartheid.[42] The corporatization of basic services—electricity, water, and housing—has meant that ten million South Africans, almost a quarter of the population, have been disconnected from water and electricity.[43] Two million have been evicted from their homes.

Meanwhile, a small white minority that has been historically privileged by centuries of brutal exploitation is more secure than ever before. They continue to control the land, the farms, the factories, and the abundant natural resources of that country. For them, the transition from apartheid to neoliberalism barely disturbed the grass. It's apartheid with a clean conscience. And it goes by the name of democracy.

Democracy has become empire's euphemism for neoliberal capitalism.

In countries of the first world, too, the machinery of democracy has been effectively subverted. Politicians, media barons, judges, powerful corporate lobbyists, and government officials are imbricated in an elaborate underhand configuration that completely undermines the lateral arrangement of checks and balances between the constitution, courts of law, parliament, the administration, and, perhaps most important of all, the independent media that form the structural basis of a parliamentary democracy. Increasingly, the imbrication is neither subtle nor elaborate.

Italian Prime Minister Silvio Berlusconi, for instance, has a controlling interest in major Italian newspapers, magazines, television channels, and publishing houses. The *Financial Times* reported that he controls about 90 percent of Italy's TV viewership.[44] Recently, during a trial on bribery charges, while insisting he was the only person who could save Italy from the left, he said, "How much longer do I have to keep living this life of sacrifices?"[45] That bodes ill for the remaining 10 percent of Italy's TV viewership. What price free speech? Free speech for whom?

In the United States, the arrangement is more complex. Clear Channel Communications is the largest radio station owner in the country. It runs more than twelve hundred channels, which together account for 9 percent of the market.[46] When hundreds of thousands of American citizens took to the streets to protest against the war on Iraq, Clear Channel organized pro-war patriotic "Rallies for America" across the country.[47] It used its radio stations to advertise the events and then sent correspondents to cover them as though they were breaking news. The era of manufacturing consent has given way to the era of manufacturing news. Soon media newsrooms will drop the pretense and start hiring theater directors instead of journalists.

As America's show business gets more and more violent and warlike, and America's wars get more and more like show business, some interesting crossovers are taking place. The designer who built the $250,000 set in Qatar from which general Tommy Franks stage-managed news coverage of Operation Shock and Awe also built sets for Disney, MGM, and *Good Morning America.*[48]

It is a cruel irony that the United States, which has the most ardent, vociferous defenders of the idea of free speech, and (until recently) the most elaborate legislation to protect it, has so circumscribed the space in which that freedom can be expressed. In a strange, convoluted way, the sound and fury that accompany the legal and conceptual defense of free speech in America serve to mask the process of the rapid erosion of the possibilities of actually exercising that freedom.

The news and entertainment industry in the United States is for the most part controlled by a few major corporations—AOL–Time Warner, Disney, Viacom, News Corporation.[49] Each of these corporations owns and controls TV stations, film studios, record companies, and publishing ventures. Effectively, the exits are sealed.

America's media empire is controlled by a tiny coterie of people. Chairman of the Federal Communications Commission Michael Powell, the son of secretary of state Colin Powell, has proposed even further deregulation of the communications industry, which will lead to even greater consolidation.[50]

So here it is—the world's greatest democracy, led by a man who was not legally elected. America's Supreme Court gifted him his job. What price have American people paid for this spurious presidency?

In the three years of George Bush the Lesser's term, the American economy has lost more than two million jobs.[51] Outlandish military expenses, corporate welfare, and tax giveaways to the rich have created a financial crisis for the US educational system. According to a survey by the National Conference of State Legislatures, US states cut $49 billion in public services, health, welfare benefits, and education in 2002. They plan to cut another $25.7 billion this year.[52] That makes a total of $75 billion. Bush's initial budget request to Congress to finance the war in Iraq was $80 billion.[53]

So who's paying for the war? America's poor. Its students, its unemployed, its single mothers, its hospital and home-care patients, its teachers, and its health workers.

And who's actually fighting the war?

Once again, America's poor. The soldiers who are baking in Iraq's desert sun are not the children of the rich. Only one of all the representatives in Congress and the Senate has a child fighting in Iraq.[54] America's "volunteer" army in fact depends on a poverty draft of poor whites, Blacks, Latinos, and Asians looking for a way to earn a living and get an education. Federal statistics show that African Americans make up 21 percent of the total armed forces and 29 percent of the US Army. They account for only 12 percent of the general population.[55] It's ironic, isn't it—the disproportionately high representation of African Americans in the army and prison? Perhaps we should take a positive view and look at this as affirmative action at its most effective. Nearly 4 million Americans (2 percent of the population) have lost the right to vote because of felony convictions.[56] Of that number, 1.4 million are African Americans, which means that 13 percent of all voting-age Black people have been disenfranchised.[57]

For African Americans there's also affirmative action in death. A study by the economist Amartya Sen shows that African Americans as a group have a lower life expectancy than people born in China, in the Indian state of Kerala (where I come from), Sri Lanka, or Costa Rica.[58] Bangladeshi men have a better chance of making it to the age of sixty-five than African American men from here in Harlem.[59]

This year, on what would have been Martin Luther King Jr.'s seventy-fourth birthday, President Bush denounced the University of Michigan's affirmative action program favoring Blacks and Latinos. He called it "divisive," "unfair," and unconstitutional.[60] The successful effort to keep Blacks off the voting rolls in the state of Florida in order that George Bush be elected was of course neither unfair nor unconstitutional. I don't suppose affirmative action for White Boys From Yale ever is.

So we know who's paying for the war. We know who's fighting it. But who will benefit from it? Who is homing in on the reconstruction contracts estimated to be worth up to $100 billion?[61] Could it be America's poor and unemployed and sick? Could it be America's single mothers? Or America's Black and Latino minorities?

Consider this: The Defense Policy Board advises the Pentagon on defense policy. Its members are appointed by the under secretary of defense and approved by Donald Rumsfeld. Its meetings are classified. No information is available for public scrutiny.

The Washington-based Center for Public Integrity found that nine out of the thirty members of the Defense Policy Board are connected to companies that were awarded defense contracts worth $76 billion between the years 2001 and 2002.[62] One of them, Jack Sheehan, a retired Marine Corps general, is a senior vice president at Bechtel, the giant international engineering outfit.[63] Riley Bechtel, the company chairman, is on the President's Export Council.[64] Former Secretary of State George Shultz, who is also on the board of directors of the Bechtel Group, is the chairman of the advisory board of the Committee for the Liberation of Iraq.[65] When asked by the *New York Times* whether he was concerned about the appearance of a conflict of interest, he said, "I don't know that Bechtel would particularly benefit from it. But if there's work to be done, Bechtel is the type of company that could do it."[66]

Bechtel has been awarded a $680 million reconstruction contract in Iraq.[67] According to the Center for Responsive Politics, Bechtel contributed $1.3 million toward the 1999–2000 Republican campaign.[68]

Arcing across this subterfuge, dwarfing it by the sheer magnitude of its malevolence, is America's antiterrorism legislation. The USA Patriot Act, passed on October 12, 2001, has become the blueprint for similar antiterrorism bills in countries across the world. It was passed in the US House of Representatives by a majority vote of 337–79. According to the *New York Times*, "Many lawmakers said it had been impossible to truly debate, or even read, the legislation."[69]

The Patriot Act ushers in an era of systemic automated surveillance. It gives the government the authority to monitor phones and computers and spy on people in ways that would have seemed completely unacceptable a few years ago.[70] It gives the FBI the power to seize all of the circulation, purchasing, and other records of library users and bookstore customers on the suspicion that they are part of a terrorist network.[71] It blurs the boundaries between speech and criminal activity, creating the space to construe acts of civil disobedience as violating the law.

Already hundreds of people are being held indefinitely as "unlawful combatants."[72] (In India, the number is also in the hundreds.[73] In Israel, five thousand Palestinians are now being detained.[74]) Noncitizens, of course, have no rights at all. They can simply be "disappeared" like the people of Chile under Washington's old ally General Pinochet. More than one thousand people, many of them Muslim or of Middle Eastern origin, have been detained, some without access to legal representatives.[75]

Apart from paying the actual economic costs of war, American people are paying for these wars of "liberation" with their own freedoms. For the ordinary American, the price of New Democracy in other countries is the death of real democracy at home.

Meanwhile, Iraq is being groomed for "liberation." (Or did they mean "liberalization" all along?) The *Wall Street Journal* reports that "the Bush administration has drafted sweeping plans to remake Iraq's economy in the U.S. image."[76]

Iraq's constitution is being redrafted. Its trade laws, tax laws, and intellectual property laws rewritten in order to turn it into an American-style capitalist economy.[77]

The United States Agency for International Development has invited US companies to bid for contracts that range from road building and water systems to textbook distribution and cell-phone networks.[78]

Soon after Bush the Second announced that he wanted American farmers to feed the world, Dan Amstutz, a former senior executive of Cargill, the biggest grain exporter in the world, was put in charge of agricultural reconstruction in Iraq. Kevin Watkin, Oxfam's policy director, said, "Putting Dan Amstutz in charge of agricultural reconstruction in Iraq is like putting Saddam Hussein in the chair of a human rights commission."[79]

The two men who have been shortlisted to run operations for managing Iraqi oil have worked with Shell, BP, and Fluor.

Fluor is embroiled in a lawsuit by Black South African workers who have accused the company of exploiting and brutalizing them during the apartheid era.[80] Shell, of course, is well known for its devastation of the Ogoni tribal lands in Nigeria.[81]

Tom Brokaw (one of America's best-known TV anchors) was inadvertently succinct about the process. "One of the things we don't want to do," he said, "is to destroy the infrastructure of Iraq because in a few days we're going to own that country."[82]

Now that the ownership deeds are being settled, Iraq is ready for New Democracy.

So, as Lenin used to ask: What Is To Be Done? Well . . . We might as well accept the fact that there is no conventional military force that can successfully challenge the American war machine. Terrorist strikes only give the US government an opportunity that it is eagerly awaiting to further tighten its stranglehold. Within days of an attack you can bet that Patriot II would be passed. To argue against US military aggression by saying that it will increase the possibilities of terrorist strikes is futile. It's like threatening Brer Rabbit that you'll throw him into the bramble bush. Anybody who has read the document called "The Project for the New American Century" can attest to that. The government's suppression of the congressional Joint Inquiry into Intelligence Community Activities before and after the terrorist attacks of September 11, 2001, which found that there was intelligence warning of the strikes that was ignored,[83] also attests to the fact that, for all their posturing, the terrorists and the Bush regime might as well be working as a team. They both hold people responsible for the actions of their governments. They both believe in the doctrine of collective guilt and collective punishment. Their actions benefit each other greatly.

The US government has already displayed in no uncertain terms the range and extent of its capability for paranoid aggression. In human psychology, paranoid aggression is usually an indicator of nervous insecurity. It could be argued that it's no different in the case of the psychology of nations. Empire is paranoid because it has a soft underbelly.

Its homeland may be defended by border patrols and nuclear weapons, but its economy is strung out across the globe. Its economic outposts are exposed and vulnerable.

Yet it would be naive to imagine that we can directly confront empire. Our strategy must be to isolate empire's working parts and disable them one by one. No target is too small. No victory too insignificant. We could reverse the idea of the economic sanctions imposed on poor countries by empire and its allies. We could impose a regime of Peoples' Sanctions on every corporate house that has been awarded a contract in postwar Iraq, just as activists in this country and around the world targeted institutions of apartheid. Each one of them should be named, exposed, and boycotted. Forced out of business. That could be our response to the Shock and Awe campaign. It would be a great beginning.

Another urgent challenge is to expose the corporate media for the boardroom bulletin that it really is. We need to create a universe of alternative information. We need to support independent media like *Democracy Now,* Alternative Radio, South End Press.

The battle to reclaim democracy is going to be a difficult one. Our freedoms were not granted to us by any governments. They were wrested from them by us. And once we surrender them, the battle to retrieve them is called a revolution. It is a battle that must range across continents and countries. It must not acknowledge national boundaries, but if it is to succeed, it has to begin here. In America. The only institution more powerful than the US government is American civil society. The rest of us are subjects of slave nations. We are by no means powerless, but you have the power of proximity. You have access to the Imperial Palace and the Emperor's chambers. Empire's conquests are being carried out in your name, and you have the right to refuse. You could refuse to fight. Refuse to move those missiles from the warehouse to the dock. Refuse to wave that flag. Refuse the victory parade.

You have a rich tradition of resistance. You need only read Howard Zinn's *A People's History of the United States* to remind yourself of this.[84]

Hundreds of thousands of you have survived the relentless propaganda you have been subjected to, and are actively fighting your own government. In the ultra-patriotic climate that prevails in the United States, that's as brave as any Iraqi or Afghan or Palestinian fighting for his or her homeland.

If you join the battle, not in your hundreds of thousands but in your millions, you will be greeted joyously by the rest of the world. And you will see how beautiful it is to be gentle instead of brutal, safe instead of scared. Befriended instead of isolated. Loved instead of hated.

I hate to disagree with your president. Yours is by no means a great nation. But you could be a great people.

History is giving you the chance. Seize the time.

WHEN THE SAINTS GO MARCHING OUT: THE STRANGE FATE OF MARTIN, MOHANDAS, AND MANDELA

WE'RE COMING UP to the fortieth anniversary of the March on Washington, when Martin Luther King Jr. gave his famous "I Have a Dream" speech. Perhaps it's time to reflect—again—on what has become of that dream.

It's interesting how icons, when their time has passed, are commodified and appropriated (some voluntarily, others involuntarily) to promote the prejudice, bigotry, and inequity they battled against. But then in an age when everything's up for sale, why not icons? In an era when all of humanity, when every creature of God's earth, is trapped between the IMF checkbook

This text is an expanded version of an essay originally broadcast by BBC Radio 4, August 25, 2003. By request of the BBC, which had determined that copyright restrictions prohibited it from broadcasting direct quotations from King's public speeches, the original used only paraphrases of King's words. In this version, direct quotations have been used.

and the American cruise missile, can icons stage a getaway?

Martin Luther King is part of a trinity. So it's hard to think of him without two others elbowing their way into the picture: Mohandas Gandhi and Nelson Mandela. The three high priests of nonviolent resistance. Together they represent (to a greater or lesser extent) the twentieth century's nonviolent liberation struggles (or should we say "negotiated settlements"?): of colonized against colonizer, former slave against slave owner.

Today the elites of the very societies and peoples in whose name the battles for freedom were waged use them as mascots to entice new masters.

Mohandas, Mandela, Martin.

India, South Africa, the United States.

Broken dreams, betrayal, nightmares.

A quick snapshot of the supposedly "Free World" today.

Last March in India, in Gujarat—Gandhi's Gujarat—right-wing Hindu mobs murdered two thousand Muslims in a chillingly efficient orgy of violence. Women were gang-raped and burned alive. Muslim tombs and shrines were razed to the ground. More than a hundred fifty thousand Muslims have been driven from their homes. The economic base of the community has been destroyed. Eyewitness accounts and several fact-finding commissions have accused the state government and the police of collusion in the violence.[1] I was present at a meeting where a group of victims kept wailing, "Please save us from the police! That's all we ask . . ."

In December 2002, the same state government was voted back to office. Narendra Modi, who was widely accused of having orchestrated the riots, has embarked on his second term as chief minister of Gujarat. On August 15, 2003, Independence Day, he hoisted the Indian flag before thousands of cheering people. In a gesture of menacing symbolism, he wore the black RSS cap—which proclaims him as a member of the Hindu nationalist guild that has not been shy of admiring Hitler and his methods.[2]

One hundred thirty million Muslims—not to mention the other minorities, Dalits, Christians, Sikhs, Adivasis—live in India under the shadow of Hindu nationalism.

As his confidence in his political future brimmed over, Narendra Modi, master of seizing the political moment, invited Nelson Mandela to Gujarat to be the chief guest at the celebration of Gandhi's birth anniversary on October 2, 2002.[3] Fortunately, the invitation was turned down.[4]

And what of Mandela's South Africa? Otherwise known as the Small Miracle, the Rainbow Nation of God? South Africans say that the only miracle they know of is how quickly the rainbow has been privatized, sectioned off, and auctioned to the highest bidders. In its rush to replace Argentina as neoliberalism's poster child, it has instituted a massive program of privatization and structural adjustment. The government's promise to redistribute agricultural land to twenty-six million landless people has remained in the realm of dark humor.[5] While more than 50 percent of the population remains landless, almost all agricultural land is owned by sixty thousand white farmers.[6] (Small wonder that George Bush on his recent visit to South Africa referred to Thabo Mbeki as his "point man" on the Zimbabwe issue.)

Post-apartheid, the income of the poorest 40 percent of Black families has diminished by about 20 percent.[7] Two million have been evicted from their homes.[8] Six hundred die of AIDS every day. Forty percent of the population is unemployed, and that number is rising sharply.[9] The corporatization of basic services has meant that millions have been disconnected from water and electricity.[10]

A fortnight ago, I visited the home of Teresa Naidoo in Chatsworth, Durban. Her husband had died the previous day of AIDS. She had no money for a coffin. She and her two small children are HIV-positive. The government disconnected her water supply because she was unable to pay her water bills and her rent arrears for her tiny council flat. The government dismisses her troubles and those of millions like her as a "culture of non-payment."[11]

In what ought to be an international scandal, this same government has officially asked the judge in a US court case to rule against forcing companies to pay reparations for the role they played during apartheid.[12] Its reasoning is that reparations—in other words, justice—will discourage foreign investment.[13] So South Africa's poorest must pay apartheid's debts, so that those who amassed profit by exploiting Black people during apartheid can profit even more from the goodwill generated by Nelson Mandela's Rainbow Nation of God. President Thabo Mbeki is still called "comrade" by his colleagues in government. In South Africa, Orwellian parody goes under the genre of Real Life.

What's left to say about Martin Luther King's America? Perhaps it's worth asking a simple question: Had he been alive today, would he have chosen to stay warm in his undisputed place in the pantheon of Great Americans? Or would he have stepped off his pedestal, shrugged off the empty hosannas, and walked out on to the streets to rally his people once more?

On April 4, 1967, one year before he was assassinated, Martin Luther King spoke at the Riverside Church in New York City. That evening he said: "I could never again raise my voice against the violence of the oppressed in the ghettos without having first spoken clearly to the greatest purveyor of violence in the world today—my own government."[14]

Has anything happened in the thirty-six years between 1967 and 2003 that would have made him change his mind? Or would he be doubly confirmed in his opinion after the overt and covert wars and acts of mass killing that successive governments of his country, both Republican and Democrat, have engaged in since then?

Let's not forget that Martin Luther King Jr. didn't start out as a militant. He began as a Persuader, a Believer. In 1964 he won the Nobel Peace Prize. He was held up by the media as an exemplary Black leader, unlike, say, the more militant Malcolm X. It was only three years later that Martin Luther King publicly connected the US government's racist war in Vietnam with its racist policies at home.

In 1967, in an uncompromising, militant speech, he denounced the American invasion of Vietnam. He said:

> *We have been repeatedly faced with the cruel irony of watching Negro and white boys on TV screens as they kill and die together for a nation that has been unable to seat them together in the same schools. So we watch them in brutal solidarity burning the huts of a poor village, but we realize that they would never live on the same block in Detroit.*[15]

The *New York Times* had some wonderful counter-logic to offer the growing antiwar sentiment among Black Americans: "In Vietnam," it said, "the Negro for the first time has been given the chance to do his share of fighting for his country."[16]

It omitted to mention Martin Luther King Jr.'s remark that "there are twice as many Negroes dying in Vietnam as whites in proportion to their size in the population."[17] It omitted to mention that when the body bags came home, some of the Black soldiers were buried in segregated graves in the Deep South.

What would Martin Luther King Jr. say today about the fact that federal statistics show that African Americans, who account for 12 percent of America's population, make up 21 percent of the total armed forces and 29 percent of the US Army?[18]

Perhaps he would take a positive view and look at this as affirmative action at its most effective?

What would he say about the fact that having fought so hard to win the right to vote, today 1.4 million African Americans, which means 13 percent of all voting-age Black people, have been disenfranchised because of felony convictions?[19]

To Black soldiers fighting in Vietnam, Martin Luther King Jr. said, "As we counsel young men concerning military service we must clarify for them our nation's role in Vietnam and challenge them with the alternative of conscientious objection."[20]

In April 1967, at a massive antiwar demonstration in Manhattan, Stokely Carmichael described the draft as "white people sending Black people to make war on yellow people in order to defend land they stole from red people."[21]

What's changed? Except of course the compulsory draft has become a poverty draft—a different kind of compulsion. Would Martin Luther King Jr. say today that the invasion and occupation of Iraq and Afghanistan are in any way morally different from the US government's invasion of Vietnam? Would he say that it was just and moral to participate in these wars? Would he say that it was right for the US government to have supported a dictator like Saddam Hussein politically and financially for years while he committed his worst excesses against Kurds, Iranians, and Iraqis—in the 1980s when he was an ally against Iran? And that when that dictator began to chafe at the bit, as Saddam Hussein did, would he say it was right to go to war against Iraq, to fire several hundred tons of depleted uranium into its fields, to degrade its water supply systems, to institute a regime of economic sanctions that resulted in the death of half a million children, to use UN weapons inspectors to force it to disarm, to mislead the public about an arsenal of weapons of mass destruction that could be deployed in a matter of minutes, and then, when the country was on its knees, to send in an invading army to conquer it, occupy it, humiliate its people, take control of its natural resources and infrastructure, and award contracts worth hundreds of millions of dollars to American corporations like Bechtel?

When he spoke out against the Vietnam War, Martin Luther King Jr. drew some connections that many these days shy away from making. He said, "The problem of racism, the problem of economic exploitation, and the problem of war are all tied together. These are the triple evils that are interrelated."[22] Would he tell people today that it is right for the US government to export its cruelties—its racism, its economic bullying, and its war machine—to poorer countries?

Would he say that Black Americans must fight for their fair share of the American pie and the bigger the pie, the better their share—never mind the terrible price that the people of Africa,

Asia, the Middle East, and Latin America are paying for the American Way of Life? Would he support the grafting of the Great American Dream onto his own dream, which was a very different, very beautiful sort of dream? Or would he see that as a desecration of his memory and everything that he stood for?

The Black American struggle for civil rights gave us some of the most magnificent political fighters, thinkers, public speakers, and writers of our times. Martin Luther King Jr., Malcolm X, Fannie Lou Hamer, Ella Baker, James Baldwin, and of course the marvelous, magical, mythical Muhammad Ali.

Who has inherited their mantle?

Could it be the likes of Colin Powell? Condoleezza Rice? Michael Powell?

They're the exact opposite of icons or role models. They *appear* to be the embodiment of Black people's dreams of material success, but in actual fact they represent the Great Betrayal. They are the liveried doormen guarding the portals of the glittering ballroom against the press and swirl of the darker races. Their role and purpose is to be trotted out by the Bush administration looking for brownie points in its racist wars and African safaris.

If these are Black America's new icons, then the old ones must be dispensed with because they do not belong in the same pantheon. If these are Black America's new icons, then perhaps the haunting image that Mike Marqusee describes in his beautiful book *Redemption Song*—an old Muhammad Ali, afflicted with Parkinson's disease, advertising a retirement pension—symbolizes what has happened to Black Power, not just in the United States but the world over.[23]

If Black America genuinely wishes to pay homage to its real heroes, and to all those unsung people who fought by their side, if the world wishes to pay homage, then it's time to march on Washington. Again. Keeping hope alive—for all of us.

IN MEMORY OF
SHANKAR GUHA
NIYOGI

WE ARE GATHERED here today exactly twelve years after the murder of your beloved leader Shankar Guha Niyogi. All these years have gone by, and we are still waiting for those who murdered him to be brought to justice.

I'm a writer, but in this time of urgent, necessary battle, it is important for everybody, even for writers, not usually given to public speaking, to stand before thousands of people and share their thoughts.

I am here on this very important day to say that I support and respect the spectacular struggle of the Chhattisgarh Mukti Morcha.

Yesterday I visited the settlement around the iron-ore mines of Dalli Rajhara where the Chhattisgarh Mukti Morcha's battle began. Now it has spread across the whole of Chhattisgarh. I was deeply moved by what I saw and the people I met. What inspired me most of all was the fact that yours is and always has

This talk was delivered in Raipur, India, September 28, 2003, and first published in Hindi in Hindustan on October 13, 2003. Shankar Guha Niyogi was a popular trade union leader of Chhattisgarh.

been a struggle not just for workers' rights and farmers' rights, not just about wages and bonuses and jobs, but a struggle that has dared to dream about what it means to be human. Whenever people's rights have been assaulted, whether they are women or children, whether they are Sikhs or Muslims during communal killings, whether they are workers or farmers who were denied irrigation, you have always stood by them.

This sharp, compelling sense of humanity will have to be our weapon in times to come, when everything—our homes, our fields, our jobs, our rivers, our electricity, our right to protest, and our dignity—is being taken from us.

This is happening not just in India but in poor countries all over the world, and in response to this the poor are rising in revolt across the world.

The culmination of the process of corporate globalization is taking place in Iraq.

Imagine if you can what we would feel if thousands of armed American soldiers were patrolling the streets of India, of Chhattisgarh, deciding where we may go, who we may meet, what we must think.

It is of utmost importance that we understand that the American occupation of Iraq and the snatching away of our fields, homes, rivers, jobs, infrastructure, and resources are products of the very same process. For this reason, any struggle against corporate globalization, any struggle for the rights and dignity of human beings must support the Iraqi people who are resisting the American occupation.

After India won independence from British rule in 1947, perhaps many of your lives did not undergo radical material change for the better. Even so, we cannot deny that it was a kind of victory, it was a kind of freedom. But today, fifty years on, even this is being jeopardized. The process of selling this country back into slavery began in the mid-1980s. The Chhattisgarh Mukti Morcha was one of the first people's resistance movements to recognize this, and so today you are an example, a beacon of light, a ray of hope for the rest of the country—and perhaps the rest of the world.

Exactly at the time when the government of India was busy undermining labor laws and dismantling the formal structures that protected workers' rights, the Chhattisgarh Mukti Morcha intensified its struggle for the rights of all workers—formal, informal, and contract laborers. For this Shankar Guha Niyogi and at least sixteen others lost their lives, killed by assassins and police bullets.[1]

When the government of India made it clear that it is not concerned with public health, the Chhattisgarh Mukti Morcha, with contributions from workers, built the wonderful Shaheed Hospital and drew attention to the urgent necessity of providing health care to the poor.

When the state made it clear that it was more than happy to keep the poor of India illiterate and vulnerable, the Chhattisgarh Mukti Morcha started schools for the children of workers. These schools don't just educate children but inculcate in them revolutionary thought and create new generations of activists. Today these children led our rally, tomorrow they'll lead the resistance. It is of immense significance that this movement is led by the workers and farmers of Chhattisgarh.

To belong to a people's movement that recognized and struggled against the project of neo-imperialism as early as the Chhattisgarh Mukti Morcha did is to shoulder a great responsibility.

But you have shown, with your courage, your wisdom, and your perseverance, that you are more than equal to this task. You know better than me that the road ahead is long and hard.

As a writer, as a human being, I salute you. *Lal Johar*.

"Another world is not only possible, she's on her way. Maybe many of us won't be here to greet her, but on a quiet day, if I listen very carefully, I can hear her breathing."

DO TURKEYS ENJOY
THANKSGIVING?

LAST JANUARY THOUSANDS of us from across the world gathered in Porto Alegre in Brazil and declared—reiterated—that "Another World Is Possible." A few thousand miles north, in Washington, George Bush and his aides were thinking the same thing.

Our project was the World Social Forum. Theirs, to further what many call "the Project for the New American Century."[1]

In the great cities of Europe and America, where a few years ago these things would only have been whispered, now people are openly talking about the good side of imperialism and the need for a strong empire to police an unruly world. The new missionaries want order at the cost of justice. Discipline at the cost of dignity. And ascendancy at any price. Occasionally some of us are invited to "debate" the issue on "neutral" platforms provided by the corporate media. Debating imperialism is a bit like debating the pros and cons of rape. What can we say? That we really miss it?

This speech was delivered at the World Social Forum in Bombay, India, on January 14, 2004.

In any case, New Imperialism is already upon us. It's a remodeled, streamlined version of what we once knew. For the first time in history, a single empire with an arsenal of weapons that could obliterate the world in an afternoon has complete, unipolar economic and military hegemony. It uses different weapons to break open different markets. Argentina's the model if you want to be the poster child of neoliberal capitalism, Iraq if you're the black sheep.

Poor countries that are geopolitically of strategic value to empire, or have a "market" of any size, or infrastructure that can be privatized, or, god forbid, natural resources of value—oil, gold, diamonds, cobalt, coal—must do as they're told or become military targets. Those with the greatest reserves of natural wealth are most at risk. Unless they surrender their resources willingly to the corporate machine, civil unrest will be fomented, or war will be waged. In this new age of empire, when nothing is as it appears to be, executives of concerned companies are allowed to influence foreign policy decisions.

This brutal blueprint has been used over and over again, across Latin America, Africa, Central and Southeast Asia. It has cost millions of lives. It goes without saying that every war empire wages becomes a just war. This, in large part, is due to the role of the corporate media. It's important to understand that the corporate media doesn't just support the neoliberal project. It *is* the neoliberal project. This is not a moral position it has chosen to take, it's structural. It's intrinsic to the economics of how the mass media works.

Most nations have adequately hideous family secrets. So it isn't often necessary for the media to lie. It's all in the editing— what's emphasized and what's ignored. Say, for example, India was chosen as the target for a righteous war. The fact that about eighty thousand people have been killed in Kashmir since 1989, most of them Muslim, most of them by Indian security forces (making the average death toll about six thousand a year); the fact that in March of 2003 more than two thousand Muslims were murdered on the streets of Gujarat, that women were gang-raped and children were burned alive and 150,000 people were driven from their homes while the police and administration watched, and sometimes actively participated; the fact that no one has been punished for these crimes and the government that oversaw them was reelected—all of this would make perfect headlines in international newspapers in the run-up to war.

Next we know, our cities will be leveled by cruise missiles, our villages fenced in with razor wire, US soldiers will patrol our streets, and Narendra Modi, Pravin Togadia, or any of our popular bigots could, like Saddam Hussein, be in US custody, having their hair checked for lice and the fillings in their teeth examined on primetime TV.

But as long as our "markets" are open, as long as corporations like Enron, Bechtel, Halliburton, Arthur Andersen are given a free hand, our "democratically elected" leaders can fearlessly blur the lines between democracy, majoritarianism, and fascism.

Our government's craven willingness to abandon India's proud tradition of being nonaligned, its rush to fight its way to the head of the queue of the completely aligned (the fashionable phrase is "natural ally"—India, Israel, and the United States are "natural allies"), has given it the legroom to turn into a repressive regime without compromising its legitimacy.

A government's victims are not only those whom it kills and imprisons. Those who are displaced and dispossessed and sentenced to a lifetime of starvation and deprivation must count among them, too. Millions of people have been dispossessed by "development" projects.

In the era of the war on terror, poverty is being slyly conflated with terrorism. In the era of corporate globalization, poverty is a crime. Protesting against further impoverishment is terrorism. And now, the Indian Supreme Court says that going on strike is a crime.[2] Criticizing the court of course is a crime, too.[3] They're sealing the exits.

Like Old Imperialism, New Imperialism too relies for its success on a network of agents—corrupt local elites who service empire. We all know the sordid story of Enron in India. The then-Maharashtra government signed a power purchase agreement that gave Enron profits that amounted to 60 percent of India's entire rural development budget. A single American company was guaranteed a profit equivalent to funds for infrastructural development for about 500 million people!

Unlike in the old days, the New Imperialist doesn't need to trudge around the tropics risking malaria or diarrhea or early death. New Imperialism can be conducted on e-mail. The vulgar, hands-on racism of Old Imperialism is outdated. The cornerstone of New Imperialism is New Racism.

The tradition of "turkey pardoning" in the United States is a wonderful allegory for New Racism. Every year since 1947, the National Turkey Federation has presented the US president with a turkey for Thanksgiving. Every year, in a show of ceremonial magnanimity, the president spares that particular bird (and eats another one). After receiving the presidential pardon, the Chosen One is sent to Frying Pan Park in Virginia to live out its natural life. The rest of the fifty million turkeys raised for Thanksgiving are slaughtered and eaten on Thanksgiving Day. ConAgra Foods, the company that has won the Presidential Turkey contract, says it trains the lucky birds to be sociable, to interact with dignitaries, schoolchildren, and the press. (Soon they'll even speak English!)

That's how New Racism in the corporate era works. A few carefully bred turkeys—the local elites of various countries, a community of wealthy immigrants, investment bankers, the occasional Colin Powell or Condoleezza Rice, some singers, some writers (like myself)—are given absolution and a pass to Frying Pan Park. The remaining millions lose their jobs, are evicted from their homes, have their water and electricity connections cut, and die of AIDS. Basically they're for the pot. But the Fortunate Fowls in Frying Pan Park are doing fine. Some of them even work for the IMF and the WTO—so who can accuse those organizations of being anti-turkey? Some serve as board members on the Turkey Choosing Committee—so who can say that turkeys are against Thanksgiving? They participate in it! Who can say the poor are anti–corporate globalization? There's a stampede to get into Frying Pan Park. So what if most perish on the way?

As part of the project of New Racism we also have New Genocide. New Genocide in this new era of economic interdependence can be facilitated by economic sanctions. New Genocide means creating conditions that lead to mass death without actually going out and killing people. Denis Halliday, who was the UN humanitarian coordinator in Iraq between 1997 and 1998 (after which he resigned in disgust), used the term *genocide* to describe the sanctions in Iraq.[4] In Iraq the sanctions outdid Saddam Hussein's best efforts by claiming more than half a million children's lives.[5]

In the new era, apartheid as formal policy is generally considered antiquated and unnecessary. International instruments of trade and finance oversee a complex system of multilateral trade laws and financial agreements that keep the poor in their Bantustans anyway. Its whole purpose is to institutionalize inequity. Why else would it be that the United States taxes a garment made by a Bangladeshi manufacturer twenty times more than it taxes a garment made in the United Kingdom?[6] Why else would it be that countries that grow 90 percent of the world's cocoa bean produce only 5 percent of the world's chocolate? Why else would it be that countries that grow cocoa bean, like the Ivory Coast and Ghana, are taxed out of the market if they try and turn it into chocolate?[7] Why else would it be that rich countries that spend over a billion dollars a day on subsidies to farmers demand that poor countries like India withdraw all agricultural subsidies, including subsidized electricity? Why else would it be that after having been plundered by colonizing regimes for more than half a century, former colonies are steeped in debt to those same regimes and repay them some $382 billion a year?[8]

For all these reasons, the derailing of trade agreements at Cancún was crucial for us.[9] Though our governments try and take the credit, we know that it was the result of years of struggle by many millions of people in many, many countries. What Cancún taught us is that in order to inflict real damage and force radical change, it is vital for local resistance movements to make international alliances. From Cancún we learned the importance of globalizing resistance.

No individual nation can stand up to the project of corporate globalization on its own. Time and again we have seen that when it comes to the neoliberal project, the heroes of our times are suddenly diminished. Extraordinary, charismatic men, giants in the opposition, when they seize power and become heads of state, they become powerless on the global stage. I'm thinking here of President Lula of Brazil. Lula was the hero of the World Social Forum (WSF) last year. This year he's busy implementing IMF guidelines, reducing pension benefits, and purging radicals from the Workers' Party. I'm thinking also of ex-president of South Africa Nelson Mandela. He instituted a program of privatization and structural adjustment, leaving millions of people homeless, jobless, and without water and electricity.

Why does this happen? There's little point in beating our breasts and feeling betrayed. Lula and Mandela are, by any reckoning, magnificent men. But the moment they cross the floor from the opposition into government, they become hostage to a spectrum of threats—most malevolent among them the threat of capital flight, which can destroy any government overnight. To imagine that a leader's personal charisma and a résumé of struggle will dent the corporate cartel is to have no understanding of how capitalism works, or for that matter how power works. Radical change will not be negotiated by governments; it can only be enforced by people.

At the WSF, some of the best minds in the world come together to exchange ideas about what is happening around us. These conversations refine our vision of the kind of world we're fighting for. It is a vital process that must not be undermined. However, if all our energies are diverted into this process at the cost of real political action, then the WSF, which has played such a crucial role in the movement for global justice, runs the risk of becoming an asset to our enemies. What we need to discuss urgently are strategies of resistance. We need to aim at real targets, wage real battles, and inflict real damage. Gandhi's Salt March was not just political theater. When, in a simple act of defiance, thousands of Indians marched to the sea and made their own salt, they broke the salt tax laws. It was a direct strike at the economic underpinning of the British Empire. It was *real*. While our movement has won some important victories, we must not allow nonviolent resistance to atrophy into ineffectual, feel-good political theater. It is a very precious weapon that needs to be constantly honed and reimagined. It cannot be allowed to become a mere spectacle, a photo opportunity for the media.

It was wonderful that on February 15, 2003, in a spectacular display of public morality, ten million people in five continents marched against the war on Iraq. It was wonderful, but it was not enough. February 15 was a weekend. Nobody had to so much as miss a day of work. Holiday protests don't stop wars. George Bush knows that. The confidence with which he disregarded overwhelming public opinion should be a lesson to us all. Bush believes that Iraq can be occupied and colonized—as Afghanistan has been, as Tibet has been, as Chechnya is being, as East Timor once was and Palestine still is. He thinks that all he has to do is hunker down and wait until a crisis-driven media, having picked this crisis to the bone, drops it, and moves on. Soon the carcass will slip off the best-seller charts and all of us outraged folks will lose interest. Or so he hopes.

This movement of ours needs a major, global victory. It's not good enough to be right. Sometimes, if only in order to test our resolve, it's important to win something. In order to win something, we need to agree on something. That something does not need to be an overarching, preordained ideology into which we force-fit our delightfully factious, argumentative selves. It does not need to be an unquestioning allegiance to one or another form of resistance to the exclusion of everything else. It could be a minimum agenda.

If all of us are indeed against imperialism and against the project of neoliberalism, then let's turn our gaze on Iraq. Iraq is the inevitable culmination of both. Plenty of antiwar activists have retreated in confusion since the capture of Saddam Hussein. Isn't the world better off without Saddam Hussein? they ask timidly.

Let's look this thing in the eye once and for all. To applaud the US Army's capture of Saddam Hussein and therefore, in retrospect, justify its invasion and occupation of Iraq is like deifying Jack the Ripper for disemboweling the Boston Strangler. And that after a quarter-century partnership in which the ripping and strangling was a joint enterprise. It's an in-house quarrel. They're business partners who fell out over a dirty deal. Jack's the CEO.

So if we are against imperialism, shall we agree that we are against the US occupation and that we believe that the United States must withdraw from Iraq and pay reparations to the Iraqi people for the damage that the war has inflicted?

How do we begin to mount our resistance? Let's start with something really small. The issue is not about *supporting* the resistance in Iraq against the occupation or discussing who exactly constitutes the resistance. (Are they old Killer Ba'athists, are they Islamic Fundamentalists?) We have to become the global resistance to the occupation.

Our resistance has to begin with a refusal to accept the legitimacy of the US occupation of Iraq. It means acting to make it materially impossible for empire to achieve its aims. It means soldiers should refuse to fight, reservists should refuse to serve, workers should refuse to load ships and aircraft with weapons. It certainly means that in countries like India and Pakistan we must block the US government's plans to have Indian and Pakistani soldiers sent to Iraq to clean up after them.

I suggest we choose by some means two of the major corporations that are profiting from the destruction of Iraq. We could then list every project they are involved in. We could locate their offices in every city and every country across the world. We could go after them. We could shut them down. It's a question of bringing our collective wisdom and experience of past struggles to bear on a single target. It's a question of the desire to win.

"The Project for the New American Century" seeks to perpetuate inequity and establish American hegemony at any price, even if it's apocalyptic. The World Social Forum demands justice and survival.

For these reasons, we must consider ourselves at war.

HOW DEEP
SHALL WE DIG?

RECENTLY A YOUNG Kashmiri friend was talking to me about life in Kashmir. Of the morass of political venality and opportunism, the callous brutality of the security forces, of the osmotic, inchoate edges of a society saturated in violence, where militants, police, intelligence officers, government servants, businessmen, and even journalists encounter each other and gradually, over time, *become* each other. He spoke of having to live with the endless killing, the mounting "disappearances," the whispering, the fear, the unresolved rumors, the insane disconnection between what is actually happening, what Kashmiris know is happening, and what the rest of us are told is happening in Kashmir. He said, "Kashmir used to be a business. Now it's a mental asylum."

This is the full text of the first I. G. Khan Memorial Lecture, delivered at Aligarh Muslim University in Aligarh, India, on April 6, 2004. It was first published in Hindi in Hindustan, April 23–24, 2004, and in English in *The Hindu*, April 25, 2004. An excerpt also appeared in the *Los Angeles Times*, April 25, 2004. On the February 14, 2003, murder of I. G. Khan, see Parvathi Menon, "A Man of Compassion," *Frontline*, March 29–April 11, 2003, www.frontline .in/static/html/fl2007/stories/20030411004511400.htm.

The more I think about that remark, the more apposite a description it seems for all of India. Admittedly, Kashmir and the Northeast are separate wings that house the more perilous wards in the asylum. But in the heartland, too, the schism between knowledge and information, between what we know and what we're told, between what is unknown and what is asserted, between what is concealed and what is revealed, between fact and conjecture, between the "real" world and the virtual world, has become a place of endless speculation and potential insanity. It's a poisonous brew which is stirred and simmered and put to the most ugly, destructive, political purpose.

Each time there is a so-called terrorist strike, the government rushes in, eager to assign culpability with little or no investigation. The burning of the Sabarmati Express in Godhra, the December 13, 2001, attack on the Parliament building, and the massacre of Sikhs by so-called terrorists in Chittisinghpura in March 2000 are only a few high-profile examples. (The so-called terrorists who were later killed by security forces turned out to be innocent villagers. The state government subsequently admitted that fake blood samples were submitted for DNA testing.)[1] In each of these cases, the evidence that eventually surfaced raised very disturbing questions and so was immediately put into cold storage. Take the case of Godhra: as soon as it happened the home minister announced it was an Inter-Services Intelligence plot. The VHP says it was the work of a Muslim mob throwing petrol bombs.[2] Serious questions remain unanswered. There is endless conjecture. Everybody believes what they want to believe, but the incident is used to cynically and systematically whip up communal frenzy.

The US government used the lies and disinformation generated around the September 11 attacks to invade not just one country but two—and heaven knows what else is in store.

The Indian government uses the same strategy, not with other countries but against its own people.

Over the last decade, the number of people who have been killed by the police and security forces runs into the thousands.

Recently several Bombay policemen spoke openly to the press about how many "gangsters" they had eliminated on "orders" from their senior officers.[3] Andhra Pradesh chalks up an average of about two hundred "extremists" in "encounter" deaths a year.[4] In Kashmir, in a situation that almost amounts to war, an estimated eighty thousand people have been killed since 1989. Thousands have simply "disappeared."[5] According to the records of the Association of Parents of Disappeared People (APDP), more than 3,000 people were killed in 2003, of whom 463 were soldiers.[6] Since the Mufti Mohammed Sayeed government came to power in October 2002 on the promise of bringing a "healing touch," the APDP says, there have been fifty-four custodial deaths.[7] In this age of hypernationalism, as long as the people who are killed are labeled gangsters, terrorists, insurgents, or extremists, their killers can strut around as crusaders in the national interest and are answerable to no one. Even if it were true (which it most certainly isn't) that every person who has been killed was in fact a gangster, terrorist, insurgent, or extremist, it only tells us there is something terribly wrong with a society that drives so many people to take such desperate measures.

The Indian state's proclivity to harass and terrorize people has been institutionalized, consecrated, by the enactment of the Prevention of Terrorism Act (POTA), which has been promulgated in ten states. A cursory reading of POTA will tell you that it is draconian and ubiquitous. It's a versatile, hold-all law that could apply to anyone—from an Al-Qaeda operative caught with a cache of explosives to an Adivasi playing his flute under a neem tree, to you or me. The genius of POTA is that it can be anything the government wants it to be. We live on the sufferance of those who govern us. In Tamil Nadu it has been used to stifle criticism of the state government.[8] In Jharkhand thirty-two hundred people, mostly poor Adivasis accused of being Maoists, have been indicted under POTA.[9] In eastern Uttar Pradesh the act is used to clamp down on those who dare to protest about the alienation of their land and livelihood rights.[10] In Gujarat and Mumbai, it is used almost exclusively against Muslims.[11] In Gujarat after the 2002 state-assisted pogrom in which an estimated 2,000 Muslims were killed and 150,000 driven from their homes, 287 people have been accused under POTA. Of these, 286 are Muslim and one is a Sikh![12] POTA allows confessions extracted in police custody to be admitted as judicial evidence. In effect, under the POTA regime, police torture tends to replace police investigation. It's quicker, cheaper, and ensures results. Talk of cutting back on public spending.

In March 2004 I was a member of a people's tribunal on POTA. Over a period of two days we listened to harrowing testimonies of what goes on in our wonderful democracy. Let me assure you that in our police stations it's everything: from people being forced to drink urine to being stripped, humiliated, given electric shocks, burned with cigarette butts, having iron rods put up their anuses to being beaten and kicked to death.

Across the country hundreds of people, including some very young children charged under POTA, have been imprisoned and are being held without bail, awaiting trial in special POTA courts that are not open to public scrutiny. A majority of those booked under POTA are guilty of one of two crimes. Either they're poor—for the most part Dalit and Adivasi—or they're Muslim. POTA inverts the accepted dictum of criminal law: that a person is innocent until proven guilty. Under POTA you cannot get bail unless you can prove you are innocent—of a crime that you have not been formally charged with. Essentially, you have to prove you're innocent even if you're unaware of the crime you are supposed to have committed. And that applies to all of us. Technically, we are a nation waiting to be accused.

It would be naive to imagine that POTA is being "misused." On the contrary. It is being used for precisely the reasons it was enacted. Of course, if the recommendations of the Malimath Committee are implemented, POTA will soon become redundant. The Malimath Committee recommends that in certain respects normal criminal law should be brought in line with the provisions of POTA.[13] There'll be no more criminals then. Only terrorists. It's kind of neat.

Today in Jammu and Kashmir and many northeastern states of India, the Armed Forces Special Powers Act allows not just officers but even junior commissioned officers and noncommissioned officers of the army to use force against (and even kill) any person on suspicion of disturbing public order or carrying a weapon.[14] On *suspicion of*! Nobody who lives in India can harbor any illusions about what that leads to. The documentation of instances of torture, disappearances, custodial deaths, rape, and gang-rape (by security forces) is enough to make your blood run cold. The fact that, despite all this, India retains its reputation as a legitimate democracy in the international community and among its own middle class is a triumph.

The Armed Forces Special Powers Act is a harsher version of the ordinance that Lord Linlithgow passed on August 15, 1942, to handle the Quit India Movement. In 1958 it was clamped on parts of Manipur, which were declared "disturbed areas." In 1965 the whole of Mizoram, then still part of Assam was declared "disturbed." In 1972 the act was extended to Tripura. By 1980, the whole of Manipur had been declared "disturbed."[15] What more evidence does anybody need to realize that repressive measures are counterproductive and only exacerbate the problem?

Juxtaposed against this unseemly eagerness to repress and eliminate people is the Indian state's barely hidden reluctance to investigate and bring to trial cases in which there is plenty of evidence: the massacre of three thousand Sikhs in Delhi in 1984 and the massacres of Muslims in Bombay in 1993 and in Gujarat in 2002 (not one conviction to date); the murder a few years ago of Chandrashekhar Prasad, former president of the Jawaharlal Nehru University student union; and the murder twelve years ago of Shankar Guha Niyogi of the Chhattisgarh Mukti Morcha are just a few examples.[16] Eyewitness accounts and masses of incriminating evidence are not enough when all of the state machinery is stacked against you.

Meanwhile, economists cheering from the pages of corporate newspapers inform us that the GDP growth rate is phenomenal, unprecedented. Shops are overflowing with consumer goods. Government storehouses are overflowing with food grain. Outside this circle of light, farmers steeped in debt are committing suicide in the hundreds. Reports of starvation and malnutrition come in from across the country. Yet the government allowed 63 million tons of grain to rot in its granaries.[17] Twelve million tons were exported and sold at a subsidized price the Indian government was not willing to offer the Indian poor.[18] Utsa Patnaik, the well-known agricultural economist, has calculated food grain availability and food grain absorption in India for nearly a century, based on official statistics. She calculates that in the period between the early 1990s and 2001, food grain absorption has dropped to levels lower than during the World War II years, including during the Bengal Famine, in which three million people died of starvation.[19] As we know from the work of professor Amartya Sen, democracies don't take kindly to starvation deaths. They attract too much adverse publicity from the "free press."[20] So dangerous levels of malnutrition and permanent hunger are the preferred model these days. Forty-seven percent of India's children below three suffer from malnutrition, 46 percent are stunted.[21] Utsa Patnaik's study reveals that about 40 percent of the rural population in India has the same food grain absorption level as sub-Saharan Africa.[22] Today, an average rural family eats about 100 kilograms less food in a year than it did in the early 1990s.[23]

But in urban India, wherever you go—shops, restaurants, railway stations, airports, gymnasiums, hospitals—you have TV monitors in which election promises have already come true. India's Shining, Feeling Good. You only have to close your ears to the sickening crunch of the policeman's boot on someone's ribs, you only have to raise your eyes from the squalor, the slums, the ragged broken people on the streets and seek a friendly TV monitor and you will be in that other beautiful world. The singing-dancing world of Bollywood's permanent pelvic thrusts, of permanently privileged, permanently happy Indians waving the tricolor flag and Feeling Good. It's becoming harder and harder to tell which one's the real world and which one's virtual. Laws like POTA are like buttons on a TV. You can use it to switch off the poor, the troublesome, the unwanted.

There is a new kind of secessionist movement taking place in India. Shall we call it New Secessionism? It's an inversion of Old Secessionism. It's when people who are actually part of a whole different economy, a whole different country, a whole different *planet*, pretend they're part of this one. It is the kind of secession in which a relatively small section of people become immensely wealthy by appropriating everything—land, rivers, water, freedom, security, dignity, fundamental rights, including the right to protest—from a large group of people. It's a vertical secession, not a horizontal, territorial one. It's the real Structural Adjustment—the kind that separates India Shining from India. India Pvt. Ltd. from India the Public Enterprise.

It's the kind of secession in which public infrastructure, productive public assets—water, electricity, transport, telecommunications, health services, education, natural resources—assets that the Indian state is supposed to hold in trust for the people it represents, assets that have been built and maintained with public money over decades, are sold by the state to private corporations. In India 70 percent of the population—70 million people—live in rural areas.[24] Their livelihoods depend on access to natural resources. To snatch these away and sell them as stock to private companies is beginning to result in dispossession and impoverishment on a barbaric scale.

India Pvt. Ltd. is on its way to being owned by a few corporations and major multinationals. The CEOs of these companies will control this country, its infrastructure and its resources, its media and its journalists, but will owe nothing to its people. They are completely unaccountable—legally, socially, morally, politically. Those who say that in India a few of these CEOs are more powerful than the prime minister know exactly what they're talking about.

Quite apart from the economic implications of all this, even if it were all that it is cracked up to be (which it isn't)—miraculous, efficient, amazing—is the *politics* of it acceptable to us? If the Indian state chooses to mortgage its responsibilities to a handful of corporations, does it mean that the theater of electoral democracy is entirely meaningless? Or does it still have a role to play?

The free market (which is actually far from free) needs the state, and needs it badly. As the disparity between the rich and poor grows in poor countries, states have their work cut out for them. Corporations on the prowl for "sweetheart deals" that yield enormous profits cannot push through those deals and administer those projects in developing countries without the active connivance of state machinery. Today corporate globalization needs an international confederation of loyal, corrupt, preferably authoritarian governments in poorer countries, to push through unpopular reforms and quell the mutinies. It's called "Creating a Good Investment Climate."

When we vote, we choose which political party we would like to invest the coercive, repressive powers of the state in.

Right now in India we have to negotiate the dangerous crosscurrents of neoliberal capitalism and communal neofascism. While the word *capitalism* hasn't completely lost its sheen yet, using the word *fascism* often causes offense. So we must ask ourselves, are we using the word loosely? Are we exaggerating our situation, does what we are experiencing on a daily basis qualify as fascism?

When a government more or less openly supports a pogrom against members of a minority community in which up to 2,000 people are brutally killed, is it fascism? When women of that community are publicly raped and burned alive, is it fascism? When authorities collude to see to it that nobody is punished for these crimes, is it fascism? When 150,000 people are driven from their homes, ghettoized, and economically and socially boycotted, is it fascism? When the cultural guild that runs hate camps across the country commands the respect and admiration of the prime minister, the home minister, the law minister, the disinvestment minister, is it fascism? When painters, writers, scholars, and filmmakers who protest are abused, threatened, and have their work burned, banned, and destroyed, is it fascism? When a government issues an edict requiring the arbitrary alteration of school history textbooks, is it fascism? When mobs attack and burn archives of ancient historical documents, when every minor politician masquerades as a professional medieval historian and archaeologist, when painstaking scholarship is rubbished using baseless populist assertion, is it fascism? When murder, rape, arson, and mob justice are condoned by the party in power and its stable of stock intellectuals as an appropriate response to a real or perceived historical wrong committed centuries ago, is it fascism? When the middle class and the well-heeled pause a moment, tut-tut, and then go on with their lives, is it fascism? When the prime minister who presides over all of this is hailed as a statesman and visionary, are we not laying the foundations for full-blown fascism?

That the history of oppressed and vanquished people remains for the most part unchronicled is a truism that does not apply only to Savarna Hindus. If the politics of avenging historical wrong is our chosen path, then surely the Dalits and Adivasis of India have the right to murder, arson, and wanton destruction?

In Russia, they say the past is unpredictable. In India, from our recent experience with school history textbooks, we know how true that is. Now all "pseudo-secularists" have been reduced to hoping that archaeologists digging under the Babri Masjid wouldn't find the ruins of a Ram temple. But even if it were true that there is a Hindu temple under every mosque in India, what was under the temple? Perhaps another Hindu temple to another god. Perhaps a Buddhist stupa. Most likely an Adivasi shrine. History didn't begin with Savarna Hinduism, did it? How deep shall we dig? How much should we overturn? And why is it that while Muslims—who are socially, culturally, and economically an unalienable part of India—are called outsiders and invaders and are cruelly targeted, the government is busy signing corporate deals and contracts for development aid with a government that colonized us for centuries? Between 1876 and 1892, during the great famines, millions of Indians died of starvation while the British government continued to export food and raw materials to England. Historical records put the figure between twelve and twenty-nine million people.[25] That should figure somewhere in the politics of revenge, should it not? Or is vengeance only fun when its victims are vulnerable and easy to target?

Successful fascism takes hard work. And so does Creating a Good Investment Climate. Do the two work well together?

Historically, corporations have not been shy of fascists. Corporations such as Siemens, I. G. Farben, Bayer, IBM, and Ford did business with the Nazis.[26] We have the more recent example of our own Confederation of Indian Industry abasing itself to the Gujarat government after the pogrom in 2002.[27] As long as our markets are open, a little homegrown fascism won't come in the way of a good business deal.

It's interesting that just around the time Manmohan Singh, then the finance minister, was preparing India's markets for neoliberalism, L. K. Advani was making his first Rath Yatra, fueling communal passion and preparing us for neo-fascism. In December 1992, rampaging mobs destroyed the Babri Masjid. In 1993 the Congress government of Maharashtra signed a power purchase agreement with Enron. It was the first private power project in India. The Enron contract, disastrous as it has turned out, kick-started the era of privatization in India. Now, as the Congress whines from the sidelines, the Bharatiya Janata Party (BJP) has wrested the baton from its hands.[28] The government is conducting an extraordinary dual orchestra. While one arm is busy selling off the nation's assets in chunks, the other, to divert attention, is arranging a baying, howling, deranged chorus of cultural nationalism. The inexorable ruthlessness of one process feeds directly into the insanity of the other.

Economically, too, the dual orchestra is a viable model. Part of the enormous profits generated by the process of indiscriminate privatization (and the accruals of "India Shining") goes into financing Hindutva's vast army—the RSS, the VHP, the Bajrang Dal, and the myriad other charities and trusts that run schools, hospitals, and social services. Between them they have tens of thousands of shakhas across the country. The hatred they preach, combined with the unmanageable frustration generated by the relentless impoverishment and dispossession of the corporate globalization project, fuels the violence of poor on poor—the perfect smoke screen to keep the structures of power intact and unchallenged.

However, directing people's frustrations into violence is not always enough. In order to Create a Good Investment Climate, the state often needs to intervene directly.

In recent years, the police has repeatedly opened fire on unarmed people, mostly Adivasis, at peaceful demonstrations. In Nagarnar, Jharkhand; in Mehndi Kheda, Madhya Pradesh; in Umergaon, Gujarat; in Rayagara and Chilika, Orissa; in Muthanga, Kerala. People are killed for encroaching on forest land, as well as when they're trying to protect forest land from dams, mining operations, steel plants.

The repression goes on and on. Jambudweep, Kashipur, Maikanj. In almost every instance of police firing, those who have been fired upon are immediately called militants.

When victims refuse to be victims, they are called terrorists and are dealt with as such. POTA is the broad-spectrum antibiotic for the disease of dissent. There are other, more specific steps that are being taken—court judgments that in effect curtail free speech, the right to strike, the right to life and livelihood.

This year, 181 countries voted in the United Nations for increased protection of human rights in the era of the war on terror. Even the United States voted in favor of the resolution.

India abstained.[29] The stage is being set for a full-scale assault on human rights.

So how can ordinary people counter the assault of an increasingly violent state?

The space for nonviolent civil disobedience has atrophied. After struggling for several years, several nonviolent people's resistance movements have come up against a wall and feel, quite rightly, they have to now change direction. Views about what that direction should be are deeply polarized. There are some who believe that an armed struggle is the only avenue left. Leaving aside Kashmir and the Northeast, huge swathes of territory, whole districts in Jharkhand, Bihar, Uttar Pradesh, and Madhya Pradesh, are controlled by those who hold that view. Others increasingly are beginning to feel they must participate in electoral politics— enter the system, negotiate from within. (Similar, is it not, to the choices people faced in Kashmir?) The thing to remember is that while their methods differ radically, both sides share the belief that, to put it crudely, Enough Is Enough. *Ya Basta*.

There is no debate taking place in India that is more crucial than this one. Its outcome will, for better or for worse, change the quality of life in this country. For everyone. Rich, poor, rural, urban.

Armed struggle provokes a massive escalation of violence from the state. We have seen the morass it has led to in Kashmir and across the Northeast.

So then, should we do what our prime minister suggests we do? Renounce dissent and enter the fray of electoral politics? Join the road show? Participate in the shrill exchange of meaningless insults that serve only to hide what is otherwise an almost absolute consensus? Let's not forget that on every major issue—nuclear bombs, Big Dams, the Babri Masjid controversy, and privatization—the Congress sowed the seeds and the BJP harvested the crop.

This does not mean that the Parliament is of no consequence and elections should be ignored. Of course there is a difference between an overtly communal party with fascist leanings and an opportunistically communal party. Of course there is a difference between a politics that openly, proudly preaches hatred and a politics that slyly pits people against each other.

But the legacy of one has led us to the horror of the other. Between them, they have eroded any real choice that parliamentary democracy is supposed to provide. The frenzy, the fairground atmosphere created around elections, takes center stage in the media because everybody is secure in the knowledge that regardless of who wins, the status quo will essentially remain unchallenged. (After the impassioned speeches in Parliament, repealing POTA doesn't seem to be a priority in any party's election campaign. They all know they need it, in one form or another.) Whatever they say during elections or when they're in the opposition, no state or national government and no political party—right, left, center, or sideways—has managed to stay the hand of neoliberalism. There will be no radical change "from within."

Personally, I don't believe that entering the electoral fray is a path to alternative politics. Not because of that middle-class squeamishness—"politics is dirty" or "all politicians are corrupt"—but because I believe that strategically battles must be waged from positions of strength, not weakness.

The targets of the dual assault of neoliberalism and communal fascism are the poor and the minority communities. As neoliberalism drives its wedge between the rich and the poor, between India Shining and India, it becomes increasingly absurd for any mainstream political party to pretend to represent the interests of both the rich and the poor, because the interests of one can only be represented at the *cost* of the other. My "interests" as a wealthy Indian (were I to pursue them) would hardly coincide with the interests of a poor farmer in Andhra Pradesh.

A political party that represents the poor will be a poor party. A party with very meager funds. Today it isn't possible to fight an election without funds. Putting a couple of well-known social activists into Parliament is interesting but not really politically meaningful. Not a process worth channeling all our energies into. Individual charisma, personality politics, cannot effect radical change.

However, being poor is not the same as being weak. The strength of the poor is not indoors in office buildings and courtrooms. It's outdoors, in the fields, the mountains, the river valleys, the city streets, and university campuses of this country. That's where negotiations must be held. That's where the battle must be waged.

Right now, those spaces have been ceded to the Hindu Right. Whatever anyone might think of their politics, it cannot be denied that they're out there, working extremely hard. As the state abrogates its responsibilities and withdraws funds from health, education, and essential public services, the foot soldiers of the Sangh Parivar have moved in. Alongside their tens of thousands of shakhas disseminating deadly propaganda, they run schools, hospitals, clinics, ambulance services, disaster management cells. They understand powerlessness. They also understand that people, and particularly powerless people, have needs and desires that are not only practical, humdrum day-to-day needs but emotional, spiritual, recreational. They have fashioned a hideous crucible into which the anger, the frustration, the indignity of daily life—and dreams of a different future—can be decanted and directed to deadly purpose. Meanwhile, the traditional, mainstream left still dreams of "seizing power" but remains strangely unbending, unwilling to address the times. It has laid siege to itself and retreated into an inaccessible intellectual space, where ancient arguments are proffered in an archaic language that few can understand.

The only ones who present some semblance of a challenge to the onslaught of the Sangh Parivar are the grassroots resistance movements scattered across the country, fighting the dispossession and violation of fundamental rights caused by our current model of "development." Most of these movements are isolated and, despite the relentless accusation that they are "foreign-funded agents," work with almost no money or resources at all. They're magnificent firefighters. They have their backs to the wall. But they have their ears to the ground, and they are in touch with grim reality. If they got together, if they were supported and strengthened, they could grow into a force to reckon with. Their battle, when it is fought, will have to be an idealistic one—not a rigidly ideological one.

At a time when opportunism is everything, when hope seems lost, when everything boils down to a cynical business deal, we must find the courage to dream. To reclaim romance. The romance of believing in justice, in freedom, and in dignity. For everybody. We have to make common cause, and to do this we need to understand how this big old machine works—who it works for and who it works against. Who pays, who profits.

Many nonviolent resistance movements fighting isolated, single-issue battles across the country have realized that their kind of special interest politics, which had its time and place, is no longer enough. That they feel cornered and ineffectual is not good enough reason to abandon nonviolent resistance as a strategy. It is, however, good enough reason to do some serious introspection. We need vision. We need to make sure that those of us who say we want to reclaim democracy are egalitarian and democratic in our own methods of functioning. If our struggle is to be an idealistic one, we cannot really make caveats for the internal injustices that we perpetrate on one another, on women, on children. For example, those fighting communalism cannot turn a blind eye to economic injustices. Those fighting dams or development projects cannot elide issues of communalism or caste politics in their spheres of influence—even at the cost of short-term success in their immediate campaign. If opportunism and expediency come at the cost of our beliefs, then there is nothing to separate us from mainstream politicians. If it is justice that we want, it must be justice and equal rights for all—not only for special interest groups with special interest prejudices. That is nonnegotiable.

We have allowed nonviolent resistance to atrophy into feel-good political theater, which at its most successful is a photo opportunity for the media, and at its least successful is simply ignored.

We need to look up and urgently discuss strategies of resistance, wage real battles, and inflict real damage. We must remember that the Dandi March was not just fine political theater. It was a strike at the economic underpinning of the British Empire.

We need to redefine the meaning of politics. The "NGO-ization" of civil society initiatives is taking us in exactly the opposite direction. It's depoliticizing us. Making us dependent on aid and handouts. We need to reimagine the meaning of civil disobedience.

Perhaps we need an elected shadow parliament *outside* the Lok Sabha, without whose support and affirmation Parliament cannot easily function. A shadow parliament that keeps up an underground drumbeat, that shares intelligence and information (all of which is increasingly unavailable in the mainstream media). Fearlessly, but nonviolently, we must disable the working parts of this machine that is consuming us.

We're running out of time. Even as we speak, the circle of violence is closing in. Either way, change will come. It could be bloody, or it could be beautiful. It depends on us.

THE ROAD TO HARSUD

VILLAGES DIE BY night. Quietly. Towns die by day, shrieking as they go. The Indian government builds walls on rivers that devastate the lives of millions of people. Since Independence, Big Dams have displaced more than thirty-five million people in India alone. What is it about our understanding of nationhood that allows governments to crush their own people with such impunity? What is it about our understanding of "progress" and "national interest" that allows (applauds) the violation of human rights on a scale so vast that it takes on the texture of everyday life and is rendered virtually invisible? But every now and then something happens to make the invisible visible, the incomprehensible comprehensible. Harsud is that something. It is literature. Theater. History.

Harsud is a seven-hundred-year-old town in Madhya Pradesh, slated to be submerged by the reservoir of the Narmada Sagar Dam. The same Harsud where in 1989 tens of thousands of activists gathered from across India, held hands in a ring around the town, and vowed to collectively resist destruction masquerading as "Development." And fifteen years on, while

First published in *Outlook*, July 26, 2004.

Harsud waits to sink, that dream endures on slender moorings. The 262-meter-high Narmada Sagar will be the highest of the high dams on the Narmada, its reservoir the largest in India. In order to irrigate 123,000 hectares of land, it will submerge 91,000 hectares. This includes 41,000 hectares of prime dry deciduous forest, 249 villages, and the town of Harsud. Thirty percent of the land slated to be serviced by irrigation canals is already irrigated. Odd math, wouldn't you say?

Those who have studied the Narmada Sagar Project—Ashish Kothari of Kalpvriksh, Claude Alvarez, and Ramesh Billorey—have warned us for years that of all the high dams on the Narmada, the Narmada Sagar would be the most destructive. The Indian Institute of Science, Bangalore, estimated that up to 40 percent of the composite command areas of the Omkareshwar and Narmada Sagar could become severely waterlogged. In a note prepared in 1993 for the Review Committee, the Ministry of Environment and Forests estimated the value of the forest that would be submerged as Rs 33,923 crore ($7 billion). The note went on to say that if these costs were included, the proportion of Cost to Benefit rendered the project unviable. The Wildlife Institute, Dehradun, warned of the loss of a vast reservoir of biodiversity, wildlife, and rare medicinal plants. Its 1994 Impact Assessment Report to the Ministry of Environment said: The compensation of the combined adversarial impacts of the Narmada Sagar Project and the Omkareshwar Project is neither possible nor is being suggested. These will have to be reckoned as the price for the perceived socioeconomic benefit.

As always, all the warnings were ignored. The construction of the dam began in 1985. For the first few years it proceeded slowly. It ran into trouble with finance and land acquisition. In 1999, after a fast by activists of the Narmada Bachao Andolan, work was suspended altogether. On May 16, 2000, in keeping with the Central Government's push to privatize the power sector and open it to global finance, the government of Madhya Pradesh signed a memorandum of understanding (MOU) with the government of

India to "affirm the joint commitment of the two parties to the reform of the power sector in Madhya Pradesh." The "reforms" involved "rationalizing" power tariffs and slashing cross-subsidies that would (and did) inevitably lead to political unrest. The same MOU promised Central Government support for the Narmada Sagar and Omkareshwar Dams by setting up a joint venture with the National Hydroelectric Power Corporation (NHPC). That contract was signed on the same day, May 16, 2000.

Both agreements will lead to the pauperization and dispossession of people in the state. The NHPC boasts that the Narmada Sagar will eventually take care of the "power needs" of the state. It's not a claim that stands up to scrutiny. The installed capacity of the Narmada Sagar dam is 1,000 megawatts (MW). Which means what it sounds like: that the power-generating machinery that has been installed is capable of producing 1,000 MW of electricity. What is produced—actual firm power—depends on actually available water flows. (A Ferrari may be able to do 300 km in an hour. But what would it do without fuel?)

The Detailed Project Report puts the actual firm power at 212 MW, coming down to 147 MW when the irrigation canals become operational. According to the NHCP's own publicity, the cost of power at the bus bar (factory gate) is Rs 4.59 (nine cents) per unit. Which means at consumer point, it will cost about Rs 9 (eighteen cents). Who can afford that? It's even more expensive than Enron's electricity in Dabhol!

When (if) the project is fully built, the NHPC says it will generate an average of 1,950 million units of power. For the sake of argument, let's accept that figure. Madhya Pradesh currently loses 44.2 percent of its electricity, 12,000 million units (the equivalent of six Narmada Sagar Projects) a year in transmission and distribution (T&D) losses. If the Madhya Pradesh government could work toward saving even half its current T&D losses, it could generate power equal to three Narmada Sagar projects, at a third of the cost, with none of the social and ecological devastation.

But instead, once again we have a Big Dam with questionable benefits and unquestionable, unviable, cruel costs. After the MOU for the Narmada Sagar was signed, the NHPC set to work with its customary callousness. The dam wall began to go up at an alarming pace. At a press conference on March 9, 2004 (after the Bharatiya Janata Party [BJP] won the assembly elections and Uma Bharati became Chief Minister of Madhya Pradesh), Yogendra Prasad, chairman and managing director of the NHPC, boasted that the project was eight to ten months ahead of schedule. He said that because of better management the costs of the project would be substantially lower. Asked to comment on the objections being raised by the Narmada Bachao Andolan (NBA) about rehabilitation, he said the objections were irrelevant. "Better management," it now turns out, is a euphemism for cheating thousands of poor people.

Yogendra Prasad, Digvijay Singh, and Uma Bharati are criminally culpable; in any society in which the powerful are accountable, they would find themselves in jail. They have willfully violated the terms of their own MOU, which legally binds them to comply with the principles of the Narmada Water Disputes Tribunal Award (NWDTA). The award specifies that in no event can submergence precede rehabilitation. (Which is about as self-evident as saying child abuse is a crime.) They have violated the government of Madhya Pradesh's Rehabilitation Policy. They have violated the conditions of environmental and forest clearance. They have violated the terms of several international covenants that India has signed: the Universal Declaration of Human Rights, the International Covenant on Civil Economic and Political Rights, and the International Labour Organization Convention. The Supreme Court says that any international treaty signed by India becomes part of our domestic and municipal law. Not a single family has been resettled according to the NWDTA or the Madhya Pradesh Rehabilitation policy. There is no excuse, no mitigating argument for the horror they have unleashed.

The road from Khandwa to Harsud is a toll road. A smooth, new private highway, littered with the carcasses of trucks, motorcycles, and cars whose speeding drivers were clearly unused to such luxury. On the outskirts of Harsud you pass row upon row of cruel, corrugated tin sheds. Tin roofs, tin walls, tin doors, tin windows. As blindingly bright on the outside as they are dark inside. A sign says, "*Baad Raahat Kendra*" (Flood Relief Center). It's largely empty except for the bulldozers, jeeps, and the government officers and police who stroll around unhurried, full of the indolent arrogance that comes with power. The Flood Relief Center has been built on acquired land marked for submergence where only a few weeks ago the government college stood. If Bargi was possible, anything's possible.

And then, under the lowering, thundery sky, Harsud . . . like a scene out of a Marquez novel.

The first to greet us was an old buffalo, blind, green-eyed with cataract. Even before we entered the town we heard the announcement repeated over and over again on loudspeakers attached to a roving matador van. Please tether your cattle and livestock. Please do not allow them to roam free. The government will make arrangements to transport them. (Where to?) People with nowhere to go are leaving. They have loosed their livestock onto Harsud's ruined streets. And the government doesn't want drowning cattle on its hands. Behind the blind buffalo, silhouetted against the sky, the bare bones of a broken town.

A town turned inside out, its privacy ravaged, its innards exposed. Personal belongings, beds, cupboards, clothes, photographs, pots and pans lie on the street. In several houses, caged parakeets hang from broken beams. An infant swaddled in a sari crib sways gently, fast asleep in a doorway leading from nowhere to nowhere in a free-standing wall. Live electric cables hang down like dangerous aerial roots. The insides of houses lie rudely exposed. It's strange to see how a bleached, colorless town on the outside was vibrant on the inside, the walls every shade of turquoise, emerald, lavender, fuchsia. Perched on the concrete frames of wrecked buildings, men, like flightless birds, are hammering, sawing, smoking, talking. If you didn't know what was happening, you could be forgiven for thinking that Harsud was being built, not broken. That it had been hit by an earthquake and its citizens were rebuilding it. But then, you notice that the trees are all still standing. And outside every house you see order in the chaos. The doorframes stacked together. Iron grills in a separate pile. Tin sheets in another. Broken bricks still flecked with colored plaster piled up in a heap. Tin boards, shop signs, leaning against lampposts. Ambika Jewelers, Lovely Beauty Parlor, Shantiniketan Dharamshala, Blood and Urine Tested Here.

On more than one house there are insanely optimistic signs: This house is for sale. Every house, every tree has a code number on it. Only the people are uncoded. The local cartoonist is exhibiting his work on a pile of stones. Every cartoon is about how the government cheated and deceived people. A group of spectators discuss the details of various ongoing rackets in town, from tenders for the tin sheets for the tin sheds, to the megaphones on the matador, to the bribes being demanded from parents for School Transfer Certificates to a nonexistent school in a nonexistent rehabilitation site. Parents are distraught and children are delighted because their school building has been torn down. Many children will lose a whole school year. The poorer ones will drop out.

The people of Harsud are razing their town to the ground. Themselves. The very young and the very old sit on heaps of broken brick. The able-bodied are frenetically busy. They're tearing apart their homes, their lives, their past, their stories. They're carting the debris away in trucks and tractors and bullock carts.

Harsud is hectic. Like a frontier town during the Gold Rush. The demise of a town is lucrative business.

People have arrived from nearby towns. Trucks, tractors, dealers in scrap-iron, timber, and old plastic throng the streets, beating down prices, driving hard bargains, mercilessly exploiting distress sales. Migrant workers camp in makeshift hovels on the edge of town. They are the poorest of the poor. They have come from Jhabua, and the villages around Omkareshwar, displaced by the other big dams on the Narmada, the Sardar Sarovar and the Omkareshwar. The better off in Harsud hire them as labor. A severely malnutritioned demolition squad.

And so the circle of relentless impoverishment closes in upon itself. In the midst of the rubble, life goes on. Private things are now public. People are cooking, bathing, chatting (and yes, crying) in their wall-less homes. Iridescent orange *jalebis* and gritty *pakoras* are being deep fried in stoves surrounded by mounds of debris. The barber has a broken mirror on a broken wall. (Perhaps the man he's shaving has a broken heart.) The man who is demolishing the mosque is trying to save the colored glass. Two men are trying to remove the Shiva *lingam* from a small shrine without chipping it. There is no method to the demolition. No safety precautions. Just a mad hammering. A house collapses on four laborers. When they are extricated one of them is unconscious and has a steel rod sticking into his temple. But they're only Adivasis. They don't matter. The show must go on.

There is an eerie, brittle numbness to the bustle. It masks the government's ruthlessness and people's despair. Everyone knows that nearby, in the Kali Machak tributary, the water has risen. The bridge on the road to Balkeshwar is under water. There are no proper estimates of how many villages will be submerged in the Narmada Sagar Reservoir, when (if) the monsoon comes to the Narmada Valley. The Narmada Control Authority website uses figures from the 1981 Census.

In newspaper reports government officials estimate it will submerge more than one hundred villages and Harsud town. Most estimates suggest that this year 30,000 families will be uprooted from their homes; 5,600 of these families (22,000 people) are from Harsud. (Remember, these are 1981 figures.) When the reservoir of the first dam on the Narmada—the Bargi dam—was filled in 1988, it submerged three times more land than government engineers said it would. One hundred and one villages were slated for submergence, but in the monsoon of 1988, when the sluice gates were closed and the reservoir was filled, 162 villages (including some of the government's own resettlement sites) were submerged.

There was no rehabilitation. Tens of thousands of people slid into destitution and abject poverty. Today, fourteen years later, irrigation canals have still not been built. So the Bargi Dam irrigates less land than it submerged and only 6 percent of the land that its planners claimed it would irrigate. All indicators suggest that the Narmada Sagar could be an even bigger disaster. Farmers who usually pray for rain, now trapped between drought and drowning, have grown to dread the monsoon.

Oddly enough, after the 1989 rally, when the anti-dam movement was at its peak, the town of Harsud never became a major site of struggle. The people chose the option of conventional, mainstream politics, and divided themselves acrimoniously between the Congress and the BJP. Like most people, they believed that dams were not intrinsically bad, provided displaced people were resettled. So they didn't oppose the dam, hoping their political mentors would see that they received just compensation. Villages in the submergence zone did try to organize resistance, but they were brutally and easily suppressed.

Time and again they appealed to the NBA (located further downstream, fighting against the Sardar Sarovar and Maheshwar Dams) for help. The NBA, absurdly overstretched and under-resourced, did make sporadic interventions but was not able to expand its zone of influence to the Narmada Sagar. In the absence of any organized resistance, and bolstered by the Supreme Court's hostile judgments on the Sardar Sarovar and Tehri Dams, the Madhya Pradesh government and its partner in crime, the NHPC, have rampaged through the region with a callousness that would shock even a seasoned cynic. The lie of rehabilitation has been punctured once and for all. Planners who peddle it do so for the most cruel, opportunistic reasons. It gives them cover. It sounds so reasonable.

In the absence of an organized resistance movement, the media in Madhya Pradesh has done a magnificent job. Local journalists have doggedly exposed the outrage for what it is. Editors have given the story the space it deserves. Sahara Samay has its OB Van parked in Harsud. Newspapers and television channels carry horror stories every day, a normally anaesthetized, unblinking public has been roused to anger.

Every day groups of people arrive to see for themselves what is happening and to express their solidarity.

The state government and the NHPC remain unmoved. Perhaps a decision has been taken to exacerbate the tragedy and wait out the storm once and for all. Perhaps they're gambling on the fickleness of public memory and the media's need for a crisis turnover. But a crime of this proportion is not going to be forgotten so easily. If it goes unpunished, it cannot but damage India's image as a benign destination for international finance: thousands of people, evicted from their homes with nowhere to go. And it's not war. It's policy.

Can it really be that twenty-two thousand people have nowhere to go? Ministers and government officials assure the press that a whole new township—New Harsud—has been built near Chhanera, 12 kilometers away. On July 12, in his budget presentation, Madhya Pradesh finance minister Shri Raghavji announced: "Rehabilitation of Harsud town which was pending for years has been completed in six months."

Lies.

New Harsud is nothing but mile upon mile of stony, barren land in the middle of nowhere. A few hundred of the poorest families of Harsud have moved there and live under tarpaulin and tin sheets. (The rest have placed themselves at the mercy of relatives in nearby towns or are using up their meager compensation on rented accommodation. In and around Chhanera, rents have skyrocketed.)

In New Harsud there's no water, no sewage system, no shelter, no school, no hospital. Plots have been marked out like cells in a prison, with mud roads that crisscross at right angles. They get water from a tanker. Sometimes they don't. There are no toilets and there is not a tree or a bush in sight for them to piss or shit behind. When the wind rises it takes the tin sheets with it. When it rains, the scorpions come out of the wet earth.

Most important of all, there's no work in New Harsud. No means of earning a livelihood. People can't leave their possessions in the open and go off in search of work. So the little money they have been paid, dwindles. Cash compensation is only given to the Head of the Family, i.e., to men. What a travesty for the thousands of women who are hit hardest by the violence of displacement.

In Chhanera the booze shops are doing brisk business. When media attention trails away so will the water tankers. People will be left in a stony desert with no option but to flee.

Again.

And this is what is being done to people from a town.

You don't need to be a rocket scientist to imagine what is happening to the villages. In circumstances such as these, how does a government get people to not just move, but to physically tear apart their own lives themselves? In Harsud so far, there has been no bulldozing, no police firing, no coercion. Only cold, brilliant strategy. The people of Harsud have known for years that their town lay in the submergence zone of the Narmada Sagar Dam. Like all "oustees" of all dams, they were promised compensation and rehabilitation. There was no sign of either. And now, while people's lives are being devastated, Uma Bharati and Digvijay Singh accuse each other of criminal negligence.

Let's look at some basic facts. In September 2003, just before the assembly elections, the Digvijay Singh government granted the NHPC permission to raise the dam wall to 245 meters. At ten o'clock in the morning on November 18, 2003, the sluice gates were closed and water began to be impounded in the reservoir.

Downstream the river dried up, fish died, and for days the riverbed was exposed.

By mid-December, when Uma Bharati took over as the new cabinet minister for drinking water and sanitation, the height of the dam was already 238 meters. Eager to partake of some of the "credit" for the Narmada Sagar without bothering to check on how rehabilitation was progressing, she allowed the dam height to be increased from 238 to 245 meters. In January 2004 she congratulated the NHPC for its "achievements." In April 2004, the NHPC began to install the radial crest gates, which will take the dam to its full height of 262 meters. Four of the twenty gates are in place.

The NHPC has announced that the project will be completed by December 2004. The responsibility of surveying the submergence zone for the purposes of compensation and rehabilitation had been transferred to the NHPC. The responsibility for actual Land Acquisition and Rehabilitation still rests with the government. The NHPC holds 51 percent of the equity in the project. Between the two "interested parties," they're in a hurry to get the job done and keep the costs down. The first, most deadly sleight of hand involves the definition of who counts as Project Affected. The absolute poorest in the villages are sloughed off at this stage.

Essentially, those who are landless—fisher people, boat people, sand quarriers, daily wage workers, and those who are considered "encroachers"—do not qualify as project affected and are done away with. In some cases, whole villages have fallen prey to this process. For example, the 1982 Detailed Project Report says that 255 villages will be submerged by the reservoir. Somewhere along the way six of those villages were taken off the list. The Narmada Control Authority now says that only 211 villages will be eligible for compensation; 38 villages have been designated as "encroachers" and are not eligible for compensation.

The next lethal blow is when rates of compensation are fixed. The fortunate people who actually qualify as Project Affected asked, quite reasonably, to be compensated for their land according to the prevailing land prices in the villages in the command area of the dam. They received almost exactly half of that: Rs 40,000 ($600) for unirrigated land, Rs 60,000 ($900) for irrigated land. The market price for irrigated land is over Rs 100,000 ($1,500).

As a result, farmers who had ten acres of land will barely manage five. Small farmers with a couple of acres become landless laborers. Rich become poor. Poor become destitute. It's called Better Management. And it gets worse. *Patwaris* and revenue inspectors descended on Harsud and the "notified" villages like a terminator virus. They held thousands of people's futures in their grasping fists. Every single person we spoke to, every farmer, every laborer, every villager, every citizen of Harsud, rich and poor, man and woman, told the same story. The technique they described is as diabolical as it is simple. Basically the patwaris and revenue inspectors undervalued everything. Irrigated land was entered as unirrigated. *Pucca* houses were shown as *kuccha*. A five-acre farm became four acres.

And so on.

This was done indiscriminately, to rich and poor alike. People had the option of challenging the award in a civil court (and spending more on lawyers' fees than the compensation they hoped to receive). The other option was to bribe the patwaris and revenue inspectors. The poor simply did not have the liquid cash to pay the going rate—"*Hum feelgood nahin kar paaye.*" (We couldn't afford to pay them any "feelgood"). So they fell out of the basket. Those who managed to make the patwaris "feelgood" managed to get their cattle sheds entered as palatial homes and received handsome compensation (in *lakhs*, or hundreds of thousands) for them.

Of course, much of this made its way back to the officials as more Feelgood. Even this unfair, absurd compensation that was promised has not been disbursed. So in the villages and in Harsud, thousands of people continued to cling to their homes.

On May 14, Uma Bharati announced a grant of Rs 25,000

(roughly $500) (or up to 10 percent of the allotted compensation) to people who demolished their houses and moved out of town before June 30. People still didn't move. On June 8, the Harsud Doobvasi Sangharsh Morcha filed a petition in the Jabalpur High Court asking that water not be impounded in the reservoir until proper compensation is paid and rehabilitation completed. Annexed to their petition were carefully compiled documents that clearly showed the extent of criminal malfeasance that took place in Harsud.

The townspeople's hopes were pinned on the court's response. At the first hearing, government lawyers cautioned the judge that there was nothing anybody could do about the fact that the water was rising and the situation could turn dangerous. It cautioned the judge that if the court intervened, it could have a disaster on its hands. The state government knew that if it could break Harsud, the despair and resignation would spread to the villages. To break Harsud once and for all, to ensure that people never came back even if the monsoon failed and the town was not fully submerged, meant demolishing the town physically. In order to create panic they simulated a flood by releasing water from the Bargi reservoir upstream.

On June 23, the water in the Kalimachak tributary rose by a meter and a half. Still people didn't move. On June 27, over three hundred police and paramilitary forces staged a flag march through the terrified town. Companies of mounted police, the Rapid Action Force, the paramilitary, and armed constabulary paraded through the streets. On June 29, the High Court issued a tepid, cautious interim order. Morale in Harsud sank. Still the deadline of June 30 passed without event. On the morning of July 1, loudspeakers mounted on vehicles crisscrossed the town announcing that the Rs 25,000 ($500) grant would be given only to those who demolished their homes that very night.

Harsud broke. All night people smashed away at their own homes with crowbars, hammers, and iron rods. By morning it looked like a suburb of modern-day Baghdad. The panic spread to the villages. Away from the gaze of the media, in place of the lure of Rs 25,000 ($500), the government resorted to good old-fashioned repression.

In fact, repression in the villages had begun a while ago. In village after village—Amba Khaal, Bhawarli, Jetpur—people told us in precise, heartbreaking detail how they had been cheated by patwaris and revenue inspectors. Fearing what lay in store for them, many had sent their children and their stocks of grain away to relatives. Families who had lived together for generations did not know when they would ever see each other again. A whole fragile economy had begun to unravel. People described how a posse of policemen would arrive in a village, dismantle hand pumps, and cut electricity connections. Those who dared to resist were beaten. (This was the same technique the Digvijay Singh government used two years ago in the submergence zone of the Mann Dam.)

In each of the villages we visited, the schools had either been demolished or occupied by the police. In Amba Khaal small children studied in the shade of a peepal tree while the police lay about in their classrooms. As we traveled further inland toward the reservoir, the road got worse and eventually disappeared. At Malud there was a boat tethered to the Police Assistance Booth overlooking a rocky outcrop. The policeman said he was waiting for the Flood.

Beyond Malud we passed ghost villages reduced to rubble. A boy with two goats told us about twenty monkeys that were marooned on a clump of trees surrounded by water. We passed Gannaur, the last village where a lone man was loading the last few bricks of his home onto a tractor. Beyond Gannaur, the land slopes down toward the edge of the reservoir. As we approached the water, it began to rain. It was quiet except for the alarm calls of frightened lapwings. In my mind, the man loading his tractor in the distance was Noah building his ark, waiting for the Deluge. The sound of the water lapping against the shore was full of menace. The violence of what we had seen and heard robbed beautiful things of their beauty. A pair of dragonflies mated in the air. I caught myself wondering if it was rape.

There was a line of froth that marked the level up to which the water had risen before it receded in the government-induced Bargi flood. There was a small child's shoe in it. On our way back we took another route. We drove down a red gravel road built by the Forest Department and traveled deep into the forest. We arrived at a village that looked as though it had been evacuated some years ago. Broken houses had been reclaimed by trees and creepers. A herd of feral cows grazed in the ruins. There was no one around to tell us the name of the village—this village that must have been loved and lived in. That must still be loved. And dreamt about.

As we turned to go, we saw a man walking toward us. His name was Baalak Ram. He was a Banjara. He told us the name of the village—Jamunia. It had been uprooted two years ago. My friend Chittaroopa from the NBA was visibly disturbed when she heard this. She remembered tractorloads of people from Jamunia who came to support NBA's rallies against the Maheshwar Dam. And now they were gone. Swallowed by their own, more terrible dam.

Baalak Ram was a laborer who had been sent back by the land-owning Patels of Jamunia to try and round up their cows. But the cows wouldn't go. "They pay me, but it's not easy, the cattle have become wild. They refuse to go. They have grass and water here, the river and the forest are close by. Why should they go?" He told us how cows and dogs had returned to Jamunia from distant places. He seemed happy, alone in the forest with the almost-wild cows. We asked him if he ever felt lonely. "This is my village," he said, and then, after a moment "Only sometimes . . . when I think where has everyone gone? Are they all dead?"

A tiny boy arrived. Dark. Glowing. He attached himself to Baalak Ram's legs. He clutched a bunch of beautiful wildflowers. We asked him who they were for. "*Khabsurat the*" (They were beautiful). As though Beautiful was someone who had died recently. At a meeting of the Harsud Doobvasi Sangharsh Morcha, desperate people discussed the possibility of filing a Public Interest Litigation in the Supreme Court. I realized with some sadness that I no longer associate that institution with the idea of justice. Power, yes. Strategy, maybe. But justice?

Phrases from justice B. N. Kirpal's judgment on the Sardar Sarovar flashed through my mind: Public Interest Litigation should not be allowed to degenerate into becoming Publicity Interest Litigation or Private Inquisitiveness Litigation.

> *Though these villages comprise a significant population of tribals and people of weaker sections, but majority will not be a victim of displacement. Instead, they will gain from shifting.*
>
> *The displacement of tribals and other persons would not per se result in the violation of their fundamental or other rights.*

Thus were the thousands displaced by the Sardar Sarovar Dam doomed to destitution.

I thought of how the same judge, one day before he retired as India's chief justice, while he was the sitting judge on another, entirely unconnected case, ordered the government of India to begin work on the River Linking Project! In an affidavit submitted in response, the central government said the project would take forty-three years to complete and would cost Rs 560,000 crore ($115 billion).

Justice Kirpal didn't quibble about the cost, only asked that the project be completed in ten years! And so, a project of Stalinist proportions, potentially more destructive than all of India's dams put together, was born. Justice Kirpal subsequently clarified that it was not an order—just a "suggestion." Meanwhile, the government began to treat it like a Supreme Court order.

How can one man, whoever he is, order the ecology of a whole country to be irreversibly altered? How can a country that calls itself a democracy function like this? (Today Justice

Kirpal heads the Indian Environmental Council of Hindustan Coca-Cola Beverage Pvt. Ltd. Earlier this year, he publicly criticized a Kerala High Court order which refused to grant a stay on the Kerala government's directive restraining Coke from mining groundwater in Plachimada. A Contempt of Court case has been filed against him.)

So. Should the people of Harsud approach the courts? It's not an easy question to answer. What should they ask for? What could they hope to achieve? The concrete section of the Narmada Sagar Dam is 245 meters high. The radial crest gates take the dam wall up to its full height of 262.13 meters.

According to the Narmada Control Authority's own figures, a huge part of the submergence will take place between 245 meters and 262 meters. Can we look to the courts to explore the possibility of blasting open the sluice gates (as was done in the case of the Mann Dam), keeping them open until the rehabilitation process is complete according to the NWDTA stipulations? Can we look to the courts to order the reopening of the diversion tunnel so that water is not impounded in the reservoir this monsoon? Can we look to the courts to arraign every politician, bureaucrat, and NHPC official who has been involved in criminal malfeasance? Can we look to the courts to order the removal of the four existing gates (and stay the installation of the rest) until every displaced family has been rehabilitated? Will the courts consider these options or will they give us more of the same?

A pseudo-rap on the government's knuckles for shoddy rehabilitation (Bad boy, Fido! Naughty dog!) and a stamp of approval for project upon project that violate the fundamental rights of fellow human beings?

What should we expect? The charade of yet another retired judge setting up yet another Grievance Redressal Authority to address the woes of yet another hundred thousand people? If so, the question must be asked. Which institution in our wonderful democracy remains accountable to people and not to power?

What are people supposed to do? Are they on their own now? Have they fallen through the grid?

We left Harsud at dusk. On the way we stopped at the Baad Raahat Kendra. There were very few people around, although a couple of families had moved into the tin sheds. One of the tin doors had a sticker that said Export Quality. It was hard to make out the man sitting on the floor in the dark. He said his name was Kallu Driver. I'm glad I met him. He was sitting on the floor. He had unstrapped his wooden leg. He used to be a driver, but fifteen years ago he lost his leg in an accident. He lived alone in Harsud. He had been given a check for Rs 25,000 ($500) in exchange for demolishing his mud hut. His pregnant daughter had come from her husband's village to help him move. He had been to Chhanera three times to try and cash his check. He ran out of money for bus fare. The fourth time he walked. The bank sent him away and asked him to come back after three days. He showed us how his wooden leg had chipped and splintered. He said every night officials threatened him and tried to make him move to New Harsud. They said that the Baad Raahat Kendra was for emergencies only. Kallu was incoherent with rage. "What will I do in that desert?" he said. "How will I live? There's nothing there." A crowd gathered at the door. His anger fueled theirs. Kallu Driver does not need to read news reports or court affidavits or sly editorials (or fly-by-night PhDs pretending to be on the inside track of people's movements) to know which side he's on. Each time anybody mentioned government officials, or Digvijay Singh or Uma Bharati, he cursed. He made no gender distinctions. Maaderchod, he said. Motherfucker. He is not aware of feminist objections to derogatory references to women's bodies.

The World Bank, however, disagrees with Kallu Driver. It has singled the NHPC out for high praise. In December 2003 a team of senior World Bank experts visited the Narmada Sagar Project. In its Draft Country Assistance Strategy (CAS 2004), the Bank said: "While for many years the hydropower business had a poor reputation, some major actors (including the NHPC) have started to improve their environmental and social practices."

Interestingly, this is the third time in six months (since January 2004—after it was clear that the Narmada Sagar Dam wall had been raised with no attention to rehabilitation) that the Bank has singled the NHPC out for praise.

Why?

Read the next sentence in the CAS: "Given this . . . the Bank will work with the Government of India and its PSU's [Public Sector Units] to seek possible new areas of support on a modest scale for hydropower development."

Then again, on February 15, 2004, in a report that praises the NHPC for "completing projects like the Narmada Sagar within time and within budget," the *Economic Times* quoted a World Bank official saying: "The NHPC is moving towards global corporate performance standards and is improving its financial performance. We have done due diligence on the corporation and are impressed by the performance."

What makes the World Bank so very solicitous? Power and Water "Reforms" in developing countries are the twenty-first century's version of the Great Game. All the usual suspects, beginning of course with the World Bank, the big private banks, and multinational corporations, are cruising around, looking for sweetheart deals.

But overt privatization has run into bad weather. It has been widely discredited and is now looking for ways in which to reincarnate itself in a new avatar. From overt invasion to covert insurgency. Over the last few years the reputation of Big Dams (both public and private) has been badly mauled. The World Bank was publicly humiliated and forced to withdraw from the Sardar Sarovar Project. But now, encouraged by the Supreme Court judgments on the Sardar Sarovar and Tehri Dams, it's back on the block and is looking for a back door entry into the industry.

Who better to cozy up to than the biggest player in India's hydropower industry—the NHPC? The NHPC, which has left a trail of human rights abuses in its wake—Loktak (Manipur), Chamera Phase I (Himachal), Koel Karo (Bihar), Omkareshwar (Madhya Pradesh). The NHPC, which is eyeing a number of other dam projects (including the Maheshwar Dam) and aims to install 32,000 MW of power over the next thirteen years.

That's the equivalent of thirty-two Narmada Sagars.

But the World Bank is by no means the only shark in the water. Here's a list of international banks that have financed NHPC projects: ANZ, Barclays, Emirates, Natwest, Standard Chartered, Sumitomo. And a list of bilateral export credit and financing agencies that support it: Coface (France); Export Development Canada and Canadian International Development Agency; Japan Bank for International Cooperation and Nippon Export and Investment Insurance (Japan); the former Official Development Assistance (now Department for International Development; United Kingdom); Swedish International Development Cooperation Agency and Swedish Export Credit Agency.

What's a few human rights abuses among friends? We're deep into the Great Game.

It is dark on the highway back to Khandwa. We pass truck upon truck carrying illegal, unmarked timber. Trucks carrying away the forest. Tractors carrying away the town. The night carrying away the dreams of hundreds of thousands of people. I agree with Kallu Driver. But I have a problem with derogatory references to women's bodies.

PUBLIC POWER IN
THE AGE OF EMPIRE

When language has been butchered and bled of meaning, how do we understand "public power"? When freedom means occupation, when democracy means neoliberal capitalism, when reform means repression, when words like *empowerment* and *peacekeeping* make your blood run cold—why, then, *public power* could mean whatever you want it to mean. A biceps building machine, or a Community Power Shower. So, I'll just have to define "public power" as I go along, in my own self-serving sort of way.

In India, the word *public* is now a Hindi word. It means *people*. In Hindi, we have *sarkar* and *public*, the government and the people. Inherent in this use is the underlying assumption that the government is quite separate from "the people." This

---

This text is based on a public address delivered to an overflow crowd at the American Sociological Association's Ninety-Ninth Annual Meeting in San Francisco on August 16, 2004. The theme of the conference was "Public Sociologies." The talk quickly aired on C-SPAN *Book TV*, *Democracy Now!*, and *Alternative Radio*, reaching audiences throughout North America and beyond, and was circulated via email around the world.

distinction has to do with the fact that India's freedom struggle, though magnificent, was by no means revolutionary. The Indian elite stepped easily and elegantly into the shoes of the British imperialists. A deeply impoverished, essentially feudal society became a modern, independent nation-state. Even today, fifty-seven years on to the day, the truly vanquished still look upon the government as *mai-baap*, the parent and provider. The somewhat more radical, those who still have fire in their bellies, see it as *chor*, the thief, the snatcher-away of all things.

Either way, for most Indians, *sarkar* is very separate from *public*. However, as you make your way up India's complex social ladder, the distinction between *sarkar* and *public* gets blurred. The Indian elite, like the elite anywhere in the world, finds it hard to separate itself from the state. It sees like the state, thinks like the state, speaks like the state.

In the United States, on the other hand, the blurring of the distinction between *sarkar* and *public* has penetrated far deeper into society. This could be a sign of a robust democracy, but unfortunately, it's a little more complicated and less pretty than that. Among other things, it has to do with the elaborate web of paranoia generated by the US *sarkar* and spun out by the corporate media and Hollywood. Ordinary people in the United States have been manipulated into imagining they are a people under siege whose sole refuge and protector is their government. If it isn't the Communists, it's Al-Qaeda. If it isn't Cuba, it's Nicaragua. As a result, this, the most powerful nation in the world—with its unmatchable arsenal of weapons, its history of having waged and sponsored endless wars, and of being the only nation in history to have actually used nuclear bombs—is peopled by a terrified citizenry, jumping at shadows. A people bonded to the state not by social services, or public health care, or employment guarantees, but by fear.

This synthetically manufactured fear is used to gain public sanction for further acts of aggression. And so it goes, building into a spiral of self-fulfilling hysteria, now formally calibrated by the US government's Amazing Technicolored Terror Alerts: fuchsia, turquoise, salmon pink.

To outside observers, this merging of *sarkar* and *public* in the United States sometimes makes it hard to separate the actions of the government from the people. It is this confusion that fuels anti-Americanism in the world. Anti-Americanism is then seized upon and amplified by the US government and its faithful media outlets. You know the routine: "Why do they hate us? They hate our freedoms," et cetera. This enhances the sense of isolation among people in the United States and makes the embrace between *sarkar* and *public* even more intimate. Like Red Riding Hood looking for a cuddle in the wolf's bed.

Two thousand one was not the first year that the US government declared a war on terrorism. As Noam Chomsky reminds us, the first war on terrorism was declared by president Ronald Reagan in the 1980s during the US-sponsored terrorist wars across Central America, the Middle East, and Africa. The Reagan administration called terrorism a "plague spread by depraved opponents of civilization itself." In keeping with this sentiment, in 1987 the United Nations General Assembly proposed a strongly worded condemnation of terrorism. One hundred fifty-three countries voted for it. Only the United States and Israel voted against it. They objected to a passage that referred to "the right to self-determination, freedom, and independence . . . of people forcibly deprived of that right . . . particularly peoples under colonial and racist regimes and foreign occupation." Remember that in 1987, the United States was a staunch ally of apartheid South Africa. The African National Congress and Nelson Mandela were listed as "terrorists." The term *foreign occupation* was taken to mean Israel's occupation of Palestine.

Over the last few years, the war on terrorism has mutated into the more generic war on terror. Using the threat of an external enemy to rally people behind you is a tired old horse that politicians have ridden into power for centuries. But could it be that ordinary people are fed up with that poor old horse and are looking for something different? There's an old Hindi film song that goes *yeh public hai, yeh sab jaanti hai* (the public, she knows it all). Wouldn't it be lovely if the song were right and the politicians wrong?

Before Washington's illegal invasion of Iraq, a Gallup International poll showed that in no European country was the support for a unilateral war higher than 11 percent. On February 15, 2003, weeks before the invasion, more than ten million people marched against the war on different continents, including North America. And yet the governments of many supposedly democratic countries still went to war.

The question is: Is "democracy" still democratic?

Are democratic governments accountable to the people who elected them? And, critically, is the *public* in democratic countries responsible for the actions of its *sarkar?*

If you think about it, the logic that underlies the war on terrorism and the logic that underlies terrorism are exactly the same. Both make ordinary citizens pay for the actions of their government. Al-Qaeda made the people of the United States pay with their lives for the actions of their government in Palestine, Saudi Arabia, Iraq, and Afghanistan. The US government has made the people of Afghanistan pay in the thousands for the actions of the Taliban, and the people of Iraq pay in the hundreds of thousands for the actions of Saddam Hussein.

The crucial difference is that nobody really elected Al-Qaeda, the Taliban, or Saddam Hussein. But the president of the United States was elected (well . . . in a manner of speaking).

The prime ministers of Italy, Spain, and the United Kingdom were elected. Could it then be argued that citizens of these countries are more responsible for the actions of their government than Iraqis were for the actions of Saddam Hussein or Afghans for the Taliban?

Whose God decides which is a "just war" and which isn't? George Bush Sr. once said: "I will never apologize for the United States. I don't care what the facts are." When the president of the most powerful country in the world doesn't *need* to care what the facts are, then we can at least be sure we have entered the Age of Empire.

So what does public power mean in the Age of Empire? Does it mean anything at all? Does it actually *exist?*

In these allegedly democratic times, conventional political thought holds that public power is exercised through the ballot. Scores of countries in the world will go to the polls this year. Most (not all) of them will get the governments they vote for. But will they get the governments they want?

In India this year, we voted the Hindu nationalists out of office. But even as we celebrated, we knew that on nuclear bombs, neoliberalism, privatization, censorship, Big Dams—on every major issue other than overt Hindu nationalism—the Congress and the BJP have no major ideological differences. We know that it is the fifty-year legacy of the Congress Party that prepared the ground culturally and politically for the Far Right. It was also the Congress Party that first opened India's markets to corporate globalization. It passed legislation that encouraged the privatization of water and power, the dismantling of the public sector, and the denationalization of public companies. It enforced cutbacks in government spending on education and health, and weakened labor laws that protected workers' rights. The BJP took this process forward with pitiless abandon.

In its election campaign, the Congress Party indicated that it was prepared to rethink some of its earlier economic policies. Millions of India's poorest people came out in strength to vote in the elections. The spectacle of the great Indian democracy was telecast live—the poor farmers, the old and infirm, the veiled women with their beautiful silver jewelry, making quaint journeys to election booths on elephants and camels and bullock carts. Contrary to the predictions of all India's experts and pollsters, Congress won more votes than any other party.

India's communist parties won the largest share of the vote in their history. India's poor had clearly voted against neoliberalism's economic "reforms" and growing fascism. As soon as the votes were counted, the corporate media dispatched them like badly paid extras on a film set. Television channels featured split screens. Half the screen showed the chaos outside the home of Sonia Gandhi, the leader of the Congress Party, as the coalition government was cobbled together. The other half showed frenzied stockbrokers outside the Bombay Stock Exchange, panicking at the thought that the Congress Party might actually honor its promises and implement its electoral mandate. We saw the Sensex stock index move up and down and sideways. The media, whose own publicly listed stocks were plummeting, reported the stock market crash as though Pakistan had launched ICBMs on New Delhi.

Even before the new government was formally sworn in, senior Congress politicians made public statements reassuring investors and the media that privatization of public utilities would continue. Meanwhile the BJP, now in opposition, has cynically, and comically, begun to oppose foreign direct investment and the further opening of Indian markets.

This is the spurious, evolving dialectic of electoral democracy.

As for the Indian poor, once they've provided the votes, they are expected to bugger off home. Policy will be decided despite them.

And what of the US elections? Do US voters have a real choice?

It's true that if John Kerry becomes president, some of the oil tycoons and Christian fundamentalists in the White House will change. Few will be sorry to see the back of Dick Cheney or Donald Rumsfeld or John Ashcroft or an end to their blatant thuggery. But the real concern is that in the new administration their policies will continue. That we will have Bushism without Bush.

Those positions of real power—the bankers, the CEOs—are not vulnerable to the vote (and in any case, they fund both sides).

Unfortunately, US elections have deteriorated into a sort of personality contest, a squabble over who would do a better job of overseeing empire. John Kerry believes in the idea of empire as fervently as George Bush does.

The US political system has been carefully crafted to ensure that no one who questions the natural goodness of the military-industrial-corporate structure will be allowed through the portals of power.

Given this, it's no surprise that in this election you have two Yale University graduates, both members of Skull and Bones, the same secret society, both millionaires, both playing at soldier-soldier, both talking up war and arguing almost childishly about who will lead the war on terror more effectively.

Like president Bill Clinton before him, Kerry will continue the expansion of US economic and military penetration into the world. He says he would have voted to authorize Bush to go to war in Iraq even if he had known that Iraq had no weapons of mass destruction. He promises to commit more troops to Iraq. He said recently that he supports Bush's policies toward Israel and Ariel Sharon "completely." He says he'll retain 98 percent of Bush's tax cuts.

So, underneath the shrill exchange of insults, there is almost absolute consensus. It looks as though even if people in the United States vote for Kerry, they'll still get Bush. President John Kerbush or president George Berry.

It's not a real choice. It's an *apparent* choice.

Like choosing a brand of detergent. Whether you buy Ivory Snow or Tide, they're both owned by Procter & Gamble.

This doesn't mean that one takes a position that is without nuance, that the Congress and the BJP, New Labor and the Tories, the Democrats and Republicans are the same. Of course they're not. Neither are Tide and Ivory Snow. Tide has oxyboosting and Ivory Snow is a gentle cleanser.

In India, there is a difference between an overtly fascist party (the BJP) and a party that slyly pits one community against another (Congress) and sows the seeds of communalism that are then so ably harvested by the BJP.

There are differences in the IQs and levels of ruthlessness between this year's US presidential candidates. The antiwar movement in the United States has done a phenomenal job of exposing the lies and venality that led to the invasion of Iraq, despite the propaganda and intimidation it faced.

This was a service not just to people here but to the whole world.

But why is it that the Democrats do not even have to pretend to be against the invasion and occupation of Iraq? If the antiwar movement openly campaigns for Kerry, the rest of the world will think that it approves of his policies of "sensitive" imperialism. Is US imperialism preferable if it is supported by the United Nations and European countries? Is it preferable if the UN asks Indian and Pakistani soldiers to do the killing and dying in Iraq instead of US soldiers? Is the only change that Iraqis can hope for that French, German, and Russian companies will share in the spoils of the occupation of their country?

Is this actually better or worse for those of us who live in subject nations? Is it better for the world to have a smarter emperor in power or a stupider one? Is that our only choice?

I'm sorry, I know that these are uncomfortable, even brutal questions, but they must be asked.

The fact is that electoral democracy has become a process of cynical manipulation. It offers us a very reduced political space today. To believe that this space constitutes real choice would be naive.

The crisis in modern democracy is a profound one. Free elections, a free press, and an independent judiciary mean little when the free market has reduced them to commodities available on sale to the highest bidder.

On the global stage, beyond the jurisdiction of sovereign governments, international instruments of trade and finance oversee a complex system of multilateral laws and agreements that have entrenched a system of appropriation that puts colonialism to shame. This system allows the unrestricted entry and exit of massive amounts of speculative capital—hot money—into and out of third world countries, which then effectively dictates their economic policy. Using the threat of capital flight as a lever, international capital insinuates itself deeper and deeper into these economies. Giant transnational corporations are taking control of their essential infrastructure and natural resources, their minerals, their water, their electricity. The World Trade Organization, the World Bank, the International Monetary Fund, and other financial institutions like the Asian Development Bank virtually write economic policy and parliamentary legislation. With a deadly combination of arrogance and ruthlessness, they take their sledgehammers to fragile, interdependent, historically complex societies, and devastate them.

All this goes under the fluttering banner of "reform."

As a consequence of this reform, in Africa, Asia, and Latin America, thousands of small enterprises and industries have closed down, millions of workers and farmers have lost their jobs and land.

Anyone who criticizes this process is mocked for being "antireform," antiprogress, antidevelopment. Somehow a Luddite.

The *Spectator* newspaper in London assures us that "we live in the happiest, healthiest and most peaceful era in human history."

Billions wonder: Who's "we"? Where does he live? What's his Christian name?

Once the economies of third world countries are controlled by the free market, they are enmeshed in an elaborate, carefully calibrated system of economic inequality. For example, Western countries that together spend more than a billion dollars a *day* on subsidies to farmers demand that poor countries withdraw all agricultural subsidies, including subsidized electricity. Then they flood the markets of poor countries with their subsidized agricultural goods and other products with which local producers cannot possibly compete.

Countries that have been plundered by colonizing regimes are steeped in debt to these same powers, and have to repay them at the rate of about $382 *billion* a year. Ergo, the rich get richer and the poor get poorer—not accidentally but by *design*. By *intention*.

To put a vulgar point on all of this—the truth is getting more vulgar by the minute—the combined wealth of the world's billionaires in 2004 (587 "individuals and family units"), according to *Forbes* magazine, is $1.9 trillion. This is more than the gross domestic product of the world's 135 poorest countries combined. The good news is that there are 111 more billionaires this year than there were in 2003. Isn't that fun?

The thing to understand is that modern democracy is safely premised on an almost religious acceptance of the nation-state. But corporate globalization is not. Liquid capital is not. So even though capital needs the coercive powers of the nation-state to put down revolts in the servants' quarters, this setup ensures that no individual nation can oppose corporate globalization on its own.

Time and again we have seen the heroes of our times, giants in opposition, suddenly diminished. President Lula of Brazil was the hero of the World Social Forum in January 2002. Now he's busy implementing IMF guidelines, reducing pension benefits, and purging radicals from the Workers' Party. Lula has a worthy predecessor in the former president of South Africa, Nelson Mandela, who instituted a massive program of privatization and structural adjustment that has left thousands of people homeless, jobless, and without water and electricity. When Harry Oppenheimer died in August 2000, Mandela called him "one of the great South Africans of our time." Oppenheimer was the head of Anglo-American, one of South Africa's largest mining companies, which made its money exploiting cheap Black labor made available by the repressive apartheid regime.

Why does this happen? It is neither true nor useful to dismiss Mandela and Lula as weak or treacherous people. It's important to understand the nature of the beast they were up against. The moment they crossed the floor from the opposition into government, they became hostage to a spectrum of threats—most malevolent among them the threat of capital flight, which can destroy any government overnight. To imagine that a leader's personal charisma and history of struggle will dent the corporate cartel is to have no understanding of how capitalism works, or for that matter, how power works.

Radical change cannot and will not be negotiated by governments; it can only be enforced by people. By the *public*. A public who can link hands *across* national borders.

So when we speak of public power in the age of empire, I hope it's not presumptuous to assume that the only thing that is worth discussing seriously is the power of a *dissenting* public. A public that *disagrees* with the very concept of empire. A public that has set itself against incumbent power—international, national, regional, or provincial governments and institutions that support and service empire.

Of course those of us who live in empire's subject nations are aware that in the great cities of Europe and the United States, where a few years ago these things would only have been whispered, there is now open talk about the benefits of imperialism and the need for a strong empire to police an unruly world. It wasn't long ago that colonialism also sanctified itself as a "civilizing mission." So we can't give these pundits high marks for originality.

We are aware that New Imperialism is being marketed as a "lesser evil" in a less-than-perfect world. Occasionally, some of us are invited to "debate" the merits of imperialism on "neutral" platforms provided by the corporate media. It's like debating slavery. It isn't a subject that deserves the dignity of a debate.

What are the avenues of protest available to people who wish to resist empire? By *resist* I don't mean only to *express* dissent but to effectively force change.

Empire has a range of calling cards. It uses different weapons to break open different markets. There isn't a country on God's earth that is not caught in the crosshairs of the US cruise missile and the IMF checkbook. Argentina's the model if you want to be the poster boy of neoliberal capitalism, Iraq if you're the black sheep.

For poor people in many countries, empire does not always appear in the form of cruise missiles and tanks, as it has in Iraq or Afghanistan or Vietnam. It appears in their lives in very local avatars—losing their jobs, being sent unpayable electricity bills, having their water supply cut, being evicted from their homes and uprooted from their land. All this overseen by the repressive machinery of the state, the police, the army, the judiciary. It is a process of relentless impoverishment with which the poor are historically familiar. What empire does is to further entrench and exacerbate already existing inequalities.

Even until quite recently, it was sometimes difficult for people to see themselves as victims of empire. But now local struggles have begun to see their role with increasing clarity. However grand it might sound, the fact is, they *are* confronting empire in their own, very different ways. Differently in Iraq, in South Africa, in India, in Argentina, and differently, for that matter, on the streets of Europe and the United States.

Mass resistance movements, individual activists, journalists, artists, and filmmakers have come together to strip empire of its sheen. They have connected the dots, turned cash-flow charts and boardroom speeches into real stories about real people and real despair. They have shown how the neoliberal project has cost people their homes, their land, their jobs, their liberty, their dignity. They have made the intangible tangible. The once seemingly incorporeal enemy is now corporeal.

This is a huge victory. It was forged by the coming together of disparate political groups, with a variety of strategies. But they all recognized that the target of their anger, their activism, and their doggedness is the same. This was the beginning of *real* globalization. The globalization of dissent.

Broadly speaking, there are two kinds of mass resistance movements in third world countries today. The landless people's movement in Brazil, the anti-dam movement in India, the Zapatistas in Mexico, the Anti-Privatization Forum in South Africa, and hundreds of others are fighting their own sovereign governments, which have become agents of the neoliberal project. Most of these are radical struggles, fighting to change the structure and chosen model of "development" of their own societies.

Then there are those fighting formal and brutal neocolonial occupations in contested territories whose boundaries and fault lines were often arbitrarily drawn last century by the imperialist powers. In Palestine, Tibet, Chechnya, Kashmir, and several states in India's Northeast provinces, people are waging struggles for self-determination.

Several of these struggles might have been radical, even revolutionary, when they began, but often the brutality of the repression they face pushes them into conservative, even retrogressive spaces where they use the same violent strategies and the same language of religious and cultural nationalism used by the states they seek to replace.

Many of the foot soldiers in these struggles will find, like those who fought apartheid in South Africa, that once they overcome overt occupation, they will be left with another battle on their hands—a battle against covert economic colonialism.

Meanwhile, the rift between rich and poor is being driven deeper and the battle to control the world's resources intensifies. Economic colonialism through formal military aggression is staging a comeback.

Iraq today is a tragic illustration of this process. An illegal invasion. A brutal occupation in the name of liberation. The rewriting of laws that allow the shameless appropriation of the country's wealth and resources by corporations allied to the occupation, and now the charade of a local "Iraqi government."

For these reasons, it is absurd to condemn the resistance to the US occupation in Iraq as being masterminded by terrorists or insurgents or supporters of Saddam Hussein. After all, if the United States were invaded and occupied, would everybody who fought to liberate it be a terrorist or an insurgent or a Bushite?

The Iraqi resistance is fighting on the frontlines of the battle against empire. And therefore that battle is our battle.

Like most resistance movements, it combines a motley range of assorted factions. Former Baathists, liberals, Islamists, fed-up collaborationists, communists, etc. Of course, it is riddled with opportunism, local rivalry, demagoguery, and criminality. But if we are only going to support pristine movements, then no resistance will be worthy of our purity.

A whole industry of development experts, academics, and consultants have built an industry on the back of global social movements in which they are not direct participants. Many of these "experts," who earn their livings studying the struggles of the world's poor, are funded by groups like the Ford Foundation, the World Bank, and wealthy universities such as Harvard, Stanford, and Cornell. From a safe distance, they offer us their insightful critiques. But the same people who tell us that we can reform the World Bank from within, that we change the IMF by working inside it, would not themselves seek to reform a resistance movement by working within it.

This is not to say that we should never criticize resistance movements. Many of them suffer from a lack of democracy, from the iconization of their "leaders," a lack of transparency, a lack of vision and direction. But most of all they suffer from vilification, repression, and lack of resources.

Before we prescribe how a pristine Iraqi resistance must conduct a secular, feminist, democratic, nonviolent battle, we should shore up our end of the resistance by forcing the US government and its allies to withdraw from Iraq.

The first militant confrontation in the United States between the global justice movement and the neoliberal junta took place famously at the WTO conference in Seattle in December 1999. To many mass movements in developing countries that had long been fighting lonely, isolated battles, Seattle was the first delightful sign that their anger and their vision of another kind of world was shared by people in the imperialist countries.

In January 2001, in Porto Alegre, Brazil, twenty thousand activists, students, filmmakers—some of the best minds in the world—came together to share their experiences and exchange ideas about confronting empire. That was the birth of the now historic World Social Forum. It was the first formal coming together of an exciting, anarchic, unindoctrinated, energetic, new kind of "public power." The rallying cry of the WSF is "Another World Is Possible." The forum has become a platform where hundreds of conversations, debates, and seminars have helped to hone and refine a vision of what kind of world it should be. By January 2004, when the fourth WSF was held in Mumbai, India, it attracted two hundred thousand delegates. I have never been part of a more electrifying gathering. It was a sign of the Social Forum's success that the mainstream media in India ignored it completely. But now the WSF is threatened by its own success. The safe, open, festive atmosphere of the Forum has allowed politicians and nongovernmental organizations that are imbricated in the political and economic systems that the Forum opposes to participate and make themselves heard.

Another danger is that the WSF, which has played such a vital role in the movement for global justice, runs the risk of becoming an end unto itself. Just organizing it every year consumes the energies of some of the best activists. If *conversations* about resistance replace real civil disobedience, then the WSF could become an asset to those whom it was created to oppose. The Forum must be held and must grow, but we have to find ways to channel our conversations there back into concrete action.

As resistance movements have begun to reach out across national borders and pose a real threat, governments have developed their own strategies of how to deal with them. They range from co-optation to repression.

I'm going to speak about three of the contemporary dangers that confront resistance movements: the difficult meeting point between mass movements and the mass media, the hazards of the NGO-ization of resistance, and the confrontation between resistance movements and increasingly repressive states.

The place in which the mass media meets mass movements is a complicated one.

Governments have learned that a crisis-driven media cannot afford to hang about in the same place for too long. Like a business needs cash turnover, the media need crisis turnover. Whole countries become old news. They cease to exist, and the darkness becomes deeper than before the light was briefly shined on them. We saw it happen in Afghanistan when the Soviets withdrew. And now, after Operation Enduring Freedom put the CIA's Hamid Karzai in place, Afghanistan has been thrown to its warlords once more.

Another CIA operative, Iyad Allawi, has been installed in Iraq, so perhaps it's time for the media to move on from there, too.

While governments hone the art of waiting out crises, resistance movements are increasingly being ensnared in a vortex of crisis production, seeking to find ways of manufacturing them in easily consumable, spectator-friendly formats.

Every self-respecting people's movement, every "issue," is expected to have its own hot-air balloon in the sky advertising its brand and purpose.

For this reason, starvation deaths are more effective advertisements for impoverishment than millions of malnourished people, who don't quite make the cut. Dams are not newsworthy until the devastation they wreak makes good television. (And by then, it's too late.)

Standing in the rising water of a reservoir for days on end, watching your home and belongings float away to protest against a big dam, used to be an effective strategy but isn't any more. The media is dead bored of that one. So the hundreds of thousands of people being displaced by dams are expected to either conjure up new tricks or give up the struggle.

Resistance as spectacle, as political theater, has a history. Gandhi's Salt March in 1931 to Dandi is among the most exhilarating examples. But the Salt March wasn't theater alone. It was the symbolic part of a larger act of real civil disobedience. When Gandhi and an army of freedom fighters marched to Gujarat's coast and made salt from seawater, thousands of Indians across the country began to make their own salt, openly defying imperial Britain's salt tax laws, which banned local salt production in favor of British salt imports. It was a direct strike at the economic underpinning of the British Empire.

The disturbing thing nowadays is that resistance as spectacle has cut loose from its origins in genuine civil disobedience and is beginning to become more symbolic than real. Colorful demonstrations and weekend marches are vital but alone are not powerful enough to stop wars. Wars will be stopped only when soldiers refuse to fight, when workers refuse to load weapons onto ships and aircraft, when people boycott the economic outposts of empire that are strung across the globe.

If we want to reclaim the space for civil disobedience, we will have to liberate ourselves from the tyranny of crisis reportage and its fear of the mundane. We have to use our experience, our imagination, and our art to interrogate those instruments of state that ensure that "normality" remains what it is: cruel, unjust, unacceptable. We have to expose the policies and processes that make ordinary things—food, water, shelter, and dignity—such a distant dream for ordinary people. The real preemptive strike is to understand that wars are the end result of a flawed and unjust peace.

As far as mass resistance movements are concerned, the fact is that no amount of media coverage can make up for mass strength on the ground. There is no option, really, to old-fashioned, backbreaking political mobilization. Corporate globalization has increased the distance between those who make decisions and those who have to suffer the effects of those decisions. Forums like the WSF enable local resistance movements to reduce that distance and to link up with their counterparts in rich countries. That alliance is a formidable one. For example, when

India's first private dam, the Maheshwar Dam, was being built, the Narmada Bachao Andolan (the NBA), the German organization Urgewald, the Berne Declaration in Switzerland, and the International Rivers Network in Berkeley worked together to push a series of international banks and corporations out of the project. This would not have been possible had there not been a rock-solid resistance movement on the ground. The voice of that local movement was amplified by supporters on the global stage, embarrassing investors and forcing them to withdraw.

An infinite number of similar alliances, targeting specific projects and specific corporations, would help to make another world possible. We should begin with the corporations that did business with Saddam Hussein and now profit from the devastation and occupation of Iraq.

A second hazard facing mass movements is the NGO-ization of resistance. It will be easy to twist what I'm about to say into an indictment of all NGOs. That would be a falsehood. In the murky waters of fake NGOs set up to siphon off grant money or as tax dodges (in states like Bihar, they are given as dowry), of course there are NGOs doing valuable work. But it's important to turn our attention away from the positive work being done by some individual NGOs and consider the NGO phenomenon in a broader political context.

In India, for instance, the funded NGO boom began in the late 1980s and 1990s. It coincided with the opening of India's markets to neoliberalism. At the time, the Indian state, in keeping with the requirements of Structural Adjustment, was withdrawing funding from rural development, agriculture, energy, transport, and public health. As the state abdicated its traditional role, NGOs moved in to work in these very areas. The difference, of course, is that the funds available to them are a minuscule fraction of the actual cut in public spending. Most large, well-funded NGOs are financed and patronized by aid and development agencies, which are in turn funded by Western governments, the World Bank, the UN, and some multinational corporations. Though they may not be the very same agencies, they are certainly part of the same loose political formation that oversees the neoliberal project and demands the slash in government spending in the first place.

Why should these agencies fund NGOs? Could it be just old-fashioned missionary zeal? Guilt? It's a little more than that.

NGOs give the *impression* that they are filling the vacuum created by a retreating state. And they are, but in a materially inconsequential way. Their *real* contribution is that they defuse political anger and dole out as aid or benevolence what people ought to have by right. They alter the public psyche. They turn people into dependent victims and blunt the edges of political resistance. NGOs form a sort of buffer between the *sarkar* and *public*. Between empire and its subjects. They have become the arbitrators, the interpreters, the facilitators of the discourse. They play out the role of the "reasonable man" in an unfair, unreasonable war.

In the long run, NGOs are accountable to their funders, not to the people they work among. They're what botanists would call an indicator species. It's almost as though the greater the devastation caused by neoliberalism, the greater the outbreak of NGOs. Nothing illustrates this more poignantly than the phenomenon of the US preparing to invade a country and simultaneously readying NGOs to go in and clean up the devastation.

In order to make sure their funding is not jeopardized and that the governments of the countries they work in will allow them to function, NGOs have to present their work—whether it's in a country devastated by war, poverty, or an epidemic of disease—within a shallow framework more or less shorn of a political or historical context. At any rate, an *inconvenient* historical or political context. It's not for nothing that the "NGO perspective" is becoming increasingly respected.

Apolitical (and therefore, actually, extremely political) distress reports from poor countries and war zones eventually make the (dark) people of those (dark) countries seem like pathological victims. *Another malnourished Indian, another starving Ethiopian, another Afghan refugee camp, another maimed Sudanese* . . . in need of the white man's help. They unwittingly reinforce racist stereotypes and reaffirm the achievements, the comforts, and the compassion (the tough love) of Western civilization, minus the guilt of the history of genocide, colonialism, and slavery. They're the secular missionaries of the modern world.

Eventually—on a smaller scale but more insidiously—the capital available to NGOs plays the same role in alternative politics as the speculative capital that flows in and out of the economies of poor countries. It begins to dictate the agenda.

It turns confrontation into negotiation. It depoliticizes resistance. It interferes with local people's movements that have traditionally been self-reliant. NGOs have funds that can employ local people who might otherwise be activists in resistance movements but now can feel they are doing some immediate, creative good (and earning a living while they're at it). Charity offers instant gratification to the giver, as well as the receiver, but its side effects can be dangerous. Real political resistance offers no such shortcuts.

The NGO-ization of politics threatens to turn resistance into a well-mannered, reasonable, salaried, 9-to-5 job. With a few perks thrown in.

Real resistance has real consequences. And no salary.

This brings us to a third danger I want to speak about tonight: the deadly nature of the actual confrontation between resistance movements and increasingly repressive states. Between public power and the agents of empire.

Whenever civil resistance has shown the slightest signs of evolving from symbolic action into anything remotely threatening, the crackdown is merciless. We've seen what happened in the demonstrations in Seattle, in Miami, in Gothenburg, in Genoa.

In the United States, you have the USA Patriot Act, which has become a blueprint for antiterrorism laws passed by governments around the world. Freedoms are being curbed in the name of protecting freedom. And once we surrender our freedoms, to win them back will take a revolution.

Some governments have vast experience in the business of curbing freedoms and still smelling sweet. The government of India, an old hand at the game, lights the path.

Over the years the Indian government has passed a plethora of laws that allow it to call almost anyone a terrorist, an insurgent, a militant. We have the Armed Forces Special Powers Act, the Public Security Act, the Special Areas Security Act, the Gangster Act, the Terrorist and Disruptive Areas Act (which has formally lapsed, but under which people are still facing trial), and, most recently, POTA (the Prevention of Terrorism Act), the broad-spectrum antibiotic for the disease of dissent.

There are other steps that are being taken, such as court judgments that in effect curtail free speech, the right of government workers to go on strike, the right to life and livelihood. Courts have begun to micromanage our lives in India. And criticizing the courts is a criminal offense.

But coming back to the counterterrorism initiatives, over the last decade the number of people who have been killed by the police and security forces runs into the tens of thousands. In the state of Andhra Pradesh (the pin-up girl of corporate globalization in India), an average of about two hundred "extremists" are killed in what are called "encounters" every year. The Bombay police boast of how many "gangsters" they have killed in "shootouts." In Kashmir, in a situation that almost amounts to war, an estimated eighty thousand people have been killed since 1989. Thousands have simply "disappeared." In the northeastern provinces, the situation is similar.

In recent years, the Indian police have opened fire on unarmed people at peaceful demonstrations, mostly Dalit and Adivasi. The preferred method is to kill them and then call them terrorists. India is not alone, though. We have seen similar things happen in countries such as Bolivia and Chile. In the era of neoliberalism, poverty is a crime, and protesting against it is more and more being defined as terrorism.

In India, the Prevention of Terrorism Act is often called the *Production* of Terrorism Act. It's a versatile, hold-all law that could apply to anyone from an Al-Qaeda operative to a disgruntled bus conductor. As with all antiterrorism laws, the genius of POTA is that it can be whatever the government wants. For example, in Tamil Nadu it has been used to imprison and silence critics of the state government. In Jharkhand 3,200 people, mostly poor Adivasis accused of being Maoists, have been named in criminal complaints under POTA. In Gujarat and Mumbai, the act is used almost exclusively against Muslims. After the 2002 state-assisted pogrom in Gujarat, in which an estimated 2,000 Muslims were savagely killed by Hindu mobs and 150,000 driven from their homes, 287 people have been accused under POTA. Of these, 286 are Muslim and *one* is a Sikh.

POTA allows confessions extracted in police custody to be admitted as judicial evidence. In effect, torture tends to replace investigation. The South Asia Human Rights Documentation Center reports that India has the highest number of torture and custodial deaths in the world. Government records show that there were 1,307 deaths in judicial custody in 2002 alone.

A few months ago, I was a member of a people's tribunal on POTA. Over a period of two days, we listened to harrowing testimonies of what is happening in our wonderful democracy. It's everything—from people being forced to drink urine, being stripped, humiliated, given electric shocks, burned with cigarette butts, having iron rods put up their anuses, to people being beaten and kicked to death.

The new government has promised to repeal POTA. I'd be surprised if that happens before similar legislation under a different name is put in place.

When every avenue of nonviolent dissent is closed down, and everyone who protests against the violation of their human rights is called a terrorist, should we really be surprised if vast parts of the country are overrun by those who believe in armed struggle and are more or less beyond the control of the state: in Kashmir, the northeastern provinces, large parts of Madhya Pradesh, Chattisgarh, Jharkhand, and Andhra Pradesh? Ordinary people in these regions are trapped between the violence of the militants and the state.

In Kashmir, the Indian Army estimates that three to four thousand militants are operating at any given time. To control them, the Indian government deploys about five hundred thousand soldiers. Clearly it isn't just the militants the army seeks to control, but a whole population of humiliated, unhappy people who see the Indian Army as an occupation force. The primary purpose of laws like POTA is not to target real terrorists or militants, who are usually simply shot. Antiterrorism laws are used to intimidate civil society. Inevitably, such repression has the effect of fueling discontent and anger.

The Armed Forces Special Powers Act allows not just officers but even junior commissioned officers and noncommissioned officers of the army to use force and even kill any person on *suspicion* of disturbing public order. It was first imposed on a few districts in the state of Manipur in 1958. Today it applies to virtually all of the Northeast and Kashmir. The documentation of instances of torture, disappearances, custodial deaths, rape, and summary execution by security forces is enough to turn your stomach.

In Andhra Pradesh, in India's heartland, the militant Marxist-Leninist People's War Group (PWG)—which for years has been engaged in a violent armed struggle and has been the principal target of many of the Andhra police's fake "encounters"—held its first public meeting in years on July 28, 2004, in the town of Warangal.

The former chief minister of Andhra Pradesh, Chandrababu Naidu, liked to call himself the CEO of the state. In return for his enthusiasm in implementing Structural Adjustment, Andhra Pradesh received millions of dollars of aid from the World Bank and development agencies such as Britain's Department for International Development. As a result of Structural Adjustment, Andhra Pradesh is now best known for two things: the hundreds of suicides by farmers who were steeped in debt and the spreading influence and growing militancy of the People's War Group. During Naidu's term in office, the PWG were not arrested or captured, they were summarily shot.

In response, the PWG campaigned actively, and, let it be said, violently, against Naidu. In May the Congress won the state elections. The Naidu government didn't just lose, it was humiliated in the polls.

When the PWG called a public meeting, it was attended by hundreds of thousands of people. Under POTA, all of them are considered terrorists.

Are they all going to be detained in some Indian equivalent of Guantánamo Bay?

The whole of the Northeast and the Kashmir valley is in ferment. What will the government do with these millions of people?

One does not endorse the violence of these militant groups. Neither morally nor strategically. But to condemn it without first denouncing the much greater violence perpetrated by the state would be to deny the people of these regions not just their basic human rights but even the right to a fair hearing. People who have lived in situations of conflict are in no doubt that militancy and armed struggle provoke a massive escalation of violence from the state. But living as they do, in situations of unbearable injustice, can they remain silent forever?

There is no discussion taking place in the world today that is more crucial than the debate about strategies of resistance. And the choice of strategy is not entirely in the hands of the *public*. It is also in the hands of *sarkar*.

After all, when the US invades and occupies Iraq in the way it has done, with such overwhelming military force, can the resistance be expected to be a conventional military one? (Of course, even if it *were* conventional, it would still be called terrorist.) In a strange sense, the US government's arsenal of weapons and unrivaled air and fire power makes terrorism an all-but-inescapable response. What people lack in wealth and power, they will make up for with stealth and strategy.

In the twenty-first century, the connection between corporate globalization, religious fundamentalism, nuclear nationalism, and the pauperization of whole populations is becoming impossible to ignore. The unrest has myriad manifestations: terrorism, armed struggle, nonviolent mass resistance, and common crime.

In this restive, despairing time, if governments do not do all they can to honor nonviolent resistance, then by default they privilege those who turn to violence. No government's condemnation of terrorism is credible if it cannot show itself to be open to change by nonviolent dissent. But instead nonviolent resistance movements are being crushed. Any kind of mass political mobilization or organization is being bought off, broken, or simply ignored.

Meanwhile, governments and the corporate media, and let's not forget the film industry, lavish their time, attention, funds, technology, research, and admiration on war and terrorism. Violence has been deified.

The message this sends is disturbing and dangerous: if you seek to air a public grievance, violence is more effective than nonviolence.

As the rift between the rich and poor grows, as the need to appropriate and control the world's resources to feed the great capitalist machine becomes more urgent, the unrest will only escalate.

For those of us who are on the wrong side of empire, the humiliation is becoming unbearable.

Each of the Iraqi children killed by the United States was our child. Each of the prisoners tortured in Abu Ghraib was our comrade. Each of their screams was ours. When they were humiliated, we were humiliated.

The US soldiers fighting in Iraq—mostly volunteers in a poverty draft from small towns and poor urban neighborhoods—are victims, just as much as the Iraqis, of the same horrendous process, which asks them to die for a victory that will never be theirs.

The mandarins of the corporate world, the CEOs, the bankers, the politicians, the judges and generals, look down on us from on high and shake their heads sternly. "There's no alternative," they say, and let slip the dogs of war.

Then, from the ruins of Afghanistan, from the rubble of Iraq and Chechnya, from the streets of occupied Palestine and the mountains of Kashmir, from the hills and plains of Colombia and the forests of Andhra Pradesh and Assam, comes the chilling reply: "There's no alternative but terrorism." Terrorism. Armed struggle. Insurgency. Call it what you want.

Terrorism is vicious, ugly, and dehumanizing for its perpetrators as well as its victims. But so is war. You could say that terrorism is the privatization of war. Terrorists are the free marketers of war. They are people who don't believe that the state has a monopoly on the legitimate use of violence.

Human society is journeying to a terrible place.

Of course, there is an alternative to terrorism. It's called justice.

It's time to recognize that no amount of nuclear weapons, or full-spectrum dominance, or daisy cutters, or spurious governing councils and *loya jirgas*, can buy peace at the cost of justice.

The urge for hegemony and preponderance by some will be matched with greater intensity by the longing for dignity and justice by others.

Exactly what form that battle takes, whether it's beautiful or bloodthirsty, depends on us.

PEACE AND THE
NEW CORPORATE
LIBERATION
THEOLOGY

IT'S OFFICIAL NOW. The Sydney Peace Foundation is neck deep in the business of gambling and calculated risk. Last year, very courageously, it chose Dr. Hanan Ashrawi of Palestine for the Sydney Peace Prize. And, as if that were not enough, this year—of all the people in the world—it goes and chooses me!

When the prize was announced, I was subjected to some pretty arch remarks from those who know me well: Why did they give it to the biggest troublemaker we know? Didn't anybody tell them that you don't have a peaceful bone in your body? And, memorably, Arundhati, *didi* (sister), what's the Sydney Peace Prize? Was there a war in Sydney that you helped to stop?

Speaking for myself, I am utterly delighted. But I must accept it as a literary prize that honors a writer for her writing, because contrary to the many virtues that are falsely attributed to me,

Sydney Peace Prize Lecture, November 4, 2004.

I'm not an activist, nor the leader of a mass movement, and I'm certainly not the "voice of the voiceless."

Today, not merely justice, but the idea of justice is under attack. The assault on fragile sections of society is at once so complete, so cruel and so clever—all-encompassing and yet specifically targeted, brutal and yet insidious—that its audacity has eroded our definition of justice. It has forced us to lower our sights and expectations.

In an alarming shift, the reduced, fragile discourse of "human rights" is replacing the magnificent concept of justice. The difference is that notions of equality have been pried loose and eased out of the equation. It's a process of attrition. Almost unconsciously, we begin to think of justice for the rich and powerful and human rights for the poor. Justice for the corporate world, human rights for its victims. Justice for the Indian upper castes, human rights for Dalits and Adivasis (if that). Justice for white Australians, human rights for Aboriginals and immigrants.

It is becoming clearer that violating human rights is an inherent and necessary part of implementing a coercive and unjust political and economic structure on the world. Without wholesale violation of human rights, the neoliberal project would remain in the dreamy realm of policy. But human rights violations increasingly are being portrayed as the unfortunate, almost accidental, fallout of an otherwise acceptable political and economic system. This is why in areas of heightened conflict—in Kashmir and in Iraq, for example—human rights professionals are regarded with suspicion.

It has been only a few weeks since Australians voted to reelect prime minister John Howard who, among other things, led Australia to participate in the illegal invasion and occupation of Iraq. The invasion of Iraq will surely go down in history as one of the most cowardly wars ever fought. It was a war in which a band of rich nations, armed with enough nuclear weapons to destroy the world several times over, rounded on a poor nation, falsely accused it of having nuclear weapons, used the United

Nations to force it to disarm, then invaded it, occupied it, and are now in the process of selling it.

Iraq is a sign of things to come, showing us the corporate–military cabal of "empire" at work. As the battle to control the world's resources intensifies, economic colonialism through formal military aggression is staging a comeback.

In 1991, US president George Bush senior mounted Operation Desert Storm. Tens of thousands of Iraqis were killed in the war. Iraq's fields were bombed with more than three hundred tons of depleted uranium, causing a fourfold increase in cancer among children. For more than thirteen years, twenty-four million Iraqi people lived in a war zone and were denied food, medicine, and clean water. In the frenzy around the US elections, let's remember that the levels of cruelty did not fluctuate whether the Democrats or the Republicans were in the White House. Half a million Iraqi children died because of economic sanctions in the run up to Operation Shock and Awe. Until recently, while there was a careful record of how many US soldiers had lost their lives, we had no idea of how many Iraqis had been killed. A new, detailed study, fast-tracked by the *Lancet* medical journal and extensively peer reviewed, estimates that one hundred thousand Iraqis have died since the invasion. And let's not forget Iraq's children. Technically, the bloodbath is called precision bombing. In ordinary language, it's called butchery.

So the civilized modern world—built painstakingly on a legacy of genocide, slavery, and colonialism—now controls most of the world's oil. And most of the world's weapons, most of the world's money, and most of the world's media. The embedded, corporate media in which the doctrine of Free Speech has been substituted by the doctrine of Free If You Agree Speech.

UN chief weapons inspector Hans Blix said he found no evidence of nuclear weapons in Iraq. Every scrap of evidence produced by the US and British governments was found to be false. And yet, in the prelude to the war, day after day the most "respectable" newspapers and TV channels in the US headlined the "evidence" of Iraq's arsenal of nuclear weapons. It now turns out that the source of the manufactured "evidence" of Iraq's arsenal of nuclear weapons was Ahmed Chalabi who—like General Suharto of Indonesia, General Pinochet of Chile, the Shah of Iran, the Taliban, and of course, Saddam Hussein himself—was bankrolled with millions of dollars from the good old CIA.

And so, a country was bombed into oblivion.

Visitors to Australia like myself are expected to answer the following question when they fill in the visa form: Have you ever committed or been involved in the commission of war crimes or crimes against humanity or human rights? Would George Bush and Tony Blair get visas to Australia? Under the tenets of international law they must surely qualify as war criminals.

Although no weapons of mass destruction have been found in Iraq—stunning new evidence has revealed that Saddam Hussein was planning a weapons program. (Like I was planning to win Olympic Gold in synchronized swimming.) No doubt all will be revealed in the free and fair trial of Saddam Hussein that's coming up soon in the New Iraq.

But we won't learn how the US and Britain plied him with money and material assistance at the time he was carrying out murderous attacks on Iraqi Kurds and Shias, or that the twelve-thousand-page report submitted by Saddam Hussein's government to the UN was censored by the United States because it lists twenty-four US corporations that participated in Iraq's pre-Gulf War nuclear and conventional weapons program. (They include Bechtel, DuPont, Eastman Kodak, Hewlett Packard, International Computer Systems, and Unisys.)

So Iraq has been "liberated," its people subjugated, and its markets "freed" in outright violation of international law. Once Iraq has been handed over to the multinationals, a mild dose of genuine democracy won't do any harm. In fact, it might be good PR for the corporate version of Liberation Theology, otherwise known as New Democracy.

Corporations like Bechtel and Halliburton, the company that US vice president Dick Cheney once headed, have won huge contracts for "reconstruction" work. A brief CV of any one of these corporations would give us a layperson's grasp of how it all works—not just in Iraq, but all over the world. Say we pick Bechtel—an old business acquaintance of Saddam Hussein. Many of its dealings were negotiated by none other than Donald Rumsfeld. In 1988, after Saddam Hussein gassed thousands of Kurds, Bechtel signed contracts with the Iraqi government to build a dual-use chemical plant in Baghdad.

Bechtel has been awarded reconstruction contracts in Iraq worth over a billion dollars, which include contracts to rebuild power generation plants, electrical grids, water supply, sewage systems, and airport facilities. Never mind revolving doors, this— if it weren't so drenched in blood—would be a bedroom farce.

And Bechtel has footprints around the world. It first attracted international attention when it signed a contract with Hugo Banzer, the Bolivian dictator, to privatize the city of Cochabamba's water supply. Bechtel immediately raised the water price, bringing hundreds of thousands of those who couldn't pay Bechtel's bills into the streets, paralyzing the city. Martial law was declared. Bechtel was forced to flee its offices, but it is now negotiating a multimillion dollar exit payment from the Bolivian government for the loss of profits.

In India, Bechtel along with General Electric are the new owners of the notorious and currently defunct Enron power project. The Enron contract, which legally binds the government of the State of Maharashtra to pay Enron a sum of $30 billion, was the largest contract ever signed in India. Enron was not shy to boast about the millions of dollars it had spent to "educate" Indian politicians and bureaucrats. The Enron contract in Maharashtra, which was India's first "fast-track" private power project, has come to be known as the most massive fraud in the country's history. (Enron was another of the Republican Party's major campaign contributors.) Enron's electricity was so expensive that the government decided it was cheaper not to buy electricity and to pay Enron damages under the contract. The government of one of the world's poorest countries was paying Enron $220 million a year not to produce electricity.

With Enron's demise, Bechtel and GE are suing the Indian government for $5.6 billion for lost profits. Enron actually invested a tiny fraction of this sum in the project. The arbitration between Bechtel, GE, and the government of India is taking place right now in London.

Think about it: The notional profits of a single corporate project would be enough to provide one hundred days of employment a year at minimum wages (calculated at a weighted average across different states) for twenty-five million people. That's five million more than the population of Australia. That is the scale of the horror of neoliberalism.

Invaded and occupied Iraq has been made to pay out $200 million in "reparations" for lost profits to corporations like Halliburton, Shell, Mobil, Nestle, Pepsi, Kentucky Fried Chicken, and Toys R Us. That's apart from its $125 billion sovereign debt forcing it to turn to the IMF.

In New Iraq, privatization has broken new ground. The US Army is increasingly recruiting private mercenaries to help in the occupation. The advantage with mercenaries is that when they're killed they're not included in the US soldiers' body count. It helps to manage public opinion. Prisons have been privatized and torture has been privatized.

Other attractions in New Iraq include newspapers being shut down. Television stations bombed. Reporters killed. US soldiers have opened fire on crowds of unarmed protestors, killing scores of people. The only kind of resistance that has managed to survive is as crazed and brutal as the occupation itself. Is there space for a secular, democratic, feminist, nonviolent resistance in Iraq? There isn't really.

That is why it falls to those of us living outside Iraq to create that mass-based, secular, and nonviolent resistance to the US occupation. If we fail to do that, then we run the risk of allowing the idea of resistance to be hijacked and conflated with terrorism, and that will be a pity because they are not the same thing.

We know very well who benefits from war in the age of empire. But we must also ask ourselves honestly: who benefits from peace in the age of empire? War mongering is criminal. But talking of peace without talking of justice could easily become advocacy for a kind of capitulation. And talking of justice without unmasking the institutions and the systems that perpetrate injustice is beyond hypocritical.

It's easy to blame the poor for being poor. It's easy to believe that the world is being caught up in an escalating spiral of terrorism and war. That's what allows the American president to say "You're either with us or with the terrorists." But we know that that is a spurious choice.

It is mendacious to make moral distinction between the unspeakable brutality of terrorism and the indiscriminate carnage of war and occupation. Both kinds of violence are unacceptable. We cannot support one and condemn the other. The real tragedy is that most people in the world are trapped between the horror of a putative peace and the terror of war. Those are the two sheer cliffs we're hemmed in by.

The question is: How do we climb out of this crevasse?

For those who are materially well-off but morally uncomfortable, the first question you must ask yourself is, do you really want to climb out of it? How far are you prepared to go? Has the crevasse become too comfortable?

If you really want to climb out, there's good news and bad news.

The good news is that the advance party began the climb some time ago. They're already halfway up. Thousands of activists across the world have been hard at work preparing footholds and securing the ropes to make it easier for the rest of us. There isn't only one path up. There are hundreds of ways of doing it. There are hundreds of battles being fought around the world that need your skills, your minds, your resources.

The bad news is that colorful demonstrations, weekend marches, and annual trips to the World Social Forum are not enough. There have to be targeted acts of real civil disobedience with real consequences. Maybe we can't flip a switch and conjure up a revolution. But there are several things we could do. For example, you could make a list of those corporations who have profited from the invasion of Iraq and have offices here in Australia. You could name them, boycott them, occupy their offices, and force them out of business. If it can happen in Bolivia, it can happen in India. It can happen in Australia. Why not?

That's only a small suggestion. But remember that if the struggle were to resort to violence, it will lose vision, beauty, and imagination. Most dangerous of all, it will marginalize and eventually victimize women. And a political struggle that does not have women at the heart of it, above it, below it, and within it is no struggle at all.

The point is that the battle must be joined. As the wonderful American historian Howard Zinn put it, "You can't be neutral on a moving train."

BREAKING THE NEWS

THIS READER GOES to press almost five years to the day since December 13, 2001, when five men (some say six) drove through the gates of the Indian Parliament in a white Ambassador car and attempted what looked like an astonishingly incompetent terrorist strike.

Consummate competence appeared to be the hallmark of everything that followed: the gathering of evidence, the speed of the investigation by the Special Cell of the Delhi police, the arrest and charge sheeting of the accused, and the forty-month-long judicial process that began with the fast-track trial court.

The operative phrase in all of this is "appeared to be." If you follow the story carefully, you'll encounter two sets of masks. First the mask of consummate competence (accused arrested, "case cracked" in two days flat), and then, when things began to come undone, the benign mask of shambling incompetence (shoddy evidence, procedural flaws, material contradictions). But underneath all of this, as each of the essays in this collection shows, is something more sinister, more worrying. Over the last

---

This chapter was the introduction to *13 December, A Reader: The Strange Case of the Attack on the Indian Parliament* (Delhi: Penguin India, 2006).

few years the worries have grown into a mountain of misgivings, impossible to ignore.

The doubts set in early on, when on December 14, 2001, the day after the Parliament attack, the police arrested S. A. R. Geelani, a young lecturer in Delhi University. He was one of four people who were arrested. His outraged colleagues and friends, certain he had been framed, contacted the well-known lawyer Nandita Haksar and asked her to take on his case. This marked the beginning of a campaign for the fair trial of Geelani. It flew in the face of mass hysteria and corrosive propaganda enthusiastically disseminated by the mass media. The campaign was successful, and Geelani was eventually acquitted, along with Afsan Guru, co-accused in the same case.

Geelani's acquittal blew a gaping hole in the prosecution's version of the Parliament attack. But in some odd way, in the public mind, the acquittal of two of the accused only confirmed the guilt of the other two. When the government announced that Mohammad Afzal Guru, Accused Number One in the case, would be hanged on October 20, 2006, it seemed as though most people welcomed the news not just with approval, but morbid excitement. But then, once again, the questions resurfaced.

To see through the prosecution's case against Geelani was relatively easy. He was plucked out of thin air and transplanted into the center of the "conspiracy" as its kingpin. Afzal was different. He had been extruded through the sewage system of the hell that Kashmir has become. He surfaced through a manhole, covered in shit (and when he emerged, policemen in the Special Cell pissed on him). The first thing they made him do was a "media confession" in which he implicated himself completely in the attack. The speed with which this happened made many of us believe that he was indeed guilty as charged. It was only much later that the circumstances under which this "confession" was made were revealed, and even the Supreme Court set it aside, saying that the police had violated legal safeguards.

From the very beginning there was nothing pristine or simple about Afzal's case. Even today Afzal does not claim complete innocence. It is the nature of his involvement that is being contested. For instance, was he coerced, tortured, and blackmailed into playing even the peripheral part he played? He didn't have a lawyer to put out his version of the story or help anyone to sift through the tangle of lies and fabrications. Various individuals worked it out for themselves. These essays by a group of lawyers, academics, journalists, and writers represent that body of work. It has fractured what—only recently—appeared to be a national consensus interwoven with mass hysteria. We're late at the barricades, but we're here.

Most people, or let's say many people, when they encounter real facts and a logical argument, do begin to ask the right questions. This is exactly what has begun to happen on the Parliament attack case. The questions have created public pressure. The pressure has created fissures, and through these fissures those who have come under the scanner—shadowy individuals, counterintelligence and security agencies, political parties—are beginning to surface. They wave flags, hurl abuse, issue hot denials, and cover their tracks with more and more untruths. Thus they reveal themselves.

Public unease continues to grow. A group of citizens has come together as a committee (chaired by Nirmala Deshpande) to publicly demand a parliamentary inquiry into the episode. There is an online petition demanding the same thing. Thousands of people have signed on. Every day new articles appear in the papers and on the Internet. At least half a dozen websites are following the developments closely. They raise questions about how Mohammad Afzal, who never had proper legal representation, can be sentenced to death, without having had an opportunity to be heard, without a fair trial. They raise questions about fabricated evidence, procedural flaws, and the outright lies that were presented in court and published in newspapers. They show how there is hardly a single piece of evidence that stands up to scrutiny.

And then, there are even more disturbing questions that have been raised, which range beyond the fate of Mohammad Afzal. Here are thirteen questions about December 13:

Question 1: For months before the attack on Parliament, both the government and the police had been saying that Parliament could be attacked. On December 12, 2001, at an informal meeting, prime minister Atal Bihari Vajpayee warned of an imminent attack on Parliament. On December 13, Parliament was attacked. Given that there was an "improved security drill," how did a car bomb packed with explosives enter the parliament complex?

Question 2: Within days of the attack, the Special Cell of Delhi police said it was a meticulously planned joint operation of Jaish-e-Mohammed and Lashkar-e-Taiba. They said the attack was led by a man called "Mohammad" who was also involved in the hijacking of IC-814 in 1998. (This was later refuted by the Central Bureau of Investigation.) None of this was ever proved in court. What evidence did the Special Cell have for its claim?

Question 3: The entire attack was recorded live on closed-circuit television (CCTV). Congress Party MP Kapil Sibal demanded in Parliament that the CCTV recording be shown to the members. He was supported by the deputy chairman of the Rajya Sabha, Najma Heptullah, who said that there was confusion about the details of the event. The chief whip of the Congress Party, Priya Ranjan Dasmunshi, said, "I counted six men getting out of the car. But only five were killed. The closed-circuit TV camera recording clearly showed the six men." If Dasmunshi was right, why did the police say that there were only five people in the car? Who was the sixth person? Where is he now? Why was the CCTV recording not produced by the prosecution as evidence in the trial? Why was it not released for public viewing?

Question 4: Why was Parliament adjourned after some of these questions were raised?

Question 5: A few days after December 13, the government declared that it had "incontrovertible proof" of Pakistan's involvement in the attack and announced a massive mobilization of almost half a million soldiers to the Indo-Pakistan border. The subcontinent was pushed to the brink of nuclear war. Apart from Afzal's "confession," extracted under torture (and later set aside by the Supreme Court), what was the "incontrovertible proof"?

Question 6: Is it true that the military mobilization to the Pakistan border had begun long before the December 13 attack?

Question 7: How much did this military standoff, which lasted for nearly a year, cost? How many soldiers died in the process? How many soldiers and civilians died because of mishandled land mines, and how many peasants lost their homes and land because trucks and tanks were rolling through their villages, and land mines were being planted in their fields?

Question 8: In a criminal investigation it is vital for the police to show how the evidence gathered at the scene of the attack led them to the accused. How did the police reach Mohammad Afzal? The Special Cell says S. A. R. Geelani led them to Afzal. But the message to look out for Afzal was actually flashed to the Srinagar police before Geelani was arrested. So how did the Special Cell connect Afzal to the December 13 attack?

Question 9: The courts acknowledge that Afzal was a surrendered militant who was in regular contact with the security forces, particularly the Special Task Force (STF) of Jammu and Kashmir police. How do the security forces explain the fact that a person under their surveillance was able to conspire in a major militant operation?

Question 10: Is it plausible that organizations like Lashkar-e-Taiba or Jaish-e-Mohammed would rely on a person who had been in and out of STF torture chambers, and was under constant police surveillance, as the principal link for a major operation?

Question 11: In his statement before the court, Afzal says that he was introduced to "Mohammad" and instructed to take him to Delhi by a man called Tariq, who was working with the STF. Tariq was named in the police charge sheet. Who is Tariq and where is he now?

Question 12: On December 19, 2001, six days after the Parliament attack, Police Commissioner S. M. Shangari, Thane (Maharashtra), identified one of the attackers killed in the Parliament attack as Mohammad Yasin Fateh Mohammad (alias Abu Hamza) of the Lashkar-e-Taiba, who had been arrested in Mumbai in November 2000 and immediately handed over to the Jammu and Kashmir police. He gave detailed descriptions to support his statement. If Police Commissioner Shangari was right, how did Mohammad Yasin, a man in the custody of the Jammu and Kashmir police, end up participating in the Parliament attack? If he was wrong, where is Mohammad Yasin now?

Question 13: Why is it that we still don't know who the five dead "terrorists" killed in the Parliament attack are?

These questions, examined cumulatively, point to something far more serious than incompetence. The words that come to mind are complicity, collusion, and involvement. There's no need for us to feign shock or shrink from thinking these thoughts and saying them out loud. Governments and their intelligence agencies have a hoary tradition of using strategies like this to further their own ends. (Look up the burning of the Reichstag and the rise of Nazi power in Germany, 1933; or Operation Gladio, in which European intelligence agencies "created" acts of terrorism, especially in Italy, in order to discredit militant groups like the Red Brigade.)

The official response to all of these questions has been dead silence. As things stand, the execution of Afzal has been postponed while the president considers his clemency petition. Meanwhile the Bharatiya Janata Party announced that it would turn "Hang Afzal" into a national campaign. The campaign was fueled by the usual stale cocktail of religious chauvinism, nationalism, and strategic falsehoods. But it doesn't seem to have taken off. Now other avenues are being explored. M. S. Bitta of the All India Anti-Terrorist Front is parading around the families of some of the security personnel who were killed during the attack. They have threatened to return the government's posthumous bravery medals if Afzal is not hanged by December 13. (On balance, it might not be a bad idea for them to turn in those medals until they really know who the attackers were working for.)

The main strategy seems to be to create confusion and po-larize the debate on communal lines. The editor of the *Pioneer* newspaper writes in his columns that Mohammad Afzal was actually one of the men who attacked Parliament, that he was the first to open fire and kill at least three security guards. The columnist Swapan Dasgupta, in an article titled "You Can't Be Good to Evil," suggests that if Afzal is not hanged there would be no point in celebrating the victory of good over evil at Dussehra or Durga Puja. It's hard to believe that falsehoods like this stem only from a poor grasp of facts.

In the business of spreading confusion, the mass media, par-ticularly television journalists, can be counted on to be perfect collaborators. On discussions, chat shows, and "special reports," we have television anchors playing around with crucial facts, like young children in a sandpit. Torturers, estranged brothers, senior police officers, and politicians are emerging from the woodwork and talking. The more they talk, the more interesting it all becomes.

At the end of November 2006, Afzal's older brother Aijaz made it onto a national news channel (CNN-IBN). He was featured on hidden camera, on what was meant to be a "sting" operation, making—we were asked to believe—stunning revelations. Aijaz's story had already been on offer to various journalists on the streets of Delhi for weeks. People were wary of him because his rift with his brother's wife and family is well known. More significantly, in Kashmir he is known to have a relationship with the STF. More than one person has suggested an audit of his newfound assets.

But here he was now, on the national news, endorsing the Supreme Court decision to hang his brother. Then, saying Afzal had never surrendered, and that it was he (Aijaz) who surrendered his brother's weapon to the Border Security Force! And since he had never surrendered, Aijaz was able to "confirm" that Afzal was an active militant with the Jaish-e-Mohammed and that Ghazi Baba, chief of operations of the Jaish, used to regularly hold meetings in their home. (Aijaz claims that when Ghazi Baba was killed, he was called in by the police to identify the body.) On the whole, it sounded as though there had been a case of mistaken identity— and that given how much he knew, and all he was admitting, Aijaz should have been the one in custody instead of Afzal.

We must keep in mind that behind both Aijaz and Afzal's "media confessions," spaced five years apart, is the invisible hand of the STF, the dreaded counterinsurgency outfit in Kashmir. They can make anyone say anything at any time. Their methods (both punitive and remunerative) are familiar to every man, woman, and child in the Kashmir valley. At a time like this, for a responsible news channel to announce that their "investigation finds that Afzal was a Jaish militant," based on totally unreliable testimony, is dangerous and irresponsible. (Since when did what our brothers say about us become admissible evidence? My brother, for instance, will testify that I'm God's gift to the universe. I could dredge up a couple of aunts who'd say I'm a Jaish militant. For a price.) How can family feuds be dressed up as breaking news?

The other character who is rapidly emerging from the shadowy periphery and wading onto center stage is deputy superintendent of police Dravinder Singh of the STF. He is the man named by Afzal as the police officer who held him in illegal detention and tortured him in the STF camp at Humhama in Srinagar, only a few months before the Parliament attack. In a letter to his lawyer Sushil Kumar, Afzal says that several of the calls made to him and Mohammad (the man killed in the attack) can be traced to Dravinder Singh. Of course no attempt was made to trace these calls.

Dravinder Singh was also showcased on the CNN-IBN show, on the by-now ubiquitous low-angle shots, camera shake and all. It seemed a bit unnecessary, because Dravinder Singh has been talking a lot these days. He's done recorded interviews, on the phone as well as face to face, saying exactly the same shocking things. Weeks before the sting operation, in a recorded interview to Parvaiz Bukhari (at that time a freelance journalist based in Srinagar), he said:

> I did interrogate and torture him [Afzal] at my camp for several days. And we never recorded his arrest in the books anywhere. His description of torture at my camp is true. That was the procedure those days and we did pour petrol in his ass and gave him electric shocks. But I could not break him. He did not reveal anything to me despite our hardest possible interrogation. We tortured him enough for Ghazi Baba but he did not break. He looked like a "bhondu" those days, what you call a "chootya" type. And I had a reputation for torture, interrogation, and breaking suspects. If anybody came out of my interrogation clean, nobody would ever touch him again. He would be considered clean for good by the whole department.

On TV this boasting spiraled into policy making. "Torture is the only deterrent for terrorism," he said, "I do it for the nation." He didn't bother to explain why or how the "bhondu" that he tortured and subsequently released allegedly went on to become the diabolical mastermind of the Parliament attack. Dravinder Singh then said that Afzal was a Jaish militant. If this is true, why wasn't the evidence placed before the courts? And why on earth was Afzal released? Why wasn't he watched? There is a definite attempt to try and dismiss this as incompetence. But given everything we know now, it would take all of Dravinder Singh's delicate professional skills to make some of us believe that.

Meanwhile, right-wing commentators have consistently taken to referring to Afzal as a Jaish-e-Mohammed militant. It's as though instructions have been issued that this is to be the party line. They have absolutely no evidence to back their claim, but they know that repeating something often enough makes it the "truth." As part of the campaign to portray Afzal as an "active" militant and not a surrendered militant, S. M. Sahai, inspector general, Kashmir, Jammu and Kashmir police, appeared on TV to say that he had found no evidence in his records that Afzal had surrendered. It would have been odd if he had, because in 1993 Afzal surrendered not to the Jammu and Kashmir police, but to the Border Security Force. But why would a TV journalist bother with that kind of detail? And why does a senior police officer need to become part of this game of smoke and mirrors?

The official version of the story of the Parliament attack is very quickly coming apart at the seams.

Even the Supreme Court judgment, with all its flaws of logic and leaps of faith, does not accuse Mohammad Afzal of being the mastermind of the attack. So who was the mastermind? If Mohammad Afzal is hanged, we may never know. But L. K. Advani, leader of the opposition, wants him hanged at once. Even a day's delay, he says, is against the national interest. Why? What's the hurry? The man is locked up in a high-security cell on death row. He's not allowed out of his cell for even five minutes a day. What harm can he do? Talk? Write, perhaps? Surely (even in L. K. Advani's own narrow interpretation of the term) it's in the national interest not to hang Afzal. At least not until there is an inquiry that reveals what the real story is and who actually attacked Parliament.

Among the people who have appealed against Mohammad Afzal's death sentence are those who are opposed to capital punishment on principle. They have asked that his death sentence be commuted to a life sentence. To sentence a man who has not had a fair trial, and has not had the opportunity to be heard, to a life sentence is less cruel but just as arbitrary as sentencing him to death. The right thing to do would be to order a retrial of Afzal's case and an impartial, transparent inquiry into the December 13 Parliament attack. It is utterly demonic to leave a man locked up alone in a prison cell, day after day, week after week, leaving him and his family to guess which day will be the last day of his life.

A genuine inquiry would have to mean far more than just a political witch hunt. It would have to look into the part played by intelligence, counterinsurgency, and security agencies as well. Offenses such as the fabrication of evidence and the blatant violation of procedural norms have already been established in the courts, but they look very much like just the tip of the iceberg. We now have a police officer admitting (boasting) on record that he was involved in the illegal detention and torture of a fellow citizen. Is all of this acceptable to the people, the government, and the courts of this country?

Given the track record of Indian governments (past and present, right, left, and center), it is naive—perhaps utopian is a better word—to hope that it will ever have the courage to institute an inquiry that will once and for all uncover the real story. A maintenance dose of pusillanimity is probably encrypted in all governments. But hope has little to do with reason.

"Ironically, the era of the free market has led to the most successful secessionist struggle ever waged in India—the secession of the middle and upper classes to a country of their own, somewhere up in the stratosphere where they merge with the rest of the world's elite. This Kingdom in the Sky is a complete universe in itself, hermetically sealed from the rest of India. It has its own newspapers, films, television programs, morality plays, transport systems, malls, and intellectuals."

"AND HIS LIFE SHOULD BECOME EXTINCT": THE VERY STRANGE STORY OF THE ATTACK ON THE INDIAN PARLIAMENT

WE KNOW THIS much: On December 13, 2001, the Indian Parliament was in its winter session. (The National Democratic Alliance government led by the Bharatiya Janata Party was under attack for yet another corruption scandal.) At 11:30 a.m., five armed men in a white Ambassador car outfitted with an improvised explosive device drove through the gates of Parliament House in New Delhi. When they were challenged, they jumped out of the car and opened fire. In the gun battle that followed, all the attackers were killed. Eight security personnel and a gardener were killed, too. The dead terrorists, the police said, had enough explosives to blow up the Parliament building and enough ammunition to take on a whole battalion of soldiers. Unlike most terrorists, these five left behind a thick

This essay first appeared in *Outlook*, October 30, 2006.

trail of evidence—weapons, mobile phones, phone numbers, ID cards, photographs, packets of dried fruit, and even a love letter.

Not surprisingly, prime minister A. B. Vajpayee seized the opportunity to compare the assault to the September 11 attacks in the United States that had happened only three months previously.

On December 14, 2001, the day after the attack on Parliament, the Special Cell of the Delhi police claimed it had tracked down several people suspected to have been involved in the conspiracy. A day later, on December 15, it announced that it had "cracked the case": the attack, the police said, was a joint operation carried out by two Pakistan-based terrorist groups, Lashkar-e-Taiba and Jaish-e-Mohammed. Twelve people were named as being part of the conspiracy: Ghazi Baba of the Jaish (Usual Suspect I); Maulana Masood Azhar, also of the Jaish (Usual Suspect II); Tariq Ahmed (a "Pakistani"); five deceased "Pakistani terrorists" (we still don't know who they are); three Kashmiri men, S. A. R. Geelani, Shaukat Hussain Guru, and Mohammad Afzal; and Shaukat's wife, Afsan Guru. These were the only four to be arrested.

In the tense days that followed, Parliament was adjourned. On December 21, India recalled its high commissioner from Pakistan; suspended air, rail, and bus communications; and banned overflights. It put into motion a massive mobilization of its war machinery and moved more than half a million troops to the Pakistan border. Foreign embassies evacuated their staff and citizens, and tourists traveling to India were issued cautionary travel advisories. The world watched with bated breath as the subcontinent was taken to the brink of nuclear war. All this cost India an estimated Rs 100 billion ($2 billion) of public money. A few hundred soldiers died just in the panicky process of mobilization.

Almost three and a half years later, on August 4, 2005, the Supreme Court delivered its final judgment in the case. It endorsed the view that the Parliament attack be regarded as an act of war. It said, "The attempted attack on Parliament is an undoubted invasion of the sovereign attribute of the State including the government of India which is its alter ego . . . the deceased terrorists were roused and impelled to action by a strong anti-Indian feeling as the writing on the fake home ministry sticker found on the car (Ex PW1/8) reveals." It went on to say, "[T]he modus operandi adopted by the hardcore 'fidayeens' are all demonstrative of launching a war against the Government of India."

The text on the fake home ministry sticker read as follows:

INDIA IS A VERY BAD COUNTRY AND WE HATE INDIA WE WANT TO DESTROY INDIA AND WITH THE GRACE OF GOD WE WILL DO IT GOD IS WITH US AND WE WILL TRY OUR BEST. THE EDIET WAJPAI AND ADVANI WE WILL KILL THEM. THEY HAVE KILLED MANY INNOCENT PEOPLE AND THEY ARE VERY BAD PERSONS THERE BROTHER BUSH IS ALSO A VERY BAD PERSON HE WILL BE NEXT TARGET HE IS ALSO THE KILLER OF INNOCENT PEOPLE HE HAVE TO DIE AND WE WILL DO IT.

This subtly worded sticker-manifesto was displayed on the windscreen of the car bomb as it drove into Parliament. (Given the amount of text, it's a wonder the driver could see anything at all. Maybe that's why he collided with the vice president's cavalcade?)

The police charge sheet was filed in a special fast-track trial court designated for cases under the Prevention of Terrorism Act. On December 16, 2002, the trial court sentenced Geelani, Shaukat, and Afzal to death. Afsan Guru was sentenced to five years of rigorous imprisonment. A year later the high court acquitted Geelani and Afsan, but it upheld Shaukat's and Afzal's death sentence. Eventually, the Supreme Court too upheld the acquittals and reduced Shaukat's punishment to ten years of rigorous imprisonment. However, it not just confirmed but also enhanced Mohammad Afzal's sentence. He has been given three life sentences and a double death sentence.

In its August 4, 2005, judgment, the Supreme Court clearly says that there was no evidence that Mohammad Afzal belonged to any terrorist group or organization. But it also says, "As is the case with most of the conspiracies, there is and could be no direct evidence of the agreement amounting to criminal conspiracy. However, the circumstances, cumulatively weighed, would unerringly point to the collaboration of the accused Afzal with the slain 'fidayeen' terrorists."

So no direct evidence, but yes, circumstantial evidence.

A controversial paragraph in the judgment goes on to say, "The incident, which resulted in heavy casualties, had shaken the entire nation, and the collective conscience of the society will only be satisfied if capital punishment is awarded to the offender."

To invoke the "collective conscience of the society" to validate ritual murder, which is what the death penalty is, skates precariously close to valorizing lynch law. It's chilling to think that this has been laid upon us not by predatory politicians or sensation-seeking journalists (though they too have done that), but as an edict from the highest court in the land.

Spelling out the reasons for awarding Afzal the death penalty, the judgment goes on to say: "The appellant, who is a surrendered militant and who was bent on repeating the acts of treason against the nation, is a menace to the society and his life should become extinct."

This sentence combines flawed logic with absolute ignorance of what it means to be a "surrendered militant" in Kashmir today.

So: Should Mohammad Afzal's life become extinct?

A small but influential minority of intellectuals, activists, editors, lawyers, and public figures have objected to the death sentence as a matter of moral principle. They also argue that there is no empirical evidence to suggest that the death sentence works as a deterrent to terrorists. (How can it, when, in this age of fedayeen and suicide bombers, death seems to be the main attraction?)

If opinion polls, letters to the editor, and the reactions of live audiences in TV studios are a correct gauge of public opinion in India, then the lynch mob is expanding by the hour. It looks as though an overwhelming majority of Indian citizens would like to see Mohammad Afzal hanged every day, weekends included, for the next few years. L. K. Advani, leader of the opposition, displaying an unseemly sense of urgency, wants him to be hanged as soon as possible, without a moment's delay.

Meanwhile in Kashmir, public opinion is equally overwhelming. Huge angry protests make it increasingly obvious that if Afzal is hanged, the consequences will be political. Some protest what they see as a miscarriage of justice, but even as they protest, they do not expect justice from Indian courts. They have lived through too much brutality to believe in courts, affidavits, and justice anymore. Others would like to see Mohammad Afzal march to the gallows like Maqbool Butt, a proud martyr to the cause of Kashmir's freedom struggle. On the whole, most Kashmiris see Mohammad Afzal as a sort of prisoner of war being tried in the courts of an occupying power. (Which it undoubtedly is.) Naturally, political parties, in India as well as in Kashmir, have sniffed the breeze and are cynically closing in for the kill.

Sadly, in the midst of the frenzy, Afzal seems to have forfeited the right to be an individual, a real person anymore. He's become a vehicle for everybody's fantasies—nationalists, separatists, and anti–capital punishment activists. He has become India's great villain and Kashmir's great hero—proving only that whatever our pundits, policy makers, and peace gurus say, all these years later, the war in Kashmir has by no means ended.

In a situation as fraught and politicized as this, it's tempting to believe that the time to intervene has come and gone. After all, the judicial process lasted forty months, and the Supreme Court has examined the evidence before it. It has convicted two of the accused and acquitted the other two. Surely this in itself is proof of judicial objectivity? What more remains to be said?

There's another way of looking at it. Isn't it odd that the prosecution's case, proved to be so egregiously wrong in one half, has been so gloriously vindicated in the other?

❖

The story of Mohammad Afzal is fascinating precisely because he is not Maqbool Butt. Yet his story too is inextricably entwined with the story of the Kashmir valley. It's a story whose coordinates range far beyond the confines of courtrooms and the limited imagination of people who live in the secure heart of a self-declared "superpower." Mohammad Afzal's story has its origins in a war zone whose laws are beyond the pale of the fine arguments and delicate sensibilities of normal jurisprudence.

For all these reasons it is critical that we consider carefully the strange, sad, and utterly sinister story of the December 13 Parliament attack. It tells us a great deal about the way the world's largest "democracy" really works. It connects the biggest things to the smallest. It traces the pathways that connect what happens in the shadowy grottos of our police stations to what goes on in the cold, snowy streets of Paradise Valley; from there to the impersonal malign furies that bring nations to the brink of nuclear war. It raises specific questions that deserve specific—not ideological or rhetorical—answers.

On October 4 this year, I was one among a very small group of people who had gathered at Jantar Mantar in New Delhi to protest against Mohammad Afzal's death sentence. I was there because I believe Mohammad Afzal is only a pawn in a very sinister game. He's not the Dragon he's being made out to be, he's only the Dragon's footprint. And if the footprint is made to "become extinct," we'll never know who the Dragon was. Is.

Not surprisingly, that afternoon there were more journalists and TV crews than there were protesters. Most of the attention was on Ghalib, Afzal's angelic-looking little son. Kind-hearted people, not sure of what to do with a young boy whose father was going to the gallows, were plying him with ice cream and cold drinks. As I looked around at the people gathered there, I noted a sad little fact. The convener of the protest, the small, stocky man who was nervously introducing the speakers and making the announcements, was S. A. R. Geelani, a young lecturer in Arabic literature at Delhi University. Accused Number Three in the Parliament attack case. He was arrested on December 14, 2001, a day after the attack, by the Special Cell of the Delhi police. Though Geelani was brutally tortured in custody, though his family—his wife, young children, and brother—were illegally detained, he refused to confess to a crime he hadn't committed. Of course you wouldn't know this if you read newspapers in the days following his arrest. They carried detailed descriptions of an entirely imaginary, nonexistent confession. The Delhi police portrayed Geelani as the evil mastermind of the Indian end of the conspiracy. Its scriptwriters orchestrated a hateful propaganda campaign against him, which was eagerly amplified and embellished by a hypernationalistic, thrill-seeking media. The police knew perfectly well that in criminal trials, judges are not supposed to take cognizance of media reports. So they knew that their entirely cold-blooded fabrication of a profile for these "terrorists" would mold public opinion and create a climate for the trial. But it would not come in for any legal scrutiny.

Here are some of the malicious outright lies that appeared in the mainstream press:

Neeta Sharma and Arun Joshi, "Case Cracked: Jaish Behind Attack," *Hindustan Times*, December 16, 2001:

"In Delhi, the Special Cell detectives detained a Lecturer in Arabic, who teaches at Zakir Hussain College (Evening) . . . after it was established that he had received a call made by militants on his mobile phone."

"DU Lecturer Was Terror Plan Hub," *Times of India*, December 17, 2001:

"The attack on Parliament on December 13 was a joint operation of the Jaish-e-Mohammed (JeM) and Lash-kar-e-Toiba (LeT) terrorist groups in which a Delhi University lecturer, Syed A. R. Gilani, was one of the key facilitators in Delhi, Police Commissioner Ajai Raj Sharma said on Sunday."

Devesh K. Pandey, "Professor Guided the 'Fidayeen,'" *Hindu*, December 17, 2001:

"During interrogation Geelani disclosed that he was in the know of the conspiracy since the day the 'fidayeen' attack was planned."

Sutirtho Patranobis, "Don Lectured on Terror in Free Time," *Hindustan Times*, December 17, 2001:

"Investigations have revealed that by evening he was at the college teaching Arabic literature. In his free time, behind closed doors, either at his house or at Shaukat Hussain's, another suspect to be arrested, he took and gave lessons on terrorism."

"Professor's Proceeds," *Hindustan Times*, December 17, 2001:

"Geelani recently purchased a house for 22 lakhs [2,200,000 rupees ($44,300)] in West Delhi. Delhi Police are investigating how he came upon such a windfall."

Sujit Thakur, "*Aligarh se England tak chaatron mein aatank-waad ke beej bo raha tha Geelani*" (From Aligarh to England Geelani Sowed the Seeds of Terrorism), *Rashtriya Sahara*, December 18, 2001:

"According to sources and information collected by investigation agencies, Geelani has made a statement to the police that he was an agent of Jaish-e-Mohammed for a long time . . . It was because of Geelani's articulation, style of working and sound planning that in 2000 Jaish-e-Mohammed gave him the responsibility of spreading intellectual terrorism." (Translation mine.)

Swati Chaturvedi, "Terror Suspect Frequent Visitor to Pak[istan] Mission," *Hindustan Times*, December 21, 2001:
"During interrogation, Geelani has admitted that he had made frequent calls to Pakistan and was in touch with militants belonging to Jaish-e-Mohammed . . . Geelani said that he had been provided with funds by some members of the Jaish and told to buy two flats that could be used in militant operations."

"Person of the Week," *Sunday Times of India*, December 23, 2001:
"A cellphone proved his undoing. Delhi University's Syed A. R. Geelani was the first to be arrested in the December 13 case—a shocking reminder that the roots of terrorism go far and deep."

Zee TV trumped them all. It produced a film called *December 13th*, a "docudrama" that claimed to be the "truth based on the police charge-sheet." (A contradiction in terms, wouldn't you say?) The film was privately screened for prime minister A. B. Vajpayee and home minister L. K. Advani. Both men applauded the film. Their approbation was widely reported by the media.

The Supreme Court dismissed an appeal to stay the broadcast of the film on the grounds that judges are not influenced by the media. (Would the Supreme Court concede that even if judges are beyond being influenced by media reports, the "collective conscience of the society" might not be?) *December 13th* was broadcast on Zee TV's national network a few days before the fast-track trial court sentenced Geelani, Afzal, and Shaukat to death. Geelani eventually spent eighteen months in jail, many of them in solitary confinement, on death row.

He was released when the high court acquitted him and Afsan Guru. (Afsan, who was pregnant when she was arrested, had her baby in prison. Her experience broke her. She now suffers from a serious psychiatric condition.) The Supreme Court upheld the acquittal. It found absolutely no evidence to link Geelani with the Parliament attack or with any terrorist organization. Not a single newspaper or journalist or TV channel has seen fit to apologize to S. A. R. Geelani for their lies. But his troubles didn't end there. His acquittal left the Special Cell with a plot but no "mastermind." This, as we shall see, becomes something of a problem.

More importantly, Geelani was a free man now—free to meet the press, talk to lawyers, clear his name. On the evening of February 8, 2005, during the course of the final hearings at the Supreme Court, Geelani was making his way to his lawyer's house. A mysterious gunman appeared from the shadows and fired five bullets into his body. Miraculously, he survived. It was an unbelievable new twist to the story. Clearly somebody was worried about what he knew, what he would say. One would imagine that the police would give this investigation top priority, hoping it would throw up some vital new leads in the Parliament attack case. Instead, the Special Cell treated Geelani as though he was the prime suspect in his own assassination. They confiscated his computer and took away his car. Hundreds of activists gathered outside the hospital and called for an inquiry into the assassination attempt, which would include an investigation into the Special Cell itself. (Of course that never happened. More than a year has passed, but nobody shows any interest in pursuing the matter. Odd.)

So here he was now, S. A. R. Geelani, having survived this terrible ordeal, standing up in public at Jantar Mantar, saying that Mohammad Afzal didn't deserve a death sentence. How much easier it would be for him to keep his head down, stay at home. I was profoundly moved, humbled, by this quiet display of courage.

Across the line from S. A. R. Geelani, in the jostling crowd of journalists and photographers, trying his best to look inconspicuous in a lemon T-shirt and gabardine pants, holding a little tape-recorder, was another Gilani. Iftikhar Gilani. He had been in prison, too. He was arrested and taken into police custody on

June 9, 2002. At the time he was a reporter for the Jammu-based *Kashmir Times*. He was charged under the Official Secrets Act. His "crime" was that he possessed obsolete information on Indian troop deployment in "Indian-held Kashmir." (This "information," it turns out, was a published monograph by a Pakistani research institute and was freely available on the Internet for anybody who wished to download it.) Iftikhar Gilani's computer was seized. Intelligence Bureau officials tampered with his hard drive, meddled with the downloaded file, changed the words "Indian-held Kashmir" to "Jammu and Kashmir" to make it sound like an Indian document, and added the words "Only for Reference. Strictly Not For Circulation," to make it seem like a secret document smuggled out of the home ministry. The directorate general of military intelligence—though it had been given a photocopy of the monograph—ignored repeated appeals from Iftikhar Gilani's counsel, kept quiet, and refused to clarify the matter for a whole six months.

Once again the malicious lies put out by the Special Cell were obediently reproduced in the newspapers. Here are a few of the lies they told:

"Iftikhar Gilani, 35-year-old son-in-law of Hurriyat hardliner Syed Ali Shah Geelani, is believed to have admitted in a city court that he was an agent of Pakistan's spy agency."—Neeta Sharma, *Hindustan Times*, June 11, 2002

"Iftikhar Gilani was the pin-point man of Syed Salahuddin of Hizbul Mujahideen. Investigations have revealed that Iftikhar used to pass information to Salahuddin about the moves of Indian security agencies. He had camouflaged his real motives behind his journalist's facade so well that it took years to unmask him, well-placed sources said."—Pramod Kumar Singh, *Pioneer*, June 2002

"*Geelani ke damaad ke ghar aaykar chhaapon mein behisaab*

sampati wa samwaidansheil dastaweiẓ baramad" (Enormous wealth and sensitive documents recovered from the house of Geelani's son-in-law during income tax raids).—*Hindustan*, June 10, 2002

Never mind that the police charge sheet recorded a recovery of only 3,450 rupees ($69) from his house. Meanwhile, other media reports said that he had a three-bedroom flat, an undisclosed income of 2,200,000 rupees ($44,300), had evaded income tax of 7,900,000 rupees ($159,000), and that he and his wife were absconding to evade arrest.

But arrested he was. In jail, Iftikhar Gilani was beaten and abjectly humiliated. In his book *My Days in Prison* he tells of how, among other things, he was made to clean the toilet with his shirt and then wear the same shirt for days. After several months of court arguments and lobbying by his colleagues, when it became obvious that if the case against him continued it would lead to serious embarrassment, he was released.

Here he was now. A free man, a reporter come to Jantar Mantar to cover a story. It occurred to me that S. A. R. Geelani, Iftikhar Gilani, and Mohammad Afzal would have been in Tihar jail at the same time (along with scores of other less well-known Kashmiris whose stories we may never learn).

It can and will be argued that the cases of both S. A. R. Geelani and Iftikhar Gilani serve only to demonstrate the objectivity of the Indian judicial system and its capacity for self-correction; they do not discredit it. That's only partly true. Both Gilani and Geelani are fortunate to be Delhi-based Kashmiris with a community of articulate, middle-class peers—journalists and university teachers—who knew them well and rallied around them in their time of need. Geelani's lawyer Nandita Haksar put together an All India Defense Committee for her client (of which I was a member). There was a coordinated campaign by activists, lawyers, and journalists to rally behind Geelani. Well-known lawyers Ram Jethmalani, K. G. Kannabiran, and Vrinda Grover represented him. They exposed the case for what it was—a pack of absurd assumptions, suppositions, and outright lies, bolstered by fabricated evidence. So of course judicial objectivity exists. But it's a shy beast that lives somewhere deep in the labyrinth of our legal system. It shows itself rarely. It takes whole teams of top lawyers to coax it out of its lair and make it come out and play. It's what in newspaper-speak would be called a Herculean task. Mohammad Afzal did not have Hercules on his side.

❖

For five months, from the time he was arrested to the day the police charge sheet was filed, Mohammad Afzal, lodged in a high-security prison, had no legal defense, no legal advice. No top lawyers, no defense committee (in India or Kashmir), and no campaign. Of all the four accused, he was the most vulnerable. His case was far more complicated than Geelani's. Significantly, during much of this time, Afzal's younger brother Hilal was illegally detained by the Special Operations Group in Kashmir. He was released after the charge sheet was filed. (This is a piece of the puzzle that will only fall into place as the story unfolds.)

In a serious lapse of procedure, on December 20, 2001, the investigating officer, assistant commissioner of police Rajbir Singh (affectionately known as Delhi's "encounter specialist" for the number of "terrorists" he has killed in "encounters") called a press conference at the Special Cell. Mohammad Afzal was made to "confess" before the media. Deputy commissioner of police Ashok Chand told the press that Afzal had already confessed to the police. This turned out to be untrue. Afzal's formal confession to the police took place only the next day (after which he continued to remain in police custody and vulnerable to torture, another serious procedural lapse). In his media "confession" Afzal incriminated himself in the Parliament attack completely.

During the course of this "media confession," a curious

thing happened. In response to a direct question, Afzal clearly said that Geelani had nothing to do with the attack and was completely innocent. At this point, assistant commissioner of police Rajbir Singh shouted at him, forced him to shut up, and requested the media not to carry this part of Afzal's "confession." And they obeyed! The story came out only three months later when the television channel Aaj Tak rebroadcast the "confession" in a program called *"Hamle Ke Sau Din"* (Hundred Days of the Attack) and somehow kept this part in. Meanwhile in the eyes of the general public—who know little about the law and criminal procedure—Afzal's public "confession" only confirmed his guilt. The verdict of the "collective conscience of the society" would not have been hard to second-guess.

The day after this "media" confession, Afzal's "official" confession was extracted from him. The flawlessly structured, perfectly fluent narrative dictated in articulate English to deputy commissioner of police Ashok Chand (in the deputy's words, "he kept on narrating and I kept on writing") was delivered in a sealed envelope to a judicial magistrate. In this confession, Afzal, now the sheet-anchor of the prosecution's case, weaves a masterful tale that connected Ghazi Baba, Maulana Masood Azhar, a man called Tariq, and the five dead terrorists; their equipment, arms, and ammunition; home ministry passes, a laptop, and fake ID cards; detailed lists of exactly how many kilos of what chemical he bought from where, the exact ratio in which they were mixed to make explosives; and the exact times at which he made and received calls on which mobile number. (For some reason, by then Afzal had also changed his mind about Geelani and implicated him completely in the conspiracy.)

Each point of the "confession" corresponded perfectly with the evidence that the police had already gathered. In other words, Afzal's confessional statement slipped perfectly into the version that the police had already offered the press days ago, like Cinderella's foot into the glass slipper. (If it were a film, you could say it was a screenplay, which came with its own box of props. Actually, as we know now, it was made into a film. Zee TV owes Afzal some royalty payments.)

Eventually, both the high court and the Supreme Court set aside Afzal's confession, citing "lapses and violations of procedural safeguards." But Afzal's confession somehow survives, the phantom keystone in the prosecution's case. And before it was technically and legally set aside, the confessional document had already served a major extralegal purpose: On December 21, 2001, when the government of India launched its war effort against Pakistan, it said it had "clear and incontrovertible proof" of Pakistan's involvement. Afzal's confession was the only "proof" of Pakistan's involvement that the government had! Afzal's confession. And the sticker-manifesto. Think about it. On the basis of this illegal confession extracted under torture, hundreds of thousands of soldiers were moved to the Pakistan border at huge cost to the public exchequer, and the subcontinent devolved into a game of nuclear brinkmanship in which the whole world was held hostage.

Big Whispered Question: Could it have been the other way around? Did the confession precipitate the war, or did the need for a war precipitate the need for the confession?

Later, when Afzal's confession was set aside by the higher courts, all talk of Jaish-e-Mohammed and Lashkar-e-Taiba ceased. The only other link to Pakistan was the identity of the five dead fedayeen. Mohammad Afzal, still in police custody, identified them as Mohammed, Rana, Raja, Hamza, and Haider. The home minister said they "looked like Pakistanis," the police said they were Pakistanis, and the trial court judge said they were Pakistanis. And there the matter rests. (Had we been told that their names were Happy, Bouncy, Lucky, Jolly, and Kidingamani from Scandinavia, we would have had to accept that, too.)

We still don't know who they really are or where they're from. Is anyone curious? Doesn't look like it. The high court said the "identity of the five deceased thus stands established. Even otherwise it makes no difference. What is relevant is the association of the accused with the said five persons and not their names."

In his Statement of the Accused (which, unlike the confession, is made in court and not police custody), Afzal says: "I had not identified any terrorist. Police told me the names of terrorists and forced me to identify them." But by then it was too late for him. On the first day of the trial, the lawyer appointed by the trial court judge agreed to accept Afzal's identification of the bodies and the postmortem reports as undisputed evidence without formal proof. This baffling move was to have serious consequences for Afzal. To quote from the Supreme Court judgment, "The first circumstance against the accused Afzal is that Afzal knew who the deceased terrorists were. He identified the dead bodies of the deceased terrorists. On this aspect the evidence remains unshattered."

Of course it's possible that the dead terrorists were foreign militants. But it is just as possible that they were not. Killing people and falsely identifying them as "foreign terrorists," or falsely identifying dead people as "foreign terrorists," or falsely identifying living people as terrorists, is not uncommon among the police or security forces either in Kashmir or even on the streets of Delhi.

The best known among the many well-documented cases in Kashmir, one that went on to become an international scandal, is the killing that took place after the Chhittisinghpura massacre. On the night of April 20, 2000, just before US president Bill Clinton arrived in New Delhi, thirty-five Sikhs were killed in the village of Chhittisinghpura by "unidentified gunmen" wearing Indian Army uniforms. (In Kashmir many people suspected that Indian security forces were behind the massacre.) Five days later the Special Operations Group and the Rashtriya Rifles, a counterinsurgency unit of the army, killed five people in a joint operation outside a village called Pathribal. The next morning they announced that the men were the Pakistan-based foreign militants who had killed the Sikhs in Chhittisinghpura. The bodies were found burned and disfigured. Under their (unburned) army uniforms, they were in ordinary civilian clothes. It turned out that they were all local people, rounded up from Anantnag district and brutally killed in cold blood.

There are others:

October 20, 2003: The Srinagar newspaper *Alsafa* printed a picture of a "Pakistani militant" who the Eighteenth Rashtriya Rifles claimed they had killed while he was trying to storm an army camp. A baker in Kupwara, Wali Khan, saw the picture and recognized it as his son, Farooq Ahmed Khan, who had been picked up by soldiers in a Gypsy (an SUV) two months earlier. His body was finally exhumed more than a year later.

April 20, 2004: The Eighteenth Rashtriya Rifles posted in the Lolab valley claimed it had killed four foreign militants in a fierce encounter. It later turned out that all four were ordinary laborers from Jammu, hired by the army and taken to Kupwara. An anonymous letter tipped off the laborers' families who traveled to Kupwara and eventually had the bodies exhumed.

November 9, 2004: The army showcased forty-seven surrendered "militants" to the press at Nagrota, Jammu, in the presence of the general officer commanding Sixteenth Corps of the Indian Army and the director general of police, Jammu and Kashmir. The Jammu and Kashmir police later found that twenty-seven of them were just unemployed men who had been given fake names and fake aliases and promised government jobs in return for playing their part in the charade.

These are just a few quick examples to illustrate the fact that in the absence of any other evidence, the police's word is just not good enough.

❖

The hearings in the fast-track trial court began in May 2002. Let's not forget the climate in which the trial took place. The frenzy over the 9/11 attacks was still in the air. The United

States was gloating over its victory in Afghanistan. Gujarat was convulsed by communal frenzy. A few months previously, coach S-6 of the Sabarmati Express had been set on fire and fifty-eight Hindu pilgrims had been burned alive inside. As "revenge," in an orchestrated pogrom, two thousand Muslims were publicly butchered and more than one hundred and fifty thousand driven from their homes.

For Afzal, everything that could go wrong went wrong. He was incarcerated in a high-security prison, with no access to the outside world, and no money to hire a lawyer professionally. Three weeks into the trial, the lawyer appointed by the court asked to be discharged from the case because she had now been professionally hired to be on the team of lawyers for S. A. R. Geelani's defense. The court appointed her junior, a lawyer with very little experience, to represent Afzal. He did not once visit his client in jail to take instructions. He did not summon a single witness for Afzal's defense and barely cross-examined any of the prosecution witnesses. Five days after he was appointed, on July 8, Afzal asked the court for another lawyer and gave the court a list of lawyers whom he hoped the court might hire for him. Each of them refused. (Given the frenzy of propaganda in the media, it was hardly surprising. At a later stage of the trial, when senior advocate Ram Jethmalani agreed to represent Geelani, Shiv Sena mobs ransacked his Mumbai office.) The judge expressed his inability to do anything about this and gave Afzal the right to cross-examine witnesses. It's astonishing for the judge to expect a layperson to be able cross-examine witnesses in a criminal trial. It's a virtually impossible task for someone who does not have a sophisticated understanding of criminal law, including new laws that had just been passed, like the Prevention of Terrorism Act, and the amendments to the Evidence Act and the Telegraph Act. Even experienced lawyers had to work overtime to bring themselves up to date.

The case against Afzal was built up in the trial court on the

strength of the testimonies of almost eighty prosecution witnesses: landlords, shopkeepers, technicians from cell-phone
companies, the police themselves. This was a crucial period
of the trial, when the legal foundation of the case was being
laid. It required meticulous, backbreaking legal work in which
evidence needed to be amassed and put on record, witnesses
for the defense summoned, and testimonies from prosecution
witnesses cross-examined. Even if the verdict of the trial court
went against the accused (trial courts are notoriously conservative), the evidence could then be worked on by lawyers in
the higher courts. Through this absolutely critical period, Afzal
went virtually undefended. It was at this stage that the bottom
fell out of his case, and the noose tightened around his neck.

Even still, during the trial, the skeletons began to clatter out
of the Special Cell's cupboard in an embarrassing heap. It became clear that the accumulation of lies, fabrications, forged
documents, and serious lapses in procedure began from the
very first day of the investigation. While the Delhi High Court
and Supreme Court judgments have pointed these things out,
they have just wagged an admonitory finger at the police, or occasionally called it a "disturbing feature," which is a disturbing
feature in itself. At no point in the trial have the police been seriously reprimanded, let alone penalized. In fact, almost every
step of the way, the Special Cell displayed an egregious disregard for procedural norms. The shoddy callousness with which
the investigations were carried out demonstrates a worrying
belief that they wouldn't be "found out," and if they were, it
wouldn't matter very much. Their confidence does not seem to
have been misplaced.

There is fudging in almost every part of the investigation.

Consider the time and place of the arrests and seizures: The
Delhi police said that Afzal and Shaukat were arrested in Srinagar based on information given to them by Geelani following his arrest. The court records show that the message to look
out for Shaukat and Afzal was flashed to the Srinagar police on

December 15 at 5:45 a.m. But according to the Delhi police's records, Geelani was only arrested in Delhi on December 15 at 10:00 a.m.—four hours after they had started looking for Afzal and Shaukat in Srinagar. They haven't been able to explain this discrepancy. The high court judgment puts it on record that the police version contains a "material contradiction" and cannot be true. It goes down as a "disturbing feature." Why the Delhi police needed to lie remains unasked—and unanswered.

When the police arrest somebody, procedure requires them to have public witnesses for the arrest who sign an arrest memo and a seizure memo for what they may have "seized" from those who have been arrested—goods, cash, documents, whatever. The police claim they arrested Afzal and Shaukat together on December 15 at 11:00 a.m. in Srinagar. They say they "seized" the truck the two men were fleeing in (it was registered in the name of Shaukat's wife). They also say they seized a Nokia mobile phone, a laptop, and one million rupees ($20,100) from Afzal. In his Statement of the Accused, Afzal says he was arrested at a bus stop in Srinagar and that no laptop, mobile phone, or money was "seized" from him.

Scandalously, the arrest memos for both Afzal and Shaukat have been signed in Delhi, by Bismillah, Geelani's younger brother, who was at the time being held in illegal confinement at the Lodhi Road Police Station. Meanwhile, the two witnesses who signed the seizure memo for the phone, the laptop, and the one million rupees ($20,100) are both from the Jammu and Kashmir police. One of them is Head Constable Mohammed Akbar (Prosecution Witness 62) who, as we shall see later, is no stranger to Mohammad Afzal, and is not just any old policeman who happened to be passing by. Even by the Jammu and Kashmir police's own admission they first located Afzal and Shaukat in Parimpura Fruit Mandi. For reasons they don't state, the police didn't arrest them there. They say they followed them to a less public place—where there were no public witnesses.

So here's another serious inconsistency in the prosecution's case. Of this the high court judgment says "the time of arrest of accused persons has been seriously dented." Shockingly, it is at this contested time and place of arrest that the police claim to have recovered the most vital evidence that implicates Afzal in the conspiracy: the mobile phone and the laptop. Once again, in the matter of the date and time of the arrests, and in the alleged seizure of the incriminating laptop and the one million rupees ($20,100), we have only the word of the police against the word of a "terrorist."

The seizures continued: The seized laptop, the police said, contained the files that created the fake home ministry pass and the fake identity cards. It contained no other useful information. They claimed that Afzal was carrying it to Srinagar in order to return it to Ghazi Baba. The investigating officer, assistant commissioner of police Rajbir Singh, said that the hard disk of the computer had been sealed on January 16, 2002 (a whole month after the seizure). But the computer shows that it was accessed even after that date. The courts have considered this but taken no cognizance of it.

(On a speculative note, isn't it strange that the only incriminating information found on the computer were the files used to make the fake passes and ID cards? And a Zee TV film clip showing the Parliament building. If other incriminating information had been deleted, why wasn't this? And why did Ghazi Baba, chief of operations of an international terrorist organization, need a laptop—with bad artwork on it—so urgently?)

Consider the mobile phone call records: Stared at for long enough, a lot of the "hard evidence" produced by the Special Cell begins to look dubious. The backbone of the prosecution's case has to do with the recovery of mobile phones, SIM cards, computerized call records, and the testimonies of officials from cell phone companies and shopkeepers who sold the phones and SIM cards to Afzal and his accomplices. The call records that were produced to show that Shaukat, Afzal, Geelani, and Mohammad (one of the dead militants) had all been in touch with each other very close to the time of the attack were uncertified computer printouts, not even copies of primary documents. They were outputs of the billing system stored as text files that could have been easily doctored and at any time. For example, the call records that were produced show that two calls had been made at exactly the same time from the same SIM card, but from separate handsets with separate International Mobile Equipment Identity numbers. This means that either the SIM card had been cloned or the call records were doctored.

Consider the SIM card: To prop up its version of the story, the prosecution relies heavily on one particular mobile phone number—9811489429. The police say it was Afzal's number—the number that connected Afzal to Mohammad, Afzal to Shaukat, and Shaukat to Geelani. The police also say that this number was written on the back of the identity tags found on the dead terrorists. Pretty convenient. Lost Kitten! Call Mom at 9811489429.

It's worth mentioning that normal procedure requires evidence gathered at the scene of a crime to be sealed. The ID cards were never sealed and remained in the custody of the police and could have been tampered with at any time.

The only evidence the police have that 9811489429 was indeed Afzal's number is Afzal's confession, which as we have seen is no evidence at all. The SIM card has never been found. The police produced a prosecution witness, Kamal Kishore, who identified Afzal and said that he had sold him a Motorola phone and a SIM card on December 4, 2001. However, the call records the prosecution relied on show that that particular SIM card was already in use on November 6, a whole month before Afzal is supposed to have bought it. So either the witness is lying, or the call records are false. The high court glosses over this discrepancy by saying that Kamal Kishore had only said that he sold Afzal a SIM card, not this particular SIM card. The Supreme Court judgment loftily says, "The SIM card should necessarily have been sold to Afzal prior to 4.12.2001."

Consider the identification of the accused: A series of prosecution witnesses, most of them shopkeepers, identified Afzal as the man to whom they had sold various things: ammonium nitrate, aluminum powder, sulfur, a Sujata mixer-grinder, packets of dried fruit, and so on. Normal procedure would require these shopkeepers to pick Afzal out from a number of people in a test identification parade. This didn't happen. Instead, Afzal was identified by them when he "led" the police to these shops while he was in police custody and introduced to the witnesses as an accused in the Parliament attack. (Are we allowed to speculate about whether he led the police or the police led him to the shops? After all he was still in their custody, still vulnerable to torture. If his confession under these circumstances is legally suspect, then why not all of this?)

The judges have pondered the violation of these procedural norms but have not taken them very seriously. They said that they did not see why ordinary members of the public would have reason to falsely implicate an innocent person. But does this hold true, given the orgy of media propaganda that ordinary members of the public were subjected to, particularly in this case? Does this hold true, if you take into account the fact that ordinary shopkeepers, particularly those who sell electronic goods without receipts in the "gray market," are completely beholden to the Delhi police?

None of the inconsistencies that I have written about so far are the result of spectacular detective work on my part. A lot of them are documented in an excellent book titled *December 13: Terror over Democracy* by Nirmalangshu Mukherji; in two reports ("Trial of Errors" and "Balancing Act") published by the People's Union for Democratic Rights, Delhi; and most important of all, in the three thick volumes of judgments of the trial court, the high court, and the Supreme Court. All these are public documents, lying on my desk. Why is it that when there is this whole murky universe begging to be revealed, our TV channels are busy staging hollow debates between uninformed people and grasping politicians? Why is it that apart from a few sporadic independent commentators, our newspapers carry front-page stories about who the hangman is going to be and macabre details about the length (60 feet) and weight (3.75 kilograms) of the rope that will be used to hang Mohammad Afzal? Shall we pause for a moment to say a few hosannas for the "free" press?

❖

It's not an easy thing for most people to do, but if you can, unmoor yourself conceptually, if only for a moment, from the Police are Good / Terrorists are Evil ideology. The evidence on offer minus its ideological trappings opens up a chasm of terrifying possibilities. It points in directions in which most of us would prefer not to look.

The prize for the Most Ignored Legal Document in the entire case goes to the Statement of the Accused Mohammad Afzal under Section 313 of the Criminal Procedure Code. In this document, the evidence against him is put to him by the court in the form of questions. He can either accept the evidence or dispute it, and he has the opportunity to put down his version of his story in his own words. In Afzal's case, given that he has never had any real opportunity to be heard, this document tells his story in his voice.

In this document, Afzal accepts certain charges made against him by the prosecution. He accepts that he met a man called Tariq. He accepts that Tariq introduced him to a man called Mohammad. He accepts that he helped Mohammad come to Delhi and helped him to buy a second-hand white Ambassador car. He accepts that Mohammad was one of the five fedayeen who was killed in the attack. The important thing about Afzal's Statement of the Accused is that he makes no effort to completely absolve himself or claim innocence. But he puts his actions in a context that is devastating. Afzal's statement explains the peripheral part he played in the Parliament attack. But it also ushers us toward an understanding of some possible reasons for why the investigation was so shoddy, why it pulls up short at the most crucial junctures, and why it is vital that we do not dismiss this as just incompetence and shoddiness. Even if we don't believe Afzal, given what we do know about the trial and the role of the Special Cell, it is inexcusable not to look in the direction he's pointing. He gives specific information—names, places, dates. (This could not have been easy, given that his family, his brothers, his wife and young son live in Kashmir and are easy meat for the people he mentions in his deposition.)

In Afzal's words:

I live in Sopre [Sopore] Jammu and Kashmir [Jammu and Kasmir] and in the year 2000 when I was there army used to harass me almost daily, then said once a week. One Raja Mohan Rai used to tell me that I should give information to him about militants. I was a surrendered militant and all militants have to mark Attendance at Army Camp every Sunday. I was not being physically torture by me. He used to only just threatened me. I used to give him small information which I used to gather from newspaper, in order to save myself. In June/July 2000 I migrated from my village and went to town Baramullah. I was having a shop of distribution of surgical instruments which I was running on commission basis. One day when I was going on my scooter S.T.F. [Special Task Force] people came and picked me up and they continuously tortured me for five days. Somebody had given information to S.T.F. that I was again indulging in militant activities. That person was confronted with me and released in my presence. Then I was kept by them in custody for about 25 days and I got myself released by paying rupees 1 lakh [one hundred thousand rupees ($2,000)]. Special Cell People had confirmed this incident. Thereafter I was given a certificate by the S.T.F. and they made me a Special Police Officer for six months. They were knowing I will not work for them. Tariq met me in Palhalan S.T.F. camp where I was in custody of S.T.F. Tariq met me later on in Sri Nagar and told me he was basically working for S.T.F. I told him I was also working for S.T.F. Mohammad who *was killed in attack on Parliament was along with Tariq. Tariq told me he was from Keran sector of Kashmir and he told me that I should take Mohammad to Delhi as Mohammad has to go out of country from Delhi after some time. I don't know why I was caught by the police of Sri Nagar on 15.12.2001 [December 15, 2001]. I was boarding bus at Sri Nagar bus stop, for going home when police caught me. Witness Akbar who had deposed in the court that he had apprehended Shaukat and me in Sri Nagar had conducted a raid at my shop about a year prior to December 2001 and told me that I was selling fake surgical instruments and he took rupees 5,000/- [roughly $100] from me. I was tortured at Special Cell and one Bhoop Singh even compelled me to take urine and I saw family of S. A. R. Geelani also there, Geelani was in miserable condition. He was not in a position to stand. We were taken to doctor for examination but instructions used to be issued that we have to tell doctor that everything was alright with a threat that if we do not do so we be again tortured.*

He then asks the court's permission to add some more information.

Mohammad the slain terrorist of Parliament attack had come along with me from Kashmir. The person who handed him over to me is Tariq. Tariq is working with Security Force and S.T.F. JK Police. Tariq told me that if I face any problem due to Mohammad he will help me as he knew the security forces and S.T.F. very well . . . Tariq had told me that I just have to drop Mohammad at Delhi and do nothing else. And if I would not take Mohammad with me to Delhi I would be implicated in some other case. I under these circumstances brought Mohammad to Delhi under a compulsion without knowing he was a terrorist.

So now we have a picture emerging of someone who could be a key player. "Witness Akbar" (Prosecution Witness 62), Mohammed Akbar, head constable, Parimpora police station, the

Jammu and Kashmir policeman who signed the seizure memo at the time of Afzal's arrest. In a letter to Sushil Kumar, his Supreme Court lawyer, Afzal describes a chilling moment at one point in the trial. In the court, Witness Akbar, who had come from Srinagar to testify about the seizure memo, reassured Afzal in Kashmiri that "his family was alright." Afzal immediately recognized that this was a veiled threat. Afzal also says that after he was arrested in Srinagar he was taken to the Parimpora police station and beaten, and he was plainly told that his wife and family would suffer dire consequences if he did not cooperate. (We already know that Afzal's brother Hilal had been held in illegal detention by the Special Operations Group during some crucial months.)

In this letter, Afzal describes how he was tortured in the Special Task Force camp—with electrodes on his genitals and chilies and petrol in his anus. He mentions the name of deputy superintendent of police Dravinder Singh who said he needed him to do a "small job" for him in Delhi. He also says that some of the phone numbers mentioned in the charge sheet can be traced to an Special Task Force camp in Kashmir.

It is Afzal's story that gives us a glimpse into what life is really like in the Kashmir valley. It's only in the Noddy book version we read about in our newspapers that security forces battle militants and innocent Kashmiris are caught in the crossfire. In the adult version, Kashmir is a valley awash with militants, renegades, security forces, double-crossers, informers, spooks, blackmailers, blackmailees, extortionists, spies, both Indian and Pakistani intelligence agencies, human rights activists, NGOs, and unimaginable amounts of unaccounted-for money and weapons. There are not always clear lines that demarcate the boundaries between all these things and people. It's not easy to tell who is working for whom.

Truth, in Kashmir, is probably more dangerous than anything else. The deeper you dig, the worse it gets. At the bottom of the pit is the Special Operations Group and Special Task Force that Afzal talks about. These are the most ruthless, undisciplined, and dreaded elements of the Indian security apparatus in Kashmir. Unlike the more formal forces, they operate in a twilight zone where policemen, surrendered militants, renegades, and common criminals do business. They prey on the local population, particularly in rural Kashmir. Their primary victims are the thousands of young Kashmiri men who rose up in revolt in the anarchic uprising of the early 1990s and have since surrendered and are trying to live normal lives.

In 1989, when Afzal crossed the border to be trained as a militant, he was only twenty years old. He returned with no training, disillusioned with his experience. He put down his gun and enrolled himself in Delhi University. In 1993 without ever having been a practicing militant, he voluntarily surrendered to the Border Security Force. Illogically enough, it was at this point that his nightmares began. His surrender was treated as a crime and his life became a hell. Can young Kashmiri men be blamed if the lesson they draw from Afzal's story is that it would be not just stupid, but also insane to surrender their weapons and submit to the vast range of myriad cruelties the Indian state has on offer for them?

The story of Mohammad Afzal has enraged Kashmiris because his story is their story, too. What has happened to him could have happened, is happening, and has happened to thousands of young Kashmiri men and their families. The only difference is that their stories are played out in the dingy bowels of joint interrogation centers, army camps, and police stations where they have been burned, beaten, electrocuted, blackmailed, and killed, their bodies thrown out of the backs of trucks for passersby to find. Whereas Afzal's story is being performed like a piece of medieval theater on the national stage, in the clear light of day, with the legal sanction of a "fair trial," the hollow benefits of a "free" press, and all the pomp and ceremony of a so-called democracy.

If Afzal is hanged, we'll never know the answer to the real question: Who attacked the Indian Parliament? Was it Lashkar-e-Taiba? Jaish-e-Mohammed? Or does the answer lie somewhere deep in the secret heart of this country that we all live in and love and hate in our own beautiful, intricate, various, and thorny ways?

There ought to be a parliamentary inquiry into the December 13 attack on Parliament. While the inquiry is pending, Afzal's family in Sopore must be protected because they are vulnerable hostages in this bizarre story.

To hang Mohammad Afzal without knowing what really happened is a misdeed that will not easily be forgotten. Or forgiven. Nor should it be.

Notwithstanding the 10 Percent Growth Rate.

CUSTODIAL
CONFESSIONS, THE
MEDIA, AND THE LAW

THE SUPREME COURT of India has sentenced Mohammad Afzal, Accused Number One in the Parliament attack case, to death. It acknowledged that the evidence against him was not direct, only circumstantial, but in its now famously controversial statement it said: "The incident, which resulted in heavy casualties, has shaken the entire nation, and the collective conscience of the society will only be satisfied if capital punishment is awarded to the offender."

Is the "collective conscience" the same as majority opinion? Would it be fair to say that it is fashioned by the information we receive? And therefore, that in this case, the mass media has played a pivotal role in determining the final court verdict? If so, has it been accurate and truthful?

Now, five years later, when disturbing questions are being raised about the Parliament attack, is the Special Cell once again cleverly exploiting the frantic hunt for "breaking news"? Suddenly spurious "exposés" are finding their way onto prime-time

This essay was first published in the *Hindustan Times* on December 22, 2006.

TV. Unfortunately, some of India's best, most responsible news channels have been caught up in this game in which carelessness and incomprehension is as deadly as malice. (A few weeks ago we had a fiasco on CNN-IBN.)

Last week (December 16), on a ninety-minute prime-time show, NDTV showcased an "exclusive" video of Mohammad Afzal's "confession" made in police custody, in the days immediately following his arrest. At no point was it clarified that the "confession" was five years old.

Much has been said about the authenticity, reliability, and legality of confessions taken in police custody, as well as the circumstances under which this particular "confession" was extracted. Because of the very real danger that custodial torture will replace real investigation, the Indian Penal Code does not admit confessions made in police custody as legal evidence in a criminal trial. The Prevention of Terrorism Act was considered an outrage on civil rights and was eventually withdrawn, primarily because it made confessions obtained in police custody admissible as legal evidence. In fact, in the case of Afzal's "confession," the Supreme Court said the Special Cell had violated even the tenuous safeguards provided under the act, and set it aside as being illegal and unreliable. Even before this, the high court had already reprimanded the Special Cell sharply for forcing Afzal to incriminate himself publicly in a "media confession."

So what made NDTV showcase this thoroughly discredited old "confession" all over again? Why now? How did the Special Cell video find its way into their hands? Does it have something to do with the fact that Afzal's clemency petition is pending with the president of India and a curative petition asking for a retrial is pending in the Supreme Court? In her column in the *Hindustan Times*, Barkha Dutt, managing editor of NDTV, said the channel spent many hours "debating what the fairest way" was to show this video. Clearly, it was a serious decision and demands to be discussed seriously.

At the start of the show, for several minutes the image of Afzal "confessing" was inset with a text that said, "*Afzal ne court mein gunaa qabool kiya tha*" (Afzal has admitted his guilt in court). This is blatantly untrue. Then, for a full fifteen minutes the "confession" ran without comment. After this, an anchor came on and said, "*Sansad par hamle ki kahani, Afzal ki ʒubaani*" (The story of the Parliament attack, in Afzal's words). This, too, is a travesty of the truth. Well into the program a reporter informed us that Afzal had since withdrawn this "confession" and had claimed it had been extracted under torture. The smirking anchor then turned to one of the panelists, S. A. R. Geelani, who was also one of the accused in the case (and who knows a thing or two about torture and the Special Cell) and remarked that if this confession was "forced," then Afzal was a very good actor.

(The anchor has clearly never experienced torture. Or even read the wonderful Uruguayan writer, Eduardo Galeano—"The electric cattle prod turns anyone into a prolific storyteller." Nor has he known what it's like to be held in police custody in Delhi while his family was hostage—as Afzal's was—in the war zone that is Kashmir.)

Later on, the "confession" was juxtaposed with what the channel said was Afzal's statement to the court, but was actually the text of a letter he wrote to his high court lawyer in which he implicates the Special Task Force (STF) in Kashmir and describes how in the months before the Parliament attack the task force illegally detained and tortured him. NDTV does not tell us that a deputy superintendent of the STF has since confirmed that he did illegally detain and torture Afzal. Instead it uses Afzal's letter to discredit him further. The bold caption at the bottom of the frame read: "*Afzal ka badalta hua baiyan*" (Afzal's changing statements).

There is another serious ethical issue. In Afzal's confession to the Special Cell in December 2001 (as opposed to his "media confession"), he implicated S. A. R. Geelani and said he was the mastermind of the conspiracy. While this was in line with the Special Cell's charge sheet, it turned out to be false, and Geelani was acquitted by the Supreme Court. Why was this portion of Afzal's confession left out? So that the confession would seem less constructed, more plausible? Who made that decision to leave it out? NDTV or the Special Cell?

All this makes the broadcast of this program a seriously prejudicial act. It wasn't surprising to watch the "collective conscience" of society forming its opinion as the show unfolded. The SMS messages on the ticker tape said:

"*Afzal ko boti boti mein kaat ke kutton ko khila do*" (Cut him into bits and feed him to the dogs).

"*Afzal ke haath aur taang kaat ke, road mein bheek mangvaney chahiye*" (Cut off his arms and legs and make him beg).

Then in English: "Hang him by his balls in Lal Chowk. Hang him and hang those who are supporting him."

Even without Sharia courts, we seem to be doing just fine.

For the record, the reporter Neeta Sharma, credited several times on the program for procuring the video, has been previously exposed for publishing falsehoods, on the "encounter" in Ansal Plaza, on the Iftikhar Gilani case, and on the S. A. R. Geelani case—and now on this one. Neeta Sharma was formerly a reporter with the *Hindustan Times*. Publishing Special Cell handouts seems to have gotten her a promotion—from print journalism to TV.

This kind of thing really makes you wonder whether media houses have an inside track on the police and intelligence agencies, or whether it's the other way around.

The quietest guest on the panel was M. K. Dhar, a former joint director of the Intelligence Bureau. He was pretty enigmatic. He certainly didn't repeat what he has said in his astonishingly frank book *Open Secrets: India's Intelligence Unveiled*: "Some day or the other, taking advantage of the weakening fabric of our democracy, some unscrupulous intelligence men may gang up with ambitious Army Brass and change the political texture of the nation."

Weakening fabric of our democracy. I couldn't have put it better.

LISTENING TO GRASSHOPPERS: GENOCIDE, DENIAL, AND CELEBRATION

I NEVER MET Hrant Dink, a misfortune that will be mine for time to come. From what I know of him, of what he wrote, what he said and did, how he lived his life, I know that had I been here in Istanbul a year ago, I would have been among the one hundred thousand people who walked with his coffin in dead silence through the wintry streets of this city, with banners saying, "We are all Armenians," "We are all Hrant Dink." Perhaps I'd have carried the one that said, "One and a half million plus one."

I wonder what thoughts would have gone through my head as I walked beside his coffin. Maybe I would have heard a reprise of the voice of Araxie Barsamian, mother of my friend David Barsamian, telling the story of what happened to her

---

This article was delivered as a lecture in Istanbul on January 18, 2008, to commemorate the first anniversary of the assassination of Hrant Dink, editor of the Turkish-Armenian paper *Agos*. It appeared in *Outlook*, February 4, 2008, and the *International Socialist Review*, Issue 58, March–April 2008.

and her family. She was ten years old in 1915. She remembered the swarms of grasshoppers that arrived in her village, Dubne, which was north of the historic Armenian city of Dikranagert, now Diyarbakir. The village elders were alarmed, she said, because they knew in their bones that the grasshoppers were a bad omen. They were right; the end came in a few months, when the wheat in the fields was ready for harvesting.

"When we left, my family was twenty-five in the family,"
Araxie Barsamian says.

They took all the men folks ... They asked my father, "Where is your ammunition?" He says, "I sold it." So they says, "Go get it." So when he went to the Kurd town, to get it, they beat him and took him all his clothes. And when he came back there—this is my mother tells me story—when he came back there, naked body, he went in the jail, they cut his arms ... So he die in the jail ... They took all the mens in the field, they tied their hands, and they shooted, killed every one of them.

Araxie, her mother, and three younger brothers were deported. All of them perished except Araxie. She was the lone survivor. This is, of course, a single testimony that comes from a history that is denied by the Turkish government and many Turks as well.

I have not come here to play the global intellectual, to lecture you, or to fill the silence in this country that surrounds the memory (or the forgetting) of the events that took place in Anatolia in 1915. That is what Hrant Dink tried to do, and paid for with his life.

The day I arrived in Istanbul, I walked the streets for many hours, and as I looked around, envying the people of Istanbul their beautiful, mysterious, thrilling city, a friend pointed out to me young boys in white caps who seemed to have suddenly appeared like a rash in the city. He explained that they were expressing their solidarity with the child assassin who was wearing a white cap when he killed Hrant. Obviously, the assassination was meant both as a punishment for Hrant and a warning to others in this country who might have been inspired by his courage—not just to say the unsayable, but to think the unthinkable.

This was the message written on the bullet that killed Hrant Dink. This is the message in the death threats received by Orhan Pamuk, Elif Shafak, and others who have dared to differ with the Turkish government's view. Before he was killed, Hrant Dink was tried three times under Article 301 of the Turkish Penal Code, which makes publicly denigrating "Turkishness" a criminal offense. Each of these trials was a signal from the Turkish state to Turkey's fascist right wing that Hrant Dink was an acceptable target. How can telling the truth denigrate Turkishness? Who has the right to limit and define what Turkishness is?

Hrant Dink has been silenced. But those who celebrate his murder should know that what they did was counterproductive. Instead of silence, it has raised a great noise. Hrant's voice has become a shout that can never be silenced again, not by bullets, or prison sentences, or insults. It shouts, it whispers, it sings, it shatters the bullying silence that has begun to gather once again like an army that was routed and is regrouping. It has made the world curious about something that happened in Anatolia more than ninety years ago. Something that Hrant's enemies wanted to bury. To forget. Well . . . speaking for myself, my first reaction was to find out what I could about 1915, to read history, to listen to testimonies. Something I might not otherwise have done. Now I have an opinion, an informed opinion about it, but, as I said, that is not what I'm here to inflict on you.

The battle with the cap-wearers of Istanbul, of Turkey, is not my battle, it's yours. I have my own battles to fight against other kinds of cap-wearers and torchbearers in my country. In a way, the battles are not all that different. There is one crucial difference, though. While in Turkey there is silence, in India there's celebration, and I really don't know which is worse. I think that silence suggests shame, and shame suggests conscience. Is that too naive and generous an interpretation? Perhaps, but why not be naive and generous? Celebration, unfortunately, does not lend itself to interpretation. It is what it says it is.

Lessons from your past have given me an insight into our future. My talk today is not about the past, it's about the future. I want to talk about the foundations that are being laid for the future of India, a country being celebrated all over the world as a role model of progress and democracy.

❖

In the state of Gujarat, there was genocide against the Muslim community in 2002. I use the word *genocide* advisedly, and in keeping with its definition contained in Article 2 of the United Nations Convention on the Prevention and Punishment of the Crime of Genocide. The genocide began as collective punishment for an unsolved crime—the burning of a railway coach in which fifty-three Hindu pilgrims were burned to death. In a carefully planned orgy of supposed retaliation, two thousand Muslims were slaughtered in broad daylight by squads of armed killers, organized by fascist militias, and backed by the Gujarat government and the administration of the day. Muslim women were gang-raped and burned alive. Muslim shops, Muslim businesses, and Muslim shrines and mosques were systematically destroyed. Two thousand were killed and more than one hundred thousand people were driven from their homes.

Even today, many of them live in ghettos—some built on garbage heaps—with no water supply, no drainage, no street lights, no health care. They live as second-class citizens, boycotted socially and economically. Meanwhile, the killers, police as well as civilian, have been embraced, rewarded, promoted. This state of affairs is now considered "normal." To seal the "normality," in 2004 both Ratan Tata and Mukesh Ambani, India's leading industrialists, praised Gujarat as a dream destination for finance capital.

The initial outcry in the national press has settled down. In Gujarat, the genocide has been brazenly celebrated as the epitome of Gujarati pride, Hindu-ness, even Indian-ness. This poisonous brew has been used twice in a row to win state elections, with campaigns that have cleverly used the language and apparatus of modernity and democracy. The helmsman, Narendra Modi, has become a folk hero, called in by the Bharatiya Janata Party (BJP) to campaign on its behalf in other Indian states.

As genocides go, the Gujarat genocide cannot compare with the people killed in the Congo, Rwanda, and Bosnia, where the numbers run into millions, nor is it by any means the first that has occurred in India. (In 1984, for instance, three thousand Sikhs were massacred on the streets of Delhi with similar impunity, by killers overseen by the Congress Party.) But the Gujarat genocide is part of a larger, more elaborate and systematic vision. It tells us that the wheat is ripening and the grasshoppers have landed in mainland India.

It's an old human habit, genocide is. It has played a sterling part in the march of civilization. Among the earliest recorded genocides is thought to be the destruction of Carthage at the end of the Third Punic War in 149 BC. The word itself—genocide—was coined by Raphael Lemkin only in 1943, and adopted by the United Nations in 1948, after the Nazi Holocaust. Article 2 of the United Nations Convention on the Prevention and Punishment of the Crime of Genocide defines it as

> any of the following acts committed with intent to destroy, in whole or in part, a national, ethnical, racial or religious group, as such:
>
> (a) Killing members of the group;
>
> (b) Causing serious bodily or mental harm to members of the group;
>
> (c) Deliberately inflicting on the group conditions of life calculated to bring about its physical destruction in whole or in part;
>
> (d) Imposing measures intending to prevent births within the group;
>
> (e) Forcibly transferring children of the group to another group.

Since this definition leaves out the persecution of political dissidents, real or imagined, it does not include some of the greatest mass murders in history. Personally, I think the definition by Frank Chalk and Kurt Jonassohn, authors of *The History and Sociology of Genocide*, is more apt. Genocide, they say, "is a form of one-sided mass killing in which a state or other authority intends to destroy a group, as that group and membership in it are defined by the perpetrator." Defined like this, genocide would include, for example, the millions killed and the monumental crimes committed by Suharto in Indonesia, Pol Pot in Cambodia, Stalin in the Soviet Union, and Mao in China.

All things considered, the word *extermination*, with its crude evocation of pests and vermin, of infestations, is perhaps the more honest, more apposite word. When a set of perpetrators faces its victims, in order to go about its business of wanton killing, it must first sever any human connection with it. It must see its victims as subhuman, as parasites whose eradication would be a service to society. Here, for example, is an account of the massacre of Pequot Indians by English Puritans led by John Mason in Connecticut in 1636:

> *Those that scaped the fire were slaine with the sword; some hewed to peeces, others rune throw with their rapiers, so as they were quickly dispatchte, and very few escaped. It was conceived they thus destroyed about four hundred at this time. It was a fearful sight to see them thus frying in the fyer, and the streams of blood quenching the same, and horrible was the stincke and sente there of, but the victory seemed a sweete sacrifice.*

And here, approximately four centuries later, is Babu Bajrangi, one of the major lynchpins of the Gujarat genocide, recorded on camera in the sting operation mounted by the Indian newsmagazine *Tehelka* a few months ago:

We didn't spare a single Muslim shop, we set everything on fire,
we set them on fire and killed them . . . hacked, burnt, set on
fire . . . We believe in setting them on fire because these bastards
don't want to be cremated, they're afraid of it.

I hardly need to say that Babu Bajrangi had the blessings of Narendra Modi, the protection of the police, and the love of his people. He continues to work and prosper as a free man in Gujarat. The one crime he cannot be accused of is Genocide Denial.

Genocide Denial is a radical variation on the theme of the old, frankly racist, bloodthirsty triumphalism. It probably evolved as an answer to the somewhat patchy dual morality that arose in the nineteenth century, when Europe was developing limited but new forms of democracy and citizens' rights at home while simultaneously exterminating people in their millions in her colonies. Suddenly countries and governments began to deny or attempt to hide the genocides they had committed. "Denial is saying, in effect," Robert J. Lifton observes, that "the murderers didn't murder. The victims weren't killed. The direct consequence of denial is that it invites future genocide."

Of course, today, when genocide politics meets the free market, official recognition—or denial—of holocausts and genocides is a multinational business enterprise. It rarely has anything to do with historical fact or forensic evidence. Morality certainly does not enter the picture. It is an aggressive process of high-end bargaining that belongs more to the World Trade Organization than to the United Nations. The currency is geopolitics, the fluctuating market for natural resources, that curious thing called futures trading, and plain old economic and military might.

In other words, genocides are often denied for the same set of reasons that genocides are prosecuted. Economic determinism marinated in racial/ethnic/religious/national discrimination. Crudely, the lowering or raising of the price of a barrel of oil (or a ton of uranium), permission granted for a military base, or the opening up of a country's economy could be the decisive factor when governments adjudicate on whether a genocide did or did not occur. Or indeed whether genocide will or will not occur. And if it does, whether it will or will not be reported, and if it is, then what slant that reportage will take. For example, the death of millions in the Congo goes virtually unreported. Why? And was the death of a million Iraqis under the sanctions regime, prior to the US invasion in 2003, genocide (which is what UN humanitarian coordinator for Iraq Denis Halliday called it) or was it "worth it," as Madeleine Albright, the US ambassador to the United Nations, claimed? It depends on who makes the rules. Bill Clinton? Or an Iraqi mother who has lost her child?

Since the United States is the richest and most powerful country in the world, in the Genocide Denial seedings it is the World's Number One. It continues to celebrate Columbus Day, the day Christopher Columbus arrived in the Americas, which marks the beginning of a holocaust that wiped out millions of Native Americans, about 90 percent of the original population. Lord Amherst, the man whose idea it was to distribute blankets infected with smallpox virus to Indians, has a university town in Massachusetts, and a prestigious liberal arts college, named after him.

In America's second holocaust, almost 30 million Africans were kidnapped and sold into slavery. Well near half of them died in transit. But in 2001, the US delegation could still walk out of the World Conference against Racism in Durban, refusing to acknowledge that slavery and the slave trade were crimes. Slavery, they insisted, was legal at the time. The United States has also refused to accept that the bombing of Tokyo, Hiroshima, Nagasaki, Dresden, and Hamburg—which killed hundreds of thousands of civilians—were crimes, let alone acts of genocide. (The argument here is that the government didn't intend to kill civilians. This was an early stage of the development of the concept of "collateral damage.") Since its first foreign conquest of Mexico in 1848, the US government has militarily intervened abroad, whether overtly or covertly, countless times. Its invasion of Vietnam, with excellent intentions of course, led to the deaths of millions of people in Indochina.

None of these actions have been acknowledged as war crimes or genocidal acts. "How much evil," asks Robert McNamara, whose career graph took him from the bombing of Tokyo in 1945 (one hundred thousand dead overnight), to being the architect of the war in Vietnam, to president of the World Bank, now sitting in his comfortable chair in his comfortable home in his comfortable country, "must we do in order to do good?"

Could there be a more perfect illustration of Robert J. Lifton's point that the denial of genocide invites more genocide?

As a friendly gesture to the government of Turkey, its ally in the volatile politics of the Middle East, the US government concurs with the Turkish government's denial of the Armenian genocide. So does the government of Israel. For the same reasons. For them the Armenian people are suffering a collective hallucination.

And what to do when the victims become perpetrators, as they did in the Congo and in Rwanda? What remains to be said about Israel, created out of the debris of one of the cruelest genocides in human history? What of its actions in the occupied territories? Its burgeoning settlements, its colonization of water, its new "security wall" that separates Palestinian people from their farms, from their work, from their relatives, from their children's schools, from hospitals and health care? It is genocide in a fishbowl, genocide in slow motion—meant especially to illustrate that section of Article 2 of the United Nations Convention on the Prevention and Punishment of the Crime of Genocide, which says genocide is any act that is designed to "deliberately inflict on the group conditions of life calculated to bring about its physical destruction in whole or part."

Perhaps the ugliest aspect of the Genocide Game is that genocides have been ranked and seeded like tennis players on the international circuit. Their victims are categorized into worthy or unworthy ones. Take for example the best-known, best-documented, most condemned genocide by far—the Jewish Holocaust, which took the lives of six million Jews. (Less publicized in books and films and Holocaust literature is the fact that the Nazis also liquidated thousands of Gypsies, communists, homosexuals, and millions of Russian prisoners of war, not all of them Jewish.) The Nazi genocide of Jews has been universally accepted as the most horrifying event of the twentieth century. In the face of this, some historians call the Armenian genocide the Forgotten Genocide, and in their fight to remind the world about it, frequently refer to it as the first genocide of the twentieth century. Peter Balakian, one of the most knowledgeable scholars of the Armenian genocide, and author of *The Burning Tigris: The Armenian Genocide and America's Response*, says that "the Armenian genocide is a landmark event. It changed history. It was unprecedented. It began the age of genocide, which we must acknowledge the twentieth century indeed was."

The professor is in error. The "era of genocide" had begun long ago. The Herero people, for example, were exterminated by the Germans in Southwest Africa only a few years into the twentieth century. In October 1904, General Adolf Lebrecht von Trotha ordered that the Herero be exterminated. They were driven into the desert, cut off from food and water, and in this way annihilated. Meanwhile, in other parts of the African continent, genocide was proceeding apace. The French, the British, the Belgians were all busy. King Leopold of Belgium was well into his "experiment in commercial expansion" in search of slaves, rubber, and ivory in the Congo. The price of his experiment: ten million human lives. It was one of the most brutal genocides of all time. (The battle to control Africa's mineral wealth rages on—scratch the surface of contemporary horrors in Africa, in Rwanda, the Congo, Nigeria, pick your country, and chances are that you will be able to trace the story back to the old colonial interests of Europe and the new colonial interests of the United States.)

In Asia, by the last quarter of the nineteenth century, the British had finished exterminating the aboriginal people in Tasmania, and most of Australia, starving them out, hunting them down. British convicts were given five pounds for every native they hunted down. The last Tasmanian woman, Truganina, died in 1876. (Her skeleton is in a museum in Hobart. Look her up when you go there next.) The Spanish, the French, and the British, of course, had by then almost finished "God's Work" in the Americas.

In the genocide sweepstakes, while pleading for justice for one people, it is so easy to inadvertently do away with the suffering of others. This is the slippery morality of the international politics of genocide. Genocide within genocide, denial within denial, on and on, like Matryoshka dolls.

The history of genocide tells us that it's not an aberration, an anomaly, a glitch in the human system. It's a habit as old, as persistent, as much a part of the human condition as love and art and agriculture. Most of the genocidal killing from the fifteenth century onward has been an integral part of Europe's search for what the Germans famously called *lebensraum*, living space. Lebensraum was a word coined by the German geographer and zoologist Friedrich Ratzel to describe what he thought of as dominant human species' natural impulse to expand their territory in their search for not just space, but sustenance. This impulse to expansion would naturally be at the cost of a less dominant species, a weaker species that Nazi ideologues believed should give way, or be made to give way, to the stronger one.

The idea of lebensraum was set out in precise terms in 1901, but Europe had already begun her quest for lebensraum four hundred years earlier, when Columbus landed in America.

Sven Lindqvist, author of *Exterminate All the Brutes*, argues that it was Hitler's quest for lebensraum—in a world that had already been carved up by other European countries—that led the Nazis to push through Eastern Europe and on toward Russia. The Jews of Eastern Europe and western Russia stood in the way of Hitler's colonial ambitions. Therefore, like the native peoples of Africa and America and Asia, they had to be enslaved or liquidated. So, Lindqvist says, the Nazis' racist dehumanization of Jews cannot be dismissed as a paroxysm of insane evil. Once again, it is a product of the familiar mix: economic determinism well marinated in age-old racism—very much in keeping with European tradition of the time.

It's not a coincidence that the political party that carried out the Armenian genocide in the Ottoman Empire was called the Committee for Union and Progress. "Union" (racial/ethnic/ religious/national) and "Progress" (economic determinism) have long been the twin coordinates of genocide.

Armed with this reading of history, is it reasonable to worry about whether a country that is poised on the threshold of "progress" is also poised on the threshold of genocide? Could the India being celebrated all over the world as a miracle of progress and democracy possibly be poised on the verge of committing genocide? The mere suggestion might sound outlandish and at this point in time, the use of the word *genocide* surely unwarranted. However, if we look to the future, and if the Tsars of Development believe in their own publicity, if they believe that There Is No Alternative to their chosen model for Progress, then they will inevitably have to kill, and kill in large numbers, in order to get their way.

In bits and pieces, as the news trickles in, it seems clear that the killing and the dying has already begun.

❖

It was in 1989, soon after the collapse of the Soviet Union, that the government of India turned in its membership in the Nonaligned Movement and signed up for membership in the Completely Aligned, often referring to itself as the "natural ally" of Israel and the United States. (They have at least this one thing in common: all three are engaged in overt, neocolonial military occupations—India in Kashmir, Israel in Palestine, the United States in Iraq and Afghanistan.)

Almost like clockwork, the two major national political parties, the BJP and the Congress, embarked on a joint program to advance India's version of Union and Progress, whose modern-day euphemisms are Nationalism and Development. Every now and then, particularly during elections, they stage some noisy familial squabbles, but have managed to gather into their fold even grumbling relatives, like the Communist Party of India (Marxist).

The Union project offers Hindu nationalism (which seeks to unite the Hindu vote, vital, you will admit, for a great democracy like India). The Progress project aims at a 10 percent annual growth rate. Both projects are encrypted with genocidal potential.

The Union project has been largely entrusted to the Rashtriya Swayamsevak Sangh (RSS), the ideological heart, the holding company of the BJP and its militias, the Vishwa Hindu Parishad and the Bajrang Dal. The RSS was founded in 1925. By the 1930s, its founder, Dr. K. B. Hedgewar, a fan of Benito Mussolini's, had begun to model it overtly along the lines of Italian fascism. Hitler, too, was and is an inspirational figure. Here are some excerpts from the RSS bible, *We, or, Our Nationhood Defined* by M. S. Golwalkar, who succeeded Dr. Hedgewar as head of the RSS in 1940:

> *Ever since that evil day, when Moslems first landed in Hindustan, right up to the present moment, the Hindu Nation has been gallantly fighting on to take on these despoilers. The Race Spirit has been awakening.*

Then:

> *In Hindustan, land of the Hindus, lives and should live the Hindu Nation . . .*
>
> *All others are traitors and enemies to the National Cause, or, to take a charitable view, idiots . . . The foreign races in Hindustan . . . may stay in the country, wholly subordinated to the Hindu Nation,*

claiming nothing, deserving no privileges, far less any preferential treatment—not even citizen's rights.

And again:

To keep up the purity of its race and culture, Germany shocked the world by her purging the country of the Semitic races—the Jews. Race pride at its highest has been manifested here . . . a good lesson for us in Hindustan to learn and profit by.

(How do you combat this kind of organized hatred? Certainly not with goofy preachings of secular love.)

By the year 2000, the RSS had more than sixty thousand shakhas (branches) and an army of more than four million swayamsevaks (volunteers) preaching its doctrine across India. They include India's former prime minister Atal Bihari Vajpayee, the former home minister and current leader of the opposition L. K. Advani, and, of course, the three-time Gujarat chief minister Narendra Modi. It also includes senior people in the media, the police, the army, the intelligence agencies, the judiciary, and the administrative services who are informal devotees of Hindutva— the RSS ideology. These people, unlike politicians who come and go, are permanent members of government machinery.

But the RSS's real power lies in the fact that it has put in decades of hard work and has created a network of organizations at every level of society, something that no other political or cultural group in India can match. The BJP is its political front. It has a trade union wing (Bharatiya Mazdoor Sangh), women's wing (Rashtra Sevika Samiti), student wing (Akhil Bharatiya Vidyarthi Parishad), and economic wing (Swadeshi Jagran Manch).

Its front organization Vidya Bharati is the largest educational organization in the nongovernmental sector. It has thirteen thousand educational institutes, including the Saraswati Vidya Mandir schools with seventy thousand teachers and more than 1.7 million students. It has organizations working with tribals (Vanavasi Kalyan Ashram), literature (Akhil Bharatiya Sahitya Parishad), intellectuals (Pragya Bharati, Deendayal Research Institute), historians (Bharatiya Itihaas Sankalan Yojanalaya), language (Sanskrit Bharti), slum dwellers (Seva Bharati, Hindu Seva Prathishtan), health (Swami Vivekanand Medical Mission, National Medicos Organization), leprosy patients (Bharatiya Kushta Nivarak Sangh), cooperatives (Sahkar Bharati), publication of newspapers and other propaganda material (Bharat Prakashan, Suruchi Prakashan, Lokhit Prakashan, Gyanganga Prakashan, Archana Prakashan, Bharatiya Vichar Sadhana, Sadhana Pustak, and Akashvani Sadhana), caste integration (Samajik Samrasta Manch), religion and proselytization (Vivekananda Kendra, Vishwa Hindu Parishad, Hindu Jagran Manch, Bajrang Dal). The list goes on and on.

On June 11, 1989, prime minister Rajiv Gandhi gave the RSS a gift. He was obliging enough to open the locks of the disputed Babri Masjid in Ayodhya, which the RSS claimed was the birthplace of Lord Ram. At the national executive of the BJP, the party passed a resolution to demolish the mosque and build a temple in Ayodhya. "I'm sure the resolution will translate into votes," said L. K. Advani. In 1990, he crisscrossed the country on his Rath Yatra, his Chariot of Fire, demanding the demolition of the Babri Masjid, leaving riots and bloodshed in his wake. In 1991, the party won 120 seats in Parliament. (It had won two in 1984.) The hysteria orchestrated by Advani peaked in 1992, when the mosque was brought down by a marauding mob. By 1998, the BJP was in power at the center.

Its first act in office was to conduct a series of nuclear tests. Across the country, fascists and corporates, princes and paupers alike, celebrated India's Hindu bomb. Hindutva had transcended petty party politics. In 2002, Narendra Modi's government planned and executed the Gujarat genocide. In the elections that took place a few months after the genocide, he was returned to power with an overwhelming majority. He ensured complete impunity for those who had participated in the killings. In the rare case where there has been a conviction, it is of course the lowly foot soldiers and not the masterminds who stand in the dock. Impunity is an essential prerequisite for genocidal killing. India has a great tradition of granting impunity to mass killers. I could fill volumes with the details.

In a democracy, for impunity after genocide, you have to "apply through proper channels." Procedure is everything. To begin with, of the 287 people accused, booked under the Prevention of Terrorism Act, 286 are Muslim and one is Sikh. No bail for them, so they're still in prison. In the case of several massacres, the lawyers that the Gujarat government appointed as public prosecutors had actually already appeared for the accused. Several of them belonged to the RSS or the Vishwa Hindu Parishad and were openly hostile to those they were supposedly representing. Survivor witnesses found that, when they went to the police to file reports, the police would record their statements inaccurately or refuse to record the names of the perpetrators. In several cases, when survivors had seen members of their families being killed (and burned alive so their bodies could not be found), the police would refuse to register cases of murder.

Ehsan Jafri, the Congress politician and poet who had made the mistake of campaigning against Modi in the Rajkot elections, was publicly butchered. (By a mob led by a fellow Congress Party worker.) In the words of a man who took part in the savagery: "Five people held him, then someone struck him with a sword . . . chopped off his hand, then his legs . . . then everything else . . . [and] after cutting him to pieces, they put him on the wood they'd piled and set him on fire. Burned him alive." While the mob that lynched Jafri, murdered seventy people, and gang-raped twelve women—before burning them alive—was gathering, the Ahmedabad commissioner of police, P. C. Pandey, was kind enough to visit the neighborhood. After Modi was reelected, Pandey was promoted and made Gujarat's director general of police. The entire killing apparatus remains in place.

The Supreme Court in Delhi made a few threatening noises but eventually put the matter into cold storage. The Congress and the Communist parties made a great deal of noise but did nothing.

In the Tehelka sting operation, broadcast recently on a news channel at prime time, apart from Babu Bajrangi, killer after killer recounted how the genocide had been planned and executed, how Modi and senior politicians and police officers had been personally involved. None of this information was new, but there they were, the butchers, on the news networks, not just admitting to but boasting about their crimes. The overwhelming public reaction to the sting was not outrage, but suspicion about its timing. Most people believed that the exposé would help Modi win the elections again. Some even believed, quite outlandishly, that he had engineered the sting. He did win the elections. And this time, on the ticket of Union and Progress. A committee all unto himself. At BJP rallies, thousands of adoring supporters now wear plastic Modi masks, chanting slogans of death. The fascist democrat has physically mutated into a million little fascists. These are the joys of democracy. (Who in Nazi Germany would have dared to put on a Hitler mask?) Preparations to re-create the "Gujarat blueprint" are currently in different stages in the BJP-ruled states of Orissa, Chhattisgarh, Jharkhand, Rajasthan, Madhya Pradesh, and Karnataka.

To commit genocide, says Peter Balakian, you have to marginalize a subgroup for a long time. This criterion has been well met in India. The Muslims of India have been systematically marginalized and have now joined the Adivasis and Dalits, who have not just been marginalized but dehumanized by caste Hindu society and its scriptures for years, for centuries. (There was a time when they were dehumanized in order to be put to work doing things that caste Hindus would not do. Now, with technology, even that labor is becoming redundant.) The RSS also pits Dalits against Muslims and Adivasis against Dalits as part of its larger project.

While the "people" were engaged with the Union project and its doctrine of hatred, India's Progress project was proceeding apace. The new regime of privatization and liberalization resulted in the sale of the country's natural resources and public infrastructure to private corporations. It has created an unimaginably wealthy upper class and growing middle class who have naturally became militant evangelists for the new dispensation.

The Progress project has its own tradition of impunity and subterfuge, no less horrific than the elaborate machinery of the Union project. At the heart of it lies the most powerful institution in India, the Supreme Court, which is rapidly becoming a pillar of Corporate Power, issuing order after order allowing for the building of dams, the interlinking of rivers, indiscriminate mining, the destruction of forests and water systems. All of this could be described as ecocide—a prelude perhaps to genocide. (And to criticize the court is a criminal offense, punishable by imprisonment.)

Ironically, the era of the free market has led to the most successful secessionist struggle ever waged in India—the secession of the middle and upper classes to a country of their own, somewhere up in the stratosphere where they merge with the rest of the world's elite. This Kingdom in the Sky is a complete universe in itself, hermetically sealed from the rest of India. It has its own newspapers, films, television programs, morality plays, transport systems, malls, and intellectuals. And in case you are beginning to think it's all joy-joy, you're wrong. It also has its own tragedies, its own environmental issues (parking problems, urban air pollution), its own class struggles. An organization called Youth for Equality, for example, has taken up the issue of reservations (affirmative action), because it feels Upper Castes are discriminated against by India's pulverized Lower Castes. This India has its own People's Movements and candlelight vigils (Justice for Jessica, the model who was shot in a bar) and even its own People's Car (the Wagon for the Volks launched by the Tata Group recently). It even has its own dreams that take the form of TV advertisements in which Indian CEOs (smeared with Fair & Lovely Face Cream) buy international corporations, including an imaginary East India Company. They are ushered to their plush new offices by fawning white women (who look as though they're longing to be laid, the final prize of conquest) and applauding white men, ready to make way for the new kings. Meanwhile the crowd in the stadium roars to its feet (with credit cards in their pockets) chanting "India! India!"

But there is a problem, and the problem is lebensraum. A Kingdom needs its lebensraum. Where will the Kingdom in the Sky find lebensraum? The Sky Citizens look toward the Old Nation. They see Adivasis sitting on the bauxite mountains of Orissa, on the iron ore in Jharkhand and Chhattisgarh. They see the people of Nandigram (Muslims, Dalits) sitting on prime land, which really ought to be a chemical hub. They see thousands of acres of farmland, and think: These really ought to be Special Economic Zones for our industries. They see the rich fields of Singur and know this really ought to be a car factory for the Tata Nano, the People's Car. They think: that's our bauxite, our iron ore, our uranium. What are these people doing on our land? What's our water doing in their rivers? What's our timber doing in their trees?

If you look at a map of India's forests, its mineral wealth, and the homelands of the Adivasi people, you'll see that they're stacked up over each other. So in reality, those whom we call poor are the truly wealthy. But when the Sky Citizens cast their eyes over the land, they see superfluous people sitting on precious resources. The Nazis had a phrase for them—*überzähligen Essern*, superfluous eaters.

The struggle for lebensraum, Friedrich Ratzel said, after closely observing the struggle between the indigenous people and their European colonizers in North America, is "an annihilating struggle." Annihilation doesn't necessarily mean the physical extermination of people—by bludgeoning, beating, burning, bayoneting, gassing, bombing, or shooting them. (Except sometimes. Particularly when they try to put up a fight.

Because then they become "terrorists.") Historically, the most efficient form of genocide has been to displace people from their homes, herd them together, and block their access to food and water. Under these conditions, they die without obvious violence and often in far greater numbers. "The Nazis gave the Jews a star on their coats and crowded them into 'reserves,'" Sven Lindqvist writes, "just as the Indians, the Hereros, the Bushmen, the Amandebele, and all the other children of the stars had been crowded together. They died on their own when food supply to the reserves was cut off."

The historian Mike Davis writes that 12.2 to 29.3 million people starved to death in India in the famines between 1876 and 1902, while Britain continued to export food and raw material from India. In a democracy, as Amartya Sen says, we are unlikely to have famine. So in place of China's Great Famine, we have India's Great Malnutrition. (India hosts more than a third of the world's undernourished children.)

With the possible exception of China, India today has the largest population of internally displaced people in the world. Dams alone have displaced more than thirty million people. The displacement is being enforced with court decrees or at gunpoint by policemen, government-controlled militias, or corporate thugs. (In Nandigram, even the Communist Party of India [Maoist] has its own armed militia.) The displaced are being herded into tenements, camps, and resettlement colonies where, cut off from a means of earning a living, they spiral into poverty.

In the state of Chhattisgarh, being targeted by corporates for its wealth of iron ore, there's a different technique. In the name of fighting Maoist rebels, hundreds of villages have been forcibly evacuated and almost forty thousand people moved into police camps. The government is arming some of them, and has created Salwa Judum, the supposedly anti-Maoist "people's" militia, created and funded by the state government. While the poor fight the poor, in conditions that approach civil war, the Tata and Essar groups have been quietly negotiating for the rights to mine iron ore in Chhattisgarh. (Can we establish a connection? We wouldn't dream of it. Even though the Salwa Judum was announced a day after the memorandum of understanding between the Tata Group and the government was signed.)

It's not surprising that very little of this account of events makes it into the version of the New India currently on the market. That's because what is on sale is another form of denial—the creation of what Robert J. Lifton calls a "counterfeit universe." In this universe, systemic horrors are converted into temporary lapses, attributable to flawed individuals, and a more "balanced," happier world is presented in place of the real one. The balance is spurious: often Union and Progress are set off against each other, a liberal secular critique of the Union project being used to legitimize the depredations of the Progress project. Those at the top of the food chain, those who have no reason to want to alter the status quo, are most likely to be the manufacturers of the "counterfeit universe." Their job is to patrol the border, diffuse rage, delegitimize anger, and negotiate a ceasefire.

Consider the response of Shah Rukh Khan (Bollywood superstar, heartthrob of millions) to a question about Narendra Modi. "I don't know him personally, I have no opinion," he says. "Personally they have never been unkind to me." Ramachandra Guha, liberal historian and founding member of the New India Foundation, advises us in his new book, *India after Gandhi: The History of the World's Largest Democracy*, that the Gujarat government is not really fascist, that the genocide was just an aberration, and that the government corrected itself after elections.

Editors and commentators in the "secular" national press, having got over their outrage at the Gujarat genocide, now assess Modi's administrative skills, which most of them are uniformly impressed by. The editor of the *Hindustan Times* said, "Modi may be a mass murderer, but he's our mass murderer," and went on to air his dilemmas about how to deal with a mass murderer who is also a "good" chief minister.

In this "counterfeit" version of India, in the realm of culture, in the new Bollywood cinema, in the boom in Indo-Anglian literature, the poor, for the most part, are simply absent. They have been erased in advance. (They only put in an appearance as the smiling beneficiaries of microcredit loans, development schemes, and charity meted out by NGOs.)

Last summer, I happened to wander into a cool room in which four beautiful young girls with straightened hair and porcelain skin were lounging, introducing their puppies to one another. One of them turned to me and said, "I was on holiday with my family and I found an old essay of yours about dams and stuff? I was asking my brother if he knew about what a bad time these Dalits and Adivasis were having, being displaced and all . . . I mean just being kicked out of their homes 'n' stuff like that? And you know, my brother's such a jerk, he said they're the ones who are holding India back. They should be exterminated. Can you imagine?"

The trouble is, I could. I can.

The puppies were sweet. I wondered whether dogs could ever imagine exterminating each other. They're probably not progressive enough.

That evening, I watched Amitabh Bachchan (another Bollywood superstar, heartthrob of millions) on TV, appearing in a commercial for the *Times of India*'s "India Poised" campaign. The TV anchor introducing the campaign said it was meant to inspire people to leave behind the "constraining ghosts of the past." To choose optimism over pessimism.

"There are two Indias in this country," Amitabh Bachchan said, in his famous baritone:

> One India is straining at the leash, eager to spring forth and live up to all the adjectives that the world has been recently showering upon us. The Other India is the leash.
>
> One India says, "Give me a chance and I'll prove myself." The Other India says, "Prove yourself first, and maybe then, you'll have a chance."

One India lives in the optimism of our hearts. The Other India lurks in the skepticism of our minds. One India wants, the Other India hopes.

One India leads, the Other India follows.

These conversions are on the rise. With each passing day, more and more people from the Other India are coming over to this side. And quietly, while the world is not looking, a pulsating, dynamic new India is emerging.

And finally:

Now in our sixtieth year as a free nation, the ride has brought us to the edge of time's great precipice. And One India, a tiny little voice in the back of the head, is looking down at the bottom of the ravine and hesitating. The Other India is looking up at the sky and saying, "It's time to fly."

Here is the counterfeit universe laid bare. It tells us that the rich don't have a choice (There Is No Alternative) but the poor do. They can choose to become rich. If they don't, it's because they are choosing pessimism over optimism, hesitation over confidence, want over hope. In other words, they're choosing to be poor. It's their fault. They are weak. (And we know what the seekers of lebensraum think of the weak.) They are the "Constraining Ghost of the Past." They're already ghosts. "Within an ongoing counterfeit universe," Robert J. Lifton says, "genocide becomes easy, almost natural."

The so-called poor have only one choice: to resist or to succumb. Bachchan is right: they are crossing over, quietly, while the world's not looking. Not to where he thinks, but across another ravine, to another side. The side of armed struggle. From there they look back at the Tsars of Development and mimic their regretful slogan: "There Is No Alternative."

They have watched the great Gandhian people's movements being reduced and humiliated, floundering in the quagmire of court cases, hunger strikes, and counter–hunger strikes. Perhaps these many million Constraining Ghosts of the Past wonder what advice Gandhi would have given the Indians of the Americas, the slaves of Africa, the Tasmanians, the Hereros, the Hottentots, the Armenians, the Jews of Germany, the Muslims of Gujarat. Perhaps they wonder how they can go on hunger strike when they're already starving. How they can boycott foreign goods when they have no money to buy any goods. How they can refuse to pay taxes when they have no earnings.

People who have taken to arms have done it with full knowledge of what the consequences of that decision will be. They have done so knowing that they are on their own. They know that the new laws of the land criminalize the poor and conflate resistance with terrorism. They know that appeals to conscience, liberal morality, and sympathetic press coverage will not help them now. They know no international marches, no globalized dissent, no famous writers will be around when the bullets fly. Hundreds of thousands have broken faith with the institutions of India's democracy. Large swathes of the country have fallen out of the government's control. (At last count it was supposed to be 25 percent.) The battle stinks of death. It's by no means pretty. How can it be when the helmsman of the Army of Constraining Ghosts is the ghost of Chairman Mao himself? (The ray of hope is that many of the foot soldiers don't know who he is. Or what he did. More Genocide Denial? Maybe.) Are they Idealists fighting for a Better World? Well ... anything is better than annihilation.

The prime minister has declared that the Maoist resistance is the "single largest threat" to internal security. There have even been appeals to call out the army. The media is agog with breathless condemnation.

Here's a typical newspaper column. Nothing out of the ordinary. "Stamp Out Naxals," it is called:

This government is at last showing some sense in tackling Naxalism. Less than a month ago Prime Minister Manmohan Singh asked

state governments to "choke" Naxal infrastructure and "cripple"
their activities through a dedicated force to eliminate the "virus."
It signaled a realization that the focus on tackling Naxalism must
be through enforcement of law, rather than wasteful expense on
development.

"Choke." "Cripple." "Virus." "Infested." "Eliminate." "Stamp out." Yes. The idea of extermination is in the air.

And people believe that faced with extermination they have the right to fight back. By any means necessary.

Perhaps they've been listening to the grasshoppers.

AZADI

FOR THE PAST sixty days or so, since about the end of June, the people of Kashmir have been free. Free in the most profound sense. They have shrugged off the terror of living their lives in the gun-sights of half a million heavily armed soldiers, in the most densely militarized zone in the world.

After eighteen years of administering a military occupation, the Indian government's worst nightmare has come true. Having declared that the militant movement has been crushed, it is now faced with a nonviolent mass protest, but not the kind it knows how to manage. This one is nourished by peoples' memory of years of repression in which tens of thousands have been killed; thousands have been "disappeared"; and hundreds of thousands tortured, injured, and humiliated. That kind of rage, once it finds utterance cannot easily be tamed, rebottled, and sent back to where it came from.

For all these years the Indian state, known among the knowing as the "deep state," has done everything it can to subvert, suppress, represent, misrepresent, discredit, interpret, intimidate,

---

This essay first appeared in the *Guardian*, on August 22, 2008, and in *Outlook*, on September 1, 2008.

purchase—and simply snuff out the voice of the Kashmiri people. It has used money (lots of it), violence (lots of it), disinformation, propaganda, torture, elaborate networks of collaborators and informers, terror, imprisonment, blackmail, and rigged elections to subdue what democrats would call "the will of the people." But now the deep state has tripped on its own hubris and bought into its own publicity, as deep states eventually tend to do. It made the mistake of believing that domination was victory, that the "normalcy" it had enforced through the barrel of a gun was indeed normal, and that the people's sullen silence was acquiescence.

The well-endowed peace industry, speaking on the people's behalf, informed us that "Kashmiris are tired of violence and want peace." What kind of peace they were willing to settle for was never clarified. Meanwhile Bollywood's cache of Kashmir/ Muslim-terrorist films has brainwashed most Indians into believing that all of Kashmir's sorrows could be laid at the door of evil, people-hating terrorists.

To anybody who cared to ask, or, more importantly, to listen, it was always clear that even in their darkest moments, people in Kashmir had kept the fires burning and that it was not peace alone they yearned for, but freedom, too. Over the last two months the carefully confected picture of an innocent people trapped between "two guns," both equally hated, has (pardon the pun) been shot to hell.

A sudden twist of fate, an ill-conceived move over the transfer of nearly one hundred acres of state forest land to the Amarnath Shrine Board (which manages the annual Hindu pilgrimage to a cave deep in the Kashmir Himalayas) suddenly became the equivalent of tossing a lit match into a barrel of petrol. Until 1989 the Amarnath pilgrimage used to attract about twenty thousand people who traveled to the Amarnath cave over a period of about two weeks. In 1990, when the overtly Islamic militant uprising in the valley coincided with the spread of virulent Hindutva in the Indian plains, the number of pilgrims began to increase exponentially. By 2008 more than five hundred thousand pilgrims visited the Amarnath cave, in large groups, their passage often sponsored by Indian business houses. To many people in the valley, this dramatic increase in numbers was seen as an aggressive political statement by an increasingly Hindu-fundamentalist Indian state. Rightly or wrongly, the land transfer was viewed as the thin edge of the wedge. It triggered an apprehension that it was the beginning of an elaborate plan to build Israeli-style settlements and change the demography of the valley. Days of massive protest forced the valley to shut down completely. Within hours the protests spread from the cities to villages. Young stone-pelters took to the streets and faced armed police who fired straight at them, killing several. For people as well as the government, it resurrected memories of the uprising in the early nineties. Throughout the weeks of protest, hartal, and police firing, while the Hindutva publicity machine charged Kashmiris with committing every kind of communal excess, the five hundred thousand Amarnath pilgrims completed their pilgrimage, not just unhurt, but touched by the hospitality they had been shown by local people.

Eventually, taken completely by surprise at the ferocity of the response, the government revoked the land transfer. But by then the land transfer had become a nonissue, and the protests had spiraled out of control.

Massive protests against the revocation erupted in Jammu. There too the issue snowballed into something much bigger. Hindus began to raise issues of neglect and discrimination by the Indian state. (For some odd reason they blamed Kashmiris for that neglect.) The protests led to the blockading of the Jammu–Srinagar highway, the only functional road link between Kashmir and India. The army was called out to clear the highway and allow safe passage of trucks between Jammu and Srinagar. But incidents of violence against Kashmiri truckers were being reported from as far away as Punjab, where there was no protection at all. As a result, Kashmiri truckers, fearing for their lives, refused to drive on the highway. Truckloads of perishable fresh fruit and valley produce began to rot. It became very obvious that the blockade had caused the situation to spin out of control. The government announced that the blockade had been cleared and that trucks were going through. Embedded sections of the Indian media, quoting the inevitable "intelligence" sources, began to refer to it as a "perceived" blockade and even suggest that there had never been one.

But it was too late for those games, the damage had been done. It had been demonstrated in no uncertain terms to people in Kashmir that they lived on sufferance and that if they didn't behave themselves they could be put under siege, starved, deprived of essential commodities and medical supplies. The real blockade became a psychological one. The last fragile link between India and Kashmir was all but snapped.

To expect matters to end there was, of course, absurd. Hadn't anybody noticed that in Kashmir even minor protests about civic issues like water and electricity inevitably turned into demands for *azadi* (freedom)? To threaten them with mass starvation amounted to committing political suicide.

Not surprisingly, the voice that the government of India has tried so hard to silence in Kashmir has massed into a deafening roar. Hundreds of thousands of unarmed people have come out to reclaim their cities, their streets and *mohallas*. They have simply overwhelmed the heavily armed security forces by their sheer numbers, and with a remarkable display of raw courage.

Raised in a playground of army camps, checkpoints, and bunkers, with screams from torture chambers for a sound track, the younger generation has suddenly discovered the power of mass protest, and above all, the dignity of being able to straighten their shoulders and speak for themselves, represent themselves. For them it is nothing short of an epiphany. They're in full flow; not even the fear of death seems to hold them back. And once that fear has gone, of what use is the largest or second largest army in the world? What threat does it hold? Who should know that better than the people of India who won their independence in the way that they did?

The circumstances in Kashmir being what they are, it is hard for the spin doctors to fall back on the same old, same old, to claim that it's all the doing of Pakistan's Inter-Services Intelligence (ISI), or that people are being coerced by militants. Since the thirties the question of who can claim the right to represent that elusive thing known as "Kashmiri sentiment" has been bitterly contested. Was it Sheikh Abdullah? The Muslim Conference? Who is it today? The mainstream political parties? The Hurriyat? The militants?

This time, the people are on the streets to represent themselves. There have been mass rallies in the past, but none in recent memory that have been so sustained and widespread. The mainstream political parties of Kashmir—National Conference, Peoples Democratic Party—feted by the deep state and the Indian media despite the pathetic voter turnout in election after election, appear dutifully for debates in New Delhi's TV studios but can't muster the courage to appear on the streets of Kashmir. The armed militants who, through the worst years of repression were seen as the only ones carrying the torch of azadi forward, if they are around at all, seem content to take a back seat and let people do the fighting for a change.

The separatist leaders who do appear and speak at the rallies are not leaders so much as followers, being guided by the phenomenal spontaneous energy of a caged, enraged people that has exploded on Kashmir's streets. The leaders, such as they are, have been presented with a full-blown revolution. The only condition seems to be that they have to do as the people say. If they say things that people do not wish to hear, they are gently persuaded to come out, publicly apologize and correct their course. This applies to all of them, including Syed Ali Shah Geelani, who at a public rally recently proclaimed himself the movement's only leader. It was a monumental political blunder that very nearly shattered the fragile new alliance between the various factions of the struggle. Within hours he retracted his statement. Like it or not, this is democracy. No democrat can pretend otherwise.

Day after day, hundreds of thousands of people swarm around places that hold terrible memories for them. They demolish bunkers, break through cordons of concertina wire, and stare straight down the barrels of soldiers' machine guns, saying what very few in India want to hear: "*Hum Kya Chahtey? Azadi!*" (What do we want? Freedom!). And, it has to be said, in equal numbers and with equal intensity: "*Jeevey Jeevey Pakistan*" (Long live Pakistan).

That sound reverberates through the valley like the drumbeat of steady rain on a tin roof, like the roll of thunder during an electric storm. It's the plebiscite that was never held, the referendum that has been indefinitely postponed.

On August 15, India's Independence Day, the city of Srinagar shut down completely. The Bakshi stadium where the governor hoisted the flag was empty except for a few officials. Hours later, Lal Chowk, the nerve center of the city (where in 1992 Murli Manohar Joshi, Bharatiya Janata Party leader and mentor of the controversial "Hinduization" of children's history textbooks, started a tradition of flag-hoisting by the Border Security Force), was taken over by thousands of people who hoisted the Pakistani flag and wished each other "Happy Belated Independence Day" (Pakistan celebrates Independence on August 14) and "Happy Slavery Day." Humor obviously has survived India's many torture centers and Abu Ghraibs in Kashmir.

On August 16, hundreds of thousands of people marched to Pampore, to the village of the Hurriyat leader Sheikh Abdul Aziz, who was shot down in cold blood five days earlier. He was part of a massive march to the Line of Control demanding that since the Jammu road had been blocked, it was only logical that the Srinagar–Muzaffarabad highway be opened for goods and people, the way it used to be before Kashmir was partitioned.

On August 18, hundreds of thousands also gathered in Srinagar in the huge TRC grounds (Tourist Reception Center, not the Truth and Reconciliation Committee) close to the United Nations Military Observer Group in India and Pakistan (UN-

MOGIP) to submit a memorandum asking for three things: the end to Indian rule, the deployment of a UN peacekeeping force, and an investigation into two decades of war crimes committed with almost complete impunity by the Indian Army and police.

The day before the rally, the deep state was hard at work. A senior journalist friend called to say that late in the afternoon the home secretary had called a high-level meeting in New Delhi. Also present were the defense secretary and intelligence chiefs. The purpose of the meeting, he said, was to brief the editors of TV news channels that the government had reason to believe that the insurrection was being managed by a small splinter cell of the ISI and to request the channels to keep this piece of exclusive, highly secret intelligence in mind while covering (or preferably not covering?) the news from Kashmir. Unfortunately for the deep state, things have gone so far that TV channels, were they to obey those instructions, would run the risk of looking ridiculous. Thankfully, it looks as though this revolution will, after all, be televised.

On the night of August 17, the police sealed the city. Streets were barricaded, thousands of armed police manned the barriers. The roads leading into Srinagar were blocked. For the first time in eighteen years the police had to plead with Hurriyat leaders to address the rally at the TRC grounds instead of marching right up to the UNMOGIP office on Gupkar Road, Srinagar's Green Zone, where, for years, the Indian establishment has barricaded itself in style and splendor.

On the morning of August 18, people began pouring into Srinagar from villages and towns across the valley. In trucks, jeeps, buses, and on foot. Once again, barriers were broken and people reclaimed their city. The police were faced with a choice of either stepping aside or executing a massacre. They stepped aside. Not a single bullet was fired.

The city floated on a sea of smiles. There was ecstasy in the air. Everyone had a banner; houseboat owners, traders, students, lawyers, doctors. One said, "We are all prisoners, set us free."

Another said, "Democracy without Justice is Demon-crazy." Demon-crazy. That was a good one. Perhaps he was referring to the twisted logic of a country that needed to commit communal carnage in order to bolster its secular credentials. Or the insanity that permits the world's largest democracy to administer the world's largest military occupation and continue to call itself a democracy.

There was a green flag on every lamppost, every roof, every bus stop, and on the top of chinar trees. A big one fluttered outside the All India Radio building. Road signs to Hazratbal, Batmaloo, Sopore were painted over. Rawalpindi, they said. Or simply Pakistan. It would be a mistake to assume that the public expression of affection for Pakistan automatically translates into a desire to accede to Pakistan. Some of it has to do with gratitude for the support—cynical or otherwise—for what Kashmiris see as their freedom struggle and the Indian state sees as a terrorist campaign. It also has to do with mischief. With saying and doing what galls India most of all.

It's easy to scoff at the idea of a "freedom struggle" that wishes to distance itself from a country that is supposed to be a democracy and align itself with another that has, for the most part, been ruled by military dictators. A country whose army has committed genocide in what is now Bangladesh. A country that is even now being torn apart by its own ethnic war. These are important questions, but right now perhaps it's more useful to wonder what this so-called democracy did in Kashmir to make people hate it so.

Everywhere there were Pakistani flags, everywhere the cry: "*Pakistan se rishta kya? La illaha illallah*" (What is our bond with Pakistan? There is no god but Allah).

"*Azadi ka matlab kya? La illaha illallah*" (What does Freedom mean? There is no god but Allah).

For somebody like myself, who is not Muslim, that interpretation of freedom is hard—if not impossible—to understand. I asked a young woman whether freedom for Kashmir would

"The Indian military occupation of Kashmir makes monsters of us all. It allows Hindu chauvinists to target and victimize Muslims in India by holding them hostage to the freedom struggle being waged by Muslims in Kashmir. It's all being stirred into a poisonous brew and administered intravenously, straight into our bloodstream."

not mean less freedom for her, as a woman. She shrugged and said, "What kind of freedom do we have now? The freedom to be raped by Indian soldiers?" Her reply silenced me.

Standing in the grounds of the TRC, surrounded by a sea of green flags, it was impossible to doubt or ignore the deeply Islamic nature of the uprising taking place around me. It was equally impossible to label it a vicious, terrorist jihad. For Kashmiris it was a catharsis. A historical moment in a long and complicated struggle for freedom with all the imperfections, cruelties, and confusions that freedom struggles have. This one cannot by any means call itself pristine and will always be stigmatized by, and will some day, I hope, have to account for, among other things, the brutal killings of Kashmiri Pandits in the early years of the uprising, culminating in the exodus of almost the entire community from the Kashmir valley.

As the crowd continued to swell I listened carefully to the slogans, because rhetoric often clarifies things and holds the key to all kinds of understanding. I'd heard many of them before a few years ago at a militant's funeral. A new one, obviously coined after the blockade was: "*Kashmir ki mandi! Rawalpindi!*" (It doesn't lend itself to translation, but it means: Kashmir's marketplace? Rawalpindi!) Another was "*Khooni lakir tod do, aar paar jod do*" (Break down the blood-soaked Line of Control, let Kashmir be united again). There were plenty of insults and humiliation for India: "*Ay jabiron ay ẓalimon, Kashmir hamara chhod do*" (Oh oppressors, oh wicked ones, get out of our Kashmir). "*Jis Kashmir ko khoon se seencha, voh Kashmir hamara hai!*" (The Kashmir we have irrigated with our blood, that Kashmir is ours!)

The slogan that cut through me like a knife and clean broke my heart was this one: "*Nanga bhookha Hindustan, jaan se pyaara Pakistan*" (Naked, starving India, more precious than life itself—Pakistan). Why was it so galling, so painful to listen to this? I tried to work it out and settled on three reasons. First, because we all know that the first part of the slogan is the embarrassing and unadorned truth about India, the emerging superpower. Second, because all Indians who are not nanga or bhooka are—and have been—complicit in complex and historical ways with the elaborate cultural and economic systems that make Indian society so cruel, so vulgarly unequal. And third, because it was painful to listen to people who have suffered so much themselves, mock others who suffer, in different ways, but no less intensely, under the same oppressor. In that slogan I saw the seeds of how easily victims can become perpetrators.

It took hours for Mirwaiz Umar Farooq and Syed Ali Shah Geelani to wade through the thronging crowds and make it onto the podium. When they arrived they were born aloft on the shoulders of young men, over the surging crowd to the podium. The roar of greeting was deafening. Mirwaiz Umar spoke first. He repeated the demand that the Armed Forces Special Powers Act, the Disturbed Areas Act, and the Public Safety Act—under which thousands have been killed, jailed, and tortured—be withdrawn. He called for the release of political prisoners, for the Srinagar–Muzaffarabad road to be opened for the free movement of goods and people, and for the demilitarization of the Kashmir valley.

Syed Ali Shah Geelani began his address with a recitation from the Koran. He then said what he has said before, on hundreds of occasions. The only way for the struggle to succeed, he said, was to turn to the Koran for guidance. He said Islam would guide the struggle and that it was a complete social and moral code that would govern the people of a free Kashmir. He said Pakistan had been created as the home of Islam and that that goal should never be subverted. He said just as Pakistan belonged to Kashmir, Kashmir belonged to Pakistan. He said minority communities would have full rights and their places of worship would be safe. Each point he made was applauded.

Oddly enough, the apparent doctrinal clarity of what he said made everything a little unclear. I wondered how the somewhat disparate views of the various factions in this freedom struggle would resolve themselves—the Jammu and Kashmir Liberation Front's vision of an independent state, Geelani's desire to merge with Pakistan and Mirwaiz Umar balanced precariously between them.

An old man with a red eye standing next to me said, "Kashmir was one country. Half was taken by India, the other half by Pakistan. Both by force. We want freedom." I wondered if, in the new dispensation, the old man would get a hearing. I wondered what he would think of the trucks that roared down the highways in the plains of India, owned and driven by men who knew nothing of history, or of Kashmir, but still had slogans on their tail gates that said, "*Doodh maango to kheer denge, Kashmir mango to chir denge*" (Ask for milk, you'll get cream; ask for Kashmir, we'll cut you open.)

Briefly, I had another thought. I imagined myself standing in the heart of a Rashtriya Swayamsevak Sangh or Vishwa Hindu Parishad rally being addressed by L. K. Advani. Replace the word "Islam" with the word "Hindutva," replace the word "Pakistan" with "Hindustan," replace the sea of green flags with saffron ones, and we would have the Bharatiya Janata Party's nightmare vision of an ideal India.

Is that what we should accept as our future? Monolithic religious states handing down a complete social and moral code, "a complete way of life"? Millions of us in India reject the Hindutva project. Our rejection springs from love, from passion, from a kind of idealism, from having enormous emotional stakes in the society in which we live. What our neighbors do, how they choose to handle their affairs does not affect our argument, it only strengthens it.

Arguments that spring from love are also fraught with danger. It is for the people of Kashmir to agree or disagree with the Islamic project (which is as contested, in equally complex ways, all over the world by Muslims, as Hindutva is contested by Hindus). Perhaps now that the threat of violence has receded and there is some space in which to debate views and air ideas, it is time for those who are part of the struggle to outline a vision for what kind of society they are fighting for. Perhaps it is time to offer people something more than martyrs, slogans, and vague generalizations. Those who wish to turn to the Koran for guidance, will, no doubt, find guidance there. But what of those who do not wish to do that, or for whom the Koran does not make any place? Do the Hindus of Jammu and other minorities also have the right to self-determination? Will the hundreds of thousands of Kashmiri Pandits living in exile, many of them in terrible poverty, have the right to return? Will they be paid reparations for the terrible losses they have suffered? Or will a free Kashmir do to its minorities what India has done to Kashmiris for sixty-one years? What will happen to homosexuals and adulterers and blasphemers? What of thieves and *lafangas* (rascals) and writers who do not agree with the "complete social and moral code"? Will we be put to death as we are in Saudi Arabia? Will the cycle of death, repression, and bloodshed continue? History offers many models for Kashmir's thinkers and intellectuals and politicians to study. What will the Kashmir of their dreams look like? Algeria? Iran? South Africa? Switzerland? Pakistan?

At a crucial time like this, few things are more important than dreams. A lazy utopia and a flawed sense of justice will have consequences that do not bear thinking about. This is not the time for intellectual sloth or a reluctance to assess a situation clearly and honestly. It could be argued that the prevarication of Maharaja Hari Singh in 1947 has been its great modern tragedy, one that eventually led to unthinkable bloodshed and the prolonged bondage of people who were very nearly free.

Already the specter of partition has reared its head. Hindutva networks are alive with rumors about Hindus in the valley being attacked and forced to flee. In response, phone calls from Jammu reported that an armed Hindu militia was threatening a massacre and that Muslims from the two Hindu majority districts were preparing to flee. (Memories of the bloodbath that ensued and claimed the lives of more than a million people when India and Pakistan were partitioned have come flooding back. That nightmare will haunt all of us forever.)

There is absolutely no reason to believe that history will repeat itself. Not unless it is made to. Not unless people actively work to create such a cataclysm. However, none of these fears of what the future holds can justify the continued military occupation of a nation and a people. No more than the old colonial argument about how the natives were not ready for freedom justified the colonial project.

Of course, there are many ways for the Indian state to continue to hold on to Kashmir. It could do what it does best. Wait. And hope the people's energy will dissipate in the absence of a concrete plan. It could try and fracture the fragile coalition that is emerging. It could extinguish this nonviolent uprising and re-invite armed militancy. It could increase the number of troops from half a million to a whole million. A few strategic massacres, a couple of targeted assassinations, some disappearances, and a massive round of arrests should do the trick for a few more years.

The unimaginable sums of public money that are needed to keep the military occupation of Kashmir going ought by right to be spent instead on schools and hospitals and food for an impoverished, malnutritioned population in India. What kind of government can possibly believe that it has the right to spend it on more weapons, more concertina wire, and more prisons in Kashmir?

The Indian military occupation of Kashmir makes monsters of us all. It allows Hindu chauvinists to target and victimize Muslims in India by holding them hostage to the freedom struggle being waged by Muslims in Kashmir. It's all being stirred into a poisonous brew and administered intravenously, straight into our bloodstream.

At the heart of it all is a moral question. Does any government have the right to take away people's liberty with military force?

India needs azadi from Kashmir just as much—if not more—than Kashmir needs azadi from India.

NINE IS NOT ELEVEN
(AND NOVEMBER
ISN'T SEPTEMBER)

WE'VE FORFEITED THE rights to our own tragedies. As the carnage in Mumbai raged on, day after horrible day, our twenty-four-hour news channels informed us that we were watching "India's 9/11." And like actors in a Bollywood rip-off of an old Hollywood film, we're expected to play our parts and say our lines, even though we know it's all been said and done before.

As tension in the region builds, US senator John McCain has warned Pakistan that, if it didn't act fast to arrest the "bad guys," he had personal information that India would launch air strikes on "terrorist camps" in Pakistan and that Washington could do nothing because Mumbai was "India's 9/11."

But November isn't September, 2008 isn't 2001, Pakistan isn't Afghanistan, and India isn't America. So perhaps we should reclaim our tragedy and pick through the debris with

This essay was published first by *Outlook*, on December 22, 2008, the *Guardian*, on December 12, 2008, and the *International Socialist Review*, Issue 63, January–February 2009.

our own brains and our own broken hearts so that we can arrive at our own conclusions.

It's odd how, in the last week of November, thousands of people in Kashmir supervised by thousands of Indian troops lined up to cast their vote, while the richest quarters of India's richest city ended up looking like war-torn Kupwara—one of Kashmir's most ravaged districts.

The Mumbai attacks are only the most recent of a spate of terrorist attacks on Indian towns and cities this year. Ahmedabad, Bangalore, Delhi, Guwahati, Jaipur, and Malegaon have all seen serial bomb blasts in which hundreds of ordinary people have been killed and wounded. If the police are right about the people they have arrested as suspects in these previous attacks, both Hindu and Muslim, all Indian nationals, it obviously indicates that something's going very badly wrong in this country.

If you were watching television, you might not have heard that ordinary people, too, died in Mumbai. They were mowed down in a busy railway station and a public hospital. The terrorists did not distinguish between poor and rich. They killed both with equal cold-bloodedness. The Indian media, however, was transfixed by the rising tide of horror that breached the glittering barricades of India Shining and spread its stench in the marbled lobbies and crystal ballrooms of two incredibly luxurious hotels and a small Jewish center.

We're told that one of these hotels is an icon of the city of Mumbai. That's absolutely true. It's an icon of the easy, obscene injustice that ordinary Indians endure every day. On a day when the newspapers were full of moving obituaries by beautiful people about the hotel rooms they had stayed in, the gourmet restaurants they loved (ironically one was called Kandahar), and the staff who served them, a small box on the top left-hand corner in the inner pages of a national newspaper (sponsored by a pizza company, I think) said, "Hungry, *kya?*" (Hungry, eh?). It then (with the best of intentions, I'm sure) informed its readers that, on the international hunger index, India ranked below

Sudan and Somalia. But of course this isn't that war. That one's still being fought in the Dalit *bastis* (settlements) of our villages; on the banks of the Narmada and the Koel Karo Rivers; in the rubber estate in Chengara; in the villages of Nandigram, Singur, and Lalgarh in West Bengal, in Chhattisgarh, Jharkhand, and Orissa, and the slums and shantytowns of our gigantic cities. That war isn't on TV. Yet. So maybe, like everyone else, we should deal with the one that is.

There is a fierce, unforgiving fault line that runs through the contemporary discourse on terrorism. On one side (let's call it Side A) are those who see terrorism, especially "Islamist" terrorism, as a hateful, insane scourge that spins on its own axis, in its own orbit, and has nothing to do with the world around it, nothing to do with history, geography, or economics. Therefore, Side A says, to try to place it in a political context, or even to try to understand it, amounts to justifying it and is a crime in itself. Side B believes that, though nothing can ever excuse or justify it, terrorism exists in a particular time, place, and political context, and to refuse to see that will only aggravate the problem and put more and more people in harm's way. Which is a crime in itself.

The sayings of Hafiz Saeed, who founded the Lashkar-e-Taiba (Army of the Pure) in 1990 and who belongs to the hard-line Salafi tradition of Islam, certainly bolsters the case of Side A. Hafiz Saeed approves of suicide bombing; hates Jews, Shias, and democracy; and believes that jihad should be waged until Islam, his Islam, rules the world. Among the things he said are: "There can't be any peace while India remains intact. Cut them, cut them—cut them so much that they kneel before you and ask for mercy." And: "India has shown us this path for jihad . . . We would like to give India a tit-for-tat response and reciprocate in the same way by killing the Hindus, just like it is killing the Muslims in Kashmir."

But where would Side A accommodate the sayings of Babu Bajrangi of Ahmedabad, India, who sees himself as a democrat, not a terrorist? He was one of the major lynchpins of the 2002 Gujarat genocide and has said (on camera):

> *We didn't spare a single Muslim shop, we set everything on fire, we set them on fire and killed them . . . hacked, burnt, set on fire . . . We believe in setting them on fire because these bastards don't want to be cremated, they're afraid of it . . . I have just . . . one last wish . . . Let me be sentenced to death . . . I don't care if I'm hanged . . . Give me two days before my hanging and I will go and have a field day in Juhapura [a Muslim-dominated area], where seven or eight lakh [seven or eight hundred thousand] of these people stay . . . I will finish them off . . . Let a few more of them die . . . At least twenty-five thousand to fifty thousand should die.*

And where in Side A's scheme of things would we place the Rashtriya Swayamsevak Sangh (RSS) bible, *We, or, Our Nationhood Defined* by M. S. Golwalkar, who became head of the RSS in 1944. It says: "Ever since that evil day, when Moslems first landed in Hindusthan, right up to the present moment, the Hindu Nation has been gallantly fighting to shake off the despoilers." Or: "To keep up the purity of the Race and its culture, Germany shocked the world by her purging of its Semitic Race, the Jews . . . Race pride at its highest has been manifested there . . . a good lesson for us in Hindusthan to learn and profit by."

Muslims are not the only people in the gun-sights of the Hindu Right. Dalits have been consistently targeted. Recently, in Kandhamal in Orissa, Christians were the target of two and a half months of violence that left at least sixteen dead. Forty thousand have been driven from their homes, many of whom now live in refugee camps.

All these years Hafiz Saeed has lived the life of a respectable man in Lahore as the head of the Jamaat-ud-Daawa, which many believe is a front organization for the Lashkar-e-Taiba. He continues to recruit young boys for his own bigoted jihad with his twisted, fiery sermons. On December 11, the United

Nations imposed sanctions on the Jamaat-ud-Daawa. The Pakistani government succumbed to international pressure and put Hafiz Saeed under house arrest. Babu Bajrangi, meanwhile, is out on bail and lives the life of a respectable man in Gujarat. A couple of years after the genocide, he left the Vishwa Hindu Parishad (a militia of the RSS) to join the Shiv Sena (another right-wing nationalist party). Narendra Modi, Bajrangi's former mentor, is still the chief minister of Gujarat. So the man who presided over the Gujarat genocide was reelected twice and is deeply respected by India's biggest corporate houses, Reliance and Tata. The policemen who supervised and sometimes even assisted the rampaging Hindu mobs in Gujarat have been rewarded and promoted.

The RSS has sixty thousand branches and more than four million volunteers preaching its doctrine of hate across India. They include Narendra Modi, but also former prime minister A. B. Vajpayee, current leader of the opposition L. K. Advani, and a host of other senior politicians, bureaucrats, and police and intelligence officers.

And if that's not enough to complicate our picture of secular democracy, we should place on record that there are plenty of Muslim organizations within India preaching their own narrow bigotry. So, on balance, if I had to choose between Side A and Side B, I'd pick Side B. We need context. Always.

On this nuclear subcontinent, that context is Partition. The Radcliffe Line, which separated India and Pakistan and tore through states, districts, villages, fields, communities, water systems, homes, and families, was drawn virtually overnight. It was Britain's final, parting kick to us.

Partition triggered the massacre of more than one million people and the largest migration of a human population in contemporary history. Eight million people, Hindus fleeing the new Pakistan, Muslims fleeing the new kind of India, left their homes with nothing but the clothes on their backs. Each of those people carries, and passes down, a story of unimaginable pain, hate, horror, but yearning, too. That wound, those torn but still un-severed muscles, that blood and those splintered bones still lock us together in a close embrace of hatred, terrifying familiarity but also love. It has left Kashmir trapped in a nightmare from which it can't seem to emerge, a nightmare that has claimed more than sixty thousand lives. Pakistan, the Land of the Pure, became the Islamic Republic of Pakistan—and then very quick-ly a corrupt, violent military state, openly intolerant of other faiths. India on the other hand declared herself an inclusive, sec-ular democracy.

It was a magnificent undertaking, but Babu Bajrangi's prede-cessors had been hard at work since the 1920s, dripping poison into India's bloodstream, undermining that idea of India even before it was born. By 1990, they were ready to make a bid for power. In 1992 Hindu mobs exhorted by L. K. Advani stormed the Babri Masjid and demolished it. By 1998, the Bharatiya Ja-nata Party was in power at the center. The US war on terror put the wind in their sails. It allowed them to do exactly as they pleased, even to commit genocide and then present their fascism as a legitimate form of chaotic democracy. This happened at a time when India had opened its huge market to international finance and it was in the interests of international corporations and the media houses they owned to project it as a country that could do no wrong. That gave Hindu nationalists all the impe-tus and the impunity they needed.

This, then, is the larger historical context of terrorism on the subcontinent—and of the Mumbai attacks. It shouldn't surprise us that Hafiz Saeed of the Lashkar-e-Taiba is from Shimla (In-dia) and L. K. Advani of the Rashtriya Swayamsevak Sangh is from Sindh (Pakistan).

In much the same way as it did after the 2001 Parliament at-tack, the 2002 burning of the Sabarmati Express, and the 2007 bombing of the Samjhauta Express, the government of India announced that it has "clear and incontrovertible proof" that the Lashkar-e-Taiba, backed by Pakistan's Inter-Services Intelligence, was behind the Mumbai strikes. The Lashkar has denied involvement but remains the prime accused. According to the police and intelligence agencies, the Lashkar operates in India through an organization called the "Indian Mujahideen." Two Indian nationals, Sheikh Mukhtar Ahmed, a special police officer working for the Jammu and Kashmir police, and Tausif Rehman, a resident of Kolkata in West Bengal, have been arrested in connection with the Mumbai attacks. So already the neat accusation against Pakistan is getting a little messy. Almost always when these stories unspool they reveal a complicated global network of foot soldiers, trainers, recruiters, middlemen, and undercover intelligence and counterintelligence operatives working not just on both sides of the India–Pakistan border, but in several countries simultaneously. In today's world, trying to pin down the provenance of a terrorist strike and isolate it within the borders of a single nation-state is very much like trying to pin down the provenance of corporate money. It's almost impossible.

In circumstances like these, air strikes to "take out" terrorist camps may take out the camps, but certainly will not "take out" the terrorists. And neither will war. (In our bid for the moral high ground, let's also try not to forget that the Liberation Tigers of Tamil Eelam (LTTE) of neighboring Sri Lanka, one of the world's most deadly militant groups, was trained by the Indian Army.)

Thanks largely to the part it was forced to play as America's ally, first in its war in support of the Afghan Islamists and then in its war against them, Pakistan, whose territory is reeling under these contradictions, is careening toward civil war. As recruiting agents for America's jihad against the Soviet Union, it was the job of the Pakistani Army and the Inter-Services Intelligence to nurture and channel funds to Islamic fundamentalist organizations. Having wired up these Frankensteins and released them into the world, the United States expected it could rein them in like pet mastiffs whenever it wanted to. Certainly it did not expect them to come calling in the heart of the homeland on

September 11. So once again, Afghanistan had to be violently remade. Now the debris of a re-ravaged Afghanistan has washed up on Pakistan's borders.

Nobody, least of all the Pakistani government, denies that it is presiding over a country that is threatening to implode. The terrorist training camps, the fire-breathing mullahs, and the maniacs who believe that Islam will, or should, rule the world are mostly the detritus of two Afghan wars. Their ire rains down on the Pakistani government and Pakistani civilians as much, if not more, than it does on India. If, at this point, India decides to go to war, perhaps the descent of the whole region into chaos will be complete. The debris of a bankrupt, destroyed Pakistan will wash up on India's shores, endangering us as never before. If Pakistan collapses, we can look forward to having millions of "non-state actors" with an arsenal of nuclear weapons at their disposal as neighbors. It's hard to understand why those who steer India's ship are so keen to replicate Pakistan's mistakes and call damnation upon this country by inviting the United States to further meddle clumsily and dangerously in our extremely complicated affairs. A superpower never has allies. It only has agents.

On the plus side, the advantage of going to war is that it's the best way for India to avoid facing up to the serious trouble building on our home front.

The Mumbai attacks were broadcast live (and exclusive!) on all or most of our sixty-seven 24-hour news channels and god knows how many international ones. TV anchors in their studios and journalists at "ground zero" kept up an endless stream of excited commentary. Over three days and three nights we watched in disbelief as a small group of very young men, armed with guns and gadgets, exposed the powerlessness of the police, the elite National Security Guard, and the Marine commandos of this supposedly mighty, nuclear-powered nation. While they did this, they indiscriminately massacred unarmed people, in railway stations, hospitals, and luxury hotels, unmindful of their class, caste, religion, or nationality. (Part of the helplessness of the security forces had to do with having to worry about hostages. In other situations, in Kashmir for example, their tactics are not so sensitive. Whole buildings are blown up. Human shields are used. The US and Israeli armies don't hesitate to send cruise missiles into buildings and drop daisy cutters on wedding parties in Palestine, Iraq, and Afghanistan.) This was different. And it was on TV.

The boy-terrorists' nonchalant willingness to kill—and be killed—mesmerized their international audience. They delivered something different from the usual diet of suicide bombings and missile attacks that people have grown inured to on the news. Here was something new. Die Hard 25. The gruesome performance went on and on. TV ratings soared. (Ask any television magnate or corporate advertiser who measures broadcast time in seconds, not minutes, what that's worth.)

Eventually the killers died, and died hard, all but one. (Perhaps, in the chaos, some escaped. We may never know.) Throughout the standoff the terrorists made no demands and expressed no desire to negotiate. Their purpose was to kill people, and inflict as much damage as they could, before they were killed themselves. They left us completely bewildered. When we say, "Nothing can justify terrorism," what most of us mean is that nothing can justify the taking of human life. We say this because we respect life, because we think it's precious. So what are we to make of those who care nothing for life, not even their own? The truth is that we have no idea what to make of them, because we can sense that even before they've died, they've journeyed to another world where we cannot reach them.

One TV channel (India TV) broadcast a phone conversation with one of the attackers, who called himself "Imran Babar." I cannot vouch for the veracity of the conversation, but the things he talked about were the things contained in the "terror emails" that were sent out before several other bomb attacks in India. Things we don't want to talk about anymore: the demolition of the Babri Masjid in 1992, the genocidal slaughter of Muslims in Gujarat in 2002, the brutal repression in Kashmir.

"You're surrounded," the anchor told him. "You're definitely going to die. Why don't you surrender?"

"We die every day," he replied in a strange, mechanical way. "It's better to live one day as a lion than die this way." He didn't seem to want to change the world. He just seemed to want to take it down with him.

If the men were indeed members of the Lashkar-e-Taiba, why didn't it matter to them that a large number of their victims were Muslim, or that their action was likely to result in a severe backlash against the Muslim community in India whose rights they claim to be fighting for? Terrorism is a heartless ideology, and like most ideologies that have their eye on the Big Picture, individuals don't figure in their calculations except as collateral damage. It has always been a part of, and often even the aim of, terrorist strategy to exacerbate a bad situation in order to expose hidden fault lines. The blood of "martyrs" irrigates terrorism. Hindu terrorists need dead Hindus, Communist terrorists need dead proletarians, Islamist terrorists need dead Muslims. The dead become the demonstration, the proof of victimhood, which is central to the project. A single act of terrorism is not in itself meant to achieve military victory; at best it is meant to be a catalyst that triggers something else, something much larger than itself, a tectonic shift, a realignment. The act itself is theater, spectacle, and symbolism, and today the stage on which it pirouettes and performs its acts of bestiality is live TV. Even as the Mumbai attacks were being condemned by TV anchors, the effectiveness of the terror strikes was being magnified a thousandfold by their broadcasts.

Through the endless hours of analysis and the endless op-ed essays, in India at least, there has been very little mention of the elephants in the room: Kashmir, Gujarat, and the demolition of the Babri Masjid. Instead, we had retired diplomats and strategic experts debate the pros and cons of a war against Pakistan. We had the rich threatening not to pay their taxes unless their security was guaranteed. (Is it all right for the poor to remain unprotected?) We had people suggest that the government step down and that each state in India be handed over to a separate corporation. We had the death of former prime minister V. P. Singh, the hero of Dalits and lower castes, and the villain of upper caste Hindus pass without a mention. We had Suketu Mehta, author of *Maximum City* and cowriter of the Bollywood film *Mission Kashmir*, give us his analysis of why religious bigots, both Hindu and Muslim, hate Mumbai: "Perhaps because Mumbai stands for lucre, profane dreams and an indiscriminate openness." His prescription: "The best answer to the terrorists is to dream bigger, make even more money, and visit Mumbai more than ever." Didn't George Bush ask Americans to go out and shop after 9/11? Ah yes. September 11, the day we can't seem to get away from.

Though one chapter of horror in Mumbai has ended, another might have just begun. Day after day, a powerful, vociferous section of the Indian elite, goaded by marauding TV anchors who make Fox News look almost radical and left wing, have taken to mindlessly attacking politicians, all politicians, glorifying the police and the army, and virtually asking for a police state. It isn't surprising that those who have grown plump on the pickings of democracy (such as it is) should now be calling for a police state. The era of "pickings" is long gone. We're now in the era of Grabbing by Force, and democracy has a terrible habit of getting in the way.

Dangerous, stupid oversimplifications like the Police Are Good / Politicians Are Bad, Chief Executives Are Good / Chief Ministers Are Bad, Army Is Good / Government Is Bad, India Is Good / Pakistan Is Bad are being bandied about by TV channels that have already whipped their viewers into a state of almost uncontrollable hysteria.

Tragically, this regression into intellectual infancy comes at a time when people in India were beginning to see that, in the business of terrorism, victims and perpetrators sometimes exchange roles. It's an understanding that the people of Kashmir, given their dreadful experiences of the last twenty years, have honed to an exquisite art. On the mainland we're still learning. (If Kashmir won't willingly integrate into India, it's beginning to look as though India will integrate/disintegrate into Kashmir.)

It was after the 2001 Parliament attack that the first serious questions began to be raised. A campaign by a group of lawyers and activists exposed how innocent people had been framed by the police and the press, how evidence was fabricated, how witnesses lied, how due process had been criminally violated at every stage of the investigation. Eventually, the courts acquitted two out of the four accused, including S. A. R. Geelani, the man whom the police claimed was the mastermind of the operation. A third, Shaukat Guru, was acquitted of all the charges brought against him, but was then convicted for a fresh, comparatively minor offense. The Supreme Court upheld the death sentence of another of the accused, Mohammad Afzal. In its judgment, the court acknowledged that there was no proof that Mohammad Afzal belonged to any terrorist group but went on to say, "The collective conscience of the society will only be satisfied if capital punishment is awarded to the offender." Even today we don't really know who the terrorists that attacked the Indian Parliament were and who they worked for.

More recently, on September 19, 2008, we had the controversial "encounter" at Batla House in Jamia Nagar, Delhi, where the Special Cell of the Delhi police gunned down two Muslim students in their rented flat under seriously questionable circumstances, claiming that they were responsible for serial bombings in Delhi, Jaipur, and Ahmedabad in 2008. An assistant commissioner of police, Mohan Chand Sharma, who played a key role in the Parliament attack investigation, lost his life as well. He was one of India's many "encounter specialists," known and rewarded for having summarily executed several "terrorists." There was an outcry against the Special Cell from a spectrum of people, ranging from eyewitnesses in the local community to senior Congress Party leaders, students, journalists, lawyers, academics, and activists, all of whom demanded a judicial inquiry into the incident. In response, the Bharatiya Janata Party and L. K. Advani lauded Mohan Chand Sharma as a "Braveheart" and launched a concerted campaign in which they targeted those who had dared to question the "integrity" of the police, saying to do so was "suicidal" and calling them "antinational." Of course there has been no inquiry.

Only days after the Batla House event, another story about "terrorists" surfaced in the news. In a report submitted to a Sessions Court, the Central Bureau of Investigation said that a team from Delhi's Special Cell (the same team that led the Batla House encounter, including Mohan Chand Sharma) had abducted two innocent men, Irshad Ali and Moarif Qamar, in December 2005, planted two kilograms of RDX (explosives) and two pistols on them, and then arrested them as "terrorists" who belonged to Al Badr (which operates out of Kashmir). Ali and Qamar, who have spent years in jail, are only two examples out of hundreds of Muslims who have been similarly jailed, tortured, and even killed on false charges.

This pattern changed in October 2008 when Maharashtra's Anti-Terrorism Squad (ATS), which was investigating the September 2008 Malegaon blasts, arrested a Hindu preacher, Sadhvi Pragya, a self-styled God man, Swami Dayanand Pande, and lieutenant colonel Prasad Purohit, a serving officer of the Indian Army. All the arrested belong to Hindu nationalist organizations, including a Hindu supremacist group called Abhinav Bharat. The Shiv Sena, the Bharatiya Janata Party, and the RSS condemned the Maharashtra ATS, and vilified its chief, Hemant Karkare, claiming he was part of a political conspiracy and declaring that "Hindus could not be terrorists." L. K. Advani changed his mind about his policy on the police and made rabble-rousing speeches to huge gatherings in which he denounced the ATS for daring to cast aspersions on holy men and women.

On November 24, 2008, newspapers reported that the ATS was considering an investigation into the high-profile Vishwa

Hindu Parishad chief Pravin Togadia's possible role in the blasts in Malegaon (a predominantly Muslim town). Two days later, in an extraordinary twist of fate, the chief of the ATS, Hemant Karkare, was killed in the Mumbai attacks. The chances are that the new chief, whoever he is, will find it hard to withstand the political pressure that is bound to be brought on him over the Malegaon investigation. While the Sangh Parivar does not seem to have come to a final decision over whether or not it is antinational and suicidal to question the police, Arnab Goswami, anchorperson of Times Now television, has stepped up to the plate. He has taken to naming, demonizing, and openly heckling people who have dared to question the integrity of the police and armed forces. My name and the name of the well-known lawyer Prashant Bhushan have come up several times. At one point, while interviewing a former police officer, Arnab Goswami turned to the camera: "I hope Arundhati Roy and Prashant Bhushan are listening," he said. "We haven't invited them to our show because we think they are disgusting." For a TV anchor to do this in an atmosphere as charged and as frenzied as the one that prevails today amounts to incitement, as well as threat, and would probably in different circumstances have cost a journalist his or her job.

So, according to a man aspiring to be the next prime minister of India, and another who is the public face of a mainstream TV channel, citizens have no right to raise questions about the police. This in a country with a shadowy history of suspicious terror attacks, murky investigations, and fake "encounters." This in a country that boasts of the highest number of custodial deaths in the world, and yet refuses to ratify the United Nations Convention against Torture. A country where the ones who make it to torture chambers are the lucky ones because at least they've escaped being "encountered" by our Encounter Specialists. A country where the line between the underworld and the Encounter Specialists virtually does not exist.

How should those of us whose hearts have been sickened by the knowledge of all this view the Mumbai attacks, and what are we to do about them? There are those who point out that US strategy has been successful inasmuch as the United States has not suffered a major attack on its home ground since 9/11. However, some would say that what America is suffering now is far worse. If the idea behind the 9/11 terror attacks was to goad America into showing its true colors, what greater success could the terrorists have asked for? The US military is bogged down in two unwinnable wars, which have made the United States the most hated country in the world. Those wars have contributed greatly to the unraveling of the American economy and who knows, perhaps eventually the American empire. (Could it be that battered, bombed Afghanistan, the graveyard of the Soviet Union, will be the undoing of this one, too?) Hundreds of thousands of people, including thousands of American soldiers, have lost their lives in Iraq and Afghanistan. The frequency of terrorist strikes on US allies/agents (including India) and US interests in the rest of the world has increased dramatically since 9/11. George W. Bush, the man who led the US response to 9/11, is a despised figure not just internationally, but also by his own people. Who can possibly claim that the United States is winning the war on terror?

Homeland security has cost the US government billions of dollars. Few countries, certainly not India, can afford that sort of price tag. But even if we could, the fact is that this vast homeland of ours cannot be secured or policed in the way the United States has been. It's not that kind of homeland. We have a hostile nuclear-weapons state that is slowly spinning out of control as a neighbor; we have a military occupation in Kashmir and a shamefully persecuted, impoverished minority of more than 150 million Muslims who are being targeted as a community and pushed to the wall, whose young see no justice on the horizon, and who, were they to totally lose hope and radicalize, will end up as a threat not just to India, but to the whole world.

If ten men can hold off the National Security Guard commandos and the police for three days, and if it takes half a million soldiers to hold down the Kashmir valley, do the math. What kind of homeland security can secure India?

Nor for that matter will any other quick fix. Antiterrorism laws are not meant for terrorists; they're for people that governments don't like. That's why they have a conviction rate of less than 2 percent. They're just a means of putting inconvenient people away without bail for a long time and eventually letting them go. Terrorists like those who attacked Mumbai are hardly likely to be deterred by the prospect of being refused bail or being sentenced to death. It's what they want.

What we're experiencing now is blowback, the cumulative result of decades of quick fixes and dirty deeds. The carpet's squelching under our feet.

The only way to contain—it would be naive to say end—terrorism is to look at the monster in the mirror. We're standing at a fork in the road. One sign points in the direction of "Justice," the other says "Civil War." There's no third sign, and there's no going back. Choose.

DEMOCRACY'S
FAILING LIGHT

WHILE WE'RE STILL arguing about whether there's life after death, can we add another question to the cart? Is there life after democracy? What sort of life will it be? By "democracy" I don't mean democracy as an ideal or an aspiration. I mean the working model: Western liberal democracy, and its variants, such as they are.

So, is there life after democracy?

Attempts to answer this question often turn into a comparison of different systems of governance and end with a somewhat prickly, combative defense of democracy. It's flawed, we say. It isn't perfect, but it's better than everything else that's on offer. Inevitably, someone in the room will say: "Afghanistan, Pakistan, Saudi Arabia, Somalia . . . is that what you would prefer?"

Whether democracy should be the utopia that all "developing" societies aspire to is a separate question altogether. (I think it should. The early, idealistic phase can be quite heady.) The question about life after democracy is addressed to those of us

---

First published in *Outlook*, July 23, 2009.

who already live in democracies or in countries that pretend to be democracies. It isn't meant to suggest that we lapse into older, discredited models of totalitarian or authoritarian governance. It's meant to suggest that the system of representative democracy—too much representation, too little democracy—needs some structural adjustment.

The question here, really, is what have we done to democracy? What have we turned it into? What happens once democracy has been used up? When it has been hollowed out and emptied of meaning? What happens when each of its institutions has metastasized into something dangerous? What happens now that democracy and the free market have fused into a single predatory organism with a thin, constricted imagination that revolves almost entirely around the idea of maximizing profit? Is it possible to reverse this process? Can something that has mutated go back to being what it used to be?

What we need today, for the sake of the survival of this planet, is long-term vision. Can governments whose very survival depends on immediate, extractive, short-term gain provide this? Could it be that democracy, the sacred answer to our short-term hopes and prayers, the protector of our individual freedoms and nurturer of our avaricious dreams, will turn out to be the endgame for the human race? Could it be that democracy is such a hit with modern humans precisely because it mirrors our greatest folly—our nearsightedness? Our inability to live entirely in the present (like most animals do), combined with our inability to see very far into the future, makes us strange in-between creatures, neither beast nor prophet. Our amazing intelligence seems to have outstripped our instinct for survival. We plunder the earth hoping that accumulating material surplus will make up for the profound, unfathomable thing that we have lost.

It would be conceit to pretend that the essays in this book provide answers to any of these questions. They only demonstrate, in some detail, the fact that it looks as though the beacon could be failing and that democracy can perhaps no longer be relied upon to deliver the justice and stability we once dreamed it would. All the essays were written as urgent, public interventions at critical moments in India—during the state-backed genocide against Muslims in Gujarat; just before the date set for the hanging of Mohammad Afzal, the accused in the December 13, 2001, Parliament attack; during US president George Bush's visit to India; during the mass uprising in Kashmir in the summer of 2008; after the November 26, 2008, Mumbai attacks. Often they were not just responses to events, they were responses to the responses.

Though many of them were written in anger, at moments when keeping quiet became harder than saying something, the essays do have a common thread. They're not about unfortunate anomalies or aberrations in the democratic process. They're about the consequences of and the corollaries to democracy; they're about the fire in the ducts. I should also say that they do not provide a panoramic overview. They're a detailed underview of specific events that I hoped would reveal some of the ways in which democracy is practiced in the world's largest democracy. (Or the world's largest "demon-crazy," as a Kashmiri protester on the streets of Srinagar once put it. His placard said: "Democracy without Justice is Demon-crazy.")

As a writer, a fiction writer, I have often wondered whether the attempt to always be precise, to try and get it all factually right, somehow reduces the epic scale of what is really going on. Does it eventually mask a larger truth? I worry that I am allowing myself to be railroaded into offering prosaic, factual precision when maybe what we need is a feral howl, or the transformative power and real precision of poetry. Something about the cunning, Brahmanical, intricate, bureaucratic, file-bound, "apply-through-proper-channels" nature of governance and subjugation in India seems to have made a clerk out of me. My only excuse is to say that it takes odd tools to uncover the maze of subterfuge and hypocrisy that cloaks the callousness and the cold, calculated violence of the world's favorite new superpower. Repression "through proper channels" sometimes engenders resistance "through proper channels." As resistance goes this isn't enough, I know. But for now, it's all I have. Perhaps someday it will become the underpinning for poetry and for the feral howl.

❖

"Listening to Grasshoppers" was a lecture I gave in Istanbul in January 2008 on the first anniversary of the assassination of the Armenian journalist Hrant Dink. He was shot down on the street outside his office for daring to raise a subject that is forbidden in Turkey—the 1915 genocide of Armenians in which more than one million people were killed. My lecture was about the history of genocide and genocide denial and the old, almost organic relationship between "progress" and genocide.

I have always been struck by the fact that the political party in Turkey that carried out the Armenian genocide was called the Committee for Union and Progress. Most of the essays in this collection are, in fact, about the contemporary correlation between Union and Progress, or, in today's idiom, between Nationalism and Development—those unimpeachable twin towers of modern, free market democracy. Both of these in their extreme form are, as we now know, encrypted with the potential of bringing about ultimate, apocalyptic destruction (nuclear war, climate change).

Though these essays were written between 2002 and 2008, the invisible marker, the starting gun, is the year 1989, when, in the rugged mountains of Afghanistan, capitalism won its long jihad against Soviet Communism. (Of course, the wheel's in spin again. Could it be that those same mountains are now in the process of burying capitalism? It's too early to tell.) Within months of the collapse of the Soviet Union and the fall of the Berlin Wall, the Indian government, once a leader of the Non-aligned Movement, performed a high-speed somersault and aligned itself completely with the United States, monarch of the new unipolar world.

The rules of the game changed suddenly and completely. Millions of people who lived in remote villages and deep in the heart of untouched forests, some of whom had never heard of Berlin or the Soviet Union, could not have imagined how events that occurred in those faraway places would affect their lives. The process of their dispossession and displacement had already begun in the early 1950s, when India opted for the Soviet-style development model in which huge steel plants (Bhilai, Bokaro) and large dams (thousands of them) would occupy the "commanding heights" of the economy. The era of Privatization and Structural Adjustment accelerated that process at a mind-numbing speed.

Today, words like "Progress" and "Development" have become interchangeable with economic "Reforms," Deregulation, and Privatization. Freedom has come to mean choice. It has less to do with the human spirit than with different brands of deodorant. Market no longer means a place where you buy provisions. The "Market" is a de-territorialized space where faceless corporations do business, including buying and selling "futures." Justice has come to mean human rights (and of those, as they say, "a few will do"). This theft of language, this technique of usurping words and deploying them like weapons, of using them to mask intent and to mean exactly the opposite of what they have traditionally meant, has been one of the most brilliant strategic victories of the tsars of the new dispensation. It has allowed them to marginalize their detractors, deprive them of a language to voice their critique and dismiss them as being "antiprogress," "antidevelopment," "antireform," and of course "antinational"—negativists of the worst sort. Talk about saving a river or protecting a forest and they say, "Don't you believe in Progress?" To people whose land is being submerged by dam reservoirs, and whose homes are being bulldozed, they say, "Do you have an alternative development model?" To those who believe that a government is duty bound to provide people with basic education, health care, and social security, they say, "You're against the market." And who except a cretin could be against markets?

To reclaim these stolen words requires explanations that are too tedious for a world with a short attention span and too expensive in an era when Free Speech has become unaffordable for the poor. This language heist may prove to be the keystone of our undoing.

Two decades of this kind of "Progress" in India has created a vast middle class punch-drunk on sudden wealth and the sudden respect that comes with it—and a much, much vaster, desperate, underclass. Tens of millions of people have been dispossessed and displaced from their land by floods, droughts, and desertification caused by indiscriminate environmental engineering and massive infrastructural projects, dams, mines, and Special Economic Zones. All developed in the name of the poor, but really meant to service the rising demands of the new aristocracy.

The battle for land lies at the heart of the "development" debate. Before he became India's finance minister, P. Chidambaram was Enron's lawyer and member of the board of directors of Vedanta, a multinational mining corporation that is currently devastating the Niyamgiri hills in Orissa. Perhaps his career graph informed his worldview. Or maybe it's the other way around. In an interview a year ago, he said that his vision was to get 85 percent of India's population to live in cities. That process is well under way and is quickly turning India into a police state in which people who refuse to surrender their land are being made to do so at gunpoint. Perhaps this is what makes it so easy for P. Chidambaram to move so seamlessly from being finance minister to being home minister. The portfolios are separated only by an osmotic membrane. Underlying this nightmare masquerading as "vision" is the plan to free up vast tracts of land and all of India's natural resources, leaving them ripe for corporate plunder—in effect, to reverse the post-Independence policy of land reforms.

Already forests, mountains, and water systems are being ravaged by marauding multinational corporations, backed by a state that has lost its moorings and is committing what can only be called ecocide. In eastern India bauxite and iron ore mining is destroying whole ecosystems, turning fertile land into desert. In the Himalayas hundreds of high dams are being planned, the consequences of which can only be catastrophic. In the plains, embankments built along rivers, ostensibly to control floods, have led to rising riverbeds, causing even more flooding, more waterlogging, more salinization of agricultural land, and the destruction of livelihoods of millions of people. Most of India's holy rivers, including the Ganga, have been turned into unholy drains that carry more sewage and industrial effluent than water. Hardly a single river runs its course and meets the ocean.

Based on the absurd notion that a river flowing into the sea is a "waste" of water, the Supreme Court, in an act of unbelievable hubris, has arbitrarily ordered that India's rivers be interlinked, like a mechanical water supply system. Implementing this would mean tunneling through mountains and forests, altering natural contours and drainage systems of river basins and destroying deltas and estuaries. In other words, wrecking the ecology of the entire subcontinent. (B. N. Kirpal, the judge who passed this order, joined the environmental board of Coca-Cola after he retired. Nice touch!)

The regime of free market economic policies, administered by people who are blissfully ignorant of the fate of civilizations that grew too dependent on artificial irrigation, has led to a worrying shift in cropping patterns. Sustainable food crops, suitable to local soil conditions and microclimates, have been replaced by water-guzzling, hybrid, and genetically modified "cash" crops, which, apart from being wholly dependent on the market, are also heavily dependent on chemical fertilizers, pesticides, canal irrigation, and the indiscriminate mining of groundwater. As abused farmland, saturated with chemicals, gradually becomes exhausted and infertile, agricultural input costs rise, ensnaring small farmers in a debt trap. Over the last few years, more than 180,000 Indian farmers have committed suicide. While state granaries are bursting with food that eventually rots, starvation and malnutrition approaching the same levels as sub-Saharan Africa stalk the land. Truly the 9 percent growth rate is beginning to look like a downward spiral. The higher the rate of this kind of growth, the worse the prognosis. Any oncologist will tell you that.

It's as though an ancient society, decaying under the weight of feudalism and caste, was churned in a great machine. The churning has ripped through the mesh of old inequalities, recalibrating some of them but reinforcing most. Now the old society has curdled and separated into a thin layer of thick cream—and a lot of water. The cream is India's "market" of many million consumers (of cars, cell phones, computers, Valentine's Day greeting cards), the envy of international business. The water is of little consequence. It can be sloshed around, stored in holding ponds, and eventually drained away.

Or so they think, the men in suits. They didn't bargain for the violent civil war that has broken out in India's heartland: Chhattisgarh, Jharkhand, Orissa, West Bengal.

❖

Coming back to 1989. As if to illustrate the connection between "Union" and "Progress," at exactly the same time that the Congress government was opening up India's markets to international finance, the right-wing Bharatiya Janata Party (BJP), then in the opposition, began its virulent campaign of Hindu nationalism (popularly known as Hindutva). In 1990, its leader, L. K. Advani, traveled across the country whipping up hatred against Muslims and demanding that the Babri Masjid, an old sixteenth-century mosque that stood on a disputed site in Ayodhya, be demolished and a Ram temple built in its place. In 1992, a mob, egged on by Advani, demolished the mosque. In early 1993, a mob rampaged through Mumbai attacking Muslims, killing almost one thousand people. As revenge, a series of bomb blasts ripped through the city, killing about 250 people. Feeding off the communal frenzy it had generated, the BJP, which had only two seats in Parliament in 1984, defeated the Congress Party in 1998 and came to power at the center.

It's not a coincidence that the rise of Hindutva corresponded with the historical moment when the United States substituted Communism with Islam as its great enemy. The radical Islamist mujahideen—whom President Reagan once entertained at the White House and compared to America's Founding Fathers—suddenly began to be called terrorists. CNN's live broadcast of the 1990–1991 Gulf War—Operation Desert Storm—made it to elite drawing rooms in Indian cities, bringing with it the early thrills of satellite TV. Almost simultaneously, the Indian government, once a staunch friend of the Palestinians, turned into Israel's "natural ally." Now India and Israel do joint military exercises, share intelligence, and probably exchange notes on how best to administer occupied territories.

By 1998, when the BJP took office, the "Progress" project of Privatization and Liberalization was eight years old. Though it had campaigned vigorously against the economic reforms, saying they were a process of "looting through liberalization," once it came to power the BJP embraced the free market enthusiastically and threw its weight behind huge corporations like Enron. (In representative democracies, once they're elected, the people's representatives are free to break their promises and change their minds.)

Within weeks of taking office, the BJP conducted a series of thermonuclear tests. Though India had thrown its hat into the nuclear ring in 1975, politically the 1998 nuclear tests were of a different order altogether. The orgy of triumphant nationalism with which the tests were greeted introduced a chilling new language of aggression and hatred into mainstream public discourse. None of what was being said was new, it's just that what was once considered unacceptable was suddenly being celebrated. Since then, Hindu communalism and nuclear nationalism, like corporate globalization, have vaulted over the stated ideologies of political parties. The venom has been injected straight into our bloodstream. It's there now—in all its violence and banality—for us to deal with in our daily lives, regardless of whether the government at the center calls itself secular or not. The Muslim community has seen a sharp decline in its fortunes and is now at the bottom of the social pyramid, along with Dalits and Adivasis.

Certain events that occur in the life of a nation have the effect of parting the curtains and giving ordinary people a glimpse into the future. The 1998 nuclear tests were one such. You don't need the gift of prophecy to tell in which direction India was heading. This is an excerpt from "The End of Imagination," an essay that I wrote after the nuclear tests:

"Explosion of Self-esteem," "Road to Resurgence," "A Moment of Pride," these were headlines in the papers in the days following the nuclear tests . . .

"These are not just nuclear tests, they are nationalism tests," we were repeatedly told.

This has been hammered home, over and over again. The bomb is India, India is the bomb. Not just India, Hindu India. Therefore, be warned, any criticism of it is not just antinational, but anti-Hindu . . . This is one of the unexpected perks of having a nuclear bomb. Not only can the government use it to threaten the enemy, it can use it to declare war on its own people. Us . . .

Why does it all seem so familiar? Is it because, even as you watch, reality dissolves and seamlessly rushes forward into the silent, black-and-white images from old films—scenes of people being hounded out of their lives, rounded up, and herded into camps? Of massacre, of mayhem, of endless columns of broken people making their way to nowhere? Why is there no soundtrack? Why is the hall so quiet? Have I been seeing too many films? Am I mad? Or am I right? Could those images be the inescapable

*culmination of what we have set into motion? Could our future be
rushing forward into our past?*

The "Us" I referred to was those of us who do not belong
to—or identify ourselves—with the "Hindu" majority. By
"past," I was referring to the Partition of India in 1947, when
more than one million Hindus and Muslims killed each other,
and eight million became refugees.

❖

In February 2002, following the burning of a train coach in which
fifty-eight Hindu pilgrims returning from Ayodhya were burned
alive, the BJP government in Gujarat, led by chief minister Narendra Modi, presided over a carefully planned genocide against
Muslims in the state. The Islamophobia generated all over the
world by the September 11, 2001, attacks put wind in their sails.
The machinery of the Gujarat state stood by and watched while
more than two thousand people were massacred. Women were
gang-raped and burned alive. One hundred and fifty thousand
Muslims were driven from their homes. The community was—
and continues to be—ghettoized, socially and economically
ostracized. Gujarat has always been a communally tense state.
There have been riots before. But this was not a riot. It was a
genocidal massacre, and though the number of victims was insignificant compared to the horror of, say, Rwanda, Sudan, or the
Congo, the Gujarat carnage was designed as a public spectacle
whose aims were unmistakable. It was a public warning to Muslim
citizens from the government of the world's favorite democracy.

After the carnage, Narendra Modi pressed for early elections.
He was returned to power with a mandate from the people of
Gujarat. Five years later he repeated his success: he is now serving a third term as chief minister, widely appreciated across the
country for his clear thinking and his faith in the free market. To
be fair to the people of Gujarat, the only alternative they had to

Narendra Modi's brand of Hindutva (nuclear) was the Congress Party's candidate, Shankarsinh Vaghela, a disgruntled former BJP chief minister. All he had to offer was Hindutva (lite and muddled). Not surprisingly, it didn't make the cut.

The Gujarat genocide is the subject of "Democracy: Who Is She When She's at Home?" written in May 2002 when murderous mobs still roamed the streets, killing and intimidating Muslims. I have deliberately not updated the text of any of the essays, because I thought it would be interesting to see how a hard look at the systemic nature of what is going on often contains within it a forecast of events that are still to come. So instead of updating the text of the essays, I've added new notes. For example, a paragraph in the essay on the Gujarat genocide says:

> *Can we expect an anniversary celebration next year? Or will there be someone else to hate by then? Alphabetically: Adivasis, Buddhists, Christians, Dalits, Parsis, Sikhs? Those who wear jeans or speak English or those who have thick lips or curly hair? We won't have to wait long.*

Mobs led by Congress Party leaders had already slaughtered thousands of Sikhs on the streets of Delhi in 1984, as revenge for the assassination of Indira Gandhi by her Sikh bodyguards. Goons belonging to the Bajrang Dal, a Hindu militia, attacked an Australian missionary, Graham Staines, and his two young sons, and burned them alive in January 1999. By December 2007, attacks on Christians by Hindu militias moved beyond stray incidents. In several states—Gujarat, Karnataka, Orissa—Christians were attacked, churches gutted. In Kandhamal, Orissa, at least sixteen Dalit and Adivasi Christians were killed by "Hindu" Dalits and Adivasis. ("Hinduizing" Dalits and Adivasis, pitting them against each other, as well as against Muslims and Maoists, is perhaps the mainstay of the Hindutva project.) Tens of thousands of Christians now live in refugee camps or hide in the surrounding forests, afraid to venture out to tend their fields and crops. (Once again, it's not a coincidence that these communities live in forests and on mineral-rich lands that corporations have their eyes on and governments want vacated. So the Hindutva *shivirs* [camps], under the pretext of bringing them into the "Hindu fold," are a means of controlling people.)

In December 2008, protected by the first-ever BJP government to come to power in a southern state, Hindu vigilante mobs in Bangalore and Mangalore—the hub of India's IT industry—began to attack women who wear jeans and western clothes. The threat is ongoing. Hindu militias have vowed to turn Karnataka into another Gujarat. That the BJP has struck roots in states like Karnataka and Gujarat, both front-runners in the globalization project, once again illustrates the organic relationship between "Union" and "Progress." Or, if you like, between fascism and the free market.

In January 2009 that relationship was sealed with a kiss at a public function. The CEOs of two of India's biggest corporations, Ratan Tata (of the Tata Group) and Mukesh Ambani (of Reliance Industries), while accepting the Gujarat Garima—Pride of Gujarat—award, celebrated the development policies of Narendra Modi, architect of the Gujarat genocide, and warmly endorsed him as a candidate for prime minister.

As this book goes to press, the nearly $2 billion 2009 general election has just been concluded. That's a lot more than the budget of the US elections. According to some media reports, the actual amount that was spent is closer to $10 billion. Where, might one ask, does that kind of money come from?

The Congress and its allies, the United Progressive Alliance (UPA), have won a comfortable majority. Interestingly, more than 90 percent of the independent candidates who stood for elections lost. Clearly, without sponsorship it's hard to win an election. And independent candidates cannot promise subsidized rice, free TVs, and cash for votes, those demeaning acts of vulgar charity that elections have been reduced to.

When you take a closer look at the calculus that underlies elections, words like "comfortable" and "majority" turn out to be deceptive, if not outright inaccurate. For instance, the actual share of votes polled by the UPA in these elections works out to only 10.3 percent of the country's population! It's interesting how the cleverly layered mathematics of electoral democracy can turn a tiny minority into a thumping mandate. Anyway, be that as it may, the point is that it will not be L. K. Advani, hatemonger incarnate, but Dr. Manmohan Singh, gentle architect of the market reforms, a man who has never won an election in his life, who will be prime minister of the world's largest democracy for a second term.

In the run-up to the polls, there was absolute consensus across party lines about the economic reforms. K. N. Govindacharya, formerly the chief ideologue of the BJP, progenitor of the Ram Janamabhoomi movement, sarcastically suggested that the Congress and BJP form a coalition. In some states they already have. In Chhattisgarh, for example, the BJP runs the government and Congress politicians run the Salwa Judum, a vicious government-backed "people's" militia. The Judum and the government have formed a joint front against the Maoists in the forests who are engaged in a deadly and often brutal armed struggle against displacement and against land acquisition by corporations waiting to set up steel factories and to begin mining iron ore, tin, and all the other wealth stashed below the forest floor. So, in Chhattisgarh, we have the remarkable spectacle of the two biggest political parties of India in an alliance against the Adivasis of Dantewara, India's poorest, most vulnerable people. Already 644 villages have been emptied. Fifty thousand people have moved into Salwa Judum camps. Three hundred thousand are hiding in the forests and are being called Maoist terrorists or sympathizers. The battle is raging, and the corporations are waiting.

It is significant that India is one of the countries that blocked a European move in the UN asking for an international probe into war crimes that may have been committed by the government of Sri Lanka in its recent offensive against the Tamil Tigers. Governments in this part of the world have taken note of

Israel's Gaza blueprint as a good way of dealing with "terrorism": keep the media out and close in for the kill. That way they don't have to worry too much about who's a "terrorist" and who isn't. There may be a little flurry of international outrage, but it goes away pretty quickly.

Things do not augur well for the forest-dwelling people of Chhattisgarh.

Reassured by the sort of "constructive" collaboration, the consensus between political parties, few were more enthusiastic about the elections than some of the major corporate houses. They seem to have realized that a democratic mandate can legitimize their pillaging in a way that nothing else can. Several corporations ran extravagant advertising campaigns on TV, some featuring Bollywood film stars urging people, young and old, rich and poor, to go out and vote. Shops and restaurants in Khan Market, Delhi's most tony market, offered discounts to those whose index (voting) fingers were marked with indelible ink. Democracy suddenly became the cool new way to be. You know how it is: the Chinese do Sport, so they had the Olympics. India does Democracy, so we had an election. Both are heavily sponsored, TV-friendly spectator sports.

The BBC commissioned a coach on a train—the India Election Special—that took journalists from all over the world on a sightseeing tour to witness the miracle of Indian elections. The train coach had a slogan painted on it: Will India's voters revive the World's Fortunes? BBC (Hindi) had a poster up in a café near my home. It featured a $100 bill (with Ben Franklin) morphing into a 500 rupee note (with Gandhi). It said: Kya India ka vote bachayega duniya ka note? (Will India's votes rescue the world's notes?) In these flagrant and unabashed ways, an electorate has been turned into a market, voters are seen as consumers, and democracy is being welded to the free market. Ergo: those who cannot consume do not matter.

What does the victory of the UPA mean in this election? Obviously myriad things. The debate is wide open. Interpreting an Indian election is about as exact a science as sorcery. Voting patterns are intricately connected with local issues and caste and community equations that vary literally from polling booth to polling booth. There can be no reliable Big Conclusion. But here's something to think about.

In its time in office, in order to mitigate the devastation caused by its economic policies, the former Congress regime passed three progressive (critics call them populist and controversial) parliamentary acts: the Forest Rights Act (which gave forest dwellers legal right to land and the traditional use of forest produce), the Right to Information Act and, most important of all, the National Rural Employment Guarantee Act (NREGA). The NREGA guarantees every rural family a hundred days of work (hard, manual labor) a year at minimum wages. It amounts to an average of 8,000 rupees (a little more than $120) per family per year. Enough for a good meal in a restaurant, including wine and dessert. Imagine how hellish times must be for even that tiny amount of money to come as a relief to millions of people who are reeling under the impact of the precipitous loss of their lands and their livelihoods. (Talk about crumbs from the high table. But then, which one of us has the heart, or the right, to argue that no crumbs are better than crumbs? Or, indeed, that no elections are better than meaningless elections?) Implementing the NREGA, seeing that the crumbs actually reach the people they're meant for, has occupied all the time and energy of some of India's finest and most committed social activists for the last several years. They have had to battle cartels of corrupt government officers, power brokers, and middlemen. They have faced threats and a fair amount of violence. One rural activist in the Jharkhand immolated himself in anger and frustration at the injustice of it all.

Ironically, the NREGA only made it through Parliament because of pressure brought to bear on the UPA government by the Left Front and, it must be said, by Sonia Gandhi. It was passed despite tremendous resistance from the mandarins of the free market within the Congress Party. The corporate media were more or less unanimously hostile to the act. Needless to say, come election time the NREGA became one of the main planks of the Congress Party's campaign. There's little doubt that the goodwill it generated among the very poor translated into votes for the Congress. But now that the elections are over, victory is being attributed to the very policies that the NREGA was passed to mitigate! The captains of industry have lost no time in claiming the "people's mandate" as their own. "It's fast forward for markets," the business papers crowed the morning after. "Vote [was] for reforms, says India Inc."

There is an even greater irony; the Left Front, acting with the duplicity that has become second nature to all parliamentary political parties, took a sharp turn to the right. Even while it criticized the government's economic policies at the center, it tried to enforce similar ones on its home turf in West Bengal. It announced that it was going to build a chemical hub in the district of Nandigram, a manufacturing unit for the Tata Nano in Singur, and a Jindal Steel plant in the forests of Lalgarh in Purulia. It began to acquire land, most of it fertile farmland, virtually at gunpoint. The massive, militant uprisings that followed were put down with bullets and lathi charges. Lumpen "party" militias ran amok among the protesters, raping women and killing people. But eventually the combination of genuine mass mobilization and militancy worked. The people prevailed. They won all three battles and forced the government to back off. The Tatas had to move the Nano project to Gujarat, that laboratory of fascism, which offered a "good investment climate." The left front was decimated in the elections in West Bengal, something that has not happened in the last thirty years.

The irony doesn't end there. In a fiendishly clever sleight of hand, the defeat of the left is being attributed to its obstructionism and antidevelopment policies! "Corporate Captains Feel Easy Without Left," the *Hindustan Times* said. The stock market surged, looking forward to "a summer of joy." CEOs on TV channels celebrated the new government's "liberation" from the left. Hectoring news anchors have announced that the UPA no longer has any excuse to prevaricate on implementing reforms, unless of course it has "closet socialists" hiding in its midst.

This is the wonderful thing about democracy. It can mean anything you want it to mean.

The absence of a genuinely left-wing party in mainstream politics is not something to celebrate. But the parliamentary left has only itself to blame for its humiliation. It's not a tragedy that it has been cut to size. Perhaps this will create the space for some truly progressive politics.

For the sake of argument, let's for a moment contemplate the absurd and accept that India Inc. and the captains of industry are right and that India's millions did in fact vote for the speeding up of market "reforms." Is that good news or bad news? Should we be celebrating the fact that millions of people who have something to teach the world, who have another imagination, another worldview, and a more sustainable way of life, have decided to embrace a discredited ideology, one that has pushed this planet into a crisis from which it may never recover?

What good will forest rights be when there are no forests? What good will the right to information be if there is no redress for our grievances? What good are rivers without water? What good are plains without mountains to water and sustain them? It's as though we're hurtling down a cliff in a bus without brakes and fighting over what songs to sing.

"Jai Ho!" perhaps?

❖

For better or for worse, the 2009 elections seem to have ensured that the "Progress" project is up and running. However, it would be a serious mistake to believe that the "Union" project has fallen by the wayside.

As the 2009 election campaign unrolled, two things got saturation coverage in the media. One was the 100,000 rupee ($2,000) "people's car," the Tata Nano—the wagon for the volks—rolling out of Modi's Gujarat. (The sops and subsidies Modi gave the Tatas had a lot to do with Ratan Tata's warm endorsement of him.) The other is the hate speech of the BJP's monstrous new debutante, Varun Gandhi (another descendant of the Nehru dynasty), who makes even Narendra Modi sound moderate and retiring. In a public speech, Varun Gandhi called for Muslims to be forcibly sterilized. "This will be known as a Hindu bastion, no ***** Muslim dare raise his head here," he said, using a derogatory word for someone who has been circumcised. "I don't want a single Muslim vote."

Varun Gandhi is a modern politician, working the democratic system, doing everything he can to create a majority and consolidate his vote bank. A politician needs a vote bank, like a corporation needs a mass market. Both need help from the mass media. Corporations buy that help. Politicians must earn it. Some earn it by dint of hard work, others with dangerous circus stunts. Varun Gandhi's hate speech bought him instant national headlines. His brief stint in prison (for violating the Election Commission's Code of Conduct), cut short by an indulgent court order, made him an instant martyr. He was gently chastised for his impetuousness by his party elders (on TV, for public consumption). But then, in order to export his coarse appeal, he, like Narendra Modi, was flown around in a chopper as a star campaigner for the BJP in other constituencies.

Varun Gandhi won his election with a colossal margin. It makes you wonder—are "the people" always right? It is worrying to think what lessons the BJP will draw from its few decisive victories and its many decisive losses in this election. In several of the constituencies where it has won, hate speech (and deed) have served it well. It still remains by far the second-largest political party, with a powerful national presence, the only real challenge to the Congress. It will certainly live to fight another day. The question is, will it turn the burners up or down?

This said, it would be a travesty to lay all the blame for divisive politics at the door of the BJP. Whether it's nuclear tests, the unsealing of the locks of the Babri Masjid, the culture of creating fissures and pitting castes and communities against each other, or passing retrograde laws, the Congress got there first and has never been shy of keeping the ball in play. In the past, both parties have used massacres to gain political mileage. Sometimes they feast off them obliquely, sometimes they accuse each other of committing mass murder. In this election, both the Congress and the BJP have brazenly fielded candidates believed to be involved in public lynchings and mass murder. At no point has either seen to it that the guilty are punished or that justice is delivered. Despite their vicious public exchange of accusations, they have colluded to protect one another from real consequences.

Eventually, the massacres get absorbed into the labyrinth of India's judicial system where they are left to bubble and ferment before being trundled out as campaign material for the next election. You could say it's all a part of the fabric of Indian democracy. Hard to see from a train window. Whether the new infusion of young blood into the Congress will change the old party's methods of doing business remains to be seen.

The hoary institutions of Indian democracy—the judiciary, the police, the "free" press, and, of course, elections—far from working as a system of checks and balances, quite often do the opposite. They provide each other cover to promote the larger interests of Union and Progress. In the process, they generate such confusion, such a cacophony, that voices raised in warning just become part of the noise. And that only helps to enhance the image of the tolerant, lumbering, colorful, somewhat chaotic democracy. The chaos is real. But so is the consensus.

❖

Speaking of consensus, there's the small and ever-present matter of Kashmir. When it comes to Kashmir the consensus in India is hard core. It cuts across every section of the establishment—including the media, the bureaucracy, the intelligentsia, and even Bollywood.

The war in the Kashmir valley is almost twenty years old now and has claimed about 70,000 lives. Tens of thousands have been tortured, several thousand have "disappeared," women have been raped, tens of thousands widowed. Half a million Indian troops patrol the Kashmir valley, making it the most militarized zone in the world. (The United States had about 165,000 active-duty troops in Iraq at the height of its occupation.) The Indian Army now claims that it has, for the most part, crushed militancy in Kashmir. Perhaps that's true. But does military domination mean victory?

How does a government that claims to be a democracy justify a military occupation? By holding regular elections, of course. Elections in Kashmir have had a long and fascinating past. The blatantly rigged state election of 1987 was the immediate provocation for the armed uprising that began in 1990. Since then elections have become a finely honed instrument of the military occupation, a sinister playground for India's deep state. Intelligence agencies have created political parties and decoy politicians, they have constructed and destroyed political careers at will. It is they more than anyone else who decide what the outcome of each election will be. After every election, the Indian establishment declares that India has won a popular mandate from the people of Kashmir.

In the summer of 2008, a dispute over land being allotted to the Amarnath Shrine Board coalesced into a massive, nonviolent uprising. Day after day, hundreds of thousands of people defied soldiers and policemen—who fired straight into the crowds, killing scores of people—and thronged the streets. From early morning to late in the night, the city reverberated to chants of "*Azadi! Azadi!*" (Freedom! Freedom!). Fruit sellers weighed fruit chanting "Azadi! Azadi!" Shopkeepers, doctors, houseboat owners, guides, weavers, carpet sellers—everybody was out with placards, everybody shouted "Azadi! Azadi!" The protests went on for several days.

The protests were massive. They were democratic, and they were nonviolent. For the first time in decades, fissures appeared in mainstream public opinion in India. The Indian state panicked. Unsure of how to deal with this mass civil disobedience, it ordered a crackdown. It enforced the harshest curfew in recent memory with shoot-on-sight orders. In effect, for days on end, it virtually caged millions of people. The major pro-freedom leaders were placed under house arrest; several others were jailed. House-to-house searches culminated in the arrests of hundreds of people. The Jama Masjid was closed for Friday prayers for an unprecedented seven weeks at a stretch.

Once the rebellion was brought under control, the government did something extraordinary—it announced elections in the state. Pro-independence leaders called for a boycott. They were rearrested. Almost everybody believed the elections would become a huge embarrassment for the Indian government. The security establishment was convulsed with paranoia. Its elaborate network of spies, renegades, and embedded journalists began to buzz with renewed energy. No chances were taken. (Even I, who had nothing to do with any of what was going on, was put under house arrest in Srinagar for two days.)

Calling for elections was a huge risk. But the gamble paid off. People turned out to vote in droves. It was the biggest voter turnout since the armed struggle began. It helped that the polls were scheduled so that the first districts to vote were the most militarized districts even within the Kashmir valley.

None of India's analysts, journalists, and psephologists cared to ask why people who had only weeks ago risked everything, including bullets and shoot-on-sight orders, should have suddenly changed their minds. None of the high-profile scholars of the great festival of democracy—who practically live in TV studios when there are elections in mainland India, picking apart every forecast and exit poll and every minor percentile swing in the vote count—talked about what elections mean in the presence of such a massive, year-round troop deployment (an armed soldier for every twenty civilians). No one speculated about the mystery of hundreds of unknown candidates who materialized out of nowhere to represent political parties that had no previous presence in the Kashmir valley. Where had they come from? Who was financing them? No one was curious.

No one spoke about the curfew, the mass arrests, the lockdown of constituencies that were going to the polls. Not many talked about the fact that campaigning politicians went out of their way to de-link azadi and the Kashmir dispute from elections, which they insisted were only about municipal issues—roads, water, electricity. No one talked about why people who have lived under a military occupation for decades—where soldiers could barge into homes and whisk away people at any time of the day or night—might need someone to listen to them, to take up their cases, to represent them.

The minute elections were over, the establishment and the mainstream press declared victory (for India) once again. The most worrying fallout was that in Kashmir, people began to parrot their colonizers' view of themselves as a somewhat pathetic people who deserved what they got. "Never trust a Kashmiri," several Kashmiris said to me. "We're fickle and unreliable." Psychological warfare, technically known as psy-ops, has been an instrument of official policy in Kashmir. Its depredations over decades—its attempt to destroy people's self-esteem—are arguably the worst aspect of the occupation.

It's enough to make you wonder whether there is any connection at all between elections and democracy.

The trouble is that Kashmir sits on the fault lines of a region that is awash in weapons and sliding into chaos. The Kashmiri freedom struggle, with its crystal-clear sentiment but fuzzy outlines, is caught in the vortex of several dangerous and conflicting ideologies—Indian nationalism (corporate as well as "Hindu," shading into imperialism), Pakistani nationalism (breaking down under the burden of its own contradictions), US imperialism (made impatient by a tanking economy), and a resurgent medieval-Islamist Taliban (fast gaining legitimacy, despite its insane brutality, because it is seen to be resisting an occupation). Each of these ideologies is capable of a ruthlessness that can range from genocide to nuclear war. Add Chinese imperial ambitions, an aggressive, reincarnated Russia, and the huge reserves of natural gas in the Caspian region and persistent whispers about natural gas, oil, and uranium reserves in Kashmir and Ladakh, and you have the recipe for a new Cold War (which, like the last one, is cold for some and hot for others).

In the midst of all this, Kashmir is set to become the conduit through which the mayhem unfolding in Afghanistan and Pakistan spills into India, where it will find purchase in the anger of the young among India's 150 million Muslims who have been brutalized, humiliated, and marginalized. Notice has been given by the series of terrorist strikes that culminated in the Mumbai attacks of 2008.

There is no doubt that the Kashmir dispute ranks right up there, along with Palestine, as one of the oldest, most intractable disputes in the world. That does not mean that it cannot be resolved. Only that the solution will not be completely to the satisfaction of any one party, one country, or one ideology. Negotiators will have to be prepared to deviate from the "party line." We haven't yet reached the stage where the government of India is even prepared to admit that there's a problem, let alone negotiate a solution. Right now it has no reason to. Internationally, its stocks are soaring. And while its neighbors deal with bloodshed, civil war, concentration camps, refugees, and army mutinies, India has just concluded a beautiful election.

However, "demon-crazy" can't fool all the people all the time. India's temporary, shotgun solutions to the unrest in

Kashmir (pardon the pun) have magnified the problem and driven it deep into a place where it is poisoning the aquifers.

❖

Perhaps the story of the Siachen Glacier, the highest battlefield in the world, is the most appropriate metaphor for the insanity of our times. Thousands of Indian and Pakistani soldiers have been deployed there, enduring chill winds and temperatures that dip to minus 40 degrees Celsius. Of the hundreds who have died there, many have died just from the cold—from frostbite and sunburn. The glacier has become a garbage dump now, littered with the detritus of war—thousands of empty artillery shells, empty fuel drums, ice axes, old boots, tents, and every other kind of waste that thousands of warring human beings generate. The garbage remains intact, perfectly preserved at those icy temperatures, a pristine monument to human folly. While the Indian and Pakistani governments spend billions of dollars on weapons and the logistics of high-altitude warfare, the battlefield has begun to melt. Right now, it has shrunk to about half its size. The melting has less to do with the military standoff than with people far away, on the other side of the world, living the good life. They're good people who believe in peace, free speech, and in human rights. They live in thriving democracies whose governments sit on the UN Security Council and whose economies depend heavily on the export of war and the sale of weapons to countries like India and Pakistan. (And Rwanda, Sudan, Somalia, the Republic of Congo, Iraq, Afghanistan . . . it's a long list.) The glacial melt will cause severe floods in the subcontinent and eventually severe drought that will affect the lives of millions of people. That will give us even more reasons to fight. We'll need more weapons. Who knows, that sort of consumer confidence may be just what the world needs to get over the current recession. Then everyone in the thriving democracies will have an even better life—and the glaciers will melt even faster.

❖

While I read "Listening to Grasshoppers" to a tense audience packed into a university auditorium in Istanbul (tense because words like "unity," "progress," "genocide," and "Armenian" tend to anger the Turkish authorities when they are uttered close together), I could see Rakel Dink, Hrant Dink's widow, sitting in the front row, crying the whole way through. When I finished, she hugged me and said, "We keep hoping. Why do we keep hoping?"

We, she said. Not you.

The words of Faiz Ahmed Faiz, sung so hauntingly by Abida Parveen, came to me:

nahin nigah main manzil to justaju hi sahi
nahin wisaal mayassar to arzu hi sahi

I tried to translate them for her (sort of):

If dreams are thwarted, then yearning must take their place
If reunion is impossible, then longing must take its place

You see what I meant about poetry?

MR. CHIDAMBARAM'S WAR

THE LOW, FLAT-TOPPED hills of south Orissa have been home to the Dongria Kondh long before there was a country called India or a state called Orissa. The hills watched over the Kondh. The Kondh watched over the hills and worshipped them as living deities. Now these hills have been sold for the bauxite they contain. For the Kondh it's as though god has been sold. They ask how much god would go for if the god were Ram or Allah or Jesus Christ?

Perhaps the Kondh are supposed to be grateful that their Niyamgiri hills, home to their Niyam Raja, God of Universal Law, has been sold to a company with a name like Vedanta (the branch of Hindu philosophy that teaches the Ultimate Nature of Knowledge). It's one of the biggest mining corporations in the world and is owned by Anil Aggarwal, the Indian billionaire who lives in London in a mansion that once belonged to the Shah of Iran. Vedanta is only one of the many multinational corporations closing in on Orissa.

First published in *Outlook*, November 9, 2009.

If the flat-topped hills are destroyed, the forests that clothe them will be destroyed, too. So will the rivers and streams that flow out of them and irrigate the plains below. So will the Dongria Kondh. So will the hundreds of thousands of tribal people who live in the forested heart of India, and whose homeland is similarly under attack.

In our smoky, crowded cities, some people say, "So what? Someone has to pay the price of progress." Some even say, "Let's face it, these are people whose time has come. Look at any developed country, Europe, the US, Australia—they all have a 'past.'" Indeed they do. So why shouldn't "we"?

In keeping with this line of thought, the government has announced Operation Green Hunt, a war purportedly against the "Maoist" rebels headquartered in the jungles of central India. Of course, the Maoists are by no means the only ones rebelling. There is a whole spectrum of struggles all over the country that people are engaged in—the landless, the Dalits, the homeless, workers, peasants, weavers.

They're pitted against a juggernaut of injustices, including policies that allow a wholesale corporate takeover of people's land and resources. However, it is the Maoists whom the government has singled out as being the biggest threat. Two years ago, when things were nowhere near as bad as they are now, the Prime Minister described the Maoists as the "single-largest internal security threat" to the country. This will probably go down as the most popular and often-repeated thing he ever said. For some reason, the comment he made on January 6, 2009, at a meeting of state chief ministers, when he described the Maoists as having only "modest capabilities," doesn't seem to have had the same raw appeal. He revealed his government's real concern on June 18, 2009, when he told Parliament: "If left-wing extremism continues to flourish in parts which have natural resources of minerals, the climate for investment would certainly be affected."

Who are the Maoists? They are members of the banned Communist Party of India (Maoist)—CPI (Maoist)—one of the several descendants of the CPI (Marxist-Leninist), which led the 1969 Naxalite uprising and was subsequently liquidated by the Indian government. The Maoists believe that the innate structural inequality of Indian society can only be redressed by the violent overthrow of the Indian state. In its earlier avatars as the Maoist Communist Centre in Jharkhand and Bihar, and the People's War Group in Andhra Pradesh, the Maoists had tremendous popular support. (When the ban on them was briefly lifted in 2004, one and a half million people attended their rally in Warangal.) But eventually their intercession in Andhra Pradesh ended badly. They left a violent legacy that turned some of their staunchest supporters into harsh critics. After a paroxysm of killing and counterkilling by the Andhra police as well as the Maoists, the People's War Group was decimated. Those who managed to survive fled Andhra Pradesh into neighboring Chhattisgarh. There, deep in the heart of the forest, they joined colleagues who had already been working there for decades.

Not many "outsiders" have any firsthand experience of the real nature of the Maoist movement in the forest. A recent interview with one of its top leaders, Comrade Ganapathy, in *Open* magazine didn't do much to change the minds of those who view the Maoists as a party with an unforgiving, totalitarian vision, which countenances no dissent whatsoever. Comrade Ganapathy said nothing that would persuade people that, were the Maoists ever to come to power, they would be equipped to properly address the almost insane diversity of India's caste-ridden society. His casual approval of the Liberation Tigers of Tamil Eelam (LTTE) of Sri Lanka was enough to send a shiver down even the most sympathetic of spines, not just because of the brutal ways in which the LTTE chose to wage its war, but also because of the cataclysmic tragedy that has befallen the Tamil people of Sri Lanka, whom it claimed to represent, and for whom it surely must take some responsibility.

Right now in central India, the Maoists' guerrilla army

is made up almost entirely of desperately poor tribal people living in conditions of such chronic hunger that it verges on famine of the kind we only associate with sub-Saharan Africa. They are people who, even after sixty years of India's so-called Independence, have not had access to education, health care, or legal redress. They are people who have been mercilessly exploited for decades, consistently cheated by small businessmen and moneylenders, the women raped as a matter of right by police and Forest Department personnel. Their journey back to a semblance of dignity is due in large part to the Maoist cadre who have lived and worked and fought by their side for decades.

If the tribals have taken up arms, they have done so because a government that has given them nothing but violence and neglect now wants to snatch away the last thing they have—their land. Clearly, they do not believe the government when it says it only wants to "develop" their region. Clearly, they do not believe that the roads as wide and flat as aircraft runways that are being built through their forests in Dantewada by the National Mineral Development Corporation are being built for them to walk their children to school on. They believe that if they do not fight for their land, they will be annihilated. That is why they have taken up arms.

Even if the ideologues of the Maoist movement are fighting to eventually overthrow the Indian state, right now even they know that their ragged, malnutritioned army, the bulk of whose soldiers have never seen a train or a bus or even a small town, are fighting only for survival.

In 2008, an expert group appointed by the Planning Commission submitted a report called "Development Challenges in Extremist Affected Areas." It said:

> [T]he Naxalite (Maoist) movement has to be recognized as a political movement with a strong base among the landless and poor peasantry and Adivasis. Its emergence and growth need to be contextualized in the social conditions and experience of people

who form a part of it. The huge gap between state policy and performance is a feature of these conditions. Though its professed long term ideology is capturing state power by force, in its day to day manifestation it is to be looked upon as basically a fight for social justice, equality, protection and local development.

A very far cry from the "single-largest internal security threat." Since the Maoist rebellion is the flavor of the week, everybody, from the sleekest fat cat to the most cynical editor of the most sold-out newspaper in this country, seems to be suddenly ready to concede that decades of accumulated injustice lie at the root of the problem. But instead of addressing that problem, which would mean putting the brakes on this twenty-first-century gold rush, they are trying to head the debate off in a completely different direction, with a noisy outburst of pious outrage about Maoist "terrorism." But they're only speaking to themselves.

The people who have taken to arms are not spending all their time watching (or performing for) TV, or reading the papers, or conducting SMS polls for the Moral Science question of the day: Is Violence Good or Bad? SMS your reply to . . .

They're out there. They're fighting. They believe they have the right to defend their homes and their land. They believe that they deserve justice.

In order to keep its better-off citizens absolutely safe from these dangerous people, the government has declared war on them. A war, which it tells us, may take between three and five years to win. Odd, isn't it, that even after the Mumbai attacks of 26/11, the government was prepared to talk with Pakistan? It's prepared to talk to China. But when it comes to waging war against the poor, it's playing hard. It's not enough that special police—with totemic names like Greyhounds, Cobras, and Scorpions—are scouring the forests with a license to kill. It's not enough that the Central Reserve Police Force, the Border Security Force, and the notorious Naga Battalion have already wreaked havoc and committed unconscionable atrocities in remote forest villages. It's not enough that the government supports and arms the Salwa Judum, the "people's militia" that has killed and raped and burned its way through the forests of Dantewada, leaving three hundred thousand people homeless or on the run. Now the government is going to deploy the Indo-Tibetan Border Police and tens of thousands of paramilitary troops. It plans to set up a brigade headquarters in Bilaspur (which will displace nine villages) and an air base in Rajnandgaon (which will displace seven). Obviously, these decisions were taken a while ago. Surveys have been done, sites chosen. Interesting. War has been in the offing for a while. And now the helicopters of the Indian air force have been given the right to fire in "self-defense," the very right that the government denies its poorest citizens.

Fire at whom? How in god's name will the security forces be able to distinguish a Maoist from an ordinary person who is running terrified through the jungle? Will Adivasis carrying the bows and arrows they have carried for centuries now count as Maoists, too? Are noncombatant Maoist sympathizers valid targets? When I was in Dantewada, the superintendent of police showed me pictures of nineteen "Maoists" whom "his boys" had killed. I asked him how I was supposed to tell they were Maoists. He said, "See Ma'am, they have malaria medicines, Dettol bottles, all these things from outside."

What kind of war is Operation Green Hunt going to be? Will we ever know? Not much news comes out of the forests. Lalgarh in West Bengal has been cordoned off. Those who try to go in are being beaten and arrested. And called Maoists, of course. In Dantewada, the Vanvasi Chetana Ashram, a Gandhian ashram run by Himanshu Kumar, was bulldozed in a few hours. It was the last neutral outpost before the war zone, a place where journalists, activists, researchers, and fact-finding teams could stay while they worked in the area.

Meanwhile, the Indian establishment has unleashed its most

potent weapon. Almost overnight, our embedded media has substituted its steady supply of planted, unsubstantiated, hysterical stories about "Islamist Terrorism" with planted, unsubstantiated, hysterical stories about "Red Terrorism." In the midst of this racket, at Ground Zero, the cordon of silence is being inexorably tightened. The "Sri Lanka Solution" could very well be in the cards. It's not for nothing that the Indian government blocked a European move in the UN asking for an international probe into war crimes committed by the government of Sri Lanka in its recent offensive against the Tamil Tigers.

The first move in that direction is the concerted campaign that has been orchestrated to shoehorn the myriad forms of resistance taking place in this country into a simple George Bush binary: If you are not with us, you are with the Maoists. The deliberate exaggeration of the Maoist "threat" helps the state to justify militarization. (And surely does no harm to the Maoists. Which political party would be unhappy to be singled out for such attention?) While all the oxygen is being used up by this new doppelganger of the war on terror, the state will use the opportunity to mop up the hundreds of other resistance movements in the sweep of its military operation, calling them all Maoist sympathizers.

I use the future tense, but this process is well under way. The West Bengal government tried to do this in Nandigram and Singur but failed. Right now in Lalgarh, the Pulishi Santrash Birodhi Janasadharaner Committee or the People's Committee Against Police Atrocities—which is a people's movement that is separate from, though sympathetic to, the Maoists—is routinely referred to as an overground wing of the CPI (Maoist). Its leader, Chhatradhar Mahato, now arrested and being held without bail, is always called a "Maoist leader." We all know the story of Dr. Binayak Sen, a medical doctor and a civil liberties activist, who spent two years in jail on the absolutely facile charge of being a courier for the Maoists. While the light shines brightly on Operation Green Hunt, in other parts of

India, away from the theater of war, the assault on the rights of the poor, of workers, of the landless, of those whose lands the government wishes to acquire for "public purpose," will pick up pace. Their suffering will deepen and it will be that much harder for them to get a hearing.

Once the war begins, like all wars, it will develop a momentum, a logic, and an economics of its own. It will become a way of life, almost impossible to reverse. The police will be expected to behave like an army, a ruthless killing machine. The paramilitary will be expected to become like the police, a corrupt, bloated administrative force. We've seen it happen in Nagaland, Manipur, and Kashmir. The only difference in the "heartland" will be that it'll become obvious very quickly to the security forces that they're only a little less wretched than the people they're fighting. In time, the divide between the people and the law enforcers will become porous. Guns and ammunition will be bought and sold. In fact, it's already happening. Whether it's the security forces or the Maoists or noncombatant civilians, the poorest people will die in this Rich People's War. However, if anybody believes that this war will leave them unaffected, they should think again. The resources it'll consume will cripple the economy of this country.

Last week, civil liberties groups from all over the country organized a series of meetings in Delhi to discuss what could be done to turn the tide and stop the war. The absence of Dr. Balagopal, one of the best-known civil rights activists of Andhra Pradesh (who died two weeks ago) closed around us like a physical pain. He was one of the bravest, wisest political thinkers of our time and left us just when we needed him most. Still, I'm sure he would have been reassured to hear speaker after speaker displaying the vision, the depth, the experience, the wisdom, the political acuity, and, above all, the real humanity of the community of activists, academics, lawyers, judges, and a range of other people who make up the civil liberties community in India. Their presence in the capital signaled that outside the arc lights of our TV studios and beyond the drumbeat of media hysteria, even among India's middle classes, a humane heart still beats. Small wonder then that these are the people whom the Union Home Minister recently accused of creating an "intellectual climate" that was conducive to "terrorism." If that charge was meant to frighten people, to cow them down, it had the opposite effect.

The speakers represented a range of opinion from the liberal to the radical left. Though none of those who spoke would describe themselves as Maoist, few were opposed in principle to the idea that people have a right to defend themselves against state violence. Many were uncomfortable about Maoist violence, about the "people's courts" that delivered summary justice, about the authoritarianism that was bound to permeate an armed struggle and marginalize those who did not have arms. But even as they expressed their discomfort, they knew that people's courts only existed because India's courts are out of reach for ordinary people and that the armed struggle that has broken out in the heartland is not the first, but the very last option of a desperate people pushed to the very brink of existence.

The speakers were aware of the dangers of trying to extract a simple morality out of individual incidents of heinous violence, in a situation that had already begun to look very much like war. Everybody had graduated long ago from equating the structural violence of the state with the violence of the armed resistance. In fact, retired justice P. B. Sawant went so far as to thank the Maoists for forcing the establishment of this country to pay attention to the egregious injustice of the system. Hargopal from Andhra Pradesh spoke of his experience as a civil rights activist through the years of the Maoist interlude in his state. He mentioned in passing the fact that in a few days in Gujarat in 2002, Hindu mobs led by the Bajrang Dal and the Vishwa Hindu Parishad had killed more people than the Maoists ever had even in their bloodiest days in Andhra Pradesh.

People who had come from the war zones, from Lalgarh, Jharkhand, Chhattisgarh, and Orissa, described the police repression, the arrests, the torture, the killing, the corruption, and the fact that in places like Orissa, they seemed to take orders directly from the officials who worked for the mining companies.

People described the dubious, malign role being played by certain NGOs funded by aid agencies wholly devoted to furthering corporate prospects. Again and again they spoke of how in Jharkhand and Chhattisgarh activists as well as ordinary people—anyone who was seen to be a dissenter—were being branded Maoists and imprisoned. They said that this, more than anything else, was pushing people to take up arms and join the Maoists. They asked how a government that professed its inability to resettle even a fraction of the fifty million people who had been displaced by "development" projects was suddenly able to identify 140,000 hectares of prime land to give to industrialists for more than three hundred Special Economic Zones, India's onshore tax havens for the rich. They asked what brand of justice the Supreme Court was practicing when it refused to review the meaning of "public purpose" in the Land Acquisition Act even when it knew that the government was forcibly acquiring land in the name of "public purpose" to give to private corporations. They asked why when the government says that "the Writ of the State must run," it seems to only mean that police stations must be put in place. Not schools or clinics or housing, or clean water, or a fair price for forest produce, or even being left alone and free from the fear of the police—anything that would make people's lives a little easier. They asked why the "Writ of the State" could never be taken to mean justice.

There was a time, perhaps ten years ago, when in meetings like these, people were still debating the model of "development" that was being thrust on them by the New Economic Policy. Now the rejection of that model is complete. It is absolute. Everyone from the Gandhians to the Maoists agree on that. The only question now is, what is the most effective way to dismantle it?

An old college friend of a friend, a big noise in the corporate world, had come along for one of the meetings out of morbid curiosity about a world he knew very little about. Even though he had disguised himself in a Fabindia *kurta*, he couldn't help looking (and smelling) expensive. At one point, he leaned across to me and said, "Someone should tell them not to bother. They won't win this one. They have no idea what they're up against. With the kind of money that's involved here, these companies can buy ministers and media barons and policy wonks, they can run their own NGOs, their own militias, they can buy whole governments. They'll even buy the Maoists. These good people here should save their breath and find something better to do."

When people are being brutalized, what "better" thing is there for them to do than to fight back? It's not as though anyone's offering them a choice, unless it's to commit suicide, like the 180,000 farmers caught in a spiral of debt have done. (Am I the only one who gets the distinct feeling that the Indian establishment and its representatives in the media are far more comfortable with the idea of poor people killing themselves in despair than with the idea of them fighting back?) For several years, people in Chhattisgarh, Orissa, Jharkhand, and West Bengal—some of them Maoists, many not—have managed to hold off the big corporations. The question now is—how will Operation Green Hunt change the nature of their struggle? What exactly are the fighting people up against?

It's true that, historically, mining companies have almost always won their battles against local people. Of all corporations, leaving aside the ones that make weapons, they probably have the most merciless past. They are cynical, battle-hardened campaigners and when people say, "*Jaan denge par jameen nahin denge*" (We'll give away our lives, but never our land), it probably bounces off them like a light drizzle on a bomb shelter. They've heard it before, in a thousand different languages, in a hundred different countries.

Right now in India, many of them are still in the First Class Arrivals lounge, ordering cocktails, blinking slowly like lazy predators, waiting for the memorandums of understanding they have signed—some as far back as 2005—to materialize into real money. But four years in a First Class lounge is enough to test the patience of even the truly tolerant. There's only that much space they're willing to make for the elaborate, if increasingly empty, rituals of democratic practice: the (rigged) public hearings, the (fake) Environmental Impact Assessments, the (purchased) clearances from various ministries, the long-drawn-out court cases. Even phony democracy is time-consuming. And time, for industrialists, is money.

So what kind of money are we talking about? In their seminal, soon-to-be-published work, *Out of This Earth: East India Adivasis and the Aluminum Cartel*, Samarendra Das and Felix Padel say that the financial value of the bauxite deposits of Orissa alone is $2.27 trillion (more than twice India's Gross Domestic Product). That was at 2004 prices. At today's prices it would be about $4 trillion. A trillion has twelve zeroes.

Of this, officially the government gets a royalty of less than 7 percent. Quite often, if the mining company is a known and recognized one, the chances are that, even though the ore is still in the mountain, it will have already been traded on the futures market. So, while for the Adivasis the mountain is still a living deity, the fountainhead of life and faith, the keystone of the ecological health of the region, for the corporation, it's just a cheap storage facility. Goods in storage have to be accessible. From the corporation's point of view, the bauxite will have to come out of the mountain. If it can't be done peacefully, then it will have to be done violently. Such are the pressures and the exigencies of the free market.

That's just the story of the bauxite in Orissa. Expand the $4 trillion to include the value of the millions of tons of high-quality iron ore in Chhattisgarh and Jharkhand and the twenty-eight other precious mineral resources, including uranium, limestone, dolomite, coal, tin, granite, marble, copper, diamond, gold, quartzite, corundum, beryl, alexandrite, silica, fluorite, and garnet. Add to that the power plants, the dams, the highways, the steel and cement factories, the aluminum smelters, and all the other infrastructure projects that are part of the hundreds of Memorandums of Understanding (more than ninety in Jharkhand alone) that have been signed. That gives us a rough outline of the scale of the operation and the desperation of the stakeholders. The forest once known as the Dandakaranya, which stretches from West Bengal through Jharkhand, Orissa, Chhattisgarh, parts of Andhra Pradesh and Maharashtra, is home to millions of India's tribal people. The media has taken to calling it the Red corridor or the Maoist corridor. It could just as accurately be called the memorandum of understanding corridor. It doesn't seem to matter at all that the Fifth Schedule of the constitution provides protection to Adivasi people and disallows the alienation of their land. It looks as though the clause is there only to make the constitution look good—a bit of window-dressing, a slash of make-up. Scores of corporations, from relatively unknown ones to the biggest mining companies and steel manufacturers in the world, are in the fray to appropriate Adivasi homelands—the Mittals, Jindals, Tata, Essar, Posco, Rio Tinto, BHP Billiton, and, of course, Vedanta. There's a memorandum of understanding on every mountain, river, and forest glade. We're talking about social and environmental engineering on an unimaginable scale.

And most of this is secret. It's not in the public domain. Somehow I don't think that the plans that are afoot to destroy one of the world's most pristine forests and ecosystems, as well as the people who live in it, will be discussed at the Climate Change Conference in Copenhagen. Our twenty-four-hour news channels that are so busy hunting for macabre stories of Maoist violence—and making them up when they run out of the real thing—seem to have no interest at all in this side of the story. I wonder why?

Perhaps it's because the development lobby to which they are so much in thrall says the mining industry will ratchet up the rate of GDP growth dramatically and provide employment to the people it displaces. This does not take into account the catastrophic costs of environmental damage. But even on its own narrow terms, it is simply untrue. Most of the money goes into the bank accounts of the mining corporations. Less than 10 percent comes to the public exchequer. A very tiny percentage of the displaced people get jobs, and those who do earn slave wages to do humiliating, backbreaking work. By caving in to this paroxysm of greed, we are bolstering other countries' economies with our ecology.

When the scale of money involved is what it is, the stakeholders are not always easy to identify. Between the CEOs in their private jets and the wretched tribal special police officers in the "people's" militias—who for a couple of thousand rupees (roughly forty dollars) a month fight their own people, rape, kill, and burn down whole villages in an effort to clear the ground for mining to begin—there is an entire universe of primary, secondary, and tertiary stakeholders. These people don't have to declare their interests, but they're allowed to use their positions and good offices to further them. How will we ever know which political party, which ministers, which members of Parliament, which politicians, which judges, which NGOs, which expert consultants, which police officers, have a direct or indirect stake in the booty? How will we know which newspapers reporting the latest Maoist "atrocity," which TV channels "reporting directly from Ground Zero"—or, more accurately, making it a point not to report from Ground Zero, or even more accurately, lying blatantly from Ground Zero— are stakeholders?

What is the provenance of the billions of dollars (several times more than India's GDP) secretly stashed away by Indian citizens in Swiss bank accounts? Where did the $2 billion spent on the last general elections come from? Where do the hundreds of millions of rupees that political parties and politicians pay the media for the "high-end," "low-end," and "live" preelection "coverage packages" that P. Sainath recently wrote about come from? (The next time you see a TV anchor haranguing a numb studio guest, shouting, "Why don't the Maoists stand for elections? Why don't they come in to the mainstream?" do SMS the channel saying, "Because they can't afford your rates.")

What are we to make of the fact that the Union Home Minister, P. Chidambaram, the CEO of Operation Green Hunt, has, in his career as a corporate lawyer, represented several mining corporations? What are we to make of the fact that he was a nonexecutive director of Vedanta—a position from which he resigned the day he became finance minister in 2004? What are we to make of the fact that, when he became finance minister, one of the first clearances he gave for foreign direct investment was to Twinstar Holdings, a Mauritius-based company, to buy shares in Sterlite, a part of the Vedanta group?

What are we to make of the fact that, when activists from Orissa filed a case against Vedanta in the Supreme Court, citing its violations of government guidelines and pointing out that the Norwegian Pension Fund had withdrawn its investment from the company alleging gross environmental damage and human rights violations committed by the company, Justice Kapadia suggested that Vedanta be substituted with Sterlite, a sister company of the same group? He then blithely announced in an open court that he too had shares in Sterlite. He gave the forest clearance to Sterlite to go ahead with the mining despite the fact that the Supreme Court's own expert committee had explicitly said that permission should be denied and that mining would ruin the forests, water sources, environment, and the lives and livelihoods of the thousands of tribals living there. Justice Kapadia gave this clearance without rebutting the report of the Supreme Court's own committee.

What are we to make of the fact that the Salwa Judum, the brutal ground-clearing operation disguised as a "spontaneous" people's militia in Dantewada, was formally inaugurated in 2005, just days after the memorandum of understanding with the Tatas was signed? And that the Jungle Warfare Training School in Bastar was set up just around then? What are we to make of the fact that two weeks ago, on October 12, 2009, the mandatory public hearing for Tata Steel's Rs 10,000 crore ($2 billion) steel project in Lohandiguda, Dantewada, was held in a small hall inside the collectorate, cordoned off with massive security, with a hired audience of fifty tribal people brought in from two Bastar villages in a convoy of government jeeps? (The public hearing was declared a success and the district collector congratulated the people of Bastar for their cooperation.)

What are we to make of the fact that just around the time the prime minister began to call the Maoists the "single-largest internal security threat" (which was a signal that the government was getting ready to go after them), the share prices of many of the mining companies in the region skyrocketed? The mining companies desperately need this "war." It's an old technique. They hope the impact of the violence will drive out the people who have so far managed to resist the attempts that have been made to evict them. Whether this will indeed be the outcome or whether it'll simply swell the ranks of the Maoists remains to be seen.

Reversing this argument, Dr. Ashok Mitra, former finance minister of West Bengal, in an article called "The Phantom Enemy" argues that the "grisly serial murders" that the Maoists are committing are a classic tactic, learned from guerrilla warfare textbooks. He suggests that they have built and trained a guerrilla army that is now ready to take on the Indian state and that the Maoist "rampage" is a deliberate attempt on their part to invite the wrath of a blundering, angry Indian state, which the Maoists hope will commit acts of cruelty that will enrage the Adivasis. That rage, Dr. Mitra says, is what the Maoists hope can be harvested and transformed into an insurrection. This, of course, is the charge of "adventurism" that several currents of the left have always leveled at the Maoists. It suggests that Maoist ideologues are not above inviting destruction on the very people they claim to represent in order to bring about a revolution that will bring them to power. Ashok Mitra is an old Communist who had a ringside seat during the Naxalite uprising of the 1960s and 1970s in West Bengal. His views cannot be summarily dismissed. But it's worth keeping in mind that the Adivasi people have a long and courageous history of resistance that predates the birth of Maoism. To look upon them as brainless puppets being manipulated by a few middle-class Maoist ideologues is to do them something of a disservice.

Presumably Dr. Mitra is talking about the situation in Lalgarh where, up to now, there has been no talk of mineral wealth. (Lest we forget—the current uprising in Lalgarh was sparked by the chief minister's visit to inaugurate a Jindal Steel factory. And where there's a steel factory, can the iron ore be very far away?) The people's anger has to do with their desperate poverty and the decades of suffering at the hands of the police and the "Harmads," the armed militia of the Communist Party of India (Marxist) that has ruled West Bengal for more than thirty years.

Even if, for argument's sake, we don't ask what tens of thousands of police and paramilitary troops are doing in Lalgarh and we accept the theory of Maoist "adventurism," it would still be only a very small part of the picture.

The real problem is that the flagship of India's miraculous "growth" story has run aground. It came at a huge social and environmental cost. And now, as the rivers dry up and forests disappear, as the water table recedes and as people realize what is being done to them, the chickens are coming home to roost. All over the country, there's unrest, there are protests by people refusing to give up their land and their access to resources, refusing to believe false promises any more. Suddenly, it's beginning to look as though the 10 percent growth rate and democracy are mutually incompatible. To get the bauxite out of the flat-topped hills, to get iron ore out from under the forest floor, to get 85 percent of India's people off their land and into the cities (which is what Mr. Chidambaram says he'd like to see), India has to become a police state. The government has to militarize. To justify that militarization, it needs an enemy. The Maoists are that enemy. They are to corporate fundamentalists what the Muslims are to Hindu fundamentalists. (Is there a fraternity of fundamentalists? Is that why the Rashtriya Swayamsevak Sangh has expressed open admiration for Mr. Chidambaram?)

It would be a grave mistake to imagine that the paramilitary troops, the Rajnandgaon air base, the Bilaspur brigade headquarters, the Unlawful Activities Act, the Chhattisgarh Special Public Security Act, and Operation Green Hunt are all being put in place just to flush out a few thousand Maoists from the forests. In all the talk of Operation Green Hunt, whether or not Mr. Chidambaram goes ahead and "presses the button," I detect the kernel of a coming State of Emergency. (Here's a math question: If it takes six hundred thousand soldiers to hold down the tiny valley of Kashmir, how many will it take to contain the mounting rage of hundreds of millions of people?)

Instead of narco-analyzing Kobad Ghandy, the recently arrested Maoist leader, it might be a better idea to talk to him.

In the meanwhile, will someone who's going to the Climate Change Conference in Copenhagen later this year please ask the only question worth asking: Can we please leave the bauxite in the mountain?

THE PRESIDENT
TOOK THE SALUTE

THE MINISTER SAYS that for India's sake, people should leave their villages and move to the cities. He's a Harvard man. He wants speed. And numbers. Five hundred million migrants, he thinks, will make a good business model.

Not everybody likes the idea of their cities filling up with the poor. A judge in Bombay called slum dwellers pickpockets of urban land. Another said, while ordering the bulldozing of unauthorized colonies, that people who couldn't afford to live in cities shouldn't live in them.

When those who had been evicted went back to where they came from, they found their villages had disappeared under great dams and dusty quarries. Their homes were occupied by hunger—and policemen. The forests were filling up with armed guerrillas. They found that the wars from the edge of India, in Kashmir, Nagaland, Manipur, had migrated to its heart. People returned to live on city streets and pavements, in

First published as the introduction to Arundhati Roy, *Broken Republic: Three Essays* (New Delhi: Hamish Hamilton/Penguin India, 2011).

hovels on dusty construction sites, wondering which corner of this huge country was meant for them.

The minister said that migrants to cities were mostly criminals and "carried a kind of behavior which is unacceptable to modern cities." The middle class admired him for his forthrightness, for having the courage to call a spade a spade. The minister said he would set up more police stations, recruit more policemen, and put more police vehicles on the road to improve law and order.

In the drive to beautify Delhi for the Commonwealth Games, laws were passed that made the poor vanish, like laundry stains. Street vendors disappeared, rickshaw pullers lost their licenses, small shops and businesses were shut down. Beggars were rounded up, tried by mobile magistrates in mobile courts, and dropped outside the city limits. The slums that remained were screened off, with vinyl billboards that said DELHIciously Yours.

New kinds of policemen patrolled the streets, better armed, better dressed, and trained not to scratch their privates in public, no matter how grave the provocation. There were cameras everywhere, recording everything.

❖

Two young criminals carrying a kind of behavior that was unacceptable to modern cities escaped the police dragnet and approached a woman sitting between her sunglasses and the leather seats of her shiny car at a traffic crossing. Shamelessly they demanded money. The woman was rich and kind. The criminals' heads were no higher than her car window. Their names were Rukmini and Kamli. Or maybe Mehrunissa and Shahbano. (Who cares.) The woman gave them money and some motherly advice. Ten rupees (twenty cents) to Kamli (or Shahbano). "Share it," she told them, and sped away when the lights changed.

Rukmini and Kamli (or Mehrunissa and Shahbano) tore into each other like gladiators, like lifers in a prison yard. Each sleek car that flashed past them, and almost crushed them, carried the reflection of their battle, their fight to the finish, on its shining door.

Eventually both girls disappeared without a trace, like thousands of children do in Delhi.

The Games were a success.

❖

Two months later, on the sixty-second anniversary of India's Republic Day, the armed forces showcased their new weapons at the Republic Day parade: a missile launcher system, Russian multibarrel rocket launchers, combat aircraft, light helicopters, and underwater weapons for the navy. The new T-90 battle tank was called Bhishma. (The older one was Arjun.) Varunastra was the name of the latest heavyweight torpedo, and Mareech was a decoy system to seduce incoming torpedoes. (Hanuman and Vajra are the names painted on the armored vehicles that patrol Kashmir's frozen streets.) The names from the Bhagavad Gita, the Ramayana, and the Mahabharata were a coincidence. Dare Devils from the army's Corps of Signals rode motorcycles in a rocket formation; then they formed a cluster of flying birds and finally a human pyramid.

The army band played the national anthem. The president took the salute.

Three Sukhoi fighter jets made a Trishul in the sky. Shiva's Trishul. Is India a Hindu republic? Only accidentally.

The thrilled crowd turned its face up to the weak winter sun and applauded the aerobatics. High in the sky, the winking silver sides of the jets carried the reflection of Rukmini and Kamli's (or Mehrunissa and Shahbano's) fight to the death.

"As a writer, a fiction writer, I have often wondered whether the attempt to always be precise, to try and get it all factually right, somehow reduces the epic scale of what is really going on. Does it eventually mask a larger truth? I worry that I am allowing myself to be railroaded into offering prosaic, factual precision when maybe what we need is a feral howl, or the transformative power and real precision of poetry."

WALKING WITH
THE COMRADES

THE TERSE, TYPEWRITTEN note slipped under my door in a sealed envelope confirmed my appointment with India's Gravest Internal Security Threat. I'd been waiting for months to hear from them. I had to be at the Ma Danteshwari mandir in Dantewada, Chhattisgarh, at any of four given times on two given days. That was to take care of bad weather, punctures, blockades, transport strikes, and sheer bad luck. The note said: "Writer should have camera, tika and coconut. Meeter will have cap, *Hindi Outlook* magazine, and bananas. Password: Namashkar Guruji."

Namashkar Guruji. I wondered whether the Meeter and Greeter would be expecting a man. And whether I should get myself a moustache.

There are many ways to describe Dantewada. It's an oxymoron. It's a border town smack in the heart of India. It's the epicenter of a war.

In Dantewada, the police wear plain clothes and the rebels wear uniforms. The jail superintendent is in jail. The prisoners

First published in *Outlook*, March 29, 2010.

are free (three hundred of them escaped from the old town jail two years ago). Women who have been raped are in police custody. The rapists give speeches in the bazaar. It's an upside down, inside out town.

Across the Indravati River, in the area controlled by the Maoists, is the place the police call "Pakistan." There the villages are empty, but the forest is full of people. Children who ought to be in school run wild. In the lovely forest villages, the concrete school buildings have either been blown up and lie in a heap, or they are full of policemen.

The deadly war that is unfolding in the jungle is a war that the government of India is both proud and shy of. Operation Green Hunt has been proclaimed as well as denied. P. Chidambaram, India's home minister (and CEO of the war), says it does not exist, that it's a media creation. And yet substantial funds have been allocated to it and tens of thousands of troops are being mobilized for it. Though the theater of war is in the jungles of Central India, it will have serious consequences for us all.

If ghosts are the lingering spirits of someone, or something, that has ceased to exist, then perhaps the new four-lane highway crashing through the forest is the opposite of a ghost. Perhaps it is the harbinger of what is still to come.

The antagonists in the forest are disparate and unequal in almost every way. On one side is a massive paramilitary force armed with the money, the firepower, the media, and the hubris of an emerging superpower. On the other, ordinary villagers armed with traditional weapons, backed by a superbly organized, hugely motivated Maoist guerrilla fighting force with an extraordinary and violent history of armed rebellion. The Maoists and the paramilitary are old adversaries and have fought older avatars of one another several times before: Telangana in the 1950s; West Bengal, Bihar, Srikakulam in Andhra Pradesh in the late 1960s and 1970s; and then again in Andhra Pradesh, Bihar, and Maharashtra from the 1980s all the way through to the present. They are familiar with one another's tactics and have studied one another's combat manuals closely. Each time, it seemed as though the Maoists (or their previous avatars) had been not just defeated, but literally, physically exterminated. Each time, they have reemerged, more organized, more determined, and more influential than ever. Today once again the insurrection has spread through the mineral-rich forests of Chhattisgarh, Jharkhand, Orissa, and West Bengal—homeland to millions of India's tribal people, dreamland to the corporate world. It's easier on the liberal conscience to believe that the war in the forests is a war between the government of India and the Maoists, who call elections a sham and Parliament a pigsty and have openly declared their intention to overthrow the Indian state. It's convenient to forget that tribal people in Central India have a history of resistance that predates Mao by centuries. (That's a truism of course. If they didn't, they wouldn't exist.) The Ho, the Oraon, the Kols, the Santhals, the Mundas, and the Gonds have all rebelled several times, against the British, against zamindars and moneylenders. The rebellions were cruelly crushed, many thousands killed, but the people were never conquered. Even after Independence, tribal people were at the heart of the first uprising that could be described as Maoist, in Naxalbari village in West Bengal (where the word Naxalite—now used interchangeably with "Maoist"—originates). Since then, Naxalite politics has been inextricably entwined with tribal uprisings, which says as much about the tribals as it does about the Naxalites.

This legacy of rebellion has left behind a furious people who have been deliberately isolated and marginalized by the Indian government. The Indian Constitution, the moral underpinning of Indian democracy, was adopted by Parliament in 1950. It was a tragic day for tribal people. The constitution ratified colonial policy and made the state the custodian of tribal homelands. Overnight, it turned the entire tribal population into squatters on their own land. It denied them their traditional rights to forest produce, it criminalized a whole way of life. In exchange for the right to vote, it snatched away their right to livelihood and dignity.

Having dispossessed them and pushed them into a downward spiral of indigence, in a cruel sleight of hand, the government began to use their own penury against them. Each time it needed to displace a large population—for dams, irrigation projects, mines—it talked of "bringing tribals into the mainstream" or of giving them "the fruits of modern development."

Of the tens of millions of internally displaced people (more than thirty million by Big Dams alone), refugees of India's "progress," the great majority are tribal people. When the government begins to talk of tribal welfare, it's time to worry. The most recent expression of concern has come from home minister P. Chidambaram, who says he doesn't want tribal people living in "museum cultures." The well-being of tribal people didn't seem to be such a priority during his career as a corporate lawyer, representing the interests of several major mining companies. So it might be an idea to enquire into the basis for his new anxiety.

Over the past five years or so, the governments of Chhattisgarh, Jharkhand, Orissa, and West Bengal have signed hundreds of memorandums of understanding with corporate houses, worth several billion dollars, all of them secret, for steel plants, sponge-iron factories, power plants, aluminum refineries, dams, and mines. In order for the memorandums to translate into real money, tribal people must be moved.

Therefore, this war.

When a country that calls itself a democracy openly declares war within its borders, what does that war look like? Does the resistance stand a chance? Should it? Who are the Maoists? Are they just violent nihilists foisting an outdated ideology on tribal people, goading them into a hopeless insurrection? What lessons have they learned from their past experience? Is armed struggle intrinsically undemocratic? Is the Sandwich Theory—

of "ordinary" tribals being caught in the cross fire between the State and the Maoists—an accurate one? Are "Maoists" and "Tribals" two entirely discrete categories as is being made out? Do their interests converge? Have they learned anything from each other? Have they changed each other?

❖

The day before I left, my mother called, sounding sleepy. "I've been thinking," she said, with a mother's weird instinct, "what this country needs is revolution."

An article on the Internet says that Israel's Mossad is training thirty high-ranking Indian police officers in the techniques of targeted assassinations, to render the Maoist organization "headless." There's talk in the press about the new hardware that has been bought from Israel: laser range-finders, thermal imaging equipment and unmanned drones, so popular with the US Army. Perfect weapons to use against the poor.

The drive from Raipur to Dantewada takes about ten hours through areas known to be "Maoist-infested." These are not careless words. "Infest/infestation" implies disease/pests. Diseases must be cured. Pests must be exterminated. Maoists must be wiped out. In these creeping, innocuous ways, the language of genocide has entered our vocabulary.

To protect the highway, security forces have "secured" a narrow bandwidth of forest on either side. Further in, it's the raj of the "Dada log." The Brothers. The Comrades.

On the outskirts of Raipur, a massive billboard advertises Vedanta (the company our home minister once worked with) Cancer Hospital. In Orissa, where it is mining bauxite, Vedanta is financing a university. In these creeping, innocuous ways, mining corporations enter our imaginations: the Gentle Giants Who Really Care. It's called Corporate Social Responsibility. It allows mining companies to be like the legendary actor and former chief minister NTR, who liked to play all the parts in

Telugu mythologicals—the good guys and the bad guys, all at once, in the same movie. This Corporate Social Responsibility masks the outrageous economics that underpins the mining sector in India. For example, according to the recent Lokayukta report for Karnataka, for every ton of iron ore mined by a private company, the government gets a royalty of Rs 27 (fifty-five cents) and the mining company makes Rs 5,000 ($102). In the bauxite and aluminum sector, the figures are even worse. We're talking about daylight robbery to the tune of billions of dollars. Enough to buy elections, governments, judges, newspapers, TV channels, NGOs, and aid agencies. What's the occasional cancer hospital here or there?

I don't remember seeing Vedanta's name on the long list of memorandums of understanding signed by the Chhattisgarh government. But I'm twisted enough to suspect that if there's a cancer hospital, there must be a flat-topped bauxite mountain somewhere. We pass Kanker, famous for its Counter Terrorism and Jungle Warfare College run by brigadier B. K. Ponwar, Rumpelstiltskin of this war, charged with the task of turning corrupt, sloppy policemen (straw) into jungle commandos (gold).

"Fight a guerrilla like a guerrilla," the motto of the warfare training school, is painted on the rocks. The men are taught to run, slither, jump on and off air-borne helicopters, ride horses (for some reason), eat snakes, and live off the jungle. The brigadier takes great pride in training street dogs to fight "terrorists." Eight hundred policemen graduate from the warfare training school every six weeks. Twenty similar schools are being planned all over India. The police force is gradually being turned into an army. (In Kashmir, it's the other way around. The army is being turned into an administrative police force.)

Upside down. Inside out. Either way, the Enemy is the People. It's late. Jagdalpur is asleep, except for the many hoardings of Rahul Gandhi asking people to join the Youth Congress. He's been to Bastar twice in recent months but hasn't said anything much about the war. It's probably too messy for the People's

Prince to meddle in at this point. His media managers must have put their foot down. The fact that the Salwa Judum—the dreaded, government-sponsored vigilante group responsible for rapes, killings, for burning down villages and driving hundreds of thousands of people from their homes—is led by Mahendra Karma, a Congress MLA, does not get much play in the carefully orchestrated publicity around Rahul Gandhi.

I arrived at the Ma Danteshwari mandir well in time for my appointment (first day, first show). I had my camera, my small coconut, and a powdery red tika on my forehead. I wondered if someone was watching me and having a laugh. Within minutes a young boy approached me. He had a cap and a backpack schoolbag. Chipped red nail polish on his fingernails. No Hindi *Outlook*, no bananas. "Are you the one who's going in?" he asked me. No Namashkar Guruji. I did not know what to say. He took out a soggy note from his pocket and handed it to me. It said, "*Outlook* nahin mila (couldn't find Outlook)."

"And the bananas?"

"I ate them," he said, "I got hungry."

He really was a security threat.

His backpack said Charlie Brown—Not your ordinary blockhead. He said his name was Mangtu. I soon learned that Dandakaranya, the forest I was about to enter, was full of people who had many names and fluid identities. It was like a balm to me, that idea. How lovely not to be stuck with yourself, to become someone else for a while. We walked to the bus stand, only a few minutes away from the temple. It was already crowded. Things happened quickly. There were two men on motorbikes. There was no conversation—just a glance of acknowledgment, a shifting of body weight, the revving of engines. I had no idea where we were going.

We passed the house of the Superintendent of Police, which I recognized from my last visit. He was a candid man: "See Ma'am, frankly speaking this problem can't be solved by us police or military. The problem with these tribals is they don't understand greed. Unless they become greedy, there's no hope for us. I have told my boss, remove the force and instead put a TV in every home. Everything will be automatically sorted out."

In no time at all we were riding out of town. No tail. It was a long ride, three hours by my watch. It ended abruptly in the middle of nowhere, on an empty road with forest on either side. Mangtu got off. I did too. The bikes left, and I picked up my backpack and followed the small internal security threat into the forest. It was a beautiful day. The forest floor was a carpet of gold. In a while we emerged on the white, sandy banks of a broad flat river. It was obviously monsoon-fed, so now it was more or less a sand flat, at the center a stream, ankle deep, easy to wade across. Across was "Pakistan." "Out there, ma'am," the candid superintendent of police had said to me, "my boys shoot to kill." I remembered that as we began to cross. I saw us in a policeman's rifle-sights—tiny figures in a landscape, easy to pick off. But Mangtu seemed quite unconcerned, and I took my cue from him.

Waiting for us on the other bank, in a lime-green shirt that said Horlicks!, was Chandu. A slightly older security threat. Maybe twenty. He had a lovely smile, a cycle, a jerry can with boiled water, and many packets of glucose biscuits for me, from the party. We caught our breath and began to walk again. The cycle, it turned out, was a red herring. The route was almost entirely noncyclable. We climbed steep hills and clambered down rocky paths along some pretty precarious ledges. When he couldn't wheel it, Chandu lifted the cycle and carried it over his head as though it weighed nothing. I began to wonder about his bemused village boy air. I discovered (much later) that he could handle every kind of weapon, "except for a light machine gun," he informed me cheerfully.

Three beautiful, sozzled men with flowers in their turbans walked with us for about half an hour, before our paths diverged. At sunset, their shoulder bags began to crow. They had roosters in them, which they had taken to market but hadn't managed to sell. Chandu seems to be able to see in the dark. I have to use my flashlight. The crickets start up and soon there's an orchestra, a dome of sound over us. I long to look up at the night sky, but I dare not. I have to keep my eyes on the ground. One step at a time. Concentrate.

I hear dogs. But I can't tell how far away they are. The terrain flattens out. I steal a look at the sky. It makes me ecstatic. I hope we're going to stop soon. "Soon," Chandu says. It turns out to be more than an hour. I see silhouettes of enormous trees. We arrive.

The village seems spacious, the houses far away from each other. The house we enter is beautiful. There's a fire, some people sitting around. More people outside, in the dark. I can't tell how many. I can just about make them out. A murmur goes around. "Lal salaam, Kaamraid" (Red salute, Comrade). "Lal salaam," I say. I'm beyond tired. The lady of the house calls me inside and gives me chicken curry cooked in green beans and some red rice. Fabulous. Her baby is asleep next to me, her silver anklets gleam in the firelight.

After dinner, I unzip my sleeping bag. It's a strange intrusive sound, the big zip. Someone puts on the radio. BBC Hindi service. The Church of England has withdrawn its funds from Vedanta's Niyamgiri project, citing environmental degradation and rights violations of the Dongria Kondh tribe. I can hear cowbells, snuffling, shuffling, cattle-farting. All's well with the world. My eyes close.

❖

We're up at 5:00 a.m. On the move by 6:00. In another couple of hours, we cross another river. We walk through some beautiful villages. Every village has a family of tamarind trees watching over it, like a clutch of huge, benevolent gods. Sweet, Bastar tamarind. By 11:00 a.m., the sun is high, and walking is less fun. We stop at a village for lunch. Chandu seems to know the people in the house. A beautiful young girl flirts with him. He looks a little shy, maybe because I'm around. Lunch is raw papaya with masoor dal and red rice. And red chili powder. We're going to wait for the sun to lose some of its vehemence before we start walking again. We take a nap in the gazebo. There is a spare beauty about the place. Everything is clean and necessary. No clutter. A black hen parades up and down the low mud wall. A bamboo grid stabilizes the rafters of the thatched roof and doubles as a storage rack. There's a grass broom, two drums, a woven reed basket, a broken umbrella, and a whole stack of flattened, empty, corrugated cardboard boxes. Something catches my eye. I need my spectacles. Here's what's printed on the cardboard: Ideal Power 90 High Energy Emulsion Explosive (Class-2) SD CAT ZZ.

We start walking again at about 2:00 p.m. In the village we are going to meet a Didi (Sister, Comrade) who knows what the next step of the journey will be. Chandu doesn't. There is an economy of information, too. Nobody is supposed to know everything. But when we reach the village, Didi isn't there. There is no news of her. For the first time, I see a little cloud of worry settling over Chandu. A big one settles over me. I don't know what the systems of communication are, but what if they've gone wrong?

We're parked outside a deserted school building, a little way out of the village. Why are all the government village schools built like concrete bastions, with steel shutters for windows and sliding folding steel doors? Why not like the village houses, with mud and thatch? Because they double up as barracks and bunkers. "In the villages in Abujhmad," Chandu says, "schools are like this . . ." He scratches a building plan with a twig in the earth. Three octagons attached to each other like a honeycomb. "So they can fire in all directions." He draws arrows to illustrate his point, like a cricket graphic—a batsman's wagon wheel. There are no teachers in any of the schools, Chandu says. They've all run away. Or have you chased them away? No, we only chase police. But why should teachers come here, to the jungle, when they get their salaries sitting at home? Good point.

He informs me that this is a "new area." The party has entered only recently. About twenty young people arrive, girls and boys. In their teens and early twenties. Chandu explains that this is the village-level militia, the lowest rung of the Maoists' military hierarchy. I have never seen anyone like them before. They are dressed in saris and lungis, some in frayed olive-green fatigues. The boys wear jewelery, headgear. Every one of them has a muzzle-loading rifle, what's called a bharmaar. Some also have knives, axes, a bow and arrow. One boy carries a crude mortar fashioned out of a heavy three-foot GI pipe. It's filled with gunpowder and shrapnel and ready to be fired. It makes a big noise but can only be used once. Still, it scares the police, they say, and giggle. War doesn't seem to be uppermost on their minds. Perhaps because their area is outside the home range of the Salwa Judum. They have just finished a day's work, helping to build fencing around some village houses to keep the goats out of the fields. They're full of fun and curiosity. The girls are confident and easy with the boys. I have a sensor for this sort of thing, and I am impressed. Their job, Chandu says, is to patrol and protect a group of four or five villages and to help in the fields, clean wells, or repair houses—doing whatever's needed.

Still no Didi. What to do? Nothing. Wait. Help out with some chopping and peeling.

After dinner, without much talk, everybody falls in line. Clearly, we are moving. Everything moves with us, the rice, vegetables, pots and pans. We leave the school compound and walk single file into the forest. In less than half an hour, we arrive in a glade where we are going to sleep. There's absolutely no noise. Within minutes everyone has spread their blue plastic sheets, the ubiquitous "*jhilli*" (without which there will be no Revolution). Chandu and Mangtu share one and spread one out for me. They find me the best place, by the best gray rock. Chandu says he has sent a message to Didi. If she gets it, she will be here first thing in the morning. If she gets it.

It's the most beautiful room I have slept in, in a long time. My private suite in a thousand-star hotel. I'm surrounded by these strange, beautiful children with their curious arsenal. They're all Maoists for sure. Are they all going to die? Is the jungle warfare training school for them? And the helicopter gunships, the thermal imaging, and the laser range-finders?

Why must they die? What for? To turn all of this into a mine? I remember my visit to the open cast iron ore mines in Keonjhar, Orissa. There was a forest there once. And children like these. Now the land is like a raw, red wound. Red dust fills your nostrils and lungs. The water is red, the air is red, the people are red, their lungs and hair are red. All day and all night trucks rumble through their villages, bumper to bumper, thousands and thousands of trucks, taking ore to Paradip port from where it will go to China. There it will turn into cars and smoke and sudden cities that spring up overnight. Into a "growth rate" that leaves economists breathless. Into weapons to make war.

Everyone's asleep except for the sentries who take one-and-a-half-hour shifts. Finally, I can look at the stars. When I was a child growing up on the banks of the Meenachal River, I used to think the sound of crickets—which always started up at twilight—was the sound of stars revving up, getting ready to shine. I'm surprised at how much I love being here. There is nowhere else in the world that I would rather be. Who should I be tonight? Kamraid Rahel, under the stars? Maybe Didi will come tomorrow.

They arrive in the early afternoon. I can see them from a distance. About fifteen of them, all in olive-green uniforms, running toward us. Even from a distance, from the way they run, I can tell they are the heavy hitters. The People's Liberation Guerrilla Army (PLGA). For whom the thermal imaging and laser-guided rifles. For whom the jungle warfare training school.

They carry serious rifles, INSAS, self-loading rifles, two have AK-47s. The leader of the squad is Comrade Madhav who has been with the party since he was nine. He's from Warangal,

Andhra Pradesh. He's upset and extremely apologetic. There was a major miscommunication, he says again and again, which usually never happens. I was supposed to have arrived at the main camp on the very first night. Someone dropped the baton in the jungle relay. The motorcycle drop was to have been at an entirely different place. "We made you wait, we made you walk so much. We ran all the way when the message came that you were here." I said it was okay, that I had come prepared, to wait and walk and listen. He wants to leave immediately, because people in the camp were waiting, and worried.

It's a few hours' walk to the camp. It's getting dark when we arrive. There are several layers of sentries and concentric circles of patrolling. There must be one hundred comrades lined up in two rows. Everyone has a weapon. And a smile. They begin to sing: "*Lal lal salaam, lal lal salaam, aane vaale saathiyon ko lal lal salaam*" (Red salute to the comrades who have arrived). It is sung sweetly, as though it was a folk song about a river or a forest blossom. With the song, the greeting, the handshake, and the clenched fist. Everyone greets everyone, murmuring "*Lalslaam, mlalslaa mlalslaam . . .*"

Other than a large blue jhilli spread out on the floor, about fifteen feet square, there are no signs of a "camp." This one has a jhilli roof as well. It's my room for the night. I was either being rewarded for my days of walking or being pampered in advance for what lay ahead. Or both. Either way it was the last time in the entire trip that I was going to have a roof over my head. Over dinner I meet Comrade Narmada, in charge of the Krantikari Adivasi Mahila Sangathan (KAMS), who has a price on her head; Comrade Saroja of the PLGA, who is only as tall as her self-loading rifle; Comrade Maase (which means Black Girl in Gondi), who has a price on her head too; Comrade Rupi, the tech wizard; Comrade Raju, who's in charge of the division I'd been walking through; and Comrade Venu (or Murali or Sonu or Sushil, whatever you would like to call him), clearly the most senior of them all. Maybe central committee, maybe even politburo. I'm not told, I don't ask. Between us we speak Gondi, Halbi, Telugu, Punjabi, and Malayalam. Only Maase speaks English. (So we all communicate in Hindi!) Comrade Maase is tall and quiet and seems to have to swim through a layer of pain to enter the conversation. But from the way she hugs me, I can tell she's a reader. And that she misses having books in the jungle. She will tell me her story only later. When she trusts me with her grief.

Bad news arrives, as it does in this jungle. A runner, with "biscuits." Handwritten notes on sheets of paper, folded and stapled into little squares. There's a bag full of them. Like chips. News from everywhere. The police have killed five people in Ongnaar village, four from the militia and one ordinary villager: Santhu Pottai (25), Phoolo Vadde (22), Kande Pottai (22), Ramoli Vadde (20), Dalsai Koram (22). They could have been the children in my star-spangled dormitory of last night.

Then good news arrives. A small contingent of people with a plump young man. He's in fatigues too, but they look brand new. Everybody admires them and comments on the fit. He looks shy and pleased. He's a doctor who has come to live and work with the comrades in the forest. The last time a doctor visited Dandakaranya was many years ago.

On the radio there's news about the home minister's meeting with chief ministers of states "affected by Left-Wing Extremism." The chief ministers of Jharkhand and Bihar are being demure and have not attended. Everybody sitting around the radio laughs. Around the time of elections, they say, right through the campaign, and then maybe a month or two after the government is formed, mainstream politicians all say things like "Naxals are our children." You can set your watch to the schedule of when they will change their minds and grow fangs.

I am introduced to Comrade Kamla. I am told that I must on no account go even five feet away from my jhilli without waking her. Because everybody gets disoriented in the dark and could get seriously lost. (I don't wake her. I sleep like a log.)

In the morning Kamla presents me with a yellow polythene packet with one corner snipped off. Once it used to contain Abis Gold Refined Soya Oil. Now it was my Loo Mug. Nothing's wasted on the Road to the Revolution. (Even now I think of Comrade Kamla all the time, every day. She's seventeen. She wears a homemade pistol on her hip. And boy, what a smile. But if the police come across her, they'll kill her. They might rape her first. No questions will be asked. Because she's an Internal Security Threat.)

❖

After breakfast, Comrade Venu (Sushil, Sonu, Murali) is waiting for me, sitting cross-legged on the jhilli, looking for all the world like a frail village schoolteacher. I'm going to get a history lesson. Or, more accurately, a lecture on the history of the last thirty years in the Dandakaranya forest, which has culminated in the war that's swirling through it today. For sure, it's a partisan's version. But then, what history isn't? In any case, the secret history must be made public if it is to be contested, argued with, instead of merely being lied about, which is what is happening now.

Comrade Venu has a calm, reassuring manner and a gentle voice that will, in the days to come, surface in a context that will completely unnerve me. This morning he talks for several hours, almost continuously. He's like a little store manager who has a giant bunch of keys with which to open up a maze of lockers full of stories, songs, and insights. Comrade Venu was in one of the seven armed squads who crossed the Godavari from Andhra Pradesh and entered the Dandakaranya forest (DK, in Partyspeak) in June 1980, thirty years ago. He is one of the original forty-niners. They belonged to People's War Group (PWG), a faction of the Communist Party of India (Marxist-Leninist; CPI [ML]), the original Naxalites. PWG was formally announced as a separate, independent party in April that year, under Kondapalli Seetharamiah. PWG had decided to build a standing army, for which it would need a base. DK was to be that base, and those first squads were sent in to reconnoiter the area and begin the process of building guerrilla zones.

The debate about whether communist parties ought to have a standing army, and whether or not a "people's army" is a contradiction in terms, is an old one. PWG's decision to build an army came from its experience in Andhra Pradesh, where its "Land to the Tiller" campaign led to a direct clash with the landlords and resulted in the kind of police repression that the party found impossible to withstand without a trained fighting force of its own. (By 2004, PWG had merged with the other CPI (ML) factions, Party Unity, and the Maoist Communist Center—which functions for the most part out of Bihar and Jharkhand. To become what it is now the Communist Party of India-Maoist.)

Dandakaranya is part of what the British, in their White Man's way, called Gondwana, land of the Gonds. Today the state boundaries of Madhya Pradesh, Chhattisgarh, Orissa, Andhra Pradesh, and Maharashtra slice through the forest. Breaking up a troublesome people into separate administrative units is an old trick. But these Maoists and Maoist Gonds don't pay much attention to things like state boundaries. They have different maps in their heads, and like other creatures of the forest, they have their own paths. For them, roads are not meant for walking on. They're meant only to be crossed, or as is increasingly becoming the case, ambushed. Though the Gonds (divided between the Koya and Dorla tribes) are by far the biggest majority, there are small settlements of other tribal communities, too. The non-Adivasi communities, traders and settlers, live on the edges of the forest, near the roads and markets.

The PWG were not the first evangelicals to arrive in Dandakaranya. Baba Amte, the well-known Gandhian, had opened his ashram and leprosy hospital in Warora in 1975. The Ramakrishna Mission had begun opening village schools in the remote forests of Abujhmad. In north Bastar, Baba Bihari Das had started an aggressive drive to "bring tribals back into the Hindu fold," which involved a campaign to denigrate tribal culture, induce self-hatred, and introduce Hinduism's great gift—caste.

The first converts, the village chiefs and big landlords—people like Mahendra Karma, founder of the Salwa Judum—were conferred the status of Dwij (twice-born) Brahmins. (Of course, this was a bit of a scam, because nobody can become a Brahmin. If they could, we'd be a nation of Brahmins by now.) But this counterfeit Hinduism is considered good enough for tribal people, just like the counterfeit brands of everything else—biscuits, soap, matches, oil—that are sold in village markets. As part of the Hindutva drive, the names of villages were changed in land records, as a result of which most have two names now, people's names and government names.

Innar village, for example, became Chinnari. On voters' lists, tribal names were changed to Hindu names. (Massa Karma became Mahendra Karma.) Those who did not come forward to join the Hindu fold were declared "*Katwas*" (by which they meant untouchables) who later became the natural constituency for the Maoists. The PWG first began work in south Bastar and Gadchiroli. Comrade Venu describes those first months in some detail: how the villagers were suspicious of them and wouldn't let them into their homes. No one would offer them food or water. The police spread rumors that they were thieves. The women hid their jewelery in the ashes of their woodstoves. There was an enormous amount of repression. In November 1980, in Gadchiroli, the police opened fire at a village meeting and killed an entire squad. That was DK's first "encounter" killing. It was a traumatic setback, and the comrades retreated across the Godavari and returned to Adilabad, but in 1981 they returned. They began to organize tribal people to demand a rise in the price they were being paid for tendu leaves (which are used to make beedis). At the time, traders paid three paise for a bundle of about fifty leaves. It was a formidable job to organize people entirely unfamiliar with this kind of politics, to lead them on strike. Eventually the strike was successful and the price was doubled, to six paise a bundle. But the real success for the party was to have been able to demonstrate the value of unity and a new way of conducting a political negotiation. Today, after several strikes and agitations, the price of a bundle of tendu leaves is Re 1. (It seems a little improbable at these rates, but the turnover of the tendu business runs into hundreds of crores of rupees [hundreds of thousands of dollars].)

Every season, the government floats tenders and gives contractors permission to extract a fixed volume of tendu leaves—usually between 1,500 and 5,000 standard bags known as manak boras. Each manak bora contains about 1,000 bundles. (Of course, there's no way of ensuring that the contractors don't extract more than they're meant to.) By the time the tendu enters the market, it is sold in kilos. The slippery arithmetic and the sly system of measurement that converts bundles into manak boras into kilos is controlled by the contractors and leaves plenty of room for manipulation of the worst kind. The most conservative estimate puts their profit per standard bag at about Rs 1,100 (twenty-three dollars). (That's after paying the party a commission of Rs 120 [two dollars and sixty cents] per bag.) Even by that gauge, a small contractor (1,500 bags) makes about Rs 16 lakh a season and a big one (5,000 bags) up to Rs 55 lakh ($118,000). A more realistic estimate would be several times this amount. Meanwhile, the Gravest Internal Security Threat makes just enough to stay alive until the next season.

We're interrupted by some laughter and the sight of Nilesh, one of the young PLGA comrades, walking rapidly toward the cooking area, slapping himself. When he comes closer, I see that he's carrying a leafy nest of angry red ants that have crawled all over him and are biting him on his arms and neck. Nilesh is laughing, too. "Have you ever eaten ant chutney?" Comrade Venu asks me. I know red ants well, from my childhood in Kerala, I've been bitten by them, but I've never eaten them. (The chapoli turns out to be nice. Sour. Lots of folic acid.)

Nilesh is from Bijapur, which is at the heart of Salwa Judum operations. Nilesh's younger brother joined the Judum on one of its looting and burning sprees and was made a special police officer. He lives in the Basaguda camp with his mother. His father refused to go and stayed behind in the village. In effect, it's a family blood feud. Later on, when I had an opportunity to talk to him, I asked Nilesh why his brother had done that. "He was very young," Nilesh said. "He got an opportunity to run wild and hurt people and burn houses. He went crazy, did terrible things. Now he is stuck. He can never come back to the village. He will not be forgiven. He knows that."

We return to the history lesson. The party's next big struggle, Comrade Venu says, was against the Ballarpur Paper Mills. The government had given the Thapars a forty-five-year contract to extract 1.5 lakh tons of bamboo at a hugely subsidized rate. (Small beer compared to bauxite, but still.) The tribals were paid 10 paise for a bundle, which contained twenty culms of bamboo. (I won't yield to the vulgar temptation of comparing that with the profits the Thapars were making.) A long agitation, a strike, followed by negotiations with officials of the paper mill in the presence of the people, tripled the price to 30 paise per bundle. For the tribal people, these were huge achievements. Other political parties had made promises but showed no signs of keeping them. People began to approach the PWG asking if they could join up.

But the politics of tendu, bamboo, and other forest produce was seasonal. The perennial problem, the real bane of people's lives, was the biggest landlord of all, the Forest Department. Every morning, forest officials, even the most junior of them, would appear in villages like a bad dream, preventing people from plowing their fields, collecting firewood, plucking leaves, picking fruit, grazing their cattle, from living. They brought elephants to overrun fields and scattered babool seeds to destroy the soil as they passed by. People would be beaten, arrested, humiliated, their crops destroyed. Of course, from the Forest Department's point of view, these were illegal people engaged in unconstitutional activity, and the department was only implementing the Rule of Law. (Their sexual exploitation of women was just an added perk in a hardship posting.)

Emboldened by the people's participation in these struggles, the party decided to confront the Forest Department. It encouraged people to take over forest land and cultivate it. The Forest Department retaliated by burning new villages that came up in forest areas. In 1986, it announced a National Park in Bijapur, which meant the eviction of sixty villages. More than half of them had already been moved out, and construction of national park infrastructure had begun when the party moved in. It demolished the construction and stopped the eviction of the remaining villages. It prevented the Forest Department from entering the area. On a few occasions, officials were captured, tied to trees, and beaten by villagers. It was cathartic revenge for generations of exploitation. Eventually, the Forest Department fled. Between 1986 and 2000, the party redistributed three hundred thousand acres of forest land. Today, Comrade Venu says, there are no landless peasants in Dandakaranya.

For today's generation of young people, the Forest Department is a distant memory, the stuff of stories mothers tell their children, about a mythological past of bondage and humiliation. For the older generation, freedom from the Forest Department meant genuine freedom. They could touch it, taste it. It meant far more than India's Independence ever did. They began to rally to the party that had struggled with them.

❖

The seven-squad team had come a long way. Its influence now ranged across a 60,000-square-kilometer stretch of forest, thousands of villages and millions of people.

But the departure of the Forest Department heralded the arrival of the police. That set off a cycle of bloodshed. Fake "encounters" by the police, ambushes by the PWG. With the redistribution of land came other responsibilities: irrigation, agricultural productivity, and the problem of an expanding population arbitrarily clearing forest land. A decision was taken to separate "mass work" and "military work."

Today, Dandakaranya is administered by an elaborate structure of Janatana Sarkars (people's governments). The organizing principles came from the Chinese revolution and the Vietnam War. Each Janatana Sarkar is elected by a cluster of villages whose combined population can range from five hundred to five thousand. It has nine departments: Krishi (agriculture), Vyapar-Udyog (trade and industry), Arthik (economic), Nyay (justice), Raksha (defense), Hospital (health), Jan Sampark (public relations), School-Riti Rivaj (education and culture), and Jungle. A group of Janatana Sarkars come under an area committee. Three area committees make up a division. There are ten divisions in Dandakaranya.

"We have a Save the Jungle department now," Comrade Venu says. "You must have read the government report that says forest has increased in Naxal areas?"

Ironically, Comrade Venu says, the first people to benefit from the party's campaign against the Forest Department were the mukhias (village chiefs)—the Dwij brigade. They used their manpower and their resources to grab as much land as they could while the going was good. But then people began to approach the party with their "internal contradictions," as Comrade Venu put it quaintly. The party began to turn its attention to issues of equity, class, and injustice within tribal society. The big landlords sensed trouble on the horizon. As the party's influence expanded, theirs had begun to wane. Increasingly, people were taking their problems to the party instead of to the mukhias. Old forms of exploitation began to be challenged. On the day of the first rain, people were traditionally supposed to till the mukhia's land instead of their own. That stopped. They no longer offered them the first day's picking of mahua or other forest produce. Obviously, something needed to be done.

Enter Mahendra Karma, one of the biggest landlords in the region and at the time a member of the CPI. In 1990, he rallied a group of mukhias and landlords and started a campaign called the Jan Jagran Abhiyaan (public awakening campaign). Their way of "awakening" the "public" was to form a hunting party of about three hundred men to comb the forest, killing people, burning houses, and molesting women. The then Madhya Pradesh government—Chhattisgarh had not yet been created—provided police back-up. In Maharashtra, something similar called "Democratic Front" began its assault. People's War responded to all of this in true People's War style, by killing a few of the most notorious landlords. In a few months, the Jan Jagran Abhiyaan, the "white terror"—Comrade Venu's term for it—faded. In 1998, Mahendra Karma, who had by now joined the Congress Party, tried to revive the Jan Jagran Abhiyaan. This time it fizzled out even faster than before.

Then, in the summer of 2005, fortune favored him. In April, the Bharatiya Janata Party (BJP) government in Chhattisgarh signed two memorandums of understanding to set up integrated steel plants (the terms of which are secret). One for Rs 7,000 crore ($1.5 billion) with Essar Steel in Bailadila, and the other for Rs 10,000 crore ($2.1 billion) with Tata Steel in Lohandiguda. That same month, prime minister Manmohan Singh made his famous statement about the Maoists being the "Gravest Internal Security Threat" to India. (It was an odd thing to say at the time, because actually the opposite was true. The Congress government in Andhra Pradesh had just outmaneuvered the Maoists, decimated them. They had lost about 1,600 of their cadre and were in complete disarray.)

The prime minister's statement sent the share value of mining companies soaring. It also sent a signal to the media that the Maoists were fair game for anyone who chose to go after them. In June 2005, Mahendra Karma called a secret meeting of mukhias in Kutroo village and announced the Salwa Judum (the Purification Hunt). A lovely mélange of tribal earthiness and Dwij/ Nazi sentiment. Unlike the Jan Jagran Abhiyaan, the Salwa Judum was a ground-clearing operation, meant to move people out of their villages into roadside camps, where they could be policed and controlled. In military terms, it's called Strategic Hamleting. It was devised by general Sir Harold Briggs in 1950 when the British were at war against the communists in Malaya. The Briggs Plan became very popular with the Indian Army, which has used it in Nagaland, Mizoram, and Telangana. The BJP chief minister of Chhattisgarh, Raman Singh, announced that as far as his government was concerned, villagers who did not move into the camps would be considered Maoists.

So, in Bastar, for an ordinary villager, just staying at home became the equivalent of indulging in dangerous terrorist activity. Along with a steel mug of black tea, as a special treat, someone hands me a pair of earphones and switches on a little MP3 player. It's a scratchy recording of Mr. Manhar, then the superintendent of police of Bijapur, briefing a junior officer over the wireless about the rewards and incentives the state and central governments are offering to *"jagrit"* (awakened) villages and to people who agree to move into camps. He then gives clear instructions that villages that refuse to surrender should be burnt and journalists who want to "cover" Naxalites should be shot on sight. (I'd read about this in the papers long ago. When the story broke, as punishment—it's not clear to whom—the superintendent was transferred to the State Human Rights Commission.)

The first village the Salwa Judum burnt (on June 18, 2005) was Ambeli. Between June and December 2005, it burned, killed, raped, and looted its way through hundreds of villages of south Dantewada. The centers of its operations were the districts of Bijapur and Bhairamgarh, near Bailadila, where Essar Steel's new plant was proposed. Not coincidentally, these were also Maoist strongholds, where the Janatana Sarkars had done a great deal of work, especially in building water-harvesting structures. The Janatana Sarkars became the special target of the Salwa Judum's attacks. Hundreds of people were killed in the most brutal ways. About sixty thousand people moved into camps, some voluntarily, others out of terror. Of these, about three thousand were appointed special police officers on a salary of Rs 1,500 (thirty-two dollars).

For these paltry crumbs, young people, like Nilesh's brother, have sentenced themselves to a life sentence in a barbed wire enclosure. Cruel as they have been, they could end up being the worst victims of this horrible war. No Supreme Court judgment ordering the Salwa Judum to be dismantled can change their fate.

The remaining hundreds of thousands of people went off the government radar. (But the development funds for these 644 villages did not. What happens to that little goldmine?) Many of them made their way to Andhra Pradesh and Orissa where they usually migrated to work as contract labor during the chili-picking season. But tens of thousands fled into the forest, where they still remain, living without shelter, coming back to their fields and homes only in the daytime.

In the slipstream of the Salwa Judum, a swarm of police stations and camps appeared. The idea was to provide carpet security for a "creeping reoccupation" of Maoist-controlled territory. The assumption was that the Maoists would not dare to attack such a large concentration of security forces. The Maoists, for their part, realized that if they did not break that carpet security, it would amount to abandoning people whose trust they had earned and with whom they had lived and worked for twenty-five years. They struck back in a series of attacks on the heart of the security grid.

❖

On January 26, 2006, the PLGA attacked the Gangalaur police camp and killed 7 people. On July 17, 2006, the Salwa Judum camp at Erabor was attacked, 20 people were killed and 150 injured. (You might have read about it: "Maoists attacked the relief camp set up by the state government to provide shelter to the villagers who had fled from their villages because of terror unleashed by the Naxalites.") On December 13, 2006, they attacked the Basaguda "relief" camp and killed 3 special police officers and a constable. On March 15, 2007, came the most audacious of them all: 120 PLGA guerrillas attacked the Rani Bodili Kanya Ashram, a girls' hostel that had been converted into a barrack for eighty Chhattisgarh Police (and special police officers) while the girls still lived in it as human shields. The PLGA entered the compound, cordoned off the annex in which the girls lived, and attacked the barracks. Some 55 policemen and special police officers were killed. None of the girls was hurt. (The candid superintendent of police of Dantewada had shown me his PowerPoint presentation with horrifying photographs of the burned, disembowelled bodies of the policemen amidst the ruins of the blown-up school building. They were so macabre, it was impossible not to look away. He looked pleased at my reaction.)

The attack on Rani Bodili caused an uproar in the country. Human rights organizations condemned the Maoists not just for their violence, but also for being antieducation and attacking schools. But in Dandakaranya, the Rani Bodili attack became a legend: songs, poems, and plays were written about it.

The Maoist counteroffensive did break the carpet security and gave people breathing space. The police and the Salwa Judum retreated into their camps, from which they now emerge—usually in the dead of night—only in packs of three hundred or one thousand to carry out cordon and search operations in villages. Gradually, except for the special police officers and their families, the rest of the people in the Salwa Judum camps began to return to their villages. The Maoists welcomed them back and announced that even special police officers could return if they genuinely, and publicly, regretted their actions. Young people began to flock to the PLGA. (The PLGA had been formally constituted in December 2000. Over the last thirty years, its armed squads had very gradually expanded into sections, sections had grown into platoons, and platoons into companies. But after the Salwa Judum's depredations, the PLGA was rapidly able to declare battalion strength.)

The Salwa Judum had not just failed, it had backfired badly.

As we now know, it was not just a local operation by a small-time hood. Regardless of the doublespeak in the press, the Salwa Judum was a joint operation by the state government of Chhattisgarh and the Congress Party, which was in power at the Center. It could not be allowed to fail. Not when all those memorandums of understanding were still waiting, like wilting hopefuls on the marriage market. The government was under tremendous pressure to come up with a new plan. They came up with Operation Green Hunt. The Salwa Judum special police officers are called Koya Commandos now. It has deployed the Chhattisgarh Armed Force, the Central Reserve Police Force, the Border Security Force, the Indo-Tibetan Border Police, the Central Industrial Security Force, Greyhounds, Scorpions, Cobras. And a policy that's affectionately called WHAM—Winning Hearts and Minds.

Significant wars are often fought in unlikely places. Free market capitalism defeated Soviet Communism in the bleak mountains of Afghanistan. Here in the forests of Dantewada, a battle rages for the soul of India. Plenty has been said about the deepening crisis in Indian democracy and the collusion between big corporations, major political parties, and the security establishment. If anybody wants to do a quick spot check, Dantewada is the place to go.

A draft report titled *State Agrarian Relations and the Unfinished Task of Land Reform (Volume 1)* said that Tata Steel and Essar Steel were the first financiers of the Salwa Judum. Because it was a government report, it created a flurry when it was reported in the press. (That fact has subsequently been dropped from the final report. Was it a genuine error, or did someone receive a gentle, integrated steel tap on the shoulder?) On October 12, 2009, the mandatory public hearing for Tata's steel plant, meant to be held in Lohandiguda where local people could come, actually took place in a small hall inside the collectorate in Jagdalpur, many miles away, cordoned off with massive security. A hired audience of fifty tribals was brought in a guarded convoy of government jeeps. After the meeting, the district collector congratulated "the people of Lohandiguda" for their cooperation. The local newspapers reported the lie, even though they knew better. (The advertisements rolled in.) Despite villagers' objections, land acquisition for the project has begun.

The Maoists are not the only ones who seek to depose the Indian state. It's already been deposed several times by Hindu fundamentalism and economic totalitarianism.

Lohandiguda, a five-hour drive from Dantewada, never used to be a Naxalite area. But it is now. Comrade Joori, who sat next to me while I ate the ant chutney, works in the area. She said they decided to move in after graffiti had begun to appear on the walls of village houses, saying, Naxali aao, hamein bachao (Naxals come and save us)! A few months ago, Vimal Meshram, president of the village panchayat, was shot dead in the market. "He was Tata's man," Joori says. "He was forcing people to give up their land and accept compensation. It's good that he's been finished. We lost a comrade, too. They shot him. D'you want more chapoli?" She's only twenty. "We won't let the Tatas come there. People don't want them." Joori is not PLGA. She's in the Chetna Natya Manch, the cultural wing of the party. She sings. She writes songs. She's from Abujhmad. (She's married to Comrade Madhav. She fell in love with his singing when he visited her village with a Chetna Natya Manch troupe.)

I feel I ought to say something at this point. About the futility of violence, about the unacceptability of summary executions. But what should I suggest they do? Go to court? Do a dharna at Jantar Mantar, New Delhi? A rally? A relay hunger strike? It sounds ridiculous. The promoters of the New Economic Policy—who find it so easy to say "There Is No Alternative"— should be asked to suggest an alternative Resistance Policy. A specific one, to these specific people, in this specific forest. Here. Now. Which party should they vote for? Which democratic institution in this country should they approach? Which door did the Narmada Bachao Andolan not knock on during the years and years it fought against Big Dams on the Narmada?

❖

It's dark. There's a lot of activity in the camp, but I can't see anything. Just points of light moving around. It's hard to tell whether they are stars or fireflies or Maoists on the move. Little Mangtu appears from nowhere. I found out that he's part of the first batch of the Young Communists Mobile School, who are being taught to read and write and tutored in basic Communist principles. ("Indoctrination of young minds!" our corporate media howls. The TV advertisements that brainwash children before they can even think are not seen as a form of indoctrination.) The young Communists are not allowed to carry guns or wear uniforms. But they trail the PLGA squads, with stars in their eyes, like groupies of a rock band.

Mangtu has adopted me with a gently proprietorial air. He has filled my water bottle and says I should pack my bag. A whistle blows. The blue jhilli tent is dismantled and folded up in five minutes flat. Another whistle and all hundred comrades fall in line. Five rows. Comrade Raju is the Director of Ops. There's a roll call. I'm in the line too, shouting out my number when Comrade Kamla, who is in front of me, prompts me. (We count to twenty and then start from one, because that's as far as most Gonds count. Twenty is enough for them. Maybe it should be enough for us, too.) Chandu is in fatigues now and carries a Sten gun. In a low voice, Comrade Raju is briefing the group. It's all in Gondi, I don't understand a thing, but I keep hearing the word "RV." Later Raju tells me it stands for Rendezvous! It's a Gondi word now. "We make RV points so that in case we come under fire and people have to scatter, they know where to regroup." He cannot possibly know the kind of panic this induces in me. Not because I'm scared of being fired on, but because I'm scared of being lost. I'm a directional dyslexic, capable of getting lost between my bedroom and my bathroom. What will I do in 60,000 square kilometers of forest? Come hell or high water, I'm going to be holding on to Comrade Raju's *pallu*.

Before we start walking, Comrade Venu comes up to me: "Okay, then, comrade. I'll take your leave." I'm taken aback. He looks like a little mosquito in a woollen cap and chappals, surrounded by his guards, three women, three men. Heavily armed. "We are very grateful to you comrade, for coming all the way here," he says. Once again the handshake, the clenched fist. "Lal Salaam Comrade." He disappears into the forest, the Keeper of the Keys. And in a moment, it's as though he was never here. I'm a little bereft. But I have hours of recordings to listen to. And as the days turn into weeks, I will meet many people who paint color and detail into the grid he drew for me.

We begin to walk in the opposite direction. Comrade Raju, smelling of Iodex from a mile off, says with a happy smile, "My knees are gone. I can only walk if I have had a fistful of pain-killers." Comrade Raju speaks perfect Hindi and has a deadpan way of telling the funniest stories. He worked as an advocate in Raipur for eighteen years. Both he and his wife Malti were party members and part of its city network. At the end of 2007, one of the key people in the Raipur network was arrested, tortured, and eventually turned informer. He was driven around Raipur in a closed police vehicle and made to point out his former colleagues. Comrade Malti was one of them. On January 22, 2008, she was arrested along with several others. The charge against her is that she mailed CDs containing video evidence of Salwa Judum atrocities to several members of Parliament. Her case rarely comes up for hearing because the police know their case is flimsy. But the new Chhattisgarh Special Public Security Act allows the police to hold her without bail for several years. "Now the government has deployed several battalions of Chhattisgarh police to protect the poor members of Parliament from their own mail," Comrade Raju says.

He did not get caught because he was in Dandakaranya at the time, attending a meeting. He's been here ever since. His two school-going children, who were left alone at home, were interrogated extensively by the police. Finally, their home was packed up and they went to live with an uncle. Comrade Raju received news of them for the first time only a few weeks ago. What gives him this strength, this ability to hold on to his acid humor? What keeps them all going, despite all they have endured? Their faith and hope—and love—for the Party. I encounter it again and again, in the deepest, most personal ways.

We're moving in single file now. Myself and one hundred "senselessly violent," bloodthirsty insurgents. I looked around at the camp before we left. There are no signs that almost one hundred people had camped here, except for some ash where the fires had been. I cannot believe this army. As far as consumption goes, it's more Gandhian than any Gandhian and has a lighter carbon footprint than any climate change evangelist. But for now, it even has a Gandhian approach to sabotage; before a police vehicle is burnt, for example, it is stripped down and every part cannibalized. The steering wheel is straightened out and made into a *bharmaar*, the rexine upholstery stripped and used for ammunition pouches, the battery for solar charging. (The new instructions from the high command are that captured vehicles should be buried and not cremated. So they can be resurrected when needed.) Should I write a play, I wonder—Gandhi Get Your Gun? Or will I be lynched?

We're walking in pitch darkness and dead silence. I'm the only one using a torch, pointed down so that all I can see in its circle of light are Comrade Kamla's bare heels in her scuffed, black chappals, showing me exactly where to put my feet. She is carrying ten times more weight than I am. Her backpack, her rifle, a huge bag of provisions on her head, one of the large cooking pots, and two shoulder bags full of vegetables. The bag on her head is perfectly balanced, and she can scramble down slopes and slippery rock pathways without so much as touching it. She is a miracle. It turns out to be a long walk. I'm grateful to the history lesson because apart from everything else it gave my feet a rest for a whole day. It's the most beautiful thing, walking in the forest at night. And I'll be doing it night after night.

❖

We're going to a celebration of the centenary of the 1910 Bhumkal rebellion in which the Koyas rose up against the British. *Bhumkal* means "earthquake." Comrade Raju says people will walk for days together to come for the celebration. The forest must be full of people on the move. There are celebrations in all the DK divisions. We are privileged because Comrade Leng, the master of ceremonies, is walking with us.

In Gondi, *Leng* means "the voice." Comrade Leng is a tall, middle-aged man from Andhra Pradesh, a colleague of the legendary and beloved singer-poet Gadar, who founded the radical cultural organization Jan Natya Manch (JNM) in 1972. Eventually, JNM became a formal part of the PWG and in Andhra Pradesh could draw audiences numbering in the tens of thousands. Comrade Leng joined in 1977 and became a famous singer in his own right. He lived in Andhra through the worst repression, the era of "encounter" killings in which friends died almost every day. He himself was picked up one night from his hospital bed, by a woman superintendent of police masquerading as a doctor. He was taken to the forest outside Warangal to be "encountered." But luckily, Gadar got the news and managed to raise an alarm.

When People's War decided to start a cultural organization in DK in 1998, Comrade Leng was sent to head the Chetna Natya Manch. And here he is now, walking with me, for some reason wearing an olive-green shirt and purple pajamas with pink bunnies on them. "There are 10,000 members in Chetna Natya Manch now," he told me. "We have 500 songs, in Hindi, Gondi, Chhattisgarhi, and Halbi. We have printed a book with 140 of our songs. Everybody writes songs." The first time I spoke to him, he sounded very grave, very single-minded. But days later, sitting around a fire, still in those pajamas, he tells us about a very successful, mainstream Telugu film director (a friend of his) who always plays a Naxalite in his own films. "I asked him," Comrade Leng said in his lovely Telugu-accented Hindi, "why do you think Naxalites are always like this?"—and he did a deft caricature of a crouched, high-stepping, hunted-looking man emerging from the forest with an AK-47 and left us screaming with laughter.

I'm not sure whether I'm looking forward to the Bhumkal celebrations. I fear I'll see traditional tribal dances stiffened by Maoist propaganda, rousing, rhetorical speeches and an obedient audience with glazed eyes. We arrive at the grounds quite late in the evening. A temporary monument, of bamboo scaffolding wrapped in red cloth, has been erected. On top, above the hammer and sickle of the Maoist Party, is the bow and arrow of the Janatana Sarkar, wrapped in silver foil. Appropriate, the hierarchy. The stage is huge, also temporary, on a sturdy scaffolding covered by a thick layer of mud plaster. Already, there are small fires scattered around the ground, people have begun to arrive and are cooking their evening meal. They're only silhouettes in the dark. We thread our way through them (lalsalaam, lalsalaam, lalsalaam) and keep going for about fifteen minutes until we reenter the forest. At our new campsite, we have to fall-in again. Another roll call. And then instructions about sentry positions and "firing arcs"—decisions about who will cover which area in the event of a police attack. RV points are fixed again. Also, a miracle.

An advance party has arrived and cooked dinner already. For dessert, Kamla brings me a wild guava that she has plucked on the walk and squirreled away for me.

From dawn, there is the sense of more and more people gathering for the day's celebration. There's a buzz of excitement building up. People who haven't seen each other in a long time meet again. We can hear the sound of mikes being tested. Flags, banners, posters, buntings are going up. A poster with the pictures of the five people who were killed in Ongnaar the day we arrived has appeared. I'm drinking tea with Comrade Narmada, Comrade Maase, and Comrade Rupi. Comrade Narmada talks about the many years she worked in Gadchiroli before becoming the DK head of the Krantikari Adivasi Mahila Sangathan. Rupi and Maase have been urban activists in Andhra Pradesh and tell me about the long years of struggle by women within the party, not just for their rights, but also to make the party see that equality between men and women is central to a dream of a just society. We talk about the 1970s and the stories of women within the Naxalite movement who were disillusioned by male comrades who thought themselves great revolutionaries but were hobbled by the same old patriarchy, the same old chauvinism. Maase says things have changed a lot since then, though they still have a way to go. (The party's central committee and politburo have no women yet.)

Around noon, another PLGA contingent arrives. This one is headed by a tall, lithe, boyish-looking man. This comrade has two names—Sukhdev and Gudsa Usendi—neither of them his. Sukhdev is the name of a very beloved comrade who was martyred. (In this war, only the dead are safe enough to use their real names.) As for Gudsa Usendi, many comrades have been Gudsa Usendi at one point or another. (A few months ago, it was Comrade Raju.) Gudsa Usendi is the name of the party's spokesperson for Dandakaranya. So even though Sukhdev spends the rest of the trip with me, I have no idea how I'd ever find him again. I'd recognize his laugh anywhere, though. He came to DK in 1988, he says, when the PWG decided to send one-third of its forces from north Telangana into DK. He's nicely dressed, in "civil" (Gondi for "civilian clothes") as opposed to "dress" (the Maoist "uniform") and could pass off as a young executive. I ask him why no uniform. He says he's been traveling and has just come back from the Keshkal ghats near Kanker. There are reports of 3 million tons of bauxite that a company called Vedanta has its eye on.

Bingo. Ten on ten for my instincts.

Sukhdev says he went there to measure the people's temperature. To see if they were prepared to fight. "They want squads now. And guns." He throws his head back and roars with laughter, "I told them it's not so easy, bhai." From the stray wisps of conversation and the ease with which he carries his AK-47, I can tell he's also high up and hands-on PLGA.

❖

Jungle post arrives. There's a biscuit for me! It's from Comrade Venu. On a tiny piece of paper, folded and refolded, he has written down the lyrics of a song he promised he would send me. Comrade Narmada smiles when she reads them. She knows this story. It goes back to the 1980s, around the time when people first began to trust the party and come to it with their problems—their "inner contradictions," as Comrade Venu put it. Women were among the first to come. One evening an old lady sitting by the fire got up and sang a song for the dada log. She was a Maadiya, among whom it was customary for women to remove their blouses and remain bare-breasted after they were married.

Jumper polo intor Dada, Dakoniley
Taane tasom intor Dada, Dakoniley
Bata papam kittom Dada, Dakoniley
Duniya kadile maata Dada, Dakoniley
(They say we cannot keep our blouses, Dada, Dakoniley
They make us take them off, Dada,
In what way have we sinned, Dada,
The world's changed, has it not Dada)

Aatum hatteke Dada, Dakoniley
Aada nanga dantom Dada, Dakoniley
Id pisval manni Dada, Dakoniley

> *Mava koyaturku vehat Dada, Dakoniley*
> *(But when we go to the market Dada,*
> *We have to go half-naked Dada,*
> *We don't want this life Dada,*
> *Tell our ancestors this Dada)*

This was the first women's issue the party decided to campaign against. It had to be handled delicately, with surgical tools. In 1986, it set up the Adivasi Mahila Sangathan, which evolved into the Krantikari Adivasi Mahila Sangathan and now has ninety thousand enrolled members. It could well be the largest women's organization in the country. (They're all Maoists by the way, all ninety thousand of them. Are they going to be "wiped out"? And what about the ten thousand members of Chetna Natya Manch? Them too?) KAMS campaigns against the Adivasi traditions of forced marriage and abduction. Against the custom of making menstruating women live outside the village in a hut in the forest. Against bigamy and domestic violence. It hasn't won all its battles, but then which feminists have? For instance, in Dandakaranya, even today women are not allowed to sow seeds. In party meetings, men agree that this is unfair and ought to be done away with. But, in practice, they simply don't allow it. So the party decided that women would sow seeds on common land, which belongs to the Janatana Sarkar. On that land, they sow seed, grow vegetables, and build check dams. A half-victory, not a whole one.

As police repression has grown in Bastar, the women of KAMS have become a formidable force and rally in their hundreds, sometimes thousands, to physically confront the police. The very fact that KAMS exists has radically changed traditional attitudes and eased many of the traditional forms of discrimination against women. For many young women, joining the party, in particular the PLGA, became a way of escaping the suffocation of their own society. Comrade Sushila, a senior office-bearer of KAMS, talks about the Salwa Judum's rage against KAMS women. She says one of their slogans was Hum do bibi layenge! Layenge! (We will have two wives! We will!). A lot of the rape and bestial sexual mutilation was directed at members of KAMS. Many young women who witnessed the savagery then joined the PLGA and now women make up 45 percent of its cadre. Comrade Narmada sends for some of them and they join us in a while.

Comrade Rinki has very short hair. A bob-cut, as they say in Gondi. It's brave of her, because here, "bob-cut" means "Maoist." For the police, that's more than enough evidence to warrant summary execution. Comrade Rinki's village, Korma, was attacked by the Naga battalion and the Salwa Judum in 2005. At that time, Rinki was part of the village militia. So were her friends Lukki and Sukki, who were also members of KAMS. After burning the village, the Naga battalion caught Lukki and Sukki and one other girl, gang-raped and killed them. "They raped them on the grass," Rinki says, "but after it was over, there was no grass left." It's been years now, the Naga battalion has gone, but the police still come. "They come whenever they need women, or chickens."

Ajitha has a bob-cut, too. The Judum came to Korseel, her village, and killed three people by drowning them in a *nallah*. Ajitha was with the militia and followed the Judum at a distance to a place close to the village called Paral Nar Todak. She watched them rape six women and shoot a man in his throat.

Comrade Laxmi, who is a beautiful girl with a long plait, tells me she watched the Judum burn thirty houses in her village, Jojor. "We had no weapons then," she says, "we could do nothing but watch." She joined the PLGA soon after. Laxmi was one of the 150 guerrillas who walked through the jungle for three and a half months in 2008, to Nayagarh in Orissa, to raid a police armory from which they captured twelve hundred rifles and two hundred thousand rounds of ammunition.

Comrade Sumitra joined the PLGA in 2004, before the Salwa Judum began its rampage. She joined, she says, because she wanted to escape from home. "Women are controlled in every way," she told me. "In our village, girls were not allowed to climb trees; if they did, they would have to pay a fine of Rs 500 (ten dollars) or a hen. If a man hits a woman and she hits him back she has to give the village a goat. Men go off to the hills for months together to hunt. Women are not allowed to go near the kill, the best part of the meat goes to men. Women are not allowed to eat eggs." Good reason to join a guerrilla army? Sumitra tells the story of two of her friends, Telam Parvati and Kamla, who worked with KAMS. Telam Parvati was from Polekaya village in south Bastar. Like everyone else from there, she too watched the Salwa Judum burn her village. She then joined the PLGA and went to work in the Keshkal ghats. In 2009, she and Kamla had just finished organizing the March 8 Women's Day celebrations in the area. They were together in a little hut just outside a village called Vadgo. The police surrounded the hut at night and began to fire. Kamla fired back, but she was killed. Parvati escaped but was found and killed the next day.

That's what happened last year on Women's Day.

And here's a press report from a national newspaper about Women's Day this year:

"Bastar rebels bat for women's rights"—Sahar Khan, *Mail Today*, Raipur, March 7, 2010

The government may have pulled out all stops to combat the Maoist menace in the country. But a section of rebels in Chhattisgarh has more pressing matters in hand than survival. With International Women's Day around the corner, Maoists in the Bastar region of the state have called for week-long "celebrations" to advocate women's rights. Posters were also put up in Bijapur, a part of Bastar district. The call by the self-styled champions of women's rights has left the state police astonished. The inspector-general of Bastar, T. J. Longkumer said, "I have never seen such an appeal from the Naxalites, who believe only in violence and bloodshed."

And then the report goes on to say: "I think the Maoists are trying to counter our highly successful Jan Jagran Abhiyaan (mass awareness campaign). We started the ongoing campaign with an aim to win popular support for Operation Green Hunt, which was launched by the police to root out Left-wing extremists," the Inspector-General said.

This cocktail of malice and ignorance is not unusual. Gudsa Usendi, chronicler of the party's present, knows more about this than most people. His little computer and MP3 recorder are full of press statements, denials, corrections, party literature, lists of the dead, TV clips, and audio and video material.

"The worst thing about being Gudsa Usendi," he says, "is issuing clarifications which are never published. We could bring out a thick book of our unpublished clarifications about the lies they tell about us." He speaks without a trace of indignation, in fact, with some amusement.

"What's the most ridiculous charge you've had to deny?"

He thinks back. "In 2007, we had to issue a statement saying, 'Nahin bhai, hamne gai ko hathode se nahin mara (No brother, we did not kill the cows with a hammer).' In 2007, the Raman Singh government announced a Gai Yojana (cow scheme), an election promise, a cow for every Adivasi. One day the TV channels and newspapers reported that Naxalites had attacked a herd of cows and bludgeoned them to death—with hammers—because they were anti-Hindu, anti-BJP. You can imagine what happened. We issued a denial. Hardly anybody carried it. Later, it turned out that the man who had been given the cows to distribute was a rogue. He sold them and said we had ambushed him and killed the cows."

And the most serious?

"Oh, there are dozens, they are running a campaign, after all. When the Salwa Judum started, the first day they attacked a village called Ambeli, burned it down and then all of them—special police officers, the Naga battalion, police—moved toward Kotrapal . . . you must have heard about Kotrapal? It's a famous village, it has been burnt twenty-two times for refusing to surrender. When the Judum reached Kotrapal, our militia

was waiting for it. They had prepared an ambush. Two officers died. We captured seven, the rest ran away. The next day
the newspapers reported that the Naxalites had massacred poor
Adivasis. Some said we had killed hundreds. Even a respectable
magazine like *Frontline* said we had killed eighteen innocent
Adivasis. Even K. Balagopal, the human rights activist, who
is usually meticulous about facts, even he said this. We sent a
clarification. Nobody published it. Later, in his book, Balagopal
acknowledged his mistake. . . . But who noticed?"

I asked what happened to the seven people who were captured. "The area committee called a jan adalat (people's court).
Four thousand people attended it. They listened to the whole
story. Two of the special police officers were sentenced to death.
Five were warned and let off. The people decided. Even with
informers—which is becoming a huge problem nowadays—
people listen to the case, the stories, the confessions and say,
"*Iska hum risk nahin le sakte*" (We're not prepared to take the
risk of trusting this person), or "*Iska risk hum lenge*" (We are
prepared to take the risk of trusting this person). The press
always reports about informers who are killed. Never about the
many who are let off.

So everybody thinks it is some bloodthirsty procedure in
which everybody is always killed. It's not about revenge, it's
about survival and saving future lives. . . . Of course, there are
problems, we've made terrible mistakes, we have even killed
the wrong people in our ambushes thinking they were policemen, but it is not the way it's portrayed in the media."

The dreaded People's Courts. How can we accept them? Or
approve this form of rude justice?

On the other hand, what about "encounters," fake and
otherwise—the worst form of summary justice—that get
policemen and soldiers bravery medals, cash awards, and
out-of-turn promotions from the Indian government?

The more they kill, the more they are rewarded. "Bravehearts"
they are called, the "Encounter Specialists." "Antinationals," we

are called, those of us who dare to question them. And what about the Supreme Court that brazenly admitted it did not have enough evidence to sentence Mohammed Afzal (accused in the December 2001 Parliament attack) to death, but did so anyway, because "the collective conscience of the society will only be satisfied if capital punishment is awarded to the offender."

At least in the case of the Kotrapal Jan Adalat, the collective was physically present to make its own decision. It wasn't made by judges who had lost touch with ordinary life a long time ago, presuming to speak on behalf of an absent collective. What should the people of Kotrapal have done, I wonder? Sent for the police?

❖

The sound of drums has become really loud. It's Bhumkal time. We walk to the grounds. I can hardly believe my eyes. There is a sea of people, the most wild, beautiful people, dressed in the most wild, beautiful ways. The men seem to have paid much more attention to themselves than the women. They have feathered headgear and painted tattoos on their faces. Many have eye make-up and white, powdered faces. There's lots of militia, girls in saris of breathtaking colors with rifles slung carelessly over their shoulders. There are old people, children, and red buntings arc across the sky. The sun is sharp and high. Comrade Leng speaks. And several officeholders of the various Janatana Sarkars. Comrade Niti, an extraordinary woman who has been with the party since 1997, is such a threat to the nation that in January 2007 more than seven hundred policemen surrounded Innar village because they heard she was there. Comrade Niti is considered to be so dangerous and is being hunted with such desperation not because she has led many ambushes (which she has), but because she is an Adivasi woman who is loved by people in the village and is a real inspiration to young people. She speaks with her AK on her shoulder. (It's a gun with a story. Almost everyone's gun has a story: who it was snatched from, how, and by whom.)

A Chetna Natya Manch troupe performs a play about the Bhumkal uprising. The evil white colonizers wear hats and golden straw for hair, and bully and beat Adivasis to pulp—causing endless delight in the audience. Another troupe from south Gangalaur performs a play called *"Nitir Judum Pito"* (Story of the Blood Hunt). Joori translates for me. It's the story of two old people who go looking for their daughter's village. As they walk through the forest, they get lost because everything is burnt and unrecognizable. The Salwa Judum has even burned the drums and the musical instruments. There are no ashes because it has been raining. They cannot find their daughter. In their sorrow, the old couple starts to sing, and hearing them, the voice of their daughter sings back to them from the ruins: the sound of our village has been silenced, she sings. There's no more pounding of rice, no more laughter by the well. No more birds, no more bleating goats. The taut string of happiness has been snapped.

Her father sings back: my beautiful daughter, don't cry today. Everyone who is born must die. These trees around us will fall, flowers will bloom and fade, one day this world will grow old. But who are we dying for? One day our looters will learn, one day Truth will prevail, but our people will never forget you, not for thousands of years.

A few more speeches. Then the drumming and the dancing begins. Each Janatana Sarkar has its own troupe. Each troupe has prepared its own dance. They arrive one by one, with huge drums, and they dance wild stories. The only character every troupe has in common is Bad Mining Man, with a helmet and dark glasses, and usually smoking a cigarette. But there's nothing stiff, or mechanical, about their dancing. As they dance, the dust rises. The sound of drums becomes deafening. Gradually, the crowd begins to sway. And then it begins to dance. They dance in little lines of six or seven, men and women separate, with their arms around each other's waists. Thousands of people. This is what they've come for. For this. Happiness is taken very seriously here, in the Dandakaranya forest. People will walk for miles, for days together to feast and sing, to put feathers in their turbans and flowers in their hair, to put their arms around each other and drink mahua and dance through the night. No one sings or dances alone. This, more than anything else, signals their defiance toward a civilization that seeks to annihilate them.

I can't believe all this is happening right under the noses of the police. Right in the midst of Operation Green Hunt. At first, the PLGA comrades watch the dancers, standing aside with their guns. But then, one by one, like ducks who cannot bear to stand on the shore and watch other ducks swim, they move in and begin to dance, too. Soon there are lines of olive-green dancers, swirling with all the other colors. And then, as sisters and brothers and parents and children and friends who haven't met for months, years sometimes, encounter each other, the lines break up and reform and the olive green is distributed among the swirling saris and flowers and drums and turbans. It surely is a People's Army. For now, at least. And what Chairman Mao said about the guerrillas being the fish and people being the water they swim in is, at this moment, literally true.

Chairman Mao. He's here, too. A little lonely, perhaps, but present. There's a photograph of him, up on a red cloth screen. Marx, too. And Charu Mazumdar, the founder and chief theoretician of the Naxalite Movement. His abrasive rhetoric fetishizes violence, blood, and martyrdom and often employs a language so coarse as to be almost genocidal. Standing here, on Bhumkal day, I can't help thinking that his analysis, so vital to the structure of this revolution, is so removed from its emotion and texture. When he said that only "an annihilation campaign" could produce "the new man who will defy death and be free from all thought of self-interest"—could he have imagined that this ancient people, dancing into the night, would be the ones on whose shoulders his dreams would come to rest?

❖

It's a great disservice to everything that is happening here that the only thing that seems to make it to the outside world is the stiff, unbending rhetoric of the ideologues of a party that has evolved from a problematic past. When Charu Mazumdar famously said, "China's Chairman is our Chairman and China's path is our path," he was prepared to extend it to the point where the Naxalites remained silent while general Yahya Khan committed genocide in East Pakistan (Bangladesh), because at the time, China was an ally of Pakistan. There was silence, too, over the Khmer Rouge and its killing fields in Cambodia. There was silence over the egregious excesses of the Chinese and Russian revolutions. Silence over Tibet. Within the Naxalite movement, too, there have been violent excesses, and it's impossible to defend much of what they've done. But can anything they have done compare with the sordid achievements of the Congress and the BJP in Punjab, Kashmir, Delhi, Mumbai, Gujarat. . . . And yet, despite these terrifying contradictions, Charu Mazumdar was a visionary in much of what he wrote and said. The party he founded (and its many splinter groups) has kept the dream of revolution real and present in India. Imagine a society without that dream. For that alone, we cannot judge him too harshly. Especially not while we swaddle ourselves with Gandhi's pious humbug about the superiority of "the nonviolent way" and his notion of trusteeship: "The rich man will be left in possession of his wealth, of which he will use what he reasonably requires for his personal needs and will act as a trustee for the remainder to be used for the good of society."

How strange it is, though, that the contemporary tsars of the Indian Establishment—the state that crushed the Naxalites so mercilessly—should now be saying what Charu Mazumdar said so long ago: China's path is our path.

Upside down. Inside out.

China's path has changed. China has become an imperial power now, preying on other countries, other people's resources. The party is still right, although the party has changed its mind.

When the party is a suitor (as it is now in Dandakaranya), wooing the people, attentive to their every need, then it genuinely is a People's Party, its army genuinely a People's Army. But after the revolution how easily this love affair can turn into a bitter marriage. How easily the People's Army can turn upon the people. Today in Dandakaranya, the party wants to keep the bauxite in the mountain. Tomorrow, will it change its mind? But can we, should we let apprehensions about the future immobilize us in the present?

The dancing will go on all night. I walk back to the camp. Maase is there, awake. We chat late into the night. I give her my copy of Neruda's *Captain's Verses* (I brought it along, just in case). She asks, again and again, "What do they think of us outside? What do students say? Tell me about the women's movement, what are the big issues now?" She asks about me, my writing. I try and give her an honest account of my chaos. Then she starts to talk about herself, how she joined the party. She tells me that her partner was killed last May, in a fake encounter. He was arrested in Nashik and taken to Warangal to be killed. "They must have tortured him badly." She was on her way to meet him when she heard he had been arrested. She's been in the forest ever since. After a long silence, she tells me she was married once before, years ago. "He was killed in an encounter, too," she says, and adds with heart-breaking precision, "but in a real one."

I lie awake on my jhilli, thinking of Maase's protracted sadness, listening to the drums and the sounds of protracted happiness from the grounds, and thinking about Charu Mazumdar's idea of protracted war, the central precept of the Maoist Party. This is what makes people think the Maoists' offer to enter "peace talks" is a hoax, a ploy to get breathing space to regroup, re-arm themselves, and go back to waging protracted war. What is protracted war? Is it a terrible thing in itself, or does it depend on the nature of the war? What if the people here in Dandakaranya had not waged their protracted war for the last thirty years, where would they be now? And are the Maoists the only ones who believe in protracted war? Almost from the moment India became a sovereign nation, it turned into a colonial power, annexing territory, waging war. It has never hesitated to use military interventions to address political problems—Kashmir, Hyderabad, Goa, Nagaland, Manipur, Telangana, Assam, Punjab, the Naxalite uprising in West Bengal, Bihar, Andhra Pradesh, and now across the tribal areas of Central India. Tens of thousands have been killed with impunity, hundreds of thousands tortured. All of this behind the benign mask of democracy. Who have these wars been waged against? Muslims, Christians, Sikhs, Communists, Dalits, Tribals, and, most of all, against the poor who dare to question their lot instead of accepting the crumbs that are flung at them. It's hard not to see that the Indian state is an essentially upper-caste Hindu State (regardless of the party in power) that harbors a reflexive hostility toward the "other." One that, in true colonial fashion, sends the Nagas and Mizos to fight in Chhattisgarh, Sikhs to Kashmir, Kashmiris to Orissa, Tamilians to Assam, and so on. If this isn't protracted war, what is?

Unpleasant thoughts on a beautiful, starry night. Sukhdev is smiling to himself, his face lit by his computer screen. He's a crazy workaholic. I ask him what's funny. "I was thinking about the journalists who came last year for the Bhumkal celebrations. They came for a day or two. One posed with my AK, had himself photographed and then went back and called us Killing Machines or something."

❖

The dancing hasn't stopped and it's daybreak. The lines are still going, hundreds of young people still dancing. "They won't stop," Comrade Raju says, "not until we start packing up." On the grounds I run into Comrade Doctor. He's been running a little medical camp on the edge of the dance floor. I want to kiss his fat cheeks. Why can't he be at least thirty people instead of just one? Why can't he be one thousand people?

I ask him what it's looking like, the health of Dandakaranya. His reply makes my blood run cold. Most of the people he has seen, he says, including those in the PLGA, have a hemoglobin count that's between five and six (when the standard for Indian women is eleven). There's TB caused by more than two years of chronic anemia. Young children are suffering from protein energy malnutrition grade II, in medical terminology called Kwashiorkor. (I looked it up later. It's a word derived from the Ga language of Coastal Ghana and means "the sickness a baby gets when the new baby comes." Basically, the old baby stops getting mother's milk, and there's not enough food to provide it nutrition.) "It's an epidemic here, like in Biafra," Comrade Doctor says, "I have worked in villages before, but I've never seen anything like this."

Apart from this, there's malaria, osteoporosis, tapeworm, severe ear and tooth infections, and primary amenorrhea— which is when malnutrition during puberty causes a woman's menstrual cycle to disappear or never appear in the first place.

"There are no clinics in this forest apart from one or two in Gadchiroli. No doctors. No medicines."

He's off now, with his little team, on an eight-day trek to Abujhmad. He's in "dress" too, Comrade Doctor. So, if they find him, they'll kill him.

❖

Comrade Raju says that it isn't safe for us to continue to camp here. We have to move. Leaving Bhumkal involves a lot of goodbyes spread over time.

Lal lal salaam, lal lal salaam,
Jaane wale saathiyon ko lal lal salaam
(Red Salute to departing comrades)
Phir milenge, phir milenge,
Dandakaranya jungle mein phir milenge
(We'll meet again, someday, in the Dandakaranya forest)

It's never taken lightly, the ceremony of arrival and departure, because everybody knows that when they say "We'll meet again" they actually mean "We may never meet again." Comrade Narmada, Comrade Maase, and Comrade Rupi are going separate ways. Will I ever see them again?

So, once again, we walk. It's becoming hotter every day. Kamla picks the first fruit of the tendu for me. It tastes like chikoo. I've become a tamarind fiend. This time we camp near a stream. Women and men take turns to bathe in batches. In the evening, Comrade Raju receives a whole packet of "biscuits."

News:

Sixty people arrested in Manpur Division at the end of January 2010 have not yet been produced in Court.

Huge contingents of police have arrived in South Bastar. Indiscriminate attacks are on.

On November 8, 2009, in Kachlaram Village, Bijapur Jila, Dirko Madka (60), and Kovasi Suklu (68) were killed.

On November 24, Madavi Baman (15) was killed in Pangodi village.

On December 3, Madavi Budram from Korenjad was also killed.

On December 11, Gumiapal village, Darba Division, seven people killed (names yet to come).

On December 15, Kotrapal village, Veko Sombar and Madavi Matti (both with KAMS) were killed.

On December 30, Vechapal village Poonem Pandu and Poonem Motu (father and son) were killed.

On January 2010 (date unknown), head of the Janatana Sarkar in Kaika village, Gangalaur, was killed.

On January 9, four people were killed in Surpangooden village, Jagargonda Area.

On January 10, three people were killed in Pullem Pulladi village (no names yet).

On January 25, seven people were killed in Takilod village, Indravati Area.

On Febuary 10 (Bhumkal Day), Kumli was raped and killed in Dumnaar Village, Abujhmad. She was from a village called Paiver.

Two thousand troops of the Indo-Tibetan Border Police are camped in the Rajnandgaon forests.

Five thousand additional Border Security Force troops have arrived in Kanker.

And then:

PLGA quota filled.

Some dated newspapers have arrived, too. There's a lot of press about Naxalites. One screaming headline sums up the political climate perfectly: "*Khadedo, Maaro, Samarpan Karao*" (Eliminate, Kill, Make Them Surrender). Below that: "*Vaarta ke liye loktantra ka dwar khula hai*" (Democracy's door is always open for talks). A second says the Maoists are growing cannabis to make money. The third has an editorial saying that the area we've camped in and are walking through is entirely under police control. The young Communists take the clips away to practice their reading. They walk around the camp reading the anti-Maoist articles loudly in radio-announcer voices.

❖

New day. New place. We're camped on the outskirts of Usir village, under huge mahua trees. The mahua has just begun to flower and is dropping its pale green blossoms like jewels on the forest floor. The air is suffused with its slightly heady smell. We're waiting for the children from the Bhatpal school, which was closed down after the Ongnaar encounter. It's been turned into a police camp. The children have been sent home. This is also true of the schools in Nelwad, Moonjmetta, Edka, Vedomakot, and Dhanora.

The Bhatpal schoolchildren don't show up.

Comrade Niti (Most Wanted) and Comrade Vinod lead us on a long walk to see the series of water-harvesting structures and irrigation ponds that have been built by the local Janatana Sarkar. Comrade Niti talks about the range of agricultural problems they have to deal with. Only 2 percent of the land is irrigated. In Abujhmad, ploughing was unheard of until ten years ago. In Gadchiroli on the other hand, hybrid seeds and chemical pesticides are edging their way in. "We need urgent help in the agriculture department," Comrade Vinod says. "We need people who know about seeds, organic pesticides, permaculture. With a little help we could do a lot."

Comrade Ramu is the farmer in charge of the Janatana Sarkar area. He proudly shows us around the fields, where they grow rice, brinjal, gongura, onions, kohlrabi. Then, with equal pride, he shows us a huge but bone-dry irrigation pond. What's this? "This one doesn't even have water during the rainy season. It's dug in the wrong place," he says, a smile wrapped around his face. "It's not ours, it was dug by the Looti Sarkar (the government that loots)." There are two parallel systems of government here, Janatana Sarkar and Looti Sarkar.

I think of what Comrade Venu said to me: they want to crush us, not only because of the minerals, but because we are offering the world an alternative model.

It's not an alternative yet, this idea of Gram Swaraj with a Gun. There's too much hunger, too much sickness here. But it has certainly created the possibilities for an alternative. Not for the whole world, not for Alaska, or New Delhi, nor even perhaps for the whole of Chhattisgarh, but for itself. For Dandakaranya. It's the world's best-kept secret. It has laid the foundations for an alternative to its own annihilation. It has defied history. Against the greatest odds it has forged a blueprint for its own survival. It needs help and imagination, it needs doctors, teachers, farmers.

It does not need war.

But if war is all it gets, it will fight back.

❖

Over the next few days, I meet women who work with KAMS, various office-bearers of the Janatana Sarkars, members of the Dandakaranya Adivasi Kisan Mazdoor Sangathan, the families of people who had been killed, and just ordinary people trying to cope with life in these terrifying times.

I met three sisters—Sukhiari, Sukdai, and Sukkali—not young, perhaps in their forties, from Narayanpur district. They have been in KAMS for twelve years. The villagers depend on them to deal with the police. "The police come in groups of two to three hundred. They steal everything: jewelry, chickens, pigs, pots and pans, bows and arrows," Sukkali says, "they won't even leave a knife." Her house in Innar has been burned twice, once by the Naga battalion and once by the Central Reserve Police Force. Sukhiari has been arrested and jailed in Jagdalpur for seven months. "Once they took away the whole village, saying the men were all Naxals." Sukhiari followed with all the women and children. They surrounded the police station and refused to leave until the men were freed. "Whenever they take someone away," Sukdai says, "you have to go immediately and snatch them back. Before they write any report. Once they write in their book, it becomes very difficult."

Sukhiari, who as a child was abducted and forcibly married to an older man (she ran away and went to live with her sister), now organizes mass rallies, speaks at meetings. The men depend on her for protection. I asked her what the party means to her. "Naxalvaad ka matlab hamara parivaar (Naxalvaad means our family). When we hear of an attack, it is like our family has been hurt," Sukhiari says.

I asked her if she knew who Mao was. She smiled shyly, "He was a leader. We're working for his vision."

I met Comrade Somari Gawde. Twenty years old, and she has already served a two-year jail sentence in Jagdalpur. She was in Innar village on January 8, 2007, the day that 740 policemen laid a cordon around it because they had information that Comrade Niti was there. (She was, but she had left by the time they arrived.) But the village militia, of which Somari was a member, was still there. The police opened fire at dawn. They killed two boys, Suklal Gawde and Kachroo Gota. Then they caught three others, two boys, Dusri Salam and Ranai, and Somari. Dusri and Ranai were tied up and shot. Somari was beaten within an inch of her life. The police got a tractor with a trailer and loaded the dead bodies into it. Somari was made to sit with the dead bodies and taken to Narayanpur.

I met Chamri, mother of Comrade Dilip who was shot on July 6, 2009. She says that after they killed him, the police tied her son's body to a pole, like an animal and carried it with them. (They need to produce bodies to get their cash rewards, before someone else muscles in on the kill.) Chamri ran behind them all the way to the police station. By the time they reached, the body did not have a scrap of clothing on it. On the way, Chamri says, they left the body by the roadside while they stopped at a dhaba to have tea and biscuits. (Which they did not pay for.) Picture this mother for a moment, following her son's corpse through the forest, stopping at a distance to wait for his murderers to finish their tea. They did not let her have her son's body back so she could give him a proper funeral. They only let her throw a fistful of earth in the pit in which they buried the others they had killed that day. Chamri says she wants revenge. Badla ku badla (Blood for blood).

I met the elected members of the Marskola Janatana Sarkar that administers six villages. They described a police raid: they come at night, three hundred, four hundred, sometimes a thousand of them. They lay a cordon around a village and lie in wait. At dawn they catch the first people who go out to the fields and use them as human shields to enter the village, to show them where the booby-traps are. ("Booby-traps" has become a Gondi word. Everybody always smiles when they say it or hear it. The forest is full of booby-traps, real and fake. Even the PLGA needs to be guided past villages.) Once the police enter a village, they loot and steal and burn houses. They come with dogs. The dogs catch those who try and run. They chase chickens and pigs, and the police kill them and take them away in sacks. Special police officers come along with the police. They're the ones who know where people hide their money and jewelry. They catch people and take them away. And extract money before they release them. They always carry some extra Naxal "dresses" with them in case they find someone to kill. They get money for killing Naxals, so they manufacture some. Villagers are too frightened to stay at home.

In this tranquil-looking forest, life seems completely militarized now. People know words like Cordon and Search, Firing, Advance, Retreat, Down, Action! To harvest their crops, they need the PLGA to do a sentry patrol. Going to the market is a military operation. The markets are full of *mukhbirs* (informers) whom the police have lured from their villages with money. I'm told there's a mukhbir mohalla (informers' colony) in Narayanpur where at least four thousand mukhbirs stay. The men can't go to market anymore. The women go, but they're watched closely. If they buy even a little extra, the police accuse them of buying it for Naxals. Chemists have been instructed not to let people buy medicines except in very small quantities. Low-price rations from the Public Distribution System, sugar, rice, kerosene, are warehoused in or near police stations, making it impossible for most people to buy.

Article 2 of the United Nations Convention on the Prevention and Punishment of the Crime of Genocide defines "genocide" as

> *any of the following acts committed with intent to destroy, in whole or part, a national, ethnic, racial, or religious group, as such: killing members of the group; causing serious bodily or mental harm to members of the group; deliberately inflicting on the group conditions of life calculated to bring about its physical destruction in whole or part; imposing measures intended to prevent births within the group; [or] forcibly transferring children of the group to another group.*

❖

All the walking seems to have finally gotten to me. I'm tired. Kamla gets me a pot of hot water. I bathe behind a tree in the dark. But I can't eat dinner and crawl into my bag to sleep. Comrade Raju announces that we have to move. This happens frequently, of course, but tonight it's hard. We have been camped in an open meadow. We'd heard shelling in the distance. There are 104 of us. Once again, single file through the night. Crickets. The smell of something like lavender. It must have been past 11:00 p.m. when we arrived at the place where we will spend the night. An outcrop of rocks. Formation. Roll call.

Someone switches on the radio. BBC says there's been an attack on a camp of Eastern Frontier Rifles in Lalgarh, West Bengal. Sixty Maoists on motorcycles. Fourteen policemen killed. Ten missing. Weapons snatched. There's a murmur of pleasure in the ranks. Maoist leader Kishenji is being interviewed. When will you stop this violence and come for talks? When Operation Green Hunt is called off. Any time. Tell Chidambaram we will talk. Next question: It's dark now, you have laid land mines, reinforcements have been called in, will you attack them, too? Kishenji: Yes, of course, otherwise people will beat me.

There's laughter in the ranks. Sukhdev the clarifier says, "They always say land mines. We don't use land mines. We use IEDs."

Another luxury suite in the thousand-star hotel. I'm feeling ill. It starts to rain. There's a little giggling. Kamla throws a jhilli over me. What more do I need? Everyone else just rolls themselves into their jhillis.

By next morning the body count in Lalgarh has gone up to twenty-one; ten are missing. Comrade Raju is considerate this morning. We don't move till evening.

❖

One night, people are crowded like moths around a point of light. It's Comrade Sukhdev's tiny computer, powered by a solar panel, and they're watching *Mother India*, the barrels of their rifles silhouetted against the sky. Kamla doesn't seem interested. I ask her if she likes watching movies. "*Nahin didi. Sirf ambush video.*" (No didi. Only ambush videos.) Later, I ask Comrade Sukhdev about these ambush videos. Without batting an eyelid, he plays one for me.

It starts with shots of Dandakaranya, rivers, waterfalls, the close-up of a bare branch of a tree, a brainfever bird calling. Then suddenly a comrade is wiring up an IED, concealing it with dry leaves. A cavalcade of motorcycles is blown up. There are mutilated bodies and burning bikes. The weapons are being snatched. Three policemen, looking shell-shocked, have been tied up.

Who's filming it? Who's directing operations? Who's reassuring the captured cops that they will be released if they surrender? (They were. I confirm that later.)

I know that gentle, reassuring voice. It's Comrade Venu.

"It's the Kudur ambush," Comrade Sukhdev says.

He also has a video archive of burned villages, testimonies from eyewitnesses and relatives of the dead. On the singed wall of a burnt house, it says, "Nagaaa! Born to Kill!" There's footage of a little boy whose fingers were chopped off to inaugurate the Bastar chapter of Operation Green Hunt. (There's even a TV interview with me. My study. My books. Strange.)

At night, on the radio, there's news of another Naxal attack. This one in Jamui, Bihar. It says 125 Maoists attacked a village and killed ten people belonging to the Kora tribe in retaliation for giving police information that led to the death of six Maoists. Of course, we know that the media report may or may not be true. But, if it is, this one's unforgivable. Comrade Raju and Sukhdev look distinctly uncomfortable.

The news that has been coming from Jharkhand and Bihar is disturbing. The gruesome beheading of the policeman Francis Induvar is still fresh in everyone's mind. It's a reminder of how easily the discipline of armed struggle can dissolve into lumpen acts of criminalized violence or into ugly wars of identity between castes and communities and religious groups. By institutionalizing injustice in the way that it does, the Indian state has turned this country into a tinderbox of massive unrest. The government is quite wrong if it thinks that by carrying out "targeted assassinations" to render the CPI (Maoist) "headless," it will end the violence. On the contrary, the violence will spread and intensify, and the government will have nobody to talk to.

❖

On my last few days, we meander through the lush, beautiful Indravati valley. As we walk along a hillside, we see another line of people walking in the same direction, but on the other side of the river. I'm told they are on their way to an anti-dam meeting in Kudur village. They're overground and unarmed. A local rally for the valley. I jump ship and join them.

The Bodhghat Dam will submerge the entire area that we have been walking in for days. All that forest, all that history, all those stories. More than one hundred villages. Is that the plan then? To drown people like rats, so that the integrated steel plant in Lohandiguda and the bauxite mine and aluminum refinery in the Keshkal ghats can have the river?

At the meeting, people who have come from miles away say the same thing we have all heard for years. We will drown, but we won't move! They are thrilled that someone from Delhi is with them. I tell them Delhi is a cruel city that neither knows nor cares about them.

Only weeks before I came to Dandakaranya, I visited Gujarat. The Sardar Sarovar Dam has more or less reached its full height now. And almost every single thing the Narmada Bachao Andolan predicted would happen has happened. People who were displaced have not been rehabilitated, but that goes without saying. The canals have not been built. There's no money. So Narmada water is being diverted into the empty riverbed of the Sabarmati (which was dammed a long time ago). Most of the water is being guzzled by cities and big industry. The downstream effects—saltwater ingress into an estuary with no river—are becoming impossible to mitigate.

There was a time when believing that Big Dams were the "temples of modern India" was misguided, but perhaps understandable. But today, after all that has happened, and when we know all that we do, it has to be said that Big Dams are a crime against humanity.

The Bodhghat dam was shelved in 1984 after local people protested. Who will stop it now? Who will prevent the foundation stone from being laid? Who will stop the Indravati from being stolen? Someone must.

❖

On the last night, we camped at the base of the steep hill we would climb in the morning, to emerge on the road from where a motorcycle would pick me up. The forest has changed even since I first entered it. The chiraunji, silk-cotton, and mango trees have begun to flower. The villagers from Kudur send a huge pot of freshly caught fish to the camp. And a list for me, of seventy-one kinds of fruit, vegetables, pulses, and insects they get from the forest and grow in their fields, along with the market price. It's just a list. But it's also a map of their world.

Jungle post arrives. Two biscuits for me. A poem and a pressed flower from Comrade Narmada. A lovely letter from Maase. (Who is she? Will I ever know?) Comrade Sukhdev asks if he can download the music from my Ipod onto his computer. We listen to a recording of Iqbal Bano singing Faiz Ahmad Faiz's *"Hum Dekhenge"* (We Will Witness the Day) at the famous concert in Lahore at the height of the repression during the Zia ul-Haq years.

> *Jab ahl-e-safa-Mardud-e-haram, Masnad pe bithaiye jayenge*
> *(When the heretics and the reviled will be seated on high)*
> *Sab taaj uchhale jayenge Sab takht giraye jayenge*
> *(All crowns will be snatched away All thrones toppled)*
> *Hum dekhenge*

Fifty thousand people in the audience in *that* Pakistan begin a defiant chant: "Inqilab zindabad! Inqilab zindabad!" (Long live the revolution!) All these years later, that chant reverberates around this forest. Strange, the alliances that get made.

The home minister's been issuing veiled threats to those who "erroneously offer intellectual and material support to Maoists." Does sharing music qualify?

At dawn, I say goodbye to Comrade Madhav and Joori, to young Mangtu and all the others. Comrade Chandu has gone to organize the bikes and will come with me to the main road. Comrade Raju isn't coming (the climb would be hell on his knees). Comrade Niti (Most Wanted), Comrade Sukhdev, Kamla, and five others will take me up the hill. As we start walking, Niti and Sukhdev casually but simultaneously unclick the safety catches of their AKs. It's the first time I've seen them do that. We're approaching the "Border." "Do you know what to do if we come under fire?" Sukhdev asks casually, as though it was the most natural thing in the world.

"Yes," I said, "immediately declare an indefinite hunger strike."

He sat down on a rock and laughed. We climbed for about an hour. Just below the road, we sat in a rocky alcove, completely concealed, like an ambush party, listening for the sound of the bikes. When it comes, the farewell must be quick. Lal Salaam Comrades. When I looked back, they were still there. Waving. A little knot. People who live with their dreams, while the rest of the world lives with its nightmares. Every night I think of this journey. That night sky, those forest paths. I see Comrade Kamla's heels in her scuffed chappals, lit by the light of my torch. I know she must be on the move. Marching, not just for herself, but to keep hope alive for us all.

TRICKLEDOWN
REVOLUTION

The law locks up the hapless felon who steals the goose from off the common, but lets the greater felon loose who steals the common from the goose.
— Anonymous, England, 1821

IN THE EARLY morning hours of July 2, 2010, in the remote forests of Adilabad, the Andhra Pradesh state police fired a bullet into the chest of a man called Chemkuri Rajkumar, known to his comrades as Azad. Azad was a member of the politburo of the banned Communist Party of India (Maoist) and had been nominated by his party as its chief negotiator for the proposed peace talks with the government of India. Why did the police fire at point-blank range and leave those tell-tale burn marks, when they could so easily have covered their tracks? Was it a mistake or was it a message?

First published in *Outlook*, September 20, 2010.

They killed a second person that morning—Hemchandra Pandey, a young journalist who was traveling with Azad when he was apprehended. Why did they kill him? Was it to make sure no eyewitness remained alive to tell the tale? Or was it just whimsy?

In the course of a war, if, in the preliminary stages of a peace negotiation, one side executes the envoy of the other side, it's reasonable to assume that the side that did the killing does not want peace. It looks very much as though Azad was killed because someone decided that the stakes were too high to allow him to remain alive. That decision could turn out to be a serious error of judgment. Not just because of who he was, but because of the political climate in India today.

Days after I said goodbye to the comrades and emerged from the Dandakaranya forest, I found myself charting a weary but familiar course to Jantar Mantar, on Parliament Street in New Delhi. Jantar Mantar is an old observatory built by Maharaja Sawai Jai Singh II of Jaipur in 1710. In those days it was a scientific marvel, used to tell the time, predict the weather, and study the planets. Today, it's a not-so-hot tourist attraction that doubles up as Delhi's little showroom for democracy.

For some years now, protests—unless they are patronized by political parties or religious organizations—have been banned in Delhi. The Boat Club on Rajpath, which has in the past seen huge, historic rallies that sometimes lasted for days, is out of bounds for political activity now and is only available for picnics, balloon-sellers and boat rides. As for India Gate, candlelight vigils and boutique protests for middle-class causes, such as "Justice for Jessica"—the model who was killed in a Delhi bar by a thug with political connections—are allowed, but nothing more. Section 144, an old nineteenth-century law that bans the gathering of more than five people—who have "a common object which is unlawful"—in a public place has been clamped on parts of the city. The law was passed by the British in 1861 to prevent a repeat of the 1857 mutiny. It was meant to be an emergency measure but has become a permanent fixture in many parts of India. Perhaps it was in gratitude for laws like these that our prime minister, while accepting an honorary degree from Oxford, thanked the British for bequeathing us such a rich legacy: "Our judiciary, our legal system, our bureaucracy and our police are all great institutions, derived from British-Indian administration, and they have served the country well."

Jantar Mantar is the only place in Delhi where Section 144 is not enforced. People from all over the country, fed up with being ignored by the political establishment and the media, converge there, desperately hoping for a hearing. Some take long train journeys. Some, like the victims of the Bhopal gas leak, have walked for weeks, all the way to Delhi. Though they had to fight each other for the best spot on the burning (or freezing) pavement, until recently protesters were allowed to camp in Jantar Mantar for as long as they liked—weeks, months, even years. Under the malevolent gaze of the police and the Special Branch, they would put up their faded *shamianas* and banners. From here they declared their faith in democracy by issuing their memorandums, announcing their protest plans and staging their indefinite hunger strikes. From here they tried (but never succeeded) to march on Parliament. From here they hoped.

Of late, though, democracy's timings have been changed. It's strictly office hours now, nine to five. No overtime. No sleepovers. No matter from how far people have come, no matter if they have no shelter in the city—if they don't leave by 6:00 p.m., they are forcibly dispersed, by the police if necessary, with batons and water cannons if things get out of hand. The new timings were ostensibly instituted to make sure that the 2010 Commonwealth Games that New Delhi is hosting go smoothly. But nobody's expecting the old timings back anytime soon. Maybe it's in the fitness of things that what's left of our democracy should be traded in for an event that was created to celebrate the British Empire. Perhaps it's only right that four hundred thousand people should have had their homes demolished and been driven out of the city overnight. Or that hundreds of thousands of roadside vendors should have had their livelihoods snatched away by order of the Supreme Court so city malls could take over their share of business. And that tens of thousands of beggars should have been shipped out of the city while more than a hundred thousand galley slaves were shipped in to build the flyovers, metro tunnels, Olympic-size swimming pools, warm-up stadiums, and luxury housing for athletes. The Old Empire may not exist. But obviously our tradition of servility has become too profitable an enterprise to dismantle.

I was at Jantar Mantar because a thousand pavement-dwellers from cities all over the country had come to demand a few fundamental rights: the right to shelter, to food (ration cards), to life (protection from police brutality and criminal extortion by municipal officers).

It was early spring, the sun was sharp, but still civilized. This is a terrible thing to have to say, but it's true: you could smell the protest from a fair distance. It was the accumulated odor of a thousand human bodies that had been dehumanized, denied the basic necessities for human (or even animal) health and hygiene for years, if not a whole lifetime. Bodies that had been marinated in the refuse of our big cities, bodies that had no shelter from the harsh weather, no access to clean water, clean air, sanitation, or medical care. No part of this great country, none of the supposedly progressive schemes, no single urban institution has been designed to accommodate them. Not the Jawaharlal Nehru National Urban Renewal Mission, not any other slum development, employment guarantee, or welfare scheme. Not even the sewage system—they shit on top of it. They are shadow people, who live in the cracks that run between schemes and institutions. They sleep on the streets, eat on the streets, make love on the streets, give birth on the streets, are raped on the streets, cut their vegetables, wash their clothes, raise their children, live and die on the streets.

If the motion picture were an art form that involved the olfactory senses—in other words, if cinema smelled—then films like *Slumdog Millionaire* would not win Oscars. The stench of that kind of poverty wouldn't blend with the aroma of warm popcorn.

The people at the protest in Jantar Mantar that day were not even slum dogs, they were pavement dwellers. Who were they? Where had they come from? They were the refugees of India's Shining, the people who are being sloshed around like toxic effluent in a manufacturing process that has gone berserk. The representatives of the more than 60 million people who have been displaced, by rural destitution; by slow starvation; by floods and drought (many of them man-made); by mines, steel factories, and aluminum smelters; by highways and expressways; by the 3,300 big dams built since Independence and now by Special Economic Zones. They're part of the 830 million people of India who live on less than Rs 20 (forty cents) a day, the ones who starve while millions of tons of food grain are either eaten by rats in government warehouses or burnt in bulk (because it is cheaper to burn food than to distribute it to poor people). They are the parents of the tens of millions of malnourished children in our country, of the 2 million who die every year before they reach the age of five. They are the millions who make up the chain gangs that are transported from city to city to build the New India. Is this what is known as enjoying the "fruits of modern development"?

What must they think, these people, about a government that sees fit to spend $9 billion of public money (2,000 percent more than the initial estimate) for a two-week sports extravaganza which, for fear of terrorism, malaria, dengue, and New Delhi's new superbug, many international athletes have refused to attend? Which the Queen of England, titular head of the Commonwealth, would not consider presiding over, not even in her most irresponsible dreams. What must they think of the fact that most of those billions have been stolen and salted away by politicians and Games officials? Not much, I guess. Because for people who live on less than twenty rupees (forty cents) a day, money on that scale must seem like science fiction. It probably doesn't occur to them that it's their money. That's why corrupt politicians in India never have a problem sweeping back into power, using the money they stole to buy elections. (Then, they feign outrage and ask, "Why don't the Maoists stand for elections?")

Standing there, in that dim crowd on that bright day, I thought of all the struggles that are being waged by people in this country—against Big Dams in the Narmada valley, Polavaram, Arunachal Pradesh; against mines in Orissa, Chhattisgarh, and Jharkhand; against the police by the Adivasis of Lalgarh; against the grabbing of their lands for industries and Special Economic Zones all over the country. How many years (and in how many ways) people have fought to avoid just such a fate. I thought of Maase, Narmada, Roopi, Nity, Mangtu, Madhav, Saroja, Raju, Gudsa Usendi, and Comrade Kamala (my young bodyguard during the time I spent with the Maoists in the jungle) with their guns slung over their shoulders. I thought of the great dignity of the forest I had so recently walked in and the rhythm of the Adivasi drums at the Bhumkal celebration in Bastar, like the soundtrack of the quickening pulse of a furious nation.

I thought of Padma with whom I traveled to Warangal. She is only in her thirties but when she walks up stairs, she has to hold the banister and drag her body behind her. She was arrested just a week after she had had an appendix operation. She was beaten until she had an internal hemorrhage and had to have several organs removed. When they cracked her knees, the police explained helpfully that it was to make sure "she would never walk in the jungle again." She was released after serving an eight-year sentence. Now she runs the Amarula Bhadhu Mitrula Committee, the Committee of Relatives and Friends of Martyrs. It retrieves the bodies of people killed in fake encounters. Padma spends her time crisscrossing northern Andhra Pradesh, in whatever transport she can find, usually a tractor, transporting the corpses of people whose parents or spouses are too poor to make the journey to retrieve the bodies of their loved ones.

The tenacity, the wisdom, and the courage of those who have

been fighting for years, for decades, to bring change, or even the whisper of justice to their lives, is something extraordinary. Whether people are fighting to overthrow the Indian State, or fighting against Big Dams, or only fighting a particular steel plant or mine or Special Economic Zone, the bottom line is that they are fighting for their dignity, for the right to live and smell like human beings. They are fighting because, as far as they are concerned, "the fruits of modern development" stink like dead cattle on the highway.

On the sixty-fourth anniversary of India's Independence, prime minister Manmohan Singh climbed into his bullet-proof soapbox in the Red Fort to deliver a passionless, bone-chillingly banal speech to the nation. Listening to him, who would have guessed that he was addressing a country that, despite having the second-highest economic growth rate in the world, has more poor people than twenty-six of Africa's poorest countries put together? "All of you have contributed to India's success," he said. "The hard work of our workers, our artisans, our farmers has brought our country to where it stands today. . . . We are building a new India in which every citizen would have a stake, an India which would be prosperous and in which all citizens would be able to live a life of honor and dignity in an environment of peace and goodwill. An India in which all problems could be solved through democratic means. An India in which the basic rights of every citizen would be protected." Some would call this graveyard humor. He might as well have been speaking to people in Finland or Sweden.

If our prime minister's reputation for "personal integrity" extended to the text of his speeches, this is what he should have said:

> *Brothers and sisters, greetings to you on this day on which we remember our glorious past. Things are getting a little expensive, I know, and you keep moaning about food prices, but look at it this way—more than 650 million of you are*

engaged in and are living off agriculture as farmers and farm labor. But your combined efforts contribute less than 18 percent of our GDP. So what's the use of you? Look at our IT sector. It employs 0.2 percent of the population and accounts for 5 percent of our GDP. Can you match that? It is true that in our country employment hasn't kept pace with growth, but fortunately 60 percent of our workforce is self-employed. Ninety percent of our labor force is employed by the unorganized sector. True, they manage to get work only for a few months in the year, but since we don't have a category called "underemployed," we just keep that part a little vague. It would not be right to enter them in our books as unemployed. Coming to the statistics that say we have the highest infant and maternal mortality in the world—we should unite as a nation and ignore bad news for the time being. We can address these problems later, after our Trickledown Revolution, when the health sector has been completely privatized. Meanwhile, I hope you are all buying medical insurance. As for the fact that the per capita food grain availability has actually decreased over the last twenty years— which happens to be the period of our most rapid economic growth—believe me, that's just a coincidence.

My fellow citizens, we are building a new India in which our hundred richest people, millionaires and billionaires, hold assets worth a full 25 percent of our GDP. Wealth concentrated in fewer and fewer hands is always more efficient. You have all heard the saying that too many cooks spoil the broth. We want our beloved billionaires, our few hundred millionaires, their near and dear ones and their political and business associates, to be prosperous and to live a life of honor and dignity in an environment of peace and goodwill in which their basic rights are protected.

I am aware that my dreams cannot come true by solely using democratic means. In fact, I have come to believe that real democracy flows through the barrel of a gun. This is why we have deployed the army, the police, the Central Reserve Police Force, the Border Security Force, the Central Industrial Security Force, the Pradeshik Armed Constabulary, the Indo-Tibetan Border Police, the Eastern Frontier Rifles—as well as the Scorpions, Greyhounds, and Cobras—to crush the misguided insurrections that are erupting in our mineral-rich areas.

Our experiments with democracy began in Nagaland, Manipur, and Kashmir. Kashmir, I need not reiterate, is an integral part of India. We have deployed more than half a million soldiers to bring democracy to the people there. The Kashmiri youth who have been risking their lives by defying curfew and throwing stones at the police for the last two months are Lashkar-e-Taiba militants who actually want employment, not aɀadi. Tragically, sixty of them have lost their lives before we could study their job applications. I have instructed the police from now on to shoot to maim rather than kill these misguided youths.

In his seven years in office, Manmohan Singh has allowed himself to be cast as Sonia Gandhi's tentative, mild-mannered underling. It's an excellent disguise for a man who, for the last twenty years, first as finance minister and then as prime minister, has powered through a regime of new economic policies that has brought India into the situation in which it finds itself now. This is not to suggest that Manmohan Singh is not an underling. Only that all his orders don't come from Sonia Gandhi. In his autobiography (*A Prattler's Tale*), Ashok Mitra, former Finance Minister of West Bengal, tells his story of how Manmohan Singh rose to power. In 1991, when India's foreign exchange reserves were dangerously low, the Narasimha Rao government approached the International Monetary Fund (IMF) for an emergency loan. The IMF agreed on two conditions. The first was Structural Adjustment and Economic Reform. The second was the appointment of a finance minister of its choice. That man, says Mitra, was Manmohan Singh.

Over the years, he has stacked his cabinet and the bureaucracy with people who are evangelically committed to the corporate takeover of everything—water, electricity, minerals, agriculture, land, telecommunications, education, health—no matter what the consequences.

Sonia Gandhi and her son play an important part in all of this. Their job is to run the Department of Compassion and Charisma and to win elections. They are allowed to make (and also to take credit for) decisions that appear progressive but are actually tactical and symbolic, meant to take the edge off popular anger and allow the big ship to keep on rolling. (The best example of this is the rally that was organized for Rahul Gandhi to claim victory for the cancellation of Vedanta's permission to mine Niyamgiri for bauxite—a battle that the Dongria Kondh tribe and a coalition of activists, local as well as international, have been fighting for years. At the rally, Rahul Gandhi announced that he was "a soldier for the tribal people." He didn't mention that the economic policies of his party are predicated on the mass displacement of tribal people. Or that every other bauxite "giri"—hill—in the neighborhood was having the hell mined out of it, while this "soldier for the tribal people" looked away. Rahul Gandhi may be a decent man. But for him to go around talking about the two Indias—the "Rich India" and the "Poor India"—as though the party he represents has nothing to do with it, is an insult to everybody's intelligence, including his own.)

The division of labor between politicians who have a mass base and win elections, and those who actually run the country but either do not need to (judges and bureaucrats) or have been freed of the constraint of winning elections (like the prime minister) is a brilliant subversion of democratic practice. To imagine that Sonia and Rahul Gandhi are in charge of the government would be a mistake. The real power has passed into the hands of a coven of oligarchs—judges, bureaucrats, and politicians. They in turn are run like prize racehorses by the few corporations who more or less own everything in the country. They may belong to different political parties and put up a great show of being political rivals, but that's just subterfuge for public consumption. The only real rivalry is the business rivalry between corporations.

A senior member of the coven is P. Chidambaram, who some say is so popular with the opposition that he may continue to be home minister even if the Congress were to lose the next election. That's probably just as well. He may need a few extra years in office to complete the task he has been assigned. But it doesn't matter if he stays or goes. The die has been rolled.

In a lecture at Harvard (his old university) in October 2007, Chidambaram outlined that task. The lecture was called "Poor Rich Countries: The Challenges of Development." He called the three decades after Independence "the lost years" and exulted about the GDP growth rate, which rose from 6.9 percent in 2002 to 9.4 percent by 2007.

What he said is important enough for me to inflict a chunk of his charmless prose on you:

> One would have thought that the challenge of development— in a democracy—will become less formidable as the economy cruises on a high growth path. The reality is the opposite. Democracy—rather, the institutions of democracy—and the legacy of the socialist era have actually added to the challenge of development.
>
> Let me explain with some examples. India's mineral resources include coal—the fourth-largest reserves in the world—iron ore, manganese, mica, bauxite, titanium ore, chromite, diamonds, natural gas, petroleum, and limestone. Common sense tells us that we should mine these resources quickly and efficiently. That requires huge capital, efficient organizations and a policy environment that will allow market forces to operate. None of these factors is present today in the mining sector. The laws in this behalf are outdated, and Parliament has been able to only tinker at the margins. Our efforts to attract private investment in prospecting and mining have, by and large, failed. Meanwhile, the sector remains virtually captive in the hands of the state

governments. Opposing any change in the status quo are groups that espouse—quite legitimately—the cause of the forests or the environment or the tribal population. There are also political parties that regard mining as a natural monopoly of the State and have ideological objections to the entry of the private sector. They garner support from the established trade unions. Behind the unions—either known or unknown to them—stand the trading mafia. The result: actual investment is low, the mining sector grows at a tardy pace and it acts as a drag on the economy.

I shall give you another example. Vast extent of land is required for locating industries. Mineral-based industries such as steel and aluminum require large tracts of land for mining, processing and production. Infrastructure projects like airports, seaports, dams, and power stations need very large extents of land so that they can provide road and rail connectivity and the ancillary and support facilities. Hitherto, land was acquired by the governments in exercise of the power of eminent domain. The only issue was payment of adequate compensation. That situation has changed. There are new stakeholders in every project, and their claims have to be recognized. We are now obliged to address issues such as environmental impact assessment, justification for compulsory acquisition, right compensation, solatium, rehabilitation, and resettlement of the displaced persons, alternative house sites and farmland, and one job for each affected family.

Allowing "market forces" to mine resources "quickly and efficiently" is what colonizers did to their colonies, what Spain and North America did to South America, what Europe did (and continues to do) in Africa. It's what the apartheid regime did in South Africa. What puppet dictators in small countries do to bleed their people. It's a formula for growth and development, but for someone else. It's an old, old, old, old story—must we really go over that ground again?

Now that mining licenses have been issued with the urgency you'd associate with a knockdown distress sale, and the scams that are emerging have run into billions of dollars, now that mining companies have polluted rivers, mined away state borders, wrecked ecosystems and unleashed civil war, the consequence of what the coven has set into motion is playing out. Like an ancient lament over ruined landscapes and the bodies of the poor.

Note the regret with which the minister in his lecture talks about democracy and the obligations it entails: "Democracy—rather, the institutions of democracy—and the legacy of the socialist era have actually added to the challenge of development." He follows that up with the standard-issue clutch of lies about compensation, rehabilitation, and jobs.

What compensation? What solatium? What rehabilitation? And what "job for each family"? (Sixty years of industrialization in India has created employment for 6 percent of the workforce.) As for being "obliged" to provide "justification" for the "compulsory acquisition" of land, a cabinet minister surely knows that to compulsorily acquire tribal land (which is where most of the minerals are) and turn it over to private mining corporations is illegal and unconstitutional under the Panchayat (Extension to Scheduled Areas) Act or PESA.

Passed in 1996, PESA is an amendment that attempts to right some of the wrongs done to tribal people by the Indian Constitution when it was adopted by Parliament in 1950. It overrides all existing laws that may be in conflict with it. It is a law that acknowledges the deepening marginalization of tribal communities and is meant to radically recast the balance of power. As a piece of legislation, it is unique because it makes the community—the collective—a legal entity and it confers on tribal societies who live in scheduled areas the right to self-governance. Under PESA, "compulsory acquisition" of tribal land cannot be justified on any count. So, ironically, those who are being called "Maoists" (which includes everyone who is resisting land acquisition) are actually fighting to uphold the constitution. While the government is doing its best to vandalize it.

Between 2008 and 2009, the Ministry of Panchayati Raj (Village Administration) commissioned two researchers to write a chapter for a report on the progress of panchayati raj in the country. The chapter is called "PESA, Left-Wing Extremism and Governance: Concerns and Challenges in India's Tribal Districts." Its authors are Ajay Dandekar and Chitrangada Choudhury.

Here are some extracts:

The Central Land Acquisition Act of 1894 has till date not been amended to bring it in line with the provisions of PESA. . . . At the moment, this colonial-era law is being widely misused on the ground to forcibly acquire individual and community land for private industry. In several cases, the practice of the state government is to sign high-profile MoUs with corporate houses and then proceed to deploy the Acquisition Act to ostensibly acquire the land for the state industrial corporation. This body then simply leases the land to the private corporation—a complete travesty of the term "acquisition for a public purpose," as sanctioned by the act. . . .

There are cases where the formal resolutions of gram sabhas expressing dissent have been destroyed and substituted by forged documents. What is worse, no action has been taken by the state against concerned officials even after the facts got established. The message is clear and ominous. There is collusion in these deals at numerous levels.

The sale of tribal lands to non-tribals in the Schedule Five areas is prohibited in all these states. However, transfers continue to take place and have become more perceptible in the post-liberalization era. The principal reasons are—transfer through fraudulent means, unrecorded transfers on the basis of oral transactions, transfers by misrepresentation of facts and misstating the purpose, forcible occupation of tribal lands, transfer through illegal marriages, collusive title suits, incorrect recording at the time of the survey, land acquisition process, eviction of encroachments and in the name of exploitation of timber and forest produce and even on the pretext of development of welfarism.

In their concluding section, they say:

The Memorandums of Understanding signed by the state governments with industrial houses, including mining companies, should be re-examined in a public exercise, with gram sabhas at the centre of this inquiry.

Here it is then—not troublesome activists, not the Maoists, but a government report calling for the mining memorandums of understanding to be reexamined. What does the government do with this document? How does it respond? On April 24, 2010, at a formal ceremony, the prime minister released the report. Brave of him, you would think. Except, this chapter wasn't in it. It was dropped.

Half a century ago, just a year before he was killed, Che Guevara wrote: "When the oppressive forces maintain themselves in power against laws they themselves established, peace must be considered already broken."

Indeed it must. In 2009, Manmohan Singh said in Parliament, "If left-wing extremism continues to flourish in parts which have natural resources of minerals, the climate for investment would certainly be affected." It was a furtive declaration of war.

(Permit me a small digression here, a moment to tell a very short Tale of Two Sikhs. In his last petition to the Punjab governor, before he was hanged by the British government in 1931, Bhagat Singh, the celebrated Sikh revolutionary—and Marxist—said: "Let us declare that the state of war does exist and shall exist so long as India's toiling masses and the natural resources are being exploited by a handful of parasites. They may be purely British Capitalist or mixed British and Indian or even purely Indian. . . . All these things make no difference.")

If you pay attention to many of the struggles taking place in India, people are demanding no more than their constitutional rights. But the government of India no longer feels the need to abide by the Indian Constitution, which is supposed to be the legal and moral framework on which our democracy rests. As constitutions go, it is an enlightened document, but its enlightenment is not used to protect people. Quite the opposite. It's used as a spiked club to beat down those who are protesting against the growing tide of violence being perpetrated by a state on its people in the name of the "public good."

In a recent article in *Outlook* (May 3), B. G. Verghese came out waving that club in defense of the state and big corporations: "The Maoists will fade away, democratic India and the Constitution will prevail, despite the time it takes and the pain involved." To this, Azad replied.

It was the last piece he wrote before he was murdered.

> *In which part of India is the constitution prevailing, Mr. Verghese? In Dantewada, Bijapur, Kanker, Narayanpur, Rajnandgaon? In Jharkhand, Orissa? In Lalgarh, Jangalmahal? In the Kashmir Valley? Manipur? Where was your constitution hiding for twenty-five long years after thousands of Sikhs were massacred? When thousands of Muslims were decimated? When lakhs of peasants are compelled to commit suicide? When thousands of people are murdered by state-sponsored Salwa Judum gangs? When Adivasi women are gang-raped? When people are simply abducted by uniformed goons? Your constitution is a piece of paper that does not even have the value of toilet paper for the vast majority of the Indian people.*

After Azad was killed, several media commentators tried to paper over the crime by shamelessly inverting what he had said in that piece, accusing him of calling the Indian constitution a piece of toilet paper.

If the government will not respect the constitution, then perhaps we should push for an amendment to the Preamble itself. "We, the People of India, having solemnly resolved to constitute India into a Sovereign Socialist Secular Democratic Republic" could be substituted with "We, the upper castes and classes of India, having secretly resolved to constitute India into a Corporate, Hindu, Satellite State . . ."

The insurrection in the Indian countryside, in particular in the tribal heartland, poses a radical challenge not only to the Indian State, but to resistance movements, too. It questions the accepted ideas of what constitutes progress, development, and indeed civilization itself. It questions the ethics as well as the effectiveness of different strategies of resistance. These questions have been asked before, yes. They have been asked persistently, peacefully, year after year, in a hundred different ways—by the Chhattisgarh Mukti Morcha, the Koel Karo and Gandhamardhan agitations—and hundreds of other people's movements. It was asked most persuasively and perhaps most visibly by the Narmada Bachao Andolan, the anti-dam movement in the Narmada valley. The government of India's only answer has been repression, deviousness, and the kind of opacity that can only come from a pathological disrespect for ordinary people. Worse, it went ahead and accelerated the process of displacement and dispossession to a point where people's anger has built up in ways that cannot be controlled. Today, the poorest people in the world have managed to stop some of the richest corporations in their tracks. It's a huge victory.

Those who have risen up are aware that their country is in a State of Emergency. They are aware that like the people of Kashmir, Manipur, Nagaland, and Assam, they too have now been stripped of their civil rights by laws like the Unlawful Activities Prevention Act and the Chhattisgarh Special Public Security Act, which criminalize every kind of dissent—by word, deed, and even intent.

During the Emergency era, grim as it was, people still allowed themselves to dream of bettering their lot, to dream of justice. When Indira Gandhi declared the Emergency on the midnight of June 25, 1975, she did it to crush an incipient revolution. The Naxalite uprising in Bengal had been more or less decimated. But then millions of people were rallying to Jayaprakash Narayan's call for "*Sampoorna Kranti*" (Total Revolution). At the heart of all the unrest was the demand for Land to the Tiller. (Even back then, it was no different—you needed a revolution to implement land redistribution, which is one of the directive principles of the constitution.)

Thirty-five years later, things have changed drastically. Justice, that grand, beautiful idea, has been whittled down to mean human rights. Equality is a utopian fantasy. The word has, more or less, been evicted from our vocabulary. The poor have been pushed to the wall. From fighting for land for the landless, revolutionary parties and resistance movements have had to lower their sights to fighting for people's rights to hold on to what little land they have. The only kind of land redistribution that seems to be in the cards is land being grabbed from the poor and redistributed to the rich, for their landbanks, which go by the name of Special Economic Zones. The landless (mostly Dalits), the jobless, the slum dwellers, and the urban working class are more or less out of the reckoning. In places like Lalgarh in West Bengal, people are only asking the police and the government to leave them alone.

The Adivasi organization called the People's Committee Against Police Atrocities (PCAPA) began with one simple demand—that the superintendent of police visit Lalgarh and apologize to the people for the atrocities his men had committed on villagers. That was considered preposterous. (How could half-naked savages expect a government officer to apologize to them?) So people barricaded their villages and refused to let the police in. The police stepped up the violence. People responded with fury. Now, two years down the line, and many gruesome rapes, killings, and fake encounters later, it's all-out war. The PCAPA has been banned and dubbed a Maoist outfit. Its leaders have been jailed or shot. (A similar fate has befallen the Chasi Mulya Adivasi Sangh in Narayanpatna in Orissa and the Visthappen Virodhi Ekta Manch in Potka in Jharkhand.)

People who once dreamt of justice and equality, who dared to demand land to the tiller, have been reduced to demanding an apology from the police for being beaten and maimed—is this progress?

During the Emergency, the saying goes, when Mrs. Gandhi asked the press to bend, it crawled. And yet, in those days, there were instances when national dailies defiantly published blank editorials to protest censorship. (Irony of ironies—one of those defiant editors was B. G. Verghese.)

This time around, in the undeclared emergency, there's not much scope for defiance because the media is the government. Nobody, except the corporations that control them, can tell it what to do. Senior politicians, ministers, and officers of the security establishment vie to appear on TV, feebly imploring Arnab Goswami or Barkha Dutt for permission to interrupt the day's sermon. Several TV channels and newspapers are overtly manning Operation Green Hunt's war room and its disinformation campaign. There was the identically worded story about the "1,500-crore Maoist industry" filed under the byline of different reporters in several different papers. Almost all newspapers and TV channels ran stories blaming the PCAPA (used interchangeably with "Maoists") for the horrific train derailment near Jhargram in West Bengal in May 2010 in which 140 people died.

Two of the main suspects have been shot down by the police in "encounters," even though the mystery around that train accident is still unraveling. The Press Trust of India put out several untruthful stories, faithfully showcased by the Indian Express, including one about Maoists mutilating the bodies of policemen they had killed. (The denial, which came from the police themselves, was published postage-stamp size hidden in the middle pages.) There are the several identical interviews, all of them billed as "exclusive," with a female guerrilla about how she had been "raped and re-raped" by Maoist leaders. She was supposed to have recently escaped from the forests, and the clutches of the Maoists, to tell the world her tale. Now it turns out that she has been in police custody for months.

The atrocity-based analyses shouted out at us from our TV screens is designed to smoke up the mirrors and hustle us into thinking: "Yes, the tribals have been neglected and are having a very bad time; yes, they need development; yes, it's the government's fault, but right now there is a crisis. We need to get rid of the Maoists, secure the land and then we can help the tribals."

As war closes in, the armed forces have announced (in the way only they can) that they too are getting into the business of messing with our heads. In June 2010, they released two "operational doctrines." One was a joint doctrine for air-land operations. The other was a doctrine on Military Psychological Operations, which "constitutes a planned process of conveying a message to select target audience, to promote particular themes that result in desired attitudes and behaviour, which affect the achievement of political and military objectives of the country. The Doctrine also provides guidelines for activities related to perception management in sub-conventional operations, especially in an internal environment wherein misguided population may have to be brought into the mainstream." The press release went on to say that "the doctrine on Military Psychological Operations is a policy, planning and implementation document that aims to create a conducive environment for the armed forces to operate by using the media available with the Services to their advantage."

A month later, at a meeting of chief ministers of Naxalite-affected states, a decision was taken to escalate the war. Thirty-six battalions of the India Reserve Force were added to the existing 105 battalions, and 16,000 special police officers (civilians armed and contracted to function as police) were added to the existing 30,000. The home secretary promised to hire 175,000 policemen over the next five years. (It's a good model for an employment guarantee scheme: hire half the population to shoot the other half. You can fool around with the ratios if you like.)

Two days later, the army chief told his senior officers to be "mentally prepared to step into the fight against Naxalism. . . . It might be in six months or in a year or two, but if we have to maintain our relevance as a tool of the state, we will have to undertake things that the nation wants us to do."

By August, newspapers were reporting that the on-again, off-again option of using the air force was on again. "The Indian air force can fire in self-defence in anti-Maoist operations," the *Hindustan Times* said. "The permission has been granted but with strict conditionalities. We cannot use rockets or the integral guns of the helicopters and we can retaliate only if fired upon. . . . To this end, we have side-mounted machine-guns on our choppers that are operated by our Garuds (IAF commandos)." That's a relief. No integral guns, only side-mounted machine-guns.

Maybe "six months or in a year or two" is about as long as it will take for the brigade headquarters in Bilaspur and the air base in Rajnandgaon to be ready. Maybe by then, in a great show of democratic spirit, the government will give in to popular anger and repeal the Armed Forces Special Powers Act (AFSPA, which allows noncommissioned officers to kill on suspicion) in Manipur, Nagaland, Assam, and Kashmir. Once the applause subsides and the celebration peters out, AFSPA will be recast, as the home minister has suggested, along the lines of the Jeevan Reddy report—to sound more humane but to be more deadly. Then it can be promulgated all over the country under a new name. Maybe that will give the armed forces the impunity they need to do what "the nation" wants them to do—to be deployed in the parts of India against the poorest of the poor who are fighting for their very survival.

Maybe that's how Comrade Kamla will die—while she's trying to bring down a helicopter gunship or a military training jet with her pistol. Or maybe by then she will have graduated to an AK-47 or a light machine gun looted from a government armory or a murdered policeman. Maybe by then the media "available to the Services" will have "managed" the perceptions of those of us who still continue to be "misguided" to receive the news of her death with equanimity.

So here's the Indian state, in all its democratic glory, willing to loot, starve, lay siege to, and now deploy the air force in "self-defense" against its poorest citizens.

Self-defense. Ah, yes. Operation Green Hunt is being waged in self-defense by a government that is trying to restore land to poor people whose land has been snatched away by Commie Corporations.

When the government uses the offer of peace talks to draw the deep-swimming fish up to the surface and then kill them, do peace talks have a future? Is either side genuinely interested in peace or justice? One question people have is, are the Maoists really interested in peace? Is there anything they can be offered within the existing system that will deflect the Maoists from their stated goal of overthrowing the Indian state? The answer to that is, of course not. The Maoists do not believe that the present system can deliver justice. The thing is that an increasing number of people are beginning to agree with them. If we lived in a society with a genuinely democratic impulse, one in which ordinary people felt they could at least hope for justice, then the Maoists would be only a small, marginalized group of militants with very little popular appeal.

The other contention is that Maoists want a ceasefire to take the heat off themselves for a while so that they can use the time to regroup and consolidate their position. Azad, in an interview to *The Hindu* (April 14, 2010), was surprisingly candid about this: "It doesn't need much of a common sense to understand that both sides will utilize the situation of a ceasefire to strengthen their respective sides." He then went on to explain that a ceasefire, even a temporary one, would give respite to ordinary people who are caught in a war zone.

The government, on the other hand, desperately needs this war. (Read the business papers to see how desperately.) The eyes of the international business community are boring holes into its back. It needs to deliver, and fast. To keep its mask from falling, it must continue to offer talks on the one hand and undermine them on the other. The elimination of Azad was an important victory because it silenced a voice that had begun to sound dangerously reasonable. For the moment, at least, peace talks have been successfully derailed.

There is plenty to be cynical about in the discussion around peace talks. The thing to remember is that for us ordinary folks no peace talks means an escalating war.

Over the last few months, the government has poured tens of thousands of heavily armed paramilitary troops into the forest. The Maoists responded with a series of aggressive attacks and ambushes. More than two hundred policemen have been killed. The bodies keep coming out of the forest. Slain policemen wrapped in the national flag; slain Maoists, displayed like hunters' trophies, their wrists and ankles lashed to bamboo poles; bullet-ridden bodies, bodies that don't look human any more, mutilated in ambushes, beheadings, and summary executions. Of the bodies being buried in the forest, we have no news. The theater of war has been cordoned off, closed to activists and journalists. So there are no body counts.

On April 6, 2010, in its biggest strike ever, the People's Liberation Guerrilla Army ambushed a Central Reserve Police Force (CRPF) company in Dantewada and killed seventy-six policemen. The party issued a coldly triumphant statement. Television milked the tragedy for everything it was worth. The nation was called upon to condemn the killing. Many of us were not prepared to—not because we celebrate killing, nor because we are all Maoists, but because we have thorny, knotty views about Operation Green Hunt. For refusing to buy shares in the rapidly growing condemnation industry, we were branded "terrorist sympathizers" and had our photographs flashed repeatedly on TV like wanted criminals.

What was a CRPF contingent doing, patrolling tribal villages with twenty-one AK-47 rifles, thirty-eight INSAS rifles, seven SLRs, six light machine guns, one Sten gun, and one two-inch mortar? To ask that question almost amounted to an act of treason.

Days after the ambush, I ran into two paramilitary commandos chatting to a bunch of drivers in a Delhi car park. They were waiting for their VIP to emerge from some restaurant or health club or hotel. Their view on what is going on involved neither grief nor patriotism. It was simple accounting. A balance sheet. They were talking about how many lakhs of rupees in bribes it takes for a man to get a job in the paramilitary forces and how most families incur huge debts to pay that bribe. That debt can never be repaid by the pathetic wages paid to a *jawan*. The only way to repay it is to do what policemen in India do—blackmail and threaten people, run protection rackets, demand payoffs, do dirty deals. (In the case of Dantewada, loot villagers, steal cash and jewelry.) But if the man dies an untimely death, it leaves the families hugely in debt. The anger of the men in the car park was directed at the government and senior police officers who make fortunes from bribes and then so casually send young men to their death. They knew that the handsome compensation that was announced for the dead in the April 6 attack was just to blunt the impact of the scandal. It was never going to be standard practice for every policeman who dies in this sordid war.

Small wonder then that the news from the war zone is that CRPF men are increasingly reluctant to go on patrol. There are reports of them fudging their daily logbooks, filling them with phantom patrols. Maybe they're beginning to realize that they are only poor khaki trash, cannon fodder in a Rich Man's War. And there are thousands waiting to replace each one of them when they are gone.

On May 17, 2010, in another major attack, the Maoists blew up a bus in Dantewada and killed about forty-four people. Of them, sixteen were special police officers (SPOs), in other words, members of the dreaded government-sponsored people's militia, the Salwa Judum. The rest of the dead were, shockingly, ordinary people, mostly Adivasis. The Maoists expressed perfunctory regret for having killed civilians, but they came that much closer to mimicking the state's "collateral damage" defense.

Last month, the Maoists kidnapped four policemen in Bihar and demanded the release of some of their senior leaders. A few days into the hostage drama, they killed one of them, an Adivasi policeman called Lucas Tete. Two days later, they released the other three. By killing a prisoner in custody, the Maoists once again harmed their own cause. It was another example of the Janus-faced morality of "revolutionary violence" that we can expect more of in a war zone, in which tactics trump rectitude and make the world a worse place.

Not many analysts and commentators who were pained by the Maoist killing of civilians in Dantewada noticed that at exactly the same time as the bus was blown up by the Maoists in Dantewada, the police had surrounded several villages in Kalinganagar in Orissa, and in Balitutha and Potko in Jharkhand, and had fired on thousands of protesters resisting the takeover of their lands by the Tatas, the Jindals, and Posco. Even now, the siege continues. The wounded cannot be taken to the hospital because of the police cordons. Videos uploaded on YouTube show armed riot police massing in the hundreds, confronted by ordinary villagers, some of whom are armed with bows and arrows.

The one favor that Operation Green Hunt has done ordinary people is that it has clarified things to them. Even the children in the villages know that the police work for the "companies" and that Operation Green Hunt isn't a war against Maoists. It's a war against the poor.

There's nothing small about what's going on. We are watching a democracy turning on itself, trying to eat its own limbs. We're watching incredulously as those limbs refuse to be eaten.

Of all the various political formations involved in the current insurrection, none is more controversial than the Communist Party of India (CPI, Maoist). The most obvious reason is its unapologetic foregrounding of armed struggle as the only path to revolution. Sumanta Banerjee's book *In the Wake of Naxalbari* is one of the most comprehensive accounts of the movement. It documents the early years, the almost harebrained manner in which the Naxalites tried to jumpstart the Indian Revolution by "annihilating the class enemy" and expecting the masses to rise up spontaneously. It describes the contortions it had to make in order to remain aligned with China's foreign policy, how Naxalism spread from state to state and how it was mercilessly crushed.

Buried deep inside the fury that is directed against them by the orthodox left as well as by the liberal intelligentsia is an unease they seem to feel with themselves and a puzzling, almost mystical, protectiveness toward the Indian state. It's as though, when they are faced with a situation that has genuine revolutionary potential, they blink. They find reasons to look away. Political parties—and individuals—who have not, in the last twenty-five years, ever lent their support to say, the Narmada Bachao Andolan, or marched in solidarity with any one of the many peaceful people's movements in the country, have suddenly begun to extol the virtues of nonviolence and Gandhian satyagraha. On the other hand, those who have been actively involved in these struggles may strongly disagree with the Maoists; they are wary, even exasperated, but they do see them as a part of the same resistance.

It's hard to say who dislikes the Maoists more: the Indian state, its army of strategic experts and its instinctively right-wing middle class, or the Communist Party of India (CPI) and Communist Party of India (Marxist), usually called the CPI(M), and the several splinter groups that were part of the original Marxist-Leninists or the liberal left. The argument begins with nomenclature. The more orthodox Communists do not believe that "Maoism" is an "ism" at all. (The Maoists, in turn, call the mainstream parliamentary Communists "social fascists" and accuse them of "economism"—basically, of gradually bargaining away the prospect of revolution.)

Each faction believes itself to be the only genuinely revolutionary Marxist party or political formation. Each believes the other has misinterpreted Communist theory and misunderstood history. Anyone who isn't a card-carrying member of one or the other group will be able to see that none of them is entirely wrong or entirely right about what it says. But bitter splits, not unlike those in religious sects, are the natural corollary of the rigid conformity to the party line demanded by all Communist parties. So they dip into a pool of insults that dates back to the Russian and Chinese revolutions, to the great debates between Lenin, Trotsky, and Stalin, to Chairman Mao's red book, and hurl them at each other. They accuse each other of the "incorrect application" of "Marxist-Leninist-Mao Zedong Thought," almost as though it's an ointment that's being rubbed in the wrong place. (My earlier essay "Walking with the Comrades" landed directly in the flight-path of this debate. It got its fair share of entertaining insults, which deserve a pamphlet of their own.)

Other than the debate about whether or not to enter electoral politics, the major disagreement between the various strands of Communism in India centers around their reading of whether conditions in the country are ripe for revolution. Is the prairie ready for the fire, as Mao announced in China, or is it still too damp for the single spark to ignite it? The trouble is that India lives in several centuries simultaneously, so perhaps the "prairie," that vast stretch of flat grassland, is the wrong analogy for India's social and political landscape. Maybe a "warren" would be a better one. To arrive at a consensus about the timing of the revolution is probably impossible. So everybody marches to their own drumbeat. The CPI and the CPI(M) have more or less postponed the revolution to the afterlife. For Charu Majumdar, founder of the Naxalite movement, it was meant to have happened thirty years ago. According to Ganapathi, current chief of the Maoists, it's about fifty years away.

Today, forty years after the Naxalbari uprising, the main charge against the Maoists by the parliamentary left continues to be what it always was. They are accused of suffering from what Lenin called an "infantile disorder," of substituting mass politics with militarism and of not having worked at building a genuinely revolutionary proletariat. They are seen as having contempt for the urban working class, of being an ideologically ossified force that can only function as a frog on the back of "innocent" (read primitive) jungle-dwelling tribal people who, according to orthodox Marxists, have no real revolutionary potential. (This is not the place perhaps to debate a vision that says people have to first become wage earners, enslaved to a centralized industrial system, before they can be considered revolutionary.)

The charge that the Maoists are irrelevant to urban working-class movements, to the Dalit movement, to the plight of farmers and agricultural workers outside the forests is true. There is no doubt that the Maoists' militarized politics makes it almost impossible for it to function in places where there is no forest cover. However, it could equally be argued that the major Communist parties have managed to survive in the mainstream only by compromising their ideologies so drastically that it is impossible to tell the difference between them and other bourgeois political parties any more. It could be argued that the smaller factions that have remained relatively uncompromised have managed to do so because they do not pose a threat to anybody.

Whatever their faults or achievements as bourgeois parties, few would associate the word "revolutionary" with the CPI or CPI(M) any more. (The CPI does play a role in some of the struggles against mining companies in Orissa.) But even in their chosen sphere of influence, they cannot claim to have done a great service to the proletariat they say they represent. Apart from their traditional bastions in Kerala and West Bengal, both of which they are losing their grip over, they have very little presence in any other part of the country, urban or rural, forest or plains. They have run their trade unions into the ground. They have not been able to stanch the massive job losses and the virtual disbanding of the formal workforce that mechanization and the new economic policies have caused. They have not been able to prevent the systematic dismantling of workers' rights. They have managed to alienate themselves almost completely from Adivasi and Dalit communities. In Kerala, many would say they have done a better job than other political parties, but their thirty-year "rule" in West Bengal has left that state in ruins.

The repression they unleashed in Nandigram and Singur, and now against the Adivasis of Jangalmahal, will probably drive them out of power for a few years. (Only for as long as it takes Mamata Banerjee to prove that she is not the vessel into which people should pour their hopes.)

Still, while listing a litany of their sins, it must be said that the demise of the mainstream Communist parties is not something to be celebrated. At least not unless it makes way for a new, more vital and genuinely left movement in India.

The Maoists (in their current as well as earlier avatars) have had a different political trajectory. The redistribution of land, by violent means if necessary, was always the centerpiece of their political activity. They have been completely unsuccessful in that endeavor. But their militant interventions, in which thousands of their cadre—as well as ordinary people—paid with their lives, shone a light on the deeply embedded structural injustice of Indian society. If nothing else, from the time of the Telangana movement, which in some ways was a precursor to the uprising in Naxalbari, the Naxalite movement, for all its faults, sparked an anger about being exploited and a desire for self-respect in some of the most oppressed communities.

In West Bengal, it led to Operation Barga (a *bargadar* is a sharecropper), and to a far lesser extent in Andhra Pradesh, it shamed governments into carrying out some land reform. Even today, all the talk about "uneven development" and "exploitation" of tribal areas by the prime minister, the government's plans to transfer Joint Forest Management funds from the Forest Department directly to the *gram panchayats*, the Planning Commission's announcement that it will allocate Rs 14,000 crore ($3 billion) for tribal development, has come as a strategy to defuse the Maoist "menace." If those funds do end up benefiting the Adivasi community, instead of being siphoned away by middlemen, then the "menace" surely ought to be given some credit. Though the Maoists have virtually no political presence outside forested areas, they do have a presence, an increasingly sympathetic one, in the popular imagination as a party that stands up for the poor against the intimidation and bullying of the state. If Operation Green Hunt eventually becomes an outright war instead of a "subconventional" one, if ordinary Adivasis start dying in huge numbers, that sympathy could ignite in unexpected ways.

Among the most serious charges leveled against the Maoists is that its leaders have a vested interest in keeping people poor and illiterate in order to retain their hold on them. Critics ask why, after working in areas like Dandakaranya for thirty years, they still do not run schools and clinics, why they don't have check-dams and advanced agriculture, and why people were still dying of malaria and malnutrition. Good question. But it ignores the reality of what it means to be a banned organization whose members—even if they are doctors or teachers—are liable to be shot on sight. It would be more useful to direct the same question to the government of India that has none of these constraints. Why is it that in tribal areas that are not overrun by Maoists, there are no schools, no hospitals, no check-dams? Why do people in Chhattisgarh suffer from such acute malnutrition that doctors have begun to call it "nutritional AIDS" because of the effect it has on the human immune system?

In their censored chapter in the Ministry of Panchayati Raj report, Ajay Dandekar and Chitrangada Choudhury (no fans of the Maoists—they call the party ideology "brutal and cynical") write:

> So the Maoists today have a dual effect on the ground in PESA areas. By virtue of the gun they wield, they are able to evoke some fear in the administration at the village/block/district level. They consequently prevent the common villager's powerlessness over the neglect or violation of protective laws like PESA, for example, warning a talati, who might be demanding bribes in return for fulfilling the duty mandated to him under the Forest Rights Act, a trader who might be paying an exploitative rate for forest produce, or a contractor who is violating the minimum

wage. The party has also done an immense amount of rural development work, such as mobilizing community labour for farm ponds, rainwater harvesting and land conservation works in the Dandakaranya region, which villagers testified had improved their crops and improved their food security situation.

In their recently published empirical analysis of the working of the National Rural Employment Guarantee Scheme (NREGA) in two hundred Maoist-affected districts in Orissa, Chhattisgarh, and Jharkhand, which appeared in the *Economic and Political Weekly*, authors Kaustav Banerjee and Partha Saha say:

The field survey revealed that the charge that the Maoists have been blocking developmental schemes does not seem to hold much ground. In fact, Bastar seems to be doing much better in terms of NREGA than some other areas . . . on top of that, the wage struggles, the enforcement of minimum wages can be traced back to the wage struggles led by the Maoists in that area. A clear result that we came across is the doubling of the wage rates for tendu leaf collection in most Maoist areas. . . . Also, the Maoists have been encouraging the conduct [sic] of social audits since this helps in the creation of a new kind of democratic practice hitherto unseen in India.

Implicit in much of the debate around Maoists is the old, patronizing tendency to cast "the masses," the Adivasi people in this case, in the role of the dim-witted horde, completely controlled by a handful of wicked "outsiders." One university professor, a well-known Maoist-baiter, accused the leaders of the party of being parasites preying on poor Adivasis. To bolster his case, he compared the lack of development in Dandakaranya to the prosperity in Kerala. After suggesting that the non-Adivasi leaders were all cowards "hiding safely in the forest," he appealed to all Adivasi Maoist guerrillas and village militia to surrender before a panel of middle-class Gandhian activists (handpicked by him). He called for the non-Adivasi leadership to be tried for war crimes. Why non-Adivasi Gandhians are acceptable, but not non-Adivasi Maoists, he did not say. There is something very disturbing about this inability to credit ordinary people with being capable of weighing the odds and making their own decisions.

In Orissa, for instance, there are a number of diverse struggles being waged by unarmed resistance movements which often have sharp differences with each other. And yet between them all, they have managed to temporarily stop some major corporations from being able to proceed with their projects—the Tatas in Kalinganagar, Posco in Jagatsinghpur, Vedanta in Niyamgiri. Unlike in Bastar, where they control territory and are well entrenched, the Maoists tend to use Orissa only as a corridor for their squads to pass through. As the security forces are closing in on people and ratcheting up the repression, they have to think very seriously about the pros and cons of involving the Maoists into their struggles. Will its armed squads stay and fight the state repression that will inevitably follow a Maoist "action"? Or will they retreat and leave unarmed people to deal with police terror? Activists and ordinary people, falsely accused of being Maoists, are already being jailed. Many have been killed in cold blood. But a tense uneasy dance continues between the unarmed resistance movements and the CPI (Maoist).

On occasion, the party has done irresponsible things, which have led to horrible consequences for ordinary people. In 2006, at the height of the tension between the Dalit and Adivasi communities in Kandhamal district, the Maoists shot dead Laxmanananda Saraswati, leader of the Vishwa Hindu Parishad, a fascist outfit of proselytizers, working among Adivasis to bring them "back into the Hindu fold." After the murder, enraged Kandha tribals who had been recently converted to Hinduism were encouraged to go on a rampage. Almost four hundred villages were convulsed with anti-Christian violence. Fifty-four Panna Dalit Christians were killed, more than two hundred churches burnt, tens of thousands had to flee their homes. Many still live in camps, unable to return. A somewhat different, but equally dangerous situation is brewing in Narayanpatna and Koraput, districts where the Chasi Mulya Adivasi Sangh (which the police say is a Maoist "front") is fighting to restore land to Adivasis that was illegally appropriated by local moneylenders and liquor dealers (many of them Dalit). These areas are reeling under police terror, with hundreds of Adivasis thrown in Koraput jail and thousands living in the forests, afraid to go home.

People who live in situations like this do not simply take instructions from a handful of ideologues who appear out of nowhere waving guns. Their decisions of what strategies to employ take into account a whole host of considerations: the history of the struggle, the nature of the repression, the urgency of the situation, and the landscape in which their struggle is taking place. The decision of whether to be a Gandhian or a Maoist, militant or peaceful, or a bit of both (like in Nandigram) is not always a moral or ideological one. Quite often, it's a tactical one. Gandhian satyagraha, for example, is a kind of political theater. In order for it to be effective, it needs a sympathetic audience, which villagers deep in the forest do not have. When a posse of eight hundred policemen lay a cordon around a forest village at night and begin to burn houses and shoot people, will a hunger strike help? (Can starving people go on a hunger strike? And do hunger strikes work when they are not on TV?)

Equally, guerrilla warfare is a strategy that villages in the plains, with no cover for tactical retreat, cannot afford. Fortunately, people are capable of breaking through ideological categories, and of being Gandhian in Jantar Mantar, militant in the plains and guerrilla fighters in the forest without necessarily suffering from a crisis of identity. The strength of the insurrection in India is its diversity, not uniformity.

Since the government has expanded its definition of "Maoist" to include anybody who opposes it, it shouldn't come as a surprise that the Maoists have moved to center stage. However, their doctrinal inflexibility, their reputed inability to countenance dissent, to work with other political formations and, most of all, their single-minded, grim, military imagination makes them too small to fill the giant pair of boots that is currently on offer.

When I met Comrade Roopi in the forest, the first thing the techie-whiz did after greeting me was to ask about an interview with me published soon after the Maoists had attacked Rani Bodili, a girls' school in Dantewada that had been turned into a police camp. More than fifty policemen and special police officers were killed. "We were glad," she said, "that you refused to condemn our Rani Bodili attack, but then in the same interview you said that if the Maoists ever come to power, the first person we would hang would probably be you. Why did you say that? Why do you think we're like that?" I was settling into my long answer but we were distracted. I would probably have started with Stalin's purges—in which millions of ordinary people and almost half of the seventy-five thousand Red Army officers were either jailed or shot and 98 out of 139 Central Committee members were arrested, and gone on to the huge price people paid for China's Great Leap Forward and the Cultural Revolution, and might have ended with the Pedamallapuram incident in Andhra Pradesh, when the Maoists, in its previous avatar as People's War, killed the village sarpanch and assaulted women activists for refusing to obey their call to boycott elections.)

Coming back to the question: Who can fill that giant pair of boots? Perhaps it cannot, and should not be, a single pair of feet. Sometimes it seems very much as though those who have a radical vision for a newer, better world do not have the steel it takes to resist the military onslaught, and those who have the steel do not have the vision.

Right now, the Maoists are the most militant end of a bandwidth of resistance movements fighting an assault on Adivasi homelands by a cartel of mining and infrastructure companies. To deduce from this that the CPI (Maoist) is in principle a party with a new way of thinking about "development" or the environment might be a little far-fetched. (The one reassuring sign is that it has cautiously said that it is against Big Dams. If it means what it says, that alone would automatically lead to a radically different development model.)

For a political party that is widely seen as opposing the onslaught of corporate mining, the Maoists' policy (and practice) on mining remains pretty woolly. In several places where people are fighting mining companies, there is a persistent view that the Maoists are not averse to allowing mining and mining-related infrastructure projects to go ahead as long as they are given protection money. From interviews and statements made by their senior leaders on the subject of mining, what emerges is just a sort of "We'll do a better job" approach. They vaguely promise "environmentally sustainable" mining, higher royalties, better resettlement for the displaced, and higher stakes for the "stakeholders." (The present minister for mining and mineral resources, too, thinking along the same lines, stood up in Parliament and promised that 26 percent of the "profits" from mining would go into "tribal development." What a feast that will be for the pigs at the trough!)

But let's take a brief look at the star attraction in the mining belt—the several trillion dollars' worth of bauxite. There is no environmentally sustainable way of mining bauxite and processing it into aluminum. It's a highly toxic process that has been exported out of their own environments by most Western countries. To produce 1 ton of aluminum, you need about 6 tons of bauxite, more than 1,000 tons of water, and a massive amount of electricity. For that amount of captive water and electricity, you need Big Dams, which, as we know, come with their own cycle of cataclysmic destruction.

Last of all—the big question—what is the aluminum for? Where is it going? Aluminum is the principal ingredient in the weapons industry—for other countries' weapons industries. Given this, what would a sane, "sustainable" mining policy be? Suppose, for the sake of argument, the CPI (Maoist) was given control of the so-called Red Corridor, the tribal homeland—with its riches of uranium, bauxite, limestone, dolomite, coal, tin, granite, marble—how would it go about the business of policy-making and governance? Would it mine minerals to put on the market in order to create revenue, build infrastructure, and expand its operations? Or would it mine only enough to meet people's basic needs? How would it define "basic needs"? For instance, would nuclear weapons be "a basic need" in a Maoist nation-state?

Judging from what is happening in Russia and China and even Vietnam, eventually communist and capitalist societies have one thing in common—the DNA of their dreams. After their revolutions, after building socialist societies that millions of workers and peasants paid for with their lives, both countries now have unbridled capitalist economies. For them, too, the ability to consume has become the yardstick by which progress is measured. For this kind of "progress" you need industry. To feed the industry you need a steady supply of raw material. For that you need mines, dams, domination, colonies, war. Old powers are waning, new ones rising. Same story, different characters—rich countries plundering poor ones. Yesterday, it was Europe and America, today it's India and China. Maybe tomorrow it'll be Africa. Will there be a tomorrow? Perhaps it's too late to ask, but hope has little to do with reason.

Can we expect that an alternative to what looks like certain death for the planet will come from the imagination that has brought about this crisis in the first place? It seems unlikely. The alternative, if there is one, will emerge from the places and the people who have resisted the hegemonic impulse of capitalism and imperialism instead of being co-opted by it.

Here in India, even in the midst of all the violence and greed, there is still immense hope. If anyone can do it, we can do it. We still have a population that has not yet been completely colonized by that consumerist dream. We have a living tradition of those who have struggled for Gandhi's vision of sustainability and self-reliance, for socialist ideas of egalitarianism and social justice. We have Ambedkar's vision, which challenges the

Gandhians as well as the socialists in serious ways. We have the most spectacular coalition of resistance movements with experience, understanding, and vision.

Most important of all, India has a surviving Adivasi population of almost one hundred million. They are the ones who still know the secrets of sustainable living. If they disappear, they will take those secrets with them. Wars like Operation Green Hunt will make them disappear. So victory for the prosecutors of these wars will contain within itself the seeds of destruction, not just for Adivasis, but eventually, for the human race. That's why the war in Central India is so important. That's why we need a real and urgent conversation between all those political formations that are resisting this war.

The day capitalism is forced to tolerate noncapitalist societies in its midst and to acknowledge limits in its quest for domination, the day it is forced to recognize that its supply of raw material will not be endless is the day when change will come. If there is any hope for the world at all, it does not live in climate change conference rooms or in cities with tall buildings. It lives low, down on the ground, with its arms around the people who go to battle every day to protect their forests, their mountains, and their rivers because they know that the forests, the mountains, and the rivers protect them.

The first step toward reimagining a world gone terribly wrong would be to stop the annihilation of those who have a different imagination—an imagination that is outside of capitalism as well as communism. An imagination that has an altogether different understanding of what constitutes happiness and fulfillment. To gain this philosophical space, it is necessary to concede some physical space for the survival of those who may look like the keepers of our past, but who may really be the guides to our future. To do this, we have to ask our rulers: Can you leave the water in the rivers? The trees in the forest? Can you leave the bauxite in the mountain?

If they say they cannot, then perhaps they should stop preaching morality to the victims of their wars.

KASHMIR'S FRUITS
OF DISCORD

A WEEK BEFORE he was elected in 2008, President Obama said that solving the dispute over Kashmir's struggle for self-determination—which has led to three wars between India and Pakistan since 1947—would be among his "critical tasks." His remarks were greeted with consternation in India, and he has said almost nothing about Kashmir since then.

But on Monday, November 8, 2010, during his visit here, he pleased his hosts immensely by saying the United States would not intervene in Kashmir and announcing his support for India's seat on the UN Security Council. While he spoke eloquently about threats of terrorism, he kept quiet about human rights abuses in Kashmir.

Whether Obama decides to change his position on Kashmir again depends on several factors: how the war in Afghanistan is going, how much help the United States needs from Pakistan, and whether the government of India goes aircraft shopping this winter. (An order for ten Boeing C-17 Globemaster III

First published in the *New York Times*, November 8, 2010.

aircraft, worth $5.8 billion, among other huge business deals in the pipeline, may ensure the president's silence.) But neither Obama's silence nor his intervention is likely to make the people in Kashmir drop the stones in their hands.

I was in Kashmir ten days ago, in that beautiful valley on the Pakistani border, home to three great civilizations—Islamic, Hindu, and Buddhist. It's a valley of myth and history. Some believe that Jesus died there, others that Moses went there to find the Lost Tribe. Millions worship at the Hazratbal shrine, where a few days a year a hair of the prophet Muhammad is displayed to believers.

Now Kashmir, caught between the influence of militant Islam from Pakistan and Afghanistan, America's interests in the region, and Indian nationalism (which is becoming increasingly aggressive and "Hinduized"), is considered a nuclear flash point. It is patrolled by more than five hundred thousand soldiers and has become the most highly militarized zone in the world.

The atmosphere on the highway between Kashmir's capital, Srinagar, and my destination, the little apple town of Shopian in the South, was tense. Groups of soldiers were deployed along the highway, in the orchards, in the fields, on the rooftops, and outside shops in the little market squares. Despite months of curfew, the "stone pelters" calling for azadi (freedom), inspired by the Palestinian intifada, were out again. Some stretches of the highway were covered with so many of these stones that you needed an SUV to drive over them.

Fortunately, the friends I was with knew alternative routes down the back lanes and village roads. The "long cut" gave me the time to listen to their stories of this year's uprising. The youngest, still a boy, told us that when three of his friends were arrested for throwing stones, the police pulled out their fingernails—every nail, on both hands.

For three years in a row now, Kashmiris have been in the streets protesting what they see as India's violent occupation. But the militant uprising against the Indian government that began with the support of Pakistan twenty years ago is in retreat. The Indian Army estimates that there are fewer than five hundred militants operating in the Kashmir Valley today. The war has left seventy thousand dead and tens of thousands debilitated by torture. Many, many thousands have "disappeared." More than two hundred thousand Kashmiri Hindus have fled the valley. Though the number of militants has come down, the number of Indian soldiers deployed remains undiminished.

But India's military domination ought not to be confused with a political victory. Ordinary people armed with nothing but their fury have risen up against the Indian security forces. A whole generation of young people who have grown up in a grid of checkpoints, bunkers, army camps, and interrogation centers, whose childhood was spent witnessing "catch and kill" operations, whose imaginations are imbued with spies, informers, "unidentified gunmen," intelligence operatives, and rigged elections, has lost its patience as well as its fear. With an almost mad courage, Kashmir's young have faced down armed soldiers and taken back their streets.

Since April, when the army killed three civilians and then passed them off as "terrorists," masked stone throwers, most of them students, have brought life in Kashmir to a grinding halt. The Indian government has retaliated with bullets, curfew, and censorship. Just in the last few months, 111 people have been killed, most of them teenagers; more than 3,000 have been wounded and one thousand arrested.

But still they come out, the young, and throw stones. They don't seem to have leaders or belong to a political party. They represent themselves. And suddenly the second-largest standing army in the world doesn't quite know what to do. The Indian government doesn't know with whom to negotiate. And many Indians are slowly realizing that they have been lied to for decades. The once solid consensus on Kashmir suddenly seems a little fragile.

I was in a bit of trouble the morning we drove to Shopian. A few days earlier, at a public meeting in Delhi, I said that

Kashmir was disputed territory, and, contrary to the Indian government's claims, it couldn't be called an "integral" part of India. Outraged politicians and news anchors demanded that I be arrested for sedition. The government, terrified of being seen as "soft," issued threatening statements, and the situation escalated. Day after day, on prime-time news, I was being called a traitor, a white-collar terrorist, and several other names reserved for insubordinate women. But sitting in that car on the road to Shopian, listening to my friends, I could not bring myself to regret what I had said in Delhi.

We were on our way to visit a man called Shakeel Ahmed Ahangar. The previous day he had come all the way to Srinagar, where I had been staying, to press me, with an urgency that was hard to ignore, to visit Shopian.

I first met Shakeel in June 2009, only a few weeks after the bodies of Nilofar, his twenty-two-year-old wife, and Asiya, his seventeen-year-old sister, were found lying a thousand yards apart in a shallow stream in a high-security zone—a floodlit area between army and state police camps. The first postmortem report confirmed rape and murder. But then the system kicked in. New autopsy reports overturned the initial findings, and after the ugly business of exhuming the bodies, rape was ruled out. It was declared that in both cases the cause of death was drowning. Protests shut Shopian down for forty-seven days, and the valley was convulsed with anger for months. Eventually, it looked as though the Indian government had managed to defuse the crisis. But the anger over the killings has magnified the intensity of this year's uprising.

Shakeel wanted us to visit him in Shopian because he was being threatened by the police for speaking out, and he hoped our visit would demonstrate that people even outside of Kashmir were looking out for him, that he was not alone.

It was apple season in Kashmir, and as we approached Shopian we could see families in their orchards, busily packing apples into wooden crates in the slanting afternoon light. I worried that a couple of the little red-cheeked children who looked so much like apples themselves might be crated by mistake. The news of our visit had preceded us, and a small knot of people were waiting on the road.

Shakeel's house is on the edge of the graveyard where his wife and sister are buried. It was dark by the time we arrived, and there was a power failure. We sat in a semicircle around a lantern and listened to him tell the story we all knew so well. Other people entered the room. Other terrible stories poured out, ones that are not in human rights reports, stories about what happens to women who live in remote villages where there are more soldiers than civilians. Shakeel's young son tumbled around in the darkness, moving from lap to lap. "Soon he'll be old enough to understand what happened to his mother," Shakeel said more than once.

Just when we rose to leave, a messenger arrived to say that Shakeel's father-in-law—Nilofar's father—was expecting us at his home. We sent our regrets; it was late and if we stayed longer it would be unsafe for us to drive back.

Minutes after we said goodbye and crammed ourselves into the car, a friend's phone rang. It was a journalist colleague of his with news for me: "The police are typing up the warrant. She's going to be arrested tonight." We drove in silence for a while, past truck after truck being loaded with apples. "It's unlikely," my friend said finally. "It's just psy-ops."

But then, as we picked up speed on the highway, we were overtaken by a car full of men waving us down. Two men on a motorcycle asked our driver to pull over. I steeled myself for what was coming. A man appeared at the car window. He had slanting emerald eyes and a salt-and-pepper beard that went halfway down his chest. He introduced himself as Abdul Hai, father of the murdered Nilofar.

"How could I let you go without your apples?" he said. The bikers started loading two crates of apples into the back of our car. Then Abdul Hai reached into a pocket of his worn brown cloak and brought out an egg. He placed it in my palm and folded my fingers over it. And then he placed another in my other hand. The eggs were still warm. "God bless and keep you," he said, and walked away into the dark. What greater reward could a writer want?

I wasn't arrested that night. Instead, in what is becoming a common political strategy, officials outsourced their displeasure to the mob. A few days after I returned home, the women's wing of the Bharatiya Janata Party (the right-wing Hindu nationalist opposition) staged a demonstration outside my house, calling for my arrest. Television vans arrived in advance to broadcast the event live. The murderous Bajrang Dal, a militant Hindu group that in 2002 spearheaded attacks against Muslims in Gujarat in which two thousand people were killed, have announced that they are going to "teach me a lesson" with all the means at their disposal, including by filing criminal charges against me in different courts across the country.

Indian nationalists and the government seem to believe that they can fortify their idea of a resurgent India with a combination of bullying and Boeing airplanes. But they don't understand the subversive strength of warm boiled eggs.

I'D RATHER NOT
BE ANNA

WHILE HIS MEANS may be Gandhian, his demands are certainly not.

If what we're watching on TV is indeed a revolution, then it has to be one of the more embarrassing and unintelligible ones of recent times. For now, whatever questions you may have about the Jan Lokpal Bill (People's Anti-Corruption Bill), here are the answers you're likely to get—tick the box: (a) "*Vande Mataram*" (I bow to thee, Mother); (b) "*Bharat Mata ki Jai*" (Victory for Mother India); (c) "India is Anna, Anna is India"; (d) "*Jai Hind*" (Hail India).

For completely different reasons, and in completely different ways, you could say that the Maoists and the Jan Lokpal Bill have one thing in common—they both seek the overthrow of the Indian state. One working from the bottom up, by means of an armed struggle, waged by a largely Adivasi army, made up of the poorest of the poor. The other from the top down, by means of a bloodless Gandhian coup, led by a freshly minted saint and

---

First published in the *Hindu*, August 21, 2011, and *Outlook*, August 22, 2011.

an army of largely urban and certainly better-off people. (In this one, the government collaborates by doing everything it possibly can to overthrow itself.)

In April 2011, a few days into Anna Hazare's first "fast unto death," searching for some way of distracting attention from the massive corruption scams that had battered its credibility, the government invited Team Anna, the brand name chosen by this "civil society" group, to be part of a joint drafting committee for a new anticorruption law. A few months down the line it abandoned that effort and tabled its own bill in Parliament, a bill so flawed that it was impossible to take seriously.

Then, on August 16, the morning of his second "fast unto death," before he had begun his fast or committed any legal offense, Anna Hazare was arrested and jailed. The struggle for the implementation of the Jan Lokpal Bill now coalesced into a struggle for the right to protest, the struggle for democracy itself. Within hours of this "Second Freedom Struggle," Anna was released. Cannily, he refused to leave prison but remained in the Tihar jail as an honored guest, where he began a fast, demanding the right to fast in a public place. For three days, while crowds and television vans gathered outside, members of Team Anna whizzed in and out of the high-security prison, carrying out his video messages to be broadcast on national TV on all channels. (Which other person would be granted this luxury?) Meanwhile 250 employees of the Municipal Commission of Delhi, fifteen trucks, and six earth movers worked around the clock to ready the slushy Ramlila grounds for the grand weekend spectacle. Now, waited upon hand and foot, watched over by chanting crowds and crane-mounted cameras, attended to by India's most expensive doctors, the third phase of Anna's fast to the death has begun. "From Kashmir to Kanyakumari, India is One," the TV anchors tell us.

While his means may be Gandhian, Anna Hazare's demands are certainly not. Contrary to Gandhiji's ideas about the decentralization of power, the Jan Lokpal Bill is a draconian anticorruption law, in which a panel of carefully chosen people will administer a giant bureaucracy, with thousands of employees, with the power to police everybody from the prime minister, the judiciary, members of Parliament, and all of the bureaucracy, down to the lowest government official. The Lokpal will have the powers of investigation, surveillance, and prosecution. Except for the fact that it won't have its own prisons, it will function as an independent administration, meant to counter the bloated, unaccountable, corrupt one that we already have. Two oligarchies, instead of just one.

Whether it works or not depends on how we view corruption. Is corruption just a matter of legality, of financial irregularity and bribery, or is it the currency of a social transaction in an egregiously unequal society, in which power continues to be concentrated in the hands of a smaller and smaller minority? Imagine, for example, a city of shopping malls, on whose streets hawking has been banned. A hawker pays the local beat cop and the man from the municipality a small bribe to break the law and sell her wares to those who cannot afford the prices in the malls. Is that such a terrible thing? In the future will she have to pay the Lokpal representative, too? Does the solution to the problems faced by ordinary people lie in addressing the structural inequality or in creating yet another power structure that people will have to defer to?

Meanwhile, the props and the choreography, the aggressive nationalism and flag-waving of Anna's Revolution are all borrowed from the antireservation protests, the World Cup victory parade, and the celebration of the nuclear tests. They signal to us that if we do not support The Fast, we are not "true Indians." The twenty-four-hour channels have decided that there is no other news in the country worth reporting.

"The Fast" of course doesn't mean Irom Sharmila's fast that has lasted for more than ten years (she's being force-fed now) against the Armed Forces Special Powers Act, which allows soldiers in Manipur to kill merely on suspicion. It does not mean the relay hunger fast that is going on by ten thousand villagers in Koodankulam protesting against the nuclear power plant. "The People" does not mean the Manipuris who support Irom Sharmila's fast. Nor does it mean the thousands who are facing down armed policemen and mining mafias in Jagatsinghpur, or Kalinganagar, or Niyamgiri, or Bastar, or Jaitapur. Nor do we mean the victims of the Bhopal gas leak, or the people displaced by dams in the Narmada valley. Nor do we mean the farmers in the New Okhla Industrial Development Area, or Pune or Haryana or elsewhere in the country, resisting the takeover of the land.

"The People" means only the audience that has gathered to watch the spectacle of a seventy-four-year-old man threatening to starve himself to death if his Jan Lokpal Bill is not tabled and passed by Parliament. "The People" are the tens of thousands who have been miraculously multiplied into millions by our TV channels, as Christ multiplied the fishes and loaves to feed the hungry. "A billion voices have spoken," we're told. "India is Anna."

Who is he really, this new saint, this Voice of the People? Oddly enough, we've heard him say nothing about things of urgent concern. Nothing about the farmers' suicides in his neighborhood or about Operation Green Hunt farther away. Nothing about Singur, Nandigram, Lalgarh, nothing about Posco, about farmers' agitations or the blight of Special Economic Zones. He doesn't seem to have a view about the government's plans to deploy the Indian Army in the forests of Central India.

He does, however, support Raj Thackeray's Marathi Manoos xenophobia and has praised the "development model" of Gujarat's chief minister, who oversaw the 2002 pogrom against Muslims. (Anna withdrew that statement after a public outcry, but presumably not his admiration.)

Despite the din, sober journalists have gone about doing what journalists do. We now have the backstory about Anna's old relationship with the right-wing Rashtriya Swayamsevak Sangh. We have heard from Mukul Sharma, who has studied Anna's village community in Ralegan Siddhi, where there have been no gram panchayat or cooperative society elections in the last twenty-five years. We know about Anna's attitude to "*harijans*": "It was Mahatma Gandhi's vision that every village should have one chamar, one sunar, one kumhar and so on. They should all do their work according to their role and occupation, and in this way, a village will be self-dependent. This is what we are practicing in Ralegan Siddhi." Is it surprising that members of Team Anna have also been associated with Youth for Equality, the antireservation (pro-"merit") movement? The campaign is being handled by people who run a clutch of generously funded NGOs whose donors include Coca-Cola and the Lehman Brothers. Kabir, run by Arvind Kejriwal and Manish Sisodia, key figures in Team Anna, has received $400,000 from the Ford Foundation in the last three years. Among contributors to the India Against Corruption campaign there are Indian companies and foundations that own aluminum plants, build ports and Special Economic Zones, run real estate businesses, and are closely connected to politicians who oversee financial empires that run into thousands of crores of rupees (hundreds of millions of dollars). Some of them are currently being investigated for corruption and other crimes. Why are they all so enthusiastic?

Remember, the campaign for the Jan Lokpal Bill gathered steam around the same time as embarrassing revelations by Wikileaks and a series of scams, including the 2G spectrum scam, broke, in which major corporations, senior journalists, and government ministers and politicians from the Congress as well as the Bharatiya Janata Party seem to have colluded in various ways as hundreds of thousands of crores of rupees were being siphoned off from the public exchequer. For the first time in years, journalist-lobbyists were disgraced, and it seemed as if some major captains of Corporate India could actually end up in prison. Perfect timing for a people's anticorruption agitation. Or was it?

At a time when the state is withdrawing from its traditional duties and corporations and NGOs are taking over government functions (water supply, electricity, transport, telecommunications, mining, health, education); at a time when the corporate-owned media with its terrifying power and reach is trying to control the public imagination, one would think that these institutions—the corporations, the media, and the NGOs—would be included in the jurisdiction of a Lokpal bill. Instead, the proposed bill leaves them out completely.

Now, by shouting louder than everyone else, by pushing a campaign that is hammering away at the theme of evil politicians and government corruption, they have very cleverly let themselves off the hook. Worse, by demonizing only the government they have built themselves a pulpit from which to call for the further withdrawal of the state from the public sphere and for a second round of reforms—more privatization, more access to public infrastructure and India's natural resources. It may not be long before Corporate Corruption is made legal and renamed a Lobbying Fee.

Will the 830 million people living on twenty rupees (forty cents) a day really benefit from the strengthening of a set of policies that is impoverishing them and driving this country to civil war?

This awful crisis has been forged out of the utter failure of India's representative democracy, in which the legislatures are made up of criminals and millionaire politicians who have ceased to represent its people. In which not a single democratic institution is accessible to ordinary people. Do not be fooled by the flag waving. We're watching India being carved up in a war for suzerainty that is as deadly as any battle being waged by the warlords of Afghanistan, only with much, much more at stake.

SPEECH TO THE
PEOPLE'S UNIVERSITY

YESTERDAY MORNING THE police cleared Zuccotti Park, but today the people are back. The police should know that this protest is not a battle for territory. We're not fighting for the right to occupy a park here or there. We are fighting for justice. Justice, not just for the people of the United States, but for everybody. What you have achieved since September 17, when the Occupy movement began in the United States, is to introduce a new imagination, a new political language, into the heart of empire. You have reintroduced the right to dream into a system that tried to turn everybody into zombies mesmerized into equating mindless consumerism with happiness and fulfillment. As a writer, let me tell you, this is an immense achievement. I cannot thank you enough.

We were talking about justice. Today, as we speak, the army of the United States is waging a war of occupation in Iraq and Afghanistan. US drones are killing civilians in Pakistan and

November 16, 2011, Washington Square Park, New York City. First published in the *Guardian*, November 17, 2011.

beyond. Tens of thousands of US troops and death squads are moving into Africa. If spending trillions of dollars of your money to administer occupations in Iraq and Afghanistan is not enough, a war against Iran is being talked up. Ever since the Great Depression, the manufacture of weapons and the export of war have been key ways in which the United States has stimulated its economy. Just recently, under President Obama, the United States made a $60 billion arms deal with Saudi Arabia. It hopes to sell thousands of bunker busters to the United Arab Emirates. It has sold $5 billion worth of military aircraft to my country, India—my country, which has more poor people than all the poorest countries of Africa put together. All these wars, from the bombing of Hiroshima and Nagasaki to Vietnam, Korea, Latin America, have claimed millions of lives—all of them fought to secure "the American way of life."

Today we know that "the American way of life"—the model that the rest of the world is meant to aspire toward—has resulted in four hundred people owning the wealth of half of the population of the United States. It has meant thousands of people being turned out of their homes and jobs while the US government bailed out banks and corporations—American International Group (AIG) alone was given $182 billion.

The Indian government worships US economic policy. As a result of twenty years of the free market economy, today one hundred of India's richest people own assets worth one-fourth of the country's GDP while more than 80 percent of the people live on less than fifty cents a day. Two hundred fifty thousand farmers driven into a spiral of death have committed suicide. We call this progress and now think of ourselves as a superpower. Like you, we are well qualified, we have nuclear bombs and obscene inequality.

The good news is that people have had enough and are not going to take it anymore. The Occupy movement has joined thousands of other resistance movements all over the world in which the poorest of people are standing up and stopping the richest corporations in their tracks. Few of us dreamed that we would see you, the people of the United States, on our side, trying to do this in the heart of empire. I don't know how to communicate the enormity of what this means.

They (the 1 percent) say that we don't have demands . . . they don't know, perhaps, that our anger alone would be enough to destroy them. But here are some things—a few "pre-revolution-ary" thoughts I had—for us to think about together.

We want to put a lid on this system that manufactures inequality.

We want to put a cap on the unfettered accumulation of wealth and property by individuals as well as corporations.

As cap-ists and lid-ites, we demand:

One: An end to cross-ownership in businesses. For example: weapons manufacturers cannot own TV stations, mining cor-porations cannot run newspapers, business houses cannot fund universities, drug companies cannot control public health funds.

Two: Natural resources and essential infrastructure—water supply, electricity, health, and education—cannot be privatized.

Three: Everybody must have the right to shelter, education, and health care.

Four: The children of the rich cannot inherit their parents' wealth.

This struggle has reawakened our imagination. Somewhere along the way, capitalism reduced the idea of justice to mean just "human rights," and the idea of dreaming of equality became blasphemous. We are not fighting to tinker with reforming a system that needs to be replaced.

As a cap-ist and a lid-ite, I salute your struggle.

Salaam and Zindabad.

CAPITALISM:
A GHOST STORY

IS IT A house or a home? A temple to the new India or a warehouse for its ghosts? Ever since Antilla arrived on Altamount Road in Mumbai, exuding mystery and quiet menace, things have not been the same. "Here we are," the friend who took me there said. "Pay your respects to our new ruler."

Antilla belongs to India's richest man, Mukesh Ambani. I'd read about this most expensive dwelling ever built, the twenty-seven floors, three helipads, nine lifts, hanging gardens, ballrooms, weather rooms, gymnasiums, six floors of parking, and six hundred servants. Nothing had prepared me for the vertical lawn—a soaring, twenty-seven-story-high wall of grass attached to a vast metal grid. The grass was dry in patches; bits had fallen off in neat rectangles. Clearly, Trickledown hadn't worked.

But Gush Up certainly has. That's why in a nation of 1.2 billion, India's one hundred richest people own assets equivalent to one-fourth of the GDP.

First published in *Outlook*, March 26, 2012.

The word on the street (and in the *New York Times*) is, or at least was, that after all that effort and gardening, the Ambanis don't live in Antilla. No one knows for sure. People still whisper about ghosts and bad luck, *Vastu* and feng shui. Maybe it's all Karl Marx's fault. (All that cussing.) Capitalism, he said, "has conjured up such gigantic means of production and of exchange, that it is like the sorcerer who is no longer able to control the powers of the netherworld whom he has called up by his spells."

In India the 300 million of us who belong to the new, post–International Monetary Fund (IMF) "reforms" middle class—the market—live side by side with spirits of the netherworld, the poltergeists of dead rivers, dry wells, bald mountains, and denuded forests; the ghosts of 250,000 debt-ridden farmers who have killed themselves and the 800 million who have been impoverished and dispossessed to make way for us. And who survive on less than twenty Indian rupees (forty cents) a day.

Mukesh Ambani is personally worth $20 billion. He holds a majority controlling share in Reliance Industries Limited (RIL), a company with a market capitalization of $47 billion and global business interests that include petrochemicals, oil, natural gas, polyester fiber, Special Economic Zones, fresh food retail, high schools, life sciences research, and stem cell storage services. RIL recently bought 95 percent shares in Infotel, a TV consortium that controls twenty-seven TV news and entertainment channels, including CNN-IBN, IBN Live, CNBC, IBN Lokmat, and ETV in almost every regional language. Infotel owns the only nationwide license for 4G broadband, a high-speed information pipeline, which, if the technology works, could be the future of information exchange. Mr. Ambani also owns a cricket team.

RIL is one of a handful of corporations that run India. Some of the others are the Tatas, Jindals, Vedanta, Mittals, Infosys, Essar, and the other Reliance, Reliance Anil Dhirubhai Ambani Group (ADAG), owned by Mukesh's brother Anil. Their race for growth has spilled across Europe, Central Asia, Africa, and Latin America. Their nets are cast wide; they are visible and invisible, overground as well as underground. The Tatas, for example, run more than one hundred companies in eighty countries. They are one of India's oldest and largest private-sector power companies. They own mines, gas fields, steel plants, telephone, and cable TV and broadband networks, and they run whole townships. They manufacture cars and trucks and own the Taj Hotel chain, Jaguar, Land Rover, Daewoo, Tetley Tea, a publishing company, a chain of bookstores, a major brand of iodized salt, and the cosmetics giant Lakme. Their advertising tagline could easily be You Can't Live Without Us.

According to the rules of the Gush-Up Gospel, the more you have, the more you can have.

The era of the Privatization of Everything has made the Indian economy one of the fastest growing in the world. However, as with any good old-fashioned colony, one of its main exports is its minerals. India's new megacorporations, Tatas, Jindals, Essar, Reliance, and Sterlite, are those that have managed to muscle their way to the head of the spigot that is spewing money extracted from deep inside the earth. It's a dream come true for businessmen—to be able to sell what they don't have to buy.

The other major source of corporate wealth comes from their land banks. All over the world, weak, corrupt local governments have helped Wall Street brokers, agribusiness corporations, and Chinese billionaires to amass huge tracts of land. (This entails commandeering water, too.) In India the land of millions of people is being acquired and handed over to private corporations for "public interest"—for Special Economic Zones, infrastructure projects, dams, highways, car manufacture, chemical hubs, and Formula One racing. (The sanctity of private property never applies to the poor.) As always, local people are promised that their displacement from their land and the expropriation of everything they ever had is actually part of employment generation. But by now we know that the connection between GDP growth and jobs is a myth. After twenty years of "growth," 60 percent of India's workforce is self-employed, and 90 percent of

India's labor force works in the unorganized sector.

Post-Independence, right up to the 1980s, people's movements, ranging from the Naxalites to Jayaprakash Narayan's Sampoorna Kranti, were fighting for land reforms, for the redistribution of land from feudal landlords to landless peasants. Today any talk of redistribution of land or wealth would be considered not just undemocratic but lunatic. Even the most militant movements have been reduced to a fight to hold on to what little land people still have. The millions of landless people, the majority of them Dalits and Adivasis, driven from their villages, living in slums and shanty colonies in small towns and megacities, do not figure even in the radical discourse.

As Gush Up concentrates wealth onto the tip of a shining pin on which our billionaires pirouette, tidal waves of money crash through the institutions of democracy—the courts, the Parliament—as well as the media, seriously compromising their ability to function in the ways they are meant to. The noisier the carnival around elections, the less sure we are that democracy really exists.

Each new corruption scandal that surfaces in India makes the last one look tame. In the summer of 2011 the 2G spectrum scandal broke. We learned that corporations had siphoned away $40 billion of public money by installing a friendly soul as the minister of communications and information who grossly underpriced the licenses for 2G telecom spectrums and illegally auctioned them to his buddies. The taped telephone conversations leaked to the press showed how a network of industrialists and their front companies, ministers, senior journalists, and a TV anchor were involved in facilitating this daylight robbery. The tapes were just an MRI that confirmed a diagnosis that people had made long ago.

The privatization and illegal sale of telecom spectrum does not involve war, displacement, and ecological devastation. The privatization of India's mountains, rivers, and forests does. Perhaps because it does not have the uncomplicated clarity of a straightforward, out-and-out accounting scandal, or perhaps because it is all being done in the name of India's "progress," it does not have the same resonance with the middle classes.

In 2005 the state governments of Chhattisgarh, Orissa, and Jharkhand signed hundreds of memorandums of understanding with a number of private corporations, turning over trillions of dollars of bauxite, iron ore, and other minerals for a pittance, defying even the warped logic of the free market. (Royalties to the government ranged between 0.5 percent and 7 percent.)

Days after the Chhattisgarh government signed a memorandum of understanding for the construction of an integrated steel plant in Bastar with Tata Steel, the Salwa Judum, a vigilante militia, was inaugurated. The government said it was a spontaneous uprising of local people who were fed up with "repression" by Maoist guerrillas in the forest. It turned out to be a ground-clearing operation, funded and armed by the government and subsidized by mining corporations. In the other states similar militias were created, with other names. The prime minister announced the Maoists were the "Single Largest Security Challenge in India." It was a declaration of war.

On January 2, 2006, in Kalinganagar, in the neighboring state of Orissa, perhaps to signal the seriousness of the government's intention, ten platoons of police arrived at the site of another Tata Steel plant and opened fire on villagers who had gathered there to protest what they felt was inadequate compensation for their land. Thirteen people, including one policeman, were killed and thirty-seven injured. Six years have gone by, and though the villages remain under siege by armed policemen, the protest has not died.

Meanwhile in Chhattisgarh, the Salwa Judum burned, raped, and murdered its way through hundreds of forest villages, evacuating 600 villages and forcing 50,000 people to come out into police camps and 350,000 people to flee. The chief minister announced that those who did not come out of the forests would be considered "Maoist terrorists." In this way, in parts of modern

India plowing fields and sowing seed came to be defined as terrorist activity. Eventually, the Salwa Judum's atrocities succeeded only in strengthening the resistance and swelling the ranks of the Maoist guerrilla army. In 2009 the government announced what it called Operation Green Hunt. Two hundred thousand paramilitary troops were deployed across Chhattisgarh, Orissa, Jharkhand, and West Bengal.

After three years of "low-intensity conflict" that has not managed to "flush" the rebels out of the forest, the central government has declared that it will deploy the Indian Army and Air Force. In India we don't call this war. We call it "Creating a Good Investment Climate." Thousands of soldiers have already moved in. A brigade headquarters and airbases are being readied. One of the biggest armies in the world is now preparing its Terms of Engagement to "defend" itself against the poorest, hungriest, most malnourished people in the world. We only await the declaration of the Armed Forces Special Powers Act, which will give the army legal impunity and the right to kill "on suspicion." Going by the tens of thousands of unmarked graves and anonymous cremation pyres in Kashmir, Manipur, and Nagaland, we might judge it to be a very suspicious army indeed.

While the preparations for deployment are being made, the jungles of Central India remain under siege, with villagers frightened to come out or to go to the market for food or medicine. Hundreds of people have been jailed, charged with being Maoists under draconian, undemocratic laws. Prisons are crowded with Adivasi people, many of whom have no idea what their crime is. Recently, Soni Sori, an Adivasi schoolteacher from Bastar, was arrested and tortured in police custody. Stones were pushed up her vagina to get her to "confess" that she was a Maoist courier. The stones were removed from her body at a hospital in Calcutta, where, after a public outcry, she was sent for a medical checkup. At a recent Supreme Court hearing, activists presented the judges with the stones in a plastic bag. The only outcome of their efforts has been that Soni Sori remains in jail, while Ankit Garg, the superintendent of police who conducted the interrogation, was conferred the President's Police Medal for Gallantry on Republic Day.

We hear about the ecological and social reengineering of Central India only because of the mass insurrection and the war. The government gives out no information. The memorandums of understanding are all secret. Some sections of the media have done what they could to bring public attention to what is happening in Central India. However, most of the Indian mass media is made vulnerable by the fact that the major share of their revenues come from corporate advertisements. If that is not bad enough, now the line between the media and big business has begun to blur dangerously. As we have seen, RIL virtually owns twenty-seven TV channels. But the reverse is also true. Some media houses now have direct business and corporate interests. For example, one of the major daily newspapers in the region, *Dainik Bhaskar*—and it is only one example—has 17.5 million readers in four languages, including English and Hindi, across thirteen states. It also owns sixty-nine companies with interests in mining, power generation, real estate, and textiles. A recent writ petition filed in the Chhattisgarh High Court accuses DB Power Ltd. (one of the group's companies) of using "deliberate, illegal and manipulative measures" through company-owned newspapers to influence the outcome of a public hearing over an open cast coal mine. Whether or not it has attempted to influence the outcome is not germane. The point is that media houses are in a position to do so. They have the power to do so. The laws of the land allow them to be in a position that lends itself to a serious conflict of interest.

There are other parts of the country from which no news comes. In the sparsely populated but militarized northeastern state of Arunachal Pradesh, 168 Big Dams are being constructed, most of them privately owned. High dams that will submerge whole districts are being constructed in Manipur and Kashmir, both highly militarized states where people can be killed merely for protesting power cuts. (That happened a few weeks ago in

Kashmir.) How can they stop a dam?

The most delusional dam of all is the Kalpasar in Gujarat. It is being planned as a 34-kilometer-long dam across the Gulf of Khambat with a ten-lane highway and a railway line running on top of it. The idea is to keep out the seawater and create a sweet-water reservoir of Gujarat's rivers. (Never mind that these rivers have already been dammed to a trickle and poisoned with chemical effluent.) The Kalpasar Dam, which would raise the sea level and alter the ecology of hundreds of kilometers of coastline, was the cause of serious concerns among scientists in a 2007 report. It has made a sudden comeback in order to supply water to the Dholera Special Investment Region (SIR) in one of the most water-stressed zones not just in India but in the world. SIR is another name for a Special Economic Zone, a self-governed corporate dystopia of industrial parks, townships, and megacities. The Dholera SIR is going to be connected to Gujarat's other cities by a network of ten-lane highways. Where will the money for all this come from?

In January 2011 in the Mahatma (Gandhi) Mandir, Gujarat's chief minister Narendra Modi presided over a meeting of ten thousand international businessmen from one hundred countries. According to media reports, they pledged to invest $450 billion in Gujarat. The meeting was deliberately scheduled to take place on the tenth anniversary of the massacre of two thousand Muslims in February 2002. Modi stands accused of not just condoning but actively abetting the killing. People who watched their loved ones being raped, eviscerated, and burned alive, the tens of thousands who were driven from their homes, still wait for a gesture toward justice. But Modi has traded in his saffron scarf and vermilion forehead for a sharp business suit and hopes that a $450 billion investment will work as blood money and square the books. Perhaps it will. Big Business is backing him enthusiastically. The algebra of infinite justice works in mysterious ways.

The Dholera SIR is only one of the smaller Matryoshka dolls, one of the inner ones in the dystopia that is being planned. It will be connected to the Delhi Mumbai Industrial Corridor (DMIC), a 1,500-kilometer-long and 300-kilometer-wide corridor with nine megaindustrial zones, a high-speed freight line, three seaports, six airports, a six-lane intersection-free expressway, and a 4,000-megawatt power plant. The DMIC is a collaborative venture between the governments of India and Japan and their respective corporate partners, and has been proposed by the McKinsey Global Institute.

The DMIC website says that approximately 180 million people will be "affected" by the project. Exactly how, it doesn't say. It envisages the building of several new cities and estimates that the population in the region will grow from the current 231 million to 314 million by 2019. That's in seven years' time. When was the last time a state, despot, or dictator carried out a population transfer of millions of people? Can it possibly be a peaceful process?

The Indian Army might need to go on a recruitment drive so that it's not taken unawares when it is ordered to deploy all over India. In preparation for its role in Central India, it publicly released its updated doctrine of military psychological operations, which outlines "a planned process of conveying a message to a select target audience, to promote particular themes that result in desired attitudes and behavior, which affect the achievement of political and military objectives of the country." This process of "perception management," it said, would be conducted by "using media available to the Services."

The army is experienced enough to know that coercive force alone cannot carry out or manage social engineering on the scale that is envisaged by India's planners. War against the poor is one thing. But for the rest of us—the middle class, white-collar workers, intellectuals, "opinion makers"—it has to be "perception management." And for this we must turn our attention to the exquisite art of Corporate Philanthropy.

Of late, the main mining conglomerates have embraced the

arts—film, art installations, and the rush of literary festivals that have replaced the 1990s obsession with beauty contests. Vedanta, currently mining the heart out of the homelands of the ancient Dongria Kond tribe for bauxite, is sponsoring a "Creating Happiness" film competition for young film students whom it has commissioned to make films on sustainable development. Vedanta's tagline is "Mining Happiness." The Jindal Group brings out a contemporary art magazine and supports some of India's major artists (who naturally work with stainless steel). Essar was the principal sponsor of the Tehelka Newsweek Think Fest that promised "high-octane debates" by the foremost thinkers from around the world, which included major writers, activists, and even the architect Frank Gehry. (All this in Goa, where activists and journalists were uncovering massive illegal mining scandals, and Essar's part in the war unfolding in Bastar was emerging.) Tata Steel and Rio Tinto (which has a sordid track record of its own) were among the chief sponsors of the Jaipur Literary Festival (Latin name: Darshan Singh Construction Jaipur Literary Festival), which is advertised by the cognoscenti as "The Greatest Literary Show on Earth." Counselage, the Tatas "strategic brand manager," sponsored the festival's press tent. Many of the world's best and brightest writers gathered in Jaipur to discuss love, literature, politics, and Sufi poetry. Some tried to defend Salman Rushdie's right to free speech by reading from his proscribed book, *The Satanic Verses*. In every TV frame and newspaper photograph, the logo of Tata Steel (and its tagline, Values Stronger than Steel) loomed behind them, a benign, benevolent host. The enemies of free speech were the supposedly murderous Muslim mobs, who, the festival organizers told us, could have even harmed the schoolchildren gathered there. (We are witness to how helpless the Indian government and the police can be when it comes to Muslims.) Yes, the hardline Darul-uloom Deobandi Islamic seminary did protest Rushdie's being invited to the festival. Yes, some Islamists did gather at the festival venue to protest, and yes, outrageously, the state government did nothing to protect the venue. That's because the whole episode had as much to do with democracy, vote banks, and the Uttar Pradesh elections as it did with Islamist fundamentalism. But the battle for free speech against Islamist fundamentalism made it to the world's newspapers. It is important that it did. But there were hardly any reports about the festival sponsors' role in the war in the forests, the bodies piling up, the prisons filling up. Or about the Unlawful Activities Prevention Act and the Chhattisgarh Special Public Security Act, which make even thinking an antigovernment thought a cognizable offense. Or about the mandatory public hearing for the Tata Steel plant in Lohandiguda, which local people complained actually took place hundreds of miles away in Jagdalpur, in the collector's office compound, with a hired audience of fifty people, under armed guard. Where was free speech then? No one mentioned Kalinganagar. No one mentioned that journalists, academics, and filmmakers working on subjects unpopular with the Indian government—like the surreptitious part it played in the genocide of Tamils in the war in Sri Lanka, or the recently discovered unmarked graves in Kashmir—were being denied visas or deported straight from the airport.

But which of us sinners was going to cast the first stone? Not me, who lives off royalties from corporate publishing houses. We all watch Tata Sky, we surf the Net with Tata Photon, we ride in Tata taxis, we stay in Tata Hotels, sip our Tata tea in Tata bone china, and stir it with teaspoons made of Tata Steel. We buy Tata books in Tata bookshops. *Hum Tata ka namak khatey hain.* We're under siege.

If the sledgehammer of moral purity is to be the criteria for stone throwing, then the only people who qualify are those who have been silenced already. Those who live outside the system; the outlaws in the forests, or those whose protests are never covered by the press, or the well-behaved Dispossessed, who go from tribunal to tribunal, bearing witness, giving testimony.

But the Litfest gave us our Aha! Moment. Oprah came. She

said she loved India, that she would come again and again. It made us proud.

This is only the burlesque end of the Exquisite Art.

Though the Tatas have been involved with corporate philanthropy for almost a hundred years now, endowing scholarships and running some excellent educational institutes and hospitals, Indian corporations have only recently been invited into the Star Chamber, the Camera stellata, the brightly lit world of global corporate government, deadly for its adversaries but otherwise so artful that you barely know it's there.

What follows in this essay might appear to some to be a somewhat harsh critique. On the other hand, in the tradition of honoring one's adversaries, it could be read as an acknowledgment of the vision, flexibility, sophistication, and unwavering determination of those who have dedicated their lives to keeping the world safe for capitalism.

Their enthralling history, which has faded from contemporary memory, began in the United States in the early twentieth century when, kitted out legally in the form of endowed foundations, corporate philanthropy began to replace missionary activity as capitalism's (and imperialism's) road-opening and systems maintenance patrol.

Among the first foundations to be set up in the United States were the Carnegie Corporation, endowed in 1911 by profits from Carnegie Steel Company, and the Rockefeller Foundation, endowed in 1914 by J. D. Rockefeller, founder of Standard Oil Company. The Tatas and Ambanis of their time.

Some of the institutions financed, given seed money, or supported by the Rockefeller Foundation are the United Nations, the CIA, the Council on Foreign Relations (CFR), New York's most fabulous Museum of Modern Art, and, of course, the Rockefeller Center in New York (where Diego Rivera's mural had to be blasted off the wall because it mischievously depicted reprobate capitalists and a valiant Lenin; free speech had taken the day off).

Rockefeller was America's first billionaire and the world's richest man. He was an abolitionist, a supporter of Abraham Lincoln, and a teetotaler. He believed his money was given to him by God, which must have been nice for him.

Here are a few verses from one of Pablo Neruda's early poems called "Standard Oil Company":

Their obese emperors from New York
are suave smiling assassins
who buy silk, nylon, cigars
petty tyrants and dictators.
They buy countries, people, seas, police, county councils,
distant regions where the poor hoard their corn
like misers their gold:
Standard Oil awakens them,
clothes them in uniforms, designates
which brother is the enemy.
The Paraguayan fights its war,
and the Bolivian wastes away
in the jungle with its machine gun.
A President assassinated for a drop of petroleum,
a million-acre mortgage,
a swift execution on a morning mortal with light, petrified,
a new prison camp for subversives,
in Patagonia, a betrayal, scattered shots
beneath a petroliferous moon,
a subtle change of ministers
in the capital, a whisper
like an oil tide,
and zap, you'll see
how Standard Oil's letters shine above the clouds,
above the seas, in your home,
illuminating their dominions.

When corporate-endowed foundations first made their appearance in the United States, there was a fierce debate about their provenance, legality, and lack of accountability. People suggested that if companies had so much surplus money, they should raise the wages of their workers. (People made these outrageous suggestions in those days, even in America.) The idea of these foundations, so ordinary now, was in fact a leap of the business imagination. Non-tax-paying legal entities with massive resources and an almost unlimited brief—wholly unaccountable, wholly nontransparent— what better way to parlay economic wealth into political, social, and cultural capital, to turn money into power? What better way for usurers to use a minuscule percentage of their profits to run the world? How else would Bill Gates, who admittedly knows a thing or two about computers, find himself designing education, health, and agriculture policies, not just for the US government but for governments all over the world?

Over the years, as people witnessed some of the genuinely good work the foundations did (running public libraries, eradicating diseases)—the direct connection between corporations and the foundations they endowed began to blur. Eventually, it faded altogether. Now even those who consider themselves left wing are not shy to accept their largesse.

By the 1920s US capitalism had begun to look outward for raw materials and overseas markets. Foundations began to formulate the idea of global corporate governance. In 1924 the Rockefeller and Carnegie Foundations jointly created what is today the most powerful foreign policy pressure group in the world—the CFR, which later came to be funded by the Ford Foundation as well. By 1947 the newly created CIA was supported by and working closely with the CFR. Over the years the CFR's membership has included twenty-two US secretaries of state. There were five CFR members in the 1943 steering committee that planned the United Nations, and an $8.5 million grant from J. D. Rockefeller bought the land on which the United Nations' New York headquarters stands.

All eleven of the World Bank's presidents since 1946—men

who have presented themselves as missionaries to the poor—have been members of the CFR. (The exception was George Woods. And he was a trustee of the Rockefeller Foundation and vice president of Chase Manhattan Bank.)

At Bretton Woods, the World Bank and IMF decided that the US dollar should be the reserve currency of the world and that in order to enhance the penetration of global capital, it would be necessary to universalize and standardize business practices in an open marketplace. It is toward that end that they spend a large amount of money promoting Good Governance (as long as they control the strings), the concept of the Rule of Law (provided they have a say in making the laws), and hundreds of anticorruption programs (to streamline the system they put in place). Two of the most opaque, unaccountable organizations in the world go about demanding transparency and account-ability from the governments of poorer countries.

Given that the World Bank has more or less directed the economic policies of the third world, coercing and cracking open the market of country after country for global finance, you could say that corporate philanthropy has turned out to be the most visionary business of all time.

Corporate-endowed foundations administer, trade, and channel their power and place their chessmen on the chessboard through a system of elite clubs and think tanks, whose members overlap and move in and out through the revolving doors. Contrary to the various conspiracy theories in circulation, particularly among left-wing groups, there is nothing secret, satanic, or Free-mason-like about this arrangement. It is not very different from the way corporations use shell companies and offshore accounts to transfer and administer their money—except that the currency is power, not money.

The transnational equivalent of the CFR is the Trilateral Commission, set up in 1973 by David Rockefeller, former US national security adviser Zbigniew Brzezinski (founder-member of the Afghan mujahidin, forefathers of the Taliban), the Chase Manhattan Bank, and some other private eminences. Its purpose was to create an enduring bond of friendship and cooperation between the elites of North America, Europe, and Japan. It has now become a pentalateral commission, because it includes members from China and India (Tarun Das of the CII; N. R. Narayana Murthy, ex-CEO of Infosys; Jamsheyd N. Godrej, managing director of Godrej; Jamshed J. Irani, director of Tata Sons; and Gautam Thapar, CEO of Avantha Group).

The Aspen Institute is an international club of local elites, businessmen, bureaucrats, and politicians, with franchises in several countries. Tarun Das is the president of the Aspen Institute, India. Gautam Thapar is chairman. Several senior officers of the McKinsey Global Institute (proposer of the Delhi Mumbai Industrial Corridor) are members of the CFR, the Trilateral Commission, and the Aspen Institute.

The Ford Foundation (liberal foil to the more conservative Rockefeller Foundation, though the two work together constantly) was set up in 1936. Though it is often underplayed, the Ford Foundation has a very clear, well-defined ideology and works extremely closely with the US State Department. Its project of deepening democracy and "good governance" is very much part of the Bretton Woods scheme of standardizing business practice and promoting efficiency in the free market. After World War II, when communists replaced fascists as the US government's Enemy Number One, new kinds of institutions were needed to deal with the Cold War. Ford funded RAND (Research and Development Corporation), a military think tank that began with weapons research for the US defense services. In 1952, to thwart "the persistent Communist effort to penetrate and disrupt free nations," it established the Fund for the Republic, which then morphed into the Center for the Study of Democratic Institutions, whose brief was to wage the Cold War intelligently, without McCarthyite excesses. It is through this lens that we need to view the work that the Ford Foundation is doing with the millions of dollars it has invested in

India—its funding of artists, filmmakers, and activists, its generous endowment of university courses and scholarships.

The Ford Foundation's declared "goals for the future of mankind" include interventions in grassroots political movements locally and internationally. In the United States it provided millions in grants and loans to support the credit union movement that was pioneered by the department store owner Edward Filene in 1919. Filene believed in creating a mass consumption society of consumer goods by giving workers affordable access to credit—a radical idea at the time. Actually, only half of a radical idea, because the other half of what Filene believed in was a more equitable distribution of national income. Capitalists seized on the first half of Filene's suggestion and, by disbursing "affordable" loans of tens of millions of dollars to working people, turned the US working class into people who are permanently in debt, running to catch up with their lifestyles.

Many years later, this idea has trickled down to the impoverished countryside of Bangladesh when Mohammed Yunus and the Grameen Bank brought microcredit to starving peasants with disastrous consequences. The poor of the subcontinent have always lived in debt, in the merciless grip of the local village usurer—the Bania. But microfinance has corporatized that, too. Microfinance companies in India are responsible for hundreds of suicides—two hundred people in Andhra Pradesh in 2010 alone. A national daily recently published a suicide note by an eighteen-year-old girl who was forced to hand over her last 150 rupees (three dollars), her school fees, to bullying employees of the microfinance company. The note read, "Work hard and earn money. Do not take loans."

There's a lot of money in poverty, and a few Nobel Prizes, too.

By the 1950s the Rockefeller and Ford Foundations, funding several NGOs and international educational institutions, began to work as quasi-extensions of the US government, which was at the time toppling democratically elected governments in Latin America, Iran, and Indonesia. (That was also around the time it made its entry into India, then nonaligned

637

but clearly tilting toward the Soviet Union.) The Ford Foundation established a US-style economics course at the Indonesian University. Elite Indonesian students, trained in counterinsurgency by US Army officers, played a crucial part in the 1965 CIA-backed coup in Indonesia that brought General Suharto to power. He repaid his mentors by slaughtering hundreds of thousands of communist rebels.

Twenty years later, young Chilean students, who came to be known as the Chicago Boys, were taken to the United States to be trained in neoliberal economics by Milton Friedman at the University of Chicago (endowed by J. D. Rockefeller), in preparation for the 1973 CIA-backed coup that killed Salvador Allende and brought in General Pinochet and a reign of death squads, disappearances, and terror that lasted for seventeen years. Allende's crime was being a democratically elected socialist and nationalizing Chile's mines.

In 1957 the Rockefeller Foundation established the Ramon Magsaysay Prize for community leaders in Asia. It was named after Ramon Magsaysay, president of the Philippines, a crucial ally in the US campaign against communism in Southeast Asia. In 2000 the Ford Foundation established the Ramon Magsaysay Emergent Leadership Award. The Magsaysay Award is considered a prestigious award among artists, activists, and community workers in India. M. S. Subulakshmi and Satyajit Ray won it, and so did Jaiprakash Narain and one of India's finest journalists, P. Sainath. But they did more for the Magsaysay Award than it did for them. In general, it has become a gentle arbiter of what kind of activism is "acceptable" and what is not.

Interestingly, Anna Hazare's anticorruption movement last summer was spearheaded by three Magsaysay Award winners—Anna Hazare, Arvind Kejriwal, and Kiran Bedi. One of Arvind Kejriwal's many NGOs is generously funded by the Ford Foundation. Kiran Bedi's NGO is funded by Coca-Cola and Lehman Brothers.

Though Anna Hazare calls himself a Gandhian, the law he

called for—the Jan Lokpal Bill—was un-Gandhian, elitist, and dangerous. An around-the-clock corporate media campaign proclaimed him to be the voice of "the people." Unlike the Occupy Wall Street movement in the United States, the Hazare movement didn't breathe a word against privatization, corporate power, or economic "reforms." On the contrary, its principal media backers successfully turned the spotlight away from massive corporate corruption scandals (which had exposed high-profile journalists, too) and used the public mauling of politicians to call for the further withdrawal of discretionary powers from government, for more reforms, more privatization. The World Bank issued a 2007 assessment from Washington saying the movement would "dovetail" with its "good governance" strategy. (In 2008 Anna Hazare received a World Bank Award for Outstanding Public Service.)

Like all good imperialists, the Philanthropoids set themselves the task of creating and training an international cadre that believed that capitalism, and by extension the hegemony of the United States, was in their own self-interest. And who would therefore help to administer the Global Corporate Government in the ways native elites had always served colonialism. So began the foundations' foray into education and the arts, which would become their third sphere of influence, after foreign and domestic economic policy. They spent (and continue to spend) millions of dollars on academic institutions and pedagogy.

Joan Roelofs, in her wonderful book *Foundations and Public Policy: The Mask of Pluralism*, describes how foundations remodeled the old ideas of how to teach political science and fashioned the disciplines of "international" and "area" studies. This provided the US Intelligence and Security Services a pool of expertise in foreign languages and culture to recruit from. The CIA and US State Department continue to work with students and professors in US universities, raising serious questions about the ethics of scholarship.

The gathering of information to control people is fundamental to any ruling power. As resistance to land acquisition and the new economic policies spreads across India, in the shadow of outright war in Central India, as a containment technique, India's government has embarked on a massive biometrics program, perhaps one of the most ambitious and expensive information gathering projects in the world—the Unique Identification Number (UID). People don't have clean drinking water, or toilets, or food, or money, but they will have election cards and UID numbers. Is it a coincidence that the UID project run by Nandan Nilekani, former CEO of Infosys, ostensibly meant to "deliver services to the poor," will inject massive amounts of money into a slightly beleaguered IT industry? To digitize a country with such a large population of the illegitimate and "illegible"—people who are for the most part slum dwellers, hawkers, Adivasis without land records—will criminalize them, turning them from illegitimate to illegal. The idea is to pull off a digital version of the Enclosure of the Commons and put huge powers into the hands of an increasingly hardening police state. Nilekani's technocratic obsession with gathering data is consistent with Bill Gates's obsession with digital databases, numerical targets, and "scorecards of progress," as though a lack of information is the cause of world hunger, and not colonialism, debt, and skewed profit-oriented corporate policy.

Corporate-endowed foundations are the biggest funders of the social sciences and the arts, endowing courses and student scholarships in development studies, community studies, cultural studies, behavioral sciences, and human rights. As US universities opened their doors to international students, hundreds of thousands of students, children of the third world elite, poured in. Those who could not afford the fees were given scholarships. Today in countries like India and Pakistan, there is scarcely a family among the upper middle classes that does not have a child who has studied in the United States. From their ranks have come good scholars and academics but also the prime ministers, finance ministers, economists, corporate law-

yers, bankers, and bureaucrats who helped to open up the economies of their countries to global corporations.

Scholars of the foundations-friendly version of economics
and political science were rewarded with fellowships, research
funds, grants, endowments, and jobs. Those with foundation-
unfriendly views found themselves unfunded, marginalized,
and ghettoized, their courses discontinued. Gradually, one
particular imagination—a brittle, superficial pretense of tolerance and multiculturalism (that morphs into racism, rabid nationalism, ethnic chauvinism, or warmongering Islamophobia
at a moment's notice) under the roof of a single overarching,
very unplural economic ideology—began to dominate the discourse. It did so to such an extent that it ceased to be perceived
as an ideology at all. It became the default position, the natural
way to be. It infiltrated normality and colonized ordinariness,
and challenging it began to seem as absurd or as esoteric as
challenging reality itself. From here it was a quick, easy step to
"There Is No Alternative."

It is only now, thanks to the Occupy movement, that another
language has appeared on US streets and campuses. To see students with banners that say "Class War" or "We don't mind you
being rich, but we mind you buying our government" is, given
the odds, almost a revolution in itself.

One century after it began, corporate philanthropy is as
much a part of our lives as Coca-Cola. There are now millions
of nonprofit organizations, many of them connected through
a byzantine financial maze to the larger foundations. Between
them, this "independent" sector has assets worth nearly $450
billion. The largest of them is the Gates Foundation with $21
billion, followed by the Lilly Endowment ($16 billion) and the
Ford Foundation ($15 billion).

As the IMF enforced structural adjustment and arm-twisted
governments into cutting back on public spending on health,
education, child care, and development, the NGOs moved in.
The Privatization of Everything has also meant the NGO-

ization of Everything. As jobs and livelihoods disappeared, NGOs have become an important source of employment, even for those who see them for what they are. And they are certainly not all bad. Of the millions of NGOs, some do remarkable, radical work, and it would be a travesty to tar all NGOs with the same brush. However, the corporate or foundation-endowed NGOs are global finance's way of buying into resistance movements, literally as shareholders buy shares in companies and then try to control them from within. They sit like nodes on the central nervous system, the pathways along which global finance flows. They work like transmitters, receivers, shock absorbers, alert to every impulse, careful never to annoy the governments of their host countries. (The Ford Foundation requires the organizations it funds to sign a pledge to this effect.) Inadvertently (and sometimes advertently), they serve as listening posts, their reports and workshops and other missionary activity feeding data into an increasingly aggressive system of surveillance of increasingly hardening states. The more troubled an area, the greater the numbers of NGOs in it.

Mischievously, when India's government or sections of its corporate press want to run a smear campaign against a genuine people's movement, like the Narmada Bachao Andolan, or the protest against the Koodankulam nuclear reactor, they accuse these movements of being NGOs receiving "foreign funding." They know very well that the mandate of most NGOs, in particular the well-funded ones, is to further the project of corporate globalization, not thwart it.

Armed with their billions, these NGOs have waded into the world, turning potential revolutionaries into salaried activists, funding artists, intellectuals, and filmmakers, gently luring them away from radical confrontation, ushering them in the direction of multiculturalism, gender equity, community development— the discourse couched in the language of identity politics and human rights.

The transformation of the idea of justice into the industry of human rights has been a conceptual coup in which NGOs and foundations have played a crucial part. The narrow focus of human rights enables an atrocity-based analysis in which the larger picture can be blocked out and both parties in a conflict—say for example the Maoists and the Indian government, or the Israeli Army and Hamas—can both be admonished as Human Rights Violators. The land grab by mining corporations and the history of the annexation of Palestinian land by the state of Israel then become footnotes with very little bearing on the discourse. This is not to suggest that human rights don't matter. They do, but they are not a good enough prism through which to view or remotely understand the great injustices in the world we live in.

Another conceptual coup has to do with foundations' involvement with the feminist movement. Why do most "official" feminists and women's organizations in India keep a safe distance between themselves and organizations like, say, the ninety-thousand-member Krantikari Adivasi Mahila Sangathan (Revolutionary Adivasi Women's Association) that is fighting patriarchy in its own communities and displacement by mining corporations in the Dandakaranya forest? Why is it that the dispossession and eviction of millions of women from land that they owned and worked is not seen as a feminist problem?

The hiving off of the liberal feminist movement from grassroots anti-imperialist and anticapitalist people's movements did not begin with the evil designs of foundations. It began with those movements' inability to adapt and accommodate the rapid radicalization of women that took place in the 1960s and 1970s. The foundations showed genius in recognizing and moving in to support and fund women's growing impatience with the violence and patriarchy in their traditional societies as well as among even the supposedly progressive leaders of left movements. In a country like India, the schism also ran along the rural–urban divide. Most radical, anticapitalist movements were located in the countryside, where patriarchy continued to rule the lives of women. Urban women activists who joined these movements (like the Naxalite movement) had been influenced and inspired by the Western feminist movement, and their own journeys toward liberation were often at odds with what their male leaders considered to be their duty: to fit in with "the masses." Many women activists were not willing to wait any longer for the "revolution" in order to end the daily oppression and discrimination in their lives, including from their own comrades. They wanted gender equality to be an absolute, urgent, and nonnegotiable part of the revolutionary process and not just a postrevolution promise. Intelligent, angry, and disillusioned women began to move away and look for other means of support and sustenance. As a result, by the late 1980s, around the time when the Indian markets were opened up, the liberal feminist movement in India had become inordinately NGO-ized. Many of these NGOs have done seminal work on queer rights, domestic violence, AIDS, and the rights of sex workers. But significantly, the liberal feminist movement has not been at the forefront of challenging the New Economic Policies, even though women have been the greatest sufferers. By manipulating the disbursement of the funds, the foundations have largely succeeded in circumscribing the range of what "political" activity should be. The funding briefs of NGOs now prescribe what counts as women's "issues" and what doesn't.

The NGO-ization of the women's movement has also made Western liberal feminism (by virtue of its being the most funded brand) the standard-bearer of what constitutes feminism. The battles, as usual, have been played out on women's bodies, extruding Botox at one end and burkas at the other. (And then there are those who suffer the double whammy, Botox and the burka.) When, as happened recently in France, an attempt is made to coerce women out of the burka rather than creating a situation in which a woman can choose what she wishes to do, it's not about liberating her but about unclothing her. It becomes an act of humiliation and cultural imperialism. Coercing a woman out of her burka is as bad as coercing her into one. It's not about the burka. It's about the coercion. Viewing gender in this way, shorn of social, political, and economic context, makes it an issue of identity, a battle of props and costumes. It's what allowed the US government to use Western feminist liberal groups as moral cover when it invaded Afghanistan in 2001. Afghan women were (and are) in terrible trouble under the Taliban. But dropping daisy cutters on them was not going to solve the problem.

In the NGO universe, which has evolved a strange anodyne language of its own, everything has become a "subject," a separate, professionalized, special interest issue. Community development, leadership development, human rights, health, education, reproductive rights, AIDS, orphans with AIDS—have all been hermetically sealed into their own silos, each with its own elaborate and precise funding brief. Funding has fragmented solidarity in ways that repression never could.

Poverty, too, like feminism, is often framed as an identity problem. As though the poor had not been created by injustice but are a lost tribe who just happen to exist and can be rescued in the short term by a system of grievance redressal (administered by NGOs on an individual, person-to-person basis), and whose long-term resurrection will come from Good Governance. Under the regime of Global Corporate Capitalism, it goes without saying.

Indian poverty, after a brief period in the wilderness while India "shone," has made a comeback as an exotic identity in the arts, led from the front by films like *Slumdog Millionaire*. These stories about the poor, their amazing spirit and resilience, have no villains—except the small ones who provide narrative tension and local color. The authors of these works are the contemporary world's equivalent of the early anthropologists, lauded and honored for working "on the ground," for their brave journeys into the unknown. You rarely see the rich being examined in these ways.

Having worked out how to manage governments, political parties, elections, courts, the media, and liberal opinion, the neoliberal establishment faced one more challenge: how to deal with growing unrest, the threat of "people's power." How do you domesticate it? How do you turn protesters into pets? How do you vacuum up people's fury and redirect it into blind alleys?

Here too, foundations and their allied organizations have a long and illustrious history. A revealing example is their role in defusing and deradicalizing the Black civil rights movement in the United States in the 1960s and the successful transformation of Black Power into Black Capitalism.

The Rockefeller Foundation, in keeping with J. D. Rockefeller's ideals, had worked closely with Martin Luther King Sr. (father of Martin Luther King Jr.). But his influence waned with the rise of the more militant organizations—the Student NonViolent Coordinating Committee and the Black Panthers. The Ford and Rockefeller Foundations moved in. In 1970 they donated $15 million to "moderate" Black organizations, giving people, grants, fellowships, scholarships, job-training programs for dropouts, and seed money for Black-owned businesses. Repression, infighting, and the honey trap of funding led to the gradual atrophying of the radical Black organizations.

Martin Luther King Jr. made the forbidden connections between capitalism, imperialism, racism, and the Vietnam War. As a result, after he was assassinated even his memory became toxic, a threat to public order. Foundations and corporations worked hard to remodel his legacy to fit a market-friendly format. The Martin Luther King Jr. Center for Nonviolent Social Change, with an operational grant of $2 million, was set up by (among others) the Ford Motor Company, General Motors, Mobil, Western Electric, Proctor and Gamble, US Steel, and Monsanto. The center maintains the King Library and Archives of the Civil Rights Movement. Among the many programs the King Center runs have been projects that "work closely with the United States Department of Defense, the Armed Forces

Chaplains Board and others." It cosponsored the Martin Luther King Jr. Lecture Series called "The Free Enterprise System: An Agent for Nonviolent Social Change."

Amen.

A similar coup was carried out in the antiapartheid struggle in South Africa. In 1978 the Rockefeller Foundation organized a Study Commission on US Policy toward Southern Africa. The report warned of the growing influence of the Soviet Union on the African National Congress (ANC) and said that US strategic and corporate interests (that is, access to South Africa's minerals) would be best served if there were genuine sharing of political power by all races.

The foundations began to support the ANC. The ANC soon turned on the more radical organizations like Steve Biko's Black Consciousness movement and more or less eliminated it. When Nelson Mandela took over as South Africa's first Black president, he was canonized as a living saint, not just because he is a freedom fighter who spent twenty-seven years in prison but also because he deferred completely to the Washington Consensus. Socialism disappeared from the ANC's agenda. South Africa's great "peaceful transition," so praised and lauded, meant no land reforms, no demands for reparation, no nationalization of South Africa's mines. Instead there was privatization and structural adjustment. Mandela gave South Africa's highest civilian award—the Order of Good Hope—to his old friend and supporter General Suharto, the killer of communists in Indonesia. Today in South Africa, a clutch of Mercedes-driving former radicals and trade unionists rule the country. But that is more than enough to perpetuate the myth of Black liberation.

The rise of Black Power in the United States was an inspirational moment for the rise of a radical, progressive Dalit movement in India, with organizations like the Dalit Panthers mirroring the militant politics of the Black Panthers. But Dalit Power, too, in not exactly the same but similar ways, has been fractured and defused and, with plenty of help from right-wing

Hindu organizations and the Ford Foundation, is well on its way to transforming into Dalit capitalism.

"Dalit Inc ready to show business can beat caste," the *Indian Express* reported in December last year. It went on to quote a mentor of the Dalit Indian Chamber of Commerce and Industry: "Getting the prime minister for a Dalit gathering is not difficult in our society. But for Dalit entrepreneurs, taking a photograph with Tata and Godrej over lunch and tea is an aspiration—and proof that they have arrived," he said. Given the situation in modern India, it would be casteist and reactionary to say that Dalit entrepreneurs oughtn't to have a place at the high table. But if this were to be the aspiration, the ideological framework of Dalit politics, it would be a great pity. And unlikely to help the one million Dalits who still earn a living off manual scavenging—carrying human shit on their heads.

Young Dalit scholars who accept grants from the Ford Foundation cannot be too harshly judged. Who else is offering them an opportunity to climb out of the cesspit of the Indian caste system? The shame as well as a large part of the blame for this turn of events also goes to India's communist movement, whose leaders continue to be predominantly upper caste. For years it has tried to force-fit the idea of caste into Marxist class analysis. It has failed miserably, in theory as well as practice. The rift between the Dalit community and the left began with a falling out between the visionary Dalit leader Bhimrao Ambedkar and S. A. Dange, trade unionist and founding member of the Communist Party of India. Dr. Ambedkar's disillusionment with the Communist Party began with the textile workers' strike in Mumbai in 1928, when he realized that despite all the rhetoric about working-class solidarity, the party did not find it objectionable that the "untouchables" were kept out of the weaving department (and qualified only for the lower-paid spinning department) because the work involved the use of saliva on the threads, which other castes considered "polluting."

Ambedkar realized that in a society where the Hindu scriptures institutionalize untouchability and inequality, the battle for "untouchables," for social and civic rights, was too urgent to wait for the promised communist revolution. The rift between the Ambedkarites and the left has come at a great cost to both. It has meant that a great majority of the Dalit population, the backbone of the Indian working class, has pinned its hopes for deliverance and dignity on constitutionalism, capitalism, and political parties like the Bahujan Samaj Party, which practices an important, but in the long run stagnant, brand of identity politics.

In the United States, as we have seen, corporate-endowed foundations spawned the culture of NGOs. In India, targeted corporate philanthropy began in earnest in the 1990s, the era of the New Economic Policies. Membership in the Star Chamber doesn't come cheap. The Tata Group donated $50 million to that needy institution, the Harvard Business School, and another $50 million to Cornell University. Nandan Nilekani of Infosys and his wife Rohini donated $5 million as a startup endowment for the India Initiative at Yale. The Harvard Humanities Center is now the Mahindra Humanities Center, after it received its largest-ever donation of $10 million from Anand Mahindra of the Mahindra Group.

At home, the Jindal Group, with a major stake in mining, metals, and power, runs the Jindal Global Law School and will soon open the Jindal School of Government and Public Policy. (The Ford Foundation runs a law school in the Congo.) The New India Foundation, funded by Nandan Nilekani, financed by profits from Infosys, gives prizes and fellowships to social scientists. The Sitaram Jindal Foundation, endowed by the chairman and managing director of Jindal Aluminum Ltd., has announced five annual cash prizes of ten million rupees ($195,000) each, to be given to those working in rural development, poverty alleviation, education and moral uplift, environment, and peace and social harmony. The Observer Research Foundation (ORF), currently endowed by Mukesh Ambani, is cast in the mold of the

Rockefeller Foundation. It has retired intelligence agents, strategic analysts, politicians (who pretend to rail against each other in Parliament), journalists, and policy makers as its research "fellows" and advisers.

ORF's objectives seem straightforward enough: "to help develop a consensus in favor of economic reforms." And to shape and influence public opinion, creating "viable, alternative policy options in areas as divergent as employment generation in backward districts and real-time strategies to counter Nuclear, Biological and Chemical threats."

I was initially puzzled by the preoccupation with "Nuclear, Biological and Chemical threats" in ORF's stated objectives. But less so when, in the long list of its "institutional partners," I found the names of Raytheon and Lockheed Martin, two of the world's leading weapons manufacturers. In 2007 Raytheon announced it was turning its attention to India. Could it be that at least part of India's $32 billion annual defense budget will be spent on weapons, guided missiles, aircraft, warships, and surveillance equipment made by Raytheon and Lockheed Martin?

Do we need weapons to fight wars? Or do we need wars to create a market for weapons? After all, the economies of Europe, the United States, and Israel depend hugely on their weapons industry. It's the one thing they haven't outsourced to China.

In the new Cold War between the United States and China, India is being groomed to play the role Pakistan played as a US ally in the Cold War with Russia. (And look what happened to Pakistan.) Many of those columnists and "strategic analysts" who are playing up the hostilities between India and China, you'll see, can be traced back directly or indirectly to the Indo-American think tanks and foundations. Being a "strategic partner" of the United States does not mean that the heads of state make friendly phone calls to each other every now and then. It means collaboration (interference) at every level. It means hosting US Special Forces on Indian soil. (A Pentagon commander recently confirmed this to the BBC.)

It means sharing intelligence, altering agriculture and energy policies, opening up the health and education sectors to global investment. It means opening up retail. It means an unequal partnership in which India is being held close in a bear hug and waltzed around the floor by a partner who will incinerate her the moment she refuses to dance.

In the list of ORF's "institutional partners," you will also find the RAND Corporation, the Ford Foundation, the World Bank, the Brookings Institution (whose stated mission is to "provide innovative and practical recommendations that advance three broad goals: strengthen American democracy; foster the economic and social welfare, security and opportunity of all Americans; and secure a more open, safe, prosperous, and cooperative international system"). You will also find the Rosa Luxemburg Foundation of Germany. (Poor Rosa, who died for the cause of communism, to find her name on a list such as this one!)

Though capitalism is meant to be based on competition, those at the top of the food chain have also shown themselves to be capable of inclusiveness and solidarity. The great Western capitalists have done business with fascists, socialists, despots, and military dictators. They can adapt and constantly innovate. They are capable of quick thinking and immense tactical cunning.

But despite having successfully powered through economic reforms, despite having waged wars and militarily occupied countries in order to put in place free market "democracies," capitalism is going through a crisis whose gravity has not revealed itself completely yet. Marx said, "What the bourgeoisie therefore produces, above all, are its own grave-diggers. Its fall and the victory of the proletariat are equally inevitable."

The proletariat, as Marx saw it, has been under continuous assault. Factories have shut down, jobs have disappeared, trade unions have been disbanded. Over the years, those making up the proletariat have been pitted against each other in every possible way. In India it has been Hindu against Muslim, Hindu against Christian, Dalit against Adivasi, caste against caste, region against region. And yet all over the world they are fighting back. In China there are countless strikes and uprisings. In India the poorest people in the world have fought back to stop some of the richest corporations in their tracks.

Capitalism is in crisis. Trickledown failed. Now Gush Up is in trouble too. The international financial meltdown is closing in. India's growth rate has plummeted to 6.9 percent. Foreign investment is pulling out. Major international corporations are sitting on huge piles of money, not sure where to invest it, not sure how the financial crisis will play out. This is a major, structural crack in the juggernaut of global capital.

Capitalism's real "gravediggers" may end up being its own delusional cardinals, who have turned ideology into faith. Despite their strategic brilliance, they seem to have trouble grasping a simple fact: Capitalism is destroying the planet. The two old tricks that dug it out of past crises—War and Shopping—simply will not work.

I stood outside Antilla for a long time watching the sun go down. I imagined that the tower was as deep as it was high. That it had a twenty-seven-story-long tap root, snaking around below the ground, hungrily sucking sustenance out of the earth, turning it into smoke and gold.

Why did the Ambanis choose to call their building Antilla?

Antilla is the name of a set of mythical islands whose story dates back to an eighth-century Iberian legend. When the Muslims conquered Hispania, six Christian Visigothic bishops and their parishioners boarded ships and fled. After days, or maybe weeks, at sea, they arrived at the isles of Antilla, where they decided to settle and raise a new civilization. They burned their boats to permanently sever their links to their barbarian-dominated homeland.

By calling their tower Antilla, do the Ambanis hope to sever their links to the poverty and squalor of their homeland and raise a new civilization? Is this the final act of the most successful secessionist movement in India: the secession of the middle and upper classes into outer space?

As night fell over Mumbai, guards in crisp linen shirts with crackling walkie-talkies appeared outside the forbidding gates of Antilla. The lights blazed on, to scare away the ghosts perhaps. The neighbors complain that Antilla's bright lights have stolen the night.

Perhaps it's time for us to take back the night.

A PERFECT DAY
FOR DEMOCRACY

WASN'T IT? YESTERDAY, I mean. Spring announced itself in Delhi. The sun was out, and the law took its course. Just before breakfast, Afzal Guru, prime accused in the 2001 Parliament attack, was secretly hanged, and his body was interred in Tihar Jail. Was he buried next to Maqbool Butt? (The other Kashmiri who was hanged in Tihar in 1984. Kashmiris will mark that anniversary tomorrow.) Afzal's wife and son were not informed. "The Authorities intimated the family through Speed Post and Registered Post," the home secretary told the press; "the Director General of J&K Police has been told to check whether they got it or not." No big deal, they're only the family of a Kashmiri terrorist.

In a moment of rare unity the Nation, or at least its major political parties, the Congress, the Bharatiya Janata Party, and the CPI(M), came together as one (barring a few squabbles about "delay" and "timing") to celebrate the triumph of the Rule of Law. The Conscience of the Nation, which broadcasts

First published in the *Hindu*, February 10, 2013.

live from TV studios these days, unleashed its collective intellect on us—the usual cocktail of papal passion and a delicate grip on facts. Like cowards that hunt in packs, they seemed to need each other to keep their courage up, even though the man was dead and gone. Perhaps because deep inside themselves they know that they all colluded to do something terribly wrong.

What are the facts?

On December 13, 2001, five armed men drove through the gates of the Parliament House in a white Ambassador fitted out with an improvised explosive device. When they were challenged they jumped out of the car and opened fire. They killed eight security personnel and a gardener. In the gun battle that followed, all five attackers were killed. In one of the many versions of confessions Afzal Guru made in police custody, he identified the men as Mohammed, Rana, Raja, Hamza, and Haider. That's all we know about them even today. L. K. Advani, the then home minister, said they "looked like Pakistanis." (He should know what Pakistanis look like, right? Being a Sindhi himself.) Based only on Afzal's confession (which the Supreme Court subsequently set aside, citing "lapses" and "violations of procedural safeguards"), the government of India recalled its ambassador from Pakistan and mobilized half a million soldiers to the Pakistan border. There was talk of nuclear war. Foreign embassies issued travel advisories and evacuated their staff from Delhi. The standoff lasted for months and cost India thousands of crores of rupees (hundreds of millions of dollars).

On December 14, 2001, the Delhi Police Special Cell claimed it had cracked the case. On December 15 it arrested the "mastermind," Professor S. A. R. Geelani, in Delhi, and Showkat Guru and Afzal Guru in a fruit market in Srinagar. Subsequently, they arrested Afsan Guru, Showkat's wife. The media enthusiastically disseminated the Special Cell's version. These were some of the headlines: "DU Lecturer Was Terror Plan Hub," "Varsity Don Guided Fidayeen," "Don Lectured on Terror in Free Time." Zee TV broadcast a "docudrama" called *December 13th*, a re-creation that claimed to be the "Truth Based on the Police Charge Sheet." (If the police version is the truth, then why have courts?) Then Prime Minister Vajpayee and L. K. Advani publicly appreciated the film. The Supreme Court refused to stay the screening, saying that the media would not influence judges. The film was broadcast only a few days before the fast-track court sentenced Afzal, Showkat, and Geelani to death. Subsequently the high court acquitted the "mastermind," Geelani, and Afsan Guru. The Supreme Court upheld the acquittal. But in its August 5, 2005, judgment it gave Mohammad Afzal three life sentences and a double death sentence.

Contrary to the lies that have been put about by some senior journalists who would have known better, Afzal Guru was not one of "the terrorists who stormed Parliament House on December 13th 2001," nor was he among those who "opened fire on security personnel, apparently killing three of the six who died." (That was the Bharatiya Janata Party member in the Rajya Sabha, Chandan Mitra, in the *Pioneer*, October 7, 2006.) Even the police charge sheet does not accuse him of that. The Supreme Court judgment says the evidence is circumstantial: "As is the case with most conspiracies, there is and could be no direct evidence amounting to criminal conspiracy." But then it goes on to say: "The incident, which resulted in heavy casualties had shaken the entire nation, and the collective conscience of society will only be satisfied if capital punishment is awarded to the offender."

Who crafted our collective conscience on the Parliament attack case? Could it have been the facts we gleaned in the papers? The films we saw on TV?

There are those who will argue that the very fact that the courts acquitted S. A. R. Geelani and convicted Afzal proves that the trial was free and fair. Was it?

The trial in the fast-track court began in May 2002. The world was still convulsed by post-9/11 frenzy. The US government was gloating prematurely over its "victory" in Afghanistan. The Gujarat pogrom was ongoing. And in the Parliament attack case, the Law was indeed taking its own course. At the most crucial stage of a criminal case, when evidence is presented, when witnesses are cross-examined, when the foundations of the argument are laid—in the high court and Supreme Court you can only argue points of law, you cannot introduce new evidence—Afzal Guru, locked in a high-security solitary cell, had no lawyer. The court-appointed junior lawyer did not visit his client even once in jail; he did not summon any witnesses in Afzal's defense and did not cross-examine the prosecution witnesses. The judge expressed his inability to do anything about the situation.

Even still, from the word go, the case fell apart. A few examples out of many:

How did the police get to Afzal? They said that S. A. R. Geelani led them to him. But the court records show that the message to arrest Afzal went out before they picked up Geelani. The high court called this a "material contradiction" but left it at that.

The two most incriminating pieces of evidence against Afzal were a cell phone and a laptop confiscated at the time of arrest. The arrest memos were signed by Bismillah, Geelani's brother, in Delhi. The seizure memos were signed by two men of the Jammu and Kashmir Police, one of them an old tormentor from Afzal's past as a surrendered "militant." The computer and cell phone were not sealed, as evidence is required to be. During the trial it emerged that the hard disk of the laptop had been accessed after the arrest. It contained only the fake home ministry passes and the fake identity cards that the "terrorists" used to access Parliament. And a Zee TV video clip of Parliament House. So according to the police, Afzal had deleted all the information except the most incriminating bits, and he was speeding off to hand it over to Ghazi Baba, whom the charge sheet described as the chief of operations.

A witness for the prosecution, Kamal Kishore, identified Afzal and told the court he had sold him the crucial SIM card that connected all the accused in the case to each other on December

4, 2001. But the prosecution's own call records showed that the SIM was actually operational from November 6, 2001.

It goes on and on, this pile-up of lies and fabricated evidence. The courts note them, but for their pains the police get no more than a gentle rap on their knuckles. Nothing more.

Then there's the backstory. Like most surrendered militants, Afzal was easy meat in Kashmir—a victim of torture, blackmail, extortion. In the larger scheme of things, he was a nobody. Anyone who was really interested in solving the mystery of the Parliament attack would have followed the dense trail of evidence that was on offer. No one did, thereby ensuring that the real authors of conspiracy will remain unidentified and uninvestigated.

Now that Afzal Guru has been hanged, I hope our collective conscience has been satisfied. Or is our cup of blood still only half full?

"*Gandhian satyagraha, for example, is a kind of political theater. In order for it to be effective, it needs a sympathetic audience, which villagers deep in the forest do not have. When a posse of eight hundred policemen lay a cordon around a forest village at night and begin to burn houses and shoot people, will a hunger strike help? (Can starving people go on a hunger strike? And do hunger strikes work when they are not on TV?)*"

THE CONSEQUENCES OF
HANGING AFZAL GURU

WHAT ARE THE political consequences of the secret and sudden hanging of Mohammad Afzal Guru, prime accused in the 2001 Parliament attack, going to be? Does anybody know?

The memo, in callous bureaucratese, with every name insultingly misspelled, sent by the superintendent of Central Jail Number 3, Tihar, New Delhi, to "Mrs. Tabassum w/o Sh Afjal Guru," reads:

> *The mercy petition of Sh Mohd Afjal Guru s/o Habibillah has been rejected by Hon'ble President of India. Hence the execution of Mohd Afjal Guru s/o Habibillah has been fixed for 09/02/2013 at 8 AM in Central Jail No-3.*
>
> *This is for your information and for further necessary action.*

The memo arrived after the execution had already taken place, denying Tabassum one last legal chance—the right to

---

First published as "Does Your Bomb-Proof Basement Have an Attached Toilet?" in *Outlook*, February 25, 2013.

challenge the rejection of the mercy petition. Both Afzal and his family, separately, had that right. Both were thwarted. Even though it is mandatory in law, the memo to Tabassum provided no reason for the president's rejection of the mercy petition. If no reason is given, on what basis do you appeal? All the other prisoners on death row in India have been given that last chance.

Since Tabassum was not allowed to meet with her husband before he was hanged, since her son was not allowed to get a few last words of advice from his father, since she was not given his body to bury, and since there can be no funeral, what "further necessary action" does the Jail Manual prescribe? Anger? Wild, irreparable grief? Unquestioning acceptance? Complete integration?

After the hanging, there were unseemly celebrations on the streets. The bereaved wives of the people who were killed in the attack were displayed on TV, with chairman of the All-India Anti-Terrorist Front M. S. Bitta and his ferocious mustaches playing the CEO of their sad little company. Will anybody tell them that the men who shot their husbands were killed at the same time, in the same place, right there and then? And that those who planned the attack will never be brought to justice because we still don't know who they are?

Meanwhile Kashmir is under curfew, once again. Its people have been locked down like cattle in a pen, once again. They have defied the curfew, once again. Three people have already been killed in three days, and fifteen more grievously injured. Newspapers have been shut down, but anybody who trawls the Internet will see that this time the rage of young Kashmiris is not defiant and exuberant as it was during the mass uprisings in the summers of 2008, 2009, and 2010—even though 180 people lost their lives on those occasions. This time the anger is cold and corrosive. Unforgiving. Is there any reason why it shouldn't be?

For more than twenty years, Kashmiris have endured a military occupation. The tens of thousands who lost their lives were killed in prisons, in torture centers, and in "encounters," genuine as well as fake. What sets the execution of Afzal Guru apart is that it has given the young, who have never had any firsthand experience of democracy, a ringside seat to watch the full majesty of Indian democracy at work. They have watched the wheels turning, they have seen all its hoary institutions, the government, police, courts, political parties, and yes, the media, collude to hang a man, a Kashmiri, whom they do not believe to have received a fair trial, and whose guilt was by no means established beyond reasonable doubt. (He went virtually unrepresented in the lower court during the most crucial stage of the trial. Not only did the state-appointed counsel never visit his client in prison, he actually admitted incriminating evidence against him. The Supreme Court deliberated on that matter and decided it was okay.) They have watched the government pull him out of the death row queue and execute him out of turn. What direction, what form will their new cold, corrosive anger take? Will it lead them to the blessed liberation they so yearn for and have sacrificed a whole generation for, or will it lead to yet another cycle of cataclysmic violence, of being beaten down and then having "normalcy" imposed on them under soldiers' boots?

All of us who live in the region know that 2014 is going to be a watershed year. There will be elections in Pakistan, in India, and in the state of Jammu and Kashmir. We know that when the United States withdraws its troops from Afghanistan, the chaos from an already seriously destabilized Pakistan will spill into Kashmir, as it has done before. By executing Afzal Guru in the way that it did, the government of India has taken a decision to fuel that process of destabilization, to actually invite it in. (As it did before, by rigging the 1987 elections in Kashmir.) After three consecutive years of mass protests in the valley ended in 2010, the government invested a great deal in restoring its version of "normalcy" (happy tourists, voting Kashmiris). The question is, why was it willing to reverse all its own efforts? Leaving aside issues of the legality, the morality, and the venality of executing Afzal Guru in the way that it did, and looking at it just politically, tactically, it is a dangerous and irresponsible thing to have done. But it was done. Clearly and knowingly. Why?

I used the word "irresponsible" advisedly. Look what happened the last time around.

In 2001, within a week of the Parliament attack (and a few days after Afzal Guru's arrest), the government recalled its ambassador from Pakistan and dispatched half a million troops to the border. On what basis was that done? The only thing the public was told is that while Afzal Guru was in the custody of the Delhi Police Special Cell, he had admitted to being a member of the Pakistan-based militant group Jaish-e-Mohammed. The Supreme Court set aside that "confession" extracted in police custody as inadmissible in law. Does a document that is inadmissible in law become admissible in war?

In its final judgment on the case, apart from the now famous statements about "satisfying collective conscience" and having no direct evidence, the Supreme Court also said there was "no evidence that Mohammad Afzal belonged to any terrorist group or organization." So what justified that military aggression, that loss of soldiers' lives, that massive hemorrhaging of public money, and the real risk of nuclear war? (Remember how foreign embassies issued travel advisories and evacuated their staff?) Was there some intelligence that preceded the Parliament attack and the arrest of Afzal Guru that we had not been told about? If so, how could the attack have been allowed to happen? And if the intelligence was accurate enough to justify such dangerous military posturing, don't people in India, Pakistan, and Kashmir have the right to know what it was? Why was that evidence not produced in court to establish Afzal Guru's guilt?

In the endless debates around the Parliament attack case, on this, perhaps the most crucial issue of all, there has been dead silence from all quarters—leftists, rightists, Hindutva-ists, secularists, nationalists, seditionists, cynics, critics. Why?

Maybe Jaish-e-Mohammed did mastermind the attack. Praveen Swami, perhaps the Indian media's best-known expert on "terrorism," who seems to have enviable sources in the Indian police and intelligence agencies, has recently cited the 2003 testimony of former Inter-Services Intelligence Chief Lieutenant General Javed Ashraf Qazi and the 2004 book by Muhammad Amir Rana, a Pakistani scholar, holding the Jaish-e-Mohammed responsible for the Parliament attack. (This belief in the veracity of the testimony of the chief of an organization whose mandate it is to destabilize India is touching.) It still doesn't explain what evidence there was in 2001, when the army mobilization took place.

For the sake of argument, let's accept that Jaish-e-Mohammed carried out the attack. Maybe the Inter-Services Intelligence was involved, too. We needn't pretend that the government of Pakistan is innocent of carrying out covert activity over Kashmir. (Just as the government of India does in Balochistan and parts of Pakistan. Remember the Indian Army trained the Mukti Bahini in East Pakistan in the 1970s. It trained six different Sri Lankan Tamil militant groups, including the Liberation Tigers of Tamil Eelam, in the 1980s.)

It's a filthy scenario all around.

What would a war with Pakistan have achieved then, and what will it achieve now? (Apart from a massive loss of life. And fattening the bank accounts of some arms dealers.) Indian hawks routinely suggest the only way to "root out the problem" is "hot pursuit" and the "taking out" of "terrorist camps" in Pakistan. Really? It would be interesting to research how many of the aggressive strategic experts and defense analysts on our TV screens have an interest in the defense and weapons industry. They don't even need war. They just need a warlike climate in which military spending remains on an upward graph. This idea of hot pursuit is even stupider and more pathetic than it sounds. What would they bomb? A few individuals? Their barracks and food supplies? Or their ideology? Look how the US government's "hot pursuit" has ended in Afghanistan. And look how a "security grid" of half a million soldiers has not been able to subdue the unarmed civilian population of Kashmir. And India is going to cross international borders to bomb a country—with nuclear arms—that is rapidly devolving into chaos? India's professional warmongers derive a great deal of satisfaction from sneering at what they see as the disintegration of Pakistan. Anyone with a rudimentary working knowledge of history and geography would know that the breakdown of Pakistan (into a gangland of crazed, nihilistic religious zealots) is absolutely no reason for anyone to rejoice.

The US presence in Afghanistan and Iraq, and Pakistan's official role as America's junior partner in the war on terror, makes that region a much-reported place. The rest of the world is at least aware of the dangers unfolding there. Less understood, and harder to read, is the perilous wind that's picking up speed in the world's favorite new superpower. The Indian economy is in considerable trouble. The aggressive, acquisitive ambition that economic liberalization unleashed in the newly created middle class is quickly turning into an equally aggressive frustration. The aircraft they were sitting in has begun to stall just after takeoff. Exhilaration is turning to panic.

The general election is due in 2014. Even without an exit poll, I can tell you what the results will be. Though it may not be obvious to the naked eye, once again we will have a Congress–Bharatiya Janata Party coalition. (Two parties, each with a mass murder of thousands of people belonging to minority communities under their belts.) The Communist Party of India–Marxist will give support from outside, even though it hasn't been asked to. Oh, and it will be a Strong State. (On the hanging front, the gloves are already off. Could the next in line be Balwant Singh Rajoana, on death row for the assassination of Punjab's chief minister Beant Singh? His execution could revive Khalistani sentiment in the Punjab and put the Akali Dal and the Bharatiya Janata Party on the mat. Perfect old-style Congress politics.)

But that old-style politics is in some difficulty. In the last few turbulent months, it is not just the image of major political parties but politics itself, the idea of politics as we know it, that has taken a battering. Again and again, whether it's about corruption, rising prices, or rape and the rising violence against women, the new, emerging middle class is at the barricades. They can be water-cannoned or lathi-charged, but they cannot be shot and imprisoned in their thousands, in the way the poor can, in the way Dalits, Adivasis, Muslims, Kashmiris, Nagas, and Manipuris can—and have been. The old political parties know that if there is not to be a complete meltdown, this aggression has to be headed off, redirected. They know that they must work together to bring politics back to what it used to be. What better way than a communal conflagration? (How else can the secular play at being secular and the communal be communal?) Maybe even a little war, so that we can play Hawks and Doves all over again.

What better solution than to aim a kick at that tried and trusted old political football—Kashmir? The hanging of Afzal Guru, its brazenness and timing, is deliberate. It has brought politics and anger back onto Kashmir's streets.

India hopes to manage it with the usual combination of brute force and poisonous Machiavellian manipulation designed to pit people against one another. The war in Kashmir is presented to the world as a battle between an inclusive secular democracy and radical Islamists. What then should we make of the fact that Mufti Bashiruddin, the so-called Grand Mufti of Kashmir (which, by the way, is a completely phantom post)—who has made the most abominable hate speeches and has issued fatwa after fatwa, intended to present Kashmir as a demonic, monolithic Wahabi society—is actually a government-anointed cleric? Kids on Facebook will be arrested, but never he. What should we make of the fact that the Indian government looks away while money from Saudi Arabia (that most steadfast partner of the United States) is pouring into Kashmir's madrassas? How different is this from what the CIA did in Afghanistan all those years ago? That whole sorry business created Osama bin

Laden, Al-Qaeda, and the Taliban. It has decimated Afghanistan and Pakistan. What sort of incubus will this unleash?

The old political football is not going to be all that easy to control. And it's radioactive. A few days ago Pakistan tested a short-range battlefield nuclear missile to protect itself against threats from "evolving scenarios." Two weeks ago the Kashmir police published "survival tips" for nuclear war. Apart from advising people to build toilet-equipped bombproof basements large enough to house their entire families for two weeks, it said: "During a nuclear attack, motorists should dive out of their cars toward the blast to save themselves from being crushed by their soon-to-be tumbling vehicles." And it warned everyone to "expect some initial disorientation as the blast wave may blow down and carry away many prominent and familiar features."

Prominent and familiar features may have already blown down.

Perhaps we should all jump out of our soon-to-be-tumbling vehicles.

THE DOCTOR
AND THE SAINT:
THE AMBEDKAR-
GANDHI DEBATE

"ANNIHILATION OF CASTE" is the nearly eighty-year-old text of a speech that was never delivered. When I first read it I felt as though somebody had walked into a dim room and opened the windows. Reading Dr. Bhimrao Ramji Ambedkar bridges the gap between what most Indians are schooled to believe in and the reality we experience every day of our lives.

My father was a Hindu, a Brahmo. I never met him until I was an adult. I grew up with my mother in a Syrian Christian family in Ayemenem, a small village in communist-ruled Kerala. And yet all around me were the fissures and cracks of caste. Ayemenem had its own separate "Paraiyar" church where "Paraiyan" priests preached to an "untouchable" congregation. Caste was implied in people's names, in the way people referred to each other, in the work they

First published as the introduction to B. R. Ambedkar, *Annihilation of Caste: The Annotated Critical Edition* (New Delhi: Navayana, 2014).

did, in the clothes they wore, in the marriages that were arranged, in the language they spoke. Even so, I never encountered the notion of caste in a single school textbook. Reading Ambedkar alerted me to a gaping hole in our pedagogical universe. Reading him also made it clear why that hole exists and why it will continue to exist until Indian society undergoes radical, revolutionary change.

Revolutions can begin, and often have begun, with reading.

If you have heard of Malala Yousafzai but not of Surekha Bhotmange, then do read Ambedkar.

Malala was only fifteen but had already committed several crimes. She was a girl, she lived in the Swat Valley in Pakistan, she was a BBC blogger, she was in a *New York Times* video, and she went to school. Malala wanted to be a doctor; her father wanted her to be a politician. She was a brave child. She (and her father) didn't take heed when the Taliban declared that schools were not meant for girls and threatened to kill her if she did not stop speaking out against them. On October 9, 2012, a gunman took her off her school bus and put a bullet through her head. Malala was flown to England, where, after receiving the best possible medical care, she survived. It was a miracle.

The US president and the secretary of state sent messages of support and solidarity. Madonna dedicated a song to her. Angelina Jolie wrote an article about her. Malala was nominated for the Nobel Peace Prize; she was on the cover of *Time*. Within days of the attempted assassination, Gordon Brown, former British prime minister and the UN special envoy for Global Education, launched an "I am Malala" petition that called on the government of Pakistan to deliver education to every girl child. The US drone strikes in Pakistan continue with their feminist mission to "take out" misogynist, Islamist terrorists.

Surekha Bhotmange was forty years old and had committed several crimes, too. She was a woman—an "Untouchable," Dalit woman—who lived in India, and she wasn't dirt poor. She was more educated than her husband, so she functioned as the head of her family. Dr. Ambedkar was her hero. Like him, her family had renounced Hinduism and converted to Buddhism. Surekha's children were educated. Her two sons Sudhir and Roshan had been to college. Her daughter Priyanka was seventeen and finishing high school. Surekha and her husband had bought a little plot of land in the village of Khairlanji in the state of Maharashtra. It was surrounded by farms belonging to castes that considered themselves superior to the Mahar caste that Surekha belonged to. Because she was Dalit and had no right to aspire to a good life, the village panchayat did not permit her to get an electricity connection or turn her thatched mud hut into a brick house. The villagers would not allow her family to irrigate their fields with water from the canal or draw water from the public well. They tried to build a public road through her land, and when she protested, they drove their bullock carts through her fields. They let their cattle loose to feed on her standing crop.

Still Surekha did not back down. She complained to the police, who paid no attention to her. Over the months, the tension in the village built to fever pitch. As a warning to her, the villagers attacked a relative of hers and left him for dead. She filed another police complaint. This time, the police made some arrests, but the accused were released on bail almost immediately. At about six in the evening of the day they were released (September 29, 2006), about seventy incensed villagers, men and women, arrived in tractors and surrounded the Bhotmanges' house. Her husband Bhaiyalal, who was out in the fields, heard the noise and ran home. He hid behind a bush and watched the mob attack his family. He ran to Dusala, the nearest town, and through a relative managed to call the police. (You need contacts to get the police to even pick up the phone.) They never came. The mob dragged Surekha, Priyanka, and the two boys, one of them partially blind, out of the house. The boys were ordered to rape their mother and sister; when they refused, their genitals were mutilated, and eventually they were lynched. Surekha and Priyanka were gang-raped and beaten to death. The four bodies were dumped in a nearby canal, where they were found the next day.

At first, the press reported it as a "morality" murder, suggesting that the villagers were upset because Surekha was having an affair with a relative (the man who had previously been assaulted). Mass protests by Dalit organizations eventually prodded the legal system into taking cognizance of the crime. Citizens' fact-finding committees reported how evidence had been tampered with and fudged. When the lower court finally pronounced a judgment, it sentenced the main perpetrators to death but refused to invoke the Scheduled Castes and Scheduled Tribes Prevention of Atrocities Act—the judge held that the Khairlanji massacre was a crime spurred by a desire for "revenge." He said there was no evidence of rape and no caste angle to the killing. For a judgment to weaken the legal framework in which it presents a crime, for which it then awards the death sentence, makes it easy for a higher court to eventually reduce, or even commute, the sentence. This is not uncommon practice in India. For a court to sentence people to death, however heinous their crime, can hardly be called just. For a court to acknowledge that caste prejudice continues to be a horrific reality in India would have counted as a gesture toward justice. Instead, the judge simply airbrushed caste out of the picture.

Surekha Bhotmange and her children lived in a market-friendly democracy. So there were no "I am Surekha" petitions from the United Nations to the Indian government, nor any fiats or messages of outrage from heads of state. Which was just as well, because we don't want daisy-cutters dropped on us just because we practice caste.

"To the Untouchables," Ambedkar said, with the sort of nerve that present-day intellectuals in India find hard to summon, "Hinduism is a veritable chamber of horrors."

For a writer to have to use terms like "Untouchable," "Scheduled Caste," "Backward Class" and "Other Backward Classes" to describe fellow human beings is like living in a chamber of horrors. Since Ambedkar used the word "Untouchable" with a cold rage, and without flinching, so must I. Today "Untouchable" has been substituted with the Marathi word "*Dalit*" (Broken People), which is, in turn, used interchangeably with "Scheduled Caste." This, as the scholar Rupa Viswanath points out, is incorrect practice, because the term "Dalit" includes Untouchables who have converted to other religions to escape the stigma of caste (like the Paraiyars in my village who had converted to Christianity), whereas "Scheduled Caste" does not. The official nomenclature of prejudice is a maze that can make everything read like a bigoted bureaucrat's file notings. To try and avoid this, I have mostly (though not always) used the word "Untouchable" when I write about the past, and "Dalit" when I write about the present. When I write about Dalits who have converted to other religions, I specifically say Dalit Sikhs, Dalit Muslims, or Dalit Christians.

Let me now return to Ambedkar's point about the chamber of horrors.

According to the National Crime Records Bureau, a crime is committed against a Dalit by a non-Dalit every sixteen minutes; every day, more than four Untouchable women are raped by Touchables; every week, thirteen Dalits are murdered and six Dalits are kidnapped. In 2012 alone, the year of the Delhi gang-rape and murder, 1,574 Dalit women were raped (the rule of thumb is that only 10 percent of rapes or other crimes against Dalits are ever reported), and 651 Dalits were murdered. That's just the rape and butchery. Not the stripping and parading naked, the forced shit-eating (literally), the seizing of land, the social boycotts, the restriction of access to drinking water. These statistics wouldn't include, say, Bant Singh of Punjab, a Mazhabi Dalit Sikh, who in 2005 had both his arms and a leg cleaved off for daring to file a case against the men who gang-raped his daughter. There are no separate statistics for triple amputees.

"If the fundamental rights are opposed by the community, no Law, no Parliament, no Judiciary can guarantee them in the real sense of the word," said Ambedkar. "What is the use of fundamental rights to the Negro in America, to the Jews in Germany and to the Untouchables in India? As Burke said, there is no method found for punishing the multitude."

Ask any village policeman in India what his job is and he'll probably tell you it is to "keep the peace." That is done, most of the time, by upholding the caste system. Dalit aspirations are a breach of peace.

Annihilation of Caste is a breach of peace.

Other contemporary abominations like apartheid, racism, sexism, economic imperialism, and religious fundamentalism have been politically and intellectually challenged at international forums. How is it that the practice of caste in India—one of the most brutal modes of hierarchical social organization that human society has known—has managed to escape similar scrutiny and censure? Perhaps because it has come to be so fused with Hinduism, and by extension with so much that is seen to be kind and good—mysticism, spiritualism, nonviolence, tolerance, vegetarianism, Gandhi, yoga, backpackers, the Beatles—that, at least to outsiders, it seems impossible to pry it loose and try to understand it.

To compound the problem, caste, unlike say apartheid, is not color-coded, and therefore not easy to see. Also unlike apartheid, the caste system has buoyant admirers in high places. They argue, quite openly, that caste is a social glue that binds as well as separates people and communities in interesting and, on the whole, positive ways. That it has given Indian society the strength and the flexibility to withstand the many challenges it has had to face. The Indian establishment blanches at the idea that discrimination and violence on the basis of caste can be compared to racism or to apartheid. It came down heavily on Dalits who tried to raise caste as an issue at the 2001 World Conference against Racism in Durban, insisting that caste was an "internal matter." It showcased theses by well-known sociologists who argued at length that the practice of caste was not the same as racial discrimination and that caste was not the same as race. Ambedkar would have agreed with them. However, in the context of the Durban conference, the point Dalit activists were making was that though caste is not the same as race, casteism and racism are indeed comparable. Both are forms of discrimination that target people because of their descent. In solidarity with that sentiment, on January 15, 2014, at a public meeting on Capitol Hill in Washington, DC, commemorating Martin Luther King Jr.'s eighty-fifth birth anniversary, African Americans signed "The Declaration of Empathy," which called for "an end to the oppression of Dalits in India."

In the current debates about identity and justice, growth and development, for many of the best-known Indian scholars, caste is at best a topic, a subheading, and, quite often, just a footnote. By force-fitting caste into reductive Marxist class analysis, the progressive and left-leaning Indian intelligentsia has made seeing caste even harder. This erasure, this Project of Unseeing, is sometimes a conscious political act, and sometimes comes from a place of such rarefied privilege that caste has not been stumbled upon, not even in the dark, and therefore it is presumed to have been eradicated, like smallpox.

The origins of caste will continue to be debated by anthropologists for years to come, but its organizing principles, based on a hierarchical, sliding scale of entitlements and duties, of purity and pollution, and the ways in which they were, and still are, policed and enforced, are not all that hard to understand. The top of the caste pyramid is considered pure and has plenty of entitlements. The bottom is considered polluted and has no entitlements but plenty of duties. The pollution–purity matrix is correlated to an elaborate system of caste-based, ancestral occupation. In "Castes in India," a paper he wrote for a Columbia University seminar in 1916, Ambedkar defined a caste as an endogamous unit, an "enclosed class." On another occasion, he described the system as an "ascending scale of reverence and a descending scale of contempt."

What we call the caste system today is known in Hinduism's founding texts as "varnashrama dharma" or "chaturvarna," the system of four varnas. The approximately four thousand endogamous castes and subcastes (jatis) in Hindu society, each with its own specified hereditary occupation, are divided into four varnas—Brahmins (priests), Kshatriyas (soldiers), Vaishyas (traders), and Shudras (servants). Outside of these varnas are the avarna castes, the Ati-Shudras, subhumans, arranged in hierarchies of their own—the Untouchables, the Unseeables, the Unapproachables—whose presence, whose touch, whose very shadow is considered to be polluting by privileged-caste Hindus. In some communities, to prevent inbreeding, each endogamous caste is divided into exogamous gotras. Exogamy is then policed with as much ferocity as endogamy—with beheadings and lynchings that have the approval of the community elders. Each region of India has lovingly perfected its own unique version of caste-based cruelty, based on an unwritten code that is much worse than the Jim Crow laws. In addition to being forced to live in segregated settlements, Untouchables were not allowed to use the public roads that privileged castes used, they were not allowed to drink from common wells, they were not allowed into Hindu temples, they were not allowed into privileged-caste schools, they were not permitted to cover their upper bodies, they were only allowed to wear certain kinds of clothes and certain kinds of jewelry. Some castes, like the Mahars, the caste to which Ambedkar belonged, had to tie brooms to their waists to sweep away their polluted footprints, others had to hang spittoons around their necks to collect their polluted saliva. Men of the privileged castes had undisputed rights over the bodies of Untouchable women. Love is polluting. Rape is pure. In many parts of India, much of this continues to this day.

What remains to be said about an imagination, human or divine, that has thought up a social arrangement such as this?

As if the dharma of varnashrama were not enough, there is also the burden of karma. Those born into the subordinated castes are supposedly being punished for the bad deeds they have done in their past lives. In effect, they are living out a prison sentence. Acts of insubordination could lead to an enhanced sentence, which would mean another cycle of rebirth as an Untouchable or as a Shudra. So it's best to behave.

"There cannot be a more degrading system of social organization than the caste system," said Ambedkar. "It is the system that deadens, paralyzes and cripples the people from helpful activity."

The most famous Indian in the world, Mohandas Karamchand Gandhi, disagreed. He believed that caste represented the genius of Indian society. At a speech at a missionary conference in Madras in 1916, he said:

> *The vast organisation of caste answered not only the religious wants of the community, but it answered too its political needs. The villagers managed their internal affairs through the caste system, and through it they dealt with any oppression from the ruling power or powers. It is not possible to deny the organising capability of a nation that was capable of producing the caste system its wonderful power of organisation.*

In 1921, in his Gujarati journal *Navajivan*, he wrote:

> *I believe that if Hindu Society has been able to stand, it is because it is founded on the caste system . . . To destroy the caste system and adopt the Western European social system means that Hindus must give up the principle of hereditary occupation which is the soul of the caste system. Hereditary principle is an eternal principle. To change it is to create disorder. I have no use for a Brahmin if I cannot call him a Brahmin for my life. It will be chaos if every day a Brahmin is changed into a Shudra and a Shudra is to be changed into a Brahmin.*

Though Gandhi was an admirer of the caste system, he believed that there should be no hierarchy between castes; that all castes should be considered equal, and that the avarna castes, the Ati-Shudras, should be brought into the varna system. Ambedkar's response to this was that "the outcaste is a by-product of the caste system. There will be outcastes as long as there are castes. Nothing can emancipate the outcaste except the destruction of the caste system."

It has been almost seventy years since the August 1947 transfer of power between the imperial British government and the government of India. Is caste in the past? How does varnashrama dharma play out in our new "democracy"?

A lot has changed. India has had a Dalit president and even a Dalit chief justice. The rise of political parties dominated by Dalits and other subordinated castes is a remarkable, and in some ways a revolutionary, development. Even if the form it has taken is that a small but visible minority—the leadership—lives out the dreams of the vast majority, given our history, the aggressive assertion of Dalit pride in the political arena can only be a good thing. The complaints about corruption and callousness brought against parties like the Bahujan Samaj Party (BSP) apply to the older political parties on an even larger scale, but charges leveled against the BSP take on a shriller, more insulting tone because its leader is someone like Mayawati, four-term chief minister of Uttar Pradesh—a Dalit, a single woman, and unapologetic about being both. Whatever the BSP's failings may be, its contribution toward building Dalit dignity is an immense political task that ought never to be minimized. The worry is that even as subordinated castes are becoming a force to reckon with in parliamentary democracy, democracy itself is being undermined in serious and structural ways.

After the fall of the Soviet Union, India, which was once at the forefront of the Nonaligned Movement, repositioned itself as a "natural ally" of the United States and Israel. In the 1990s, the Indian government embarked on a process of dramatic economic reforms, opening up a previously protected market to global capital, with natural resources, essential services, and national infrastructure that had been developed over fifty years with public money now turned over to private corporations. Twenty years later, despite a spectacular GDP growth rate (which has recently slowed down), the new economic policies have led to the concentration of wealth in fewer and fewer hands. Today, India's one hundred richest people own assets equivalent to one-fourth of its celebrated GDP. In a nation of 1.2 billion, more than 800 million people live on less than Rs 20 (forty cents) a day. Giant corporations virtually own and run the country. Politicians and political parties have begun to function as subsidiary holdings of big business.

How has this affected traditional caste networks? Some argue that caste has insulated Indian society and prevented it from fragmenting and atomizing like Western society did after the Industrial Revolution. Others argue the opposite; they say that the unprecedented levels of urbanization and the creation of a new work environment have shaken up the old order and rendered caste hierarchies irrelevant if not obsolete. Both claims deserve serious attention. Pardon the somewhat unliterary interlude that follows, but generalizations cannot replace facts.

A recent list of dollar billionaires published by *Forbes* magazine features fifty-five Indians. The figures, naturally, are based on revealed wealth. Even among these dollar billionaires the distribution of wealth is a steep pyramid in which the cumulative wealth of the top ten outstrips the forty-five below them. Seven out of those top ten are Vaishyas, all of them CEOs of major corporations with business interests all over the world. Between them they own and operate ports, mines, oil fields, gas fields, shipping companies, pharmaceutical companies, telephone networks, petrochemical plants, aluminum plants, cellphone networks, television channels, fresh food outlets, high schools, film production companies, stem cell storage systems, electricity supply networks, and Special Economic Zones. They are: Mukesh Ambani (Reliance Industries Ltd.), Lakshmi Mittal (Arcelor Mittal), Dilip Shanghvi (Sun Pharmaceuticals), the Ruia brothers (Ruia Group), K. M. Birla (Aditya Birla Group), Savitri Devi Jindal (O. P. Jindal Group), Gautam Adani (Adani Group), and Sunil Mittal (Bharti Airtel). Of the remaining forty-five, nineteen are Vaishyas, too. The rest are for the most part Parsis, Bohras, and Khattris (all mercantile castes) and

Brahmins. There are no Dalits or Adivasis in this list.

Apart from big business, Banias (Vaishyas) continue to have a firm hold on small trade in cities and on traditional rural moneylending across the country, which has millions of impoverished peasants and Adivasis, including those who live deep in the forests of Central India, caught in a spiraling debt trap. The tribal-dominated states in India's Northeast—Arunachal Pradesh, Manipur, Mizoram, Tripura, Meghalaya, Nagaland, and Assam—have, since "Independence," witnessed decades of insurgency, militarization, and bloodshed. Through all this, Marwari and Bania traders have settled there, kept a low profile, and consolidated their businesses. They now control almost all the economic activity in the region.

In the 1931 census, which was the last to include caste as an aspect of the survey, Vaishyas accounted for 2.7 percent of the population (while the Untouchables accounted for 12.5 percent). Given their access to better health care and more secure futures for their children, the figure for Vaishyas is likely to have decreased rather than increased. Either way, their economic clout in the new economy is extraordinary. In big business and small, in agriculture as well as industry, caste and capitalism have blended into a disquieting, uniquely Indian alloy. Cronyism is built into the caste system.

Vaishyas are only doing their divinely ordained duty. The Arthashastra (circa 350 BCE) says usury is the Vaishya's right. The Manusmriti (circa 150 CE) goes further and suggests a sliding scale of interest rates: 2 percent per month for Brahmins, 3 percent for Kshatriyas, 4 percent for Vaishyas, and 5 percent for Shudras. On an annual basis, the Brahmin was to pay 24 percent interest and the Shudra and Dalit, 60 percent. Even today, for moneylenders to charge a desperate farmer or landless laborer an annual interest of 60 percent (or more) for a loan is quite normal. If they cannot pay in cash, they have to pay what is known as "bodily interest," which means they are expected to toil for the moneylender from generation to generation to repay impossible debts. It goes without saying that according to the Manusmriti no one can be forced into the service of anyone belonging to a "lower" caste.

Vaishyas control Indian business. What do the Brahmins—the bhudevas (gods on earth)—do? The 1931 census puts their population at 6.4 percent, but, like the Vaishyas and for similar reasons, that percentage too has probably declined. According to a survey by the Centre for the Study of Developing Societies (CSDS), from having a disproportionately high number of representatives in Parliament, Brahmins have seen their numbers drop dramatically. Does this mean Brahmins have become less influential?

According to Ambedkar, Brahmins, who were 3 percent of the population in the Madras Presidency in 1948, held 37 percent of the gazetted posts and 43 percent of the nongazetted posts in government jobs. There is no longer a reliable way to keep track of these trends because after 1931 the Project of Unseeing set in. In the absence of information that ought to be available, we have to make do with what we can find. In a 1990 piece called "Brahmin Power," the writer Khushwant Singh observed:

> Brahmins form no more than 3.5 per cent of the population of our country . . . today they hold as much as 70 per cent of government jobs. I presume the figure refers only to gazetted posts. In the senior echelons of the civil service from the rank of deputy secretaries upward, out of 500 there are 310 Brahmins, i.e. 63 per cent; of the 26 state chief secretaries, 19 are Brahmins; of the 27 Governors and Lt Governors, 13 are Brahmins; of the 16 Supreme Court Judges, 9 are Brahmins; of the 330 judges of High Courts, 166 are Brahmins; of 140 ambassadors, 58 are Brahmins; of the total 3,300 IAS officers, 2,376 are Brahmins. They do equally well in electoral posts; of the 508 Lok Sabha members, 190 were Brahmins; of 244 in the Rajya Sabha, 89 are Brahmins. These statistics clearly prove that this 3.5 per cent of Brahmin community of India holds between 36 per cent to 63 per cent of all the plum jobs available in the country. How this has come about I do not know. But I can scarcely

believe that it is entirely due to the Brahmin's higher IQ.

The statistics Khushwant Singh cites may be flawed, but they are unlikely to be drastically flawed. They are a quarter of a century old now. Some new census-based information would help but is unlikely to be forthcoming.

According to the CSDS study, 47 percent of all Supreme Court chief justices between 1950 and 2000 were Brahmins. During the same period, 40 percent of the associate justices in the high courts and lower courts were Brahmin. The Backward Classes Commission, in a 2007 report, said that 37.17 percent of the Indian bureaucracy was made up of Brahmins. Most of them occupied the top posts.

Brahmins have also traditionally dominated the media. Here too, what Ambedkar said in 1945 still has resonance:

> *The Untouchables have no Press. The Congress Press is closed to them and is determined not to give them the slightest publicity. They cannot have their own Press and for obvious reasons. No paper can survive without advertisement revenue. Advertisement revenue can come only from business and in India all business, both high and small, is attached to the Congress and will not favour any Non-Congress organisation. The staff of the Associated Press in India, which is the main news distributing agency in India, is entirely drawn from the Madras Brahmins—indeed the whole of the Press in India is in their hands—and they, for well-known reasons, are entirely pro-Congress and will not allow any news hostile to the Congress to get publicity. These are reasons beyond the control of the Untouchables.*

In 2006, the CSDS did a survey on the social profile of New Delhi's media elite. Of the 315 key decision makers surveyed from thirty-seven Delhi-based Hindi and English publications and television channels, almost 90 percent of the decision makers in the English language print media and 79 percent in television were found to be "upper caste." Of them, 49 percent were Brahmins. Not one of the 315 was a Dalit or an Adivasi; only 4 percent belonged to castes designated as Shudra, and 3 percent were Muslim (who make up 13.4 percent of the population).

That's the journalists and the "media personalities." Who owns the big media houses that they work for? Of the four most important English national dailies, three are owned by Vaishyas and one by a Brahmin family concern. The Times Group (Bennett, Coleman Company, Ltd.), the largest mass media company in India, whose holdings include the *Times of India* and the twenty-four-hour news channel Times Now, is owned by the Jain family (Banias). The *Hindustan Times* is owned by the Bhartiyas, who are Marwari Banias; the *Indian Express* by the Goenkas, also Marwari Banias; the *Hindu* is owned by a Brahmin family concern; the *Dainik Jagran* Hindi daily, which is the largest-selling newspaper in India with a circulation of fifty-five million, is owned by the Gupta family, Banias from Kanpur. *Dainik Bhaskar*, among the most influential Hindi dailies with a circulation of 17.5 million, is owned by Agarwals, Banias again. Reliance Industries, Ltd. (owned by Mukesh Ambani, a Gujarati Bania) has controlling shares in twenty-seven major national and regional TV channels. The Zee TV network, one of the largest national TV news and entertainment networks, is owned by Subhash Chandra, also a Bania. (In southern India, caste manifests itself somewhat differently. For example, the Eenadu Group—which owns newspapers, the largest film city in the world, and a dozen TV channels, among other things—is headed by Ramoji Rao of the Kamma peasant caste of Andhra Pradesh, which bucks the trend of Brahmin–Bania ownership of Big Media. Another major media house, the Sun TV group, is owned by the Marans, who are designated as a "backward" caste but are politically powerful today.)

After Independence, in an effort to right a historic wrong, the Indian government implemented a policy of reservation (positive discrimination) in universities and for jobs in state-run bodies for those who belong to Scheduled Castes and Scheduled Tribes. Reservation is the only opportunity the Scheduled Castes have to break into the mainstream. (Of course, the policy does not apply to Dalits who have converted to other religions but continue to face discrimination.) To be eligible for the reservation policy, a Dalit needs to have completed high school. According to government data, 71.3 percent of Scheduled Caste students drop out before they matriculate, which means that even for low-end government jobs, the reservation policy only applies to one in every four Dalits. The minimum qualification for a white-collar job is a graduate degree. According to the 2001 Census, only 2.24 percent of the Dalit population are graduates. The policy of reservation, however minuscule the percentage of the Dalit population it applies to, has nevertheless given Dalits an opportunity to find their way into public services, to become doctors, scholars, writers, judges, policemen, and officers of the civil services. Their numbers are small, but the fact that there is some Dalit representation in the echelons of power alters old social equations. It creates situations that were unimaginable even a few decades ago in which, say, a Brahmin clerk may have to serve under a Dalit civil servant. Even this tiny opportunity that Dalits have won for themselves washes up against a wall of privileged-caste hostility.

The National Commission for Scheduled Castes and Scheduled Tribes, for example, reports that in Central Public Sector Enterprises, only 8.4 percent of the A-Grade officers (pardon the horrible term) belong to the Scheduled Castes, when the figure should be 15 percent.

The same report has some disturbing statistics about the representation of Dalits and Adivasis in India's judicial services: among Delhi's twenty high court judges, not one belonged to the Scheduled Castes, and in all other judicial posts, the figure was 1.2 percent; similar figures were reported from Rajasthan; Gujarat had no Dalit or Adivasi judges; in Tamil Nadu, with its legacy of social justice movements, only four out of thirty-eight high court judges were Dalit; Kerala, with its Marxist legacy, had one Dalit high court judge among twenty-five. A study of the prison population would probably reveal an inverse ratio.

Former President K. R. Narayanan, a Dalit himself, was mocked by the judicial fraternity when he suggested that Scheduled Castes and Scheduled Tribes, who according to the 2011 Census make up 25 percent of India's 1.2 billion population, should find proportionate representation as judges in the Supreme Court. "Eligible persons from these categories are available and their under-representation or non-representation would not be justifiable," he said in 1999. "Any reservation in judiciary is a threat to its independence and the rule of law," was the response of a senior Supreme Court advocate. Another high-profile legal luminary said: "Job quotas are a vexed subject now. I believe the primacy of merit must be maintained."

"Merit" is the weapon of choice for an Indian elite that has dominated a system by allegedly divine authorization and denied knowledge—of certain kinds—to the subordinated castes for thousands of years. Now that it is being challenged, there have been passionate privileged-caste protests against the policy of reservation in government jobs and student quotas in universities. The presumption is that "merit" exists in an ahistorical social vacuum and that the advantages that come from privileged-caste social networking and the establishment's entrenched hostility toward the subordinated castes are not factors that deserve consideration. In truth, "merit" has become a euphemism for nepotism.

In Jawaharlal Nehru University (JNU)—which is regarded as a bastion of progressive social scientists and historians—only 3.29 percent of the faculty is Dalit and 1.44 percent Adivasi, while the quotas are meant to be 15 percent and 7.5 percent, respectively. This, despite having supposedly implemented reservation for twenty-seven years. In 2010, when the subject was raised, some of its professors emeritus said that implementing the constitutionally mandated reservation policy would "prevent JNU from remaining one of the premier centres of excellence." They argued that if reservation was implemented in faculty positions at JNU, "the well-to-do will move to foreign and private universities, and the disadvantaged will no longer be able to get world class education which JNU has been so proud to offer them so far." B. N. Mallick, a professor of life sciences, was less shy: "Some castes are genetically malnourished and so very little can be achieved in raising them up; and if they are, it would be undoing excellence and merit." Year after year, privileged-caste students have staged mass protests against reservation across India.

That's the news from the top. At the other end of New India, the Sachar Committee Report tells us that Dalits and Adivasis still remain at the bottom of the economic pyramid where they always were, below the Muslim community. We know that Dalits and Adivasis make up the majority of the millions of people displaced by mines, dams, and other major infrastructure projects. They are the pitifully low-paid farm workers and the contract laborers who work in the urban construction industry. Seventy percent of Dalits are by and large landless. In states like Punjab, Bihar, Haryana, and Kerala, the figure is as high as 90 percent.

There is one government department in which Dalits are over-represented by a factor of six. Almost 90 percent of those designated as sweepers—who clean streets, who go down manholes and service the sewage system, who clean toilets and do menial jobs—and employed by the government of India are Dalits. (Even this sector is up for privatization now, which means private companies will be able to subcontract jobs on a temporary basis to Dalits for less pay and with no guarantee of job security.)

While janitors' jobs in malls and in corporate offices with swanky toilets that do not involve "manual scavenging" go to non-Dalits, there are (officially) 1.3 million people, mostly women, who continue to earn their living by carrying baskets of human shit on their heads as they clean out traditional-style toilets that use no water. Though it is against the law, the Indian

Railways is one of the biggest employers of manual scavengers. Its 14,300 trains transport 25 million passengers across 65,000 kilometers every day. Their shit is funneled straight onto the railway tracks through 172,000 open-discharge toilets. This shit, which must amount to several tons a day, is cleaned by hand, without gloves or any protective equipment, exclusively by Dalits. While the Prohibition of Employment as Manual Scavengers and their Rehabilitation Bill, 2012, was cleared by the Cabinet and by the Rajya Sabha in September 2013, the Indian Railways has ignored it. With deepening poverty and the steady evaporation of government jobs, a section of Dalits has to fiercely guard its "permanent" state employment as hereditary shit-cleaners against predatory interlopers.

A few Dalits have managed to overcome these odds. Their personal stories are extraordinary and inspirational. Some Dalit businessmen and women have come together to form their own institution, the Dalit Indian Chamber of Commerce and Industry, which is praised and patronized by big business and given plenty of play on television and big media because it helps to give the impression that as long as you work hard, capitalism is intrinsically egalitarian.

Time was when a caste Hindu crossing the oceans was said to have lost caste and become polluted. Now, the caste system is up for export. Wherever Hindus go, they take it with them. It exists among the brutalized Tamils in Sri Lanka; it exists among upwardly mobile Indian immigrants in the "Free World," in Europe as well as in the United States. For about ten years, Dalit-led groups in the UK have been lobbying to have caste discrimination recognized by British law as a form of racial discrimination. Caste-Hindu lobbies have managed to scuttle it for the moment.

Democracy hasn't eradicated caste. It has entrenched and modernized it. This is why it's time to read Ambedkar.

Ambedkar was a prolific writer. Unfortunately, his work, unlike the writings of Gandhi, Nehru, or Vivekananda, does not shine out at you from the shelves of libraries and bookshops.

Of his many volumes, *Annihilation of Caste* is his most radical text. It is not an argument directed at Hindu fundamentalists or extremists, but at those who considered themselves moderate, those whom Ambedkar called "the best of Hindus"—and some academics call "left-wing Hindus." Ambedkar's point is that to believe in the Hindu shastras and to simultaneously think of oneself as liberal or moderate is a contradiction in terms. When the text of *Annihilation of Caste* was published, the man who is often called the "Greatest of Hindus"—Mahatma Gandhi—responded to Ambedkar's provocation.

Their debate was not a new one. Both men were their generation's emissaries of a profound social, political, and philosophical conflict that had begun long ago and has still by no means ended. Ambedkar, the Untouchable, was heir to the anti-caste intellectual tradition that goes back to 200–100 BCE. The practice of caste, which is believed to have its genesis in the Purusha Sukta hymn in the Rig Veda (1200–900 BCE), faced its first challenge only a thousand years later, when the Buddhists broke with caste by creating sanghas that admitted everybody, regardless of which caste they belonged to. Yet caste endured and evolved. In the mid-twelfth century, the Veerashaivas led by Basava challenged caste in South India and were crushed. From the fourteenth century onward, the beloved Bhakti poet-saints—Cokhamela, Ravidas, Kabir, Tukaram, Mira, Janabai—became, and still remain, the poets of the anti-caste tradition. In the nineteenth and early twentieth centuries came Jotirao Phule and his Satyashodhak Samaj in western India; Pandita Ramabai, perhaps India's first feminist, a Marathi Brahmin who rejected Hinduism and converted to Christianity (and challenged that, too); Swami Achhutanand Harihar, who led the Adi Hindu movement, started the Bharatiya Achhut Mahasabha (Parliament of Indian Untouchables), and edited *Achhut*, the first Dalit journal; Ayyankali and Sree Narayana Guru, who shook up the old order in Malabar and Travancore; and the iconoclast Iyothee Thass and his Sakya Buddhists, who ridiculed Brahmin supremacy in the Tamil world. Among Ambedkar's contemporaries in the anti-caste tradition were E. V. Ramasamy Naicker, known as "Periyar" in the Madras presidency; Jogendranath Mandal of Bengal; and Babu Mangoo Ram, who founded the Ad Dharm movement in the Punjab that rejected both Sikhism and Hinduism. These were Ambedkar's people.

Gandhi, a Vaishya, born into a Gujarati Bania family, was the latest in a long tradition of privileged-caste Hindu reformers and their organizations—Raja Ram Mohan Roy, who founded the Brahmo Samaj in 1828; Swami Dayananda Saraswati, who founded the Arya Samaj in 1875; Swami Vivekananda, who established the Ramakrishna Mission in 1897; and a host of other, more contemporary reformist organizations.

Putting the Ambedkar–Gandhi debate into context for those unfamiliar with its history and its protagonists will require detours into their very different political trajectories. For this was by no means just a theoretical debate between two men who held different opinions. Each represented very separate interest groups, and their battle unfolded in the heart of India's national movement. What they said and did continues to have an immense bearing on contemporary politics. Their differences were (and remain) irreconcilable. Both are deeply loved and often deified by their followers. It pleases neither constituency to have the other's story told, though the two are inextricably linked. Ambedkar was Gandhi's most formidable adversary. He challenged him not just politically or intellectually, but also morally. To have excised Ambedkar from Gandhi's story, which is the story we all grew up on, is a travesty. Equally, to ignore Gandhi while writing about Ambedkar is to do Ambedkar a disservice, because Gandhi loomed over Ambedkar's world in myriad and un-wonderful ways.

The Indian national movement, as we know, had a stellar cast. It has even been the subject of a Hollywood blockbuster that won eight Oscars. In India, we have made a pastime of holding opinion polls and publishing books and magazines in which our constellation of founding fathers (mothers don't make the cut) are arranged and rearranged in various hierarchies and formations. Mahatma Gandhi does have his bitter critics, but he still tops the charts. For others to even get a look-in, the Father of the Nation has to be segregated, put into a separate category: Who, after Mahatma Gandhi, is the greatest Indian?

Dr. Ambedkar (who, incidentally, did not even have a walk-on part in Richard Attenborough's *Gandhi*, though the film was co-funded by the Indian government) almost always makes it into the final heat. He is chosen more for the part he played in drafting the Indian Constitution than for the politics and the passion that were at the core of his life and thinking. You definitely get the sense that his presence on the lists is the result of positive discrimination, a desire to be politically correct. The caveats continue to be murmured: "opportunist" (because he served as Labour Member of the British Viceroy's Executive Council, 1942–46), "British stooge" (because he accepted an invitation from the British government to the First Round Table Conference in 1930 when congressmen were being imprisoned for breaking the salt laws), "separatist" (because he wanted separate electorates for Untouchables), "antinational" (because he endorsed the Muslim League's case for Pakistan, and because he suggested that Jammu and Kashmir be trifurcated).

Notwithstanding the name-calling, the fact, as we shall see, is that neither Ambedkar nor Gandhi allows us to pin easy labels on them that say "pro-imperialist" or "anti-imperialist." Their conflict complicates and perhaps enriches our understanding of imperialism as well as the struggle against it.

History has been kind to Gandhi. He was deified by millions of people in his own lifetime. Gandhi's godliness has become a universal and, so it seems, an eternal phenomenon. It's not just that the metaphor has outstripped the man. It has entirely reinvented him. (Which is why a critique of Gandhi need not automatically be taken to be a critique of all Gandhians.) Gandhi has become all things to all people: Obama loves him and so does the Occupy movement. Anarchists love him and so does the Establishment. Narendra Modi loves him and so does Rahul Gandhi. The poor love him and so do the rich.

He is the Saint of the Status Quo.

Gandhi's life and his writing—48,000 pages bound into ninety-eight volumes of collected works—have been disaggregated and carried off, event by event, sentence by sentence, until no coherent narrative remains, if indeed there ever was one. The trouble is that Gandhi actually said everything and its opposite. To cherry pickers, he offers such a bewildering variety of cherries that you have to wonder if there was something the matter with the tree.

For example, there's his well-known description of an arcadian paradise in "The Pyramid vs. the Oceanic Circle," written in 1946:

> *Independence begins at the bottom. Thus every village will be a republic or panchayat having full powers. It follows, therefore, that every village has to be self-sustained and capable of managing its affairs even to the extent of defending itself against the whole world . . . In this structure composed of innumerable villages there will be ever-widening, never-ascending circles. Life will not be a pyramid with the apex sustained by the bottom. But it will be an oceanic circle whose centre will be the individual always ready to perish for the village . . . Therefore the outermost circumference will not wield power to crush the inner circle but will give strength to all within and derive its own strength from it.*

Then there is his endorsement of the caste system in 1921 in Navajivan. It is translated from Gujarati by Ambedkar (who suggested more than once that Gandhi "deceived" people and that his writings in English and Gujarati could be productively compared):

> *Caste is another name for control. Caste puts a limit on enjoyment. Caste does not allow a person to transgress caste limits in pursuit of his enjoyment. That is the meaning of such caste restrictions*

> *as inter-dining and inter-marriage . . . These being my views I*
> *am opposed to all those who are out to destroy the Caste System.*

Is this not the very antithesis of "ever-widening and never-ascending circles"?

It's true that these statements were made twenty-five years apart. Does that mean that Gandhi reformed? That he changed his views on caste? He did, at a glacial pace. From believing in the caste system in all its minutiae, he moved to saying that the four thousand separate castes should "fuse" themselves into the four varnas (what Ambedkar called the "parent" of the caste system). Toward the end of Gandhi's life (when his views were just views and did not run the risk of translating into political action), he said that he no longer objected to interdining and intermarriage between castes. Sometimes he said that though he believed in the varna system, a person's varna ought to be decided by their worth and not their birth (which was also the Arya Samaj position). Ambedkar pointed out the absurdity of this idea: "How are you going to compel people who have acquired a higher status based on birth, without reference to their worth, to vacate that status? How are you going to compel people to recognise the status due to a man, in accordance to his worth, who is occupying a lower status based on his birth?" He went on to ask what would happen to women, whether their status would be decided upon their own worth or their husbands' worth.

Notwithstanding stories and anecdotes from Gandhi's followers about Gandhi's love for Untouchables and the intercaste weddings he attended, in the ninety-eight volumes of his writing, Gandhi never decisively and categorically renounced his belief in chaturvarna, the system of four varnas. Though he was given to apologizing and agonizing publicly and privately over things like the occasional lapses in his control over his sexual desire, he never agonized over the extremely damaging things he had said and done on caste.

Still, why not eschew the negative and concentrate instead

on what was good about Gandhi, use it to bring out the best in people? It is a valid question, and one that those who have built shrines to Gandhi have probably answered for themselves. After all, it is possible to admire the work of great composers, writers, architects, sportspersons, and musicians whose views are inimical to our own. The difference is that Gandhi was not a composer or writer or musician or a sportsman. He offered himself to us as a visionary, a mystic, a moralist, a great humanitarian, the man who brought down a mighty empire armed only with Truth and Righteousness. How do we reconcile the idea of the nonviolent Gandhi, the Gandhi who spoke Truth to Power, Gandhi the Nemesis of Injustice, the Gentle Gandhi, the Androgynous Gandhi, Gandhi the Mother, the Gandhi who (allegedly) feminized politics and created space for women to enter the political arena, the eco-Gandhi, the Gandhi of the ready wit and some great one-liners—how do we reconcile all this with Gandhi's views (and deeds) on caste? What do we do with this structure of moral righteousness that rests so comfortably on a foundation of utterly brutal, institutionalized injustice? Is it enough to say that Gandhi was complicated and let it go at that? There is no doubt that Gandhi was an extraordinary and fascinating man, but during India's struggle for freedom, did he really speak Truth to Power? Did he really ally himself with the poorest of the poor, the most vulnerable of his people?

"It is foolish to take solace in the fact that because the Congress is fighting for the freedom of India, it is, therefore, fighting for the freedom of the people of India and of the lowest of the low," Ambedkar said. "The question whether the Congress is fighting for freedom has very little importance as compared to the question for whose freedom is the Congress fighting."

In 1931, when Ambedkar met Gandhi for the first time, Gandhi questioned him about his sharp criticism of the Congress (which, it was assumed, was tantamount to criticizing the struggle for the homeland). "Gandhiji, I have no homeland," was Ambedkar's famous reply. "No Untouchable worth the name will be proud of this land."

History has been unkind to Ambedkar. First it contained him, and then it glorified him. It has made him India's Leader of the Untouchables, the King of the Ghetto. It has hidden away his writings. It has stripped away the radical intellect and the searing insolence.

All the same, Ambedkar's followers have kept his legacy alive in creative ways. One of those ways is to turn him into a million mass-produced statues. The Ambedkar statue is a radical and animate object. It has been sent forth into the world to claim the space—both physical and virtual, public and private—that is the Dalit's due. Dalits have used Ambedkar's statue to assert their civil rights—to claim land that is owed them, water that is theirs, commons they are denied access to. The Ambedkar statue that is planted on the commons and rallied around always holds a book in its hand. Significantly, that book is not *Annihilation of Caste* with its liberating, revolutionary rage. It is a copy of the Indian Constitution that Ambedkar played a vital role in conceptualizing—the document that now, for better or for worse, governs the life of every single Indian citizen.

Using the constitution as a subversive object is one thing. Being limited by it is quite another. Ambedkar's circumstances forced him to be a revolutionary and to simultaneously put his foot in the door of the establishment whenever he got a chance to. His genius lay in his ability to use both these aspects of himself nimbly and to great effect. Viewed through the prism of the present, however, it has meant that he left behind a dual and sometimes confusing legacy: Ambedkar the Radical, and Ambedkar the Father of the Indian Constitution. Constitutionalism can come in the way of revolution. And the Dalit revolution has not happened yet. We still await it. Before that there cannot be any other, not in India.

This is not to suggest that writing a constitution cannot be a radical act. It can be, it could have been, and Ambedkar tried his best to make it one. However, by his own admission, he did not entirely succeed.

As India hurtled toward independence, both Ambedkar and Gandhi were seriously concerned about the fate of minorities, particularly Muslims and Untouchables, but they responded to the approaching birth of the new nation in very different ways. Gandhi distanced himself more and more from the business of nation building. For him, the Congress Party's work was done. He wanted the party dissolved. He believed (quite rightly) that the state represented violence in a concentrated and organized form, that because it was not a human entity, because it was soulless, it owed its very existence to violence. In Gandhi's understanding, *swaraj* (self-rule) lived in the moral heart of his people, though he made it clear that by "his people" he did not mean the majority community alone:

> It has been said that Indian swaraj will be the rule of the majority community, i.e., the Hindus. There could not be a greater mistake than that. If it were to be true, I for one would refuse to call it swaraj and would fight it with all the strength at my command, for to me Hind Swaraj is the rule of all the people, is the rule of justice.

For Ambedkar, "the people" was not a homogeneous category that glowed with the rosy hue of innate righteousness. He knew that, regardless of what Gandhi said, it would inevitably be the majority community that decided what form swaraj would take. The prospect of India's Untouchables being ruled by nothing other than the moral heart of India's predominantly Hindu people filled him with foreboding. Ambedkar became anxious, even desperate, to maneuver himself into becoming a member of the Constituent Assembly, a position that would enable him to influence the shape and the spirit of the constitution for the emerging nation in real and practical ways. For this he was even prepared to set aside his pride and his misgivings about his old foe, the Congress Party.

Ambedkar's main concern was to privilege and legalize

"constitutional morality" over the traditional, social morality of the caste system. Speaking in the Constituent Assembly on November 4, 1948, he said, "Constitutional morality is not a natural sentiment. It has to be cultivated. We must realise that our people have yet to learn it. Democracy in India is only a top-dressing on an Indian soil which is essentially undemocratic."

Ambedkar was seriously disappointed with the final draft of the constitution. Still, he did succeed in putting in place certain rights and safeguards that would, as far as the subordinated castes were concerned, make it a document that was more enlightened than the society it was drafted for. (For others, however, like India's Adivasis, the constitution turned out to be just an extension of colonial practice. We'll come to that later.) Ambedkar thought of the constitution as a work in progress. Like Thomas Jefferson, he believed that unless every generation had the right to create a new constitution for itself, the earth would belong to "the dead and not the living." The trouble is that the living are not necessarily more progressive or enlightened than the dead. There are a number of forces today, political as well as commercial, that are lobbying to rewrite the constitution in utterly regressive ways.

Though Ambedkar was a lawyer, he had no illusions about law making. As law minister in post-independence India, he worked for months on a draft of the Hindu Code Bill. He believed that the caste system advanced itself by controlling women, and one of his major concerns was to make Hindu personal law more equitable for women. The bill he proposed sanctioned divorce and expanded the property rights of widows and daughters. The Constituent Assembly dragged its feet over it for four years (from 1947 to 1951) and then blocked it. The president, Rajendra Prasad, threatened to stall the bill's passage into law. Hindu sadhus laid siege to Parliament. Industrialists and zamindars warned they would withdraw their support in the coming elections. Eventually, Ambedkar resigned as law minister. In his resignation speech he said: "To leave inequality between class and class, between sex and sex, which is the soul of Hindu society, and to go on passing legislation relating to economic problems is to make a farce of our Constitution and to build a palace on a dung heap."

More than anything else, what Ambedkar brought to a complicated, multifaceted political struggle, with more than its fair share of sectarianism, obscurantism, and skullduggery, was intelligence.

Annihilation of Caste is often called (even by some Ambedkarites) Ambedkar's utopia—his impracticable, unfeasible dream. He was rolling a boulder up a cliff, they say. How can a society so steeped in faith and superstition be expected to be open to such a ferocious attack on its most deeply held beliefs? After all, for millions of Hindus of all castes, including Untouchables, Hinduism in its practice is a way of life that pervades everything—birth, death, war, marriage, food, music, poetry, dance. It is their culture, their very identity. How can Hinduism be renounced only because the practice of caste is sanctioned in its foundational texts, which most people have never read?

Ambedkar's point is—how can it not be? How can such institutionalized injustice, even if it is divinely ordained, be acceptable to anyone?

> *It is no use seeking refuge in quibbles. It is no use telling people that the shastras do not say what they are believed to say, if they are grammatically read or logically interpreted. What matters is how the shastras have been understood by people. You must take the stand that Buddha took. . . . You must not only discard the shastras, you must deny their authority as did Buddha and Nanak. You must have the courage to tell the Hindus that what is wrong with them is their religion—the religion which has produced in them this notion of the sacredness of caste. Will you show that courage?*

Gandhi believed that Ambedkar was throwing the baby out with the bathwater. Ambedkar believed the baby and the bathwater were a single, fused organism.

Let us concede—but never accept—that *Annihilation of Caste* is indeed a piece of utopian thinking. If it is, then let us concede and accept how reduced, how depleted, and how pitiable we would be as a people if even this—this rage, this audacious denunciation—did not exist in our midst. Ambedkar's anger gives us all a little shelter, a little dignity.

The utopianism that Ambedkar is charged with was very much part of the tradition of the anti-caste movement. The poetry of the Bhakti movement is replete with it. Unlike the nostalgia-ridden, mythical village republics in Gandhi's "*Ram Rajya*" (The Reign of Lord Ram), the subaltern Bhakti saints sang of towns. They sang of towns in timeless places, where Untouchables would be liberated from ubiquitous fear, from unimaginable indignity and endless toil on other peoples' land. For Ravidas (also known as Raidas, Ruhidas, Rohidas), that place was Be-gham-pura, the City without Sorrow, the city without segregation, where people were free to go wherever they wanted:

> *Where there is no affliction or suffering*
> *Neither anxiety nor fear, taxes nor capital*
> *No menace, no terror, no humiliation . . .*
> *Says Raidas the emancipated Chamar:*
> *One who shares with me that city is my friend.*

For Tukaram, the city was Pandharpur, where everybody was equal, where the headman had to work as hard as everyone else, where people danced and sang and mingled freely. For Kabir, it was Premnagar, the City of Love.

Ambedkar's utopia was a pretty hard-nosed one. It was, so to speak, the City of Justice—worldly justice. He imagined an enlightened India, Prabuddha Bharat, that fused the best ideas of the European Enlightenment with Buddhist thought. Prabuddha Bharat was, in fact, the name he gave to the last of the four newspapers he edited in his lifetime.

If Gandhi's radical critique of Western modernity came

from a nostalgic evocation of a uniquely Indian pastoral bliss, Ambedkar's critique of that nostalgia came from an embrace of pragmatic Western liberalism and its definitions of progress and happiness. (Which, at this moment, is experiencing a crisis from which it may not recover.)

Gandhi called modern cities an "excrescence" that "served at the present moment the evil purpose of draining the life-blood of the villages." To Ambedkar, and to most Dalits, Gandhi's ideal village was, understandably, "a sink of localism, a den of ignorance, narrow-mindedness and communalism." The impetus toward justice turned Ambedkar's gaze away from the village toward the city, toward urbanism, modernism, and industrialization—big cities, big dams, big irrigation projects. Ironically, this is the very model of "development" that hundreds of thousands of people today associate with injustice, a model that lays the environment to waste and involves the forcible displacement of millions of people from their villages and homes by mines, dams, and other major infrastructural projects. Meanwhile, Gandhi—whose mythical village is so blind to appalling, inherent injustice—has, as ironically, become the talisman for these struggles for justice.

While Gandhi promoted his village republic, his pragmatism, or what some might call his duality, allowed him to support and be supported by big industry and Big Dams as well.

The rival utopias of Gandhi and Ambedkar represented the classic battle between tradition and modernity. If utopias can be said to be "right" and "wrong," then both were right, and both were also grievously wrong. Gandhi was prescient enough to recognize the seed of cataclysm that was implanted in the project of Western modernity:

> *God forbid that India should ever take to industrialism after the manner of the West. The economic imperialism of a single tiny island kingdom is today keeping the world in chains. If an entire nation of 300 millions took to similar economic exploitation it*

would strip the world bare like locusts.

As the earth warms up, as glaciers melt, and forests disappear, Gandhi's words have turned out to be prophetic. But his horror of modern civilization led him to eulogize a mythical Indian past that was, in his telling, just and beautiful. Ambedkar, on his part, was painfully aware of the iniquity of that past, but in his urgency to move away from it, he failed to recognize the catastrophic dangers of Western modernity.

Ambedkar's and Gandhi's very different utopias ought not to be appraised or assessed by the "end product" alone—the village or the city. Equally important is the impetus that drove those utopias. For Ambedkarites to call mass struggles against contemporary models of development "eco-romantic" and for Gandhians to hold Gandhi out as a symbol of justice and moral virtue are shallow interpretations of the very different passions that drove the two men.

The towns the Bhakti poet-saints dreamed of—Beghampura, Pandharpur, Premnagar—had one thing in common. They all existed in a time and space that was liberated from the bonds of Brahminism. "Brahminism" was the term that the anti-caste movement preferred over "Hinduism." By Brahminism, they didn't mean Brahmins as a caste or a community. They meant the domino effect, what Ambedkar called the "infection of imitation," that the caste that first "enclosed" itself—the Brahmins—set off. "Some closed the door," he wrote, "others found it closed against them."

The "infection of imitation," like the half-life of a radioactive atom, decays exponentially as it moves down the caste ladder but never quite disappears. It has created what Ambedkar describes as a system of "graded inequality" in which "there is no such class as a completely unprivileged class except the one which is at the base of the social pyramid. The privileges of the rest are graded. Even the low is privileged as compared with lower. Each class being privileged, every class is interested in maintaining the system."

The exponential decay of the radioactive atom of caste means that Brahminism is practiced not just by the Brahmin against the Kshatriya or the Vaishya against the Shudra, or the Shudra against the Untouchable, but also by the Untouchable against the Unapproachable, the Unapproachable against the Unseeable. It means there is a quotient of Brahminism in everybody, regardless of which caste they belong to. It is the ultimate means of control in which the concept of pollution and purity and the perpetration of social as well as physical violence—an inevitable part of administering an oppressive hierarchy—is not just outsourced, but implanted in everybody's imagination, including those at the bottom of the hierarchy. It's like an elaborate enforcement network in which everybody polices everybody else. The Unapproachable polices the Unseeable, the Malas resent the Madigas, the Madigas turn upon the Dakkalis, who sit on the Rellis; the Vanniyars quarrel with the Paraiyars, who in turn could beat up the Arundhatiyars.

Brahminism makes it impossible to draw a clear line between victims and oppressors, even though the hierarchy of caste makes it more than clear that there are victims and oppressors. (The line between Touchables and Untouchables, for example, is dead clear.) Brahminism precludes the possibility of social or political solidarity across caste lines. As an administrative system, it is pure genius. "A single spark can light a prairie fire" was Mao Zedong's famous message to his guerrilla army. Perhaps. But Brahminism has given us in India a labyrinth instead of a prairie. And the poor little single spark wanders, lost in a warren of firewalls. Brahminism, Ambedkar said, "is the very negation of the spirit of Liberty, Equality and Fraternity."

Annihilation of Caste is the text of a speech Ambedkar was supposed to deliver in Lahore in 1936 to an audience of privileged-caste Hindus. The organization that had been bold enough to invite him to deliver its presidential address was the Jat-Pat Todak Mandal (Forum for Break-up of Caste) of Lahore, a "radical" offshoot of the Arya Samaj. Most of its members were privileged-caste Hindu reformers. They asked to be provided the text of the speech in advance, so that they could print and distribute it. When they read it and realized that Ambedkar was going to launch an intellectual assault on the Vedas and shastras, on Hinduism itself, they wrote to him:

> [T]hose of us who would like to see the conference terminate without any untoward incident would prefer that at least the word "Veda" be left out for the time being. I leave this to your good sense. I hope, however, in your concluding paragraphs you will make it clear that the views expressed in the address are your own and that the responsibility does not lie on the Mandal.

Ambedkar refused to alter his speech, and so the event was canceled. His text ought not to have come as such a surprise to the Mandal. Just a few months previously, on October 13, 1935, at the Depressed Classes Conference in Yeola in the Bombay Presidency (now in the state of Maharashtra), Ambedkar had told an audience of more than ten thousand people:

> Because we have the misfortune of calling ourselves Hindus, we are treated thus. If we were members of another faith none would treat us so. Choose any religion which gives you equality of status and treatment. We shall repair our mistake now. I had the misfortune of being born with the stigma of an Untouchable. However, it is not my fault; but I will not die a Hindu, for this is in my power.

At that particular moment in time, the threat of religious conversion by an Untouchable leader of Ambedkar's standing came as the worst possible news to Hindu reformers.

Conversion was by no means new. Seeking to escape the stigma of caste, Untouchable and other degraded laboring castes had begun to convert to other religions centuries ago. Millions had converted to Islam during the years of Muslim rule. Later, millions more had taken to Sikhism and Christianity. (Sadly, caste prejudice in the subcontinent trumps religious belief. Though their scriptures do not sanction it, elite Indian Muslims, Sikhs, and Christians all practice caste discrimination. Pakistan, Bangladesh, and Nepal all have their own communities of Untouchable sweepers. So does Kashmir. But that's another story.)

The mass conversion of oppressed-caste Hindus, particularly to Islam, continues to sit uncomfortably with Hindu supremacist history writing, which dwells on a golden age of Hinduism that was brought to naught by the cruelty and vandalism of Muslim rule. Vandalism and cruelty there certainly was. Yet it meant different things to different people. Here is Jotiba Phule (1827–90), the earliest of the modern anti-caste intellectuals, on the subject of the Muslim rule and of the so-called golden age of the Arya Bhats (Brahmins):

> *The Muslims, destroying the carved stone images of the cunning Arya Bhats, forcibly enslaved them and brought the Shudras and Ati-Shudras in great numbers out of their clutches and made them Muslims, including them in the Muslim Religion. Not only this, but they established inter-dining and intermarriage with them and gave them all equal rights. They made them all as happy as themselves and forced the Arya Bhats to see all this.*

By the turn of the century, however, religious conversion came to have completely different implications in India. A new set of unfamiliar considerations entered the mix. Opposing an unpopular regime was no longer just a question of a conquering army riding into the capital, overthrowing the monarch and taking the throne. The old idea of empire was metamorphosing into the new idea of the nation-state. Modern governance now involved addressing the volatile question of the right to representation: Who had the right to represent the Indian people? The Hindus, the Muslims, the Sikhs, the Christians, the privileged castes, the oppressed castes, the farmers, the workers? How would the "self" in self-rule—the "swa" in swaraj—be constituted? Who would decide? Suddenly, a people who belonged to an impossibly diverse range of races, castes, tribes, and religions—who, between them, spoke more than one thousand languages—had to be transformed into modern citizens of a modern nation. The process of synthetic homogenization began to have the opposite effect. Even as the modern Indian nation constituted itself, it began to fracture.

Under the new dispensation, demography became vitally important. The empirical taxonomy of the British census had solidified and freeze-dried the rigid but not entirely inflexible hierarchy of caste, adding its own prejudices and value judgments to the mix, classifying entire communities as "criminals" and "warriors" and so on. The Untouchable castes were entered under the accounting head "Hindu." (In 1930, according to Ambedkar, the Untouchables numbered about 44.5 million. The population of African Americans in the US around the same time was 8.8 million.) The large-scale exodus of Untouchables from the "Hindu fold" would have been catastrophic for the "Hindu" majority. In pre-Partition, undivided Punjab, for example, between 1881 and 1941, the Hindu population dropped from 43.8 percent to 29.1 percent, due largely to the conversion of the subordinated castes to Islam, Sikhism, and Christianity.

Hindu reformers hurried to stem this migration. The Arya Samaj, founded in 1875 in Lahore by Dayananda Saraswati (born Mool Shankar, a Gujarati Brahmin from Kathiawar), was one of the earliest. It preached against the practice of untouchability and banned idol worship. Dayananda Saraswati initiated the Shuddhi program in 1877, to "purify the impure," and, in the early twentieth century, his disciples took this up on a mass scale in North India.

In 1899, Swami Vivekananda of the Ramakrishna Math—the man who became famous in 1893 when he addressed the Parliament of the World's Religions in Chicago in his sadhu's robes—said, "Every man going out of the Hindu pale is not only a man less, but an enemy the more." A raft of new reformist outfits appeared in Punjab, committed to saving Hinduism by winning the "hearts and minds" of Untouchables: the Shradhananda Dalituddhar Sabha, the All-India Achhutodhar Committee, the Punjab Achhut Udhar Mandal, and the Jat-Pat Todak Mandal, which was part of the Arya Samaj.

The reformers' use of the words "Hindu" and "Hinduism" was new. Until then, they had been used by the British as well as the Mughals, but it was not the way people who were described as Hindus chose to describe themselves. Until the panic over demography began, they had always foregrounded their jati, their caste identity. "The first and foremost thing that must be recognised is that Hindu society is a myth. The name Hindu is itself a foreign name," said Ambedkar.

> It was given by the Mohammedans to the natives [who lived east of the river Indus] for the purpose of distinguishing themselves. It does not occur in any Sanskrit work prior to the Mohammedan invasion. They did not feel the necessity of a common name, because they had no conception of their having constituted a community. Hindu society as such does not exist. It is only a collection of castes.

When reformers began to use the word "Hindu" to describe themselves and their organizations, it had less to do with religion than with trying to forge a unified political constitution out of a divided people. This explains the reformers' constant references to the "Hindu nation" or the "Hindu race." This political Hinduism later came to be called Hindutva.

The issue of demography was addressed openly and head-on. "In this country, the government is based on numbers," wrote the editor of *Pratap*, a Kanpur newspaper, on January 10, 1921.

> Shuddhi has become a matter of life and death for Hindus. The Muslims have grown from negative quantity into 70 million. The Christians number four million. 220 million Hindus are finding it hard to live because of 70 million Muslims. If their numbers

increase only God knows what will happen. It is true that Shuddhi
should be for religious purposes alone, but the Hindus have been
obliged by other considerations as well to embrace their other
brothers. If the Hindus do not wake up now, they will be finished.

Conservative Hindu organizations like the Hindu Mahasabha took the task beyond rhetoric, and against their own deeply held beliefs and practice began to proselytize energetically against untouchability. Untouchables had to be prevented from defecting. They had to be assimilated, their proteins broken down. They had to be brought into the Big House, but kept in the servants' quarters. Here is Ambedkar on the subject:

It is true that Hinduism can absorb many things. The beef-eating
Hinduism (or strictly speaking Brahminism which is the proper
name of Hinduism in its earlier stage) absorbed the non-violence
theory of Buddhism and became a religion of vegetarianism.
But there is one thing which Hinduism has never been able to
do—namely to adjust itself to absorb the Untouchables or to
remove the bar of untouchability.

While the Hindu reformers went about their business, anti-caste movements led by Untouchables began to organize themselves, too. Swami Achhutanand Harihar presented the Prince of Wales with a charter of seventeen demands including land reform, separate schools for Untouchable children, and separate electorates. Another well-known figure was Babu Mangoo Ram. He was a member of the revolutionary, anti-imperialist Ghadar Party established in 1913, predominantly by Punjabi migrants in the United States and Canada. Ghadar (Revolt) was an international movement of Punjabi Indians who had been inspired by the 1857 Mutiny, also called the First War of Independence. Its aim was to overthrow the British by means of armed struggle. (It was, in some ways, India's first communist party. Unlike the Congress, which had an urban, privileged-caste leadership, the Ghadar Party was closely linked to the Punjab peasantry. Though it has ceased to exist, its memory continues to be a rallying point for several left-wing revolutionary parties in Punjab.) However, when Babu Mangoo Ram returned to India after a decade in the United States, the caste system was waiting for him. He found he was Untouchable again. In 1926, he founded the Ad Dharm movement, with Ravidas, the Bhakti saint, as its spiritual hero. Ad Dharmis declared that they were neither Sikh nor Hindu. Many Untouchables left the Arya Samaj to join the Ad Dharm movement. Babu Mangoo Ram went on to become a comrade of Ambedkar's.

The anxiety over demography made for turbulent politics. There were other lethal games afoot. The British government had given itself the right to rule India by imperial fiat and had consolidated its power by working closely with the Indian elite, taking care never to upset the status quo. It had drained the wealth of a once-wealthy subcontinent—or, shall we say, drained the wealth of the elite in a once-wealthy subcontinent. It had caused famines in which millions had died while the British government exported food to England. None of that stopped it from also lighting sly fires that ignited caste and communal tension. In 1905, it partitioned Bengal along communal lines. In 1909, it passed the Morley–Minto reforms, granting Muslims a separate electorate in the Central as well as Provincial Legislative Councils. It began to question the moral and political legitimacy of anybody who opposed it. How could a people who practiced something as primitive as untouchability talk of self-rule? How could the Congress Party, run by elite, privileged-caste Hindus, claim to represent the Muslims? Or the Untouchables? Coming from the British government, it was surely wicked, but even wicked questions need answers.

The person who stepped into the widening breach was perhaps the most consummate politician the modern world has ever known—Mohandas Karamchand Gandhi. If the British had their imperial mandate to raise them above the fray, Gandhi had his Mahatmahood.

Gandhi returned to India in 1915 after twenty years of political activity in South Africa and plunged into the national movement. His first concern, as any politician's would be, was to stitch together the various constituencies that would allow the Indian National Congress to claim it was the legitimate and sole representative of the emerging nation. It was a formidable task. The temptations and contradictions of attempting to represent everybody—Hindus, Muslims, Christians, Sikhs, privileged castes, subordinated castes, peasants, farmers, serfs, zamindars, workers, and industrialists—were all absorbed into the other-worldly provenance of Gandhi's Mahatmahood.

Like Shiva in the myth, who swallowed poison to save the world in the story of the Samudra Manthan—the churning of the Ocean of Milk—Gandhi stood foremost among his peers and fellow-churners and tried to swallow the poison that rose up from the depths as he helped to roil the new nation into existence. Unfortunately, Gandhi was not Shiva, and the poison eventually overwhelmed him. The greater the Congress Party's impulse to hegemony, the more violently things blew apart.

The three main constituencies it had to win over were the conservative, privileged-caste Hindus; the Untouchables; and the Muslims.

For the conservative Hindus, the Congress Party's natural constituency, Gandhi held aloft the utopia of Ram Rajya and the Bhagavad Gita, his "spiritual dictionary." (It's the book most Gandhi statues hold.) He called himself a "Sanatani Hindu." Sanatan dharma, by virtue of being "eternal law," positions itself as the origin of all things, the "container" of everything. Spiritually, it is a generous and beautiful idea, the very epitome of tolerance and pluralism. Politically, it is used in the opposite way, for the very narrow purpose of assimilation and domination, in which all religions—Islam, Buddhism, Jainism, Sikhism, Christianity—are sought to be absorbed. They're expected to function like small concerns under the umbrella of a larger holding company.

To woo its second major constituency, the Untouchables, the Indian National Congress passed a resolution in 1917 abolishing untouchability. Annie Besant of the Theosophical Society, a founding member of the Congress, presided over the meeting. Ambedkar called it "a strange event." He republished Besant's essay (published in the *Indian Review* in 1909), in which she had made a case for segregating Untouchable children from the children of "purer" castes in schools:

> *Their bodies at present are ill-odorous and foul with the liquor and strong-smelling food out of which for generations they have been built up; it will need some generations of purer food and living to make their bodies fit to sit in the close neighbourhood of a school room with children who have received bodies trained in habits of exquisite personal cleanliness and fed on pure food stuffs. We have to raise the Depressed Classes to a similar level of purity, not drag the clean to the level of the dirty, and until that is done, close association is undesirable.*

The third big constituency the Congress Party needed to address was the Muslims (who, for caste Hindus, counted on the purity–pollution scale as *mleccha*—impure; sharing food and water with them was forbidden). In 1920, the Congress decided to ally with conservative Indian Muslims who were leading the pan-Islamist agitation against the partitioning of the Ottoman territories by the Allies after World War I. The sultan of the defeated Ottomans was the caliph, the spiritual head of Sunni Islam. Sunni Muslims equated the partition of the Ottoman Empire with a threat to the Islamic Caliphate itself. Led by Gandhi, the Congress Party leapt into the fray and included the Khilafat (Caliphate) agitation in its first national *satyagraha*. The satyagraha had been planned to protest the Rowlatt Act passed in 1919 to extend the British government's wartime emergency powers.

Whether or not Gandhi's support for the Khilafat movement

was just ordinary political opportunism is a subject that has been debated endlessly. The historian Faisal Devji argues convincingly that at this point Gandhi was acting with a certain internationalism; as a responsible "imperial subject" (which was how he saw himself in his years in South Africa), he was attempting to morally transform empire and hold it accountable to all its subjects. Gandhi called Khilafat an "ideal" and asked that the struggle of "Non-cooperation be recognised as a struggle of 'religion against irreligion.'" By this he meant that Hinduism and Islam should join forces to transform a Christianity that, as Gandhi saw it, was losing its moral core. It was during the first Non-Cooperation Movement that Gandhi made religion and religious symbolism the central tenet of his politics. Perhaps he thought he was lighting a wayside fire for pilgrims to warm their souls. But it ended in a blaze that has still not been put out.

By expressing solidarity with a pan-Islamic movement, Gandhi was throwing his turban into a much larger ring. Though he went to great lengths to underline his "Hinduness," he was staking his claim to be more than just a Hindu or even an Indian leader—he was aspiring to be the leader of all the subjects of the British Empire. Gandhi's support for Khilafat, however, played straight into the hands of Hindu extremists, who had by then begun to claim that Muslims were not "true" Indians because the center of gravity of Muslim fealty lay outside of India. The Congress Party's alliance with conservative Muslims angered conservative Hindus as well as moderate Muslims.

In 1922, when the Non-Cooperation Movement was at its peak, things went out of control. A mob killed twenty-two policemen and burnt down a police station in Chauri Chaura in the United Provinces (today's Uttar Pradesh). Gandhi saw this violence as a sign that people had not yet evolved into true satyagrahis, that they were not ready for nonviolence and noncooperation. Without consulting any other leaders, Gandhi unilaterally called off the satyagraha. Since the Non-Cooperation Movement and the Khilafat movement were conjoined, it meant an end to the Khilafat movement, too. Infuriated by this arbitrariness, the leaders of the Khilafat movement parted ways with the Congress. Things began to unravel.

By 1925, Dr. K. B. Hedgewar had founded the Rashtriya Swayamsevak Sangh (RSS), a Hindu nationalist organization. B. S. Moonje, one of the early ideologues of the RSS, traveled to Italy in 1931 and met Mussolini. Inspired by European fascism, the RSS began to create its own squads of storm troopers. (Today they number in the millions. RSS members include former prime minister Atal Bihari Vajpayee, former home minister L. K. Advani, and four-time chief minister of Gujarat Narendra Modi.) By the time World War II broke out, Hitler and Mussolini were the RSS's spiritual and political leaders (and so they still remain). The RSS subsequently declared that India was a Hindu nation and that Muslims in India were the equivalent of the Jews in Germany. In 1939, M. S. Golwalkar, who succeeded Hedgewar as the head of the RSS, wrote in what is regarded as the RSS bible, *We, or Our Nationhood Defined*:

> *To keep up the purity of its race and culture, Germany shocked the world by purging the country of the semitic races—the Jews. Race pride at its highest has been manifested here . . . a good lesson for us in Hindustan to learn and profit by.*

By 1940, the Muslim League, led by M. A. Jinnah, had passed the Pakistan Resolution.

In 1947, in what must surely count as one of the most callous, iniquitous acts in history, the British government drew a hurried border through the country that cut through communities and people, villages and homes, with less care than it might have taken to slice up a leg of lamb.

Gandhi, the Apostle of Peace and Nonviolence, lived to see the movement he thought he led dissolve into a paroxysm of genocidal violence in which half a million people (a million, according to Stanley Wolpert in *A New History of India*) lost their lives and almost twelve million people lost their homes, their past, and everything they had ever known. Through the horror of Partition, Gandhi did all he could to still the madness and bloodlust. He traveled deep into the very heart of the violence. He prayed, he pleaded, he fasted, but the incubus had been unleashed and could not be recalled. The hatred spilled over and consumed everything that came in its path. It continues to branch out, overground and underground. It has bequeathed the subcontinent a dangerous, deeply wounded psyche.

Amidst the frenzy of killing, ethnic cleansing, and chest-thumping religious fundamentalism on both sides, the government of Pakistan kept its head about one thing: it declared that Untouchable municipal sweepers were part of the country's "essential services" and impounded them, refusing them permission to move to India. (Who else was going to clean people's shit in the Land of the Pure?) Ambedkar raised the matter with prime minister Jawaharlal Nehru in a letter in December 1947. With great difficulty Ambedkar managed to help at least a section of the "essential services" get across the border. Even today in Pakistan, while various Islamist sects slaughter each other over who is the better, more correct, more faithful Muslim, there does not seem to be much heartache over the very un-Islamic practice of untouchability.

Five months after Partition, in January 1948, Gandhi was shot dead at a prayer meeting on the lawns of Birla House, where he usually lived when he visited Delhi. His assassin was Nathuram Godse, a Brahmin and a former activist of the Hindu Mahasabha and the RSS. Godse was, if such a thing is possible, a most respectful assassin. First he saluted Gandhi for the work he had done to "awaken" people, and then he shot him. After pulling the trigger, he stood his ground. He made no attempt to escape or to kill himself. In his book, *Why I Assassinated Mahatma Gandhi*, he said:

[But] in India communal franchise, separate electorates and the

> *like had already undermined the solidarity of the nation, more of
> such were in the offing and the sinister policy of communal favour-
> itism was being pursued by the British with the utmost tenacity and
> without any scruple. Gandhiji therefore found it most difficult to
> obtain the unquestioned leadership of the Hindus and Muslims as
> in South Africa. But he had been accustomed to be the leader of all
> Indians. And quite frankly he could not understand the leadership
> of a divided country. It was absurd for his honest mind to think of
> accepting the generalship of any army divided against itself.*

Gandhi's assassin seemed to feel that he was saving the Mahatma
from himself. Godse and his accomplice, Narayan Apte, climbed
the gallows carrying a saffron flag, a map of undivided India
and, ironically, a copy of the Bhagavad Gita, Gandhi's "spiritual
dictionary."

The Gita, essentially Krishna's counsel to Arjuna during the
battle of the Mahabharata (in which brothers fought brothers),
is a philosophical and theological treatise on devotion and
ethical practice on a battlefield. Ambedkar wasn't enamoured
of the Bhagavad Gita. His view was that the Gita contained "an
unheard of defence of murder." He called it a book that "offers
a philosophic basis to the theory of Chaturvarna by linking it to
the theory of innate, inborn qualities in men."

Mahatma Gandhi died a sad and defeated man. Ambedkar
was devastated. He wanted his adversary exposed, not killed.
The country went into shock.

All that came later. We're getting ahead of the story.

For more than thirty-five years before that, Gandhi's
Mahatmahood had billowed like a sail in the winds of the national
movement. He captured the world's imagination. He roused
hundreds of thousands of people into direct political action. He
was the cynosure of all eyes, the voice of the nation. In 1931, at the
Second Round Table Conference in London, Gandhi claimed—
with complete equanimity—that he represented all of India. In
his first public confrontation with Ambedkar (over Ambedkar's

proposal for a separate electorate for Untouchables), Gandhi felt able to say, "I claim myself in my own person to represent the vast mass of Untouchables."

How could a privileged-caste Bania claim that he, in his own person, represented 45 million Indian Untouchables unless he believed he actually was a Mahatma? Mahatmahood provided Gandhi with an amplitude that was not available to ordinary mortals. It allowed him to use his "inner voice" affectively, effectively, and often. It allowed him the bandwidth to make daily broadcasts on the state of his hygiene, his diet, his bowel movements, his enemas, and his sex life and to draw the public into a net of prurient intimacy that he could then use and manipulate when he embarked on his fasts and other public acts of self-punishment. It permitted him to contradict himself constantly and then say: "My aim is not to be consistent with my previous statements on a given question, but to be consistent with the truth as it may present itself to me in a given moment. The result has been that I have grown from truth to truth."

Ordinary politicians oscillate from political expediency to political expediency. A Mahatma can grow from truth to truth.

How did Gandhi come to be called a Mahatma? Did he begin with the compassion and egalitarian instincts of a saint? Did they come to him along the way?

In his recent biography of Gandhi, the historian Ramachandra Guha argues that it was the two decades he spent working in South Africa that made Gandhi a Mahatma. His canonization—the first time he was publicly called Mahatma— was in 1915, soon after he returned from South Africa to begin work in India, at a meeting in Gondal, close to his hometown, Porbandar, in Gujarat. At the time, few in India knew more than some very sketchy, rather inaccurate accounts of the struggles he had been engaged in. These need to be examined in some detail because whether or not they made him a Mahatma, they certainly shaped and defined his views on caste, race, and imperialism. His views on race presaged his views on caste. What happened in South Africa continues to have serious implications for the Indian community there. Fortunately, we have the Mahatma's own words (and inconsistencies) to give us the detail and texture of those years. To generations who have been raised on a diet of Gandhi hagiographies (including myself), to learn of what happened in South Africa is not just disturbing, it is almost stupefying.

THE SHINING PATH

Gandhi, twenty-four years old and trained as a lawyer in London's Inner Temple, arrived in South Africa in May 1893. He had a job as legal adviser to a wealthy Gujarati Muslim merchant. Imperial Britain was tightening its grip on the African continent. Gandhi was unkindly jolted into political awakening a few months after he arrived. Half the story is legendary: Gandhi was thrown out of a "Whites only" first-class coach of a train in Pietermaritzburg. The other half of the story is less known: Gandhi was not offended by racial segregation. He was offended that "passenger Indians"—Indian merchants who were predominantly Muslim but also privileged-caste Hindus—who had come to South Africa to do business, were being treated on a par with native Black Africans. Gandhi's argument was that passenger Indians came to Natal as British subjects and were entitled to equal treatment on the basis of Queen Victoria's 1858 proclamation, which asserted the equality of all imperial subjects.

In 1894, he became secretary of the Natal Indian Congress, founded and funded by rich Indian merchants and traders. The membership fee, of three pounds, was a princely sum that meant the Natal Indian Congress would remain an elite club. (For a sense of proportion—twelve years later, the Zulus would rise in rebellion against the British for imposing an unaffordable one-pound poll tax on them.)

One of the earliest political victories for the Natal Indian

Congress came in 1895 with a "solution" to what was known as the Durban Post Office problem. The post office had only two entrances: one for Blacks and one for Whites. Gandhi petitioned the authorities and had a third entrance opened so that Indians did not need to use the same entrance as the "Kaffirs." In an open letter to the Natal Legislative Assembly dated December 19, 1894, he says that both the English and the Indians "spring from common stock, called the Indo-Aryan," and cites Max Müller, Arthur Schopenhauer, and William Jones to buttress his argument. He complains that the "Indian is being dragged down to the position of a raw Kaffir." As spokesman for the Indian community, Gandhi was always careful to distinguish—and distance—passenger Indians from indentured (bonded) workers:

> *Whether they are Hindus or Mahommedans, they are absolutely without any moral or religious instruction worthy of the name. They have not learned enough to educate themselves without any outside help. Placed thus, they are apt to yield to the slightest temptation to tell a lie. After some time, lying with them becomes a habit and a disease. They would lie without any reason, without any prospect of bettering themselves materially, indeed, without knowing what they are doing. They reach a stage in life when their moral faculties have completely collapsed owing to neglect.*

The Indian indentured labor whose "moral faculties" were in such a state of collapse were largely from the subordinated castes and lived and worked in conditions of virtual slavery, incarcerated on sugarcane farms. They were flogged, starved, imprisoned, often sexually abused, and died in great numbers.

Gandhi soon became the most prominent spokesperson for the cause of the passenger Indians. In 1896, he traveled to India where he addressed packed—and increasingly indignant—meetings about the racism that Indians were being subjected to in South Africa. At the time, the white regime was getting increasingly anxious about the rapidly expanding Indian population. For them Gandhi was the leader of the "coolies"—their name for all Indians. In a perverse sense, their racism was inclusive. It didn't notice the distinctions that Gandhi went to such great lengths to make.

When Gandhi returned to Durban in January 1897, the news of his campaign had preceded him. His ship was met by thousands of hostile white demonstrators, who refused to let it dock. It took several days of negotiation before Gandhi was allowed to disembark. On his way home, on January 12, 1897, he was attacked and beaten. He bore the attack with fortitude and dignity. Two days later, in an interview with the *Natal Advertiser*, Gandhi once again distanced himself from the "coolies":

> *I have said most emphatically, in the pamphlets and elsewhere, that the treatment of the indentured Indians is no worse or better in Natal than they receive in any other parts of the world. I have never endeavoured to show that the indentured Indians have been receiving cruel treatment.*

In 1899, the British went to war with Dutch settlers over the spoils of South Africa. Diamonds had been discovered in Kimberley in 1870 and gold on the Witwatersrand in 1886. The Anglo-Boer War, as it was called then, is known more properly today as the South African War or the White Man's War. Thousands of Black Africans and indentured Indian laborers were dragooned into the armies on either side. The Indians were not given arms, so they worked as menials and stretcher-bearers. Gandhi and a band of passenger Indians, who felt it was their responsibility as imperial subjects, volunteered their services to the British. Gandhi was enlisted in the Ambulance Corps.

It was a brutal war in which British troops fought Boer guerrillas. The British burnt down thousands of Boer farms, slaughtering people and cattle as they swept through the land. Tens of thousands of Boer civilians, mostly women and children, were moved into concentration camps, in which almost thirty thousand people died. Many simply starved to death. These concentration camps were the first of their kind, the progenitors of Hitler's extermination camps for Jews. Several years later, after he returned to India, when Gandhi wrote about the South African war in his memoirs, he suggested that the prisoners in the camps were practicing a cheerful form of satyagraha (which was the course of action he prescribed to the Jews of Germany too):

> *Boer women understood that their religion required them to suffer in order to preserve their independence, and therefore, patiently and cheerfully endured all hardships. . . . They starved, they suffered biting cold and scorching heat. Sometimes a soldier intoxicated by liquor or maddened by passion might even assault these unprotected women. Still the brave women did not flinch.*

After the war, the British announced that their troops would be given a slab each of "Queen's Chocolate" as a reward for their bravery. Gandhi wrote a letter to the colonial secretary to ask for the largesse to be extended to the Ambulance Corps leaders, who had volunteered without pay: "It will be greatly appreciated by them and prized as a treasure if the terms under which the gift has been graciously made by Her Majesty would allow of its distribution among the Indian leaders." The colonial secretary replied curtly to say that the chocolate was only for noncommissioned officers.

In 1901, with the Boer War now behind him, Gandhi spoke of how the objective of the Natal Indian Congress was to achieve a better understanding between the English and the Indians. He said he was looking forward to an "Imperial Brotherhood," toward which "everyone who was the friend of the Empire should aim."

This was not to be. The Boers managed to outmaneuver and out-brotherhood Gandhi. In 1902, they signed the Treaty of Vereeniging with the British. According to the treaty, the Boer republics of the Transvaal and the Orange Free State became colonies of the British Empire under the sovereignty of the

British Crown. In return, the British government agreed to give the colonies self-rule. The Boers became the British government's brutal lieutenants. Jan Smuts, once a dreaded Boer "terrorist," switched sides and eventually led the British Army of South Africa in World War I. The white folks made peace. They divided the diamonds, the gold, and the land between themselves. Blacks, Indians, and "coloreds" were left out of the equation.

Gandhi was not deterred. A few years after the South African War, he once again volunteered for active service.

In 1906, the Zulu chief Bhambatha kaMancinza led his people in an uprising against the British government's newly imposed one-pound poll tax. The Zulus and the British were old enemies and had fought each other before. In 1879, the Zulus had routed the British Army when it attacked the Zulu kingdom, a victory that put the Zulu on the world map. Eventually, over the years, because they could not match the firepower of British troops, they were conquered and driven off their land. Still, they refused to work on the white man's farms, which is why bonded, indentured labor was shipped in from India. Time and again, the Zulus had risen up. During the Bhambatha Rebellion, the rebels, armed only with spears and cowhide shields, fought British troops equipped with modern artillery.

As the news of the rebellion came in, Gandhi published a series of letters in *Indian Opinion*, a Gujarati–English newspaper he had started in 1903. (One of its chief benefactors was Sir Ratanji Jamsetji Tata of the Tata industrial empire.) In a letter dated November 18, 1905, Gandhi said:

> *At the time of the Boer War, it will be remembered, the Indians volunteered to do any work that might be entrusted to them, and it was with great difficulty that they could get their services accepted even for ambulance work. General Butler has certified as to what kind of work the Natal Indian Volunteer Ambulance Corps did. If the Government only realised what reserve force is being wasted, they would make use of it and would give Indians a thorough*

training for actual warfare.

On April 14, 1906, Gandhi wrote again in *Indian Opinion* (translated from Gujarati):

> *What is our duty during these calamitous times in the Colony? It is not for us to say whether the revolt of the Kaffirs [Zulus] is justified or not. We are in Natal by virtue of British Power. Our very existence depends on it. It is therefore our duty to render whatever help we can. There was a discussion in the Press as to what part the Indian community would play in the event of an actual war. We have already declared in the English columns of this journal that the Indian community is prepared to play its part; and we believe what we did during the Boer War should also be done now.*

The rebellion was eventually contained. Chief Bhambatha was captured and beheaded. Four thousand Zulus were killed, thousands more flogged and imprisoned. Even Winston Churchill, Master of War, at the time under secretary of state, was disturbed by the violence. He said: "It is my duty to warn the Secretary of State that this further disgusting butchery will excite in all probability great disapproval in the House of Commons . . . The score between black and white stands at present at about 3500 to 8."

Gandhi, on his part, never regretted the role he played in the White Man's War and in the Bhambatha uprising. He just reimagined it. Years later, in 1928, in *Satyagraha in South Africa*, the memoirs he wrote in Yerawada Central Jail, both stories had, shall we say, evolved. By then the chessmen on the board had moved around. Gandhi had turned against the British. In his new account, the "Truth" about the stretcher-bearer corps in the Bhambatha Rebellion had "grown" into another "Truth":

> *The Zulu "rebellion" broke out just while attempts were being made to impose further disabilities upon Indians in the Transvaal . . . therefore I made an offer to the Government to*

raise a Stretcher-bearer Corps for service with the troops. . . . The corps was on active service for a month. . . . We had to cleanse the wounds of several Zulus which had not been attended to for as many as five or six days and were therefore stinking horribly. We liked the work. The Zulus could not talk to us, but from their gestures and the expression in their eyes they seemed to feel as if God had sent them our succour.

The retrospectively constructed image of the flogged, defeated Zulu—a dumb animal conveying his gratitude to God's missionaries of peace—is completely at odds, as we shall see, with his views about Zulus that were published in the pages of his newspapers during those years. In Gandhi's reimagining of the story of the Bhambatha Rebellion, the broken Zulu becomes the inspiration for another of his causes: celibacy.

While I was working with the Corps, two ideas which had long been floating in my mind became firmly fixed. First, an aspirant after a life exclusively devoted to service must lead a life of celibacy. Second, he must accept poverty as a constant companion through life. He may not take up any occupation which would prevent him or make him shrink from undertaking the lowliest of duties or largest risks.

Gandhi's experiments with poverty and celibacy began in the Phoenix Settlement, a commune he had set up in 1904. It was built on a hundred-acre plot of land in the heart of Natal amidst the sugar fields that were worked by Indian indentured labor. The members of the commune included a few Europeans and (nonindentured) Indians, but no Black Africans.

In September 1906, only months after the Bhambatha Rebellion, despite his offers of friendship and his demonstrations of loyalty, Gandhi was let down once again. The British government passed the Transvaal Asiatic Law Amendment Act. Its purpose was to control Indian merchants (who were regarded as competition to white traders) from entering the Transvaal. Every male Asian had to register himself and produce on demand a thumbprinted certificate of identity. Unregistered people were liable to be deported. There was no right of appeal. Suddenly, a community whose leader had been dreaming of an "Imperial Brotherhood" had been once again reduced "to a status lower than that of the aboriginal races of South Africa and the Coloured People."

Gandhi led the struggle of the passenger Indians bravely and from the front. Two thousand people burned their passes in a public bonfire; Gandhi was assaulted mercilessly, arrested, and imprisoned. And then his worst nightmares became a reality. The man who could not bear to even share the entrance to a post office with "Kaffirs" now had to share a prison cell with them:

> We were all prepared for hardships, but not quite for this experience. We could understand not being classed with the Whites, but to be placed on the same level with the Natives seemed to be too much to put up with. I then felt that Indians had not launched our passive resistance too soon. Here was further proof that the obnoxious law was meant to emasculate the Indians . . . Apart from whether or not this implies degradation, I must say it is rather dangerous. Kaffirs as a rule are uncivilised—the convicts even more so. They are troublesome, very dirty and live almost like animals.

A year later, the sixteenth of the twenty years he would spend in South Africa, he wrote "My Second Experience in Gaol" in *Indian Opinion* (January 16, 1909):

> I was given a bed in a cell where there were mostly Kaffir prisoners who had been lying ill. I spent the night in this cell in great misery and fear. . . . I read the Bhagvad Gita which I had carried with me. I read the verses which had a bearing on my situation and meditating on them, managed to compose myself. The reason why I felt so uneasy was that the Kaffir and

Chinese prisoners appeared to be wild, murderous and given to immoral ways. . . . He [the Chinese] appeared to be worse. He came near the bed and looked closely at me. I kept still. Then he went to a Kaffir lying in bed. The two exchanged obscene jokes, uncovering each other's genitals. . . . I have resolved in my mind on an agitation to ensure that Indian prisoners are not lodged with Kaffirs or others. We cannot ignore the fact that there is no common ground between them and us. Moreover those who wish to sleep in the same room as them have ulterior motives for doing so.

From inside jail Gandhi began to petition the white authorities for separate wards in prisons. He led battles demanding segregation on many counts: he wanted separate blankets because he worried that "a blanket that has been used by the dirtiest of Kaffirs may later fall to an Indian's lot." He wanted prison meals specially suited to Indians—rice served with ghee—and refused to eat the "mealie pap" that the "Kaffirs" seemed to relish. He also agitated for separate lavatories for Indian prisoners.

Twenty years later, in 1928, the "Truth" about all this had transmogrified into another story altogether. Responding to a proposal for segregated education for Indians and Africans in South Africa, Gandhi wrote:

Indians have too much in common with the Africans to think of isolating themselves from them. They cannot exist in South Africa for any length of time without the active sympathy and friendship of the Africans. I am not aware of the general body of the Indians having ever adopted an air of superiority towards their African brethren, and it would be a tragedy if any such movement were to gain ground among the Indian settlers of South Africa.

Then, in 1939, disagreeing with Jawaharlal Nehru, who believed that Black Africans and Indians should stand together against the white regime in South Africa, Gandhi contradicted himself once more: "However much one may sympathise with the Bantus, Indians cannot make common cause with them."

Gandhi was an educated, well-traveled man. He would have been aware of the winds that were blowing in other parts of the world. His disgraceful words about Africans were written around the same time W. E. B. Du Bois wrote *The Souls of Black Folk*: "One ever feels this two-ness—an American, a Negro; two souls, two thoughts, two un-reconciled strivings; two warring ideals in one dark body, whose dogged strength alone keeps it from being torn asunder."

Gandhi's attempts to collaborate with a colonial regime were taking place at the same time that the anarchist Emma Goldman was saying:

> *The centralisation of power has brought into being an international feeling of solidarity among the oppressed nations of the world; a solidarity which represents a greater harmony of interests between the working man of America and his brothers abroad than between the American miner and his exploiting compatriot; a solidarity which fears not foreign invasion, because it is bringing all the workers to the point when they will say to their masters, "Go and do your own killing. We have done it long enough for you."*

Pandita Ramabai (1858–1922), Gandhi's contemporary from India, did not have his unfortunate instincts. Though she was born a Brahmin, she renounced Hinduism for its patriarchy and its practice of caste, became a Christian, and quarreled with the Anglican Church too, earning a place of pride in India's anti-caste tradition. She traveled to the US in 1886 where she met Harriet Tubman, who had once been a slave, whom she admired more than anybody she had ever met. Contrast Gandhi's attitude toward the African people to Pandita Ramabai's description of her meeting with Harriet Tubman:

> *Harriet still works. She has a little house of her own, where she*

and her husband live and work together for their own people . . .
Harriet is very large and strong. She hugged me like a bear and
shook me by the hand till my poor little hand ached!

In 1873, Jotirao Phule dedicated his *Gulamgiri* (Slavery) to

The good people of the United States as a token of admiration
for their sublime disinterested and self sacrificing devotion in
the cause of Negro Slavery; and with an earnest desire, that
my countrymen may take their noble example as their guide in
the emancipation of their Shudra Brothers from the trammels of
Brahmin thraldom.

Phule—who, among other things, campaigned for
widow remarriage, girls' education, and started a school for
Untouchables—described how "the owners of slaves treated
the slaves as beasts of burden, raining kicks and blows on them
all the time and starving them," and how they would "harness
the slaves as bullocks and make them plough the fields in the
blazing sun." Phule believed that the Shudra and Ati-Shudra
would understand slavery better than anyone else because "they
have a direct experience of slavery as compared to the others
who have never experienced it so; the Shudras were conquered
and enslaved by the Brahmins."

The connection between racism and casteism was made more
than a century before the 2001 Durban conference. Empathy
sometimes achieves what scholarship cannot.

Despite all of Gandhi's suffering in unsegregated South
African prisons, the satyagraha against the Pass Laws did not
gain much traction. After leading a number of protests against
registering and fingerprinting, Gandhi suddenly announced that
Indians would agree to be fingerprinted as long as it was voluntary. It would not be the first time that he would make a deal
that contradicted what the struggle was about in the first place.

Around this time, his wealthy architect friend Hermann

Kallenbach gifted him 1,100 acres of farmland just outside Johannesburg. Here he set up his second commune, Tolstoy Farm, with one thousand fruit trees on it. On Tolstoy Farm he began his experiments in purity and spirituality and developed his home-grown protocol for the practice of satyagraha.

Given Gandhi's proposals to partner with the British in their colonization of South Africa—and British reluctance to accept that partnership—satyagraha, appealing to your opponent with the force of Truth and Love, was the perfect political tool. Gandhi was not trying to overwhelm or destroy a ruling structure; he simply wanted to be friends with it. The intensity of his distaste for the "raw Kaffir" was matched by his affection and admiration for the British. Satyagraha seemed to be a way of reassuring them, a way of saying: "You can trust us. Look at us. We would rather harm ourselves than harm you." (This is not to suggest that satyagraha is not, and cannot be, in certain situations, an effective means of political resistance. I am merely describing the circumstances in which Gandhi began his experiments with satyagraha.)

Essentially, his idea of satyagraha revolved around a regimen of renunciation and purification. Renunciation naturally segued into a missionary approach to politics. The emphasis on purity and purification obviously derived from the caste system, though Gandhi inverted the goalposts and called his later ministrations to Untouchables a process of "self-purification." On the whole, it was a brand of hair-shirt Christianity combined with his own version of Hinduism and esoteric vegetarianism (which ended up underlining the "impurity" of Dalits, Muslims, and all the rest of us meat-eaters—in other words, the majority of the Indian population). The other attraction was brahmacharya—celibacy. The practice of semen retention and complete sexual abstinence became the minimum qualification for a "pure" satyagrahi. Crucifixion of the flesh, denial of pleasure and desire—and eventually almost every normal human instinct—became a major theme. Even eating came in for some serious stick: "Taking food is as dirty an act as answering the call of nature."

Would a person who was starving think of eating as a "dirty act"?

Gandhi always said that he wanted to live like the poorest of the poor. The question is, can poverty be simulated? Poverty, after all, is not just a question of having no money or no possessions. Poverty is about having no power. As a politician, it was Gandhi's business to accumulate power, which he did effectively. Satyagraha wouldn't have worked, even as much as it did, if it wasn't for his star power. If you are powerful, you can live simply, but you cannot be poor. In South Africa, it took a lot of farmland and organic fruit trees to keep Gandhi in poverty.

The battle of the poor and the powerless is one of reclamation, not renunciation. But Gandhi, like many successful godmen, was an astute politician. He understood that the act of renunciation by someone who has plenty to renounce has always appealed to the popular imagination. (Gandhi would eventually discard his Western suit and put on a dhoti in order to dress like the poorest of the poor. Ambedkar, on the other hand, born unmoneyed, Untouchable, and denied the right to wear clothes that privileged-caste people wore, would show his defiance by wearing a three-piece suit.)

The irony is that while Gandhi was performing the rituals of poverty in Tolstoy Farm, he was not questioning the accumulation of capital or the unequal distribution of wealth. He was not holding out for improved working conditions for the indentured, or for the return of land to those it had been stolen from. He was fighting for Indian merchants' right to expand their businesses to the Transvaal and to compete with British merchants.

For centuries before Gandhi and for years after him, Hindu rishis and yogis have practiced feats of renunciation far more arduous than Gandhi's. However, they have usually done it alone, on a snowy mountainside or in a cave set in a windblown cliff. Gandhi's genius was that he yoked his otherworldly search for *moksha* to a very worldly, political cause and performed both, like a fusion dance, for a live audience, in a live-in theater. Over the years, he expanded his strange experiments to include his wife as well as other people, some of them too young to know what they were being subjected to. Toward the end of his life, as an old man in his seventies, he took to sleeping with two young girls, Manu, his seventeen-year-old grand-niece, and Abha (who were known as his "walking sticks"). He did this, he said, in order to gauge the degree of success or failure of his conquest over sexual desire. Leaving aside the very contentious, disturbing issues of consent and propriety, leaving aside the effect it had on the girls, the "experiment" raises another distressing, almost horrifying question. For Gandhi to extrapolate from the "results" of sleeping with two (or three, or four) women that he had, or had not, conquered heterosexual desire suggests that he viewed women not as individuals, but as a category. That, for him, a very small sample of a few physical specimens, including his own grand-niece, could stand in for the whole species.

Gandhi wrote at length about the experiments he conducted at Tolstoy Farm. On one occasion, he describes how he slept with young boys and girls spread around him, "taking care to arrange the order of the beds" but knowing full well that "any amount of such care would have been futile in case of a wicked mind." Then:

> I sent the boys reputed to be mischievous and the innocent young girls to bathe in the same spot at the same time. I had fully explained the duty of self-restraint to the children, who were all familiar with my Satyagraha doctrine. I knew, and so did the children, that I loved them with a mother's love ... Was it a folly to let the children meet there for bath and yet to expect them to be innocent?

The "trouble" that Gandhi had been anticipating—spoiling for, actually—with a mother's prescience, took place:

> One day, one of the young men made fun of two girls, and the girls themselves or some child brought me the information. The news made me tremble. I made inquiries and found that the report

was true. I remonstrated with the young men, but that was not enough. I wished the two girls to have some sign on their person as a warning to every young man that no evil eye might be cast upon them, and as a lesson to every girl that no one dare assail their purity. The passionate Ravana could not so much as touch Sita with evil intent while Rama was thousands of miles away. What mark should the girls bear so as to give them a sense of security and at the same time to sterilise the sinner's eye? This question kept me awake for the night.

By morning, Gandhi had made his decision. He "gently suggested to the girls that they might let him cut off their fine long hair." At first they were reluctant. He kept the pressure up and managed to win the elderly women of the farm over to his side. The girls came around after all, "and at once the very hand that is narrating this incident set to cut off their hair. And afterwards analysed and explained my procedure before my class, with excellent results. I never heard of a joke again."

There is no mention of what punishment the same mind that had thought up the idea of cutting the girls' hair had thought up for the boys.

Gandhi did indeed make the space for women to participate in the national movement. But those women had to be virtuous; they had to, so to speak, bear "marks" upon their person that would "sterilise the sinner's eye." They had to be obedient women who never challenged the traditional structures of patriarchy.

Gandhi may have enjoyed and learned a great deal from his "experiments." But he's gone now, and left his followers with a legacy of a joyless, joke-free world: no desire, no sex—which he described as a poison worse than snakebite—no food, no beads, no nice clothes, no dance, no poetry. And very little music. It is true that Gandhi fired the imagination of millions of people. It's also true that he has debilitated the political imagination of millions with his impossible standards of "purity" and righteousness as a minimum qualification for political engagement:

> *Chastity is one of the greatest disciplines without which the mind*
> *cannot attain the requisite firmness. A man who loses stamina*
> *becomes emasculated and cowardly. . . . Several questions arise:*
> *How is one to carry one's wife with one? Yet those who wish to take*
> *part in great work are bound to solve these puzzles.*

No questions seem to have arisen as to how one was to carry one's husband with one. Nor any thoughts on whether satyagraha would be effective, for example, against the hoary tradition of marital rape.

In 1909, Gandhi published his first and most famous political tract, *Hind Swaraj*. It was written in Gujarati and translated into English by Gandhi himself. It is considered to be a piece of genuinely original thinking, a classic. Gandhi himself remained pleased with it to the end of his days. *Hind Swaraj* defines Gandhi in the way *Annihilation of Caste* defines Ambedkar. Soon after it was published, copies of it were seized in Bombay, and it was banned for being seditious. The ban was lifted only in 1938.

It was conceived of as Gandhi's response to Indian socialists, impatient young nihilists and nationalists he had met in London. Like the Bhagavad Gita (and Jotirao Phule's *Gulamgiri*), *Hind Swaraj* is written as a conversation between two people. Its best and most grounded passages are those in which he writes about how Hindus and Muslims would have to learn to accommodate each other after swaraj. This message of tolerance and inclusiveness between Hindus and Muslims continues to be Gandhi's real, lasting, and most important contribution to the idea of India.

Nevertheless, in *Hind Swaraj*, Gandhi (like many rightwing Hindu nationalists would do in the future) superimposes Hinduism's spiritual map—the map of its holy places—on the territorial map of India and uses that to define the boundaries of the country. By doing so, consciously or unconsciously, Gandhi presents the homeland as unmistakably Hindu. But he goes on, in the manner of a good host, to say that "a country must have a faculty for assimilation" and that "the Hindus, the Mohammedans, the Parsees and the Christians who have made India their country, are fellow countrymen." The time Gandhi spent in South Africa—where the majority of his clients, and later his political constituency, were wealthy Muslim businessmen—seems to have made him more attentive to the Muslim question than he might have otherwise been. For the sin of this attentiveness, this obviously unforgivable complexity, he paid with his life.

The rest of *Hind Swaraj* is a trenchant (some say lyrical) denunciation of modernity. Like the Luddites, but with no calls for machine smashing, it indicts the Industrial Revolution and modern machinery. It calls the British Parliament a "sterile woman" and a "prostitute." It condemns doctors, lawyers, and the railways and dismisses Western civilization as "satanic." It might not have been a crude or even excessive adjective to use from the point of view of the genocide of tens of millions of people in the Americas, in Australia, the Congo, and West Africa that was an inalienable part of the colonial project. But it was a little odd, considering Gandhi's proposals for an "Imperial Brotherhood." And even odder, considering his respect for the British and his disdain for the uncivilized "raw Kaffir."

"What then is civilisation?" the "Reader" eventually asks the "Editor." The Editor then launches into an embarrassing, chauvinistic reverie of a mythical India: "I believe that the civilisation India has evolved is not to be beaten in the world." It's tempting to reproduce the whole chapter, but since that isn't possible, here are some key passages:

> *A man is not necessarily happy because he is rich or unhappy because he is poor. The rich are often seen to be unhappy, the poor to be happy. Millions will always remain poor . . . Observing all this our ancestors dissuaded us from luxuries and pleasures. We have managed with the same kind of plough as it existed thousands of years ago. We have retained the same kind of cottages we had*

> *in former times and our indigenous education remains the same as*
> *before. We have had no system of life-corroding competition. Each*
> *followed his own occupation or trade. And charged a regulation*
> *wage. It was not that we did not know how to invent machinery,*
> *but our forefathers knew that, if we set our hearts after such things*
> *we would become slaves and lose our moral fibre. . . . A nation with*
> *a constitution like this is fitter to teach others than to learn from*
> *others. This nation had courts, lawyers and doctors, but they were*
> *all within bounds. . . . Justice was tolerably fair.*

Gandhi's valorization of the mythic village came at a point in his
life when he does not seem to have even visited an Indian village.
And yet his faith in it is free of doubt or caveats.

> *The common people lived independently, and followed their agri-*
> *cultural occupation. They enjoyed true Home Rule. And where*
> *this cursed modern civilisation has not reached, India remains as*
> *it was before . . . I would certainly advise you and those like you*
> *who love the motherland to go into the interior that has yet not*
> *been polluted by the railways, and to live there for at least six*
> *months; you might be patriotic and speak of Home Rule. Now*
> *you see what I consider to be real civilisation. Those who want*
> *to change conditions such as I have described are enemies of the*
> *country and are sinners.*

Other than the vague allusion to the idea of people following an
ancestral occupation or trade that was rewarded by a "regulation
wage," caste is absent in Gandhi's reverie. Though Gandhi later
insisted that untouchability had troubled him since he was a boy,
in *Hind Swaraj* he makes absolutely no mention of it.

Around the time *Hind Swaraj* was published, the first biographies of Gandhi were also published: *M. K. Gandhi: An Indian
Patriot in South Africa* by Reverend Joseph Doke (a minister of
the Johannesburg Baptist Church) in 1909, and *M. K. Gandhi: A
Sketch of His Life and Work* in 1910 by Henry S. L. Polak, one of

Gandhi's closest friends and most admiring of disciples. These contained the first intimations of coming Mahatmahood.

In 1910, the separate British colonies of Natal, the Cape, the Transvaal, and the Orange Free State united to become the Union of South Africa, a self-governing Dominion under the British crown, with Louis Botha as its first prime minister. Segregation began to harden.

Around then, only three years before he was to leave South Africa, Gandhi condescendingly began to admit that Africans were the original inhabitants of the land:

> *The negroes alone are the original inhabitants of this land. We have not seized the land from them by force; we live here with their goodwill. The whites, on the other hand, have occupied the country forcibly and appropriated it to themselves.*

By now he seems to have forgotten that he had actively collaborated with the whites in their wars to forcibly occupy the country, appropriate the land, and enslave Africans. Gandhi chose to ignore the scale and extent of the brutality that was taking place around him. Did he really believe that it was the "negroes' goodwill" that allowed Indian merchants to ply their trade in South Africa, and not, despite its racist laws, British colonialism? In 1906, during the Zulu rebellion, he had been less woolly about things like "goodwill" when he said, "We are in Natal by virtue of British Power. Our very existence depends on it."

By 1911, the anxiety of the white folks about the burgeoning Indian population led to legislation that stopped the import of labor from India. Then came 1913—the year the first volume of Marcel Proust's *À la recherche du temps perdu* was first published, the year Rabindranath Tagore won the Nobel Prize for literature—South Africa's year of blood. It was the year the foundations for apartheid were laid, the year of the Land Act, legislation that created a system of tenure that deprived the majority of South Africa's inhabitants of the right to own land. It was the year African women marched against the Pass Laws that herded them into townships and restricted interprovince movement, the year white mine workers and railway workers, and then African mine workers, went on strike. It was the year Indian workers rose against a new three-pound tax and against a new marriage law that made their existing marriages illegal and their children illegitimate. The year the three-pound tax was imposed on those who had worked off their indenture and wanted to live on in South Africa as free citizens. Being unaffordable, the tax would have forced workers to re-indenture and lock themselves into a cycle of servitude.

For the first time in twenty years, Gandhi aligned himself politically with the people he had previously taken care to distance himself from. He stepped in to "lead" the Indian workers' strike. In fact, they did not need "leading." For years before, during, and after Gandhi, they had waged their own heroic resistance. It could be argued that they were fortunate to have escaped Gandhi's attentions, because they did not just wage a resistance, they also broke caste in the only way it can be broken—they transgressed caste barriers, got married to each other, made love, and had babies.

Gandhi traveled from town to town, addressing coal miners and plantation workers. The strike spread from the collieries to the sugar plantations. Nonviolent satyagraha failed. There was rioting, arson, and bloodshed. Thousands were arrested as they defied the new immigration bill and crossed the border into the Transvaal. Gandhi was arrested, too. He lost control of the strike. Eventually, he signed a settlement with Jan Smuts. The settlement upset many in the Indian community, who saw it as a pyrrhic victory. One of its most controversial clauses was the one in which the government undertook to provide free passage to Indians who wished to return permanently to India. It reinforced and formalized the idea that Indians were sojourners who could be repatriated. (In their 1948 election manifesto, the apartheid National Party called for the repatriation of all Indians. Indians finally became full-fledged citizens only in 1960, when South Africa became a republic.)

P. S. Aiyar, an old adversary of Gandhi's, had accused him of being primarily concerned with the rights of the passenger Indians. (During the struggle against the first proposal of the draft Immigration Bill in 1911, while some Indians, including Aiyar, were agitating for the free movement of all Indians to all provinces, Gandhi and Henry Polak were petitioning for six new entrants a year to be allowed into the Transvaal.) Aiyar was editor of the *African Chronicle*, a newspaper with a predominantly Tamil readership that reported the terrible conditions in which indentured laborers worked and lived. About the Gandhi–Smuts settlement, Aiyar said that Gandhi's "ephemeral fame and popularity in India rest on no glorious achievement for his countrymen, but on a series of failures, which has resulted in causing endless misery, loss of wealth, and deprivation of existing rights." He added that Gandhi's leadership over the previous two decades had "resulted in no tangible good to anyone." On the contrary, Gandhi and his band of passive resisters had made themselves "an object of ridicule and hatred among all sections of the community in South Africa." (A joke among some Blacks and Indians goes like this: Things were good then, back in 1893. Gandhi only got thrown off a train. By 1920, we couldn't even get on one.)

Though it was not put down in writing, part of the Gandhi–Smuts settlement seems to have been that Gandhi would have to leave South Africa.

In all his years in South Africa, Gandhi maintained that Indians deserved better treatment than Africans. The jury is still out on whether or not Gandhi's political activity helped or harmed the Indian community in the long run. But his consistent attempts to collaborate with the British government certainly made the Indian community vulnerable during the rise of African nationalism. When Indian political activists joined the liberation movement under African leadership in the 1950s and saw their freedom as being linked to the freedom of African people, they were breaking with Gandhi's politics, not carrying on his legacy. When Indians joined the Black Consciousness Movement in the 1970s seeking to build a broader Black identity, they were actually upending Gandhian politics. It is these people, many of whom did their time in Robben Island with Nelson Mandela and other African comrades, who have saved the South African Indian community from being painted as a race of collaborators and from being isolated, even expelled, like the Indians in Uganda were in 1972.

That Gandhi is a hero in South Africa is as undeniable as it is baffling. One possible explanation is that after he left South Africa, Gandhi was reimported, this time as the shining star of the freedom struggle in India. The Indian community in South Africa, already cut adrift from its roots, was, after Gandhi left, further isolated and brutalized by the apartheid regime. Gandhi's cult status in India and his connection to South Africa would have provided South African Indians with a link to their history and their motherland.

In order for Gandhi to be a South African hero, it became necessary to rescue him from his past and to rewrite it. Gandhi himself began that project. Some writers of history completed it. Toward the end of Gandhi's stay in South Africa, the first few biographies had spread the news, and things were moving fast on the messiah front. The young reverend Charles Freer Andrews traveled to South Africa and fell on his knees when he met Gandhi at the Durban dock. Andrews, who became a lifelong devotee, went on to suggest that Gandhi, the leader of the "humblest, the lowliest and lost," was a living avatar of Christ's spirit. Europeans and Americans vied with one another to honor him.

In 1915, Gandhi returned to India via London where he was awarded something far better than the Queen's chocolate. For his services to the British Empire, he was honored with the Kaisar-i-Hind Gold Medal for Public Service, presented to him by Lord Hardinge of Penshurst. (He returned it in 1920 before the first national Non-Cooperation Movement.) Honored thus, he arrived in India fitted out as the Mahatma—Great Soul—who had fought racism and imperialism and had stood up for the rights of Indian workers in South Africa. He was forty-six years old.

To honor the returning hero, G. D. Birla, a leading Indian industrialist (and a fellow Bania), organized a grand reception in Calcutta. The Birlas ran an export–import business based in Calcutta and Bombay. They traded in cotton, wheat, and silver. G. D. Birla was a wealthy man who was chafing at the bit, offended by the racism he had personally encountered at the hands of the British. He had had several run-ins with the colonial government. He became Gandhi's chief patron and sponsor and paid him a generous monthly retainer to cover the costs of running his ashrams and for his Congress Party work. There were other industrialist sponsors as well, but Gandhi's arrangement with G. D. Birla lasted for the rest of his days. In addition to mills and other businesses, G. D. Birla owned a newspaper, *Hindustan Times*, where Gandhi's son, Devdas, eventually worked as managing editor.

So the Mahatma who promoted homespun khadi and the wooden charkha was sponsored by a millowner. The man who raged against the machine was kept afloat by industrialists. This arrangement was the precursor to the phenomenon of the corporate-sponsored NGO.

Once the finances were in place and the ashrams were up and running, Gandhi set off on his mission of rallying people against the British government, yet never harming the old hierarchies that he (and his sponsors) intrinsically believed in. He traveled the length and breadth of the country to get to know it. His first satyagraha was in Champaran, Bihar, in 1917. Three years prior to his arrival there, landless peasants living on the verge of famine, laboring on British-owned indigo plantations, had risen in revolt against a new regime of British taxes. Gandhi traveled to Champaran and set up an ashram from where he backed their struggle. The people were not sure exactly who he was. Jacques Pouchepadass, who studied the Champaran Satyagraha, writes: "Rumours . . . reported that Gandhi had been sent into Champaran by the Viceroy, or even the King, to redress all the grievances of the raiyats [farmers] and that his mandate overruled all the local officials and the courts." Gandhi stayed in Champaran for a year and then left. Says Pouchepadass, "It is a fact that from 1918 onwards, after Gandhi had left and the planters' influence had begun to fade away, the hold of the rural oligarchy grew stronger than ever."

To rouse people against injustice and yet control them and persuade them to his view of injustice, Gandhi had to make some complicated maneuvers. In 1921, when peasants (*kisans*) rose against their Indian landlords (*zamindars*) in the United Provinces, Gandhi sent them a message:

> *Whilst we will not hesitate to advise kisans when the moment comes to suspend payment of taxes to Government, it is not contemplated that at any stage of non-cooperation we would seek to deprive the zamindars of their rent. The kisan movement must be confined to the improvement of the status of the kisans and the betterment of the relations between the zamindars and them. The kisans must be advised scrupulously to abide by the terms of their agreement with the zamindars, whether such agreement is written or inferred from custom.*

Inferred from custom. We needn't guess what that means. It's the whole ball of wax.

Though Gandhi spoke of inequality and poverty, though he sometimes even sounded like a socialist, at no point in his political career did he ever seriously criticize or confront an Indian industrialist or the landed aristocracy. This was of a piece with his doctrine of trusteeship or what today goes by the term Corporate Social Responsibility (CSR). Expanding on this in an essay called "Equal Distribution," Gandhi said: "The rich man will be left in possession of his wealth, of which he will use what he reasonably requires for his personal needs and will act as a trustee for the remainder to be used for society. In this argument, honesty on the part of the trustee is assumed." To justify the idea of the rich becoming the "guardians of the poor," he argued that "the rich cannot accumulate wealth without the co-operation of the poor in society." And then, to empower the poor wards of the rich guardians: "If this knowledge were to penetrate to and spread amongst the poor, they would become strong and would learn how to free themselves by means of non-violence from the crushing inequalities which have brought them to the verge of starvation." Gandhi's ideas of trusteeship echo almost verbatim what American capitalists—the Robber Barons—like J. D. Rockefeller and Andrew Carnegie were saying at the time. Carnegie writes in *The Gospel of Wealth* (1889):

> *This, then, is held to be the duty of the man of Wealth: First, to set an example of modest, unostentatious living, shunning display or extravagance; to provide moderately for the legitimate wants of those dependent upon him; and after doing so to consider all surplus revenues which come to him simply as trust funds, which he is called upon to administer, and strictly bound as a matter of duty to administer, in the manner which, in his judgement, is best calculated to produce the most beneficial results for the community—the man of wealth thus becoming the mere agent and trustee for his poorer brethren, bringing to their service his superior wisdom, experience and ability to administer, doing for them better than they would or could do for themselves.*

The contradictions mattered little, because by then Gandhi was far beyond all that. He was a Sanatani Hindu (which is how he described himself) and an avatar of Christ (which is how he allowed himself to be described). The trains he traveled in were mobbed by devotees seeking "*darshan*" (a sighting). The biographer D. G. Tendulkar, who traveled with him, describes the phenomenon as "mass conversions to the new creed."

This simple faith moved India's millions who greeted him everywhere with cries of "Mahatma Gandhi ki Jai." Prostitutes of Barisal, the Marwari merchants of Calcutta, Oriya coolies, railway strikers, Santhals eager to present khadi chaadars, all claimed his attention . . . wherever he went he had to endure the tyranny of love.

In his classic essay, "Gandhi as Mahatma," the historian Shahid Amin describes how the combination of cleverly planted rumors by local Congress leaders, adulatory—and sometimes hallucinatory—newspaper reporting, a gullible people, and Gandhi's extraordinary charisma built up mass hysteria which culminated in the deification of Mahatma Gandhi. Even back then, not everyone was convinced. An editorial in *The Pioneer* of April 23, 1921, said, "The very simple people in the east and south of the United Provinces afford a fertile soil in which a belief in the power of the 'mahatmaji', who is after all little more than a name of power to them, may grow." The editorial was criticizing an article that had appeared in *Swadesh*, a Gorakhpur newspaper, that had published rumors about the miracles that surrounded Gandhi: he had made fragrant smoke waft up from a well, a copy of the Holy Koran had appeared in a locked room, a buffalo that belonged to an Ahir who refused money to a sadhu begging in the Mahatma's name had perished in a fire, and a Brahmin who had defied Gandhi's authority had gone mad.

The taproot of Gandhi's Mahatmahood had found its way into a fecund rill, where feudalism met the future, where miracles met modernity. From there it drew sustenance and prospered.

The skeptics were few and did not count for much. Gandhi was by now addressing rallies of up to two hundred thousand people. The hysteria spread abroad. In 1921, the Unitarian minister John Haynes Holmes of the Community Church in New York in a sermon called "Who is the Greatest Man in the World?" introduced Gandhi to his congregation as "The Suffering Christ of the twentieth century." Years later, in 1958, Martin Luther King, Jr. would do the same: "Christ furnished the spirit and motivation, while Gandhi furnished the method." They presented Gandhi with a whole new constituency: a paradoxical gift for a man who so feared and despised Africans.

Perhaps because the Western Christian world was apprehensive about the spreading influence of the Russian Revolution, and was traumatized by the horror of World War I, Europeans and Americans vied to honor the living avatar of Christ. It didn't seem to matter that unlike Gandhi, who was from a well-to-do family (his father was the prime minister of the princely state of Porbandar), Jesus was a carpenter from the slums of Jerusalem who stood up against the Roman Empire instead of trying to make friends with it. And he wasn't sponsored by big business.

The most influential of Gandhi's admirers was the French dramatist Romain Rolland, who won the Nobel Prize for literature in 1915. He had not met Gandhi when in 1924 he published *Mahatma Gandhi: The Man Who Became One with the Universal Being*. It sold more than a hundred thousand copies and was translated into several European languages. It opens with Tagore's invocation from the Upanishads:

> He is the One Luminous, Creator of All, Mahatma,
> Always in the hearts of the people enshrined,
> Revealed through Love, Intuition and Thought,
> Whoever knows him, Immortal becomes

Gandhi said he found a "real vision of truth" in the book. He called Rolland his "self-chosen advertiser" in Europe. By 1924, on the list of executives of his own organization, All-India Spinners Association, his name appeared as Mahatma Gandhi. Sad then, for him to say in the first paragraph of his response to *Annihilation of Caste*: "Whatever label he wears in the future, Dr. Ambedkar is not the man to allow himself to be forgotten."

As though pointing to the profound horrors of the caste system was just a form of self-promotion for Ambedkar.

This is the man, or, if you are so inclined, the Saint, that Doctor Bhimrao Ramji Ambedkar, born in 1891 into an Untouchable Mahar family, presumed to argue with.

THE CACTUS GROVE

Ambedkar's father, Ramji Sakpal, and both his grandfathers were soldiers in the British Army. They were Mahars from the Konkan, then a part of the Bombay Presidency and, at the time, a hotbed of nationalist politics. The two famous congressmen, Bal Gangadhar Tilak of the *"garam dal"* (militant faction) and Gandhi's mentor, Gopal Krishna Gokhale, of the *"naram dal"* (moderate faction), were both Chitpavan Brahmins from the Konkan. (It was Tilak who famously said, "Swaraj is my birthright, and I shall have it.")

The Konkan coast was also home to Ambedkar's political forebear, Jotirao Phule, who called himself Joti Mali, the Gardener. Phule was from Satara, the town where Ambedkar spent his early childhood. The Mahars were considered Untouchables and, though they were landless agricultural laborers, they were comparatively better off than the other Untouchable castes. In the seventeenth century, they served in the army of Shivaji, the Maratha king of western India. After Shivaji's death, they served the Peshwas, an oppressive Brahminical regime that treated them horribly. (It was the Peshwas who forced Mahars to hang pots around their necks and tie brooms to their hips.) Unwilling to enter into a "trusteeship" of this sort, the Mahars shifted their loyalty to the British. In 1818, in the Battle of Koregaon, a small British regiment of Mahar soldiers defeated the massive army of the last Peshwa ruler, Bajirao II. The British subsequently raised a Mahar Regiment, which is still part of the Indian Army.

Over time, a section of the Mahar population left their villages and moved to the city. They worked in the Bombay mills and as casual, unorganized labor in the city. The move widened their horizons and perhaps accounts for why the Mahars were politicized quicker than other Untouchable communities in the region.

Ambedkar was born on April 14, 1891, in the cantonment town of Mhow near Indore in Central India. He was the fourteenth and last child of Ramji Sakpal and Bhimabai Murbadkar Sakpal. His mother died when he was two years old, the same year that his father retired from the army. The family was brought up in the Bhakti tradition of Kabir and Tukaram, but Ramji Sakpal also educated his children in the Hindu epics. As a young boy, Ambedkar was skeptical about the Ramayana and the Mahabharata and their capricious lessons in morality. He was particularly distressed by the story of the killing and dismembering of the "low-born" Karna. (Karna was born of Surya, the Sun God, and the unmarried Kunti. Abandoned by his mother, he was brought up by a lowly charioteer. Karna was killed while he was repairing his chariot wheel on the battlefield by his half-brother Arjun on the advice of Krishna.) Ambedkar argued with his father: "Krishna believed in fraud. His life is nothing but a series of frauds. Equal dislike I have for Rama." Later, in a series of essays called *Riddles in Hinduism*, published posthumously, he would expand on the themes of what he saw as inexcusable misogyny in Rama's and Krishna's slippery ethics.

Ambedkar's encounters with humiliation and injustice began from his early childhood. When Gandhi was serving in the South African War, Ambedkar was ten years old, living with his aunt and going to a local government school in Satara. Thanks to a new British legislation, he was allowed to go to a Touchable school, but he was made to sit apart from his classmates, on a scrap of gunnysack, so that he would not pollute the classroom floor. He remained thirsty all day because he was not allowed to drink from the Touchables' tap. Satara's barbers would not cut his hair, not even the barbers who sheared goats and buffaloes.

This cruelty continued in school after school. His older brothers were not allowed to learn Sanskrit because it was the language of the Vedas, and the colonization of knowledge was a central tenet of the caste system. (If a Shudra listens intentionally to the Vedas, the Gautama Dharma Sutra says, his ears must be filled with molten tin or lac.) Much later, in the 1920s, Ambedkar studied Sanskrit (and in the 1940s also studied Pali) and became familiar with Brahminical texts—and when he wrote *Annihilation of Caste*, he deployed this knowledge explosively.

Eventually, in 1897, the family moved to a chawl in Bombay. In 1907, Ambedkar matriculated, the only Untouchable student in Elphinstone High School. It was an exceptional achievement for a Mahar boy. Soon after, he was married to nine-year-old Ramabai (not to be confused with Pandita Ramabai) in a ceremony that took place in a shed built over a city drain. While he was doing his bachelor's degree at Elphinstone College, a well-wisher introduced him to Sayajirao Gaekwad, the progressive Maharaja of Baroda. The Maharaja gave him a scholarship of Rs 25 (fifty cents) a month to complete his graduation. The Maharaja was one of a number of unusual, privileged-caste Hindu individuals who helped or allied with Ambedkar in times of adversity and in his political confrontations.

The times were turbulent. The Morley–Minto reforms, which advocated a separate electorate for Muslims, had been passed. Nationalists were infuriated and saw the reforms as a British ploy to undermine the unity of the growing national movement. Tilak was convicted of sedition and deported to Mandalay. In 1910, Vinayak Damodar Savarkar, a young follower of Tilak, was arrested for organizing an armed revolt against the Morley–Minto reforms. (In prison Savarkar turned toward political Hinduism and in 1923 wrote *Hindutva: Who Is a Hindu?*)

When Ambedkar graduated, he became one of three students who was given a scholarship by Sayajirao Gaekwad to travel abroad to continue his studies. In 1913 (Gandhi's last year in South Africa), the boy who had to sit on a gunnysack on his classroom floor was admitted to Columbia University in New York. It was while he was there, under the tutelage of John Dewey (of "Deweyan liberalism" fame), Edwin Seligman, James Shotwell, James Harvey Robinson, and A. A. Goldenweiser, that he wrote his original, path-breaking paper on caste, "Castes in India: Their Mechanism, Genesis and Development," in which he argued that caste could not be equated with either race or class, but was a unique social category in itself—an enclosed, endogamous class. When he wrote it, Ambedkar was only twenty-five years old. He returned briefly to India and then went to London to study economics at the London School of Economics and simultaneously take a degree in law at Gray's Inn in London—a degree he had to abandon halfway but completed later.

Ambedkar returned to Baroda in 1917. To repay his scholarship, he was expected to serve as military secretary to the Maharaja. He came back to a very different reception from the one Gandhi received. There were no glittering ceremonies, no wealthy sponsors. On the contrary, from spending hours reading in the university library with its endless books, and eating at dining tables with napkins and cutlery, Ambedkar returned to the thorny embrace of the caste system. Afraid of even accidentally touching Ambedkar, clerks and peons in his office would fling files at him. Carpets were rolled up when he walked in and out of office so that they would not be polluted by him. He found no accommodation in the city: his Hindu, Muslim, and Christian friends, even those he had known at Columbia, turned him down. Eventually, by masquerading as a Parsi, he got a room at a Parsi inn. When the owners discovered he was an Untouchable, he was thrown onto the street by armed men. "I can even now vividly recall it and never recall it without tears in my eyes," Ambedkar wrote. "It was then for the first time I learnt that a person who is Untouchable to a Hindu is also Untouchable to a Parsi."

Unable to find accommodation in Baroda, Ambedkar returned to Bombay, where, after initially teaching private tutorials, he got a job as a professor at Sydenham College.

In 1917, Hindu reformers were wooing Untouchables with an edge of desperation. The Congress had passed its resolution against untouchability. Both Gandhi and Tilak called untouchability a "disease" that was antithetical to Hinduism. The first All-India Depressed Classes Conference was held in Bombay, presided over by Ambedkar's patron and mentor, Maharaja Sayajirao Gaekwad, and attended by several luminaries of the time, including Tilak. They passed the All-India Anti-Untouchability Manifesto, which was signed by all of them (except Tilak, who managed to find a way around it).

Ambedkar stayed away from these meetings. He had begun to grow sceptical about these very public but completely out-of-character displays of solicitude for Untouchables. He saw that these were ways in which, in the changing times, the privileged castes were maneuvering to consolidate their control over the Untouchable community. While his audience, his constituency, and his chief concern were the Untouchables, Ambedkar believed that it was not just the stigma, the pollution–purity issues around untouchability, but caste itself that had to be dismantled. The practice of untouchability, cruel as it was—the broom tied to the waist, the pot hung around the neck—was the performative, ritualistic end of the practice of caste. The real violence of caste was the denial of entitlement: to land, to wealth, to knowledge, to equal opportunity. (The caste system is the feudal version of the doctrine of trusteeship: the entitled must be left in possession of their entitlement and be trusted to use it for the public good.)

How can a system of such immutable hierarchy be maintained if not by the threat of egregious, ubiquitous violence? How do landlords force laborers, generation after generation, to toil night and day on subsistence wages? Why would an Untouchable laborer, who is not allowed to even dream of being a landowner one day, put his or her life at the landlord's disposal, to plough the land, to sow seed, and harvest the crop, if it were not out of sheer terror of the punishment that awaits the wayward? (Farmers, unlike industrialists, cannot afford strikes. Seed must be sown when it must be sown, the crop must be harvested when it must be harvested. The farmworker must be terrorized into abject submission, into being available when he must be available.) How were African slaves forced to work on American cotton fields? By being flogged, by being lynched, and if that did not work, by being hung from a tree for others to see and be afraid. Why are the murders of insubordinate Dalits even today never simply murders but ritual slaughter? Why are they always burnt alive, raped, dismembered, and paraded naked? Why did Surekha Bhotmange and her children have to die the way they did?

Ambedkar tried to provide an answer:

> *Why have the mass of people tolerated the social evils to which they have been subjected? There have been social revolutions in other countries of the world. Why have there not been social revolutions in India, is a question that has incessantly troubled me. There is only one answer which I can give and it is that the lower classes of Hindus have been completely disabled for direct action on account of this wretched caste system. They could not bear arms, and without arms they could not rebel. They were all ploughmen—or rather condemned to be ploughmen—and they were never allowed to convert their ploughshares into swords. They had no bayonets, and therefore everyone who chose, could and did sit upon them. On account of the caste system, they could receive no education. They could not think out or know the way to their salvation. They were condemned to be lowly; and not knowing the way of escape, and not having the means of escape, they became reconciled to eternal servitude, which they accepted as their inescapable fate.*

In rural areas, the threat of actual physical violence sometimes paled before the specter of the "social boycott" that orthodox Hindus would proclaim against any Untouchable who dared to defy the system. (This could mean anything from daring to buy a piece of land, wearing nice clothes, smoking a bidi in the presence of a caste Hindu, or having the temerity to wear shoes or ride a mare in a wedding procession. The crime could even be an attitude, a posture that was less craven than an Untouchable's is meant to be.) It's the opposite of the boycott that the civil rights movement in the US used as a campaign tool; the American Blacks at least had a modicum of economic clout to boycott buses and businesses that held them in contempt. Among privileged castes, the social boycott in rural India traditionally means "*hukka-pani bandh*"—no *hukka* (tobacco) and no *pani* (water) for a person who has annoyed the community. Though it's called a "social boycott," it is an economic as well as social boycott. For Dalits, that is lethal. The "sinners" are denied employment in the neighborhood, denied the right to food and water, denied the right to buy provisions in the village Bania's shop. They are hounded out and left to starve. The social boycott continues to be used as a weapon against Dalits in Indian villages. It is noncooperation by the powerful against the powerless—noncooperation, as we know it, turned on its head.

In order to detach caste from the political economy, from conditions of enslavement in which most Dalits lived and worked, in order to elide the questions of entitlement, land reforms, and the redistribution of wealth, Hindu reformers cleverly narrowed the question of caste to the issue of untouchability. They framed it as an erroneous religious and cultural practice that needed to be reformed.

Gandhi narrowed it even further to the issue of "*bhangis*"—scavengers, a mostly urban and therefore somewhat politicized community. From his childhood, he resurrected the memory of Uka, the boy scavenger who used to service the household's lavatory, and often spoke of how the Gandhi family's treatment of Uka had always troubled him. Rural Untouchables—ploughmen, potters, tanners, and their families—lived in scattered, small communities, in hutments on the edges of villages (beyond polluting distance). Urban Untouchables—bhangis, Chuhras, and Mehtars—scavengers, as Gandhi liked to call them, lived together in numbers and actually formed a political constituency. In order to discourage them from converting to Christianity, Lala Mulk Raj Bhalla, a Hindu reformer of the Punjabi Khatri caste, rebaptized them in 1910, and they came to collectively be called Balmikis. Gandhi seized upon the Balmikis and made them his show window for untouchability. Upon them he performed his missionary acts of goodness and charity. He preached to them how to love and hold on to their heritage and how to never aspire toward anything more than the joys of their hereditary occupation. All through his life, Gandhi wrote a great deal about the importance of "scavenging" as a religious duty. It did not seem to matter that people in the rest of the world were dealing with their shit without making such a fuss about it.

Delivering the presidential address at the Kathiawar Political Conference in Bhavnagar on January 8, 1925, Gandhi said:

> *If at all I seek any position it is that of a bhangi. Cleansing of dirt is sacred work which can be done by a Brahmin as well as a bhangi, the former doing it with and the latter without the knowledge of its holiness. I respect and honour both of them. In the absence of either of the two, Hinduism is bound to face extinction. I like the path of service; therefore, I like the bhangi. I have personally no objection to sharing my meal with him, but I am not asking you to inter-dine with or inter-marry him. How can I advise you?*

Gandhi's attentiveness toward the Balmikis, his greatly publicized visits to "bhangi colonies," paid dividends, despite the fact that he treated them with condescension and contempt. When he stayed in one such colony in 1946

> *half the residents were moved out before his visit and the shacks of the residents torn down and neat little huts constructed in their place. The entrances and windows of the huts were screened with matting, and during the length of Gandhi's visit, were kept*

sprinkled with water to provide a cooling effect. The local temple was white-washed and new brick paths were laid. In an interview with Margaret Bourke-White, a photo-journalist for Life magazine, one of the men in charge of Gandhi's visit, Dinanath Tiang of the Birla Company, explained the improvements in the untouchable colony, "We have cared for Gandhiji's comfort for the last twenty years."

In his history of the Balmiki workers of Delhi, the scholar Vijay Prashad says when Gandhi staged his visits to the Balmiki Colony on Mandir Marg (formerly Reading Road) in 1946, he refused to eat with the community:

"You can offer me goat's milk," he said, "but I will pay for it. If you are keen that I should take food prepared by you, you can come here and cook my food for me". . . . Balmiki elders recount tales of Gandhi's hypocrisy, but only with a sense of uneasiness. When a dalit gave Gandhi nuts, he fed them to his goat, saying that he would eat them later, in the goat's milk. Most of Gandhi's food, nuts and grains, came from Birla House; he did not take these from the dalits. Radical Balmikis took refuge in Ambedkarism which openly confronted Gandhi on these issues.

Ambedkar realized that the problem of caste would only be further entrenched unless Untouchables were able to organize, mobilize, and become a political constituency with their own representatives. He believed that reserved seats for Untouchables within the Hindu fold, or within the Congress, would just produce pliable candidates—servants who knew how to please their masters. He began to develop the idea of a separate electorate for Untouchables. In 1919, he submitted a written testimony to the Southborough Committee on electoral reforms. The committee's brief was to propose a scheme of territorial constituencies based on existing land revenue districts and separate communal representation for Muslims, Christians, and Sikhs, for a new constitution that was to be drafted to prepare for Home Rule. The Congress boycotted the committee. To his critics, who called him a collaborator and a traitor, Ambedkar said that Home Rule was as much the right of the Untouchable as it was of the Brahmin, and it was the duty of privileged castes to do what they could to put everybody on an equal plane. In his testimony, Ambedkar argued that Untouchables were as separate a social group from Touchable Hindus as Muslims, Christians, and Sikhs:

> *The right of representation and the right to hold office under the State are the two most important rights that make up citizenship. But the untouchability of the untouchables puts these rights far beyond their reach. In a few places they do not even possess such insignificant rights as personal liberty and personal security, and equality before law is not always assured to them. These are the interests of the Untouchables. And as can be easily seen they can be represented by the Untouchables alone. They are distinctively their own interests and none else can truly voice them. . . . Hence it is evident that we must find the Untouchables to represent their grievances which are their interests and, secondly, we must find them in such numbers as will constitute a force sufficient to claim redress.*

The British government did not, at that point, pay much attention to his testimony, though his presentation did perhaps provide the basis for Ambedkar being invited to the First Round Table Conference ten years later, in 1930.

Around this time, Ambedkar started his first journal, *Mook Nayak* (Leader of the Voiceless). Tilak's newspaper, *Kesari*, refused to carry even a paid advertisement announcing the publication of *Mook Nayak*. The editor of *Mook Nayak* was P. N. Bhatkar, the first Mahar to matriculate and go to college. Ambedkar wrote the first thirteen editorials himself. In the first one, he described Hindu society in a chilling metaphor—as a multistoried tower with no staircase and no entrance. Everybody had to die in the story they were born in.

In May 1920, backed by Chhatrapati Shahu, the Maharaja of Kolhapur, known for his anti-Brahmin views and for pioneering the policy of reservation in education and jobs as far back as 1902, Ambedkar and his colleagues organized the first All-India Depressed Classes Conference in Nagpur. It was agreed that no Untouchable representative chosen by a caste-Hindu majority could (or would) genuinely work against chaturvarna.

The 1920s marked the beginning of an era of direct action by Untouchables for the right to use wells, schools, courts, offices, and public transport. In 1924, in what came to be known as the Vaikom Satyagraha, the Ezhavas, a community-designated Shudra, and the Pulayas, who were Untouchables, agitated to use the public roads that skirted the Mahadeva temple in Vaikom, twenty miles from Kottayam in Travancore (now in the state of Kerala). One of the leaders of the Vaikom Satyagraha was George Joseph, a Syrian Christian, and an admirer of Gandhi. Gandhi, on his part, disapproved of a "non-Hindu" intervening in what he believed to be an "internal matter" of the Hindus. (The same logic had not applied three years before, when he "led" the Khilafat Movement.) He was also reluctant to support a full-blown satyagraha in an "Indian-ruled" state. During the course of the Vaikom Satyagraha, George Joseph was imprisoned. He became deeply disillusioned by what he saw as Gandhi's inexcusable ambivalence on the issue of caste. As the tension in Vaikom rose, C. Rajagopalachari, Congress leader and Gandhi's chief lieutenant, traveled to Vaikom to oversee matters. On May 27, 1924, he reassured the worried privileged-caste Hindus of Vaikom in a public speech:

> *Let not the people of Vykom or any other place fear that Mahatmaji wants caste abolished. Mahatmaji does not want the caste system abolished but holds that untouchability should be abolished. . . . Mahatmaji does not want you to dine with Thiyas or Pulayas. What he wants is that we must be prepared to touch*

or go near other human beings as you go near a cow or a horse . . .
Mahatmaji wants you to look upon so-called untouchables as you
do at the cow and the dog and other harmless creatures.

Gandhi himself arrived in Vaikom in March 1925 to arbitrate.
He consulted with the Brahmin priests of the temple—who did
not allow him, a non-Brahmin, to enter the sanctum—and the
Queen of Travancore, and negotiated a compromise: the roads
were realigned so that they were no longer within "polluting"
distance from the temple. The contentious portion of the road
remained closed to Christians and Muslims as well as avarnas
(Untouchables) who continued to have no right to enter the
temple. Saying he was "unable to satisfy the orthodox friends"
Gandhi advised the "withdrawal of satyagraha," but the local
satyagrahis continued with their struggle. Twelve years later,
in November 1936, the Maharaja of Travancore issued the first
Temple Entry Proclamation in India.

If one of Gandhi's first major political actions was the "solution" to the problem of the Durban Post Office, Ambedkar's was
the Mahad Satyagraha of 1927.

In 1923, the Legislative Council of Bombay (whose elections
had been boycotted by the Congress) passed a resolution, the
Bole Resolution, that allowed Untouchables to use public tanks,
wells, schools, courts, and dispensaries. In the town of Mahad,
the municipality declared that it had no objection if Untouchables
used the Chavadar Tank in the town. Passing a resolution was one
thing, acting on it quite another. After four years of mobilization,
the Untouchables gathered courage and, in March 1927, held a
two-day conference in Mahad. Money for the conference was
raised by public contribution. In an unpublished manuscript, the
scholar Anand Teltumbde quotes Anant Vinayak Chitre, one of
the organizers of the Mahad Satyagraha, saying that forty villages
contributed Rs 3 (six cents) each, and a play about Tukaram was
staged in Bombay that made Rs 23 (forty-seven cents), making
the total collection Rs 143 (two dollars and ninety-three cents).

Contrast this with Gandhi's troubles. Just a few months before the Mahad Satyagraha, on January 10, 1927, Gandhi wrote to his industrialist-patron, G. D. Birla:

> *My thirst for money is simply unquenchable. I need at least Rs 200,000—for Khadi, Untouchability and education. The dairy work makes another 50,000. Then there is the Ashram expenditure. No work remains unfinished for want of funds, but God gives after severe trials. This also satisfies me. You can give as you like for whatever work you have faith in.*

The Mahad conference was attended by about three thousand Untouchables, and a handful of progressive members of the privileged castes. (V. D. Savarkar, out of jail by now, was one of the supporters of the Mahad Satyagraha.) Ambedkar presided over the meeting. On the morning of the second day people decided to march to the Chavadar Tank and drink water. The privileged castes watched in horror as a procession of Untouchables walked through the town, four abreast, and drank water from the tank. After the shock subsided came the violent counterattack, with clubs and sticks. Twenty Untouchables were injured. Ambedkar urged his people to stay firm and not to strike back. A rumor was deliberately spread that the Untouchables planned to enter the Veereshwar temple, which added a hysterical edge to the violence. The Untouchables scattered. Some found shelter in Muslim homes. For his own safety, Ambedkar spent the night in the police station. Once calm returned, the Brahmins "purified" the tank with prayers, and with 108 pots of cow dung, cow urine, milk, curd, and ghee. The symbolic exercise of their rights did not satisfy the Mahad satyagrahis. In June 1927, an advertisement appeared in *Bahishkrit Bharat* (Excluded India), a fortnightly Ambedkar had founded, asking those members of the Depressed Classes who wished to take the agitation further to enlist themselves. The orthodox Hindus of Mahad approached the sub-judge of the town and got a temporary legal injunction against the Untouchables using the tank. Still, the

Untouchables decided to hold another conference and regrouped in Mahad in December. Ambedkar's disenchantment with Gandhi was still some years away. Gandhi had, in fact, spoken approvingly of the Untouchables' composure in the face of the attacks from the orthodoxy, so his portrait was put up on stage.

Ten thousand people attended the second Mahad conference. On this occasion Ambedkar and his followers publicly burnt a copy of the *Manusmriti*, and Ambedkar gave a stirring speech:

> *Gentlemen, you have gathered here today in response to the invitation of the Satyagraha Committee. As the Chairman of that Committee, I gratefully welcome you all. . . . This lake at Mahad is public property. The caste Hindus of Mahad are so reasonable that they not only draw water from the lake themselves but freely permit people of any religion to draw water from it, and accordingly people of other religions, such as Islam, do make use of this permission. Nor do the caste Hindus prevent members of species considered lower than the human, such as birds and beasts, from drinking at the lake. Moreover, they freely permit beasts kept by untouchables to drink at the lake.*
>
> *The caste Hindus of Mahad prevent the untouchables from drinking the water of the Chavadar Lake not because they suppose that the touch of the Untouchables will pollute the water or that it will evaporate and vanish. Their reason for preventing the Untouchables from drinking it is that they do not wish to acknowledge by such permission that castes declared inferior by sacred tradition are in fact their equals.*
>
> *It is not as if drinking the water of the Chavadar Lake will make us immortal. We have survived well enough all these days without drinking it. We are not going to the Chavadar Lake merely to drink its water. We are going to the Lake to assert that we too are human beings like others. It must be clear that this meeting has been called to set up the norm of equality . . .*

Time and again, Ambedkar returned to the theme of equality.

THE DOCTOR AND THE SAINT

Men may not all be equal, he said, but equality was the only possible governing principle because the classification and assortment of human society was impossible.

> To sum up, untouchability is not a simple matter; it is the mother of all our poverty and lowliness and it has brought us to the abject state we are in today. If we want to raise ourselves out of it, we must undertake this task. We cannot be saved in any other way. It is a task not for our benefit alone; it is also for the benefit of the nation.
>
> Even this will not be enough. The inequality inherent in the four-castes system must be rooted out.... Our work has been begun to bring about a real social revolution. Let no one deceive himself by supposing that it is a diversion to quieten minds entranced with sweet words. The work is sustained by strong feeling, which is the power that drives the movement. No one can now arrest it. I pray to god that the social revolution that begins here today may fulfil itself by peaceful means. We say to our opponents too: please do not oppose us. Put away the orthodox scriptures. Follow justice. And we assure you that we shall carry out our programme peacefully.

The thousands attending the conference were in a militant mood and wanted to defy the court injunction and march to the tank. Ambedkar decided against it, hoping that after hearing the matter, the courts would declare that Untouchables had the right to use public wells. He thought that a judicial order would be a substantial step forward from just a municipal resolution. Although the high court did eventually lift the injunction, it found a technical way around making a legal declaration in favor of the Untouchables (like the judge who, almost eighty years later, wrote the Khairlanji verdict).

That same month (December 1927), Gandhi spoke at the All-India Suppressed Classes Conference in Lahore, where he preached a gospel opposite to Ambedkar's. He urged Untouchables to fight for their rights by "sweet persuasion and not by Satyagraha which becomes Duragraha when it is intended to give rude shock to the deep-rooted prejudices of the people." He defined duragraha as "devilish force," which was the polar opposite of Satyagraha, "soul force."

Ambedkar never forgot Gandhi's response to the Mahad Satyagraha. Writing in 1945, in *What Congress and Gandhi Have Done to the Untouchables*, he said:

> *The Untouchables were not without hope of getting the moral support of Mr Gandhi. Indeed they had very good ground for getting it. For the weapon of satyagraha—the essence of which is to melt the heart of the opponent by suffering—was the weapon which was forged by Mr Gandhi, and who had led the Congress to practise it against the British Government for winning swaraj. Naturally the Untouchables expected full support from Mr Gandhi to their satyagraha against the Hindus the object of which was to establish their right to take water from public wells and to enter public Hindu temples. Mr Gandhi however did not give his support to the satyagraha. Not only did he not give his support, he condemned it in strong terms.*

Logically, the direction in which Ambedkar was moving ought to have made him a natural ally of the Communist Party of India, founded in 1925, two years before the Mahad Satyagraha. Bolshevism was in the air. The Russian Revolution had inspired communists around the world. In the Bombay Presidency, the trade union leader S. A. Dange, a Maharashtrian Brahmin, organized a large section of the Bombay textile workers into a breakaway union—the Girni Kamgar Union, India's first communist trade union, with seventy thousand members. At the time a large section of the workforce in the mills were Untouchables, many of them Mahars, who were employed only in the much lower paid spinning department, because in the weaving department workers had to hold thread in their mouths, and the Untouchables' saliva was believed to be polluting to the product. In 1928, Dange led the Girni Kamgar Union's first major strike. Ambedkar suggested that one of the issues that ought to be raised was equality and equal entitlement within the ranks of workers. Dange did not agree, and this led to a long and bitter falling out.

Years later, in 1949, Dange, who is still a revered figure in the communist pantheon, wrote a book, *Marxism and Ancient Indian Culture: India from Primitive Communism to Slavery*, in which he argued that ancient Hindu culture was a form of primitive communism in which "Brahman is the commune of Aryan man and yagnya [ritual fire sacrifice] is its means of production, the primitive commune with the collective mode of production." D. D. Kosambi, the mathematician and Marxist historian, said in a review: "This is so wildly improbable as to plunge into the ridiculous."

The Bombay mills have since closed down, though the Girni Kamgar Union still exists. Mill workers are fighting for compensation and housing and resisting the takeover of mill lands for the construction of malls. The Communist Party has lost its influence, and the union has been taken over by the Shiv Sena, a party of militant Maharashtrian Hindu chauvinists.

Years before Ambedkar and Dange were disagreeing about the internal inequalities between laborers, Gandhi was already an established labor organizer. What were his views on workers and strikes?

Gandhi returned from South Africa at a time of continuous labor unrest. The textile industry had done well for itself during World War I, but the prosperity was not reflected in workers' wages. In February 1918, millworkers in Ahmedabad went on strike. To mediate the dispute, Ambalal Sarabhai, president of the Ahmedabad Mill Owners' Association, turned to Gandhi, who had set up his ashram in Sabarmati, just outside Ahmedabad. It was the beginning of Gandhi's lifelong career as a labor union organizer in India. By 1920, he had managed to set up a labor union called the Majoor Mahajan Sangh—which translates as the Workers and Mill Owners Association. The English name was the Textile Labour Union. Anusuyaben, Ambalal Sarabhai's sister, a labor organizer, was elected president for life, and Gandhi became a pivotal member of the advisory committee, also for life. The union did work at improving the hygiene and living conditions of workers, but no worker was ever elected to the union leadership. No worker was permitted to be present at closed-door arbitrations between the management and the union. The union was divided up into a federation of smaller, occupation-based unions whose members worked in the different stages of the production process. In other words, the structure of the union institutionalized caste divisions. According to a worker interviewed by the scholar Jan Breman, Untouchables were not allowed into the common canteen; they had separate drinking water tanks and segregated housing.

In the union, Gandhi was the prime organizer, negotiator, and decision maker. In 1921, when workers did not turn up for work for three days, Gandhi was infuriated:

> *Hindu and Muslim workers have dishonoured and humiliated themselves by abstaining from mills. Labour cannot discount me. I believe no one in India can do so. I am trying to free India from bondage and I refuse to be enslaved by workers.*

Here is a 1925 entry from a report of the Textile Labour Union. We don't know who wrote it, but its content and its literary cadence are unmistakably similar to what Gandhi had said about indentured labor in South Africa more than thirty years before:

> *They are not as a rule armed with sufficient intelligence and moral development to resist the degrading influences which surround them on all sides in a city like this. So many of them sink in one way or another. A large number of them lose their moral balance and become slaves to liquor habits, many go down as physical wrecks and waste away from tuberculosis.*

Since Gandhi's main sponsor was a mill owner and his main

constituency was supposed to be the laboring class, Gandhi developed a convoluted thesis on capitalists and the working class:

> *The mill-owner may be wholly in the wrong. In the struggle between capital and labour, it may be generally said that more often than not capitalists are in the wrong box. But when labour comes fully to realise its strength, I know it can become more tyrannical than capital. The mill-owners will have to work on the terms dictated by labour, if the latter could command the intelligence of the former. It is clear, however, that labour will never attain to that intelligence. . . . It would be suicidal if the labourers rely upon their numbers or brute-force, i.e., violence. By doing so they would do harm to industries in the country. If on the other hand they take their stand on pure justice and suffer in their person to secure it, not only will they always succeed but they will reform their masters, develop industries, and both masters and men will be as members of one and the same family.*

Gandhi took a dim view of strikes. But his views on sweepers' strikes, which he published in 1946, were even more stringent than those on other workers' strikes:

> *There are certain matters on which strikes would be wrong. Sweepers' grievances come in this category. My opinion against sweepers' strikes dates back to about 1897 when I was in Durban. A general strike was mooted there, and the question arose as to whether scavengers should join it. My vote was registered against the proposal. Just as a man cannot live without air, so too he cannot exist for long if his home and surroundings are not clean. One or the other epidemic is bound to break out, especially when modern drainage is put out of action. . . . A bhangi [scavenger] may not give up his work even for a day. And there are many other ways open to him for securing justice.*

It's not clear what the "other" ways were for securing justice:

Untouchables on satyagraha were committing duragraha. Sweepers on strike were sinning. Everything other than "sweet persuasion" was unacceptable.

While workers could not strike for fair wages, it was perfectly correct for Gandhi to be generously sponsored by big industrialists. (It was with this same sense of exceptionalism that in his reply to *Annihilation of Caste* he wrote, as point number one, "He [Ambedkar] has priced it at 8 annas, I would have advised 2 or at least 4 annas.")

The differences between Ambedkar and the new Communist Party of India were not superficial. They went back to first principles. Communists were people of The Book, and The Book was written by a German Jew who had heard of, but had not actually encountered, Brahminism. This left Indian communists without theoretical tools to deal with caste. Since they were people of The Book, and since the caste system had denied Shudra and Untouchable castes the opportunity of learning, by default the leaders of the Communist Party of India and its subsequent offshoots belonged to (and by and large continue to belong to) the privileged castes, mostly Brahmin. Despite intentions that may have been genuinely revolutionary, it was not just theoretical tools they lacked, but also a ground-level understanding and empathy with "the masses" who belonged to the subordinated castes. While Ambedkar believed that class was an important—and even primary—prism through which to view and understand society, he did not believe it was the only one. Ambedkar believed that the two enemies of the Indian working class were capitalism (in the liberal sense of the word) and Brahminism. Reflecting perhaps on his experience in the 1928 textile workers' strike, he asks in *Annihilation of Caste*:

> *That seizure of power must be by a proletariat. The first question I ask is: Will the proletariat of India combine to bring about this revolution? . . . Can it be said that the proletariat of India, poor*

as it is, recognises no distinctions except that of the rich and poor?
Can it be said that the poor in India recognise no such distinctions
of caste or creed, high or low?

To Indian communists, who treated caste as a sort of folk dialect
derived from the classical language of class analysis, rather than
as a unique, fully developed language of its own, Ambedkar
said, "[T]he caste system is not merely a division of labour. *It is
also a division of labourers.*"

Unable to reconcile his differences with the communists, and
still looking for a political home for his ideas, Ambedkar decided
to try and build one himself. In 1938, he founded his own political party, the Independent Labour Party. As its name suggests,
the program of the ILP was broad-based, overtly socialist,
and not limited to issues of caste. Its manifesto announced
"the principle of State management and State ownership of
industry whenever it may become necessary in the interests
of the people." It promised a separation between the judiciary
and the executive. It said it would set up land mortgage banks,
agriculturist producers' cooperatives, and marketing societies.
Though it was a young party, the Independent Labour Party
did extremely well in the 1937 elections, winning sixteen of the
eighteen seats it contested in the Bombay Presidency and the
Central Provinces and Berar. In 1939, the British government,
without consulting any Indians, declared that India was at war
with Germany. In protest, the Congress Party resigned from all
provincial ministries, and the provincial assemblies were dissolved. The brief but vigorous political life of the Independent
Labour Party came to an abrupt end.

Angered by Ambedkar's display of independence, the communists denounced him as an "opportunist" and an "imperial
stooge." In his book *History of the Indian Freedom Struggle*, E.
M. S. Namboodiripad, the (Brahmin) former chief minister of
Kerala and head of the first ever democratically elected communist government in the world, wrote about the conflict between

Ambedkar and the left: "However, this was a great blow to the freedom movement. For this led to the diversion of the people's attention from the objective of full independence to the *mundane cause* of uplift of Harijans [Untouchables]."

The rift has not mended and has harmed both sides mortally. For a brief period in the 1970s, the Dalit Panthers in Maharashtra tried to bridge the gap. They were the progeny of Ambedkar the radical (as opposed to Ambedkar the writer of the constitution). They gave the Marathi word "Dalit"—oppressed, broken—an all-India currency, and used it to refer not just to Untouchable communities, but to "the working people, the landless and poor peasants, women and all those who are being exploited politically and economically and in the name of religion." This was a phenomenal and politically confident act of solidarity on their part. They saw Dalits as a Nation of the Oppressed. They identified their friends as "revolutionary parties set to break down the caste system and class rule" and "left parties that are left in the true sense"; and their enemies as "landlords, capitalists, moneylenders and their lackeys." Their manifesto, essential reading for students of radical politics, fused the thinking of Ambedkar, Phule, and Marx. The founders of the Dalit Panthers—Namdeo Dhasal, Arun Kamble, and Raja Dhale—were writers and poets, and their work created a renaissance in Marathi literature.

It could have been the beginning of the revolution that India needed and is still waiting for, but the Dalit Panthers swiftly lost their bearings and disintegrated.

The caste–class question is not an easy one for political parties to address. The Communist Party's theoretical obtuseness to caste has lost it what ought to have been its natural constituency. The Communist Party of India and its offshoot, the Communist Party of India (Marxist), have more or less become bourgeois parties enmeshed in parliamentary politics. Those that split away from them in the late 1960s and independent Marxist-Leninist parties in other states (collectively known as the "Naxalites," named after the first uprising in the village of Naxalbari in West Bengal) have tried to address the issue of caste and to make common cause with Dalits, but with little success. The few efforts they made to seize land from big zamindars and redistribute it to laborers failed because they did not have the mass support or the military firepower to see it through. Their sidelong nod to caste as opposed to a direct engagement with it has meant that even radical communist parties have lost the support of what could have been a truly militant and revolutionary constituency.

Dalits have been fragmented and pitted against each other. Many have had to move either into mainstream parliamentary politics or—with the public sector being hollowed out, and job opportunities in the private sector being denied to them—into the world of NGOs, with grants from the European Union, the Ford Foundation, and other funding agencies with a long, self-serving history of defusing radical movements and harnessing them to "market forces." There is no doubt that this funding has given a few Dalits an opportunity to be educated in what are thought to be the world's best universities. (This, after all, is what made Ambedkar the man he was.) However, even here, the Dalits' share in the massive NGO money-pie is minuscule. And within these institutions (some of which are generously funded by big corporations to work on issues of caste discrimination, like Gandhi was), Dalits can be treated in unfair and ugly ways.

In his search for primitive communism, S. A. Dange would have been better advised to look toward indigenous Adivasi communities rather than toward the ancient Vedic Brahmins and their yagnyas. Gandhi too could have done the same. If anybody was even remotely living out his ideal of frugal village life, of stepping lightly on the earth, it was not the Vedic Hindus, it was the Adivasis. For them, however, Gandhi showed the same level of disdain that he did for Black Africans. Speaking in 1896 at a public meeting in Bombay, he said: "The Santhals of Assam will be as useless in South Africa as the natives of that country."

On the Adivasi question, Ambedkar too stumbles. So quick to

react to slights against his own people, Ambedkar, in a passage in *Annihilation of Caste*, echoes the thinking of colonial missionaries and liberal ideologues and adds his own touch of Brahminism:

> *Thirteen million people living in the midst of civilisation are still in a savage state, and are leading the life of hereditary crimi-nals.... The Hindus will probably seek to account for this savage state of the aborigines by attributing to them congenital stupidity. They will probably not admit that the aborigines have remained savages because they made no effort to civilise them, to give them medical aid, to reform them, to make them good citizens. . . . Civilising the aborigines means adopting them as your own, living in their midst, and cultivating fellow-feeling—in short, loving them . . .*
>
> *The Hindu has not realised that these aborigines are a source of potential danger. If these savages remain savages, they may not do any harm to the Hindus. But if they are reclaimed by non-Hindus and converted to their faiths, they will swell the ranks of the enemies of the Hindus.*

Today, Adivasis are the barricade against the pitiless march of modern capitalism. Their very existence poses the most radical questions about modernity and "progress"—the ideas that Ambedkar embraced as one of the ways out of the caste system. Unfortunately, by viewing the Adivasi community through the lens of Western liberalism, Ambedkar's writing, which is otherwise so relevant in today's context, suddenly becomes dated.

Ambedkar's opinions about Adivasis betrayed a lack of information and understanding. First of all, Hindu evangelists like the Hindu Mahasabha had been working to "assimilate" the Adivasis since the 1920s (just like they were Balmiki-izing castes that were forced into cleaning and scavenging work). Tribes like the Ho, the Oraon, the Kols, the Santhals, the Mundas, and the Gonds did not wish to be "civilized" or "assimilated." They had rebelled time and again against the British as well as against zamindars and Bania moneylenders and had fought fiercely to protect their land, culture, and heritage. Thousands had been killed in these uprisings, but unlike the rest of India, they were never conquered. They still have not been. Today, they are the armed, militant end of a spectrum of struggles. They are waging nothing short of a civil war against the Indian state, which has signed over Adivasi homelands to infrastructure and mining corporations. They are the backbone of the decades-long struggle against Big Dams in the Narmada valley. They make up the ranks of the People's Liberation Guerrilla Army of the Communist Party of India (Maoist) that is fighting tens of thousands of paramilitary forces that have been deployed by the government in the forests of Central India.

In a 1945 address in Bombay ("The Communal Deadlock and a Way to Solve It"), discussing the issue of proportionate representation, Ambedkar brought up the issue of Adivasi rights once again. He said:

> *My proposals do not cover the Aboriginal Tribes although they are larger in number than the Sikhs, Anglo-Indians, Indian Christians and Parsis. . . . The Aboriginal Tribes have not as yet developed any political sense to make the best use of their political opportunities and they may easily become mere instruments in the hands either of a majority or a minority and thereby disturb the balance without doing any good to themselves.*

This unfortunate way of describing a community was sometimes aimed at non-Adivasis, too, in an equally troubling manner. At one point in *Annihilation of Caste* Ambedkar resorts to using the language of eugenics, a subject that was popular with European fascists: "Physically speaking the Hindus are a C3 people. They are a race of pygmies and dwarfs, stunted in stature and wanting in stamina."

His views on Adivasis had serious consequences. In 1950, the Indian Constitution made the state the custodian of Adivasi homelands, thereby ratifying British colonial policy. The Adivasi population became squatters on their own land. By denying them their traditional rights to forest produce, it criminalized a whole way of life. It gave them the right to vote, but snatched away their livelihood and dignity.

How different are Ambedkar's words on Adivasis from Gandhi's words on Untouchables when he said:

> *Muslims and Sikhs are all well organised. The "Untouchables" are not. There is very little political consciousness among them, and they are so horribly treated that I want to save them against themselves. If they had separate electorates, their lives would be miserable in villages which are the strongholds of Hindu orthodoxy. It is the superior class of Hindus who have to do penance for having neglected the "Untouchables" for ages. That penance can be done by active social reform and by making the lot of the "Untouchables" more bearable by acts of service, but not by asking for separate electorates for them.*

Gandhi said this at the Second Round Table Conference in London in 1931. It was the first public face-to-face encounter between Ambedkar and Gandhi.

THE CONFRONTATION

The Congress had boycotted the First Round Table Conference in 1930 but nominated Gandhi as its representative in the second. The aim of the conference was to frame a new constitution for self-rule. The princely states and representatives of various minority communities—Muslims, Sikhs, Christians, Parsis, and Untouchables—were present. Adivasis went unrepresented. For Untouchables, it was a historic occasion. It was the first time that they had been invited as a separately represented constituency. One of the several committees that made up the conference was the Minority Committee, charged with the task of finding a workable solution to the growing communal question. It was potentially the most inflammable and, perhaps for that reason, was chaired by the British prime minister, Ramsay MacDonald.

It was to this committee that Ambedkar submitted his memorandum, "A Scheme of Political Safeguards for the Protection of the Depressed Classes in the Future Constitution of a Self-Governing India." It was, for its time, within the framework of liberal debates on rights and citizenship, a revolutionary document. In it, Ambedkar tried to do in law what he dreamt of achieving socially and politically. This document was an early draft of some of the ideas that Ambedkar eventually managed to put into the constitution of post-1947 India.

Under "Condition No. 1: Equal Citizenship," it says:

> The Depressed Classes cannot consent to subject themselves to majority rule in their present state of hereditary bondsmen. Before majority rule is established, their emancipation from the system of untouchability must be an accomplished fact. It must not be left to the will of the majority. The Depressed Classes must be made free citizens entitled to all the rights of citizenship in common with other citizens of the State.

The memorandum went on to delineate what would constitute Fundamental Rights and how they were to be protected. It gave Untouchables the right to access all public places. It dwelt at length on social boycotts and suggested they be declared a criminal offense. It prescribed a series of measures by which Untouchables would be protected from social boycotts and caste Hindus punished for instigating and promoting them. Condition No. 5 asked that a Public Service Commission be set up to ensure Untouchables "Adequate Representation in the Services." This is what has eventually evolved into the system of reservation in educational institutions and government jobs, against which privileged castes in recent times have militantly agitated.

The most unique aspect of Ambedkar's memorandum was his proposal for a system of positive discrimination within the electoral system. Ambedkar did not believe that universal adult franchise alone could secure equal rights for Untouchables. Since the Untouchable population was scattered across the country in little settlements on the outskirts of Hindu villages, Ambedkar realized that within the geographical demarcation of a political constituency, they would always be a minority and would never be in a position to elect a candidate of their own choice. He suggested that Untouchables, who had been despised and devalued for so many centuries, be given a separate electorate so that they could, without interference from the Hindu orthodoxy, develop into a political constituency with a leadership of its own. In addition to this, and in order that they retain their connection with mainstream politics, he suggested that they be given the right to vote for general candidates, too. Both the separate electorate and the double vote were to last for a period of only ten years. Though the details were not agreed upon, when the conference concluded, all the delegates unanimously agreed that the Untouchables should, like the other minorities, have a separate electorate.

While the First Round Table Conference was in session in London, India was in turmoil. In January 1930, the Congress had declared its demand for Poorna Swaraj—complete independence. Gandhi showcased his genius as a political organizer and launched his most imaginative political action yet—the Salt Satyagraha. He called on Indians to march to the sea and break the British salt tax laws. Hundreds of thousands of Indians rallied to his call. Jails filled to overflowing. Ninety thousand people were arrested. Between salt and water, between the Touchables' satyagraha and the Untouchables' "duragraha" lay a sharply divided universe—of politics, of philosophy, and of morality.

At its Karachi Session in March 1931, the Congress passed a Resolution of Fundamental Rights for a free India. It was a valuable, enlightened document, and it included some of the rights Ambedkar had been campaigning for. It laid the foundation for a modern, secular, and largely socialist state. The rights included the freedoms of speech, press, assembly and association, equality before law, universal adult franchise, free and compulsory primary education, a guaranteed living wage for every citizen, and limited hours of work. It underlined the protection of women and peasants and state ownership or control of key industries, mines, and transport. Most important, it created a firewall between religion and the state.

Notwithstanding the admirable principles of the Resolution of Fundamental Rights that had been passed, the view from the bottom was slightly different. The 1930 elections to the provincial legislatures coincided with the Salt Satyagraha. The Congress had boycotted the elections. In order to embarrass "respectable" Hindus who did not heed the boycott and stood as independent candidates, the Congress fielded mock candidates who were Untouchables—two cobblers, a barber, a milkman, and a sweeper. The idea was that no self-respecting, privileged-caste Hindu would want to be part of an institution where he or she was put on a par with Untouchables. Putting up Untouchables as mock candidates was a Congress Party tactic that had begun with the 1920 elections and went on right up to 1943. Ambedkar says:

> What were the means adopted by the Congress to prevent Hindus from standing on an independent ticket? The means were to make the legislatures objects of contempt. Accordingly, the Congress, in various provinces, started processions carrying placards saying, "Who will go to the Legislatures? Only barbers, cobblers, potters and sweepers." In the processions, one man would utter the question as part of the slogan and the whole crowd would repeat as answer the second part of the slogan.

At the Round Table Conference, Gandhi and Ambedkar clashed, both claiming that they were the real representatives of the Untouchables. The conference went on for weeks. Gandhi eventually agreed to separate electorates for Muslims and Sikhs but would not countenance Ambedkar's argument for a separate electorate for Untouchables. He resorted to his usual rhetoric: "I would far rather that Hinduism died than that Untouchability lived."

Gandhi refused to acknowledge that Ambedkar had the right to represent Untouchables. Ambedkar would not back down, either. Nor was there a call for him to. Untouchable groups from across India, including Mangoo Ram of the Ad Dharm movement, sent telegrams in support of Ambedkar. Eventually Gandhi said, "Those who speak of the political rights of Untouchables do not know their India, do not know how Indian society is today constructed, and therefore I want to say with all the emphasis that I can command that if I was the only person to resist this thing I would resist it with my life." Having delivered his threat, Gandhi took the boat back to India. On the way, he dropped in on Mussolini in Rome and was extremely impressed by him and his "care of the poor, his opposition to super-urbanisation, his efforts to bring about co-ordination between capital and labour."

A year later, Ramsay MacDonald announced the British government's decision on the Communal Question. It awarded the Untouchables a separate electorate for a period of twenty years. At the time, Gandhi was serving a sentence in Yerawada Central Jail in Poona. From prison, he announced that unless the provision of separate electorates for Untouchables was revoked, he would fast to death.

He waited for a month. When he did not get his way, Gandhi began his fast from prison. This fast was completely against his own maxims of satyagraha. It was barefaced blackmail, nothing less manipulative than the threat of committing public suicide. The British government said it would revoke the provision only if the Untouchables agreed. The country spun like a top. Public statements were issued, petitions signed, prayers offered, meetings held, appeals made. It was a preposterous situation:

privileged-caste Hindus, who segregated themselves from Untouchables in every possible way; who deemed them unworthy of human association; who shunned their very touch; who wanted separate food, water, schools, roads, temples and wells; now said that India would be balkanized if Untouchables had a separate electorate. And Gandhi, who believed so fervently and so vocally in the system that upheld that separation, was starving himself to death to deny Untouchables a separate electorate.

The gist of it was that the caste Hindus wanted the power to close the door on Untouchables, but on no account could Untouchables be given the power to close the door on themselves. The masters knew that choice was power.

As the frenzy mounted, Ambedkar became the villain, the traitor, the man who wanted to dissever India, the man who was trying to kill Gandhi. Political heavyweights of the *garam dal* (militants) as well as the *naram dal* (moderates), including Tagore, Nehru, and C. Rajagopalachari, weighed in on Gandhi's side. To placate Gandhi, privileged-caste Hindus made a show of sharing food on the streets with Untouchables, and many Hindu temples were thrown open to them, albeit temporarily. Behind those gestures of accommodation, a wall of tension built up, too. Several Untouchable leaders feared that Ambedkar would be held responsible if Gandhi succumbed to his fast, and this in turn, could put the lives of ordinary Untouchables in danger. One of them was M. C. Rajah, the Untouchable leader from Madras, who, according to an eyewitness account of the events, said:

> For thousands of years we had been treated as Untouchables, downtrodden, insulted, despised. The Mahatma is staking his life for our sake, and if he dies, for the next thousands of years we shall be where we have been, if not worse. There will be such a strong feeling against us that we brought about his death, that the mind of the whole Hindu community and the whole civilised community will kick us downstairs further still. I am not going to stand by you any longer. I will join the conference and find a

solution and I will part company from you.

What could Ambedkar do? He tried to hold out with his usual arsenal of logic and reason, but the situation was way beyond all that. He didn't stand a chance. After four days of the fast, on September 24, 1932, Ambedkar visited Gandhi in Yerawada prison and signed the Poona Pact. The next day in Bombay he made a public speech in which he was uncharacteristically gracious about Gandhi: "I was astounded to see that the man who held such divergent views from mine at the Round Table Conference came immediately to my rescue and not to the rescue of the other side."

Later, though, having recovered from the trauma, Ambedkar wrote:

> *There was nothing noble in the fast. It was a foul and filthy act. . . . [I]t was the worst form of coercion against a helpless people to give up the constitutional safeguards of which they had become possessed under the Prime Minister's Award and agree to live on the mercy of the Hindus. It was a vile and wicked act. How can the Untouchables regard such a man as honest and sincere?*

According to the pact, instead of separate electorates, the Untouchables would have reserved seats in general constituencies. The number of seats they were allotted in the provincial legislatures increased (from 78 to 148), but the candidates, because they would now have to be acceptable to their privileged caste–dominated constituencies, lost their teeth. Uncle Tom won the day. Gandhi saw to it that leadership remained in the hands of the privileged castes.

In *The New Jim Crow*, Michelle Alexander describes how, in the United States, criminalization and mass incarceration have led to the disenfranchisement of an extraordinary percentage of the African American population. In India, in a far slyer way, an apparently generous form of enfranchisement has ensured the virtual disenfranchisement of the Dalit population.

Nevertheless, what to Ambedkar was a foul and filthy act appeared to others as nothing less than a divine miracle. Louis Fischer, author of perhaps the most widely read biography of Gandhi ever written, said:

> *The fast could not kill the curse of untouchability which was more than three thousand years old . . . but after the fast, untouchability forfeited its public approval; the belief in it was destroyed. . . . Gandhi's "Epic Fast" snapped a long chain that stretched back into antiquity and had enslaved tens of millions. Some links of the chain remained. Many wounds from the chain remained. But nobody would forge new links, nobody would link the links together again. . . . It [the Poona Pact] marked a religious reformation, a psychological revolution. Hinduism was purging itself of a millennial sickness. The mass purified itself in practice. . . . If Gandhi had done nothing else in his life but shatter the structure of untouchability he would have been a great social reformer. . . . Gandhi's agony gave vicarious pain to his adorers who knew they must not kill God's messenger on earth. It was evil to prolong his suffering. It was blessed to save him by being good to those whom he had called "The Children of God."*

On the great occasion of the Poona Pact, contradicting the stand he took at the Round Table Conference, Gandhi was quite willing to accept Ambedkar's signature on the pact as the representative of the Untouchables. Gandhi himself did not sign the pact, but the list of the other signatories is interesting: G. D. Birla, Gandhi's industrialist-patron; Pandit Madan Mohan Malaviya, a conservative Brahmin leader and founder of the right-wing Hindu Mahasabha (of which Gandhi's future assassin, Nathuram Godse, was a member); V. D. Savarkar, accused of conspiracy in Gandhi's assassination, who also served as president of the Mahasabha; Palwankar Baloo, an Untouchable cricketer of the Chambhar caste, who was celebrated earlier as a sporting idol by Ambedkar and whom the Congress and the Hindu Mahasabha propped up as an opponent of Ambedkar; and, of course, M. C. Rajah (who would, much later, regret his collusion with Gandhi, the Hindu Mahasabha, and the Congress).

Among the (many) reasons that criticism of Gandhi is not just frowned upon, but often censored in India, "secularists" tell us, is that Hindu nationalists (from whose midst Gandhi's assassins arose, and whose star is on the ascendant in India these days) will seize upon such criticism and turn it to their advantage. The fact is there was never much daylight between Gandhi's views on caste and those of the Hindu right. From a Dalit point of view, Gandhi's assassination could appear to be more a fratricidal killing than an assassination by an ideological opponent. Even today, Narendra Modi, Hindu nationalism's most aggressive proponent and a possible future prime minister, is able to invoke Gandhi in his public speeches without the slightest discomfort. (Modi invoked Gandhi to justify the introduction of two antiminority legislations in Gujarat—the anticonversion law of 2003, called the Gujarat Freedom of Religion Act, and the amendment to the old cow-slaughter law in 2011.) Many of Modi's pronouncements are delivered from the Mahatma Mandir in Gandhinagar, a spanking new convention hall whose foundation contains sand brought in special urns from each of Gujarat's eighteen thousand villages, many of which continue to practice egregious forms of untouchability.[247]

After the Poona Pact, Gandhi directed all his energy and passion toward the eradication of untouchability. For a start, he rebaptized Untouchables and gave them a patronizing name: Harijans. "Hari" is the name for a male deity in Hinduism, "jan" is people. So Harijans are People of God, though in order to infantilize them even further, in translation they are referred to as "Children of God." In this way, Gandhi anchored Untouchables firmly to the Hindu faith. He founded a new newspaper called *Harijan*. He started the Harijan Sevak Sangh (Harijan Service Society), which he insisted would be manned only by privileged-caste Hindus who had to do penance for their past sins against Untouchables. Ambedkar saw all this as the Congress's plan to "kill Untouchables by kindness."

Gandhi toured the country, preaching against untouchability. He was heckled and attacked by Hindus even more conservative than himself, but he did not swerve from his purpose. Everything that happened was harnessed to the cause of eradicating caste. In January 1934, there was a major earthquake in Bihar. Almost twenty thousand people lost their lives. Writing in the *Harijan* on February 24, Gandhi shocked even his colleagues in the Congress when he said it was God's punishment to the people for the sin of practicing untouchability. None of this stopped the Congress Party from continuing with a tradition it had invented: it once again fielded mock Untouchable candidates in the 1934 elections to the Central Legislature.

Gandhi could not, it appears, conceive of a role for Untouchables other than as victims in need of ministration. That they had also been psychologically hardwired into the caste system, that they too might need to be roused out of thousands of years of being conditioned to think of themselves as subhuman, was an antithetical, intimidating idea to Gandhi. The Poona Pact was meant to defuse or at least delay the political awakening of Untouchables.

What Gandhi's campaign against untouchability did, and did effectively, was to rub balm on injuries that were centuries old. To a vast mass of Untouchables, accustomed only to being terrorized, shunned, and brutalized, this missionary activity would have induced feelings of gratitude and even worship. Gandhi knew that. He was a politician. Ambedkar was not. Or, at any rate, not a very good one. Gandhi knew how to make charity an event, a piece of theater, a spectacular display of fireworks. So, while the Doctor was searching for a more lasting cure, the Saint journeyed across India distributing a placebo.

The chief concern of the Harijan Sevak Sangh was to persuade privileged castes to open up temples to Untouchables—ironic, because Gandhi was no temple-goer himself. Nor was his sponsor G. D. Birla, who, in an interview with Margaret

Bourke-White, said, "Frankly speaking, we build temples but we don't believe in temples. We build temples to spread a kind of religious mentality." The opening of temples had already begun during the days of Gandhi's epic fast. Under pressure from the Harijan Sevak Sangh, hundreds of temples were thrown open to Untouchables. (Some, like the Guruvayur temple in Kerala, refused point-blank. Gandhi contemplated a fast but soon changed his mind.) Others announced that they were open to Untouchables but found ways of humiliating them and making it impossible for them to enter with any sort of dignity.

A Temple Entry Bill was tabled in the Central Legislature in 1933. Gandhi and the Congress supported it enthusiastically. But when it became apparent that the privileged castes were seriously opposed to it, they backed out.

Ambedkar was sceptical about the temple entry program. He saw that it had a tremendous psychological impact on Untouchables, but he recognized temple entry as the beginning of "assimilation"—of Hinduizing and Brahminizing Untouchables, drawing them further into being partners in their own humiliation. If the "infection of imitation" of Brahminism had been implanted in Untouchables even when they had been denied entry into temples for centuries, what would temple entry do for them? On February 24, 1933, Ambedkar issued a statement on temple entry:

> *What the Depressed Classes want is a religion that will give them equality of social status . . . nothing can be more odious and vile than that admitted social evils should be sought to be justified on the ground of religion. The Depressed Classes may not be able to overthrow inequities to which they are subjected. But they have made up their mind not to tolerate a religion that will lend its support to the continuance of these inequities.*

Ambedkar was only echoing what a fourteen-year-old Untouchable Mang girl, Muktabai Salve, had said long ago. She was a student in the school for Untouchable children that Jotirao and Savitri

Phule ran in Poona. In 1855, she said, "Let that religion, where only one person is privileged and the rest are deprived, perish from the earth and let it never enter our minds to be proud of such a religion."

Ambedkar had learned from experience that Christianity, Sikhism, Islam, and Zoroastrianism were not impervious to caste discrimination. In 1934, he had a reprise of his old experiences. He was visiting the Daulatabad fort, in the princely state of Hyderabad, with a group of friends and co-workers. It was the month of Ramzan. Dusty and tired from their journey, Ambedkar and his friends stopped to drink water and wash their faces from a public tank. They were surrounded by a mob of angry Muslims calling them "*Dheds*" (a derogatory term for Untouchables). They were abused, nearly assaulted, and prevented from touching the water. "This will show," Ambedkar writes in his *Autobiographical Notes*, "that a person who is Untouchable to a Hindu, is also Untouchable to a Mohammedan."

A new spiritual home was nowhere in sight.

Still, at the 1935 Yeola conference, Ambedkar renounced Hinduism. In 1936, he published the incendiary (and overpriced, as Gandhi patronizingly commented) text of *Annihilation of Caste* that set out the reasons for why he had done so.

That same year, Gandhiji too made a memorable contribution to literature. He was by now sixty-eight years old. He wrote a classic essay called "The Ideal Bhangi":

The Brahmin's duty is to look after the sanitation of the soul, the Bhangi's that of the body of society . . . and yet our woebegone Indian society has branded the Bhangi as a social pariah, set him down at the bottom of the scale, held him fit only to receive kicks and abuse, a creature who must subsist on the leavings of the caste people and dwell on the dung heap.

If only we had given due recognition to the status of the Bhangi as equal to that of the Brahmin, our villages, no less their inhabitants would have looked a picture of cleanliness and order.

I therefore make bold to state without any manner of hesitation or doubt that not till the invidious distinction between Brahmin and Bhangi is removed will our society enjoy health, prosperity and peace and be happy.

He then outlined the educational requirements, practical skills, and etiquette an ideal bhangi should possess:

What qualities therefore should such an honoured servant of society exemplify in his person? In my opinion an ideal Bhangi should have a thorough knowledge of the principles of sanitation. He should know how a right kind of latrine is constructed and the correct way of cleaning it. He should know how to overcome and destroy the odour of excreta and the various disinfectants to render them innocuous. He should likewise know the process of converting urine and night soil into manure. But that is not all. My ideal Bhangi would know the quality of night soil and urine. He would keep a close watch on these and give timely warning to the individual concerned . . .

The *Manusmriti* says a Shudra should not amass wealth even if he has the ability, for a Shudra who amasses wealth annoys the Brahmin. Gandhi, a Bania, for whom the Manusmriti prescribes usury as a divine calling, says: "Such an ideal Bhangi, while deriving his livelihood from his occupation, would approach it only as a sacred duty. In other words, he would not dream of amassing wealth out of it."

Seventy years later, in his book *Karmayogi* (which he withdrew after the Balmiki community protested), Narendra Modi proved he was a diligent disciple of the Mahatma:

I do not believe they have been doing this job just to sustain their livelihood. Had this been so, they would not have continued with this kind of job generation after generation. . . . At some point of time somebody must have got the enlightenment that it is their

(Balmikis') duty to work for the happiness of the entire society and the Gods; that they have to do this job bestowed upon them by Gods; and this job should continue as internal spiritual activity for centuries.

The naram dal and the garam dal may be separate political parties today, but ideologically they are not as far apart from one another as we think they are.

Like all the other Hindu reformers, Gandhi too was alarmed by Ambedkar's talk of renouncing Hinduism. He adamantly opposed the religious conversion of Untouchables. In November 1936, in a now-famous conversation with John Mott—an American evangelist and chairman of the International Missionary Council—Gandhi said:

> *It hurt me to find Christian bodies vying with the Muslims and Sikhs in trying to add to the numbers of their fold. It seemed to me an ugly performance and a travesty of religion. They even proceeded to enter into secret conclaves with Dr. Ambedkar. I should have understood and appreciated your prayers for the Harijans, but instead you made an appeal to those who had not even the mind and intelligence to understand what you talked; they have certainly not the intelligence to distinguish between Jesus and Mohammed and Nanak and so on. . . . If Christians want to associate themselves with this reform movement they should do so without any idea of conversion.*
>
> *J. M.: Apart from this unseemly competition, should they not preach the Gospel with reference to its acceptance?*
>
> *G: Would you, Dr. Mott, preach the Gospel to a cow? Well, some of the untouchables are worse than cows in understanding. I mean they can no more distinguish between the relative merits of Islam and Hinduism and Christianity than a cow. You can only preach through your life. The rose does not say: "Come and smell me."*

It's true that Gandhi often contradicted himself. It's also true that he was capable of being remarkably consistent. For more than half a century—throughout his adult life—his pronouncements on the inherent qualities of Black Africans, Untouchables, and the laboring classes remained consistently insulting. His refusal to allow working-class people and Untouchables to create their own political organizations and elect their own representatives (which Ambedkar considered to be fundamental to the notion of citizenship) remained consistent, too.

Gandhi's political instincts served the Congress Party extremely well. His campaign of temple entry drew the Untouchable population in great numbers to the Congress.

Though Ambedkar had a formidable intellect, he didn't have the sense of timing, the duplicity, the craftiness, and the ability to be unscrupulous—qualities that a good politician needs. His constituency was made up of the poorest, most oppressed sections of the population. He had no financial backing. In 1942, Ambedkar reconfigured the Independent Labour Party into the much more self-limiting Scheduled Castes Federation. The timing was wrong. By then, the national movement was reigniting. Gandhi had announced the Quit India Movement. The Muslim League's demand for Pakistan was gaining traction, and for a while caste identity became less important that the Hindu–Muslim issue.

By the mid-1940s, as the prospect of partition loomed, the subordinated castes in several states had been "assimilated" into Hinduism. They began to participate in militant Hindu rallies; in Noakhali in Bengal, for instance, they functioned as an outlying vigilante army in the run-up to the bloodbath of Partition.

In 1947 Pakistan became the world's first Islamic republic. More than six decades later, as the war on terror continues in its many avatars, political Islam is turning inward, narrowing and hardening its precincts. Meanwhile, political Hinduism is expanding and broadening. Today, even the Bhakti movement has been "assimilated" as a form of popular, folk Hinduism. The naram dal, often dressed up as "secular nationalism," has recruited Jotirao Phule, Pandita Ramabai, and even Ambedkar, all of whom denounced Hinduism, back into the "Hindu fold" as people Hindus can be "proud" of. Ambedkar is being assimilated in another way, too—as Gandhi's junior partner in their joint fight against untouchability.

The anxiety around demography has by no means abated. Hindu supremacist organizations like the Rashtriya Swayamsevak Sangh and the Shiv Sena are working hard (and successfully) at luring Dalits and Adivasis into the "Hindu fold." In the forests of Central India, where a corporate war for minerals is raging, the Vishwa Hindu Parishad and the Bajrang Dal (both organizations that are loosely linked to the RSS) run mass conversion programs called *"ghar wapsi"*—the return home—in which Adivasi people are "reconverted" to Hinduism. Privileged-caste Hindus, who pride themselves on being descendants of Aryan invaders, are busy persuading people who belong to indigenous, autochthonous tribes to return "home." It makes you feel that irony is no longer a literary option in this part of the world.

Dalits who have been harnessed to the "Hindu fold" serve another purpose: even if they have not been part of the outlying army, they can be used as scapegoats for the crimes the privileged castes commit.

In 2002, in the Godhra railway station in Gujarat, a train compartment was mysteriously burned down, and fifty-eight Hindu pilgrims were charred to death. With not much evidence to prove their guilt, some Muslims were arrested as the perpetrators. The Muslim community as a whole was collectively blamed for the crime. Over the next few days, the Vishwa Hindu Parishad and the Bajrang Dal led a pogrom in which more than two thousand Muslims were murdered, women were mob-raped and burnt alive in broad daylight, and a hundred and fifty thousand people were driven from their homes. After the pogrom, 287 people were arrested under the Prevention of Terrorism Act (POTA). Of them, 286 were Muslim and one was a Sikh. Most of them are still in prison.

If Muslims were the "terrorists," who were the "rioters"? In his essay "Blood under Saffron: The Myth of Dalit–Muslim Confrontation," Raju Solanki, a Gujarati Dalit writer who studied the pattern of arrests, says that of the 1,577 "Hindus" who were arrested (not under POTA, of course), 747 were Dalits and 797 belonged to "Other Backward Classes." Nineteen were Patels, two were Banias, and two were Brahmins. The massacres of Muslims occurred in several cities and villages in Gujarat. However, Solanki points out that not a single massacre took place in bastis where Dalits and Muslims lived together.

Narendra Modi, the chief minister of Gujarat who presided over the pogrom, has since won the state elections three times in a row. Despite being a Shudra, he has endeared himself to the Hindu right by being more blatantly and ruthlessly anti-Muslim than any other Indian politician. When he was asked in a recent interview whether he regretted what happened in 2002, he said, "[I]f we are driving a car, we are a driver, and someone else is driving a car and we're sitting behind, even then if a puppy comes under the wheel, will it be painful or not? Of course it is. If I'm a Chief Minister or not, I'm a human being. If something bad happens anywhere, it is natural to be sad."

As blatantly casteist and communal as the Hindu right is, in their search for a foothold in mainstream politics, even radical Dalits have made common cause with it. In the mid-1990s, the remarkable Dalit poet Namdeo Dhasal, one of the founders of the Dalit Panthers, joined the Shiv Sena. In 2006, Dhasal shared the dais with RSS chief K. S. Sudarshan at a book launch and praised the RSS's efforts at equality.

It is easy to dismiss what Dhasal did as an unforgivable compromise with fascists. However, in parliamentary politics, after the Poona Pact—or rather, because of the Poona Pact—Dalits as a political constituency have had to make alliances with those whose interests are hostile to their own. For Dalits, as we have seen, the distance between the Hindu "right" and the Hindu "left" is not as great as it might appear to be to others.

Despite the debacle of the Poona Pact, Ambedkar didn't entirely give up the idea of separate electorates. Unfortunately, his second party, the Scheduled Castes Federation, was defeated in the 1946 elections to the Provincial Legislature. The defeat meant that Ambedkar lost his place on the Executive Council in the Interim Ministry that was formed in August 1946. It was a serious blow, because Ambedkar desperately wanted to use his position on the Executive Council to become part of the committee that would draft the Indian Constitution. Worried that this was not going to be possible, and in order to put external pressure on the Drafting Committee, Ambedkar, in March 1947, published a document called States and Minorities—his proposed constitution for a "United States of India" (an idea whose time has perhaps come). Fortunately for him, the Muslim League chose Jogendranath Mandal, a colleague of Ambedkar's and a Scheduled Castes Federation leader from Bengal, as one of its candidates on the Executive Council. Mandal made sure that Ambedkar was elected to the Constituent Assembly from the Bengal province. But disaster struck again. After Partition, East Bengal went to Pakistan and Ambedkar lost his position once more. In a gesture of goodwill, and perhaps because there was no one as equal to the task as he was, the Congress appointed Ambedkar to the Constituent Assembly. In August 1947, Ambedkar was appointed India's first law minister and chairman of the Drafting Committee for the Constitution. Across the new border, Jogendranath Mandal became Pakistan's first law minister. It was extraordinary that, through all the chaos and prejudice, the first law ministers of both India and Pakistan were Dalits. Mandal was eventually disillusioned with Pakistan and returned to India. Ambedkar was disillusioned too, but he really had nowhere to go.

The Indian Constitution was drafted by a committee and reflected the views of its privileged-caste members more than Ambedkar's. Still, several of the safeguards for Untouchables that he had outlined in States and Minorities did find their way in. Some of Ambedkar's more radical suggestions, such as nationalizing agriculture and key industries, were summarily dropped. The drafting process left Ambedkar more than a little unhappy. In March 1955, he said in the Rajya Sabha (India's Upper House of Parliament): "The Constitution was a wonderful temple we built for the gods, but before they could be installed, the devils have taken possession." In 1954, Ambedkar contested his last election as a Scheduled Castes Federation candidate and lost.

Ambedkar was disillusioned with Hinduism, with its high priests, its saints and its politicians. Yet the response to temple entry probably taught him how much people long to belong to a spiritual community, and how inadequate a charter of civil rights or a constitution is to address those needs.

After twenty years of contemplation, during which he studied Islam as well as Christianity, Ambedkar turned to Buddhism. This, too, he entered in his own, distinct, angular way. He was wary of classical Buddhism, of the ways in which Buddhist philosophy could, had, and continues to be used to justify war and unimaginable cruelty. (The most recent example is the Sri Lankan government's version of state Buddhism, which culminated in the genocidal killing of at least forty thousand ethnic Tamils and the internal displacement of three hundred thousand people in 2009.) Ambedkar's Buddhism, called "Navayana Buddhism" or the Fourth Way, distinguished between religion and dhamma. "The purpose of Religion is to explain the origin of the world," Ambedkar said, sounding very much like Karl Marx, "the purpose of Dhamma is to reconstruct the world." On October 14, 1956, in Nagpur, only months before his death, Ambedkar, Sharda Kabir, his (Brahmin) second wife, and half a million supporters took the vow of the Three Jewels and Five Precepts and converted to Buddhism. It was his most radical act. It marked his departure from Western liberalism and its purely materialistic vision of a society based on "rights," a vision whose origin coincided with the rise of modern capitalism.

Ambedkar did not have enough money to print his major work on Buddhism, *The Buddha and His Dhamma*, before he died.

He wore suits, yes. But he died in debt.

Where does that leave the rest of us?

Though they call the age we are living through the Kali Yuga, Ram Rajya could be just around the corner. The fourteenth-century Babri Masjid, supposedly built on the birthplace of Lord Ram in Ayodhya, was demolished by Hindu storm troopers on December 6, 1992, Ambedkar's death anniversary. We await with apprehension the construction of a grand Ram temple in its place. As Mahatma Gandhi desired, the rich man has been left in possession of his (as well as everybody else's) wealth. Chaturvarna reigns unchallenged: the Brahmin largely controls knowledge; the Vaishya dominates trade. The Kshatriyas have seen better days, but they are still, for the most part, rural landowners. The Shudras live in the basement of the Big House and keep intruders at bay. The Adivasis are fighting for their very survival. And the Dalits—well, we've been through all that.

Can caste be annihilated?

Not unless we show the courage to rearrange the stars in our firmament. Not unless those who call themselves revolutionary develop a radical critique of Brahminism. Not unless those who understand Brahminism sharpen their critique of capitalism.

And not unless we read Babasaheb Ambedkar. If not inside our classrooms, then outside them. Until then we will remain what he called the "sick men" and women of Hindustan, who seem to have no desire to get well.

"For Ambedkar, 'the people' was not a homogeneous category that glowed with the rosy hue of innate righteousness."

PROFESSOR, P.O.W

MAY 9, 2015, marks one year since Dr. G. N. Saibaba, lecturer of English at Ramlal Anand College, Delhi University, was abducted by unknown men on his way home from work. When her husband went missing and did not respond to calls to his cell phone, Vasantha, Dr. Saibaba's wife, filed a missing person's complaint in the local police station. Subsequently, the unknown men identified themselves as the Maharashtra Police and described the abduction as an arrest.

Why did they abduct him in this way when they could easily have arrested him formally, this professor who happens to be wheelchair bound and paralyzed from his waist down since he was five years old? There were two reasons: First, because they knew from their previous visits to his house that if they picked him up from his home on the Delhi University campus, they would have to deal with a crowd of angry people—professors, activists, and students who loved and admired Professor Saibaba not just because he was a dedicated teacher but also because of his fearless political worldview. Second, because abducting him made it look as though they, armed only with their wit and

First published in *Outlook*, May 18, 2015.

daring, had tracked down and captured a dangerous terrorist.

The truth is more prosaic. Many of us had known for a long time that Professor Saibaba was likely to be arrested. It had been the subject of open discussion for months. Never in all those months, right up to the day of his abduction, did it ever occur to him or to anybody else that he should do anything else but face up to it fair and square. In fact, during that period, he put in extra hours and wrote his doctoral thesis on the politics of the discipline of Indian English writing. Why did we think he would be arrested? What was his crime?

In September 2009, the then home minister P. Chidambaram announced a war called Operation Green Hunt in what is known as India's Red Corridor. It was advertised as a cleanup operation by paramilitary forces against Maoist "Terrorists" in the jungles of Central India. In reality it was the official name for what had so far been a scorched-earth battle being waged by state-sponsored vigilante militias (the Salwa Judum in Bastar and unnamed militias in other states). The mandate was to clear the forests of its troublesome residents so that mining and infrastructure-building corporations could move ahead with their stalled projects. The fact that signing over Adivasi homelands to private corporations is illegal and unconstitutional did not bother the United Progressive Alliance government of the time. (The present government's new Land Acquisition Act proposes to exalt that lawlessness into law.) Thousands of paramilitary troops accompanied by vigilante militias invaded the forests, burning villages, murdering villagers, and raping women. Tens of thousands of Adivasis were forced to flee from their homes and hide in the jungle for months under the open sky. The backlash against this brutality was that hundreds of local people signed up to join the People's Liberation Guerrilla Army (PLGA) raised by the Communist Party of India (Maoist), whom former prime minister Manmohan Singh famously described as India's "single largest internal security threat." Even now, the whole region remains convulsed by what can only be called a civil war.

As is the case with any protracted war, the situation has become far from simple. While some in the resistance continue to fight the good fight, others have become opportunists, extortionists, and ordinary criminals. It is not always easy to tell one group from another, and that makes it easy to tar them all with the same brush. Horrible atrocities have taken place. One set of atrocities is called Terrorism and the other, Progress.

In 2010 and 2011 when Operation Green Hunt was at its most brutal, a campaign against it began to gather speed. Public meetings and rallies took place in several cities. As word of what was happening in the forest spread, the international media began to pay attention. One of the main mobilizers of this public and entirely un-secret campaign against Operation Green Hunt was Dr. Saibaba. The campaign was, at least temporarily, successful. The government was shamed into pretending that there was no such thing as Operation Green Hunt, that it was merely a media creation. (Of course, the assault on the Adivasi homelands continues, largely unreported, because now it is an Operation Without a Name. This week, on May 5, 2015, Chhavindra Karma, the son of the founder of Salwa Judum Mahendra Karma, who was killed in a Maoist ambush, announced the inauguration of Salwa Judum-2. This despite the Supreme Court judgment declaring Salwa Judum-1 to be illegal and unconstitutional and ordering that it be disbanded.)

In Operation No-Name anybody who criticizes or impedes the implementation of state policy is called a Maoist. Thousands of Dalits and Adivasis, thus labeled, are in jail absurdly charged with crimes like Sedition and Waging War against the State under the Unlawful Activities Prevention Act—a law which would make any intelligent human being bust a gut laughing if only the uses to which it is being put were not so tragic. While villagers languish for years in prison, with no legal help and no hope of justice, often not even sure what crime they have been accused of, the state has turned its attention to what it calls Overground Workers in the cities.

Determined not to allow a repeat of the situation it found itself in earlier, the Ministry of Home Affairs spelled out its intentions clearly in its 2013 affidavit filed in the Supreme Court. It said: "The ideologues and supporters of the Communist Party of India (Maoist) in cities and towns have undertaken a concerted and systematic propaganda against the State to project it in a poor light . . . it is these ideologues who have kept the Maoist movement alive and are in many ways more dangerous than the cadres of the People's Liberation Guerrilla Army."

Enter Dr. Saibaba.

We knew he was a marked man when several clearly planted, hyperbolic stories about him began appear in the papers. (When they don't have real evidence, their next best option—tried and tested—is to create a climate of suspicion around their quarry.)

On September 12, 2013, his home was raided by fifty policemen armed with a search warrant for stolen property from a magistrate in Aheri, a small town in Maharashtra. They did not find any stolen property. Instead, they took away (stole?) his personal laptop, hard disks, and pen drives. Two weeks later Suhash Bawache (the investigating officer for the case) rang Dr. Saibaba and asked him for the passwords to access the hard disks. He gave it to them. On January 9, 2014, a team of policemen interrogated him at his home for several hours. And on May 9 they abducted him. That same night they flew him to Nagpur and from there drove him to Aheri and then back to Nagpur with hundreds of policemen escorting the convoy of jeeps and mine-proof vehicles. He was incarcerated in the Nagpur Central jail in its notorious "Anda Cell," adding his name to the three hundred thousand under-trials who crowd our country's prisons. In the midst of all the high theater, his wheel-chair was damaged. Dr. Saibaba is what is known as "90 percent disabled." In order to prevent his physical condition from further deteriorating, he needs constant care, physiotherapy, and medi-cation. Despite this he was thrown into a bare cell (where he still remains) with nobody to assist him even to use the bathroom. He had to crawl around on all fours. None of this would fall under the definition of torture. Of course not. The great advantage the state has over this particular prisoner is that he is not equal among prisoners. He can be cruelly tortured, perhaps even killed, without anybody having to so much as lay a finger on him.

The next morning's papers in Nagpur had front-page pictures of the heavily armed team of Maharashtra Police proudly posing with their trophy—the dreaded terrorist, Professor P.O.W., in his damaged wheelchair.

He has been charged under the Unlawful Activities Prevention Act, Section 13 (taking part in/advocating/abetting/inciting the commission of unlawful activity); Section 18 (conspiring/ attempting to commit a terrorist act); Section 20 (being a member of a terrorist gang or organization), Section 38 (associating with a terrorist organization with intention to further its activities); and Section 39 (inviting support and addressing meetings for the purpose of encouraging support for a terrorist organization.) He has been accused of giving a computer chip to Hem Mishra, a Jawaharlal Nehru University student, to deliver to Comrade Narmada of the CPI (Maoist). Hem Mishra was arrested at the Ballarshah railway station in August 2013 and is in Nagpur jail along with Dr. Saibaba. The three others accused with them in this "conspiracy" are out on bail.

Another of the serious offenses listed in the charge sheet is that Dr. Saibaba is the joint-secretary of the Revolutionary Democratic Front (RDF), an organization that is banned in Orissa and Andhra Pradesh where it is suspected to be a Maoist Front organization. It is not banned in Delhi. Or Maharashtra. The president of RDF is the well-known poet Varavara Rao who lives in Hyderabad.

Dr. Saibaba's trial has not begun. When it does, it is likely to take months, if not years. The question is, can a person with a 90 percent disability survive in those abysmal prison conditions for so long?

In the year he's been in prison, his physical condition has deteriorated alarmingly. He is in constant, excruciating pain.

(The jail authorities have helpfully described this as "quite normal" for polio victims.) His spinal cord has degenerated. It has buckled and is pushing up against his lungs. His left arm has stopped functioning. The cardiologist at the local hospital where the jail authorities took him for a test has asked that he be given an angioplasty urgently. If he does undergo an angioplasty, given his condition and the conditions in prison, the prognosis is dire. If he does not, and remains incarcerated, it is dire, too. Time and again the jail authorities have disallowed him medication that is vital not just to his well-being, but to his survival. When they do allow the medicines, they disallow the special diet that is meant to go with it.

Although India is party to international covenants on disability rights and Indian law expressly forbids the incarceration of a person who is disabled as an under-trial for a prolonged period, Dr. Saibaba has been denied bail twice by the sessions court. On the second occasion bail was denied based on the jail authorities demonstrating to the court that they were giving him the specific, special care a person in his condition required. (They did allow his family to replace his wheelchair.) In a letter from prison, Dr. Saibaba said that the day the order denying him bail came, the special care was withdrawn. Driven to despair he went on a hunger strike. Within a few days he was taken to the hospital unconscious.

For the sake of argument let's leave to the courts the decision about whether Dr. Saibaba is guilty or innocent of the charges leveled against him. And for just a moment, let's turn our attention solely to the question of bail, because for him that is quite literally a question of life and death.

No matter what the charges against him are, should Professor Saibaba get bail? Here's a list of a few well-known public figures and government servants who have been given bail.

On April 23, 2015, Babu Bajrangi, convicted and sentenced to life imprisonment for his role in the 2002 Naroda Patiya massacre in which ninety-seven people were murdered in broad daylight, was released on bail by the Gujarat High Court for an "urgent eye operation." This is Babu Bajrangi in his own words speaking about the crime he committed: "We didn't spare a single Muslim shop, we set everything on fire, we set them on fire and killed them . . . hacked, burnt, set on fire . . . We believe in setting them on fire because these bastards don't want to be cremated. They're afraid of it" ("After Killing Them I Felt Like Maharana Pratap" *Tehelka*, September 1, 2007).

Eye-operation, huh? Well, maybe on second thought it is urgent to replace the murderous lenses he seems to view the world through with something less stupid and less dangerous.

On July 30, 2014, Maya Kodnani, a former minister of the Modi government in Gujarat, convicted and serving a twenty-eight-year sentence for being the "kingpin" of that same Naroda Patiya massacre, was granted bail by the Gujarat High Court. Kodnani is a medical doctor and says she suffers from intestinal tuberculosis, a heart condition, clinical depression, and a spinal problem. Her sentence has been suspended.

Amit Shah, also a former minister in the Modi government in Gujarat, was arrested in July 2010, accused of ordering the extrajudicial killing of three people—Sohrabuddin Sheikh; his wife, Kausar Bi; and Tulsiram Prajapati. The Central Bureau of Investigation produced phone records showing that Shah was in constant touch with the police officials who held the victims in illegal custody before they were murdered and that the number of phone calls between him and those police officials spiked sharply during those days. Amit Shah was released on bail three months after his arrest. (Subsequently, after a series of disturbing and mysterious events, he has been let off altogether.) He is currently the president of the Bharatiya Janata Party and the right-hand man of prime minister Narendra Modi.

On May 22, 1987, forty-two Muslim men rounded up in a truck by the Police Armed Constabulary (PAC) were shot dead in cold blood on the outskirts of Hashimpura; their bodies were dumped in a canal. Nineteen members of the PAC were accused in the case. All of them were allowed to continue in service, receiving their promotions and bonuses like everybody else. Thirteen years later, in the year 2000, sixteen of them surrendered (three had died). They were released on bail immediately. A few weeks ago, in March 2015, all sixteen were acquitted for lack of evidence.

Hany Babu, a teacher in Delhi University and a member of the Committee for the Defense and Release of Saibaba, was recently able to meet Dr. Saibaba for a few minutes in the hospital. At a press conference (on April 23, 2015) that went more or less unreported, Hany Babu described the circumstances of the meeting: Dr. Saibaba, on a saline drip, sat up in bed and spoke to him. A security guard stood over him with an AK-47 pointed at his head. It was his duty to make sure the prisoner did not run away on his paralyzed legs.

Will Dr. Saibaba come out of the Nagpur Central jail alive? Do they want him to? There is much to suggest that they do not.

This is what we put up with, what we vote for, what we agree to.

This is us.

MY SEDITIOUS HEART

ON A BALMY February night, aware that things were not going well, I did what I rarely do. I put in earplugs and switched on the television. Even though I had said nothing about the spate of recent events—murders and lynchings, police raids on university campuses, student arrests, and enforced flag-waving—I knew that my name was still on the A-list of "antinationals."

That night, I began to worry that, in addition to the charge of criminal contempt of court I was already facing (for "interfering in the administration of justice," "bashing the Central Government, State Governments, the Police Machinery, so also the Judiciary," and "demonstrating a surly, rude and boorish attitude"),[1] I would also be charged with causing the death of the eternally indignant news anchor on Times Now. I thought he might succumb to an apoplectic fit as he stabbed the air and spat out my name, suggesting that I was a part of some shadowy cabal behind the ongoing "antinational" activity in the country. My crime, according to him, is that I have written about the struggle for freedom in Kashmir, questioned the execution of Mohammad

First published as the foreword to Arundhati Roy, *The End of Imagination* (Chicago: Haymarket Books, 2016) and in *Caravan*, April 30, 2016.

Afzal Guru, walked with the Maoist guerrillas ("terrorists" in television speak) in the forests of Bastar, connected their armed rebellion to my reservations about India's chosen model of "development," *and*—with a hissy, sneering pause—even questioned the country's nuclear tests.

Now it's true that my views on these matters are at variance with those of the ruling establishment. In better days, that used to be known as a critical perspective or an alternative worldview. These days in India, it's called sedition.

Sitting in Delhi, somewhat at the mercy of what looks like a democratically elected government gone rogue, I wondered whether I should rethink some of my opinions. I thought back, for instance, on a talk I gave in 2004 at the annual meeting of the American Sociological Association, just before the Bush-versus-Kerry election, in which I joked about how the choice between the Democrats and the Republicans—or their equivalents in India, the Congress and the Bharatiya Janata Party—was like having to choose between Tide and Ivory Snow, two brands of washing powder both actually owned by the same company. Given all that is going on, can I honestly continue to believe that?

On merit, when it comes to pogroms against non-Hindu communities, or looking away while Dalits are slaughtered, or making sure the levers of power and wealth remain in the hands of the tiny minority of dominant castes, or smuggling in neoliberal economic reforms on the coat-tails of manufactured communal conflict, or banning books, there's not much daylight between the Congress and the BJP. (When it comes to the horrors that have been visited upon places like Kashmir, Nagaland, and Manipur, all the parliamentary parties, including the two major left parties, stand united in their immorality.)

Given this track record, does it matter that the stated ideologies of the Congress and the BJP are completely different? Whatever its practice, the Congress *says* it believes in a secular, liberal democracy, while the BJP mocks secularism and believes that India is essentially a "Hindu Rashtra"—a Hindu nation.

Hypocrisy, Congress-style, is serious business. It's clever—it smokes up the mirrors and leaves us groping around. However, to proudly declare your bigotry, to bring it out into the sunlight as the BJP does, is a challenge to the social, legal, and moral foundations on which modern India (supposedly) stands. It would be an error to imagine that what we are witnessing today is just business as usual between unprincipled, murderous political parties.

Although the idea of India as a Hindu Rashtra is constantly being imbued with an aura of ancientness, it's a surprisingly recent one. And, ironically, it has more to do with representative democracy than it does with religion. Historically, the people who now call themselves Hindu only identified themselves by their *jati*, their caste names. As a community, they functioned as a loose coalition of endogamous castes organized in a strict hierarchy. (Even today, for all the talk of unity and nationalism, only 5 percent of marriages in India cut across caste lines. Transgression can still get young people beheaded.) Since each caste could dominate the ones below it, all except those at the very bottom were inveigled into being a part of the system. *Brahmanvaad*—Brahminism—is the word that the anti-caste movement has traditionally used to describe this taxonomy. Though it has lost currency (and is often erroneously taken to refer solely to the practices and beliefs of Brahmins as a caste group), it is, in fact, a more accurate term than "Hinduism" for this social and religious arrangement, because it is as ancient as caste itself and pre-dates the idea of Hinduism by centuries.

This is a volatile assertion, so let me shelter behind Bhimrao Ambedkar. "The first and foremost thing that must be recognized," he wrote in *Annihilation of Caste* in 1936, "is that Hindu society is a myth. The name Hindu is itself a foreign name. It was given by the Mohammedans to the natives [who lived east of the river Indus] for the purpose of distinguishing themselves."[2]

So how and why did the people who lived east of the Indus begin to call themselves Hindus? Toward the end of the nineteenth century, the politics of representative governance (paradoxically, introduced to its colony by the imperial British government), began to replace the politics of emperors and kings. The British marked the boundaries of the modern nation-state called India, divided it into territorial constituencies, and introduced the idea of elected bodies for local self-government. Gradually, subjects became citizens, citizens became voters, and voters formed constituencies that were assembled from complicated networks of old as well as new allegiances, alliances, and loyalties. Even as it came into existence, the new nation began to struggle against its rulers. But it was no longer a question of overthrowing a ruler militarily and taking the throne. The new rulers, whoever they were, would need to be legitimate representatives of the people. The politics of representative governance set up a new anxiety: Who could legitimately claim to represent the aspirations of the freedom struggle? Which constituency would make up the majority?

This marked the beginning of what we now call "vote bank" politics. Demography turned into an obsession. It became imperative that people who previously identified themselves only by their caste names band together under a single banner to make up a majority. That was when they began to call themselves Hindu. It was a way of crafting a political majority out of an impossibly diverse society. "Hindu" was the name of a political constituency more than of a religion, one that could define itself as clearly as other constituencies—Muslim, Sikh, and Christian—could. Hindu nationalists, as well as the officially "secular" Congress party, staked their claims to the "Hindu vote."

It was around this time that a perplexing contestation arose around the people then known as "Untouchables" or "Outcastes," who, though they were outside the pale of the caste system, were also divided into separate castes arranged in a strict hierarchy. To even begin to understand the political chaos we are living through now, at the centre of which is the suicide of the Dalit scholar Rohith Vemula, it's important to understand, at least conceptually, this turn-of-the-century contestation.

Over the previous centuries, in order to escape the scourge of caste, millions of Untouchables (I use this word only because Ambedkar used it, too) had converted to Buddhism, Islam, Sikhism, and Christianity. In the past, those conversions had not been a cause of anxiety for the privileged castes. However, when the politics of demography took centre stage, this haemorrhaging became a source of urgent concern. People who had been shunned and cruelly oppressed were now viewed as a population who could greatly expand the numbers of the Hindu constituency. They had to be courted and brought into the "Hindu fold."

That was the beginning of Hindu evangelism. What we know today as *ghar wapsi*, or "returning home," was a ceremony that dominant castes devised to "purify" Untouchables and Adivasis, whom they considered "polluted." The idea was (and is) to persuade these ancient and autochthonous peoples that they were formerly Hindus, and that Hinduism was the original, indigenous religion of the subcontinent.

It was not only Hindu nationalists among the privileged castes that tried to embrace the Untouchables politically while continuing to valorize the caste system. Their counterparts in the Congress did the same thing, too. This was the reason for the legendary standoff between Bhimrao Ambedkar and Mohandas Gandhi, and continues to be the cause of serious disquiet in Indian politics. Even today, to properly secure its idea of a Hindu Rashtra, the BJP has to persuade a majority of the Dalit population to embrace a creed that stigmatizes and humiliates them. It has been surprisingly successful, and has even managed to draw in some militant Ambedkarite Dalits. It is this paradox that has made the political moment we are living through so incandescent, so highly inflammable, and so unpredictable.

Ever since the Rashtriya Swayamsevak Sangh was founded, in 1925, this ideological holding company of Hindu nationalism (and of the BJP) has set itself the task of making myriad castes, communities, tribes, religions, and ethnic groups submerge their identities and line up behind the banner of the Hindu Rashtra.

Which is a little like trying to sculpt a gigantic, immutable stone statue of Bharat Mata—the Hindu right's ideal of Mother India—out of a stormy sea. Turning water into stone may not be a practical ambition, but the RSS's long years of trying have polluted the sea and endangered its flora and fauna in irreversible ways. Its ruinous ideology—known as Hindutva, and inspired by the likes of Benito Mussolini and Adolf Hitler—openly proposes Nazi-style purges of Indian Muslims. In RSS doctrine (theorized by M. S. Golwalkar, the organization's second *sarsanghchalak*, or supreme leader), the three main enemies obstructing the path to the Hindu Rashtra are Muslims, Christians, and Communists. And now, as the RSS races toward that goal, although what's happening around us may look like chaos, everything is actually going strictly by the book.

Of late, the RSS has deliberately begun to conflate nationalism with Hindu nationalism. It uses the terms interchangeably, as though they mean the same thing. Naturally, it chooses to gloss over the fact that it played absolutely no part in the struggle against British colonialism. But while the RSS left the battle of turning a British colony into an independent nation to other people, it has, since then, worked far harder than any other political or cultural organization to turn this independent nation into a Hindu nation. Before the BJP was founded, in 1980, the political arm of the RSS was the Bharatiya Jan Sangh. However, the RSS's influence cut across party lines, and in the past its shadowy presence has even been evident in some of the more nefarious and violent activities of the Congress. The organization now has a network of tens of thousands of *shakhas* (branches) and hundreds of thousands of workers. It has its own trade union, its own educational institutions where millions of students are indoctrinated, its own teachers' organization, a women's wing, a media and publications division, its own organizations dedicated to Adivasi welfare, its own medical missions, its own sad stable of historians (who produce their own hallucinatory version of history), and, of course, its own army of trolls on social media.

Its sister concerns, the Bajrang Dal and the Vishwa Hindu Parishad, provide the storm troopers that carry out organized attacks on anyone whose views they perceive to be a threat. In addition to creating its own organizations (which, together with the BJP, make up the Sangh Parivar—the Saffron Family), the RSS has also worked patiently to place its chessmen in public institutions: on government committees, in universities, the bureaucracy, and, crucially, the intelligence services.

That all this farsightedness and hard work was going to pay off one day was a foregone conclusion. Still, it took imagination and ruthlessness to come this far. Most of us know the story, but given the amnesia that is being pressed upon us, it might serve to put down a chronology of the recent present. Who knows, things that appeared unconnected may, when viewed in retrospect, actually be connected. And vice versa. So forgive me if, in an attempt to decipher a pattern, I go over some familiar territory.

The journey to power began with the Ram Janmabhoomi movement. In 1990, L. K. Advani, a BJP leader and a member of the RSS, traveled the length and breadth of the country in an air-conditioned *rath*—chariot—exhorting "Hindus" to rise up and build a temple on the hallowed birthplace of Lord Ram. The birthplace, people were told, was the exact same spot on which a sixteenth-century mosque, the Babri Masjid, stood in the town of Ayodhya. In 1992, just two years after his *rath yatra*, Advani stood by and watched as an organized mob reduced the Babri Masjid to rubble. Riots, massacres, and serial bombings followed. The country was polarized in a way it had not been since Partition. By 1998, the BJP (which had only two seats in Parliament in 1984) had formed a coalition government at the centre.

The first thing the BJP did was to realize a long-standing desire of the RSS by conducting a series of nuclear tests. From being an organization that had been banned three times (after the assassination of Gandhi, during the Emergency, and after the demolition of the Babri Masjid), the RSS was finally in a position to dictate government policy. We can call it the Year of the Ascension.

It wasn't the first time India had conducted nuclear tests, but the exhibitionism of the 1998 ones was different. It was like a rite of passage. The "Hindu bomb" was meant to announce the imminent arrival of the Hindu Rashtra. Within days, Pakistan (already ahead of the curve, having declared itself an Islamic republic in 1956) showed off its "Muslim bomb." And now we're stuck with these two strutting, nuclear-armed roosters, who are trained to hate each other, who hold their minority populations hostage as they mimic each other in a competing horror show of majoritarianism and religious chauvinism. And they have Kashmir to fight over.

The nuclear tests altered the tone of public discourse in India. They coarsened and, you could say, weaponized it. In the months that followed, we were force-fed Hindu nationalism. Then, like now, articles circulated predicting that a mighty, all-conquering Hindu Rashtra was about to emerge—that a resurgent India would "burst forth upon its former oppressors and destroy them completely." Absurd as it all was, having nuclear weapons made thoughts like these seem feasible. It *created* thoughts like these.

You didn't have to be a visionary to see what was coming.

The Year of the Ascension, 1998, witnessed gruesome attacks on Christians (essentially Dalits and Adivasis), Hindutva's most vulnerable foes. Swami Aseemanand, the head of the RSS-affiliated Vanvasi Kalyan Ashram's religious wing (who would make national news as the main accused in the 2007 Samjhauta Express train bombing), was sent to the remote, forested Dang district in western Gujarat to set up a headquarters. The violence began on Christmas Eve. Within a week, more than twenty churches in the region were burned down or otherwise destroyed by mobs of thousands led by the Hindu Dharma Jagran Manch, an organization affiliated to the Vishwa Hindu Parishad and the Bajrang Dal. Soon, Dang district became a major centre of ghar wapsi. Tens of thousands of Adivasis were "returned" to Hinduism. The violence spread to other states.

In Keonjhar district in Odisha, an Australian Christian

missionary, Graham Staines, who had been working in India for thirty-five years, was burned alive along with his two sons, aged six and ten. The man who led the attack was Dara Singh, a Bajrang Dal activist.

In April 2000, US president Bill Clinton was on an official visit to Pakistan, after which he was due in Delhi. It was less than a year since the war in the Kargil district of Ladakh, in which India had pushed back the Pakistani Army after it, in an aggressive, provocative move, sent soldiers across the Line of Control to occupy a strategic post. The Indian government was keen for the international community to recognize that Pakistan was a "terrorist state." On April 20, the night before Clinton was expected to arrive, thirty-five Sikhs were shot down in cold blood in Chittisinghpora, a village in south Kashmir. The killers were said to be Pakistan-based militants disguised in Indian Army uniforms. It was the first time Sikhs had been targeted by militants in Kashmir. Five days later, the Special Operations Group and the Rashtriya Rifles claimed to have tracked down and killed five of the militants. The burnt, disfigured bodies of the dead men were dressed in fresh, unburnt army uniforms. It turned out they were all local Kashmiri villagers who had been abducted by the army and killed in a staged encounter.

In October 2001, just weeks after the 9/11 attacks in the United States, the BJP installed Narendra Modi as the chief minister of Gujarat. At the time, Modi was more or less unknown. His main political credential was that he had been a long-time and loyal member of the RSS.

On the morning of December 13, 2001, in Delhi, when the Indian parliament was in its winter session, five armed men in a white Ambassador car fitted with an improvised explosive device drove through its gates. Apparently, they got through security because they had a fake home ministry sticker on their windscreen, the back of which read:

INDIA IS A VERY BAD COUNTRY AND WE HATE INDIA WE WANT TO DESTROY INDIA AND WITH THE GRACE OF GOD WE WILL DO

*IT GOD IS WITH US AND WE WILL TRY OUR BEST. THE EDIET
WAJPAI AND ADVANI WE WILL KILL THEM. THEY HAVE KILLED
MANY INNOCENT PEOPLE AND THEY ARE VERY BAD PERSONS
THERE BROTHER BUSH IS ALSO A VERY BAD PERSON HE WILL BE
NEXT TARGET HE IS ALSO THE KILLER OF INNOCENT PEOPLE HE
HAVE TO DIE AND WE WILL DO IT.*

When the men were eventually challenged, they jumped out
and opened fire. In the gun battle that ensued, all the attackers,
eight security personnel, and a gardener were killed. The then
prime minister Atal Bihari Vajpayee (also a member of the RSS),
had, only the previous day, expressed a worry that the parliament
might be attacked. L. K. Advani, who was the home minister by
then, compared the assault to the 9/11 attacks. He said the men
"looked like Pakistanis." Fourteen years later, we still don't know
who they really were. They are yet to be properly identified.

Within days, on December 16, the Special Cell of the Delhi
police announced that it had cracked the case. It said that the attack
was a joint operation by two Pakistan-based terrorist outfits,
Lashkar-e-Taiba and Jaish-e-Mohammed. Three Kashmiri men,
SAR Geelani, Shaukat Hussain Guru, and Mohammad Afzal
Guru, were arrested. Shaukat's wife, Afsan Guru, was arrested
too. The mastermind at the Indian end, the Special Cell told
the media, was Geelani, a young professor of Arabic at Delhi
University. (He was subsequently acquitted by the courts.) On
December 21, based on these intelligence inputs, the Indian
government suspended air, rail, and bus communications with
Pakistan, banned overflights, and recalled its ambassador. More
than half a million troops were moved to the border, where they
remained on high alert for several months. Foreign embassies
issued travel advisories to their citizens and evacuated their staff,
apprehending a war that could turn nuclear.

On February 27, 2002, while Indian and Pakistani troops eye-
balled each other on the border and communal polarization was
at fever pitch, 58 *kar sevaks*—Hindu pilgrims—traveling home

from Ayodhya, were burned alive in their train coach just outside the train station in the town of Godhra, Gujarat. The Gujarat police said the coach had been firebombed from the outside by an angry mob of local Muslims. (Later, a report by the State Forensic Lab showed that this was not the case.) L. K. Advani said that "outside elements" may have also been involved. The kar sevaks' bodies, burnt beyond recognition, were transported to Ahmedabad for the public to pay their respects.

What happened next is well known. (And well forgotten too, because the bigots of yesterday are being sold to us as the moderates of today.) So, briefly: in February and March 2002, while police stood by, Gujarat burned. In cities and in villages, organized Hindutva mobs murdered two thousand Muslims in broad daylight. Women were raped and burned alive. Infants were put to the sword. Men were dismembered. Whole localities were burned down. Tens of thousands of Muslims were driven from their homes and into refugee camps. The killing went on for several weeks.

There have been pogroms in India before, equally heinous, equally unpardonable, in which the numbers of people killed have been far higher: the massacre of Muslims in Nellie, Assam, in 1983, under a Congress state government (estimates of the number killed vary between two thousand, officially, and more than double that figure, unofficially); the massacre of almost three thousand Sikhs following the assassination of Indira Gandhi in 1984, by Congress-led mobs in Delhi (which Rajiv Gandhi, who then went on to become prime minister, justified by saying, "When a big tree falls, the ground shakes"); the massacre, in 1993, of hundreds of Muslims by the Shiv Sena in Mumbai, following the demolition of the Babri Masjid. In these pogroms too, the killers were protected and given complete impunity.

But Gujarat 2002 was a massacre in the time of mass media. Its ideological underpinning was belligerently showcased, and the massacre justified in ways that marked a departure from the past. It was perpetuation, as well as a commencement. We, the public, were being given notice in no uncertain terms.

The era of dissimulation had ended.

The Gujarat pogrom dovetailed nicely with the international climate of Islamophobia. The war on terror had been declared. Afghanistan had been bombed. Iraq was already on the radar. Within months of the massacre, a fresh election was announced in Gujarat. Modi won it hands down. A few years into his first tenure, some of those involved in the 2002 pogrom were caught on camera boasting about how they had hacked, burned, and speared people to death. The footage was broadcast on the national news. It only seemed to enhance Modi's popularity in the state, where he won the next two elections as well, securing the backing of several heads of major corporations along the way, and remained chief minister for twelve years.

While Modi moved from strength to strength, his party faltered at the center. Its "India Shining" campaign in the 2004 general election was received by people as a cruel joke, and the Congress made a stunning comeback. The BJP remained out of power at the center for the next ten years.

The RSS showed itself to be an organization that thrives in the face of adversity. The climate was what is known as "vitiated." Between 2003 and 2009, a series of bombings and terror strikes on trains, buses, marketplaces, mosques, and temples, by what were thought to be Islamist terror groups, killed scores of innocent people. The worst of them all were the 2008 Mumbai attacks, in which Lashkar-e-Taiba militants from Pakistan shot 164 people and wounded more than 300.

Not all the attacks were what they were made out to be. What follows is just a sampling, an incomplete list of some of those events: On June 15, 2004, a young woman called Ishrat Jahan and three Muslim men were shot dead by the Gujarat police, who said they were Lashkar-e-Taiba operatives on a mission to assassinate Modi. The Central Bureau of Investigation has since said that the "encounter" was staged, and that all four victims were captured and then killed in cold blood. On November 23, 2005, a Muslim couple, Sohrabuddin Sheikh and his wife, Kausar Bi, were taken off a public bus by the Gujarat police.

Three days later, Sheikh was reported killed in an "encounter" in Ahmedabad. The police said that he worked for Lashkar-e-Taiba, and that they suspected he was on a mission to assassinate Modi. Kausar Bi was killed two days later. A witness to the Sheikh killing, Tulsiram Prajapati, was shot dead a year later, in a police encounter. Several senior officers of the Gujarat police are standing trial for these killings. (One of them, P. P. Pandey, has just been appointed as the director general of police for Gujarat.) On February 18, 2007, the Samjhauta Express, a "friendship train" that ran twice a week between Delhi and Attari in Pakistan, was bombed, killing sixty-eight people, most of them Pakistanis. In September 2008, three bombs went off in the towns of Malegaon and Modassa. Several of those arrested in these cases, including Swami Aseemanand of the Vanvasi Kalyan Ashram, were members of the RSS. (Hemant Karkare, the police officer who headed the Maharashtra Anti-Terrorism Squad, which led the investigations, was shot dead in 2008, during the course of the Mumbai attacks. For the story within the story, read *Who Killed Karkare?* by S. M. Mushrif, a retired inspector general of the Maharashtra police.)

The assaults on Christians continued, too. The most ferocious of them was in Kandhamal, Odisha, in 2008. Ninety Christians (all Dalits) were murdered, and more than fifty thousand people were displaced. Tragically, the mobs that attacked them were made up of newly "Hinduised" Adivasis freshly dragooned into the Sangh Parivar's vigilante militias. Kandhamal's Christians continue to live under threat, and most of them cannot return to their homes. In other states too, like Chhattisgarh and Jharkhand, Christians live in constant danger.

In 2013, the BJP announced that Modi would be its prime ministerial candidate for the 2014 general election. During his campaign, he was asked if he regretted what had happened on his watch in Gujarat in 2002. "Any person if we are driving a car, we are a driver, and someone else is driving a car and we're sitting behind," he told a Reuters journalist, "even then if a puppy comes under the wheel, will it be painful or not? Of course it is. If I'm a Chief Minister or not, I'm a human being. If something bad happens anywhere, it is natural to be sad."

The media dutifully filed the Gujarat pogrom away as old news. The campaign went well. Modi was allowed to reinvent himself as the architect of the "Gujarat model"—supposedly an example of dynamic economic development. He became corporate India's most favored candidate—the embodiment of the aspirations of the new India, architect of an economic miracle waiting to happen. His election broke the bank, costing $115 million—more than Rs 700 crore—according to the election commission.

But behind the advertising blitz and the 3D dioramas, things hadn't really changed all that much. In a district called Muzaffarnagar, in Uttar Pradesh, the tried and tested version of the *real* Gujarat model was revived as a poll strategy. Technology played a part. (This would become a recurring theme.) It began with an altercation over what was, at the time, being called "love-jihad"—a notion that played straight into that old anxiety about demography. The Muslim "love-jihad" campaign, Hindus were told, involved entrapping Hindu girls romantically and persuading them to convert to Islam. In August 2013, a Muslim boy accused of teasing a Hindu girl was killed by two Jats. Two Jats were killed in retaliation. A video of an obviously Muslim mob beating a man to death began to circulate on Facebook and over cell-phone networks. In reality, the incident had taken place in Sialkot, Pakistan. But it was put about that the video documented a local incident in which Muslims had beaten a Hindu boy to death. Provoked by the video, Hindu Jat farmers armed with swords and guns turned on local Muslims, with whom they had lived and worked for centuries. Between August and September 2013, according to official estimates, sixty-two people were killed—forty-two Muslims and twenty Hindus.

Unofficial estimates put the number of Muslims killed at more than two hundred.[3] Tens of thousands of Muslims were forced off their lands and into refugee camps. And, of course, many women were raped.

In April 2014, just before the general election, Amit Shah, a general secretary of the BJP at the time, and now the party president (he had been arrested in the Sohrabuddin Sheikh case, but was discharged by a special court), spoke at a meeting of Jats in a district bordering Muzaffarnagar. "In Uttar Pradesh, especially western UP, it is an election for honour," he said. "It is an election to take revenge for the insult. It is an election to teach a lesson to those who have committed injustice." Once again, the strategy paid off. The BJP swept Uttar Pradesh—the state with the largest share of seats in parliament.

In the midst of all this, the slew of genuinely progressive legislation which the Congress-led government had pushed through—like the Right to Information Act and the National Rural Employment Guarantee Act, which brought a modicum of real relief to the poorest of the poor—seemed to count for nothing. After ten years out of power at the centre, the BJP won a massive single-party majority. Narendra Modi became the prime minister of the world's largest democracy. In an election campaign in which optics was everything, he flew from Ahmedabad to Delhi for his swearing-in on a private jet belonging to the Adani Group. The victory was so decisive, the celebrations so aggressive, that it seemed the establishment of the Hindu Rashtra was only weeks away.

Modi's ascent to power came at a time when much of the rest of the world was descending into chaos. There was civil war in Afghanistan, Iraq, Libya, Somalia, South Sudan, and Syria. The Arab Spring had happened and un-happened. ISIS, the macabre progeny of the war on terror, which makes even the Taliban and al-Qaeda seem like moderates, was on the rise. The European refugee crisis had begun, even if it had not yet peaked. Pakistan was in serious trouble. In contrast, India looked like the warm, cuddly, unruly, Bollywoody, free-market-friendly democracy that *works*. But that was the view from the outside.

As soon as he was sworn in, the new prime minister began to display the kind of paranoia you might expect from a man who knows he has a lot of enemies, and who does not trust his own organization. His first move was to disempower and make redundant a faction within the BJP led by Advani, whom he now viewed as a threat. He usurped a great deal of the decision making in the government, and then set off on a dizzying world tour (which hasn't ended yet), with a few pit stops in India.

Modi's personal ambition, his desire to be seen as a global leader, soon began to overshadow the organization that had mentored him, and which does not take kindly to self aggrandizement. In January 2015, he greeted the visiting US president, Barack Obama, in a suit that cost over a million rupees ($15,000), with his name woven into the pin stripes: arendradamodardasmodin-arendradamodardasmodi. This was clearly a man who was in love with himself—no longer just a worker bee, no longer merely a humble servant. It began to look as though the ladders that had been used to climb into the clouds were being kicked away.

The ModiModi suit was eventually auctioned, and bought by an admirer for Rs 4.3 crore ($680,000). Meanwhile, it became the delight of cartoonists and the butt of some seriously raucous humour on social media. A man who had been feared was being laughed at for the first time. A month after his wardrobe malfunction, Modi experienced his first major shock. In the February 2015 Delhi state election, even though he campaigned tirelessly, the fledgling Aam Aadmi Party won sixty-seven of seventy seats. It was the first election Modi had lost since 2002. Suddenly, the new leader began to look brittle and unsure of himself.

Nevertheless, in the rest of the country, thugs and vigilante assassins, sure of political backing from the people they had brought into power, continued about their bloody business.

In February 2015, Govind Pansare, a writer and a prominent member of the Communist Party of India, was shot dead in Kolhapur, in Maharashtra. On August 30, 2015, M. M. Kalburgi, a well-known Kannada rationalist and scholar, was assassinated outside his home in Dharwad, in Karnataka. Both men had been threatened several times by extremist right-wing Hindu organizations, and told to stop their writing.

In September 2015, a mob gathered outside the home of a Muslim family in Dadri, a village near Delhi, claiming that they had been eating beef (a violation of the ban on cow slaughter that had been imposed in Uttar Pradesh, as well as in several other states). The family denied it. The mob refused to believe them. Mohammad Akhlaq was pulled out of his home and bludgeoned to death. The thugs of the new order were unapologetic. After the murder, when the Sangh Parivar's apparatchiks spoke to the press about "illegal slaughter," they meant the imaginary cow. When they talked about "taking evidence for forensic examination," they meant the food in the family's fridge, not the body of the lynched man. The meat taken from Akhlaq's house turned out not to be beef after all. But so what?

For days after that, the Twitter-loving prime minister said nothing. Under pressure, he issued a weak, watery admonishment. Since then, similar rumors have led to others being beaten to within an inch of their lives, even hanged. With their tormentors assured of complete impunity, Muslims now know that even a minor skirmish can ignite a full-scale massacre. A whole population is expected to hunch its shoulders and live in fear. And that, as we know, is not a feasible proposition. We are talking about approximately 170 million people.

Then, quite suddenly, just when hope was failing, something extraordinary began to happen. Despite, or perhaps *because* of, the fact that the BJP's massive majority in Parliament had reduced the opposition to a rump, a new kind of resistance made itself known. Ordinary people began to show discomfort with what was going on. That feeling soon hardened into a stubborn resilience. In protest against the lynching of Akhlaq and the murders of Kalburgi and Pansare, as well as that of the rationalist and author Narendra Dabholkar, murdered in Pune in 2013, one by one, several well-known writers and filmmakers began to return various national awards they had received. By the end of 2015, dozens of them had done so. The returning of awards—which came to be known as award-wapsi, an ironic reference to ghar wapsi—was an unplanned, spontaneous, and yet deeply political gesture, by artists and intellectuals who did not belong to any particular group or subscribe to any particular ideology, or even agree with each other about most things. It was powerful and unprecedented, and probably has no historical parallel. It was politics plucked out of thin air.

Award-wapsi was widely reported by the international press. Precisely because it was spontaneous, and could not be painted into a corner as any sort of conspiracy, it enraged the government. If this was not enough, around the same time, in November 2015, the BJP suffered another massive electoral defeat, this time in the state of Bihar, at the hands of two wily, old-school politicians—Nitish Kumar and Lalu Prasad Yadav. Lalu is a doughty foe of the Sangh Parivar, and, way back in 1990, he was one of the few politicians to show some steel and arrest Advani when the rath yatra passed through Bihar. Losing the Bihar election was a personal as well as political humiliation for Modi, who had spent weeks campaigning there. The BJP was quick to suggest some sort of collusion between its opponents and "antinational" intellectuals.

As a party that can mass-produce trolls but finds it hard to produce a single real thinker, this humiliating setback sharpened its instinctive hostility toward intellectual activity. It was never just dissent that our current rulers wished to crush. It was thought—intelligence—itself. Not surprisingly, the prime targets in the attack on our collective IQ have been some of India's best universities.

The first signs of trouble came when, in May 2015, the administration of the Indian Institute of Technology in Chennai "de-recognized" a student organization called the Ambedkar-Periyar Study Circle (APSC). Its members are Dalit Ambedkarites, who have a sharp critique of Hindutva politics but also of neoliberal economics, and of the rapid corporatization and privatization that is putting higher education out of the reach of the poor. The order banning the APSC accused it of trying to "de-align" Dalit and Adivasi students, to "make them protest against the Central government" and create hatred against the "Prime Minister and Hindus."[4]

Why should a tiny student organization with only a couple of dozen members have been seen as such a threat? Because by making connections between caste, capitalism, and communalism, the APSC was straying into forbidden territory—the sort of territory into which the South African antiapartheid activist Steve Biko and the US civil-rights leader Martin Luther King had strayed, and paid for with their lives. The de-recognition led to public protests, and was quickly rescinded, although the APSC continues to be harassed and its activity remains seriously impeded.

The next confrontation came at India's best-known film school, the Film and Television Institute of India (FTII) in Pune, where BJP and RSS cronies were appointed to the institute's governing council. Among these "persons of eminence," one had until recently been the state president of the Akhil Bharatiya Vidyarthi Parishad (ABVP), the student wing of the RSS. Another was a filmmaker who had made a documentary called *Narendra Modi: A Tale of Extraordinary Leadership*. An actor by the name of Gajendra Chauhan was appointed the council's chairman. His credential for the post, apart from his loyalty to the BJP, was his less than mediocre performance as Yudhishthira in a television version of the Mahabharata. (Of the rest of his acting career, the less said the better. You can find him on YouTube.)

The students went on strike, demanding to know on what basis a chairman with no qualifications for the job could be foisted on them. They demanded that Chauhan be removed from his post. Their real fear was that, by stacking the governing council with its cohorts, the government was setting up a coup, preparing (for the nth time) to privatize the FTII, and turn it into yet another institution exclusively for the rich and privileged.

The strike lasted for 140 days. The students were attacked by off-campus Hindutva activists, but were supported by trade unions, civil-society groups, filmmakers, artists, intellectuals, and fellow students from across the country. The government refused to back down. The strike was eventually called off, but the unrest just moved to a bigger arena.

For several years now, the University of Hyderabad (UOH) has been a charged place, particularly around Dalit politics. Among the many student groups active on the campus is the Ambedkar Students Association (ASA). As a formation of Ambedkarites, like the APSC in Chennai, the ASA was asking some profound and disturbing questions. For obvious reasons, its main antagonist on campus was the ABVP, which is emerging as the eyes and ears of the RSS, and its agent provocateur, on almost every campus in the country. When, in August, the ASA, quoting Ambedkar's views on capital punishment, protested the hanging of Yakub Memon—convicted for the 1993 serial blasts in Mumbai that followed the Shiv Sena–led pogrom against Muslims—the ABVP branded them "antinational." Following a head-on confrontation between the two groups over the documentary film *Muzaffarnagar Baaqi Hain* (Muzaffarnagar Is Still Standing), which the ASA screened on campus, five students—all Dalits, and all members of the ASA—were suspended, and told to leave their hostels. Young Dalits reaching out to the Muslim community was not something the Sangh Parivar was going to allow if it could help it.

These were first-generation students, whose parents had toiled all their lives to scrape together enough money to get their children an education. It's hard for middle-class people who take the education of their children for granted to imagine what it means to have such painstakingly cultivated hope so callously snuffed out.

One of the five suspended students was Rohith Vemula, a PhD scholar. He was the son of a poor single mother, and had no means of supporting himself without his scholarship. Driven to despair, on January 17, 2016, he hanged himself. He left behind a suicide note of such extraordinary power and poignancy that—like a piece of great literature should—his words ignited a tinderbox of accumulated fury.

Rohith wrote:

> *I always wanted to be a writer. A writer of science, like Carl Sagan.*
>
> *I loved Science, Stars, Nature, but then I loved people without knowing that people have long since divorced from nature. Our feelings are second handed. Our love is constructed. Our beliefs coloured. Our originality valid through artificial art. It has become truly difficult to love without getting hurt.*
>
> *The value of a man was reduced to his immediate identity and nearest possibility. To a vote. To a number. To a thing. Never was a man treated as a mind. As a glorious thing made up of star dust. In every field, in studies, in streets, in politics, and in dying and living.*
>
> *I am writing this kind of letter for the first time. My first time of a final letter. Forgive me if I fail to make sense.*
>
> *Maybe I was wrong, all the while, in understanding* [the] *world. In understanding love, pain, life, death. . . . My birth is my fatal accident. I can never recover from my childhood loneliness. The unappreciated child from my past.*[5]

Imagine this. We live in a culture that shunned a man like Rohith Vemula and treated him as an Untouchable. A culture that shut him down and made a mind like his extinguish itself. Rohith was a Dalit, an Ambedkarite, a Marxist (who was disillusioned with the Indian left), a student of science, an aspiring writer, and a seasoned political activist. But beyond all these identities, he was, like all of us, a unique human being, with a unique set of joys and sorrows. We might never know what that last secret sadness was that made him take his life. Perhaps that's just as well. We must make do with his farewell letter.

The things that make it revolutionary might not be immediately obvious. Despite all that was done to him, it contains sorrow but not victimhood. Though everything we know about him tells us that he was ferocious about his identity and his politics, he refuses to box himself in and define himself by the tags that others had given him. Despite bearing the weight of an oppression and cultural conditioning that is centuries old, Rohith gives himself—wrests for himself—the right to be magnificent, to dream of being stardust, of being loved as an equal, as all men and women ought to be.

Rohith was only the latest of the many Dalit students who end their lives every year. His story resonated with thousands of Dalits in universities across the country—students who had been traumatized by the medieval horrors of the caste system, and the segregation, discrimination, and injustice that follow them into the most modern university campuses, into India's premier medical and engineering colleges, into their hostels, canteens, and lecture rooms. (About half of all Dalit students drop out of school before they matriculate. Under 3 percent of the Dalit population are graduates.) They saw Rohith Vemula's suicide for what it was—a form of institutionalized murder. His suicide—and, it has to be said, the power of his prose—made people stop in their tracks, and think and rage about the criminal arrangement known as the caste system, that ancient engine that continues to run modern Indian society.

The fury over Vemula's suicide was, and is, an insurrectionary moment for a thus far marginalized, radical political vision. It saw Ambedkarites, Ambedkarite Marxists, and a coalition of left parties and social movements march together. Alert to the fact that if this configuration was allowed to consolidate it could grow into a serious threat, the BJP moved to defuse it. Its clumsy, outrageous response—claiming that Rohith Vemula was not a

Dalit—backfired badly, and pushed the party into what looked like (and could still turn out to be) a tailspin.

Attention had to be diverted. Another crisis was urgently required. The gun-sights swung around. The target had been marked a while ago.

Jawaharlal Nehru University (JNU), long known to be a "bastion of the left," was the focus of a front-page story in the November 2015 issue of *Panchajanya*, the RSS's weekly paper. It described JNU as a den of Naxalites, a "huge anti-national block which has the aim of disintegrating India." Naxalites had been a long-standing problem for the Sangh Parivar—Enemy Number Three in its written doctrine. But now, evidently, it had another, more worrying one, too.

Over the last few years, the student demography in JNU has changed dramatically. From being in a small minority, students from disadvantaged backgrounds—Dalits, Adivasis, and the many castes and subcastes that come under the capacious category known as Other Backward Classes (OBC), formerly called Shudras—now make up almost half the student body. This has radically changed campus politics. What troubles the Parivar more than the presence of the left on the JNU campus, perhaps, are the rising voices of this section of students. They are, for the most part, followers of Ambedkar, of the Adivasi hero Birsa Munda, who fought the British and died in prison in 1900, and of the radical thinker and reformer Jotirao Phule, who was a Shudra and called himself a *mali* (gardener). Phule renounced, in fact denounced, Hinduism—most trenchantly in his famous book *Gulamgiri* (Slavery), published in 1873. In much of his writing and poetry, Phule deconstructs Hindu myths to show how they are really stories grounded in history, and how they glorify the idea of an Aryan conquest of an indigenous, Dravidian culture. Phule writes of how Dravidians were demonized and turned into *asuras*, while the conquering Aryans were exalted and conferred divinity. In effect, he frames Hinduism as a colonial narrative.

In 2012, an organization of Dalit and OBC students in JNU

began to observe what it calls Mahishasur Martyrdom Day. Mahishasur, Hindus believe, is a mythical half-human half-demon entity that the goddess Durga vanquished in battle—a victory that is celebrated every year during Durga Puja. These young intellectuals said that Mahishasur was actually a Dravidian king, beloved of the Asur, Santhal, Gond, and Bhil tribes in West Bengal and Jharkhand, and others. The students declared that they would mourn the day Mahishasur was martyred, not celebrate it. Another group, that called itself the "New Materialists," began to hold a "free food festival" on Mahishasur Martyrdom Day, at which it served beef and pork, saying these were the traditional foods of the oppressed castes and tribes of India.

OBCs make up the majority of India's population, and are vitally important to every major political party. It is for this reason that Modi, in his 2014 election campaign, went out of his way to foreground the fact that he was an OBC. (Most people think of "Modi" as a bania surname.) OBCs have traditionally been used by the dominant castes as henchmen, to hold the line against Dalits (just as Dalits have been used as foot soldiers in attacks on Muslims, and Adivasis are pitted against Dalits—as they were in Kandhamal in 2008.) These signs of a section of OBCs breaking rank with Hinduism set off the RSS's extremely alert early-warning system.

If this were not trouble enough, a tentative conversation (or perhaps just an argument that was prelude to a conversation) had started between some young communists—who seemed to have begun to understand the past errors of India's major communist parties—and the followers of Birsa Munda, Ambedkar, and Phule. These groups have a vexed history, and had every reason to be wary of each other. As long as each of these loose constituencies remained hostile to the other, they did not constitute a real threat to the Sangh Parivar.

The RSS recognized that if what was going on in JNU was not stopped, it could one day pose an intellectual and existential threat to the fundamental principles and politics of Hindutva.

Why so? Because such an alliance proposes, even if only conceptually, the possibility of a countermobilization, a sort of reverse engineering of the Hindutva project. It envisions an altogether different coalition of castes, one that is constituted from the ground up, instead of organized and administered from the top down: Dalit-Bahujanism instead of Brahminism. A powerful movement, contemporary and yet rooted in India's unique social and cultural context, that has people like Ambedkar, Jotirao Phule, Savitribai Phule, Periyar, Ayyankali, Birsa Munda, Bhagat Singh, Marx, and Lenin as the stars in its constellation. A movement that challenges patriarchy, capitalism, and imperialism, that dreams of a caste-less, classless society, whose poets would be the poets of the people, and would include Kabir, Tukaram, Ravidas, Pash, Gaddar, Lal Singh Dil, and Faiz. A movement of Adivasi-Dalit-Bahujans in the sense championed by the Dalit Panthers (who, in the 1970s, took "Dalit" to connote "Members of the scheduled castes and tribes, neo-Buddhists, the working people, the landless and poor peasants, women and all those who are being exploited politically, economically and in the name of religion.")[6] A movement whose comrades would include those from the privileged castes who no longer want to claim their privileges. A movement spiritually generous enough to embrace all those who believe in justice, whatever their creed or religion.

Small wonder, then, that the *Panchajanya* story went on to say that JNU was an institution where "Innocent Hindu youth are lured after being fed wrong facts about the Varna system, which is an integral part of Hindu society." It wasn't really the "disintegrating" of India that the RSS was worried about. It was the disintegration of Hindutva. And not by a new political party, but by a new way of thinking. Had all this hinged on a formal political alliance, its leaders could have been killed or jailed. Or simply bought out, like any number of *swamis, sufis, maulanas,* and other charlatans have been. But what do you do with an idea that has begun to drift around like smoke?

You try and snuff it out at its source.

The battle lines could not have been marked more clearly. It was to be a battle between those who dream of equality and those who believe in institutionalizing inequality. Rohith Vemula's suicide made the conversation that had begun in JNU more important, more urgent, and very real. And it probably brought forward the date of an attack that was already on the cards.

The ambush was built around an obstinate old ghost who refuses to go away. The harder they try to exorcise it, the more stubbornly it persists with its haunting.

The third anniversary of the hanging of Mohammad Afzal Guru fell on February 9, 2016. Although Afzal was not accused of direct involvement in the 2001 attack on the Indian Parliament, he was convicted by the Delhi high court and given three life sentences and a double death sentence for being part of the conspiracy.

In August 2005, the Supreme Court upheld this judgment, and famously said:

> *As is the case with most conspiracies, there is and could be no direct evidence amounting to criminal conspiracy. . . . The incident which resulted in heavy casualties had shaken the entire nation, and the collective conscience of the society will only be satisfied if capital punishment is awarded to the offender.*[7]

The controversy over the Parliament attack, over the Supreme Court judgment, and over Afzal's sudden, secret execution is by no means a new one. Several books and essays by scholars, journalists, lawyers, and writers (including myself) have been published on the subject. Some of us believe that there are grave questions about the attack that remain unanswered, and that Afzal was framed and did not receive a fair trial. Others believe that the manner of his execution was a miscarriage of justice.

After the Supreme Court judgment, Afzal remained in solitary confinement in Tihar Jail for several years. The BJP, which was out of power at the center during those years, made frequent and aggressive demands that he be pulled out of the queue of those awaiting execution and hanged. The issue became a central theme in its election campaigns. Its slogan was: "*Desh abhi sharminda hai, Afzal abhi bhi zinda hai*" (The country hangs its head in shame because Afzal is still alive).

As the 2014 general election approached, the Congress-led government in power at the center—weakened by a series of corruption scandals and terrified of being outflanked by the BJP in this contest of competitive nationalism, one that the Congress is doomed to lose—pulled Afzal out of his cell one morning and hurriedly hanged him. His family was not even informed, let alone permitted a last visit. For fear that his grave would become a monument and a political rallying point for the struggle in Kashmir, he was buried inside Tihar Jail, next to Maqbool Butt, the Kashmiri separatist hero, who was hanged in 1984. (P. Chidambaram, who served the Congress-led government as home minister from 2008 to 2012, now says that Afzal's case was "perhaps not correctly decided." When I was in Class IV, we had a saying: Sorry doesn't make a dead man alive.)

Every year since then, on the anniversary of Afzal Guru's hanging, the Kashmir valley shuts down in protest. Leave alone the Kashmiri nationalists, even the mainstream, pro-India Peoples Democratic Party, currently the BJP's coalition partner in the state of Jammu and Kashmir, continues to demand that Afzal's mortal remains be returned to his family for a proper burial.

A few days prior to the third anniversary of his death, notices appeared on the JNU campus inviting students to a cultural evening "Against the Brahmanical 'collective conscience,' against the judicial killing of Afzal Guru and Maqbool Butt," and "in solidarity with the struggle of Kashmiri people for their democratic right to self-determination."

It was not the first time JNU students had met to discuss these issues. Only this time, the February 9 anniversary fell three weeks after Rohith Vemula's suicide. The atmosphere was politically

charged. Once again, the ABVP was the cat's paw. It complained
to the university authorities, and then invited the Delhi police to
intervene in what it said was "antinational activity." A camera
crew from Zee TV was on hand to record the event. The first
batch of footage in that Zee broadcast showed two groups of
students confronting each other on the JNU campus, shouting
slogans. In response to the ABVP's *"Bharat Mata ki Jai!"*
(Victory to Mother India!), another group of students, most of
them Kashmiris, some of them wearing masks, began to chant
what Kashmiris chant every day at every street-corner protest
and at every militant's funeral:

Hum kya chahatey?
Azadi!
Chheen ke lengey—
Azadi!
(What do we want?
Freedom!
We will snatch it—
Freedom!)

There were also some less familiar slogans:

Bandook ke dum pe!
Azadi!
(At gunpoint if need be!
Freedom!)

Kashmir ki azadi tak, Bharat ki barbaadi tak,
Jung ladengey! Jung ladengey!
(Until freedom comes to Kashmir, until destruction comes to
India,
War will be waged! War will be waged!)

And:

Pakistan Zindabad!
(Long live Pakistan!)

From the Zee TV footage, it wasn't clear who the students actually chanting the slogans were. Sure, it riled viewers, but winding people up about Kashmir or getting them to rail at unknown students who looked and sounded like Kashmiris was not the point, and would have served no purpose. Especially not when the BJP's negotiations with the People's Democratic Party about forming a new government in Jammu and Kashmir had run into rough weather. (That problem has subsequently been resolved.) In the JNU ambush, Kashmir was just the trigger-wire. The real goal was (and is) to tarnish the reputation of JNU, in order to eventually shut it down.

It was an easy problem to solve. The soundtrack of the confrontation was grafted onto the video of another meeting that took place two days later, this one addressed by Kanhaiya Kumar, the president of the JNU Students' Union. Kanhaiya belongs to the All India Students' Federation, the student wing of the Communist Party of India. At the meeting he addressed, the refrain of "Azadi!" was the same, only the slogans raised were completely different. They demanded azadi from poverty, from caste, from capitalism, from the Manusmriti, from Brahminism. It was a whole other ball of wax.

The doctored video was broadcast to millions by major news channels, including Zee TV, Times Now, and News X. It was shameful, unprofessional, and possibly criminal. These broadcasts set off a frenzy. First Kanhaiya Kumar, and then, two weeks later, two other students accused of organizing the Afzal Guru meeting, Umar Khalid and Anirban Bhattacharya, formerly members of the left-wing Democratic Students' Union, were arrested and charged with sedition. Posters went up across Delhi putting a price on these students' heads. One even offered a cash reward for Kanhaiya Kumar's tongue.

The Kashmiri students who were actually seen raising

slogans in the Zee TV footage remained unidentified. But they were only doing what thousands of people do every day in Kashmir. Can there be separate standards for sloganeering in Delhi and Srinagar? Perhaps you could say yes, if you argue, as many Kashmiris do, that all of Kashmir is a giant prison, and you can't arrest the already incarcerated. In any case, did those students' slogans really deliver a mortal blow to this mighty, nuclear-powered Hindu nation?

Matters continued to escalate in ever more ludicrous ways. Based on a joke on a parody Twitter account ("Hafeez Muhamad Saeed"), the home minister, Rajnath Singh, announced that the protest at JNU was backed by Hafiz Saeed, the head of Lashkar-e-Taiba and India's equivalent of Osama bin Laden. Television channels began to suggest that Umar Khalid, a self-declared Marxist–Leninist, was a Jaish-e-Mohammed terrorist. (The hard evidence this time was that his name was Umar.)

Smriti Irani, the unstoppable minister of Human Resource and Development, who is in charge of higher education, said the nation would not tolerate an insult to Mother India. The saffron-robed Yogi Adityanath, a BJP member of Parliament from Gorakhpur, said that "JNU has become a blot on education," and that it "should be closed down in the interest of the nation." Another self-styled man of god, the BJP MP Sakshi Maharaj, also clad in saffron, called the students "traitors," and said they "should be hanged instead of being lodged in jail for life or they should be killed by police bullet."[8] Gyandev Ahuja, a BJP member of the Rajasthan legislative assembly and empiricist extraordinaire, informed the world that "More than 10,000 butts of cigarettes and 4000 pieces of *beedis* are found daily in the JNU campus. 50,000 big and small pieces of bones are left by those eating non-vegetarian food. They gorge on meat . . . these anti-nationals. 2,000 wrappers of chips and *namkeen* are found, as also 3000 used condoms—the misdeeds they commit with our sisters and daughters there. And 500 used contraceptive injections are also found." In other words, JNU students were meat-eating, chip-crunching, cigarette-smoking, beer-swilling, sex-obsessed antinationals. (Does that sound so terrible?)

The prime minister said nothing.

The students of JNU and UOH, on the other hand, had plenty to say. The protests on those campuses spread to the streets, and then to universities in other parts of the country. In Delhi, on the day Kanhaiya Kumar was to be produced before a magistrate, the war zone shifted to the courts. On two days in a row, sheltering under an oversized national flag, a group of lawyers who boasted openly of their affiliation to the BJP beat up students, professors, journalists, and finally Kanhaiya Kumar himself inside a courthouse. They threatened and abused a committee of senior lawyers that the Supreme Court had urgently constituted to look into the matter. The police stood by and watched. The Delhi police chief called it a minor scuffle. The lawyers gloated to the press about how they "thrashed" Kanhaiya and forced him to say *"Bharat Mata ki Jai."* For a few days, it looked as though every last institution in the country was helpless in the face of this insane attack.

The RSS has now declared that anybody who refuses to say *"Bharat Mata ki Jai!"* is an antinational. The yoga and health-food tycoon Baba Ramdev announced that, were it not illegal, he would behead anybody who refused to say it.

What would these people have done to Ambedkar? In 1931, when questioned by Gandhi about his sharp critique of the Congress—which was seen as a critique of the party's struggle for an independent homeland—Ambedkar said, "Gandhiji, I have no homeland. No Untouchable worth the name would be proud of this land." Would they have charged him with sedition? (On the other hand, garlanding portraits of Ambedkar, as the Sangh Parivar has done, and suggesting that he—the man who called Hinduism "a veritable chamber of horrors"—is one of the founding fathers of the Hindu Rashtra, is probably much worse.)

The other tactic the BJP and its media partners have used to silence people is an absurd false binary—the Brave Soldiers versus the Evil Antinationals. In February, just when the JNU crisis was at its peak, an avalanche on the Siachen Glacier killed ten soldiers, whose bodies were flown down for military funerals. For days and nights, screeching television anchors and their studio guests inserted their own words into the mouths of the dead men, and grafted their tin-pot ideologies onto lifeless bodies that couldn't talk back. Of course they neglected to mention that most Indian soldiers are poor people looking for a means of earning a living. (You don't hear the patriotic rich asking for the draft, so that they and their children are forced to serve as ordinary soldiers.)

They also forgot to tell their viewers that soldiers are not just deployed on the Siachen Glacier or on the borders of India. That there has not been a single day since Independence in 1947 when the Indian Army and other security forces have not been deployed *within* India's borders against what are meant to be their "own" people—in Kashmir, Nagaland, Manipur, Mizoram, Assam, Junagadh, Hyderabad, Goa, Punjab, Telangana, and West Bengal, and now Chhattisgarh, Odisha, and Jharkhand.

Tens of thousands of people have lost their lives in conflicts in these places. An even greater number have been brutally tortured, many of them crippled for life. There have been documented cases of mass rape in Kashmir in which the accused have been protected by the Armed Forces Special Powers Act, as though rape is a necessary and unavoidable part of battle.[9] The aggressive insistence on unquestioning soldier-worship, even by self-professed "liberals," is a sick, dangerous game that's been dreamt up by a cynical oligarchy. It doesn't help either soldiers or civilians. And if you take a hard look at the list of places within India's current borders in which its security forces have been deployed, an extraordinary fact emerges—the populations in those places are mostly Muslim, Christian, Adivasi, Sikh, and Dalit. What we are being asked to salute obediently and unthinkingly is a reflexively dominant-caste Hindu state that nails together its territory with military might.

What if some of us dream instead of creating a society to which people *long* to belong? What if some of us dream of living in a society that people are not *forced* to be part of? What if some of us don't have colonialist, imperialist dreams? What if some of us dream instead of justice? Is it a criminal offense?

So what is this new bout of flag-waving and chest-thumping all about, really? What is it trying to hide?

The usual stuff: A tanking economy and an abject betrayal of the election promises the BJP made to gullible people, as well as to its corporate sponsors. During his election campaign, Modi burned his candle at both ends. He vulgarly promised poor villagers that 15 lakh rupees (roughly $22,500) would magically appear in their bank accounts when he came to power. He was going to bring home the illegal billions that rich Indians had parked in offshore tax havens and distribute it to the poor. How much of that illegal money was brought back? Not a lot. How much was redistributed? Approximately zero point zero zero, whatever that is in rupees. Meanwhile, corporations were eagerly looking forward to a new Land Acquisition Act that would make it easier for businessmen to acquire villagers' land. That legislation did not make it past the upper house. In the countryside, the crisis in agriculture has deepened. While big business has had tens of thousands of crores of rupees (billions of dollars) worth of loans written off, tens of thousands of small farmers trapped in a cycle of debt—that will never be written off—continue to kill themselves. In 2015, in the state of Maharashtra alone, more than 3,200 farmers committed suicide. Their suicides too are a form of institutionalized murder, just as Rohith Vemula's was.

What the new government has to offer in lieu of its wild election promises is the kind of deal that is usually available only on the saffron stock exchange: trade in your hopes for a decent livelihood and buy into an exciting life of perpetual hysteria. A life in which you are free to hate your neighbor, and if things get really bad, and if you really want to, you can get together with friends and even beat her or him to death.

The manufactured crisis in JNU has also, extremely successfully, turned our attention away from a terrible tragedy that has befallen some of the most vulnerable people in this country. The war for minerals in Bastar, Chhattisgarh, is gearing up again. Operation Green Hunt—the previous government's attempt at clearing the forest of its troublesome inhabitants in order to hand it over to mining and infrastructure companies—was largely unsuccessful. Many of the hundreds of memorandums of understanding that the government signed with private companies regarding this territory have not been actualized. Bastar's people, among the poorest in the world, have, for years, stopped the richest corporations in their tracks.

Now, in preparation for the as yet unnamed Operation Green Hunt II, thousands of Adivasis are in jail once again, most of them accused of being Maoists.

The forest is being cleared of all witnesses—journalists, activists, lawyers, and academics. Anybody who muddies the tidy delineation of the state-versus-"Maoist terrorists" paradigm is in a great deal of danger. The extraordinary Adivasi schoolteacher and activist Soni Sori, who was imprisoned in 2011 but went straight back to her organizing work after being released in 2014, was recently attacked, and had her face smeared with a substance that burnt her skin. She has since gone back to work in Bastar once again. With a burnt face.

The Jagdalpur Legal Aid Group, a tiny team of women lawyers that offered legal aid to incarcerated Adivasis, and Malini Subramaniam, whose series of investigative reports from Bastar were a source of embarrassment to the local police, have been evicted and forced to leave. Lingaram Kodopi, Bastar's first Adivasi journalist, who was horribly tortured and imprisoned for three years, is being threatened, and has despairingly announced that he will kill himself if the intimidation does not stop. Four other local journalists have been arrested on specious charges, including one who posted comments against the police on WhatsApp. Bela Bhatia, a researcher, has had the village she lives in visited by mobs shouting slogans against her and threatening her landlords. Paramilitary troops and vigilante militias, confident of impunity, have once again begun to storm villages and terrorize people, forcing them to abandon their homes and flee into the forest as they did in the time of Operation Green Hunt I. Horrific accounts of rape, molestation, looting, and robbery are trickling in. The Indian Air Force has begun "practising" air-to-ground firing from helicopters.

Anybody who criticizes the corporate takeover of Adivasi land is called an antinational "sympathizer" of the banned Maoists. Sympathy is a crime, too. In television studios, guests who try to bring a semblance of intelligence into the debate are shouted down and compelled to demonstrate their loyalty to the nation. This is a war against people who have barely enough to eat one square meal a day. What particular brand of nationalism does this come under? What exactly are we supposed to be proud of?

Our lumpen nationalists don't seem to understand that the more they insist on this hollow sloganeering, the more they force people to say *"Bharat Mata ki Jai!"* and to declare that "Kashmir is an integral part of India," the less sure of themselves they sound. The nationalism that is being rammed down our throats is more about hating another country—Pakistan—than loving our own. It's more about securing territory than loving the land and its people. Paradoxically, those who are branded antinational are the ones who speak about the deaths of rivers and the desecration of forests. They are the ones who worry about the poisoning of the land and the falling of water tables. The "nationalists," on the other hand, go about speaking of mining, damming, clear-felling, blasting, and selling. In their rule book, hawking minerals to multinational companies is patriotic activity. They have privatized the flag and wrested the microphone.

The three JNU students who were arrested are all out on interim bail. In Kanhaiya Kumar's case, the bail order by a high court judge caused more apprehension than relief: "Whenever some infection is spread in a limb, effort is made to cure the same by giving antibiotics orally and if that does not work, by following second line of treatment. Sometimes it may require surgical intervention also. However, if the infection results in infecting the limb to the extent that it becomes gangrene, amputation is the only treatment."[10] *Amputation?* What could she mean?

As soon as he was released, Kanhaiya appeared on the JNU campus and gave his now famous speech to a crowd of thousands of students. It doesn't matter whether or not you agree with every single thing he said. I didn't. But it's the spirit with which he said it that was so enchanting. It dissipated the pall of fear and gloom that had dropped on us like a fog. Overnight, Kanhaiya *and* his cheeky audience became beloved of millions. The same thing happened with the other two students, Umar Khalid and Anirban Bhattacharya. Now, people from all over the world have heard the slogan the BJP wanted to silence: "*Jai Bhim! Lal salaam!*" (Salute Bhimrao Ambedkar! Red salute!).

And with that call, the spirit of Rohith Vemula and the spirit of JNU have come together in solidarity. It's a fragile, tenuous coming together, that will most likely—if it hasn't already— come to an unhappy end, exhausted by mainstream political parties, NGOs, and its own inherent contradictions. Obviously, neither "the left" nor the "Ambedkarites" nor "OBCs" are remotely homogenous categories in themselves. However, even broadly speaking, the present left is, for the most part, doctrinally opaque to caste, and, by *unseeing* it, perpetuates it. (The outstanding exception to this, it must be said, are the writings of the late Anuradha Ghandy.) This has meant that many Dalits and OBCs who do lean toward the left have had bitter experiences, and are now determined to isolate themselves, thereby inadvertently deepening caste divisions and strengthening a system that sustains itself by precluding all forms of solidarity.

All these old wounds will act up, we'll tear each other to shreds, arguments and accusations will fly around in maddening ways. But even after this moment has passed, the radical ideas that have emerged from this confrontation with the agents of Hindutva are unlikely to ever go away. They will stay around, and will continue to be built upon. They must, because they are our only hope.

Already the real meanings, the real politics behind the refrain of "Azadi" are being debated. Did Kanhaiya pinch the slogan from the Kashmiris? He did. (And where did the Kashmiris get it? From the feminists or the French Revolution, maybe.) Is the slogan being diluted? Most definitely, as far as those who chant it in Kashmir are concerned. Is it being deepened? Yes, that too. Because fighting for azadi from patriarchy, from capitalism, and from Brahminvaad is as radical as any struggle for national self-determination.

Perhaps while we debate the true, deep meanings of freedom, those who have been so shocked by what is happening in the mainland over the last few months will be moved to ask themselves why, when far worse things happen in other places, it leaves them so untroubled? Why is it all right for us to ask for azadi in our university campuses while the daily lives of ordinary people in Kashmir, Nagaland, and Manipur are overseen by the army, and their traffic jams managed by uniformed men waving AK 47s? Why is it easy for most Indians to accept the killing of 112 young people on the streets of Kashmir in the course of a single summer?

Why do we care so much about Kanhaiya and Rohith Vemula, but so little about students like Shaista Hameed and Danish Farooq, who were shot dead in Kashmir the day before the smear campaign against JNU was launched? "Azadi" is an immense word, and a beautiful one, too. We need to wrap our minds around it, not just play with it. This is not to suggest some sort of high-mindedness in which we all fight each other's battles side by side and feel each other's pain with equal intensity. Only to say that if we do not acknowledge each other's yearning for azadi, if we do not acknowledge injustice when it is looking us straight in the eye, we will all go down together in the quicksand of moral turpitude.

The end result of the BJP's labors is that students, intellectuals, and even sections of the mainstream media, have seen how we are being torn apart by its manifesto of hate. Little by little, people have begun to stand up to it. Afzal's ghost has begun to travel to other university campuses.

As often happens after episodes like this, everybody who has been involved can, and usually does, claim victory. The BJP's assessment seems to be that the polarization of the electorate into "nationalists" and "antinationals" has been successful, and brought it substantial political gain. Far from showing signs of contrition, it has moved to turn all the knobs to high.

Kanhaiya, Umar, and Anirban's lives are in real danger from rogue assassins seeking approbation from the Sangh Parivar's high command. Thirty-five students of the FTII (one in every five) have had criminal cases filed against them. They're out on bail, but are required to report regularly to the police. Appa Rao Podile, the much-hated vice chancellor of UOH, who went on leave in January and had a case filed against him, laying responsibility at his door for the circumstances that led to Rohith Vemula's suicide, has reappeared on the campus, enraging students. When they protested, police invaded the campus, brutally beat them, arrested twenty-five students and two faculty members, and held them for days. The campus has been cordoned off by police— ironically, the police of the state of Telangana, which so many of the students on the campus fought so long and so hard to create. The arrested UOH students too have serious cases filed against them now. They need lawyers, and money to pay them with. Even if they are eventually acquitted, their lives can be destroyed by the sheer harassment involved.

It isn't just students. All over the country, lawyers, activists, writers, and filmmakers—any who criticize the government—are being arrested, imprisoned, or entangled in spurious legal cases. We can expect serious trouble, all sorts of trouble, as we head toward state elections—in particular the 2017 contest in Uttar Pradesh—and the general election in 2019. We must anticipate false-flag terrorist strikes, and perhaps even what is being optimistically called a "limited war" with Pakistan. At a public meeting in Agra, on February 29, Muslims were warned of a "final battle." A fired-up, five-thousand-strong crowd chanted: *"Jis Hindu ka khoon na khaule, khoon nahin woh pani hai"* (Any Hindu whose blood isn't boiling has water in the veins, not blood).

Regardless of who wins elections in the years to come, can this sort of venom be counteracted once it has entered the blood stream? Can any society mend itself after having its fabric slashed and rent apart in this way?

What is happening right now is actually a systematic effort to *create* chaos, an attempt to arrive at a situation in which the civil rights enshrined in the Indian Constitution can be suspended. The RSS has never accepted the constitution. It has now, finally, manoeuvered itself into a position where it has the power to subvert it. It is waiting for an opportunity. We might well be witnessing preparations for a coup—not a military coup, but a coup nevertheless. It could be only a matter of time before India will officially cease to be a secular, democratic republic. We may find ourselves looking back fondly on the era of doctored videos and parody Twitter handles.

Our forests are full of soldiers and our universities full of police. The University Grants Commission's new guidelines for higher educational institutions suggest that campuses have high boundary walls topped by concertina wire, armed guards at entrances, police stations, biometric tests, and security cameras. Smriti Irani has ordered that all public universities must fly the national flag from 207-foot-high flagpoles for students to "worship." (Who'll get the contracts?) She has also announced plans to rope in the army to instill patriotism in the minds of students.

In Kashmir, the presence of an estimated half a million troops ensures that, whatever its people may or may not want today, Kashmir has been made an integral part of India. But now, with soldiers and barbed wire and enforced flag-worshipping in the mainland, it looks more and more as though India is becoming an integral part of Kashmir.

As symbols of countries, flags are powerful objects, worthy of contemplation. But what of those like Rohith Vemula, who have imaginations that predate the idea of countries by hundreds of thousands of years? The earth is 4.5 billion years old. Human beings appeared on it about 200,000 years ago. What we call "human civilization" is just a few thousand years old. India as a country with its present borders is less than 80 years old. Clearly, we could do with a little perspective.

Worship a flag? My soul is either too modern or too ancient for that.

I'm not sure which.

Maybe both.

APPENDIX

THE GREAT INDIAN
RAPE-TRICK I

AT THE PREMIERE screening of *Bandit Queen* in Delhi, Shekhar Kapur introduced the film with these words: "I had a choice between Truth and Aesthetics. I chose Truth, because Truth is Pure."

To insist that the film tells the Truth is of the utmost commercial (and critical) importance to him. Again and again, we are assured, in interviews, in reviews, and eventually in writing on the screen before the film begins: "This is a True Story."

If it weren't the "Truth," what would redeem it from being just a classy version of your run-of-the-mill Rape n' Retribution theme that our film industry churns out every now and then? What would save it from the familiar accusation that it doesn't show India in a Proper Light? Exactly nothing.

It's the "Truth" that saves it. Every time. It dives about like Superman with a Swiss knife and snatches the film straight from the jaws of unsavory ignominy. It has bought headlines. Blunted argument. Drowned criticism.

If you say you found the film distasteful, you're told—

First published in *Sunday*, August 22, 1994.

well, that's what truth is—distasteful. Manipulative? That's Life—manipulative.

Go on. Now you try. Try . . . Exploitative. Or . . . Gross. Try Gross.

It's a little like having a dialogue with the backs of trucks. God is Love. Life is Hard. Truth is Pure. Sound Horn.

Whether or not it is the Truth is no longer relevant. The point is that it will (if it hasn't already) become the Truth.

Phoolan Devi the woman has ceased to be important. (Yes, of course she exists. She has eyes, ears, limbs, hair, etc. Even an address now.) But she is suffering from a case of Legenditis. She's only a version of herself. There are other versions of her that are jostling for attention. Particularly Shekhar Kapur's "Truthful" one, which we are currently being bludgeoned into believing.

"It has the kind of story, which, if it were a piece of fiction, would be difficult to credit. In fact, it is the true story of Phoolan Devi, the Indian child bride . . . ." Derek Malcolm writes in the *Guardian*.

But is it? The True Story? How does one decide? Who decides? Shekhar Kapur says that the film is based on Mala Sen's book—*India's Bandit Queen: The True Story of Phoolan Devi*. The book reconstructs the story, using interviews, newspaper reports, meetings with Phoolan Devi, and extracts from Phoolan's written account, smuggled out of prison by her visitors, a few pages at a time.

Sometimes various versions of the same event—versions that totally conflict with each other, that is, Phoolan's version, a journalist's version, or an eyewitness's version—are all presented to the reader in the book. What emerges is a complex, intelligent, and human book. Full of ambiguity, full of concern, full of curiosity about who this woman called Phoolan Devi really is.

Shekhar Kapur wasn't curious.

He has openly admitted that he didn't feel that he needed to meet Phoolan. His producer Bobby Bedi supports this decision: "Shekhar would have met her if he had felt a need to do so."

It didn't matter to Shekhar Kapur who Phoolan Devi really was. What kind of person she was. She was a woman, wasn't she? She was raped, wasn't she? So what did that make her? A Raped Woman! You've seen one, you've seen 'em all.

He was in business. What the hell would he need to meet her for?

Did he not stop to think that there must have been something very special about her? That if this was the normal career graph of a low-caste village woman who was raped, our landscapes would be teeming with female gangsters?

If there is another biographer anywhere in the world who has not done a living subject the courtesy of meeting her even once—will you please stand up and say your name? And having done that, will you (and your work) kindly take a running jump?

What does Shekhar Kapur mean when he says the film is based on Mala Sen's book? How has he decided which version of which event is "True"? On what basis has he made these choices? There's a sort of loutish arrogance at work here. A dunce's courage. Unafraid of what it doesn't know. What he has done is to rampage through the book, picking up what suits him, ignoring and even altering what doesn't.

I am not suggesting that a film should include every fact that's in the book.

I am suggesting that if you take a long hard look at the choices he has made—at his inclusions, his omissions, and his blatant alterations—a truly dreadful pattern emerges.

Phoolan Devi (in the film version) has been kept on a tight leash. Each time she strays toward the shadowy marshlands that lie between Victimhood and Brutishness, she has been reined in. Brought to heel.

It is of consummate importance to the Emotional Graph of the film that you never, ever stop pitying her. That she never threatens the Power Balance.

I would have thought that this was anathema to the whole point of the Phoolan Devi story. That it went way beyond the

You-Rape-Me, I'll-Kill-You equation. That the whole point of it was that she got a little out of control. That the Brutalized became the Brute.

The film wants no part of this. Because of what it would do to the Emotional Graph. To understand this, you must try and put Rape into its correct perspective. The Rape of a nice Woman (saucy, headstrong, foul-mouthed perhaps, but basically moral, sexually moral)—is one thing. The rape of a nasty/perceived-to-be-immoral woman is quite another. It wouldn't be quite so bad. You wouldn't feel quite so sorry. Perhaps you wouldn't feel sorry at all.

Any policeman will tell you that. Whenever the police are accused of custodial rape, they immediately set to work. Not to prove that she wasn't raped. But to prove that she wasn't nice. To prove that she was a loose woman. A prostitute. A divorcee. Or an Elopee—i.e.: she asked for it. Same difference.

Bandit Queen, the film, does not make a case against rape. It makes its case against the rape of nice (read moral) women. (Never mind the rest of us who aren't "nice.")

It's on the lookout, like a worried hen, saving Phoolan Devi from herself. Meanwhile we, the audience, are herded along, like so much trusting cattle. We cannot argue (because Truth is Pure—and you can't mess with that).

Every time the director has been faced with something that could disrupt the simple, prefabricated calculations of his cloying morality play, it has been tampered with and forced to fit. I'm not accusing him of having planned this. I believe that it comes from a vision that has been distorted by his own middle-class outrage, which he has then turned on his audience like a firefighter's hose.

According to Shekhar Kapur's film, every landmark—every decision, every turning point in Phoolan Devi's life, starting with how she became a dacoit in the first place, has to do with having been raped or avenging rape.

He has just blundered through her life like a Rape-diviner. You cannot but sense his horrified fascination at the havoc that a wee willie can wreak. It's a sort of reversed male self-absorption.

Rape is the main dish. Caste is the sauce that it swims in.

The film opens with a pre-credit sequence of Phoolan Devi the child being married off to an older man who takes her away to his village where he rapes her, and she eventually runs away. We see her next as a young girl being sexually abused by Thakur louts in her village. When she protests, she is publicly humiliated, externed from the village, and when she returns to the village, ends up in prison. Here too she is raped and beaten and eventually released on bail. Soon after her release, she is carried away by dacoits.

She has in effect become a criminal who has jumped bail. And so has little choice but to embark on a life in the ravines.

He has the caste-business and the rape-business neatly intertwined to kickstart that "swift, dense, dramatic narrative."

Mala's book tells a different story.

Phoolan Devi stages her first protest against injustice at the age of ten. Before she is married off. In fact, it's the reason that she's married off so early. To keep her out of trouble. She didn't need to be raped to protest. Some of us don't. She had heard from her mother the story of how her father's brother Biharilal and his son Maiyadeen falsified the land records and drove her father and mother out of the family house, forcing them to live in a little hut on the outskirts of the village.

The angry little girl accompanied by a frightened older sister marches into her uncle's hora field where the two of them hang around with a combative air, munching hora nuts and plucking flowers (combatively). Their cousin Maiyadeen, a young man in his twenties, orders the children off his premises. Phoolan refuses to move. Instead this remarkable child taunts him and questions his claim to the land. She was special. She is beaten unconscious with a brick.

Phoolan Devi's first war, like almost every dacoit's first war, was fought for territory. It was the classic beginning of the journey into dacoitdom. But does it have rape in it? Nope. Caste violence? Nope. So is it worth including in the film? Nope.

According to the book, her second protest, too, has to do

with territory. And it is this (not the sexual harassment by the village louts, though that happens, too) that lands Phoolan Devi in jail and enters her name in the police records. Maiyadeen, the book says, was enraged because the property dispute (thanks to Phoolan's pleas to the village panchayat) had been reopened and transferred to the Allahabad High Court. As revenge he destroys Devideen's (Phoolan's father) crop and is in the process of hacking down their Neem tree when Phoolan intervenes and throws a stone at him. She is attacked, trussed up, and handed to the police. Soon after she's released on bail, she is kidnapped by dacoits. This too, according to Phoolan's version (up to this point, there is no other version), is engineered by Maiyadeen as a ruse to get her out of his hair. Maiyadeen does not figure in the film.

Already some pretty big decisions have been made. What stays, what goes. What is highlighted, what isn't. Life is Rape. The rest is just details.

We then see Phoolan in the ravines, being repeatedly raped by Babu Singh Gujar, the Thakur leader of the gang she has been kidnapped by. Vikram Mallah, the second-in-command, is disgusted by his behavior and puts a bullet through him. According to the book, the killing happens as a drunken Babu Gujar is threatening to assault Phoolan. In the film he's actually at it, lying on top of her, his naked bottom jerking. As he breathes his last, Phoolan blinks the blood out of her eyes and looks long into the eyes of her redeemer. Just so that we get the point.

After this we are treated to a sequence of After-rape romance. The touching bits about the first stirrings of sexual desire in a much-raped woman. The way it works in the film is If-you-touch-me-I'll-slap-you-but-I-really-do-want-to-touch-you.

It's choreographed like a dusty dance in which they rub against each other, but whenever he touches her she swats his hand away, but nevertheless quivers with desire. It is such a crude, obvious, doltish depiction of conflict in a woman who is attracted to a man but associates sex with humiliation. It's not in the book, so I'm not sure whose version Shekhar has used. From the looks of it, probably Donald Duck's.

Vikram Mallah and Phoolan Devi become lovers. While the book and the film agree that he was her one true love, the book does not suggest that he was her only lover.

The film does. She has to be portrayed as a One-Man Woman. Otherwise who's going to pity her? So it's virtue or bust. One lover (a distant cousin) is eliminated completely. The other (Man Singh) is portrayed as what used to be known in college as a Rakhi-brother.

From all accounts, Vikram Mallah seems to have been the midwife of Phoolan's birth into dacoitdom. He supervises her first act of retribution against her husband Puttilal. The film shows him bound and gagged, being beaten by Phoolan Devi with the butt of her gun, whimpering and crying with remembered rage.

At having been raped. In the Retribution bits, she is allowed a little latitude. Otherwise, (as we shall see) none at all.

But there's a sly omission here. According to the book, according to Phoolan Devi herself, there were two victims that day. Not one.

The second one was a woman. Vidya, Puttilal's second wife.

The film hasn't told us about a second experience Phoolan has with Puttilal. The time that Maiyadeen forced her to return to Puttilal. Phoolan arrived at her husband's house to find that he had taken a second wife. Vidya harassed and humiliated Phoolan and eventually forced Puttilal to send her away. Her humiliation at Vidya's hands is more recent in Phoolan's memory. Phoolan, in her written version, says she wanted to kill them both and leave a note saying that this will be the fate of any man who takes two wives. Later she changed her mind and decided to leave them alive to tell the tale. She beat them both. And broke Puttilal's hands and legs.

But what nice woman would do that? Beat up another woman? How would you feel sorry for someone like that?

So, in the film, Vidya is dumped.

Phoolan's affair with Vikram Mallah ends tragically when he is shot. She is captured by his Thakur killers, gagged, bound, and transported to Behmai. The stage is set for what has come to be referred to as the "centerpiece" of the film. The gang rape. It is the scene by which the film is judged. Not surprisingly, Phoolan herself is reticent about what happened. All she says is "*Un logo ne mujhse bahut maẓaak ki*" (Those people behaved badly with me). She mentions being beaten, humiliated, and paraded from village to village. She mentions another woman dacoit, Kusuma, who disliked her and taunted and abused her. (Of course, there's no sign of her in the film. It would only serve to confuse the Woman-as-victim moral arithmetic.)

Since Phoolan isn't forthcoming, it is the vivid (vicarious) account in *Esquire* by an American journalist, Jon Bradshaw, that has been enlisted to structure this scene.

Phoolan screamed, striking out at him, but he was too strong. Holding her down, the stranger raped her. They came in one by one after that. Tall, silent Thakur men—and raped her until Phoolan lost consciousness. For the next three weeks Phoolan was raped several times a night, and she submitted silently turning her face to the wall . . . she lost all sense of time . . . a loud voice summoned her outside. Sri Ram ordered Phoolan to fetch water from the well. When she refused, he ripped off her clothes and kicked her savagely . . . at last she limped to the well while her tormentors laughed and spat at her. The naked girl was dragged back to the hut and raped again.

Whatever Shekhar Kapur's other failings are, never let it be said that he wasn't a trier. He did his bit, too. He locked himself up in a room—the door opening and closing as one man after another strode in—imagining himself being sodomized!!! After this feat of intersexual empathy, he arrives at some radical, definitive conclusions. "There is no pain in a gang-rape, no physical pain after a while," he assures us. "It is about something as dirty as the abject humiliation of a human being and the complete domination of its soul."

Thanks, baby. I would never have guessed.

It's hard to match the self-righteousness of a filmmaker with a cause. Harder when the filmmaker is a man and the cause is rape. And when it's the gang-rape of a low-caste woman by high-caste men . . . Don't even try it. Go with the feeling.

We see a lot of Phoolan's face, in tight close-up, contorted into a grimace of fear and pain as she is raped and mauled and buggered. The overwhelming consensus in the press has been that the rape was brilliantly staged and chilling.

That it wasn't exploitative. Now what does that mean? Should we be grateful to Shekhar Kapur for not showing us the condition of her breasts and genitals? Or theirs? That he leaves so much to our imagination? That he gave us a tasteful rape? But I thought the whole point of this wonderful film was its no-holds-barred brutality? So why stop now? Why the sudden coyness? I'll tell you why. Because it's all about regulating the Rape-meter. Adjusting it enough to make us a little green-at-the-gills. Skip dinner, perhaps. But not miss work.

It's us, We-the-Audience, stuck in our voyeuristic middle-class lives who really make the decisions about how much or how little rape/violence we can take/will applaud, and therefore, are given. It isn't about the story. (There are ways and ways of telling a story.) It isn't about the Truth. (There are ways around that too. Right?) It isn't about what Really Happened. It's none of that high falutin' stuff. It's good old Us. We make the decisions about how much we would like to see. And when the mixture's right, it thrills us. And we purr with approbation.

It's a class thing. If the controls are turned up too high, the hordes will get excited and arrive. To watch the centerpiece. They might even whistle. They won't bother to cloak their eagerness in concern like we do. This way, it's fine, it's just Us and our Imagination. But hey, I have news for you—the hordes have heard and are on their way. They'll even pay to watch. It'll make money, the centerpiece. It's hot stuff.

How does one grade film-rapes on a scale from Exploitative to Nonexploitative? Does it depend on how much skin we see? Or is it a more complex formula that juggles exposed skin, genitalia, and bare breasts? Exploitative, I'd say, is when the whole point of the exercise is to stand on high moral ground and inform us (as if we didn't know) that rape is about abject humiliation. And, as in the case of this film, when it exploits exploitation. Phoolan has said that she thinks they're no better than the men who raped her.

And they've done it without dirtying their hands. What was that again? The complete domination of the soul? I guess you don't need hands to hold souls down.

After the centerpiece, the film rushes through to its conclusion. Phoolan manages to escape from her captors and arrives at a cousin's house, where she recuperates and then eventually teams up with Man Singh who later becomes her lover (though of course the film won't admit it). On one foray into a village with her new gang (one of the only times we see her indulging in some non-rape-related banditry), we see her wandering through a village in a daze, with flaring nostrils, while the men loot and plunder. She isn't even scared when the police arrive. Before she leaves she smashes a glass case, picks out a pair of silver anklets, and gives it to a little girl. Sweet.

When Phoolan and her gang arrive in Behmai for the denouement, everybody flees indoors except for a baby that is for some reason left by the well. The gang fans out and gathers the Thakurs who have been marked for death. Suddenly the color seeps out of the film and everything becomes bleached and dream sequency. It all turns very conceptual. No brutal close-ups. No bestiality.

A girl's gotta do what a girl's gotta do. The twenty-two men are shot. The baby wallows around in rivers of blood. Then color leaches back into the film.

And with that, according to the film, she's more or less through with her business. The film certainly is more or less through with her. Because there's no more rape. No more retribution.

According to the book, it is really only after the Behmai massacre that Phoolan Devi grows to fit her legend. There's a price on her head, people are baying for her blood, the gang splinters. Many of them are shot by the police. Ministers and chief ministers are in a flap. The police are in a panic. Dacoits are being shot down in fake encounters and their bodies are publicly displayed like game. Phoolan is hunted like an animal. But ironically, it is now, for the first time, that she is in control of her life. She becomes a leader of men. Man Singh becomes her lover, but on her terms. She makes decisions. She confounds the police. She evades every trap they set for her. She plays daring little games with them. She undermines the credibility of the entire Uttar Pradesh police force. And all this time, the police don't even know what she really looks like. Even when the famous Malkhan Singh surrenders, Phoolan doesn't.

This goes on for two whole years. When she finally does decide to surrender, it is after several meetings with a persuasive policeman called Rajendra Chaturvedi, the superintendent of police of Bhind, with whom she negotiates the terms of her surrender to the government of Madhya Pradesh.

Is the film interested in any of this? Go on. Take a wild guess.

In the film, we see her and Man Singh on the run, tired, starved, and out of bullets. Man Singh seems concerned, practical, and stoical. Phoolan is crying and asking for her mother!!!

The next thing we know is that we're at surrender. As she gives up her gun, she looks at Man Singh and he gives her an approving nod. Good girl! Clever girl! Good Clever Girl.

Phoolan Devi spent three and a half years in the ravines. She was wanted on forty-eight counts of major crime, twenty-two murder, the rest kidnaps-for-ransom and looting. Even simple mathematics tells me that we've been told just half the story. But the cool word for Half-truth is Greater Truth. Other signs of circular logic are beginning to surface.

Such as: Life is Art.

Art is not Real.

How about changing the title of the film to: *Phoolan Devi's Rape and Abject Humiliation: The True Half-Truth*? How about sending it off to an underwater film festival with only one entry?

What responsibility does a biographer have to his subject? Particularly to a living subject? None at all? Does it not matter what she thinks or how this is going to affect her life?

Is he not even bound to show her the work before it is released for public consumption?

If the issues involved are culpable criminal offenses such as Murder and Rape—if some of them are still pending in a court of law—legally, is he allowed to present conjecture, reasonable assumption and hearsay as the unalloyed "Truth"?

Shekhar Kapur has made an appeal to the Censor Board to allow the film through without a single cut. He has said that the Film, as a work of Art, is a whole, and that if it were censored it wouldn't be the same film. What about the Life that he has fashioned his Art from? He has a completely different set of rules for that.

It's been several months since the film premiered at Cannes. Several weeks since the showings in Bombay and Delhi. Thousands of people have seen the film. It's being invited to festivals all over the world. Phoolan Devi hasn't seen the film. She wasn't invited.

I met her yesterday. In the morning papers Bobby Bedi had dismissed Phoolan's statements to the press—"Let Phoolan sit with me and point out inaccuracies in the film, I will counter her accusations effectively." What is he going to do? Explain to her how it really happened? But it's deeper than that. His story to the press is one thing. To Phoolan it's quite another. In front of me she rang him up and asked him when she could see the film. He would not give her a definite date. What's going on?

Private screenings have been organized for powerful people. But not for her. They hadn't bargained for this. She was supposed to be safely in jail. She wasn't supposed to matter. She isn't supposed to have an opinion. "Right now," the *Sunday Observer* says, "Bobby Bedi is more concerned about the Indian Censor Board than a grumbling Phoolan Devi."

Legally, as things stand, in Uttar Pradesh the charges against her haven't been dropped. (Mulayam Singh has tried, but an appeal against this is pending in the high court.) There are several versions of what happened at Behmai. Phoolan denies that she was there. More importantly, two of the men who were shot at but didn't die say she wasn't there. Other eyewitnesses say she was. Nothing has been proved. Everything is conjecture.

By not showing her the film but keeping her quiet until it's too late to protest (until it has been passed by the censors and the show hits the road), what are they doing to Phoolan? By appearing to remain silent, is she concurring with the film version of the massacre at Behmai? Which states, unequivocally, that Phoolan was there. Will it appear as though she is admitting evidence against herself? Does she know that whether or not the film tells the Truth it is only a matter of time before it becomes the Truth? And that public sympathy for being shown as a rape victim doesn't get you off the hook for murder?

Are they helping her to put her head in a noose?

On the one hand, the concerned cowboys Messrs Bedi & Kapur are so eager to share with us the abject humiliation and the domination of Phoolan Devi's "soul," and on the other they seem to be so totally uninterested in her. In what she thinks of the film, or what their film will do to her life and future.

What is she to them? A concept? Or just a cunt?

One last terrifying thing. While she was still in jail, Phoolan was rushed to hospital bleeding heavily because of an ovarian cyst. Her womb was removed. When Mala Sen asked why this had been necessary, the prison doctor laughed and said, "We don't want her breeding any more Phoolan Devis."

The state removed a woman's uterus! Without asking her. Without her knowing. It just reached into her and plucked out a part of her! It decided to control who was allowed to breed and who wasn't. Was this even mentioned in the film? No. Not even in the rolling titles at the end.

When it comes to getting bums on seats, a hysterectomy just doesn't measure up to rape.

THE GREAT INDIAN
RAPE-TRICK II

I'VE TRIED. BUT I'm afraid I simply cannot see another point of view on this whole business. The question is not whether *Bandit Queen* is a good film or a bad film. The question is, should it exist at all? If it were a work of fiction, if the filmmakers had taken the risk that every fiction writer takes, and told a story, then we could begin to discuss the film—its artistic merit, its performances, its editing, the conviction behind its social comment, and so on. If this had been the case, I, as the writer of films that have been infinitely less successful, would not have commented.

The trouble is that *Bandit Queen* claims nothing less than "Truth." The filmmakers have insured themselves against accusations of incompetence, exaggeration, even ignorance, by using a living human being.

Unfortunately, to protect themselves from these (comparatively) small risks, they had to take one big one. The dice were loaded in their favor. It nearly paid off. But then, the wholly unanticipated happened. Phoolan Devi spoiled everything by

First published in *Sunday*, September 23, 1994.

being released from prison on bail. And now, before our eyes, in delicious slow motion, the house of cards is collapsing.

As it folds softly to the floor, it poses the Big Questions. Of Truth. Of Justice. Of Liberty.

A man who read my essay of last week, came up to me and said, "She's scum. Why are you getting involved with her?"

I'm not sure I know how one defines scum. But for the sake of the argument, let's assume that she is. Phoolan Devi (Scum)—like a degree from an unknown university. Does Scum have civil rights? It took a Salman Rushdie to make the world discuss the freedom of expression. Not an Enid Blyton. And so, to discuss an individual's right to Justice, it takes a Phoolan Devi. Not the Pope.

In yesterday's papers, the chairman of the Censor Board defended the delay in clearing some films on Rajiv Gandhi. "The trouble with political films," he said, "is that they are about real people. They must be absolutely true." In the eyes of the Law, are Rajiv Gandhi and Phoolan Devi equally real? Or is one a little more real than the other? As we watch the drama unfold in the press, one thing has become absolutely clear. The most elusive, the most enigmatic, the most intangible character of all is the "Truth." She hardly appears. She has no lines. Perhaps it's safe to assume that the play isn't about her at all. If so, then what are we left with? Versions. Versions of the story. Versions of the woman herself.

We have the version of her in the film: Poor Phoolan. Raped and re-raped and re-re-raped until she takes to crime and guns down twenty-two Thakur Rapists. (Forgive her, the film says to us.) We have the version of her painted by the producers now that she's protested about their film: manipulative, cunning, trying to hit them for more money. (Look at the greedy bitch!) We have the version of her that appears in the papers: Ex-jailbird. Flirting with politics. Trying to adjust to married life, manipulated by her husband and her French biographers.

And these are only some of them.

We have versions of her story. Phoolan's version. Mala Sen's book that claims to be based on Phoolan's "writings." This film that claims to be based on Mala Sen's book. And these are only some of them.

As always, when we cannot agree, we must turn to law. Study contracts. Examine promises. Scrutinize signatures.

What does Phoolan's contract say? Or, more accurately, what do Phoolan's contracts say? They say quite simply, all three of them, that the film was to be based on Phoolan's writings; the film was to be Phoolan Devi's version of her story. Not Mala Sen's version. Not Shekhar Kapur's version. Not your or my version. Not even the "True" version (if such a thing exists), but Phoolan's version.

You see, it turns out that Mala Sen's book was published long after the first contract with Phoolan was signed.

The first agreement for the purchase of the rights to Phoolan's version was with Jalal Agha's company called Anancy Films. It was signed in 1988. The contract clearly states (underlined right across the top) that it was to be a documentary film "relating to Indian banditry and your role therein." Having made this clear, the contract refers to it as "the Film."

Another agreement was signed in 1989 informing Phoolan that the rights to her "writings" now belonged to Channel Four.

The third letter was issued in 1992 by BV Videographics, S. S. Bedi's company, affirming the agreement between Phoolan Devi and Channel Four and informing her that they were the latest in the line of succession to the rights of her story.

The contracts, smuggled in and out of prison by Phoolan's family in tiffin carriers, are vague and cursory. Couched in this vagueness there is a sort of disdain. Of the educated for the illiterate. Of the rich for the poor. Of the free for the incarcerated. It's like the attitude of a *memsahib* getting her *ayah* to undertake to vacate the servants' quarter in the event that she's sacked. Essentially, Phoolan Devi seems to have given Channel Four the rights to film her version of the story of her life, in return for the sum of a little over

5,000 pounds. Less than 1 percent of the 650,000-pound budget of the film. (What was that about her being greedy?)

Anyway, let us assume that it all started out in good faith. That they intended to make a Documentary Film. Somewhere along the way it became a Feature film. They took care of that in the small print. Okay. In the last clause of the agreement(s), they gave themselves the right to "cut, alter and adapt the writings and use alone or with other material and/or accompanied by editorial comment."

Herein (they believe) lies their salvation. What did they mean by this clause? What did they intend when they included this in the contract? To me, as a writer of films, it seems fair enough. You must have the right to cut, alter, and adapt your source material. Of course you must. Unless you want to make a film that is exactly as long as the life of your subject. But does "cut, alter, and adapt" include Distort and Falsify?

The producers' (by now public, and written) refusal to show Phoolan the original version of the film (the one that has been seen and reviewed and is now on its World Tour) suggests that they know they have done her a terrible injustice. But they say they are not worried because they have a "fool-proof" contract with her. What does this imply? That they deliberately set out to cheat and mislead her? That they conned an illiterate woman into signing away her rights? I don't know. I'm asking.

Surely the fact that they were dealing with an illiterate woman only increases their obligation to her? Surely it was up to them, to check and countercheck the facts with her? To read her the script, to fine-tune the details, to show her the rough cut before the film was shown to the rest of the world? Instead what do they do? They never meet her once. Not even to sign the contracts. They reinvent her life. Her loves. Her rapes. They implicate her in the murder of twenty-two men that she denies having committed. Then they try to slither out of showing her the film!

"Cut, alter, and adapt"? Is that what it's called?

Could it be that the film's success, and the producers' (and director's) blatant exploitation of this person, both have to do with the same thing? That she's a woman, that she's poor, and illiterate, and has (they assume) no court of appeal? Which is why she became a bandit in the first place? Which they haven't got yet. The point that they seem to keep on missing (in the film, and otherwise) is that she's no victim. She's a fighter. Unfortunately for her, this time she's on their territory. Not hers.

After I saw the film, which was about three weeks ago, I met Phoolan several times. Initially, I did not speak of the film to her, because I believed that it would have been wrong of me to influence her opinion. The burden of my song so far has been: Show her the film. I only supported her demand that she had a right, a legal right to see the film that claims to be the true story of her life. My opinion of the film has nothing to do with her opinion. Mine doesn't matter. Hers does. More than anyone else's.

Two days ago, on September 1, when the producer replied to Phoolan's legal notice, making it absolutely clear that he would not show her the original, international version of the film (the version that has been written about, and so glowingly reviewed), I sat with her and told the sequence of events, scene by scene. The discrepancies, the departures, the outright fabrications are frightening. I wrote about some of them last week. I didn't know then just how bad it really was.

Phoolan didn't write any prison diaries. She couldn't. She narrated them to someone who was with her in jail. The writings were smuggled out and given to Mala Sen. Mala Sen pieced them together and wrote first a script, then a book. The book presents several versions of the story, including Phoolan's. The film doesn't. Mala Sen's book and *Bandit Queen* the film differ radically, not just in fact, but in spirit. I believe that her film script was altered by the makers of the film. Substantially altered. It departs from the book as well as from Phoolan's version of her story.

Since I have not seen Phoolan's diaries, I can only read the extracts published in Mala Sen's book and assume that they are accurate. Mala Sen quotes her: "What I am writing is read by many, and written by those I do not know so well . . ." What a terrible position to be in! What easy meat for jackals!

According to Mala Sen, Phoolan Devi was reluctant to even discuss rape:

> *There are various versions of what happened to Phoolan Devi after Vikram Mallah's death. When I spoke to her she was reluctant to speak of her beʐathi (dishonor) as she put it, at the hands on the Thakurs. She did not want to dwell on the details and merely said, "Un logo ne mujhse bahut maʐak ki" (Those people behaved badly with me). I was not surprised at her reticence to elaborate. First of all, because we had an audience, including members of her family, other prisoners and their relatives. Secondly because we live in societies where a woman who is abused sexually ends up feeling deeply humiliated, knowing that many will think that it was her fault, or partly her fault. That she provoked the situation in the first place. Phoolan Devi, like many other women all over the world, feels she will only add to her own shame if she speaks of this experience.*

Does this sound like a woman who would have agreed to have her humiliation recreated for the world to watch? Does this sound like the book that a film replete with rape could be based on? Every time Mala Sen quotes Phoolan as saying, "Un logo ne mujhse bahut mazak ki," the director of the film has assumed that she meant that she was raped. "How else can a woman be expected to express the shame heaped on her . . ." asks Kapur. And in the film he does not shy away from dwelling on details. Oh, no. That's woman stuff. When Phoolan won't provide him with the details, he goes ahead and uses the wholly vicarious account of some American journalist from *Esquire*. The man writes with skill and feeling. Almost as though he was there. (I've quoted from this at length in "The Great Indian Rape-Trick I.")

Assuming, for the sake of argument, that whenever Phoolan says "mujhse mazak ki" she does in fact mean that she was raped. Do they have the right to show it? In all its explicit detail? This raises the question of an Individual's Right to Privacy. In Phoolan Devi's case, not just Privacy, Sexual Privacy. And not just infringement. Outright assault.

In the rape scenes in the film (Phoolan Devi is shown being raped by her husband, raped by Babu Gujjar, raped by the police, and gang-raped by the Thakurs of Behmai), her humiliation and degradation could not possibly be more explicit.

While I watched this, I remember feeling that using the identity of a living woman, recreating her degradation and humiliation for public consumption, was totally unacceptable to me. Doing it without her consent, without her specific, written, repeated, whole-hearted, unambiguous consent, is monstrous. I cannot believe that it has happened. I cannot believe that it is being condoned.

I cannot believe that it is not a criminal offense.

If it were a fictional film, where rape was being examined as an issue, if it were a fictional character who was being raped, it would be an entirely different issue. I would be glad to enter into an argument about whether showing the rape was necessary, whether or not it was "exploitative."

The Accused, a film that challenges accepted norms about what constitutes rape and what doesn't, hardly shows the act of rape at all! *Bandit Queen*, on the other hand, has nothing intelligent to say about the subject beyond the fact that Rape is degrading and humiliating. Dwelling on the Degradation and the Humiliation is absolutely essential for the commercial success of the film. Without it, there would be no film. The intensity of these emotions is increased to fever pitch because we're told: She's real. This happened. And faithfully, our critics go home and write about it. Praise it to the skies. Who are we to assess a living woman's rape? Who are we to decide how well done it was? How Brutal? How Chilling? How true-to-life? Who the hell are we?

Had I been raped, perhaps I would devote my every waking hour to call for stiffer legislation, harsher punishment for rapists.

Perhaps I'd take lessons from Lorena Bobbitt. What I would never ever do, and I don't imagine that anyone else (even those who loved the film so much) would either, is to agree to have it recreated as entertainment cloaked in the guise of concern, for an audience that was going to pay to watch. It would be like being raped all over again. And ironically, the more skillful the director, the greater would be my shame and humiliation.

I am disgusted that I was invited to Siri Fort to watch Phoolan Devi being raped—without her permission. Had I known that she had not seen the film, I would never have gone. I know that there are videotapes of *Bandit Queen* doing the rounds in Delhi drawing rooms. If any of you who read this essay has a tape—please do the right thing. Show it to Phoolan Devi (since the producers won't). Ask her whether she minds your watching or not. Given all this, to call Phoolan Devi's protests and demands to see the film "tantrums" and "grumbling" is so small-minded, so blinkered that it's unbelievable. And unforgiveable.

I've tried so hard to understand how it could possibly be that so many intelligent people have not seen through this charade. I can only think that to them, a "True Story" is just another kind of story. That "Truth" is merely a more exciting form of fiction.

They don't believe that Phoolan Devi is real. That she actually exists. That she has feelings. Opinions. A mind. A Past. A father that she loved (who didn't sell her for a secondhand bicycle). Her life, or what they know of it, is so implausible, so far-fetched. So unlike what Life means to them. It has very little to do with what they associate with being "human." They cannot put themselves in her shoes—and think what they'd feel if the film had done to them what it has done to her.

The more "touched" among them don't denigrate her. They exalt her with their pity. From "Woman" to "Womanhood."

Indeed, the strength of the film is that it goes much beyond Phoolan Devi, who is of course the original peg . . .

Kapur's film is not the story of one extraordinary woman: it is a manifesto about Indian womanhood.

When a woman becomes Womanhood, she ceases to be real.

I don't need to argue this any further, because my work has been done for me. Every time they open their mouths—the producer, the director, and even the actress of this incredible film—every time they open their mouths, they damn themselves.

The West has lapped up the film. It has been very tightly edited and the essence of child abuse and caste discrimination comes out very strongly. Phoolan is just a vehicle for the expression of these.

The film was a means of finding deeper meaning in the world. It was a means of discovering myself. It helped me discover new aspects of myself.

When I was selected for the role, I read every report on Phoolan and looked at her picture for hours on end to understand her. When I was done with all this, I realized that I had formed an image of her and worked out why she had reacted the way she did. After this I did not want to meet her because I did not want any contradictions to the image I had formed of her.

In their quest for Classic Cinema, they've stripped a human being of her Rights. Her Dignity. Her Privacy. Her Freedom. And perhaps, as I will argue later, of her Right to Life itself.

And so we move from Rape to Murder.

Phoolan Devi denies having murdered twenty-two Thakurs at Behmai. She has denied it in her statement to the Police. She has denied it in her "writings." She has denied it to Mala Sen.

Bandit Queen shows her present and responsible for the massacre of twenty-two Thakurs at Behmai.

What does this mean? Essentially, I did not kill these twenty-two men.

Yes, you did.

No, I didn't.

Yes, you did.

Cut, Alter, and Adapt?

Does *Bandit Queen* the film constitute an Interference with the Administration of Justice? It certainly does.

This February, after eleven years in prison, Phoolan Devi was released on bail. Two days after her release, the widows of Behmai filed an appeal against Mulayam Singh Yadav's plans to drop the charges against Phoolan Devi for the massacre of their husbands. Phoolan's trial is still pending in Indian courts. If she's found guilty, she could be hanged.

Very few know what really happened in Behmai on that cold February night. There was gunfire. There were twenty-two corpses. Those are the facts.

Was Phoolan Devi there? Did she kill those men? Two of the men who were shot but didn't die have said she wasn't there. Other eyewitnesses say that she was. There is plenty of room for doubt. Certainly there is that. All we have for sure, is a Definite Maybe.

Faced with this dilemma, with this great big hole in their story line (Rape n' Retribution), what does our "Greatest Indian Film Ever Made" do? It haggles with the "Truth" like a petty shopkeeper.

"The case against Phoolan was sub-judice and so we took her statements about the Behmai massacre where she said she had shot a few people. But in the film we have not shown her killing anybody as we did not want it to affect her case."

But what if she did in fact kill those men? Is that not a terrible injustice to the murdered men and their families?

Never mind the fact that according to the law, showing Phoolan Devi present, supervising and responsible for the massacre, whether or not she actually pulled the trigger, does not make her any less culpable. So, in effect, the result of their little arrangement with the "Truth" is that they've managed something quite remarkable. They've got it wrong both ways. They've done both sides an injustice.

Apart from this, in other, more subtle ways, the Interference in the Administration of Justice has already begun.

Phoolan Devi knows that the people who made the film have a lot at stake. She also knows that they have the Media supporting them. She knows that they are powerful, influential people. From where she comes from, they look as though they own the world. They fly around it all the time.

And who is she? What has she got to say for herself? That she's India's best known bandit?

She's not even a free woman. She's a prisoner, out on bail. She is terrified. She feels cornered. She cannot be expected to be coherent in her protest. She believes that all it would take would be a nudge here, a wink there, and she could land right back in jail. Perhaps her fears are unfounded. But as far as she's concerned, they could.

So what are her options? She's caught between a rock and a hard place. Should she accept this public reenactment of her rape, her humiliation, her by now immortal walk to the well? Should she leave uncontested the accusation that she did indeed kill twenty-two men? What could she expect in return? A little bit of Liberty? Somewhat shaky, somewhat dangerous, somewhat temporary?

When *Bandit Queen* is released in India, the people who see it will believe that it is the Truth. It will be seen by people in cities and villages. By lawyers, by judges, by journalists, by Phoolan Devi's family, by the relatives of the men who were murdered in Behmai. By people whose vision and judgment will directly affect Phoolan Devi's life.

It will influence Courts of Law. It could provoke retribution from the Thakur community, which has every right to be outraged at the apparent condoning of this massacre. And they, judging by the yardstick of this film, would be entirely justified were they to take the law into their own hands. Perhaps not here, in the suburbs of Delhi. But away from here. Where these things are real and end in death.

Bandit Queen the film seriously jeopardizes Phoolan Devi's life. It passes judgments that ought to be passed in Courts of

Law. Not in Cinema Halls. The threads that connect Truth to Half-Truths to Lies could very quickly tighten into a noose around Phoolan Devi's neck. Or put a bullet through her head. Or a knife in her back.

While We-the-Audience peep saucer-eyed out of our little lives. Not remotely aware of the fact that our superficial sympathy, our ignorance of the facts, and our intellectual sloth could grease her way to the gallows.

We makes me sick.

ACKNOWLEDGMENTS

AS MUCH AS the fiction I write comes from solitude, this book comes from companionship. From walking, talking, and breaking bread with comrades and friends who are so much a part of my life that thanking them feels as though I am thanking parts of myself.

Still, for the record, and for their friendship, insight, support, and solidarity, I say their names out loud. . .

Himanshu Thakker, Shripad Dharmadhikary, Nandini Oza, Chittaroopa Palit, Alok Aggarwal, Medha Patkar, Prashant Bhushan, Nikhil De, Jharana Jhaveri, Anurag Singh, S. Anand, Ashwin Desai, G. N. Saibaba, Rona Wislon, Savitri, Ravikumar, Sunil Sardar, Jawed Naqvi, Jitendra Yadav, Rebecca John, Chander Uday Singh, Jawahar Raja, John Berger, Pankaj Mishra, Vinod Mehta, N. Ram, Arjun Raina, Tarun Bhartiya, Eve Ensler, Shohini Ghosh, Parvaiz Bukhari, and Aijaz Hussain.

Pradip Krishen, who always added that perfect final touch.

David Godwin, who is always there. Lisette Verhagen, who I hope always will be.

Maya Palit, who compiled and organized this manuscript.

Mayank Austen Soofi, for the cover photograph.

Antoine Gallimard, Luigi Brioschi, Simon Prosser, Ravi

Singh, and Meru Gokhale, who have, over the years, published almost every essay in this book. No writer could ask for better publishers.

And finally, Sanjay Kak and Anthony Arnove, who walked the whole way, who know every sentence, every footnote, every joy and sorrow that went into this twenty-year journey.

GLOSSARY

Adivasis: tribal, literally original inhabitants of India.

L. K. Advani: leader of the BJP and former Indian home minister (and later deputy prime minster) who led the agitation for the demolition of the Babri Masjid.

Mukesh Ambani: CEO of Reliance Industries Ltd. India's richest industrialist.

B. R. Ambedkar: (1891–1956), an icon of Dalit awakening. He renounced Hinduism and, toward the end of his life embraced Buddhism. He was chairman of the drafting committee for the constitution and India's first law minister. He is the author of several revolutionary essays, including *Annihilation of Caste*, *Riddles in Hinduism*, and *The Buddha and His Dhamma*.

Azadi: Freedom. A popular slogan of the movement for self-determination in Kashmir.

Babri Masjid: On December 6, 1992, violent mobs of Hindu fundamentalists converged on the town of Ayodhya and demolished the Babri Masjid, an old Muslim mosque. Initiated by the BJP leader L. K. Advani, this was the culmination of a nationwide campaign to "arouse the pride" of Hindus. Plans for replacing the mosque with a huge Hindu temple are under way. See Ram Mandir, below.

Bajrang Dal: militant Hindu fundamentalist organization named after the Hindu god Hanuman; allied with the BJP and the Vishwa Hindu Parishad (VHP), and, with them, instrumental in the destruction of the Babri Masjid in Ayodhya in 1992.

Bastar: district in the state of Chhattisgarh, parts of which are a Maoist stronghold.

Bharatiya Janata Party (BJP): literally, the Indian People's Party. It espouses a Hindu nationalist ideology, and its support is concentrated mostly in northern India. Since the elections of 2014, it has been the single largest party of the governing coalition.

Bharat Mata ki Jai: Victory to Mother India.

Chhattisgarh: heavily forested state in central India, rich in minerals and a growth area for industry. It has a large Adivasi population.

P. Chidambaram: former Indian finance minister and home minister, as well as member of parliament.

Congress Party: Indian National Congress. The main parliamentary expression of the Indian national independence struggle and the dominant national political party after independence in 1947.

crore: ten million (one hundred lakhs).

Dalit: those who are oppressed or literally "ground down"; the preferred term for those people who used to be called "Untouchables" in India. Gandhi coined the term *harijan* (children of God) as a euphemism for these castes, but *Dalit* has a more explicit political meaning and is preferred today.

Dandakaranya: Dandak Forest, in the Bastar district of Chhattisgarh, considered sacred in Hindu mythology.

dargah: Muslim tomb.

dharna: peaceful protest or sit-in.

lakh: one hundred thousand.

Mohandas Gandhi: (1869–1948), a world icon and household name. He was a member of the Congress Party and one of the main leaders of the Indian national independence movement. His practice of satyagraha (see below) and nonviolent civil disobedience has elevated him in the eyes of millions to the status of a saint or a mahatma—a great soul.

Godhra train burning: On February 27, 2002, fifty-nine people died after a fire broke out on the Sabarmati Express train near the Godhra railway station in the Indian state of Gujarat. A number of Muslims belonging to the town of Godhra were arrested for the crime. The incident was followed by the Gujarat pogrom. The actual cause of the fire has never been indisputably established.

Gujarat pogrom: After the Godhra train burning, violent riots took more than two thousand Muslim lives. Narendra Modi was chief minister of Gujarat at the time.

Afzal Guru: (1969–2013) was sentenced to death and hanged over his alleged role in the Indian parliament attack of 2002.

Anna Hazare: Kisan Baburao Hazare, a social activist, known for his hunger strikes against corruption in India.

Hindutva: ideology seeking to strengthen "Hindu identity" and create a Hindu state, advocated by the BJP, Shiv Sena, and other communalist parties.

hydel: hydroelectric power.

ISI: Inter-Services Intelligence, the Pakistani intelligence agency.

khadi: hand-spun cotton cloth popularized by Gandhi during the independence struggle as a defiant statement of self-reliance and a badge of membership in the Congress movement. Khadi is still worn today by many politicians and Gandhian workers.

khichdi: a rice and lentil dish.

LTTE: Liberation Tigers of Tamil Eelam, a Sri Lankan Tamil separatist guerrilla group.

Mahatma Gandhi National Rural Employment Guarantee Act: a 2005 act of parliament that aimed to enhance the livelihood of people in rural areas by providing at least one hundred days of paid employment to every rural household.

Mandal Commission: commission constituted by the Janata Party government under the chairmanship of B. P. Mandal in 1977 to look into the issue of reservations for "backward" castes in government jobs and educational institutions. The report was submitted in 1980, and its recommendations led to a huge backlash from upper castes, with violent protests across the country.

mandir: temple.

Manusmriti: an ancient code of conduct, attributed to Manu, sometimes viewed as a book of Hindu laws.

Maoists: A label applied to a number of political movements and organizations in India that trace their politics in part to the politics of Chairman Mao (1893–1976) in China, particularly insofar as his view of communism diverged from the Soviet model in the mid-1950s and early 1960s to emphasize peasant rebellion and struggles of popular classes in the so-called third world.

masjid: mosque.

Mayawati: Dalit leader of the Bahujan Samaj Party. She has served as chief minister of Uttar Pradesh, the largest state in India, for four terms.

Narendra Modi: Chief Minister of Gujarat; presided over the state government when violent riots took more than two thousand Muslim lives in 2002. He became prime minister in 2014.

Narmada: a river that flows through Gujarat, Madhya Pradesh, and Maharashtra, and a site of major contestations over dam construction.

Narmada Bachao Andolan: Save the Narmada Movement.

Naxalites: label applied to a number of left-wing groups in India that are linked to the Communist Party of India (Marxist-Leninist), named after a rebellion that took place in 1967 in the village Naxalbari in West Bengal.

Jawaharlal Nehru: (1889–1964), one of the most important leaders of the Indian national independence movement. He became the first prime minister after independence.

Shankar Guha Niyogi: trade union leader of the Chhattisgarh Mukti Morcha, killed in September 1991 by hired assassins.

Parliament attack: On December 13, 2001, gunmen attacked the Parliament House in Delhi. The attackers, one civilian, and six military personnel were killed in the attack.

Parsis: A small community of Persian descent who practice the Zoroastrian faith.

Sardar Vallabhbhai Patel: (1875–1950), prominent leader of the Indian National Congress party who served as India's first deputy prime minister after independence.

Prasad: sacred food, shared by devotees in an act of seeking benediction.

PWG: Peoples' War Group, an extreme left-wing armed group, present in many states in India.

Ram Mandir: a temple to the Hindu god Ram. See Babri Masjid, above.

Rashtriya Swayamsevak Sangh (RSS): literally, the National Self-Help Group; a right-wing militaristic organization founded in 1925, with a clearly articulated anti-Muslim stand and a nationalistic notion of Hindutva. The RSS is the ideological backbone of the BJP.

Rath Yatra: literally, the Chariots' Journey, a long road rally led by a campaign bus dressed up as a chariot, undertaken first in 1990 by L. K. Advani to "mobilize Hindu sentiment" for the building of the Ram Mandir at Ayodhya. It culminated in widespread violence in many parts of northern India. Two years after the Rath Yatra, a Hindu vigilante mob demolished the Babri Masjid.

Reliance Industries Ltd.: India's richest corporation—led by Mukesh Ambani— dominant in energy, petrochemicals, textiles, and telecommunications, among other industries.

Sangh Parivar: literally, family group, an undefined group of closely linked right-wing Hindu fundamentalist organizations in India that includes the Bajrang Dal, BJP, RSS, and VHP.

Saraswati shishu mandirs: literally, temples for children, schools run by the RSS and named after Saraswati, the Hindu goddess of learning.

Satyagraha: literally "life force," Gandhi's term for civil disobedience. The term is now commonly applied to any movement that confronts its foe—typically, the state—nonviolently.

Savarna Hinduism: that part of caste Hindu society that excludes Dalits and so-called backward castes.

Amit Shah: the current president of the BJP.

shakha: an RSS branch (literally) or center. RSS shakhas are training camps or cells.

Shiv Sena: a right-wing regional Hindu chauvinist party in the state of Maharashtra.

shloka: stanzas, or verse in general, that are prayers to the deities.

Manmohan Singh: Indian prime minister from 2004 to 2014 and finance minister from 1991 to 1996 as a member of the Congress Party.

stupa: a Buddhist religious monument.

swadeshi: nationalist.

Tata Group: One of India's largest conglomerates, dominant in chemicals, energy, consumer goods, steel, and engineering, among other industries.

Atal Bihari Vajpayee: (1924–2018), served three times as prime minister of India as a member of the BJP.

Vedanta: a Hindu philosophical tradition rooted in the ancient Sanskrit texts known as the Upanishads. Also the name of a major mining company.

VHP: Vishwa Hindu Parishad, literally the World Hindu Council, self-appointed leaders of the Hindu community and part of the "Sangh" family of Hindu nationalist organizations to which the BJP also belongs. The VHP was in the forefront of the move to destroy the Babri Masjid and build a temple to Lord Ram at Ayodhya.

Yatra: literally, pilgrimage; can be translated as any journey "with purpose."

NOTES

FOREWORD

1. https://www.livemint.com/Companies/z9KNZfDJBIFtkYn207pRVN/Sardar-Patels-Statue-of-Unity-inauguration-today-Worlds-t.html.

THE GREATER COMMON GOOD

1. Jawaharlal Nehru, *Modern Temples of India: Selected Speeches of Jawaharlal Nehru at Irrigation and Power Projects*, ed. C. V. J. Sharma (Delhi: Central Board of Irrigation and Power, 1989), 40–49.
2. Patrick McCully, *Silenced Rivers: The Ecology and Politics of Large Dams* (Hyderabad: Orient Longman, 1998), 80.
3. From (uncut) film footage of Bargi Dam oustees, Anurag Singh and Jharana Jhaveri, Jan Madhyam, New Delhi, 1995.
4. J. Nehru, *Modern Temples*, 52–56. In a speech given before the Twenty-Ninth Annual Meeting of the Central Board of Irrigation and Power (November 17, 1958) Nehru said, "For some time past, however, I have been beginning to think that we are suffering from what we may call 'the disease of gigantism.' We want to show that we can build big dams and do big things. This is a dangerous outlook developing in India . . . the idea of big—having big undertakings and doing big things for the sake of showing that we can do big things—is not a good outlook at all." And "it is . . . the small irrigation projects, the small

industries and the small plants for electric power, which will change the face of the country far more than half a dozen big projects in half a dozen places."

5. Centre for Science and Environment (CSE), *Dying Wisdom: Rise, Fall, and Potential of India's Traditional Water Harvesting Systems* (New Delhi: CSE, 1997), 399; Madhav Gadgil and Ramachandra Guha, *Ecology and Equity* (New Delhi: Penguin India, 1995), 39.

6. Indian Water Resources Society, *Five Decades of Water, Resources Development in India* (1998), 7.

7. World Resource Institute, *World Resources 1998–99* (Oxford: Oxford University Press, 1998), 251.

8. McCully, *Silenced Rivers*, 26–29. See also *The Ecologist Asia* 6, no. 5 (September–October 1998): 50–51, for excerpts of speech by Bruce Babbitt, US interior secretary, in August 1998.

9. Besides McCully, *Silenced Rivers*, see the CSE's *State of India's Environment*, 1999, 1985, and 1982; Nicholas Hildyard and Edward Goldsmith, *The Social and Environmental Impacts of Large Dams* (Cornwall, UK: Wadebridge Ecological Centre, 1984); Satyajit Singh, *Taming the Waters: The Political Economy of Large Dams* (New Delhi: Oxford University Press, 1997); World Bank, *India: Irrigation Sector Review* (1991); and Anthony H. J. Dorcey, ed., *Large Dams: Learning from the Past, Looking to the Future* (1997).

10. Mihir Shah, Debashis Banerji, P. S. Vijayshankar, and Pramathesh Ambasta, *India's Drylands: Tribal Societies and Development through Environmental Regeneration* (New Delhi: Oxford University Press, 1998), 51–103.

11. Ann Danaiya Usher, *Dams as Aid: A Political Anatomy of Nordic Development Thinking* (London: Routledge, 1997).

12. $1 US = Rs 43.35. A crore is 10 million. Equal to Rs 2,200,000 crore, at constant 1996–97 prices.

13. D. K. Mishra and R. Rangachari, *The Embankment Trap and Some Disturbing Questions*, Seminar 478 (June 1999), 46–48 and 62–63, respectively; CSE, *Floods, Floodplains and Environmental Myths*.

14. Shah et al., *India's Drylands*, 51–103.

15. Singh, *Taming the Waters*, 188–90; also, government of India (GOI) figures for actual displacement.

16. At a January 21, 1999, meeting in New Delhi organized by the Union Ministry of Rural Areas and Employment, for discussions on the draft National Resettlement and Rehabilitation Policy and the amendment to the draft Land Acquisition Act.

17. Bradford Morse and Thomas Berger, *Sardar Sarovar: The Report of the Independent Review* (Ottawa: Resource Futures International [RFI], 1992), 62.

18. GOI, *28th and 29th Report of the Commissioner for Scheduled Castes and Scheduled Tribes* (New Delhi, 1988–89).

19. *Indian Express* (New Delhi), April 10, 1999, front page.

20. GOI, *Ninth Five Year Plan, 1997–2002* (1999), 2:437.

21. Siddharth Dube, *Words like Freedom* (New Delhi: Harper Collins, 1998); Centre for Monitoring the Indian Economy, 1996. See also *World Bank Poverty Update*, quoted in *Business Line*, June 4, 1999.

22. National Human Rights Commission, *Report of the Visit of the Official Team of the NHRC to the Scarcity Affected Areas of Orissa*, December 1996.

23. GOI, *Award of the Narmada Water Disputes Tribunal*, 1978–79.

24. GOI, *Report of the FMG-2 on SSP* (1995); also see various affidavits of the government of India and government of Madhya Pradesh before the Supreme Court of India, 1994–98.

25. Central Water Commission, *Monthly Observed Flows of the Narmada at Garudeshwar* (New Delhi: Hydrology Studies Organisation, Central Water Commission, 1992).

26. Written Submission on Behalf of Union of India, February 1999, p. 7, clause 1.7.

27. *Tigerlink News* 5, no. 2 (June 1999): 28.

28. *World Bank Annual Reports*, 1993–98.

29. McCully, *Silenced Rivers*, 274.

30. Ibid., 21. The World Bank started funding dams in China in 1984. Since then it has lent around $3.4 billion (not adjusted for inflation) to finance thirteen Big Dams that will cause the displacement of 360,000 people. The centerpiece of the World Bank's dam financing in China is the Xiaolangdi dam on the Yellow River, which will singlehandedly displace 181,000 people.

31. Ibid., 278.

32. J. Vidal and N. Cumming-Bruce, "The Curse of Pergau," *Economist*, March 5, 1994; "Dam Price Jumped 81 Million Pounds Days after Deal," *Guardian*, January 19, 1994; "Whitehall Must Not Escape Scot Free," *Guardian*, February 12, 1994; quoted in McCully, *Silenced Rivers*, 291.

33. McCully, *Silenced Rivers*, 62.

34. For example, see Sardar Sarovar Narmada Nigam (SSNNL), *Planning for Prosperity* (1989); Babubhai J. Patel, *Progressing amidst Challenges* (1992); C. C. Patel, *SSP, What It Is and What It Is Not* (1991); and P. A. Raj, *Facts: Sardar Sarovar Project* (Gujarat: Sardar Sarovar Narmada Nigam, 1989, 1990, 1991 editions).

35. Ibid.; also Rahul Ram, *Muddy Waters: A Critical Assessment of the Benefits of the Sardar Sarovar Project* (New Delhi: Kalpavriksh, 1993).

36. Morse and Berger, *Sardar Sarovar*, 319. According to official statistics (Narmada Control Authority, *Benefits to Saurashtra and Kutch Areas in Gujarat* [Indore: NCA, 1992]), 948 villages in Kutch and 4,877 villages in Saurashtra are to get drinking water from the Sardar Sarovar Projects. However, according to the 1981 census there are only 887 inhabited villages in Kutch and 4,727 villages in the whole of Saurashtra. The planners had simply hoovered up the names of villages from a map, thereby including the names of 211 deserted villages! Cited

in Ram, *Muddy Waters.*

37. For example, the minutes of the various meetings of the Rehabilitation and Resettlement subgroups of the Narmada Control Authority, 1998–99. Also, Morse and Berger, *Sardar Sarovar*, 51.

38. Ram, *Muddy Waters*, 34.

39. See for example, the petition filed by the NBA in the Supreme Court, 1994.

40. SSNNL, *Planning for Prosperity*; government of Gujarat.

41. S. Dharmadhikary, "Hydropower at Sardar Sarovar: Is It Necessary, Justified, and Affordable?" in *Towards Sustainable Development? Struggling over India's Narmada River*, ed. William F. Fisher (Armonk, NY: M. F. Sharpe, 1995), 141.

42. McCully, *Silenced Rivers*, 87.

43. Ibid., 185.

44. World Bank, *Resettlement and Development: The Bankwide Review of Projects Involving Resettlement 1986–1993* (Washington, DC, 1994).

45. World Bank, *Resettlement and Rehabilitation of India: A Status Update of Projects Involving Involuntary Resettlement* (Washington, DC, 1994).

46. Ibid.

47. Letter to the president in Morse and Berger, *Sardar Sarovar*, xii, xxiv, xxv.

48. Morse and Berger, *Sardar Sarovar*, xxv.

49. Minimum conditions included unfinished appraisal of social and environmental impacts. For details, see Lori Udall, "The International Narmada Campaign," in *Toward Sustainable Development? Struggling over India's Narmada River*, ed. William F. Fisher (Armonk, NY: M. F. Sharpe, 1995); Patrick McCully, "Cracks in the Dam: The World Bank in India," *Multinational Monitor*, December 1992, http://www.multinationalmonitor.org /hyper/issues/1992/12/mm1292_08.html.

50. See the letter from the GOI to the World Bank, March 29, 1993; press release of the World Bank dated March 30, 1993, a copy of which can be found in the campaign information package of International Rivers Network, *Narmada Valley Development Project* 1 (August 1998).

51. The date was November 14, 1992. Venue: outside the Taj Mahal Hotel, Bombay, where Lewis Preston, president of the World Bank, was staying. See Lawyers Committee for Human Rights, *Unacceptable Means: India's Sardar Sarovar Project and Violations of Human Rights: Oct. 1992–Feb. 1993*, 10–12.

52. On the night of March 20, 1994, the NBA Office at Baroda was attacked by hoodlums simply because of a (baseless) rumor that one member of the Five Member Group Committee was sitting inside with members of the NBA. Some NBA activists were manhandled, and a large collection of NBA documents was burned and destroyed.

53. Ministry of Water Resources, GOI, *Report of the Five Member Group on Sardar Sarovar Project*, 1994.

54. Writ Petition 319 of 1994 argued that the Sardar Sarovar Projects violated the

fundamental rights of those affected by the project and that the project was not viable on social, environmental, technical (including seismic and hydrological), financial, or economic grounds. The Writ Petition asked for a comprehensive review of the project, pending which construction on the project should cease.

55. *Frontline*, January 27, 1995, and January 21, 1995.

56. In January 1995 the Supreme Court took on record the statement of the Counsel for the Union of India that no further work on the Sardar Sarovar Dam would be done without informing the court in advance. On May 4, 1995, the court allowed construction of "humps" on the dam, on the plea of the Union of India that they were required for reasons of safety. The court, however, reiterated its order of January 1995 that no further construction will be done without the express permission of the court.

57. *Report of the Narmada Water Disputes Tribunal with Its Decision* (1979), 2:102; cited in Morse and Berger, *Sardar Sarovar*, 250.

58. Morse and Berger, *Sardar Sarovar*, 323–29.

59. Raj, *Facts: Sardar Sarovar Project*.

60. Medha Patkar, "The Struggle for Participation and Justice: A Historical Narrative," in *Toward Sustainable Development? Struggling over India's Narmada River*, ed. William F. Fisher (Armonk, NY: M. F. Sharpe, 1995), 159–78; S. Parasuraman, "The Anti-Dam Movement and Rehabilitation Policy," in *The Dam and the Nation*, ed. Jean Drèze, Meera Samson, and Satyajit Singh (Oxford: Oxford University Press, 1997), 26–65; and minutes of various meetings of the R & R subgroup of the Narmada Control Authority.

61. On my visit to the valley in March 1999, I was told this by villagers at Mokhdi who had returned from their resettlement colonies.

62. *Kaise Jeebo Re*, documentary film directed by Anurag Singh and Jharana Jhaveri, Jan Madhyam, 1997; also, unedited footage in the NBA archives.

63. Letter to *Independent Review* from a resident of Parveta resettlement colony, cited in https://www.facebook.com/attn/videos/1006281599407299/159-160.

64. Narmada Manavadhikar Yatra, which traveled from the Narmada Valley to Delhi via Bombay. It reached Delhi on April 7, 1999.

65. Told to me by Mohan Bhai Tadvi, in Kevadia Colony, March 1999.

66. Morse and Berger, *Sardar Sarovar*, 89–94; NBA interviews, March 1999.

67. NBA interviews, March 1999.

68. Morse and Berger, *Sardar Sarovar*, 277–94.

69. McCully, *Silenced Rivers*, 46–49.

70. For a discussion on the subject, see the World Bank, *India Irrigation Sector Review* (1991); A. Vaidyanathan, *Food, Agriculture and Water* (Madras: MIDS, 1994); and McCully, *Silenced Rivers*, 182–207.

71. World Bank, *India Irrigation Sector Review*, 2:7.

72. Cited in McCully, *Silenced Rivers*, 187.

73. Shaheen Rafi Khan, "The Kalabagh Controversy" (Pakistan, 1998), http://www.sanalist.org/kalabagh/a-14.htm; E. Goldsmith, "Learning to Live with Nature: The Lessons of Traditional Irrigation," *Ecologist* 6, no. 5 (September–October 1998).

74. Shah et al., *India's Drylands*, 51; also in Goldsmith, "Learning to Live with Nature."

75. Operations Research Group (ORG), *Critical Zones in Narmada Command: Problems and Prospects* (Baroda, 1981); ORG, *Regionalisation of Narmada Command* (Gandhinagar, 1982); World Bank, *Staff Appraisal Report, India, Narmada River Development—Gujarat, Water Delivery and Drainage Project*, Report 5108-IN (1985); Core Consultants, *Main Report: Narmada Mahi Doab Drainage Study*, commissioned by Narmada Planning Group, government of Gujarat (1985).

76. Robert Wade, "Greening the Bank: The Struggle over the Environment, 1970–1995," in *The World Bank: Its First Half Century*, ed. Devesh Kapur, John P. Lewis, and Richard Webb (Washington, DC: Brookings Institution Press, 1997), 661–62.

77. Khan, "Kalabagh Controversy."

78. CES, *Pre-Feasibility Level Drainage Study for SSP Command beyond River Mahi* (New Delhi: CES Water Resources Development and Management Consultancy for government of Gujarat, 1992).

79. Rahul Ram, "The Best-Laid Plans . . . ," *Frontline*, July 14, 1995, 78.

80. Core Consultants, *Main Report*, 66.

81. Ibid.

82. For example, see GOI, *Report of the FMG-2*; or Ram, "Best-Laid Plans."

83. Called the Economic Regeneration Programme, formulated to generate funds for the cash-strapped Sardar Sarovar Narmada Nigam. Under the program, land along the main canal of the Narmada Project will be acquired and sold for tourist facilities, hotels, water parks, fun world sites, garden restaurants, etc. Cf. *Times of India* (Ahmedabad), May 17, 1998.

84. World Bank, *India Irrigation Sector Review*.

85. Written Submissions on Behalf of the Petitioners (NBA) in the Supreme Court, January 1999, 63; *Times of India* (Ahmedabad), May 23, 1999.

86. Ismail Serageldin, *Water Supply, Sanitation and Environmental Sustainability* (Washington, DC: World Bank, 1994), 4.

87. Morse and Berger, *Sardar Sarovar*, xxiii.

88. Ibid., 317–19.

89. McCully, *Silenced Rivers*, 167.

POWER POLITICS: THE REINCARNATION
OF RUMPELSTILTSKIN

1. Stephen Fidler and Khozem Merchant, "US, India Announce Deals of Dollars 4bn," *Financial Times*, March 25, 2000, 10.

2. Peter Popham, "Clinton's Visit Seals Future for Controversial Indian Dam," *Independent*, March 28, 2000, 16; "S. Kumars Ties Up with Ogden for MP Project," *Economic Times of India*, December 14, 1999.

3. See 39–40, above; World Commission on Dams, *Dams and Development: A New Framework for Decision-Making—The Report of the World Commission on Dams* (London: Earthscan, 2000), 117 (hereafter WCD Report); Steven A. Brandt and Fekri Hassan, "Dams and Cultural Heritage Management: Final Report—August 2000," WCD Working Paper, http://www.dams.org/docs/html/contrib/soc212.htm; and WCD, "Flooded Fortunes: Dams and Cultural Heritage Management," press release, September 26, 2000. See also "Do or Die: The People versus Development in the Narmada Valley," *New Internationalist* 336 (July 2001), http://newint.org/issues/2001/07/01/; documentation at the Friends of the River Narmada site, http://www.narmada.org/nvdp.dams/.

4. Second World Water Forum: From Vision to Action, The Hague, March 17–22, 2000.

5. One billion people in the world have no access to safe drinking water: United Nations Development Program, *Human Development Report 2000: Human Rights and Human Development* (New York: Oxford University Press, 2000), 4 (hereafter UNDP 2000).

6. See chapter 8, note 5, above.

7. "Bolivian Water Plan Dropped after Protests Turn into Melees," *New York Times*, April 11, 2000.

8. "Develop Infrastructure to Cope with Digital Revolution: John Welch," *Hindu*, September 17, 2000; "Welch Makes a Power Point," *Economic Times of India*, September 17, 2000.

9. World Resource Institute, *World Resources 1998–1999* (Oxford: Oxford University Press, 1998), 251; UNDP 2000, table 4, Human Poverty in Developing Countries, 170.

10. Peter Marsh, "Big Four Lead the Field in Power Stakes: The Main Players," *Financial Times*, June 4, 2001, 2.

11. US Department of Energy, Energy Information Administration, *International Energy Outlook 1998*, Electricity Report (DOE/EIA-0484[98]), http://www.eia.doe.gov/oiaf/archive/ieo98/elec.html.

12. "India: Bharat Heavy Electricals–GE's Refurbishment Centre," *Hindu*, March 17, 2001; "BHEL Net Rises 10% to Rs 599 Crore," *Economic Times of India*, September 30, 2000.

13. Abhay Mehta, *Power Play: A Study of the Enron Project* (Hyderabad, India:

Orient Longman, 2000), 15; Irfan Aziz, "The Supreme Court Upheld the Ruling That the Jain Diary Constituted Insufficient Evidence," Rediff.com, July 22, 2000, http://www.rediff.com/news/2000/jul/22spec.htm; and Ritu Sarin, "Ex-CBI Official Accuses Vijaya Rama Rao," *Financial Express*, May 11, 1997.

14. See figures in "Clinton's India Sojourn: Industry Hopes Doubling of FDI, Better Access to US Markets," DHAN.com News Track, March 27, 2000; and George Pickart (senior adviser, Bureau for South Asian Affairs), "Address to the Network of South Asian Professionals," Washington, DC, August 9, 1997 http://www.indiainc.org.in/h0809971.htm.

15. P. R. Kumaramangalam, speech at the Conference of the Power Minister of India, March 2, 2000. See also "India: Power Problems," *Business Line*, June 21, 2000.

16. Ritu Sarin, "Disappearing Power," *Indian Express*, March 28, 2000. Hereafter Sarin, "Disappearing Power."

17. Neeraj Mishra, "Megawatt Thieves," *Outlook*, July 31, 2000, 54; Sarin, "Disappearing Power"; "India: Power Problems," *Business Line*, June 21, 2000; Louise Lucas, "Survey—India: Delays and Bureaucracy Force Investors to Flee: Power," *Financial Times*, November 6, 2000; and "India's Power Generation to Increase over Next 3 Years: Minister," *Asia Pulse*, April 27, 2001.

18. Sarin, "Disappearing Power"; "Red Tape and Blue Sparks," *Economist* 359, no. 8224 (June 2–8, 2001); "A Survey of India's Economy," *Economist* 359, no. 8224 (June 2–8, 2001), 9–10; and Sunil Saraf, "At Last, the Selloff Gets Underway," Survey—Power in Asia 1996, *Financial Times*, September 16, 1996, 5.

19. Mehta, *Power Play*; Human Rights Watch, *The Enron Corporation: Corporate Complicity in Human Rights Violations* (New York: Human Rights Watch, 1999), https://www.hrw.org/report/1999/01/01/enron-corporation/corporate -complicity-human-rights-violations; Tony Allison, "Enron's Eight-Year Power Struggle in India," Asia Times Online, January 18, 2001, http:// www.atimes.com/reports/CA13Ai01.html; Scott Baldauf, "Plug Pulled on Investment in India," *Christian Science Monitor*, July 9, 2001, 9; S. N. Vasuki, "The Search for a Middle Ground," *Business Times* (Singapore), August 6, 1993; Agence France-Presse, "Work to Start in December on India's Largest Power Plant," September 14, 1993; and Agence France-Presse, "Work on Enron Power Project to Resume on May 1," February 23, 1996.

20. Scott Neuman, "More Power Reviews Likely in India," United Press International, August 5, 1995.

21. Agence France-Presse, "India, Enron Deny Payoff Charges over Axed Project," August 7, 1995, which acknowledges "a remark by an Enron official that the company spent 20 million dollars on 'educating Indians' about the controversial deal."

22. "Former US Amabassador to India Joins Enron Oil Board," *Asia Pulse*, October 30, 1997; Girish Kuber, "US Delegation to Meet Ministers on Enron

Row," *Economic Times of India*, January 23, 2001; and Vijay Prashad, "The Power Elite: Enron and Frank Wisner," *People's Democracy*, November 16, 1997.

23. Mark Nicholson, "Elections Cloud Investment in India: Opening the Economy Has Wide Support Despite Recent Events," *Financial Times*, August 21, 1995; Agence France-Presse, "Hindu Leader Ready for Talks on Scrapped Enron Project," August 31, 1995; BBC Summary of World Broadcasts, "Maharashtra Government Might Consider New Enron Proposal," September 2, 1995; Suzanne Goldenberg, "India Calls on Left Bloc as BJP Cedes Power," *Guardian*, May 29, 1996; Mark Nicholson, "Delhi Clears Way for Dollars 2.5bn Dabhol Power Plant," *Financial Times*, July 10, 1996, 4; and Associated Press, "Enron Can Resume Big Indian Power Project," *New York Times*, July 10, 1996, D19.

24. Mehta, *Power Play*, xv, 20–21, 151–58; Agence France-Presse, "Massive US-Backed Power Project Awaits Indian Court Ruling," August 25, 1996; Kenneth J. Cooper, "Foreign Power Plant Blooms; Low-Key India Venture Avoids Enron's Woes," *International Herald Tribune*, September 11, 1996; Praful Bidwai, "Enron Judgment: Blow to Energy Independence," *Times of India*, May 22, 1997; and Praful Bidwai, "The Enron Deal Must Go: Albatross round Public's Neck," *Times of India*, May 4, 1995.

25. Agence France-Presse, "Enron Power Project Survives Court Challenge," May 3, 1997.

26. "The Dabhol Backlash," *Business Line*, December 5, 2000; Sucheta Dalai, "No Power May End Up Being Better Than That High Cost Power," *Indian Express*, December 3, 2000; Soma Banerjee, "State Plans to Move Court on Tariff Revision Proposal," *Economic Times of India*, May 26, 2000; Madhu Nainan, "Indian State Says It Has No Money to Pay Enron for Power," Agence France-Presse, January 8, 2001; Khozem Merchant, "Enron Invokes Guarantee to Retrieve Fees from Local Unit," *Financial Times*, January 31, 2001, 7; S. N. Roy, "The Shocking Truth about Power Reforms," *Indian Express*, February 28, 2000; and Anthony Spaeth, "Bright Lights, Big Bill," *Time* (Asian edition) 157 (February 26, 2001): 8, http://www.time.com/time/asia/biz/magazine/0,9754,99899,00.html.

27. "India: Maharashtra State Electricity Board Stops Buying Power," *Hindu*, May 30, 2001; Celia W. Dugger, "High-Stakes Showdown: Enron's Fight over Power Plant Reverberates beyond India," *New York Times*, March 20, 2001, C1 (hereafter Dugger, "High-Stakes Showdown").

28. Mehta, *Power Play*, 3; Dugger, "High-Stakes Showdown"; "Red Tape and Blue Sparks"; "A Survey of India's Economy," 9–10; GOI, *Ninth Five Year Plan, 1997–2002*; and GOI, Press Information Bureau, fact sheet.

29. S. Balakrishnan, "FIS in U.S. Press Panic Button as MSEB Fails to Pay Enron," *Times of India*, January 7, 2001; Madhu Nainan, "Indian State Says It Has No Money to Pay Enron for Power," Agence France-Presse, January 8, 2001; and Khozem Merchant, "Enron Invokes Guarantee to Retrieve Fees from

Local Unit," *Financial Times*, January 31, 2001, 7.

30. Pratap Chatterjee, "Meet Enron, Bush's Biggest Contributor," *Progressive* 64 (September 2000): 9. See also Dugger, "High-Stakes Showdown."

31. Dugger, "High-Stakes Showdown"; Praful Bidwai, "Congentrix = (Equals) Bullying Tricks," *Kashmir Times*, December 27, 1999.

32. Center for Science and Environment, *State of India's Environment: The Citizens' Fifth Report*, pt. 2, *Statistical Database* (New Delhi: Center for Science and Environment, 1999), 203; Union Power Minister Suresh Prabhu, press conference, Hyderabad, cited in *Business Line*, July 21, 2001; and Abusaleh Shariff, *India: Human Development Report—A Profile of Indian States in the 1990s* (New Delhi: National Council of Applied Economic Research/Oxford University Press, 1999), 238.

33. UNDP 2000, table 18, Aid and Debt by Recipient Country, p. 221. See also ENS Economic Bureau, "India Inching towards Debt Trap," *Indian Express*, February 23, 1999. See also Economist Intelligence Unit, "India: External Debt."

34. WCD Report, p. 11 and table 1.2.

35. See 29–30, above; WCD Report, table 1.1, Dams Currently under Construction, p. 10, and table V.1, Top 20 Countries by Number of Large Dams, p. 370; and the website of the International Commission on Large Dams, http://www.icold-cigb.org/home.asp.

36. *Modern Temples of India: Selected Speeches of Jawaharlal Nehru at Irrigation and Power Projects*, ed. C. V. J. Sharma (Delhi: Central Board of Irrigation and Power, 1989), 40–49. See 25, 28, above.

37. PTI News Agency (New Delhi), "India: Construction Begins on 'Controversial' Narmada Dam," BBC Worldwide Monitoring, October 31, 2000; Vinay Kumar, "People Cheer as Work on Narmada Dam Resumes," *Hindu*, November 1, 2000; "Violence Mars Gujarat Govt's Narmada Bash," *Times of India*, November 1, 2000; and "Ministers Attacked, Cars Burnt at Narmada Dam Site," *Hindustan Times*, November 1, 2000.

38. WCD Fact Sheet, "Dams and Water: Global Statistics: India: 4,291 Large Dams and 9% of the World Dam Population." See also Himanshu Thakker, "Performance of Large Dams in India: The Case of Irrigation and Flood Control," paper presented at the World Commission on Dams Regional Consultation, Sri Lanka, December 1998.

39. R. Rangachari et al., "Large Dams—India's Experience: A WCD Case Study Prepared as an Input to the World Commission on Dams," World Commission on Dams Country Review Paper, November 2000 (hereafter Rangachari et al., "Large Dams—India's Experience").

40. Ibid., 25.

41. Ashok Gulati, "Overflowing Granaries, Empty Stomachs," *Economic Times of India*, April 27, 2000; UNDP 2000, table 4, Human Poverty in Developing Countries, p. 170.

42. Gail Omvedt, "Editorial: Rotting Food," *Hindu*, October 23, 1999. See also Shri Sriram Chuahan, Minister of States for Food and Public Distribution, Ministry of Consumer Affairs, Food, and Public Distribution, GOI, "Loss of Foodgrains," press release, August 8, 2000.

43. See 32, above; "Indian Govt to Protest World Commission on Dams Report," *Asia Pulse*, February 5, 2001; Kalpana Sharma, "Misconceptions about Dams Commission," *Hindu*, September 11, 1998; "Keshubhai Warns Dam Inspection Team May Be Held," *Indian Express*, September 9, 1998; "Gujarat Bans Visit of 'Anti-dam' Body," *Hindu*, September 5, 1998; Kalpana Sharma, "Damning All Dissent," *Hindu*, September 21, 1998; WCD website, http://www.internationalrivers.org/; "Medium and Large Dams Damned," *Business Standard*, September 23, 2000; "SC Wants Time Limit on Closure of Polluting Units," *Times of India*, January 25, 2001; and Rangachari et al., "Large Dams—India's Experience," 116.

44. Ibid.

45. US Department of Energy, Energy Information Administration, *International Energy Outlook 1998*; see 30, 65–67, above; and Rangachari et al., "Large Dams—India's Experience," 132.

46. "The Human Cost of the Bargi Dam," http://www.narmada.org/nvdp.dams/bargi/bargi.html; "Dam Ousters to Go on Hunger-Strike," *Statesman*, August 13, 1997.

47. WCD Report, 106–07; Sanjay Sangvai, *The River and Life: People's Struggle in the Narmada Valley* (Mumbai: Earthcare Books, 2000), 28; and "Human Cost of the Bargi Dam."

48. See 44, above.

49. WCD Report, 104–05; see 44, above; Robert Marquand, "Indian Dam Protests Evoke Gandhi," *Christian Science Monitor*, August 5, 1999, 1; "The Sardar Sarovar Dam: A Brief Introduction," http://www.narmada.org/sardarsarovar.html; Narmada Bachao Andolan (NBA), "Displacement, Submergence, and Rehabilitation in Sardar Sarovar Project: Ground Reality Indicating Utter Injustice," http://www.narmada.org/sardar-sarovar/sc.ruling/Displacement.rehab.html; and Free the Narmada Campaign, India, "Who Pays? Who Profits? A Short Guide to the Sardar Sarovar Project," http://www.narmada.org/sardar-sarovar/faq/whopays.html.

50. International Rivers Network, "Confidential World Bank Evaluation Admits Future of Narmada Dam Uncertain," press release, May 16, 1995; Office of Director-General, Operations Evaluation, World Bank, Memorandum to the Executive Directors and the President, March 29, 1995; MNC Masala, "The World Bank and Sardar Sarovar Project: A Story of Unacceptable Means towards Unacceptable Ends," CorpWatch, n.d.; WCD Report, 26; and Morse and Berger, *Sardar Sarovar*.

51. Celia W. Dugger, "Opponents of India Dam Project Bemoan Green Light

from Court," *New York Times*, October 20, 2000, A9.

52. Free the Narmada Campaign, "Who Pays? Who Profits?"

53. "The Maheshwar Dam: A Brief Introduction" and related links, http://www.narmada.org/maheshwar.html; Meena Menon, "Damned by the People: The Maheshwar Hydro-Electricity Project in Madhya Pradesh," *Business Line*, June 15, 1998; Sangvai, *River and Life*, 81–84; and Richard E. Bissell, Shekhar Singh, and Hermann Warth, *Maheshwar Hydroelectric Project: Resettlement and Rehabilitation—An Independent Review Conducted for the Ministry of Economic Cooperation and Development (BMZ), Government of Germany*, June 15, 2000 (hereafter Bissell Report).

54. Mardana Resolution, http://www.narmada.org/maheshwar/mardana .declaration.html; NBA, "Hundreds of Maheshwar Dam Affected People Demonstrate at IFCI, Delhi," press note, November 16, 2000, http://www .narmada.org/nba-press-releases/november-2000/ifci.demo.html; and Sangvai, *River and Life*, Annexure 4, 194–97, and Annexure 6, 200–201.

55. Heffa Schücking, "The Maheshwar Dam in India," March 1999, http://www .narmada.org/urg990421.3.html.

56. Menon, "Damned by the People."

57. "S. Kumars Forays into Ready-to-Wear Apparel," *India Info*, December 10, 2000, and "S. Kumars Ups Ads-Spend by 66% with Kapil Dev on Board," *India Express*, July 8, 1999.

58. Menon, "Damned by the People"; "Do or Die: The People versus Development in the Narmada Valley."

59. "German Firms Pull Out of MP Dam Project," *Statesman*, April 21, 1999. See also Desikan Thirunarayanapuram, "Siemens Role in Dam Project Doubtful," *Statesman*, June 30, 2000.

60. Bissell Report.

61. "Leaked Letter Shows German Company Quits Bid for Dam Credit," *Deutsche Presse-Agentur*, August 25, 2000; "US Firm Pulls Out of Narmada Hydel Project," *Statesman*, December 13, 2000.

62. "PM's Is Going to Be a 'Power Trip,'" *Indian Express*, September 4, 2000.

63. "Ogden Pulls Out from Maheshwar Hydel Unit," *Indian Express*, December 8, 2000.

64. Mark Landler, "Hi, I'm in Bangalore (But I Can't Say So)," *New York Times*, March 21, 2001, A1.

65. David Gardiner, "Impossible India's Improbable Chance," in *The World in 2001* (London: Economist, 2000), 46.

66. Prabhakar Sinha, "Tatas Plan Foray into Call Centre Business," *Times of India*, October 7, 2000.

THE LADIES HAVE FEELINGS, SO . . .
SHALL WE LEAVE IT TO THE EXPERTS?

1. Roger Cohen, "Germans Seek Foreign Labor for New Era of Computers," *New York Times*, April 9, 2000, 1.

2. Report at Rediff.com, http://www.rediff.com/news/2001/may/26pic3.htm.

3. For data on poverty and illiteracy in India, see UNDP 2000, table 1, Human Development Index, p. 159; table 4, Human Poverty in Developing Countries, p. 170; and table 19, Demographic Trends, p. 225. Reports also available online at http://www.undp.org and at the site of the UNDP Program in India, http://www.undp.org.in/.

4. Arundhati Roy, *The Cost of Living* (New York: Modern Library, 1999), which includes "The End of the Imagination," published in *Outlook* and *Frontline* magazines in August 1998, and "The Greater Common Good," published by *Outlook* and *Frontline* in May–June 1999. "Power Politics: The Reincarnation of Rumpelstiltskin," appeared originally in *Outlook*, November 27, 2000. See http://www.frontlineonline.com and http://www.outlookindia.com/ Arundhati Roy, *The God of Small Things* (New York: HarperPerennial, 1998).

5. UNDP 2000, table 19, Demographic Trends, p. 225.

6. Ashok Gulati, "Overflowing Granaries, Empty Stomachs," *Economic Times of India*, April 27, 2000.

7. UNDP 2000, table 4, Human Poverty in Developing Countries, p. 170, and table 19, Demographic Trends, p. 225. See also Gardiner, "Impossible India's Improbable Chance," 46.

8. Joseph Kahn, "U.S.-India Agreement," *New York Times*, January 11, 2000, 4.

9. Dev Raj, "Land Acquisition Bill Worse Than Colonial Law," Inter Press Service, December 3, 1998; S. Gopikrishna Warrier, "India: NGOs for Including Relief, Rehab Provisions in Land Act," *Business Line*, February 13, 2001.

10. Associated Press, "Anti-dam Activists Vow to Protest India's Supreme Court Ruling," October 20, 2000. For more on the Sardar Sarovar Dam project, see "The Greater Common Good"; "The Sardar Sarovar Dam: A Brief Introduction," Friends of the River Narmada, http://www.narmada.org/sardarsarovar.html, and related links; and Sangvai, *River and Life*.

11. Frederick Noronha, "Dam Protesters Battle Police for Access to World Bank President," Environment News Service, Global News Wire, November 13, 2000.

12. See 32, above; Rangachari et al., "Large Dams—India's Experience," 116–17, 130–31. For additional information on Big Dams, see Patrick McCully, *Silenced Rivers: The Ecology and Politics of Large Dams*, enlarged and updated edition (London: Zed Books, 2001), and the website of the International Rivers Network, http://www.internationalrivers.org/.

13. For more information on displacement from Sardar Sarovar, see WCD

Report, box 4.3, p. 104. See also Rangachari et al., "Large Dams—India's Experience," 116–17; Planning Commission, GOI, "Irrigation, Flood Control, and Command Area Development: Rehabilitation and Resettlement," chap. 4 in *Mid-term Appraisal of the Ninth Five Year Plan: Final Document (1997–2002)* (Delhi: Planning Commission, 2000), 89, para. 68; see 33, above; Morse and Berger, *Sardar Sarovar*, 62; and GOI, *28th and 29th Report of the Commissioner for Scheduled Castes and Scheduled Tribes* (New Delhi: Government of India, 1988).

14. "Indian Govt to Protest World Commission on Dams Report"; Sharma, "Misconceptions about Dams Commission"; "Keshubhai Warns Dam Inspection Team May Be Held"; "Gujarat Bans Visit of 'Anti-Dam' Body"; and Sharma, "Damning All Dissent."

15. WCD Report. See the WCD website, http://www.internationalrivers .org/; "Medium and Large Dams Damned."

16. Peter Popham, "Squalid, Disgusting, Toxic: Is This the Dirtiest City on the Planet?" *Independent*, October 27, 1997, E9; World Bank, "World Bank Says World's Worst Slums Can Be Transformed," press release, June 3, 1996, web.worldbank.org/WBSITE/EXTERNAL/NEWS/0,,contentMDK :20011723~piPK:4607,00.html.

17. GOI, Ministry of Environment and Forests, White Paper on Pollution in Delhi: With an Action Plan (New Delhi: Ministry of Environment and Forests, 1997), http://envfor.nic.in/divisions/cpoll/delpolln.html.

18. WCD Report, p. 11 and table 1.2.

19. "NBA Case: Supreme Court Adjourns Hearing on Gujarat Plea," *Hindu*, July 30, 1999; T. Padmanabha Rao, "India: Supreme Court Unhappy with NBA Leaders, Arundhati Roy," *Hindu*, October 16, 1999.

THE ALGEBRA OF INFINITE JUSTICE

1. Fox News, September 17, 2001.

2. Marc Levine, "New Suspect Arrested, but Doubts Grow over Terrorists' Identities," Agence France-Presse, September 21, 2001.

3. President George W. Bush, "September 11, 2001, Terrorist Attacks on the United States."

4. Elsa Brenner, "Hoping to Fill the Need for Office Space," *New York Times*, Westchester Weekly ed., September 23, 2001, 3.

5. Leslie Stahl, "Punishing Saddam," produced by Catherine Olian, *60 Minutes*, CBS, May 12, 1996.

6. Tamim Ansary, "Bomb Afghanistan Back to Stone Age? It's Been Done," *Providence Journal-Bulletin*, September 22, 2001, B7.

7. Thomas E. Ricks, "Land Mines, Aging Missiles Pose Threat," *Washington Post*, September 25, 2001, A15. See also Danna Harman, "Digging up Angola's

Deadly Litter," *Christian Science Monitor*, July 27, 2001, 6.

8. Barry Bearak, "Misery Hangs over Afghanistan after Years of War and Drought," *New York Times*, September 24, 2001, B3; Rajiv Chandrasekaran and Pamela Constable, "Panicked Afghans Flee to Border Area," *Washington Post*, September 23, 2001, A30; Catherine Solyom, "Exhibit a Glimpse into Refugee Life," *Gazette* (Montreal), September 21, 2001, A13; and Raymond Whitaker, Agence France-Presse, "Pakistan Fears for Seven Million Refugees as Winter Looms," *Independent* (London), September 27, 2001, 4.

9. BBC, "Aid Shortage Adds to Afghan Woes," September 22, 2001, http://news.bbc.co.uk/2/hi/south_asia/1556117.stm.

10. Ansary, "Bomb Afghanistan Back to Stone Age?"

11. Paul Leavitt, "Maps of Afghanistan Now in Short Supply," *USA Today*, September 18, 2001, 13A.

12. *Washington Post*, February 7, 1985, quoted in Raja Anwar, *The Tragedy of Afghanistan: A First-Hand Account*, trans. Khalid Hasan (New York: Verso, 1988), 232; "Inside the Taliban: U.S. Helped Cultivate the Repressive Regime Sheltering bin Laden," *Seattle Times*, September 19, 2001, A3; and Andrew Duffy, "Geographic Warriors," *Ottawa Citizen*, September 23, 2001, C4.

13. On the CIA connection, see Steve Coll, "Anatomy of a Victory: CIA's Covert Afghan War," *Washington Post*, July 19, 1992, A1; Steve Coll, "In CIA's Covert Afghan War, Where to Draw the Line Was Key," *Washington Post*, July 20, 1992, A1; Tim Weiner, "Blowback from the Afghan Battlefield," *New York Times Magazine*, March 13, 1994, 6: 53; and Ahmed Rashid, "The Making of a Terrorist," *Straits Times* (Singapore), September 23, 2001, 26.

14. Scott Baldauf, "Afghans Try Opium-Free Economy," *Christian Science Monitor*, April 3, 2001, 1.

15. David Kline, "Asia's 'Golden Crescent' Heroin Floods the West," *Christian Science Monitor*, November 9, 1982, 1; David Kline, "Heroin's Trail from Poppy Fields to the West," *Christian Science Monitor*, November 10, 1982, 1; and Rahul Bedi, "The Assassins and Drug Dealers Now Helping US Intelligence," *Daily Telegraph* (London), September 26, 2001, 10.

16. Peter Popham, "Taliban Monster That Was Launched by the US," *Independent* (London), September 17, 2001, 4.

17. Suzanne Goldenberg, "Mullah Keeps Taliban on a Narrow Path," *Guardian* (London), August 17, 1998, 12.

18. David K. Willis, "Pakistan Seeks Help from Abroad to Stem Heroin Flow," *Christian Science Monitor*, February 28, 1984, 11.

19. Farhan Bokhari, survey in "Pakistan: Living in Shadow of Debt Mountain," *Financial Times* (London), March 6, 2001, 4.

20. Douglas Frantz, "Sentiment in Pakistani Town Is Ardently Pro-Taliban," *New York Times*, September 27, 2001, B1; Rahul Bedi, "The Assassins and Drug Dealers Now Helping US Intelligence," *Daily Telegraph* (London),

September 26, 2001, 10.

21. Edward Luce, "Pakistan Nervousness Grows as Action Nears," *Financial Times* (London), September 27, 2001, 6.

22. Angus Donald and Khozem Merchant, "Concern at India's Support for US," *Financial Times* (London), September 21, 2001, 14.

23. Jeff Greenfield and David Ensor, "America's New War: Weapons of Terror," *Greenfield at Large*, CNN, September 24, 2001.

24. Jim Drinkard, "Bush Vows to 'Rid the World of Evildoers,'" *USA Today*, September 17, 2001, 1A.

25. Secretary of Defense Donald Rumsfeld, "Developments concerning Attacks on the Pentagon and the World Trade Center Last Week," special defense briefing, Federal News Service, September 20, 2001.

26. Robert Fisk, "This Is Not a War on Terror, It's a Fight against America's Enemies," *Independent* (London), September 25, 2001, 4.

27. George Monbiot, "The Need for Dissent," *Guardian* (London), September 18, 2001, 17.

28. Michael Slackman, "Terrorism Case Illustrates Difficulty of Drawing Tangible Ties to Al Qaeda," *Los Angeles Times*, September 22, 2001, A1.

29. Tim Russert, "Secretary of State Colin Powell Discusses America's Preparedness for the War on Terrorism," *Meet the Press*, NBC, September 23, 2001.

30. T. Christian Miller, "A Growing Global Chorus Calls for Proof," *Los Angeles Times*, September 24, 2001, A10; Dan Rather, "President Bush's Address to Congress and the Nation," *CBS News Special Report*, September 20, 2001.

31. Nityanand Jayaraman and Peter Popham, "Work Halts at Indian Unilever Factory after Poisoning Alert," *Independent* (London), March 11, 2001, 19.

32. Jack Hitt, "Battlefield: Space," *New York Times Magazine*, August 5, 2001, 6.

33. Colin Nickerson and Indira A. R. Lakshmanan, "America Prepares the Global Dimension," *Boston Globe*, September 27, 2001, A1; Barbara Crossette, "Taliban's Ban on Poppy a Success, U.S. Aides Say," *New York Times*, May 20, 2001, 1, 7; and Christopher Hitchens, "Against Rationalization," *Nation* 273, no. 10 (October 8, 2001): 8.

34. Bush, "September 11, 2001, Terrorist Attacks on the United States."

WAR IS PEACE

1. Alexander Nicoll, "US Warplanes Can Attack at All Times, Says Forces Chief," *Financial Times* (London), October 10, 2001, 2.

2. Noam Chomsky, "US Iraq Policy: Motives and Consequences," in *Iraq under Siege: The Deadly Impact of Sanctions and War*, ed. Anthony Arnove (Cambridge, MA: South End; London: Pluto, 2000), 54.

3. Slackman, "Terrorism Case Illustrates Difficulty of Drawing Tangible Ties to Al Qaeda," A1.

4. "Bush's Remarks on U.S. Military Strikes on Afghanistan," *New York Times*, October 8, 2001, B6; Ellen Hale, "'To Safeguard Peace, We Have to Fight,' Blair Emphasizes to Britons," *USA Today*, October 8, 2001, 6A.

5. "Remarks by President George W. Bush at an Anti-Terrorism Event," Washington, DC, Federal News Service, October 10, 2001.

6. Tom Pelton, "A Graveyard for Many Armies," *Baltimore Sun*, September 18, 2001, 2A.

7. Dave Newbart, "Nowhere to Go but Up," *Chicago Sun-Times*, September 18, 2001, 10.

8. Edward Epstein, "U.S. Seizes Skies over Afghanistan," *San Francisco Chronicle*, October 10, 2001, A1.

9. Steven Mufson, "For Bush's Veteran Team, What Lessons to Apply?" *Washington Post*, September 15, 2001, A5.

10. Donald H. Rumsfeld, "Defense Department Special Briefing Re: Update on U.S. Military Campaign in Afghanistan," Arlington, VA, Federal News Service, October 9, 2001.

11. Epstein, "U.S. Seizes Skies over Afghanistan."

12. Human Rights Watch, "Military Assistance to the Afghan Opposition: Human Rights Watch Backgrounder," October 2001, http://www.hrw.org /backgrounder/asia/afghan-bck1005.htm. See also Gregg Zoroya, "Northern Alliance Has Bloody Past, Critics Warn," *USA Today*, October 12, 2001, 1A.

13. David Rohde, "Visit to Town Where 2 Linked to bin Laden Killed Afghan Rebel," *New York Times*, September 26, 2001, B4.

14. Zahid Hussain and Stephen Farrell, "Tribal Chiefs See Chance to Be Rid of Taliban," *Times* (London), October 2, 2001.

15. Alan Cowell, "Afghan King Is Courted and Says, 'I Am Ready,'" *New York Times*, September 26, 2001, A4.

16. Said Mohammad Azam, "Civilian Toll Mounts as Bush Signals Switch to Ground Assault," Agence France-Presse, October 19, 2001; Indira A. R. Lakshmanan, "UN's Peaceful Mission Loses 4 to War," *Boston Globe*, October 10, 2001, A1; and Steven Lee Myers and Thom Shanker, "Pilots Told to Fire at Will in Some Zones," *New York Times*, October 17, 2001, B2.

17. UN documents and reports summarized in Center for Economic and Social Rights, "Afghanistan Fact Sheet 3: Key Human Vulnerabilities," http://www .cesr.org/downloads/Afghanistan%20Fact%20Sheet%203.pdf.

18. David Rising, "U.S. Military Defends Its Food Drops in Afghanistan from Criticism by Aid Organizations," Associated Press, October 10, 2001; Luke Harding, "Taliban Say Locals Burn Food Parcels," *Guardian* (London), October 11, 2001, 9; and Tyler Marshall and Megan Garvey, "Relief Efforts Trumped by Air War," *Los Angeles Times*, October 17, 2001, A1.

19. Martin Merzer and Jonathan S. Landay, Knight Ridder News Service, "Second Phase of Strikes Begins," *Milwaukee Journal Sentinel*, October 10, 2001, 1A.

20. Jennifer Steinhauer, "Citing Comments on Attack, Giuliani Rejects Saudi's Gift," *New York Times*, October 12, 2001, B13.

21. Robert Pear, "Arming Afghan Guerrillas: A Huge Effort Led by U.S.," *New York Times*, April 18, 1988, A1. See also Coll, "Anatomy of a Victory," A1; Coll, "In CIA's Covert Afghan War, Where to Draw the Line Was Key," A1; Weiner, "Blowback from the Afghan Battlefield"; and Rashid, "Making of a Terrorist," 26.

22. "Voices of Dissent and Police Action," *Hindu*, October 13, 2001.

23. "Vajpayee Gets Tough, Says No Compromise with Terrorism," *Economic Times of India*, October 15, 2001.

24. Howard Fineman, "A President Finds His True Voice," *Newsweek*, September 24, 2001, 50.

25. Aaron Pressman, "Former FCC Head Follows the Money," *IndustryStandard.com*, May 2, 2001.

26. Alice Cherbonnier, "Republican-Controlled Carlyle Group Poses Serious Ethical Questions for Bush Presidents, but *Baltimore Sun* Ignores It," *Baltimore Chronicle and Sentinel*, n.d. See also Leslie Wayne, "Elder Bush in Big G.O.P. Cast Toiling for Top Equity Firm," *New York Times*, March 5, 2001, A1.

27. "America, Oil and Afghanistan," editorial, *Hindu*, October 13, 2001.

28. Tyler Marshall, "The New Oil Rush: High Stakes in the Caspian," *Los Angeles Times*, February 23, 1998, A1.

29. Ahmed Rashid, *Taliban: Militant Islam, Oil, and Fundamentalism in Central Asia* (New Haven, CT: Yale Nota Bene / Yale University Press, 2001), 143–82.

ON CITIZENS' RIGHTS TO EXPRESS DISSENT

1. Nadja Vancauwenberghe and Maurice Frank, "New Media: If You Take a Bribe, We'll Nail You," *Guardian*, June 4, 2001; "Egg on Congress's Face," *Statesman*, April 10, 2001; "Chief Justice Turns Down Request for Sitting Judge for Arms Scandal Inquiry," BBC Summary of World Broadcasts, March 20, 2001; and "CJI Refuses to Spare Sitting Judge," *Times of India*, March 20, 2001.

2. PTI, "Ex-SC Judge to Hold Probe," *Tribune*, March 19, 2001, http://www.tribuneindia.com/20010320/main3.htm.

DEMOCRACY: WHO IS SHE WHEN SHE'S AT HOME?

1. Violence was directed especially at women. See, for example, the following report by Laxmi Murthy: "A doctor in rural Vadodara said that the wounded

who started pouring in from February 28 had injuries of a kind he had never witnessed before even in earlier situations of communal violence. In a grave challenge to the Hippocratic oath, doctors have been threatened for treating Muslim patients, and pressurised to use the blood donated by RSS volunteers only to treat Hindu patients. Sword injuries, mutilated breasts and burns of varying intensity characterised the early days of the massacre. Doctors conducted post-mortems on a number of women who had been gang raped, many of whom had been burnt subsequently. A woman from Kheda district who was gang raped had her head shaved and 'Om' cut into her head with a knife by the rapists. She died after a few days in the hospital. There were other instances of 'Om' engraved with a knife on women's backs and buttocks." From Laxmi Murthy, "In the Name of Honour," CorpWatch India, April 23, 2002.

2. See "Stray Incidents Take Gujarat Toll to 544," *Times of India*, March 5, 2002.

3. Edna Fernandes, "India Pushes through Anti-Terror Law," *Financial Times* (London), March 27, 2002, 11; "Terror Law Gets President's Nod," *Times of India*, April 3, 2002; Scott Baldauf, "As Spring Arrives, Kashmir Braces for Fresh Fighting," *Christian Science Monitor*, April 9, 2002, 7; Howard W. French and Raymond Bonner, "At Tense Time, Pakistan Starts to Test Missiles," *New York Times*, May 25, 2002, A1; Edward Luce, "The Saffron Revolution," *Financial Times* (London), May 4, 2002, 1; Martin Regg Cohn, "India's 'Saffron' Curriculum," *Toronto Star*, April 14, 2002, B4; and Pankaj Mishra, "Holy Lies," *Guardian* (London), April 6, 2002, 24.

4. See Edward Luce, "Battle over Ayodhya Temple Looms," *Financial Times* (London), February 2, 2002, 7.

5. "Gujarat's Tale of Sorrow: 846 Dead," *Economic Times*, April 18, 2002; see also Celia W. Dugger, "Religious Riots Loom over Indian Politics," *New York Times*, July 27, 2002, A1; Edna Fernandes, "Gujarat Violence Backed by State, Says EU Report," *Financial Times* (London), April 30, 2002, 12; and Human Rights Watch, "'We Have No Orders to Save You': State Participation and Complicity in Communal Violence in Gujarat," vol. 14, no. 3(C), April 2002, www.hrw.org /reports/2002/india/ (hereafter HRW Report). See also Human Rights Watch, "India: Gujarat Officials Took Part in Anti-Muslim Violence," press release, New York, April 30, 2002.

6. "A Tainted Election," *Indian Express*, April 17, 2002; Meena Menon, "A Divided Gujarat Not Ready for Snap Poll," Inter Press Service, July 21, 2002.

7. See HRW Report, 27–31. Dugger, "Religious Riots Loom over Indian Politics," A1; "Women Relive the Horrors of Gujarat," *Hindu*, May 18, 2002; Harbaksh Singh Nanda, "Muslim Survivors Speak in India," United Press International, April 27, 2002; and "Gujarat Carnage: The Aftermath—Impact of Violence on Women," 2002, www.onlinevolunteers.org/gujarat/women/index.htm.

8. HRW Report, 15–16, 31; Justice A. P. Ravani, Submission to the National Human Rights Commission, New Delhi, March 21, 2002, appendix 4. See also

Dugger, "Religious Riots Loom over Indian Politics," A1.

9. HRW Report, 31; and "Artists Protest Destruction of Cultural Landmarks," Press Trust of India, April 13, 2002.

10. HRW Report, 7, 45. Rama Lakshmi, "Sectarian Violence Haunts Indian City: Hindu Militants Bar Muslims from Work," *Washington Post*, April 8, 2002, A12.

11. *Communalism Combat* (March–April 2002) recounted Jaffri's final moments: "Ehsan Jaffri is pulled out of his house, brutally treated for 45 minutes, stripped, paraded naked, and asked to say, 'Vande Maataram!' and 'Jai Shri Ram!' He refuses. His fingers are chopped off, he is paraded around in the locality, badly injured. Next, his hands and feet are chopped off. He is then dragged, a fork-like instrument clutching his neck, down the road before being thrown into the fire." See also "50 Killed in Communal Violence in Gujarat, 30 of Them Burnt," Press Trust of India, February 28, 2002.

12. HRW Report, 5. See also Dugger, "Religious Riots Loom over Indian Politics," A1.

13. "ML Launches Frontal Attack on Sangh Parivar," *Times of India*, May 8, 2002.

14. HRW Report, 21–27. See also the remarks of Kamal Mitra Chenoy of Jawaharlal Nehru University, who led an independent fact-finding mission to Gujarat, "Can India End Religious Revenge?" CNN International, "Q&A with Zain Verjee," April 4, 2002.

15. See Tavleen Sigh, "Out of Tune," *India Today*, April 15, 2002, 21. See also Sharad Gupta, "BJP: His Excellency," *India Today*, January 28, 2002, 18.

16. Khozem Merchant, "Gujarat: Vajpayee Visits Scene of Communal Clashes," *Financial Times* (London), April 5, 2002, 10. See also Pushpesh Pant, "Atal at the Helm, or Running on Auto?" *Times of India*, April 8, 2002.

17. See Bharat Desai, "Will Vajpayee See through All the Window Dressing?" *Economic Times*, April 5, 2002.

18. Agence France-Press, "Singapore, India to Explore Closer Economic Ties," April 8, 2002.

19. See "Medha Files Charges against BJP Leaders," *Economic Times*, April 13, 2002.

20. HRW Report, 30. See also Burhan Wazir, "Militants Seek Muslim-Free India," *Observer* (London), July 21, 2002, 20.

21. See Mishra, "Holy Lies," 24.

22. The Home Minister, L. K Advani, made a public statement claiming that the burning of the train was a plot by Pakistan's Inter-Services Intelligence (ISI). Months later, the police have not found a shred of evidence to support that claim. The Gujarat government's forensic report says that sixty liters of petrol were poured onto the floor by someone who was inside the carriage. The doors were locked, possibly from the inside. The burned bodies of the passengers were

found in a heap in the middle of the carriage. So far, nobody knows who started the fire. There are theories to suit every political position: It was a Pakistani plot. It was Muslim extremists who managed to get into the train. It was the angry mob. It was a VHP / Bajrang Dal plot staged to set off the horror that followed. No one really knows. See HRW Report, 13–14; Siddharth Srivastava, "No Proof Yet on ISI Link with Sabarmati Attack: Officials," *Times of India*, March 6, 2002; "ISI behind Godhra Killings, Says BJP," *Times of India*, March 18, 2002; Uday Mahurkar, "Gujarat: Fuelling the Fire," *India Today*, July 22, 2002, 38; "Bloodstained Memories," *Indian Express*, April 12, 2002; and Celia W. Dugger, "After Deadly Firestorm, India Officials Ask Why," *New York Times*, March 6, 2002, A3.

23. "Blame It on Newton's Law: Modi," *Times of India*, March 3, 2002. See also Fernandes, "Gujarat Violence Backed by State," 12.

24. "RSS Cautions Muslims," Press Trust of India, March 17, 2002. See also Sanghamitra Chakraborty, "Minority Guide to Good Behaviour," *Times of India*, March 25, 2002.

25. P. R. Ramesh, "Modi Offers to Quit as Gujarat CM," *Economic Times*, April 13, 2002; "Modi Asked to Seek Mandate," *Statesman* (India), April 13, 2002.

26. See M. S. Golwalkar, *We, or Our Nationhood Defined* (Nagpur: Bharat, 1939); Vinayak Damodar Savarkar, *Hindutva* (New Delhi: Bharti Sadan, 1989). See also "Saffron Is Thicker Than . . . ," editorial, *Hindu*, October 22, 2000; David Gardner, "Hindu Revivalists Raise the Question of Who Governs India," *Financial Times* (London), July 13, 2000, 12.

27. See Arundhati Roy, *Power Politics*, 2nd ed. (Cambridge, MA: South End Press, 2001), 57 and notes (p. 159).

28. See Noam Chomsky, "Militarizing Space 'to Protect U.S. Interests and Investment,'" *International Socialist Review* 19 (July–August 2001), www.isreview .org/issues/19/NoamChomsky.shtml.

29. Pankaj Mishra, "A Mediocre Goddess," *New Statesman*, April 9, 2001, a review of Katherine Frank, *Indira: A Life of Indira Nehru Gandhi* (London: HarperCollins, 2001).

30. William Claiborne, "Gandhi Urges Indians to Strengthen Union," *Washington Post*, November 20, 1984, A9. See also Tavleen Singh, "Yesterday, Today, Tomorrow," *India Today*, March 30, 1998, 24.

31. HRW Report, 39–44.

32. President George W. Bush, "September 11, 2001, Terrorist Attacks on the United States," address to Joint Session of Congress, Federal News Service, September 20, 2001.

33. John Pilger, "Pakistan and India on Brink," *Mirror* (London), May 27, 2002, 4.

34. Alison Leigh Cowan, Kurt Eichenwald, and Michael Moss, "Bin Laden Family, with Deep Western Ties, Strives to Re-Establish a Name," *New York*

Times, October 28, 2001, 1, 9.

35. Sanjeev Miglani, "Opposition Keeps Up Heat on Government over Riots," Reuters, April 16, 2002.

36. "Either Govern or Just Go," *Indian Express*, April 1, 2002. Parekh is CEO of HDFC, the Housing Development Finance Corporation Limited.

37. "It's War in Drawing Rooms," *Indian Express*, May 19, 2002.

38. Ranjit Devraj, "Pro-Hindu Ruling Party Back to Hardline Politics," Inter Press Service, July 1, 2002; "An Unholy Alliance," *Indian Express*, May 6, 2002.

39. Nilanjana Bhaduri Jha, "Congress [Party] Begins Oust-Modi Campaign," *Economic Times*, April 12, 2002.

40. Richard Benedetto, "Confidence in War on Terror Wanes," *USA Today*, June 25, 2002, 19A; David Lamb, "Israel's Invasions, 20 Years Apart, Look Eerily Alike," *Los Angeles Times*, April 20, 2002, A5.

41. See "The End of Imagination," above.

42. "I would say it is a weapon of peace guarantee, a peace guarantor," said Abdul Qadeer Khan of Pakistan's nuclear bomb. See Imtiaz Gul, "Father of Pakistani Bomb Says Nuclear Weapons Guarantee Peace," Deutsche Presse-Agentur, May 29, 1998. See also Raj Chengappa, *Weapons of Peace: The Secret Story of India's Quest to Be a Nuclear Power* (New Delhi: HarperCollins, 2000).

43. The 1999 Kargil War between India and Pakistan claimed hundreds of lives. See Edward Luce, "Fernandes Hit by India's Coffin Scandal," *Financial Times* (London), December 13, 2001, 12.

44. See "Arrested Growth," *Times of India*, February 2, 2000.

45. Dugger, "Religious Riots Loom over Indian Politics," A1.

46. Edna Fernandes, "EU Tells India of Concern over Violence in Gujarat," *Financial Times* (London), May 3, 2002, 12; Alex Spillius, "'Please Don't Say This Was a Riot. It Was Genocide, Pure and Simple,'" *Daily Telegraph* (London), June 18, 2002, 13.

47. "Gujarat is an internal matter and the situation is under control," said Jaswant Singh, India's foreign affairs minister. See Shishir Gupta, "The Foreign Hand," *India Today*, May 6, 2002, 42 and sidebar.

48. "Laloo Wants Use of POTA [Prevention of Terrorism Act] against VHP, RSS," *Times of India*, March 7, 2002.

WAR TALK: SUMMER GAMES WITH NUCLEAR BOMBS

1. *Prophecy*, directed by Susumu Hani (1982; Nagasaki, Japan: Nagasaki Publishing Committee), 16mm.

2. See Aruna Roy and Nikhil Dey, "Words and Deeds," *India Together*, June 2002, and "Stand-Off at Maan River: Dispossession Continues to Stalk the Narmada Valley," *India Together*, May 2002, www.indiatogether.org/campaigns

/narmada/. See also "Maan Dam," Friends of River Narmada, www.narmada
.org/nvdp.dams/maan/.

3. "Nobel laureate Amartya Sen may think that health and education are the reasons why India has lagged behind in development in the past 50 years, but I think it is because of defence," said Home Minister L. K. Advani. See "Quote of the Week, Other Voices," India Today, June 17, 2002, 13.

4. See Human Rights Watch, "Behind the Kashmir Conflict: Abuses by Indian Security Forces and Militant Groups Continue," 1999, www.hrw.org/reports /1999/kashmir/summary.htm.

5. See Pilger, "Pakistan and India on Brink," 4; Neil Mackay, "Cash from Chaos: How Britain Arms Both Sides," Sunday Herald (Scotland), June 2, 2002, 12.

6. See Richard Norton-Taylor, "UK Is Selling Arms to India," Guardian (London), June 20, 2002, 1; Tom Baldwin, Philip Webster, and Michael Evans, "Arms Export Row Damages Peace Mission," Times (London), May 28, 2002; and Agence France-Presse, "Blair Peace Shuttle Moves from India to Pakistan," January 7, 2002.

7. Pilger, "Pakistan and India on Brink."

AHIMSA (NONVIOLENT RESISTANCE)

1. The government of India plans to build 30 large, 135 medium, and 3,000 small dams on the Narmada to generate electricity, displacing 400,000 people in the process. For more information, see www.narmada.org.

2. The activists ended their fast on June 18, 2002, after an independent committee was set up to look into the issue of resettlement. For more information, see www.narmada.org/nba-press-releases/jun-2002/fast.ends.html.

COME SEPTEMBER

1. See John Berger, G. (New York: Vintage International, 1991), 123.

2. See Damon Johnston, "U.S. Hits Back Inspirations," Advertiser, September 22, 2001, 7.

3. See John Pomfret, "Chinese Working Overtime to Sew U.S. Flags," Washington Post, September 20, 2001, A14.

4. See "Democracy: Who Is She When She's at Home?" above.

5. See David E. Sanger, "Bin Laden Is Wanted in Attacks, 'Dead or Alive,' President Says," New York Times, September 18, 2001, A1; John F. Burns, "10-Month Afghan Mystery: Is Bin Laden Dead or Alive?" New York Times, September 30, 2002, A1.

6. See the Associated Press list, available on the website of the *Toledo Blade*, of those confirmed dead, reported dead, or reported missing in the September 11 terrorist attacks, www.toledoblade.com/Nation/2011/09/11/list-of-2977 -victims-of-Sept-11-2001-terror-attacks.html.

7. Quoted in Seymour M. Hersh, *The Price of Power: Kissinger in the Nixon White House* (New York: Summit Books, 1983), 265.

8. See Pilar Aguilera and Ricardo Fredes, eds., *Chile: The Other September 11* (New York: Ocean, 2002); Amnesty International, "The Case of Augusto Pinochet."

9. Clifford Krauss, "Britain Arrests Pinochet to Face Charges by Spain," *New York Times*, October 18, 1998, 1; National Security Archive, "Chile: 16,000 Secret U.S. Documents Declassified," press release, November 13, 2000, nsarchive.gwu.edu/news/20001113/; and selected documents on the National Security Archive website, nsarchive.gwu.edu/news/20001113/#docs.

10. Kissinger told this to Pinochet at a meeting of the Organization of American States in Santiago, Chile, on June 8, 1976. See Lucy Kosimar, "Kissinger Covered Up Chile Torture," *Observer*, February 28, 1999, 3.

11. Among other histories, see Eduardo Galeano, *Open Veins of Latin America: Five Centuries of the Pillage of a Continent*, trans. Cedric Belfrage, 2nd ed. (New York: Monthly Review Press, 1998); Noam Chomsky, *Turning the Tide: U.S. Intervention in Central America and the Struggle for Peace*, 2nd ed. (Boston: South End, 1985); Noam Chomsky, *The Culture of Terrorism* (Boston: South End, 1983); and Gabriel Kolko, *Confronting the Third World: United States Foreign Policy, 1945–1980* (New York: Pantheon, 1988).

12. In a public relations move, the SOA renamed itself the Western Hemisphere Institute for Security Cooperation (WHINSEC) on January 17, 2001. See Jack Nelson-Pallmeyer, *School of Assassins: Guns, Greed, and Globalization*, 2nd ed. (New York: Orbis Books, 2001); Michael Gormley, "Army School Faces Critics Who Call It Training Ground for Assassins," Associated Press, May 2, 1998; and School of the Americas Watch, www.soaw.org.

13. On these interventions, see, among other sources, Noam Chomsky, *American Power and the New Mandarins*, 2nd ed. (New York: New Press, 2002); Noam Chomsky, *At War with Asia* (New York: Vintage Books, 1970); and Howard Zinn, *Vietnam: The Logic of Withdrawal*, 2nd ed. (Cambridge, MA: South End, 2002).

14. See Samih K. Farsoun and Christina E. Zacharia, *Palestine and the Palestinians* (Boulder, CO: Westview, 1997), 10.

15. The Balfour Declaration is included in ibid., appendix 2, 320.

16. Quoted in Noam Chomsky, *Fateful Triangle: The United States, Israel, and the Palestinians*, 2nd ed. (Cambridge, MA: South End, 2000), 90.

17. Quoted in "Scurrying towards Bethlehem," editorial, *New Left Review* 10 (July/August 2001), 9n5.

18. Quoted in Farsoun and Zacharia, *Palestine and the Palestinians*, 10, 243.

19. Ibid., 111, 123.

20. Ibid., 116.

21. See Chomsky, *Fateful Triangle*, 103–07, 118–32, 156–60.

22. From 1987 to 2002 alone, more than two thousand Palestinians were killed. See statistics from B'Tselem (Israeli Information Center for Human Rights in the Occupied Territories) at www.btselem.org/statistics.

23. See Naseer H. Aruri, *Dishonest Broker: The United States, Israel, and the Palestinians* (Cambridge MA: South End, 2003); Noam Chomsky, *World Orders Old and New*, 2nd ed. (New York: Columbia University Press, 1996).

24. In addition to more than $3 billion annually in official Foreign Military Financing, the US government supplies Israel with economic assistance, loans, technology transfers, and arms sales. See Nick Anderson, "House Panel Increases Aid for Israel, Palestinians," *Los Angeles Times*, May 10, 2002, A1; Aruri, *Dishonest Broker*; and Anthony Arnove and Ahmed Shawki, foreword to *The Struggle for Palestine*, ed. Lance Selfa (Chicago: Haymarket Books, 2002), xxv.

25. Article 27 of the Charter of the Islamic Resistance Movement (Hamas), quoted in Farsoun and Zacharia, *Palestine and the Palestinians*, appendix 13, 339.

26. George H. W. Bush, "Text of Bush's Speech: 'It Is Iraq against the World,'" *Los Angeles Times*, September 12, 1990, A7.

27. See Glenn Frankel, "Iraq Long Avoided Censure on Rights," *Washington Post*, September 22, 1990, A1.

28. See Christopher Dickey and Evan Thomas, "How Saddam Happened," *Newsweek*, September 23, 2002, 35–37.

29. See Anthony Arnove, introduction to *Iraq under Siege*, 20.

30. Arnove, *Iraq under Siege*, 221–22.

31. Ibid., 17, 205.

32. See Thomas J. Nagy, "The Secret behind the Sanctions: How the U.S. Intentionally Destroyed Iraq's Water Supply," *Progressive* 65, no. 9 (September 2001).

33. See Arnove, *Iraq under Siege*, 121, 185–203. See also Nicholas D. Kristof, "The Stones of Baghdad," *New York Times*, October 4, 2002, A27.

34. Leslie Stahl, "Punishing Saddam," produced by Catherine Olian, *60 Minutes*, CBS, May 12, 1996.

35. Elisabeth Bumiller, "Bush Aides Set Strategy to Sell Policy on Iraq," *New York Times*, September 7, 2002, A1.

36. Richard Perle, "Why the West Must Strike First against Saddam Hussein," *Daily Telegraph* (London), August 9, 2002, 22.

37. See Alan Simpson and Glen Rangwala, "The Dishonest Case for a War on Iraq," September 27, 2002, www.grassrootspeace.org/counter-dossier.html; Glen Rangwala, "Notes Further to the Counter-Dossier," September 29, 2002, grassrootspeace.org/archivecounter-dossierII.html.

38. George Bush, "Bush's Remarks on U.S. Military Strikes in Afghanistan," *New York Times*, October 8, 2001, B6.

39. See Paul Watson, "Afghanistan Aims to Revive Pipeline Plans," *Los Angeles Times*, May 30, 2002, A1; Ilene R. Prusher, Scott Baldauf, and Edward Girardet, "Afghan Power Brokers," *Christian Science Monitor*, June 10, 2002, 1.

40. See Lisa Fingeret et al., "Markets Worry That Conflict Could Spread in Area That Holds Two-Thirds of World Reserves," *Financial Times* (London), April 2, 2002, 1.

41. Thomas L. Friedman, "Craziness Pays," *New York Times*, February 24, 1998, A21.

42. Thomas L. Friedman, *The Lexus and the Olive Tree: Understanding Globalization* (New York: Farrar, Strauss, and Giroux, 1999), 373.

43. Statistics from Joseph E. Stiglitz, *Globalization and Its Discontents* (New York: W. W. Norton, 2002), 5; Noam Chomsky, *Rogue States: The Rule of Law in World Affairs* (Cambridge, MA: South End, 2000), 214; and Noreena Hertz, "Why Consumer Power Is Not Enough," *New Statesman*, April 30, 2001.

44. Among the many treaties and international agreements the United States has not signed, ignores, violates, or has broken are the UN International Covenant on Economic, Social and Cultural Rights (1966); the UN Convention on the Rights of the Child (CRC); the UN Convention on the Elimination of All Forms of Discrimination Against Women (CEDAW); agreements setting the jurisdiction for the International Criminal Court (ICC); the 1972 Anti-Ballistic Missile Treaty with Russia; the Comprehensive Test Ban Treaty (CTBT); and the Kyoto Protocol regulating greenhouse gas emissions.

45. See David Cole and James X. Dempsey, *Terrorism and the Constitution: Sacrificing Civil Liberties in the Name of National Security* (New York: New Press, 2002).

46. Luke Harding, "Elusive Mullah Omar 'Back in Afghanistan,'" *Guardian* (London), August 30, 2002, 12.

47. See Human Rights Watch, "Opportunism in the Face of Tragedy: Repression in the Name of Anti-terrorism," http://www.hrw.org/legacy/campaigns/september11/opportunismwatch.htm.

48. See "Power Politics," 76–105, above, and related notes.

THE LONELINESS OF NOAM CHOMSKY

1. R. W. Apple, Jr., "Bush Appears in Trouble despite Two Big Advantages," *New York Times*, August 4, 1988, A1. Bush made this remark in refusing to apologize for the shooting down of an Iranian passenger plane, killing 290 passengers. See Lewis Lapham, *Theater of War* (New York: New Press, 2002), 126.

2. Chomsky would be the first to point out that other pioneering media analysts include his frequent coauthor Edward Herman, Ben Bagdikian (whose 1983 classic *The Media Monopoly* recounts the suppression of Chomsky and

Herman's *Counter-Revolutionary Violence: Bloodbaths in Fact and Propaganda*), and Herbert Schiller.

3. Paul Betts, "Ciampi Calls for Review of Media Laws," *Financial Times* (London), July 24, 2002, 8. For an overview of Berlusconi's holdings, see Ketupa.net Media Profiles: www.ketupa.net/berlusconi1.htm.

4. See Sabin Russell, "U.S. Push for Cheap Cipro Haunts AIDS Drug Dispute," *San Francisco Chronicle*, November 8, 2001, A13; Frank Swoboda and Martha McNeil Hamilton, "Congress Passes $15 Billion Airline Bailout," *Washington Post*, September 22, 2001, A1.

5. President George W. Bush Jr., "President Bush's Address on Terrorism before a Joint Meeting of Congress," *New York Times*, September 21, 2001, B4.

6. Dan Eggen, "Ashcroft Invokes Religion in U.S. War on Terrorism," *Washington Post*, February 20, 2002, A2.

7. President George W. Bush Jr., "Bush's Remarks on U.S. Military Strikes in Afghanistan," *New York Times*, October 8, 2001, B6.

8. President George W. Bush Jr., remarks at FBI Headquarters, Washington, DC, October 10, 2001, Federal Document Clearinghouse.

9. See Howard Zinn, *A People's History of the United States: 1492–Present*, 20th anniv. ed. (New York: HarperCollins, 2001).

10. Bob Marley and N. G. Williams (aka King Sporty), "Buffalo Soldier."

11. Noam Chomsky, "The Manufacture of Consent," in *The Chomsky Reader*, ed. James Peck (New York: Pantheon, 1987), 121–22.

12. See Jim Miller, "Report from the Inferno," *Newsweek*, September 7, 1981, 72; review of Committee for the Compilation of Materials on Damage Caused by the Atomic Bombs in Hiroshima and Nagasaki, *Hiroshima and Nagasaki: The Physical, Medical, and Social Effects of the Atomic Bombings* (New York: Basic, 1981).

13. David E. Sanger, "Bush to Formalize a Defense Policy of Hitting First," *New York Times*, June 17, 2002, A1; David E. Sanger, "Bush Renews Pledge to Strike First to Counter Terror Threats," *New York Times*, July 20, 2002, A3.

14. See Terence O'Malley, "The Afghan Memory Holds Little Room for Trust in U.S.," *Irish Times*, October 15, 2001, 16.

15. Arnove, *Iraq under Siege*.

16. See Noam Chomsky, "Memories," review of *In Retrospect* by Robert McNamara (New York: Times Books, 1995), *Z Magazine* (July–August 1995), www.zmag.org/.

17. "Myth and Reality in Bloody Battle for the Skies," *Guardian* (London), October 13, 1998, 15.

18. Bill Keller, "Moscow Says Afghan Role Was Illegal and Immoral," *New York Times*, October 24, 1989, A1.

19. Noam Chomsky, "Afghanistan and South Vietnam," in *Chomsky Reader*, ed. Peck, 225.

20. Samuel P. Huntington, "The Bases of Accommodation," *Foreign Affairs*

46, no. 4 (1968): 642–56. Quoted in Noam Chomsky, *At War with Asia* (New York: Vintage Books, 1970), 87.

21. Samuel P. Huntington, "The Clash of Civilizations?" *Foreign Affairs* 72, no. 3 (Summer 1993): 22–49.

22. Huntington, "The Bases of Accommodation," quoted in Chomsky, *At War with Asia*, 87.

23. T. D. Allman, "The Blind Bombers," *Far Eastern Economic Review* 75, no. 5 (January 29, 1972): 18–20, quoted in Chomsky, *For Reasons of State*, 72.

24. Chomsky, *For Reasons of State*, 72; Chomsky, *At War with Asia*, 87; and Lapham, *Theater of War*, 145.

25. T. D. Allman, "The War in Laos: Plain Facts," *Far Eastern Economic Review* 75, no. 2 (January 8, 1972): 16ff.

26. Chomsky, *For Reasons of State*, 18. See also Noam Chomsky, "The Pentagon Papers as Propaganda and as History," in *The Pentagon Papers: The Defense Department History of United States Decisionmaking on Vietnam; The Senator Gravel Edition—Critical Essays*, ed. Noam Chomsky and Howard Zinn (Boston: Beacon, 1971–72), 5:79–201.

27. Chomsky, *For Reasons of State*, 67, 70.

28. William Pfaff, *Condemned to Freedom: The Breakdown of Liberal Society* (New York: Random House, 1971), 75–77, quoted in Chomsky, *For Reasons of State*, 94.

29. Pfaff, *Condemned to Freedom*, 75–77, quoted in Chomsky, *For Reasons of State*, 94–95.

30. *Pentagon Papers*, 4:43, quoted in Chomsky, *For Reasons of State*, 67.

31. Philip Jones Griffiths, *Vietnam Inc.*, 2nd ed. (New York: Phaidon, 2001), 210. First edition quoted in Chomsky, *For Reasons of State*, 3–4.

32. Noam Chomsky, interview with James Peck, in *Chomsky Reader*, ed. Peck, 14.

CONFRONTING EMPIRE

1. See Ranjit Devraj, "Asia's 'Outcast' Hurt by Globalization," Inter Press Service, January 6, 2003; Statesman News Service, "Farm Suicide Heat on Jaya," *Statesman* (India), January 9, 2003; and "'Govt. Policies Driving Farmers to Suicide,'" *Times of India*, February 4, 2002.

2. See "Govt.'s Food Policy Gets a Reality Check from States," *Indian Express*, January 11, 2003; Parul Chandra, "Victims Speak of Hunger, Starvation across Country," *Times of India*, January 11, 2003.

3. See "Democracy: Who Is She When She's at Home?" 160–76, above; see also Pankaj Mishra, "The Other Face of Fanaticism," *New York Times*, February 2, 2003, 42–46; Concerned Citizens Tribunal, *Crime against Humanity: An Inquiry into the Carnage in Gujarat*, 2 vols. (Mumbai: Citizens for Justice and Peace, 2002).

4. See Edward Luce, "Gujarat Win Likely to Embolden Hindu Right," *Financial Times* (London), December 16, 2002, 8.

5. Oscar Olivera, "The War over Water in Cochabamba, Bolivia," trans. Florencia Belvedere, presented at "Services for All?" Municipal Services Project Conference, South Africa, May 15–18, 2002.

6. Tom Lewis, "Contagion in Latin America," *International Socialist Review* 24 (July–August 2002).

7. Julian Borger and Alex Bellos, "U.S. 'Gave the Nod' to Venezuelan Coup," *Guardian* (London), April 17, 2002, 13.

8. David Sharrock, "Thousands Protest in Buenos Aires as Economic Woes Persist," *Times* (London), December 21, 2002, 18.

9. See Mary McGrory, "'A River of Peaceful People,'" *Washington Post*, January 23, 2003, A21.

PEACE IS WAR: THE COLLATERAL DAMAGE OF BREAKING NEWS

1. Mohammed Shehzad, "'Killing Hindus' Better than Dialogue with India: Lashkar-e-Taiba Chief," Agence France-Presse, April 3, 2003.

2. Ben H. Bagdikian, *The New Media Monopoly* (Boston: Beacon, 2004).

3. Edward Helmore, "Who Sets the TV Control? Battle Is Raging over a Decision to Allow US Media Giants to Own Even More," *Observer* (London), June 8, 2003, 6.

4. Howard Rheingold, "From the Screen to the Streets," *In These Times*, November 17, 2003, 34; Stephen Labaton, "Debate/Monopoly on Information: It's a World of Media Plenty; Why Limit Ownership?" *New York Times*, October 12, 2003, 4.

5. See Connie Koch, *2/15: The Day the World Said No to War* (New York: Hello NYC; Oakland: AK Press, 2004).

6. See Edward Luce, "Battle over Ayodhya Temple Looms," *Financial Times* (London), February 2, 2002, 7.

7. Pankaj Mishra, "A Mediocre Goddess," *New Statesman*, April 9, 2001; John Ward Anderson, "The Flame That Lit An Inferno: Hindu Leader Creates Anti-Muslim Frenzy," *Washington Post*, August 11, 1993, A14. See also "Democracy: Who Is She When She's at Home?" 160–76, above.

8. See "In Memory of Shankar Guha Niyogi," 280–83.

9. Raja Bose, "A River Runs Through It," *Times of India*, February 25, 2001.

10. C. Rammanohar Reddy, "At Loggerheads over Resources," *Hindu*, May 27, 2001; Kata Lee (Project Coordinator of Hotline Asia), "India: Unarmed Tribals Killed by Jharkhand Police," Asian Center for the Progress of Peoples, Asian Human Rights Commission, March 3, 2003.

11. Gurbir Singh, "Guj[arat] Police Cane Protesters of NATELCO-UNOCAL Port," *Economic Times*, April 12, 2000; "Human Rights Defenders Persecuted in India: Amnesty [International]," Press Trust of India, April 26, 2000. See also Rosa Basanti, "Villagers Take On Giant Port Project," Inter Press Service, June 7, 2000.

12. Sanjay Kumar, "The Adivasis of Orissa," *Hindu*, November 6, 2001; Anu Kumar, "Orissa: A Continuing Denial of Adivasi Rights," InfoChange News and Features, Centre for Communication and Development Studies, November 2003. See also "When Freedom Is Trampled Upon," *Hindu*, January 24, 1999.

13. Danielle Knight, "The Destructive Impact of Fish Farming," Inter Press Service, October 13, 1999.

14. "Eviction of Tribals by Force in Kerala to Be Taken Up with NHRC," *Hindu*, February 26, 2003.

15. On the Nagarnar attacks, see Kuldip Nayar, "Pushing the POTO," *Hindu*, November 28, 2001.

16. People's War Group (PWG), Maoist Communist Centre (MCC), Pakistan's Inter-Services Intelligence (ISI), and the Liberation Tigers of Tamil Eelam (LTTE).

17. "Mr. [Vakkom] Purushothaman said he was of the view that the Adivasis who had 'tried to establish a parallel government should have been suppressed or shot.'" Quoted in "Opposition Boycotts Assembly," *Hindu*, February 22, 2003.

18. Mari Marcel Thekaekara, "What Really Happened," *Frontline*, March 15–28, 2003.

19. Sanjay Nigam, Mangat Verma, and Chittaroopa Palit, "Fifteen Thousand Farmers Gather in Mandleshwar to Protest against Electricity Tariff Hikes in Madhya Pradesh," Nimad Malwa Kisan Mazdoor Sangathan press release, February 27, 2003, www.narmada.org/nba-press-releases/february-2003/antitariff.html.

20. WCD Report, box 4.3, 104.

21. "The Greater Common Good" and "Power Politics," above.

22. L. S. Aravinda, "Supreme Court Majority Judgment: Mockery of Modern India," Association for India's Development.

23. World Bank Water Resources Management Group, *Water Resources Sector Strategy: Strategic Directions for World Bank Engagement* (Washington, DC: International Bank for Reconstruction and Development/World Bank, 2004), documents.worldbank.org/curated/en/2004/01/3030614/water-resources-sector-strategy-strategic-directions-world-bank-engagement; Peter Bosshard et al., "Gambling with People's Lives: What the World Bank's New 'High-Risk/High-Reward' Strategy Means for the Poor and the Environment," Environmental Defense, Friends of the Earth and International Rivers Network, September 19, 2003. See also Carrieann Davies, "From the Editor:

Back to the Future," *Water Power and Dam Construction*, April 30, 2003, 3.

24. "Major Rivers to Be Linked by 2016," Press Trust of India, December 17, 2002. See also Medha Patkar, ed., *River Linking: A Millennium Folly?* (Pune, India: National Alliance of People's Movements/Initiative, 2004).

25. See "Tribals' Promised Land Is Kerala Sanctuary," *Indian Express*, February 6, 2003.

26. "Call to Prosecute Grasim Management for Pollution," *Business Line*, February 1, 1999.

27. R. Krishnakumar, "Closure of Grasim Industries," *Frontline*, July 21–August 3, 2001.

AN ORDINARY PERSON'S GUIDE TO EMPIRE

1. CNN International, March 21, 2003.

2. Ibid.

3. Ibid. See also Dexter Filkins, "In the Field Marines: Either Take a Shot or Take a Chance," *New York Times*, March 29, 2003, A1. Filkins interviewed Sergeant Eric Schrumpf, aged twenty-eight, of the Fifth Marine Regiment. "'We had a great day,' Sergeant Schrumpf said. 'We killed a lot of people.' . . . 'We dropped a few civilians, . . . but what do you do?' . . . He recalled watching one of the women standing near the Iraqi soldier go down. 'I'm sorry,' the sergeant said. 'But the chick was in the way.'"

4. Patrick E. Tyler and Janet Elder, "Threats and Responses—The Poll: Poll Finds Most in U.S. Support Delaying a War," *New York Times*, February 14, 2003, A1.

5. Maureen Dowd, "The Xanax Cowboy," *New York Times*, March 9, 2003, 4, 13.

6. George W. Bush, joint statement with Tony Blair after the Azores summit. See "Excerpts from Remarks by Bush and Blair: 'Iraq Will Soon Be Liberated,'" *New York Times*, April 9, 2003, B7.

7. "You Cannot Hide, Hoon Tells Saddam," *Birmingham Evening Mail*, March 20, 2003, 2; Charles Reiss, "We Had No Option But to Use Force to Disarm Saddam, Says Straw," *Evening Standard* (London), March 20, 2003, 11.

8. General Vince Brooks, deputy director of operations, United States Central Command Daily Press Briefing, Federal News Service, March 27, 2003.

9. CNN International, March 25, 2003.

10. Remarks by President George W. Bush to Troops at MacDill Air Force Base, Tampa, FL, Federal News Service, March 26, 2003.

11. See David Cole, *Enemy Aliens: Double Standards and Constitutional Freedoms in the War on Terrorism* (New York: New Press, 2003).

12. Charles Lane, "Justices to Rule on Detainees' Rights; Court Access for

660 Prisoners at Issue," *Washington Post*, November 11, 2003, 1; David Rohde, "U.S. Rebuked on Afghans in Detention," *New York Times*, March 8, 2004, A6. See also Cole, *Enemy Aliens*, 39–45.

13. Jeremy Armstrong, "Field of Death—Total Slaughter: Amnesty [International] Demands Probe Be over Bloody Massacre of Taliban Prisoners," *Mirror* (London), November 29, 2001, 6.

14. "Injustice in Afghanistan," editorial, *Washington Post*, March 21, 2004, B6.

15. Bill O'Reilly, "Talking Points Memo," *The O'Reilly Factor*, Fox News, March 24, 2003. See also Bill O'Reilly, "Unresolved Problems: Interview with Kenneth Roth," *The O'Reilly Factor*, Fox News, March 27, 2003.

16. See Rageh Omaar, *Revolution Day: The Human Story of the Battle for Iraq* (London: Viking, 2004).

17. Martin Bright, Ed Vulliamy, and Peter Beaumont, "Revealed: US Dirty Tricks to Win Vote on Iraq War," *Observer* (London), March 2, 2003, 1.

18. Marc Santora, "Aid Workers Fear Dangers of Delay: Basra, without Power and Water, Is at Risk," *International Herald Tribune*, March 25, 2003, 1; John Pilger, "Gulf War 2: Six Days of Shame," *Mirror* (London), March 26, 2003, 14.

19. Patrick Nicholson, "The Cans and Buckets Are Empty and People Are Desperate," *Independent* (London), April 5, 2003, 8.

20. Agence France-Presse, "Iraq's Weekly Oil Production Reaches New Levels," July 23, 2002.

21. Mark Nicholson, "Troops Prepare to Deliver Supplies," *Financial Times* (London), March 27, 2003, 2.

22. Nick Guttmann, "Humanitarian Aid—Wanted: 32 Galahads a Day," *Independent on Sunday* (London), March 30, 2003, 26.

23. Quoted in Noam Chomsky, *For Reasons of State* (New York: New Press, 2003), 67–69.

24. Juan J. Walte, "Greenpeace: 200,000 Died in Gulf," *USA Today*, May 30, 1991, 1A.

25. Kim Cobb, "Vets Warn of Risks to Soldiers' Health: Critics Fear Repeat of Gulf War Illnesses," *Houston Chronicle*, February 9, 2003, 1.

26. James Meikle, "'Health Will Suffer for Years,'" *Guardian* (London), November 12, 2003, 17.

27. Joel Brinkley, "American Companies Rebuilding Iraq Find They Are Having to Start from the Ground Up," *New York Times*, February 22, 2004, 11; Tucker Carlson, "Hired Guns," *Esquire*, March 2004, 130–38.

28. Felicity Barringer, "Security Council Votes to Revive Oil-for-Food Program in Iraq," *New York Times*, March 29, 2003, B7.

29. Dan Morgan and Karen DeYoung, "Hill Panels Approve War Funds, with Curbs: Most Restrictions Aimed at Pentagon," *Washington Post*, April 2, 2003, A26.

30. Lou Dobbs, *Lou Dobb's Moneyline*, CNN, March 27, 2003.

31. Greg Wright, "French Fries? Mais Non, Congress Calls Em Freedom Fries," Gannett News Service, March 12, 2003, www.gannettonline.com/gns /faceoff2/20030312-18100.shtml.

32. Serge Bellanger, "Of Wal-Marts, BMWs and Brie," *Chicago Tribune*, April 27, 2003, 9.

33. George W. Bush, Camp David, Maryland, press briefing, September 16, 2001: "We're going to do it. We will rid the world of the evildoers. We will call together freedom-loving people to fight terrorism. And so on this day of—on the Lord's day, I say to my fellow Americans, thank you for your prayers, thank you for your compassion, thank you for your love for one another, and tomorrow when you get back to work, work hard like you always have. But we've been warned. We've been warned there are evil people in this world. We've been warned so vividly and we'll be alert. Your government is alert. The governors and mayors are alert that evil folks still lurk out there."

INSTANT-MIX IMPERIAL DEMOCRACY
(BUY ONE, GET ONE FREE)

1. Molly Moore, "The USS *Vincennes* and a Deadly Mistake: Highly Sophisticated Combat Ship at Center of Defense Department Investigation," *Washington Post*, July 4, 1988, A23.

2. Apple, "Bush Appears in Trouble," A1. See Lapham, *Theater of War*, 126.

3. Tyler and Elder, "Threats and Responses," A1.

4. Dowd, "The Xanax Cowboy," 13.

5. President George W. Bush, address to the nation, State Floor Cross Hallway, the White House, Federal News Service, March 17, 2003.

6. President George W. Bush, speech at the Cincinnati Museum Center, Cincinnati, Ohio, Federal News Service, October 7, 2002.

7. See Saïd K. Aburish, *Saddam Hussein: The Politics of Revenge* (London: Bloomsbury, 2001). See also the PBS *Frontline* interview with Aburish, "Secrets of His Life and Leadership," from *The Survival of Saddam*, www .pbs.org/wgbh/pages/frontline/shows/saddam/interviews/aburish.html.

8. See Anthony Arnove, "Indonesia: Crisis and Revolt," *International Socialist Review* 5 (Fall 1998).

9. Originally stated in a May 1980 interview on the *MacNeil/Lehrer Report* on PBS. Quoted in Philip Geyelin, "Forget Gunboat Diplomacy," *Washington Post*, September 29, 1980, A13.

10. See Arnove, *Iraq under Seige*, especially the chapter by Noam Chomsky, "US Iraq Policy: Consequences and Motives," 65–74, and Arnove's introduction, 11–31.

11. See, among many other of Bush's speeches, his address to the Wings over the Rockies Air and Space Museum, Denver, Colorado, Federal News Service, October 28, 2002, in which he reminded his audience that Hussein "is a person who has gassed his own people. . . . He's anxious to have, once again to develop a nuclear weapon. He's got connections with al Qaeda." Bush also commented: "We love life, everybody matters as far as we're concerned, everybody is precious. They have no regard for innocent life whatsoever. (Applause.) They hate the fact that we love freedom. We love our freedom of religion, we love our freedom of speech, we love every aspect of freedom. (Applause.) And we're not changing. (Applause.) We're not intimidated. As a matter of fact, the more they hate our freedoms, the more we love our freedoms. (Applause.)"

12. See Arnove, *Iraq under Siege*, 68–69.

13. "We are a nation called to defend freedom—a freedom that is not the grant of any government or document, but is our endowment from God." See Eggen, "Ashcroft Invokes Religion," A2.

14. Michael R. Gordon, "Baghdad's Power Vacuum Is Drawing Only Dissent," *New York Times*, April 21, 2003, A10.

15. Peter Beaumont, "Anger Rises as US Fails to Control Anarchy," *Observer* (London), April 13, 2003, 3.

16. Jim Dwyer, "Troops Endure Blowing Sands and Mud Rain," *New York Times*, March 26, 2003, A1; Neela Banerjee, "Army Depots in Iraqi Desert Have Names of Oil Giants," *New York Times*, March 27, 2003, C14.

17. Secretary of Defense Donald H. Rumsfeld, Defense Department operational update briefing, Pentagon Briefing Room, Arlington, VA, Federal News Service, April 11, 2003.

18. Reuters, "Number Imprisoned Exceeds 2 Million, Justice Dept. Says," *Washington Post*, April 7, 2003, A4; Sentencing Project, "U.S. Prison Populations: Trends and Implications," May 2003, 1.

19. Sentencing Project, "U.S. Prison Populations."

20. Fox Butterfield, "Prison Rates among Blacks Reach a Peak, Report Finds," *New York Times*, April 7, 2003, A12.

21. Richard Willing, "More Seeking President's Pardon," *USA Today*, December 24, 2002, 3A.

22. Paul Martin, Ed Vulliamy, and Gaby Hinsliff, "US Army Was Told to Protect Looted Museum," *Observer* (London), April 20, 2003, 4; Frank Rich, "And Now: 'Operation Iraqi Looting,'" *New York Times*, April 27, 2003, 2.

23. See Scott Peterson, "Iraq: Saladin to Saddam," *Christian Science Monitor*, March 4, 2003, 1.

24. Rumsfeld, Defense Department briefing.

25. Martin, Vulliamy, and Hinsliff, "US Army Was Told to Protect Looted Museum," 4.

26. See Robert Fisk, "Americans Defend Two Untouchable Ministries from the Hordes of Looters," *Independent* (London), April 14, 2003, 7:

Iraq's scavengers have thieved and destroyed what they have been allowed to loot and burn by the Americans—and a two-hour drive around Baghdad shows clearly what the US intends to protect. After days of arson and pillage, here's a short but revealing scorecard. US troops have sat back and allowed mobs to wreck and then burn the Ministry of Planning, the Ministry of Education, the Ministry of Irrigation, the Ministry of Trade, the Ministry of Industry, the Ministry of Foreign Affairs, the Ministry of Culture and the Ministry of Information. They did nothing to prevent looters from destroying priceless treasures of Iraq's history in the Baghdad Archaeological Museum and in the museum in the northern city of Mosul, or from looting three hospitals.

The Americans have, though, put hundreds of troops inside two Iraqi ministries that remain untouched—and untouchable—because tanks and armoured personnel carriers and Humvees have been placed inside and outside both institutions. And which ministries proved to be so important for the Americans? Why, the Ministry of Interior, of course—with its vast wealth of intelligence information on Iraq—and the Ministry of Oil.

27. Carlotta Gall, "In Afghanistan, Violence Stalls Renewal Effort," *New York Times*, April 26, 2003, A1. See also Rohde, "U.S. Rebuked on Afghans in Detention," A6.

28. Scott Lindlaw, "Accommodating TV-Friendly Presidential Visit Caused a Few Changes in Navy Carrier's Routine," Associated Press, May 2, 2003.

29. Walter V. Robinson, "1-Year Gap in Bush's Guard Duty: No Record of Airman at Drills in 1972–73," *Boston Globe*, May 23, 2000, A1.

30. David E. Sanger, "Bush Declares 'One Victory in a War on Terror,'" *New York Times*, May 2, 2003, A1.

31. James Harding, "Bush to Hail Triumph but Not Declare a US Victory," *Financial Times* (London), May 1, 2003, 8.

32. Quoted in John R. MacArthur, "In the Psychological Struggle, Nations Wield Their Weapons of Mass Persuasion," *Boston Globe*, March 9, 2003, D12.

33. General Tommy Franks, *Sunday Morning*, CBS, March 23, 2003.

34. "'Non' Campaigner Chirac Ready to Address French," *Daily Mail* (London), March 20, 2003, 13.

35. Robert J. McCartney, "Germany Stops Short of Saying 'I Told You So': Opposition to War Vindicated, Officials Say," *Washington Post*, April 3, 2003, A33: "Although Germany formally opposes the war, it is supporting the U.S. effort through such steps as overflight rights and special security at U.S. bases in Germany. Officials say Germany is doing more for the war than any country except Britain." See also Giles Tremlett and John Hooper, "War in the Gulf: Clampdown on Coverage of Returning Coffins," *Guardian* (London), March 27, 2003, 3.

36. Judy Dempsey and Robert Graham, "Paris Gives First Signs of Support to Coalition," *Financial Times* (London), April 4, 2003, 4.

37. Interfax, "Putin Wants US Victory," *Hobart Mercury* (Australia), April 4, 2003.

38. Morton Abramowitz, "Turkey and Iraq, Act II," *Wall Street Journal*, January 16, 2003, A12.

39. Noam Chomsky, *Hegemony or Survival: America's Quest for Global Dominance* (New York: Metropolitan Books, 2004), 131.

40. Angelique Chrisafis et al., "Millions Worldwide Rally for Peace," *Guardian* (London), February 17, 2003, 6, http://www.theguardian.com/world/2003/feb/17/politics.uk.

41. Richard W. Stevenson, "Antiwar Protests Fail to Sway Bush on Plans for Iraq," *New York Times*, February 19, 2003, A1.

42. David McDonald and John Pape, "South Africa: Cost Recovery Is Not Sustainable," Africa News, August 30, 2002; David McDonald and John Pape, eds., *Cost Recovery and the Crisis of Service Delivery in South Africa* (London: Zed Press, 2002). See also Ashwin Desai, *We Are the Poors: Community Struggles in Post-Apartheid South Africa* (New York: Monthly Review Press, 2002).

43. "Africa's Engine," *Economist*, January 17, 2004.

44. Betts, "Ciampi Calls for Review of Media Laws," 8. For an overview of Berlusconi's holdings, see Ketupa.net Media Profiles: www.ketupa.net/berlusconi1.htm.

45. Frank Bruni, "Berlusconi, in a Rough Week, Says Only He Can Save Italy," *New York Times*, May 10, 2003, A1.

46. Tim Burt, "Mays on a Charm Offensive: The Clear Channel Chief Is Seeking to Answer His Group's Critics," *Financial Times* (London), October 27, 2003, 27. See also John Dunbar and Aron Pilhofer, "Big Radio Rules in Small Markets," Center for Public Integrity, October 1, 2003, https://www.publicintegrity.org/2003/10/01/6587/big-radio-rules-small-markets.

47. Douglas Jehl, "Across Country, Thousands Gather to Back U.S. Troops and Policy," *New York Times*, March 24, 2003, B15.

48. Frank Rich, "Iraq around the Clock," *New York Times*, March 30, 2003, 2.

49. Bagdikian, *New Media Monopoly*.

50. Tom Shales, "Michael Powell and the FCC: Giving Away the Marketplace of Ideas," *Washington Post*, June 2, 2003, C1; Paul Davidson and David Lieberman, "FCC Eases Rules for Media Mergers," *USA Today*, June 3, 2003, 1A.

51. David Leonhardt, "Bush's Record on Jobs: Risking Comparison to a Republican Ghost," *New York Times*, July 3, 2003, C1.

52. Robert Tanner, "Report Says State Budget Gaps Jumped by Nearly 50 Percent, with Next Year Looking Worse," Associated Press, February 5, 2003.

53. Dana Milbank and Mike Allen, "Bush to Ask Congress for $80 Billion: Estimate of War's Cost Comes as Thousands March in Protest," *Washington Post*, March 23, 2003, A1.

54. Sheryl Gay Stolberg, "Senators' Sons in War: An Army of One," *New York Times*, March 22, 2003, B10. See also David M. Halbfinger and Steven A. Holmes, "Military Mirrors a Working-Class America," *New York Times*, March 30, 2003, A1.

55. Darryl Fears, "Draft Bill Stirs Debate over the Military, Race, and Equity," *Washington Post*, February 4, 2003, A3.

56. David Cole, "Denying Felons Vote Hurts Them, Society," *USA Today*, February 3, 2000, 17A; "From Prison to the Polls," editorial, *Christian Science Monitor*, May 24, 2001, 10.

57. See Cole, "Denying Felons" and sidebar, "Not at the Ballot Box."

58. Kenneth J. Cooper, "In India's Kerala, Quality of Life Is High but Opportunity Is Limited," *Washington Post*, January 3, 1997, A35; Amartya Sen, *Development as Freedom* (New York: Alfred A. Knopf, 1999). See also Fareed Zakaria, "Beyond Money," *New York Times Book Review*, November 28, 1999, 14.

59. Linda Villarosa, "As Black Men Move into Middle Age, Dangers Rise," *New York Times*, September 23, 2002, F1.

60. Amy Goldstein and Dana Milbank, "Bush Joins Admissions Case Fight: U-Mich. Use of Race Is Called 'Divisive,'" *Washington Post*, January 16, 2003, A1; James Harding, "Bush Scrambles to Bolster Civil Rights Credibility," *Financial Times* (London), January 21, 2003, 10.

61. Elizabeth Becker and Richard A. Oppel Jr., "Bechtel Top Contender In Bidding over Iraq," *New York Times*, March 29, 2003, B6.

62. André Verlöy and Daniel Politi, with Aron Pilhofer, "Advisors of Influence: Nine Members of the Defense Policy Board Have Ties to Defense Contractors," Center for Public Integrity, March 28, 2003, https://www.publicintegrity.org/2003/03/28/3157/advisors-influence-nine-members-defense-policy-board-have-ties-defense-contractors.

63. Laura Peterson, "Bechtel Group Inc.," Center for Public Integrity, http://www.publicintegrity.org/wow/bio.aspx?act=pro&ddlC=6.

64. Ibid.

65. Bob Herbert, "Spoils of War," *New York Times*, April 10, 2003, A27.

66. Quoted in ibid.

67. Karen DeYoung and Jackie Spinner, "Contract for Rebuilding of Iraq Awarded to Bechtel: U.S. Firm 1 of 6 Invited to Bid for $680 Million Project," *Washington Post*, April 18, 2003, A23. In December 2003 the contract was raised by $350 million, to $1.03 billion. In January 2004 Bechtel won a contract worth another $1.8 billion. See Elizabeth Douglass and John Hendren, "Bechtel Wins Another Iraq Deal," *Los Angeles Times*, January 7, 2004, C2.

68. Stephen J. Glain, "Bechtel Wins Pact to Help Rebuild Iraq: Closed-Bid Deal Could Total $680M," *Boston Globe*, April 18, 2003, A1.

69. Robin Toner and Neil A. Lewis, "House Passes Terrorism Bill Much Like

Senate's, but with 5-Year Limit," *New York Times*, October 13, 2001, B6.

70. See Cole, *Enemy Aliens*, 57–69.

71. Evelyn Nieves, "Local Officials Rise Up to Defy the Patriot Act," *Washington Post*, April 21, 2003, A1.

72. See Cole, *Enemy Aliens*.

73. Amnesty International, "India: Abuse of the Law in Gujarat: Muslims Detained Illegally in Ahmedabad," November 6, 2003, AI index no. ASA 20/029/2003, https://www.amnesty.org/en/documents/asa20/029/2003/en/. See also "People's Tribunal"; Sanghamitra Chakraborty et al., "Slaves in Draconia: Ordinary Folks—Minors, Farmers, Minorities—Fall Prey to POTA for No Fault of Theirs," *Outlook India*, March 22, 2004.

74. Greg Myre, "Shootout in West Bank Kills an Israeli Soldier and a Palestinian," *New York Times*, March 13, 2003, A5.

75. Wayne Washington, "More Opposition to Detentions in Terror Probe," *Boston Globe*, May 13, 2002, A1; Tamar Lewin, "As Authorities Keep Up Immigration Arrests, Detainees Ask Why They Are Targets," *New York Times*, February 3, 2002, 14.

76. Neil King, Jr., "Bush Officials Draft Broad Plan for Free-Market Economy in Iraq," *Wall Street Journal*, May 1, 2003, A1.

77. Naomi Klein, "Iraq Is Not America's to Sell," *Guardian* (London), November 7, 2003, 27. See also Jeff Madrick, "The Economic Plan for Iraq Seems Long on Ideology, Short on Common Sense," *New York Times*, October 2, 2003, C2.

78. David Usborne, "US Firm Is Hired to Purge Schools of Saddam's Doctrine," *Independent* (London), April 22, 2003, 10; Steve Johnson, "Scramble to Win the Spoils of War," *Financial Times* (London) April 23, 2003, 27; and Paul Richter and Edmund Sanders, "Contracts Go to Allies of Iraq's Chalabi," *Los Angeles Times*, November 7, 2003, A1.

79. Heather Stewart, "Iraq—After the War: Fury at Agriculture Post for US Grain Dealer," *Guardian* (London), April 28, 2003, 11.

80. Alan Cowell, "British Ask What a War Would Mean for Business," *New York Times*, March 18, 2003, W1; "Spoils of War," editorial, *San Francisco Chronicle*, March 29, 2003, A14; Jan Hennop, "S. African Apartheid Victims File Lawsuit in US Court, Name Companies," Agence France-Presse, November 12, 2002; and Nicol Degli Innocenti, "African Workers Launch Dollars 100bn Lawsuit," *Financial Times* (London), October 13, 2003, 9.

81. John Vidal, "Shell Fights Fires as Strife Flares in Delta," *Guardian* (London), September 15, 1999, 15; Vidal, "Oil Wealth Buys Health in Country within a Country," *Guardian* (London), September 16, 1999, 19. See also Ike Okonta and Oronto Douglas, *Where Vultures Feast: Shell, Human Rights, and Oil* (New York: Verso, 2003); Al Gedicks, *Resource Rebels: Native Challenges to Mining and Oil Corporations* (Cambridge, MA: South End, 2001).

82. Tom Brokaw, speaking to Vice Admiral Dennis McGinn, *NBC News Special Report: Target Iraq*, March 19, 2003.

83. Bryan Bender, "Roadblocks Seen in Sept. 11 Inquiry," *Boston Globe*, July 9, 2003, A2. See also Josh Meyer, "Terror Not a Bush Priority before 9/11, Witness Says," *Los Angeles Times*, March 25, 2004, A1; Edward Alden, "Tale of Intelligence Failure Above and Below," *Financial Times* (London), March 26, 2004, 2.

84. Zinn, *A People's History of the United States*. See also Anthony Arnove and Howard Zinn, *Voices of a People's History of the United States* (New York: Seven Stories, 2004).

WHEN THE SAINTS GO MARCHING OUT: THE STRANGE FATE OF MARTIN, MOHANDAS, AND MANDELA

1. See "Democracy: Who Is She When She's at Home?" 160–76 above.

2. "Cong[ress Party] Ploy Fails, Modi Steals the Show in Pain," *Indian Express*, August 16, 2003.

3. Agence France-Presse, "Indian Activists Urge Mandela to Snub Gujarat Government Invite," August 4, 2003; "Guj[arat]–Mandela," Press Trust of India, August 5, 2003; and "Battle for Gujarat's Image Now on Foreign Soil," *Times of India*, August 7, 2003.

4. Agence France-Presse, "Relax, Mandela Isn't Coming, He's Working on a Book," August 5, 2003.

5. Michael Dynes, "Mbeki Can Seize White Farms under New Law," *Times* (London), January 31, 2004, 26.

6. Ibid.

7. Patrick Laurence, "South Africa Fights to Put the Past to Rest," *Irish Times*, December 28, 2000, 57.

8. Anthony Stoppard, "South Africa: Water, Electricity Cutoffs Affect 10 Million," Inter Press Service, March 21, 2002.

9. Henri E. Cauvin, "Hunger in Southern Africa Imperils Lives of Millions," *New York Times*, April 26, 2002, A8; James Lamont, "Nobody Says 'No' to Mandela," *Financial Times* (London), December 10, 2002, 4; and Patrick Laurence, "South Africans Sceptical of Official Data," *Irish Times*, June 6, 2003, 30.

10. See Ashwin Desai, *We Are the Poors: Community Struggles in Post-Apartheid South Africa* (New York: Monthly Review Press, 2002).

11. South African Press Association, "Gauteng Municipalities to Target Service Defaulters," May 4, 1999; Alison Maitland, "Combining to Harness the Power of Private Enterprise," *Financial Times* (London), August 23, 2002, survey: "Sustainable Business," 2.

12. Nicol Degli Innocenti and John Reed, "SA Govt Opposes Reparations

Lawsuit," *Financial Times* (London), May 19, 2003, 15.

13. South African Press Association, "SAfrica Asks US Court to Dismiss Apartheid Reparations Cases," BBC Worldwide Monitoring, July 30, 2003.

14. Martin Luther King, Jr., *A Testament of Hope: The Essential Writings and Speeches of Martin Luther King, Jr.*, ed. James M. Washington (New York: HarperCollins, 1991), 233.

15. Ibid., 233.

16. "Men of Vietnam," *New York Times*, April 9, 1967, Week in Review, 2E. Quoted in Mike Marqusee, *Redemption Song: Muhammad Ali and the Spirit of the Sixties* (New York: Verso, 1999), 217.

17. King, *Testament of Hope*, 245.

18. David M. Halbfinger and Steven A. Holmes, "Military Mirrors a Working-Class America," *New York Times*, March 30, 2003, A1; Darryl Fears, "Draft Bill Stirs Debate over the Military, Race, and Equity," *Washington Post*, February 4, 2003, A3.

19. David Cole, "Denying Felons Vote Hurts Them, Society," *USA Today*, February 3, 2000, 17A; "From Prison to the Polls," editorial, *Christian Science Monitor*, May 24, 2001, 10.

20. King, *Testament of Hope*, 239.

21. Quoted in Marqusee, *Redemption Song*, 218.

22. King, *Testament of Hope*, 250.

23. Marqusee, *Redemption Song*, 1–4, 292.

IN MEMORY OF SHANKAR GUHA NIYOGI

1. Human Rights Watch, "India: Human Rights Developments," *Human Rights Watch World Report 1993*, www.hrw.org/reports/1993/WR93/Asw-06.htm.

DO TURKEYS ENJOY THANKSGIVING?

1. See André Verlöy and Daniel Politi, with Aron Pilhofer, "Advisors of Influence: Nine Members of the Defense Policy Board Have Ties to Defense Contractors," Center for Public Integrity, March 28, 2003, https://www.publicintegrity.org/2003/03/28/3157/advisors-influence-nine-members-defense-policy-board-have-ties-defense-contractors.

2. "Strike Not Your Right Anymore: SC [Supreme Court] to Govt Staff," *Indian Express*, August 7, 2003; "Trade Unions Protest against SC [Supreme Court] Order on Strikes," *Times of India*, August 8, 2003.

3. See "On Citizens' Rights to Express Dissent," in the current volume.

4. Michael Jensen, "Denis Halliday: Iraq Sanctions Are Genocide," *Daily Star*,

Lebanon, July 7, 2000. See also the interview with Halliday and Phyllis Bennis in *Iraq under Siege*, 53–64.

5. Arnove, *Iraq under Siege*, 103–04.

6. Joseph E. Stiglitz, *Globalization and Its Discontents* (New York: W. W. Norton, 2002), 7, 61, 253–54.

7. "World Trade Special Report," *Independent* (London), September 10, 2003, 1; Thompson Ayodele, "Last Chance for Fair Go on Trade," *Australian Financial Review*, September 11, 2003, B63.

8. George Monbiot, *The Age of Consent* (New York: New Press, 2004), 158. See also UN General Assembly, *External Debt Crisis and Development: Report to the Secretary-General*, A/57/253, 2003, 2, https://documents-dds-ny.un.org/doc/UNDOC/GEN/N02/503/65/PDF/N0250365.pdf?OpenElement.

9. The Fifth WTO Ministerial Conference was held in Cancún, Mexico, September 10–14, 2003. Sue Kirchhoff and James Cox, "WTO Talks Break Down, Threatening Future Pact," *USA Today*, September 15, 2003, 1B.

HOW DEEP SHALL WE DIG?

1. Hina Kausar Alam and P. Balu, "J&K [Jammu and Kashmir] Fudges DNA Samples to Cover Up Killings," *Times of India*, March 7, 2002.

2. See "Democracy: Who Is She When She's at Home?" 160–76, above.

3. Somit Sen, "Shooting Turns Spotlight on Encounter Cops," *Times of India*, August 23, 2003.

4. W. Chandrakanth, "Crackdown on Civil Liberties Activists in the Offing?" *Hindu*, October 4, 2003: "Several activists have gone underground fearing police reprisals. Their fears are not unfounded, as the State police have been staging encounters at will. While the police frequently release the statistics on naxalite violence, they avoid mentioning the victims of their own violence. The Andhra Pradesh Civil Liberties Committee (APCLC), which is keeping track of the police killings, has listed more than 4,000 deaths, 2,000 of them in the last eight years alone." See also K. T. Sangameswaran, "Rights Activists Allege Ganglord-Cop Nexus," *Hindu*, October 22, 2003.

5. David Rohde, "India and Kashmir Separatists Begin Talks on Ending Strife," *New York Times*, January 23, 2004, A8; Deutsche Presse-Agentur, "Thousands Missing, Unmarked Graves Tell Kashmir Story," October 7, 2003.

6. Unpublished reports from the Association of Parents of Disappeared People (APDP), Srinagar.

7. See also Edward Luce, "Kashmir's New Leader Promises 'Healing Touch,'" *Financial Times* (London), October 28, 2002, 12.

8. Ray Marcelo, "Anti-Terrorism Law Backed by India's Supreme Court," *Financial Times* (London), December 17, 2003, 2.

9. People's Union for Civil Liberties, "In Jharkhand All the Laws of the Land Are Replaced by POTA," Delhi, India, May 2, 2003, www.pucl.org/Topics /Law/2003/poto-jharkhand.htm.

10. "People's Tribunal Highlights Misuse of POTA," *Hindu*, March 18, 2004.

11. "People's Tribunal." See also "Human Rights Watch Ask Centre to Repeal POTA," Press Trust of India, September 8, 2002.

12. Leena Misra, "240 POTA Cases, All against Minorities," *Times of India*, September 15, 2003; "People's Tribunal." The *Times of India* misreported the testimony presented. As the Press Trust of India article notes, in Gujarat "the only non-Muslim in the list is a Sikh, Liversingh Tej Singh Sikligar, who figured in it for an attempt on the life of Surat lawyer Hasmukh Lalwala, and allegedly hung himself in a police lock-up in Surat in April [2003]." On Gujarat, see "Democracy: Who Is She," above.

13. "A Pro-Police Report," *Hindu*, March 20, 2004; Amnesty International, "India: Report of the Malimath Committee on Reforms of the Criminal Justice System: Some Comments," September 19, 2003 (ASA 20/025/2003).

14. "J&K [Jammu and Kashmir] Panel Wants Draconian Laws Withdrawn," *Hindu*, March 23, 2003. See also South Asian Human Rights Documentation Center, "Armed Forces Special Powers Act: A Study in National Security Tyranny," November 1995.

15. "Growth of a Demon: Genesis of the Armed Forces (Special Powers) Act, 1958" and related documents in *Manipur Update*, December 1999.

16. On the lack of any convictions for the massacres in Gujarat, see Edward Luce, "Master of Ambiguity," *Financial Times* (London), April 3–4, 2004, 16. On the March 31, 1997, murder of Chandrashekhar Prasad, see Andrew Nash, "An Election at JNU," *Himāl*, December 2003. For more information on the additional crimes listed here, see 287–90, above.

17. N. A. Mujumdar, "Eliminate Hunger Now, Poverty Later," *Business Line*, January 8, 2003.

18. "Foodgrain Exports May Slow Down This Fiscal [Year]," *India Business Insight*, June 2, 2003; "India—Agriculture Sector: Paradox of Plenty," *Business Line*, June 26, 2001; and Ranjit Devraj, "Farmers Protest against Globalization," Inter Press Service, January 25, 2001.

19. Utsa Patnaik, "Falling Per Capita Availability of Foodgrains for Human Consumption in the Reform Period in India," *Akhbar* 2 (October 2001); P. Sainath, "Have Tornado, Will Travel," *Hindu Magazine*, August 18, 2002; Sylvia Nasar, "Profile: The Conscience of the Dismal Science," *New York Times*, January 9, 1994, 8; and Maria Misra, "Heart of Smugness: Unlike Belgium, Britain Is Still Complacently Ignoring the Gory Cruelties of Its Empire," *Guardian* (London), July 23, 2002, 15. See also Utsa Patnaik, "On Measuring 'Famine' Deaths: Different Criteria for Socialism and Capitalism?" *Akhbar* 6 (November–December 1999), www.indowindow.com/akhbar/article.php

?article=74&category=8&issue=9.

20. Amartya Sen, *Development as Freedom* (New York: Alfred A. Knopf, 1999).

21. "The Wasted India," *Statesman* (India), February 17, 2001; "Child-Blain," *Statesman* (India), November 24, 2001.

22. Utsa Patnaik, "The Republic of Hunger," lecture, Jawaharlal Nehru University, New Delhi, April 10, 2004, macroscan.com/fet/apro4 /fet210404Republic_Hunger.htm.

23. Praful Bidwai, "India amidst Serious Agrarian Crisis," *Central Chronicle* (Bhopal), April 9, 2004.

24. See "Power Politics," 76–105, above.

25. See Mike Davis, *Late Victorian Holocausts: El Niño Famines and the Making of the Third World* (New York: Verso, 2002).

26. Among other sources, see Edwin Black, *IBM and the Holocaust: The Strategic Alliance between Nazi Germany and America's Most Powerful Corporation* (New York: Three Rivers, 2003).

27. "For India Inc., Silence Protects the Bottom Line," *Times of India*, February 17, 2003; "CII Apologises to Modi," *Hindu*, March 7, 2003.

28. In May 2004, the right-wing BJP-led coalition was not just voted out of power, it was humiliated by the Indian electorate. None of the political pundits had predicted this decisive vote against communalism and neoliberalism's economic "reforms." Yet even as we celebrate, we know that on every major issue other than overt Hindu nationalism—nuclear bombs, Big Dams, privatization—the newly elected Congress Party and the BJP have no major ideological differences. We know that it was the legacy of the Congress that led us to the horror of the BJP. Still we celebrated, because surely a darkness has passed. Or has it? Even before it formed a government, the Congress made overt reassurances that "reforms" would continue. Exactly what kind of reforms, we'll have to wait and see. Fortunately, the Congress will be hobbled by the fact that it needs the support of left parties—the only parties to be overtly (if ineffectively) critical of the reforms—to make up a majority in order to form a government. The left parties have been given an unprecedented mandate. Hopefully, things will change. A little. It's been a pretty hellish six years.

29. India was the only country to abstain on December 22, 2003, from UN General Assembly Resolution, "Protection of Human Rights and Fundamental Freedoms While Countering Terrorism," A/RES/58/187, http://www.un .org/en/ga/search/view_doc.asp?symbol=A/RES/58/187&Area=UNDOC. Quoted in Amnesty International India, "Security Legislation and State Accountability: A Presentation for the POTA People's Hearing, March 13–14, New Delhi."

BREAKING THE NEWS

1.Statement of Mohammad Afzal to the Court under Section 313 Criminal Procedure Code, September 2002.

2. "'Terrorists Were Close-Knit Religious Fanatics'" and "Police Impress with Speed But Show Little Evidence," both published in *The Times of India*, December 21, 2001.

3. Judgment of the Supreme Court of India on Mohammad Afzal v. the State (NCT of Delhi), August 4, 2005.

4. "Book on December 13 Parliament Attack," ptinews.com, December 13, 2006.

5. Speech made by Manmohan Singh (at the time the leader of the opposition, and later prime minister) on December 18, 2001, in the Rajya Sabha. See the full text in Rajya Sabha, Official Day's Proceedings, December 18, 2001, paragraph 4, 430.

6. Davinder Kumar, "The Ham Burger—Did Delhi Police Sleuths Jump the Gun with the Wrong One?" *Outlook*, January 21, 2002.

7. Priya Ranjan Dasmunshi, "'Advaniji Too Was Confused,'" *Outlook*, December 24, 2001.

8. For the full text of the Parliament attack charge sheet, see Nirmalangshu Mukherji, *December 13: Terror over Democracy* (New Delhi: Promilla, 2005), Annexure 1.

9. See "Scandal," *Economist*, August 28, 1999; and Sarah Delaney and Michael Evans, "Britain Joined Plot to Overthrow a Communist Italian Government," *Times* (London), January 14, 2008, 31. On the political context, see Noam Chomsky, *Turning the Tide: U.S. Intervention in Central America and the Struggle for Peace*, 2nd ed. (Cambridge, MA: South End Press, 1987), 67, 195.

10. "Show No Mercy, Hang Afzal: BJP," *Indian Express*, November 23, 2006.

11. Chandan Mitra, editor of the *Pioneer* newspaper, reviewed the book *13 December: A Reader* in *India Today* (January 22, 2007, "Trapped in Half-Truths"). An edited version of my letter in response was published in the Letters section of *India Today* (February 5, 2007). Here is the full text:

> Sir—This is regarding Chandan Mitra's review of the book *13 December: A Reader*. An interesting choice of reviewer—someone who has brazenly falsified facts on the Parliament attack case and has been exposed for doing so in the book he reviews. He asks for a "source" for my statement: "On December 12, 2001, at an informal meeting, Prime Minister Atal Bihari Vajpayee warned of an imminent attack on Parliament."
>
> Please refer to the speech made by the Prime Minster Manmohan Singh (then leader of the opposition) on December 18, 2001, in the Rajya Sabha. He said: "Yet, it is a fact that an attack on parliament was quite anticipated . . . In fact, one day before this attack took place, i.e., on 12th December, while speaking at Mumbai, the Hon. Prime Minister himself had referred to the existence of this threat, such a threat to our Parliament."

In his own article, "Celebrating Treason" (*Pioneer*, October 7, 2006) cited in my Introduction, Chandan Mitra says, "Afzal Guru was one of the terrorists who stormed Parliament House on December 13th 2001, and it was he who first opened fire on security personnel, apparently killing three of the six who died protecting the majesty of democracy that morning."

None of the three court judgments sentencing Mohammad Afzal to death have accused him (leave alone found him guilty) of killing anybody, of being directly involved in the attack on Parliament, or indeed of being anywhere near the parliament building on December 13, 2001. Even the police charge sheet clearly states that at the time of the attack, Afzal was somewhere else. The Supreme Court judgment explicitly says there was no direct evidence against him, nor any evidence that he was a member of a terrorist organization. Can Chandan Mitra cite a source for his outlandish assertion? Or tell us how he knows what the police and the courts do not? And why he has suppressed this "evidence" for all these years?

See Chandan Mitra, "Celebrating Treason," *Pioneer*, October 7, 2006.

12. Swapan Dasgupta, "You Can't Be Good to Evil," *Pioneer*, October 1, 2006.

13. Siddhartha Gautam, "The Other Side of Afzal's Surrender," CNN-IBN, November 27, 2006. See also Narendra Nag, "Afzal Gets Mixed Bag from Politcos," CNN-IBN, November 28, 2006.

14. Siddhartha Gautam, "Tortured, but Kept Alive for a Deal," CNN-IBN, November 27, 2006.

15. Dravinder Singh, interview by Parvaiz Bukhari, October 2006, in Srinagar, unpublished manuscript, provided in personal correspondence to the author dated March 7, 2009.

16. Gautam, "Tortured, but Kept Alive for a Deal."

17. Gautam, "The Other Side of Afzal's Surrender."

18. "Advani Criticizes Delay in Afzal Execution," *Hindu*, November 13, 2006.

19. See Judgment of the Supreme Court of India on Mohammad Afzal vs. the State (NCT of Delhi), August 4, 2005.

"AND HIS LIFE SHOULD BECOME EXTINCT"

1. The high court claimed that "the fire power was awesome enough to engage a battalion and had the attack succeeded, the entire building with all inside would have perished." See the court's verdict of October 29, 2003. For details of the Parliament attack and the subsequent trial, see Nandita Haksar, *Framing Geelani, Hanging Afzal: Patriotism in the Time of Terror* (New Delhi: Promilla, 2007); Praful Bidwai et al., *13 December: A Reader: The Strange Case of the Attack on the Indian Parliament*, revised and updated ed. (New Delhi: Penguin Books India, 2007); Syed Bismillah Geelani, *Manufacturing Terrorism: Kashmiri Encounters with Media and the Law* (New Delhi: Promilla, 2006); Mukherji, *December 13;*

People's Union for Democratic Rights, "Balancing Act: High Court Judgment on the 13th December 2001 Case," New Delhi, December 19, 2003; and People's Union for Democratic Rights, "Trial of Errors: A Critique of the POTA Court Judgment on the 13 December Case," New Delhi, February 15, 2003.

2. Judge S. N. Dhingra, Judgment of the Special Prevention of Terrorism Act Court, Mohammad Afzal vs. the State (NCT of Delhi), December 16, 2002.

3. "Statement Made by Shri L. K. Advani, Union Home Minister on Tuesday, the 18th December, 2001, in Lok Sabha in Connection with the Terrorist Attack on Parliament House," Ministry of External Affairs, https://www.mea.gov.in/articles-in-indian-media.htm?dtl/16856Satement+made+by+Shri+LK+Advani+Union+Home+Minister+on+Tuesday+the+18th+December+2001+In+Lok+Sabha+in+Connection+with+the+terrorist+attack+on+Parliament+House.

4. See Susan Milligan, "Despite Diplomacy, Kashmir Troops Brace," *Boston Globe*, January 20, 2002, A1; Farah Stockman and Anthony Shadid, "Sanctions Fueling Ire between India, Pakistan," *Boston Globe*, December 28, 2001, A3; Zahid Hussai, "Tit-for-Tat Bans Raise Tension on Kashmir," *Times* (London), December 28, 2001; and Ghulam Hasnain and Nicholas Rufford, "Pakistan Raises Kashmir Nuclear Stakes," *Sunday Times* (London), December 30, 2001.

5. Dhingra, Judgment of the Special Prevention of Terrorism Act Court.

6. See Somini Sengupta, "Indian Opinion Splits on Call for Execution," *International Herald Tribune*, October 9, 2006; and Somini Sengupta and Hari Kumar, "Death Sentence in Terror Attack Puts India on Trial," *New York Times*, October 10, 2006, A3.

7. "Advani Criticizes Delay in Afzal Execution," *Hindu*, November 13, 2006.

8. Maqbool Butt, a founder of the Jammu and Kashmir Liberation Front, was hanged in New Delhi on February 11, 1984. See "India Hangs Kashmiri for Slaying Banker," *New York Times*, February 12, 1984, sec. 1, 7.

9. Lakshmi Balakrishnan, "Reliving a Nightmare," *Hindu*, December 12, 2002, 2. See also Shuddhabrata Sengupta, "Media Trials and Courtroom Tribulations," in Bidwai et al., *13 December*, 46.

10. Press Trust of India, "S[upreme]C[ourt] Allows Zee [TV] to Air Film on Parliament Attack," IndiaInfo.com, December 13, 2002.

11. "Five Bullets Hit Geelani, Says Forensic Report," *Hindustan Times*, February 25, 2005.

12. See "Police Force," *Indian Express*, July 15, 2002; "Editor's Guild Seeks Fair Trial for Iftikhar," *Indian Express*, June 20, 2002; and "Kashmir Time Staffer's Detention Issue Raised in Lok Sabha," *Business Recorder*, August 4, 2002.

13. Iftikar Gilani, *My Days in Prison* (New Delhi: Penguin Books India, 2005). In 2008 the Urdu translation of this book received one of India's highest literary awards from the Sahitya Akademi, http://www.indianexpress.com/news/iftikhar-gilani-wins-sahitya-akademiaward/424871.

14. Doordarshan Television (New Delhi), "Court Releases Kashmir Times Journalist from Detention," BBC Monitoring South Asia, January 13, 2003.

15. Statement of Sayed Abdul Rahman Geelani, New Delhi, August 4, 2005; http://www.revolutionarydemocracy.org/ parl/geelanistate.htm. See also Basharat Peer, "Victims of December 13," *Guardian* (London), July 5, 2003, 29.

16. "Special Cell, ACP Face Charges of Excesses, Torture," *Hindustan Times*, July 31, 2005. Singh was later murdered, in March 2008, in what is widely believed to be an underworld property dispute. See Press Trust of India, "Encounter Specialist Rajbir Singh Shot Dead," *Hindustan Times*, March 25, 2008.

17. See the articles "'Terrorists Were Close-Knit Religious Fanatics,'" and "Police Impress with Speed But Show Little Evidence," *Times of India*, December 21, 2001.

18. Emily Wax and Rama Lakshmi, "Indian Official Points to Pakistan," *Washington Post*, December 6, 2008, A8.

19. Mukherji, *December 13*, 43.

20. Statement of Mohammad Afzal to the Court under Section 313 Criminal Procedure Code in the Court of Shri S. N. Dhingra, ASJ, New Delhi S/V Afzal Guru and Others, FIR 417/01, September 2002, http://www.revolutionarydemocracy .org/afzal/azfal6.htm.

21. Aijaz Hussain, "Killers in Khaki," *India Today*, June 11, 2007. See also "PUDR Picks Several Holes in Police Version on Pragati Maidan Encounter," *Hindu*, May 3, 2005; People's Union for Democratic Rights, "An Unfair Verdict: A Critique of the Red Fort Judgment," New Delhi, December 22, 2006; and "Close Encounter: A Report on Police Shoot-Outs in Delhi," New Delhi, October 21, 2004.

22. See "A New Kind of War," *Asia Week*, April 7, 2000, and Ranjit Dev Raj, "Tough Talk Continues Despite Peace Demands," Inter Press Service, April 19, 2000.

23. See "'Five Killed after Chattisinghpora Massacre Were Civilians,'" Press Trust of India, July 16, 2002, and "Judicial Probe Ordered into Chattisinghpora Sikh Massacre," Press Trust of India, October 31, 2000.

24. Public Commission on Human Rights, "State of Human Rights in Jammu and Kashmir 1990–2005" (Srinagar: Jammu and Kashmir Coalition of Civil Society, 2006), 21.

25. "Probe Into Alleged Fake Killings Ordered," *Daily Excelsior* (Janipura), August 30, 2005.

26. M. L. Kak, "Army Quiet on Fake Surrender by Ultras," *Tribune* (Chandigarh), December 14, 2006.

27. "Appeal to the President of India," March 5, 2002, https://www.sabrang. com/gujarat/statement/statement.htm#SAHMAT%20CALLS%20MODI %20A%20%E2%80%98MASS%20MURDERER; Mark Oliver and Luke Harding, "He Is Blamed for the Death of 2,000 Muslims in India. So Why Is

Narendra Modi in Wembley?" *The Guardian*, August 18, 2003. "Genocide," Communalism Combat, March–April 2002, https://sabrang.com/cc/archive/2002/marapril/edinote.htm; Amnesty Internationa, "Equal Protection to All Citizens Must be Ensured in Gujarat," March 1, 2002.

28. "Storm over a Sentence," *Statesman* (India), February 12, 2003.

29. The analysis that follows is based on the judgments of the Supreme Court of India, the Delhi High Court, and the Prevention of Terrorism Act Trial Court cited earlier.

30. "As Mercy Petition Lies with Kalam, Tihar Buys Rope for Afzal Hanging," *Indian Express*, October 16, 2006.

CUSTODIAL CONFESSIONS, THE MEDIA, AND THE LAW

1. Somini Sengupta, "Indian Opinion Splits on Call for Execution," *New York Times*, October 9, 2006.

2. See the letter of N. D. Pancholi to NDTV, December 26, 2006, http://www.sacw.net/free/pancholitoNDTV.html.

3. Despite the court judgments, the media continues to publish custodial confessions. See Mihir Srivastava, "Inside the Mind of the Bombers," *India Today*, October 2, 2008.

4. Barkha Dutt, "Death of the Middle Ground," *Hindustan Times*, December 16, 2006.

5. Maloy Krishna Dhar, *Open Secrets: India's Intelligence Unveiled* (New Delhi: Manas Publications, 2005), 20.

LISTENING TO GRASSHOPPERS: GENOCIDE, DENIAL, AND CELEBRATION

1. One and a half million is the number of Armenians who were systematically murdered by the Ottoman Empire in the genocide in Anatolia in the spring of 1915. The Armenians, the largest Christian minority living under Islamic Turkic rule in the area, had lived in Anatolia for more than 2,500 years. Figures given by Peter Balakian, talk at the World Affairs Forum, San Francisco, California, November 2, 2003. Audio and transcript available from Alternative Radio, http://www.alternativeradio.org/programs/BALP 002.shtml.

2. Araxie Barsamian, speaking at the University of Colorado at Denver, Colorado, September 26, 1986. Audio and transcript available from Alternative Radio, http://www.alternativeradio.org/programs/BAAR-FISR001.shtml.

3. See Susanne Fowler, "Turkey, a Touchy Critic, Plans to Put a Novel on Trial," *New York Times*, September 15, 2006, A4, and Nicholas Birch, "Speaking

Out in the Shadow of Death," *Guardian* (London), April 7, 2007, 30.

4. "Appeal to the President of India," March 5, 2002, https://www.sabrang.com /gujarat/statement/statement.htm#SAHMAT%20CALLS%20MODI%20A %20%E2%80%98MASS%20MURDERER%E2%80%99; Mark Oliver and Luke Harding, "He Is Blamed for the Death of 2,000 Muslims in India. So Why is Narendra Modi in Wembley?" *The Guardian*, August 18, 2003; "Genocide," Communalism Combat, March–April 2002, https://sabrang.com/cc/archive /2002/marapril/edinote.htm; Amnesty Internationa, "Equal Protection to All Citizens Must be Ensured in Gujarat," March 1, 2002.

5. See Dionne Bunsha, *Scarred*: *Experiments with Violence in Gujarat* (New Delhi: Penguin Books India, 2006).

6. "Tata, Ambani Bag Gujarat Garima Awards," *Business Standard* (India), January 13, 2004.

7. Pankaj Mishra, "A Mediocre Goddess," *New Statesman*, April 9, 2001.

8. United Nations Convention on the Prevention and Punishment of the Crime of Genocide, approved and proposed for signature and ratification or accession by General Assembly resolution 260 A (III) of December 9, 1948, and entered into force on January 12, 1951.

9. Frank Chalk and Kurt Jonassohn, *The History and Sociology of Genocide: Analyses and Case Studies* (New Haven: Yale University Press, 1990), 23.

10. Quoted in Howard Zinn, *A People's History of the United States: 1492– Present* (New York: Harper Perennial Classics, 2001), 15.

11. Babu Bajrangi, "'After Killing Them, I Felt Like Maharana Pratap,'" *Tehelka*, September 1, 2007.

12. Talk by Robert J. Lifton, Center for the Study of Violence and Human Survival, John Jay College, City University of New York, January 29, 1996. See also Robert J. Lifton and Greg Mitchell, *Hiroshima in America: A Half Century of Denial* (New York: Harper Perennial, 1996).

13. See Mahmood Mamdani, "The Politics of Naming: Genocide, Civil War, Insurgency," *London Review of Books*, March 8, 2007.

14. See Anthony Arnove, ed., *Iraq Under Siege: The Deadly Impact of Sanctions and War* (Cambridge, MA: South End Press, 2002), 63 and 145.

15. See Rachel L. Swarns, "Overshadowed, Slavery Debate Boils in Durban," *New York Times*, September 6, 2001, A1, and Chris McGreal Durban, "Africans Back Down at the UN Race Talks," *Observer* (London), September 9, 2001, 16.

16. See Sven Linqvist, *A History of Bombing* (New York: New Press, 2003); Marilyn B. Young and Yuki Tanaka, eds., *Bombing Civilians: A Twentieth-Century History* (New York: New Press, 2009); and Gabriel Kolko, *Century of War: Politics, Conflict, and Society since 1914* (New York: New Press, 1995).

17. See Marilyn B. Young, *The Vietnam Wars: 1945–1990* (New York: Harper Perennial, 1991); Stephen Kinzer, *Overthrow: America's Century of Regime Change from Hawaii to Iraq* (New York: Times Books, 2007); and Chalmers

Johnson's trilogy, *Blowback: The Costs and Consequences of American Empire*, 2nd ed.; *The Sorrows of Empire: Militarism, Secrecy, and the End of the Republic;* and *Nemesis: The Last Days of the American Republic* (New York: Metropolitan Books, 2004, 2004, and 2008).

18. Robert McNamara, interview by Errol Morris, in *The Fog of War: Eleven Lessons from the Life of Robert S. McNamara* (Sony Pictures, 2004), 95 minutes, http://www.errolmorris.com/film/fow_transcript.html.

19. See Carl Hulse, "U.S. and Turkey Thwart Armenian Genocide Bill," *New York Times*, October 26, 2007, A12. Similar resolutions have also been consistently defeated in the Knesset in Israel. See, for example, Gideon Alon, "Knesset Opts Not to Discuss Armenian Genocide at P[rime] M[inister]'s Request," *Ha'aretz*, March 15, 2007.

20. See Heinz Heger, *The Men with the Pink Triangle: The True Life-and-Death Story of Homosexuals in the Nazi Death Camps*, 2nd ed. (New York: Alyson Books, 1994); Daniel Guérin, *The Brown Plague: Travels in Late Weimar and Early Nazi Germany* (Durham, NC: Duke University Press, 1994); Guenter Lewy, *The Nazi Persecution of the Gypsies* (New York: Oxford University Press, 2000); and Catherine Merridale, *Ivan's War: Life and Death in the Red Army, 1939–1945* (New York: Picador, 2007).

21. Balakian, World Affairs Forum. See also Peter Balakian, *The Burning Tigris: The Armenian Genocide and America's Response* (New York: Harper Perennial, 2004).

22. Sven Lindqvist, *"Exterminate All the Brutes": One Man's Odyssey into the Heart of Darkness and the Origins of European Genocide* (New York: New Press, 1997).

23. See Adam Hochschild, *King Leopold's Ghost: A Story of Greed, Terror, and Heroism in Colonial Africa* (New York: Mariner Books, 1999). Leonard Courtney, president of the Royal Statistical Society in London, gave a lecture titled "An Experiment in Commercial Expansion" on December 13, 1898, at the society's annual meeting. See "Colonial Lessons from the Congo Free State," *Public Opinion* (New York), January 5, 1899, 11.

24. Lindqvist, *"Exterminate All the Brutes."*

25. See "RSS Aims for a Hindu Nation," BBC News, March 10, 2003, and Press Trust of India, "RSS Might Get Trendy Uniform Next Year," Rediff. com, July 23, 2004.

26. Leena Misra, "240 POTA Cases, All against Minorities," *Times of India*, September 15, 2003; "People's Tribunal Highlights Misuse of POTA," March 18, 2004. The *Times of India* misreported the testimony presented. As the Press Trust of India article notes, in Gujarat, "The only non-Muslim in the list is a Sikh, Liversingh Tej Singh Sikligar, who figured in it for an attempt on the life of Surat lawyer Hasmukh Lalwala, and allegedly hung himself in a police lock-up in Surat in April [2003]."

27. On the violence in Nandigram, West Bengal, see the archives of the site Sanhati: Fighting Neoliberalism in Bengal and Beyond, http://sanhati.com/november-2007-violence-in-nandigram-archive-of-events.

28. Quoted in Lindqvist, *"Exterminate All the Brutes,"* 154. See also Woodruff D. Smith, "Friedrich Ratzel and the Origins of Lebensraum," *German Studies Review* 3, no. 1 (February 1980): 1–68.

29. Lindqvist, *"Exterminate All the Brutes,"* xx.

30. Mike Davis, *Late Victorian Holocausts: El Niño Famines and the Making of the Third World* (London: Verso, 2002), 7.

31. Neeta Lal, "Malnutrition Rampant, May Trigger Crisis," *India Together*, April 2, 2007.

32. See "The Greater Common Good," 25–75, above; it was also published in Arundhati Roy, *The Algebra of Infinite Justice* (New Delhi: Penguin Books India), 2001; and Roy, *The Cost of Living* (New York: Modern Library, 1999). See also R. Rangachari et al., "Large Dams: India's Experience," World Commission on Dams, November 2002.

33. See "Chhattisgarh Govt. Risking Civilian Lives Through Anti-Naxal Camps: ACHR," *Hindustan Times*, March 17, 2006.

34. See Aman Sethi, "New Battle Zones," *Frontline* (India), September 8–21, 2007.

35. Lifton, "Turkish Denial of Armenian Genocide," City University of New York, January 29, 1996.

36. Shah Rukh Khan, interview by Namrata Joshi, "'Films Are for Entertainment, Messages Are for the Post Office,'" *Outlook*, October 22, 2007.

37. Ramachandra Guha, *India after Gandhi: The History of the World's Largest Democracy* (New York: Harper Perennial, 2008), 743. See the review by Sanjay Kak, "A Chronicle of 'India Shining,'" *Biblio: A Review of Books*, July–August 2007, 1–3.

38. "The Denial of an American Visa Is a Political Boon for Narendra Modi," *Economist*, March 26, 2005, quoting Vir Sanghvi.

39. Amitabh Bachchan, "'India Poised' Anthem," https://www.youtube.com/watch?v=wP-TwHwLc98.

40. Lifton, "Turkish Denial of Armenian Genocide," City University of New York, January 29, 1996.

41. Sudeep Chakravarti, *Red Sun: Travels in Naxalite Country* (New Delhi: Penguin Books India, 2007).

42. Quoted in "Naxal March: Timebomb Ticks at Home," *Hindustan Times*, August 8, 2006.

43. Hartosh Singh Bal, "Stamp Out Naxals," *Mail Today*, January 10, 2008.

AZADI

1. See Yaroslav Trofimov, "A New Tack in Kashmir," *Wall Street Journal*, December 15, 2008, A1.

2. Human Rights Watch, "India's Secret Army in Kashmir: New Patterns of Abuse Emerge in the Conflict," Washington, DC, May 1996. See also reports by the International Crisis Group (http://www.crisisgroup.org) and Amnesty International (http://www.amnesty.org).

3. See Sonia Jabbar, "Politics of Pilgrimage," *Hindustan Times*, June 29, 2008.

4. Gautam Navlakha, "State Cultivation of the Amarnath Yatra," *Economic and Political Weekly* (Mumbai), July 26, 2008. See also Navlakha, "Jammu and Kashmir: Pilgrim's Progress Causes Regression," *Economic and Political Weekly* (Mumbai), July 8, 2006.

5. See Indo-Asian News Service, "Amid Amarnath Land Row, Pilgrimage Keeps Its Peace," *Hindustan Times*, August 14, 2008; and Indo-Asian News Service, "Muslims Holding Makeshift Kitchens for Stranded Amarnath Pilgrims," *Hindustan Times*, July 1, 2008.

6. Andrew Buncombe, "Kashmir Tries to Defuse Shrine Riots by Revoking Deal," *Independent* (London), July 2, 2008, 26.

7. Indo-Asian News Service, "Amid Amarnath Land Row, Pilgrimage Keeps Its Peace."

8. "On Punjab–J&K Border, Parivar Pitches Tent, Calls the Shots," *Indian Express*, August 6, 2008 (about Jammu and Kashmir). See also Indo-Asian News Service, "Land Row Makes Kashmir Economy Bleed," *Hindustan Times*, August 7, 2008.

9. "'No Highway Blockade, It's Only Propaganda,'" *Times of India*, August 17, 2008; "Gov[ernmen]t Counters Blockade Propaganda with Bulletins," *Economic Times* (India), August 14, 2008; and Karan Thapar, "Jammu Discriminated and Kashmir Favoured: Jaitley," CNN-IBN, August 24, 2008.

10. "Hawk Geelani Says He's 'Sole' Azadi Leader, Then Apologises," *Indian Express*, August 19, 2008. See also interview with Rediff, "'I Do Not Want to Be Compared with Osama [bin Laden],'" Rediff News, August 25, 2008.

11. Aijaz Hussain, "Kashmiri Muslims March in Call for Freedom," Associated Press, August 17, 2008, and "Indian Kashmir Separatists Announce Protests to Continue Till Demands Met," BBC Monitoring South Asia, August 17, 2008.

12. "Protestors March to UN Office in Kashmir Capital Srinagar," Deutsche Presse-Agentur, August 18, 2008.

NINE IS NOT ELEVEN
(AND NOVEMBER ISN'T SEPTEMBER)

1. Rezaul H. Laskar, "India May Carry Out Surgical Strikes on Pak[istan], Warns McCain," Press Trust of India, December 7, 2008.

2. Yossi Melman, "Mumbai Terrorists Badly Tortured Chabad House Victims," Ha'aretz, December 26, 2008.

3. Quoted in Patrick French, "They Hate Us—and India Is Us," New York Times, December 8, 2008, A29.

4. Quoted in Mohammad Shah, "'Killing Hindus' Better than Dialogue with India: Lashkar-e-Taiba Chief," Agence France-Presse, April 3, 2003.

5. Bajrangi, "'After Killing Them, I Felt Like Maharana Pratap.'"

6. Golwalkar, We, or, Our Nationhood Defined, 35, 37, and 62, and quoted in William Dalrymple, "India: The War Over History," New York Review of Books, April 7, 2005.

7. Angana Chatterji, "Hindutva's Violent History," Tehelka, September 13, 2008. See also Hari Kumar and Heather Timmons, "Violence in India Is Fueled by Religious and Economic Divide," New York Times, September 4, 2008, A6.

8. "Situation in Kandhamal Out of Control: Archbishop," Hindu, September 29, 2008.

9. Wax and Lakshmi, "Indian Official Points to Pakistan."

10. Damien McElroy, "At Least Two More Terrorists Are on the Run, Police Admit," Sunday Telegraph (London), December 7, 2008, 30.

11. V. K. Shashikumar, "Recruited by RAW, Trained by Army: LTTE," CNNIBN, July 2, 2006, http://ibnlive.in.com/news/recruitedby-raw-trained -by-army-ltte/14462-3-1.html.

12. Emily Wax, "Calls Shed Light on Gunmen's Motives," Washington Post, December 16, 2008, A14.

13. Suketu Mehta, "What They Hate about Mumbai," New York Times, November 28, 2008, A23.

14. See "Batla House Residents Speak Out," Hindustan Times, September 27, 2008, and Hamari Jamatia, "Jamia Teachers' Group Points Finger at Batla House Encounter," IndianExpress.com, February 21, 2009. See also Jamia Teachers' Solidarity Group, "'Encounter' at Batla House: Unanswered Questions," February 24, 2009, http://www.sacw.net/article691.html.

15. L. K. Advani, Inauguration of National Seminar on Terrorism, New Delhi, October 4, 2008. See also "Advani Cautions against President's Rule," Hindu, October 6, 2008, and "Braveheart Delhi Cop Sharma Laid to Rest," Times of India, September 20, 2008.

16. Parul Abrol, "CBI Wants Action Against Delhi Police Special Officer," Indo-Asian News Service, November 18, 2008.

17. United News of India, "Malegaon Bomb Blast," November 14, 2008.

18. F. Ahmed, "ATS Is Lying, Hindus Can't Be Terrorists: V. K. Malhotra," Indo-Asian News Service, November 17, 2008.

19. Press Trust of India, "Togadia Denies Links with Malegaon Blast Case: CBI Too Distances Itself," *Financial Express*, November 25, 2008.

20. See Shoma Chaudhury, "Is Kali a Wimp?" *Tehelka*, December 13, 2008.

21. See Asian Centre for Human Rights, "Torture in India 2008: A State of Denial," New Delhi, India, June 2008; "Is Torture Ever Justified?" *Economist*, September 22, 2007. The United Nations Convention against Torture and Other Cruel, Inhuman or Degrading Treatment or Punishment was opened for discussion on February 4, 1985.

DEMOCRACY'S FAILING LIGHT

1. See P. Chidambaram's interview with Shoma Chaudhury and Shantanu Guha Ray, *Tehelka* 5, no. 21 (May 31, 2008).

2. P. Sainath, "Neo-Liberal Terrorism in India: The Largest Wave of Suicides in History," *CounterPunch*, February 12, 2009.

3. See United Nations Children's Fund (UNICEF), *The State of Asia-Pacific's Children 2008* (May 2008), https://www.unicef.org/publications/files/SOAPC_2008_080408.pdf .

4. For a detailed account of the Mumbai riots of 1993, see the Report of the Justice B. N. Srikrishna Commission of Enquiry, http://www.sabrang.com/srikrish/sri%20main.htm.

5. Sachar Committee Report, November 2006.

6. Arundhati Roy, "The End of Imagination," 1–23, above.

7. See the Rejoinder Affidavit of the Citizens for Justice and Peace through its president vs The Dist. Collector, Ahmedabad & Ors . . . Respondents in Writ Petition Civil 3770/2003. Rejoinder filed October 3, 2006.

8. See Celia W. Dugger, "India Orders Inquiry into Missionary's Killing," *New York Times*, January 29, 1999, A9.

9. See Chatterji, "Hindutva's Violent History." See also Angana P. Chatterji, *Violent Gods: Hindu Nationalism in India's Present; Narratives from Orissa* (Gurgaon: Three Essays Collective, 2009).

10. See Somini Sengupta, "Attack on Women at an Indian Bar Intensifies a Clash of Cultures," *New York Times*, February 8, 2009, A5.

11. "Lok Sabha Polls to Cost More Than US Presidential Poll," *Times of India*, March 1, 2009.

12. See Shantanu Guha Ray, "Offer Valid Till Votes Last," *Tehelka*, May 27, 2009.

13. See online results from the Election Commission of India at http://www.eci.nic.in.

14. Of India's population of one billion, the registered voter base is 672

million. In 2009, only 356 million Indians voted, a turnout of 53 percent. Of this the United Progressive Alliance vote share was approximately 33 percent, that is, less than 120 million voted for the alliance, http://eciresults.nic.in /frmPercentVotesParty-WiseChart.aspx.

15. See "BJP, Congress Should Join Hands, Says Govindacharya," Press Trust of India, Indore, May 15, 2009.

16. See "India, Pak Unite to Block Anti-Lanka Move at UN," *Indian Express*, May 28, 2009.

17. See "Journalism on Wheels," photo by Rajeev Bhatt of BBC's India Election Special Train, *Hindu*, April 26, 2009.

18. See "Vote for Reforms, Says India Inc," *Sunday Hindustan Times*, May 17, 2009.

19. See "Corporate Captains Feel Easy Without Left," *Sunday Hindustan Times*, May 17, 2009.

20. The theme song from the hit film *Slumdog Millionaire* was bought by the Congress Party for its election campaign for a sum of Rs 1 crore ($200,000).

21. See Uday Khandeparkar, "Behind the Nano Hype," *Wall Street Journal*, March 19, 2009.

22. D. K. Singh, "'In logon ko pakad pakad ke nasbandi karana padega'" (These people must be caught and sterilized), *Indian Express*, March 22, 2009.

23. See Pratap Bhanu Mehta, "A Country in 40 Acres," *Indian Express*, August 6, 2008. See also Vir Sanghvi, "Think the Unthinkable," *Hindustan Times*, August 16, 2008, and Swaminathan Iyer, "Pushing Kashmir Towards Pakistan," *Economic Times*, August 13, 2008.

24. For an appraisal of the recently concluded elections in Jammu and Kashmir, see Gautam Navlakha, "Jammu and Kashmir Elections: A Shift in Equations," and Rekha Chowdhary, "Separatist Sentiments and Deepening of Democracy," *Economic and Political Weekly*, January 17–23, 2009.

25. For a detailed report, see Rajeev Upadhyay, "The Melting of the Siachen Glacier," *Current Science* (March 10, 2009): 646–48.

THE PRESIDENT TOOK THE SALUTE

1. Express News Service, "Migrants Blamed for Surging Crimes in Cities," *Indian Express*, April 2, 2013.

TRICKLEDOWN REVOLUTION

1. P. Chidambaram, "Poor Rich Countries," *Outlook*, October 22, 2007.

2. Ajay Dandekar and Chitrangada Choudhury, "PESA, Left-Wing Extremism

and Governance: Concerns and Challenges in India's Tribal Districts," 2010, https://www.researchgate.net/publication/265000754_PESA_Left-Wing _Extremism_and_Governance_Concerns_and_Challenges_in_India's _Tribal_Districts.

3. B. G. Verghese, "Daylight at the Thousand Star Hotel," *Outlook*, May 3, 2010.

4. Sumanta Banerjee, *In the Wake of Naxalbari: Four Decades of a Simmering Revolution* (Kolkata, West Bengal: Sahitya Samsad, 2009).

5. Dandekar and Choudhury, "PESA, Left-Wing Extremism and Governance."

6. Kaustav Banerjee and Partha Saha, "The NREGA, the Maoists and the Developmental Woes of the Indian State," *Economic and Political Weekly* 45, no. 28 (July 10, 2010): 42–47; retrieved from http://www.indiaenvironmentportal .org.in/files/The%20NREGA.pdf.

KASHMIR'S FRUITS OF DISCORD

1. Joe Klein, "The Full Obama Interview," *Time*, October 23, 2008.

2. Sheryl Gay Stolberg and Jim Yardley, "Countering China, Obama Backs India for U.N. Council," *New York Times*, November 8, 2010.

3. Yusuf Jameel and Lydia Polgreen, "Indian Agency Insists 2 Kashmiri Women Drowned," *New York Times*, December 14, 2009. Human Rights Watch Asia authored a report on the high incidence of rape by Indian security personnel. See "Rape in Kashmir: A Crime of War," AsiaWatch (division of Human Rights Watch) and Physicians for Human Rights, vol. 5, no. 9 (2009), http://www.hrw.org/sites/default/files/reports/INDIA935.PDF.

4. Special correspondent, "Bajrang Dal's Warning to Arundhati Roy," *Hindu*, October 28, 2010.

I'D RATHER NOT BE ANNA

1. "Anna Hazare Himself Involved in Corruption, Says Congress," *Economic Times*, August 14, 2011. See also "Had Held Hazare Guilty of Corruption: PB Sawant," *IBNLive*, August 14, 2011.

2. Shortly after Hazare's release from prison, the *Telegraph* reported that Hazare was sustained with glucose and electrolyte powder during his second "fast unto death." Of the possible fraud, the physician who examined him, Abhijit Vaidya, offered an analysis: "I fear Hazare is being used as a tool to destabilise the government. . . . Corruption obviously needs to be fought but Hazare has never addressed other social issues such as economic inequality, extreme poverty and farmers' suicides that are equally hurting the country." "Secret of Fast? Hear It from a Pune Doctor," *Telegraph*, August 16, 2011. See also "The Anna Hazare

Scam," *Analytical Monthly Review*, April 15, 2011, http://mrzine.monthlyreview.org/2011/amr150411.html.

3. Manas Dasgupta, "Hazare Clarifies Remarks on Modi, but Activists Unrelenting," *Hindustan*, April 13, 2011.

4. "Hazare Failed to Recognise Workers' Contribution: RSS," *Hindu*, February 5, 2012.

5. Mukul Sharma, "The Making of Moral Authority: Anna Hazare and Watershed Management Programme in Ralegan Siddhi," *Economic and Political Weekly* 41, no. 20 (May 2006): 1981–88.

6. Lola Nayar, "Flowing the Way of Their Money," *Outlook*, September 19, 2011.

SPEECH TO THE PEOPLE'S UNIVERSITY

1. Andrea Shalai-Esa, "Saudi Deals Boosted US Arms Sales to Record 66.3 Billion in 2011," Reuters UK, August 27, 2012.

2. Sunil Dasgupta and Stephen P. Cohen, "Arms Sales for India," *Foreign Affairs*, March/April 2011.

3. "Mukesh Ambani Tops for the Third Year as India's Richest," *Forbes Asia*, news release, September 30, 2010. The article notes, "The combined net worth of India's 100 richest people is $300 billion, up from $276 billion last year. This year, there are 69 billionaires on the India Rich List, 17 more than last year." India's 2009 GDP was $1.2 trillion.

4. P. Sainath, "Farm Suicides Rise in Maharashtra, State Still Leads the List," *Hindu*, July 3, 2012.

CAPITALISM: A GHOST STORY

1. "Mukesh Ambani Tops for the Third Year as India's Richest," *Forbes Asia*, news release, September 30, 2010.

2. Vikas Bajaj, "For Wealthy Indian Family, Palatial House Is No Home," *New York Times*, October 18, 2011.

3. Frederick Engels and Karl Marx, *Manifesto of the Communist Party*, trans. Samuel Moore (Torfaen, UK: Merlin, 1998), 17.

4. P. Sainath, "Farm Suicides Rise in Maharashtra, State Still Leads the List."

5. National Commission for Enterprises in the Unorganised Sector (NCEUS), Report on Conditions of Work and Promotion of Livelihoods in the Unorganised Sector, Government of India, August 2007, https://ruralindiaonline.org/resources/report-on-conditions-of-work-and-promotion-of-livelihoods-in-the-unorganised-sector/. The state-supported study notes that though a "buoyancy

in the economy did lead to a sense of euphoria by the turn of the last century . . . a majority of the people . . . were not touched by this euphoria. At the end of 2004–5, about 836 million or 77 per cent of the population were living below Rs. 20 a day and constituted most of India's informal economy" (1).

6. As of March 2013, Mukesh Ambani was worth $21.5 billion, according to a *Forbes* profile: http://www.forbes.com/profile/mukesh-ambani/.

7. "RIL Buys 95% Stake in Infotel Broadband," *Times of India*, June 11, 2010.

8. Depali Gupta, "Mukesh Ambani–Owned Infotel Broadband to Set Up over 1,000,000 Towers for 4G Operations," *Economic Times*, August 23, 2012.

9. Brinda Karat, "Of Mines, Minerals, and Tribal Rights," *Hindu*, May 15, 2012.

10. See Michael Levien, "The Land Question: Special Economic Zones and the Political Economy of Dispossession in India," *Journal of Peasant Studies* 39, nos. 3–4 (2012): 933–69.

11. S. Sakthivel and Pinaki Joddar, "Unorganised Sector Workforce in India: Trends, Patterns, and Social Security Coverage," *Economic and Political Weekly*, May 27, 2006, 2107–14.

12. "India Approves Increase in Royalties on Mineral Mining," *Wall Street Journal*, August 12, 2009.

13. From a 2009 Ministry of Rural Development report titled "State Agrarian Relations and Unfinished Task of Land Reforms," commissioned by the Government of India: "The new approach came about with the *Salwa Judum*. . . . [Its] first financiers . . . were Tata and the Essar. . . . 640 villages as per official statistics were laid bare, burnt to the ground and emptied with the force of the gun and the blessings of the state. 350,000 tribals, half the total population of Dantewada district are displaced, their womenfolk raped, their daughters killed, and their youth maimed. Those who could not escape into the jungle were herded together into refugee camps run and managed by the *Salwa Judum*. Others continue to hide in the forest or have migrated to the nearby tribal tracts in Maharashtra, Andhra Pradesh and Orissa. 640 villages are empty. Villages sitting on tons of iron ore are effectively de-peopled and available for the highest bidder. The latest information that is being circulated is that both Essar Steel and Tata Steel are willing to take over the empty landscape and manage the mines" (161). The report is available at http://southasia.oneworld.net/Files/MRD%20Commitee%20Report.pdf

14. P. Pradhan, "Police Firing at Kalinganagar," People's Union for Civil Liberties (PUCL) report, Orissa. April 2006.

15. Ibid.

16. Sudha Ramachandran, "India's War on Maoists under Attack," *Asia Times Online*, May 26, 2010.

17. "Anti-Naxal Operations: Gov't to Deploit 10,000 CRPF Troopers," Zeenews. com, October 30, 2012. "Chhattisgarh HM Wants Army to Tackle Naxalism," webindia, November 15, 2012; Soumittra S. Bose, "Naxals Gear up to Take on

the Indian Army, *Times of India*, June 2, 2012.

18. See Human Rights Watch, "Getting Away with Murder: 50 Years of the Armed Forces Special Powers Act (AFSPA)," August 2008. The report states that AFSPA's ability to act "on suspicion" has led to thousands of disappearances in Jammu and Kashmir. Many of those who've disappeared are believed to be in "unmarked graves that security forces say are the burials of unidentified militants. Human rights groups have long called for an independent investigation and forensic tests to establish the identity of those in the graves, but the government has yet to respond to that demand" (12).

19. J. Balaji, "Soni Sori Case: HRW Wants PM to Order Impartial Probe on Torture," *Hindu*, March 8, 2011. Although Soni Sori has been acquitted in six of the eight cases filed against her, she remains in a Chhattisgarh jail. See Suvojit Bagchi, "Soni Sori Acquitted in a Case of Attack on Congress Leader," *Hindu*, May 1, 2013.

20. Aman Sethi, "High Court Stays Clearance for DB Power Coal Mine in Chhattisgarh," *Hindu*, December 12, 2001.

21. Sanjib Kr Baruah, "Dam Wrong," *Hindustan Times*, September 2, 2010.

22. "Kashmir Power Cut Protest Turns Deadly," *Aljazeera*, January 3, 2012.

23. "Report Raised Fears about Proximity of Kalpasar Dam and Mithivirdi N-Project," *Indian Express*, May 3, 2013.

24. Vinod K. Jose, "The Emperor Uncrowned: The Rise of Narendra Modi," *Caravan Magazine*, March 1, 2012.

25. Maj. Gen. Dhruv Katoch et al., "Perception Management of the Indian Army," Centre for Land Warfare Studies seminar, Delhi, February 21, 2012.

26. Lydia Polgreen, "High Ideals and Corruption Dominate Think Festival Agenda," *New York Times*, November 1, 2011. While Tehelka held a "Summit of the Powerless" conference in 2006, initiating discussions of Naxalism and farmer suicides, the 2011 Think Fest, hosted by the same magazine, was a "glitzy and glamorous celebration" with guests including Thomas Friedman and India's "mining barons and real estate tycoons" held "at a five-star resort . . . allegedly owned by men in jail awaiting charges involving the 2G telecommunications scam."

27. Raman Kirpal, "How Goa's Illegal Ore Miners Are in League with CM Kamat," *First Post Politics*, September 5, 2011.

28. Purnima S. Tripathi, "Battle of Bastar," *Frontline* 29, no. 8 (April/May 2012), http://www.frontline.in/navigation/?type=static&page=flonnet&rdurl=fl2908/stories/20120504290803200.htm.

29. "PIL on India Role in 'Genocide,'" *Telegraph India*, March 21, 2013. Peter Cobus, "Indian Kashmir to ID Bodies from Unmarked Graves," *Voice of America*, September 26, 2011.

30. Jaipur Sun, "Jaipur Lit Fest: Oprah Winfrey Charms Chaotic India," *Indian Express*, January 22, 2012.

31. Gerard Colby, *Thy Will Be Done: Conquest of the Amazon; Nelson Rockefeller and Evangelism in the Age of Oil* (New York: Harper Collins, 1996).

32. "Introduction: The Rockefellers," *American Experience*, Corporation for Public Broadcasting, http://www.pbs.org/wgbh/americanexperience/features /introduction/rockefellers-introduction/. "Because of the ruthless war he waged to crush his competitors, Rockefeller was to many Americans the embodiment of an unjust and cruel economic system. Yet he lived a quiet and virtuous life. 'I believe the power to make money is a gift of God,' Rockefeller once said. 'It is my duty to make money and even more money and to use the money I make for the good of my fellow men.'"

33. Pablo Neruda, "Standard Oil Company," in *Canto General*, trans. Jack Schmitt (Berkeley: University of California Press, 1991), 176.

34. For further analysis of the Gates Foundation's involvement in privatizing education, coupled with drastic reductions in government spending, see Jeff Bale and Sara Knopp, "Obama's Neoliberal Agenda for Public Education," in *Education and Capitalism: Struggles for Learning and Liberation* (Chicago: Haymarket Books, 2012).

35. Joan Roelofs, "The Third Sector as a Protective Layer for Capitalism," *Monthly Review* 47, no. 4 (September 1995): 16.

36. Joan Roelofs, *Foundations and Public Policy: The Mask of Pluralism* (Albany, NY: SUNY Press, 2003).

37. Eric Toussaint, *Your Money or Your Life: The Tyranny of Global Finance* (Chicago: Haymarket Books, 2005).

38. Roelofs, "The Third Sector as a Protective Layer for Capitalism."

39. Ibid.

40. Ibid.

41. Ibid.

42. Erika Kinetz, "Small Loans Add Up to Lethal Debts." *Hindu*, February 25, 2012.

43. David Ransom, "Ford Country: Building an Elite in Indonesia," in *The Trojan Horse: A Radical Look at Foreign Aid*, ed. Steve Weissman with members of the Pacific Studies Center and the North American Congress on Latin America (Palo Alto, CA: Ramparts, 1975), 93–116.

44. Juan Gabriel Valdés, *Pinochet's Economists: The Chicago School of Economics in Chile* (New York: Cambridge University Press, 1995).

45. Rajander Singh Negi, "Magsaysay Award: Asian Nobel, Not So Noble," *Economic and Political Weekly* 43, no. 34 (2008): 14–16.

46. Narayan Lakshman,"World Bank Needs Anti-Graft Policies," *Hindu*, September 1, 2011. Speaking to the *Hindu*, Navin Girishankar, one of the main authors of the World Bank's Independent Evaluation Group study, said that "on the one hand there is a need to foster demand for good governance by helping improve the government responsiveness to pressures through

greater transparency and more disclosure policies. . . . The Indian experience, including the Lokpal bills, might dovetail with this type of strategy."

47. Alejandra Viveros, "World Bank Announces Winners of Award for Outstanding Public Service," April 15, 2008, http://africa.gm/north-america/united-states/washington-dc/article/2008/4/17/world-bank-announces-winners-of-award-for-outstanding-public-service.

48. Joan Roelofs, *Foundations and Public Policy: The Mask of Pluralism* (Albany: State University of New York Press, 2003).

49. See Roelofs, "Third Sector as a Protective Layer for Capitalism."

50. Press Trust of India, "Infosys to Bid for UID Projects, Sees No Conflict of Interest," *Indian Express*, June 27, 2009

51. Justin Gillis, "Bill Gates Calls for More Accountability on Food Programs," *New York Times*, February 23, 2012.

52. Robert Arnove, ed., *Philanthropy and Cultural Imperialism: The Foundations at Home and Abroad* (Boston: G. K. Hall, 1980). In the essay "American Philanthropy and the Social Sciences," Donald Fisher outlines US foundations' role in shaping political thought through influence over university disciplines worldwide.

53. See Foundation Center, "Foundation Stats," 2014, http://foundationcenter.org/findfunders/topfunders/top100assets.html.

54. See Roelofs, *Foundations and Public Policy*.

55. Manning Marable, *Race, Reform, and Rebellion: The Second Reconstruction and Beyond in Black America, 1945–2006* (Jackson: University of Mississippi Press, 2007).

56. Devin Fergus, *Liberalism, Black Power, and the Making of American Politics, 1965–1980* (Athens: University of Georgia Press, 2009).

57. The Department of Defense links to the King Center's website and continues to play an active role in shaping how the United States celebrates King's legacy.

58. See Roelofs, "Third Sector as a Protective Layer for Capitalism."

59. P. Vaidyanathan Iyer, "Dalit Inc. Ready to Show Business Can Beat Caste," *Indian Express*, December 15, 2011.

60. The ORF has also been directly involved in Modi's ascent: of Modi's participation in a conference hosted by Google, one ORF fellow said, "He is trying to project himself as a modern person who is keen on developmental issues and this summer offers him a platform to reach out to people of the younger generation—what we call aspirational India." See Neha Thirani Bagri, "Google Hosts Narendra Modi at Tech Summit," *New York Times*, March 20, 2013.

61. See "Raytheon Aligns with Indian Companies to Pursue Emerging Opportunities," Raytheon.com, November 13, 2007.

62. Engels and Marx, *Manifesto of the Communist Party*.

A PERFECT DAY FOR DEMOCRACY

1. Sandeep Joshi and Ashok Kumar, "Afzal Guru Hanged in Secrecy, Buried in Tihar Jail," *Hindu*, February 9, 2013. Even the lawyers who argued for his death sentence decried the secret hanging as a "human rights violation." See Manoj Mitta, "Afzal Guru's Secret Hanging a Human Rights Violation: Prosecutor," *Times of India*, February 13, 2013.

2. See Joshi and Kumar, "Afzal Guru Hanged in Secrecy."

3. Sumegha Gulati, "SAR Geelani, Iftikhar among Those Placed under Detention," *Indian Express*, February 10, 2013. During the trial, Geelani was presented as the mastermind of the 2001 attack, though he was eventually acquitted.

4. Mohammad Ali, "Muslim Groups See Political Motives," *Hindu*, February 11, 2013.

THE CONSEQUENCES OF HANGING AFZAL GURU

1. Ahmed Ali Fayyaz, "Two Days after Hanging, Letter Reaches Azfal's Wife," *Hindu*, February 11, 2013. Fayyaz notes, "Seals and signatures on the communication make it clear that the letter was written on February 6, or three days after the mercy petition was rejected, and dispatched only a day before the execution," making it clear that the late notice was deliberate.

2. News desk, "Kashmir's One Month since Afzal Guru's Hanging: 350 Civilians, 150 Cops Injured, 4 Dead," *Kashmir Walla*, March 10, 2013.

3. See "Afzal Guru Papers" online: "Full Text: Supreme Court Judgement on Parliament Attack Convict Afzal Guru." IBNlive.in.com, February, 9, 2013. See also Arundhati Roy, ed., *A Reader: The Strange Case of the Attack on the Indian Parliament* (New Delhi: Penguin Books India, 2006), and Mukherji, *December 13*.

4. "Short of Participating in the Actual Attack, He Did Everything . . . ," *Indian Express*, February 10, 2013.

5. "Afzal Guru Papers": "There is no evidence that [Afzal] is a member of a terrorist gang or a terrorist organization, once the confessional statement is excluded. Incidentally, we may mention that even going by confessional statement, it is doubtful whether the membership of a terrorist gang or organization is established."

6. Praveen Swami, "Terrorism in Jammu and Kashmir in Theory and Practice," *India Review* 2 (July 2003). See also Muhammad Amir Rana, *A to Z of Jehadi Organizations in Pakistan* (Lahore, Pakistan: Mashal Books, 2004).

7. See Yug Mohit Chaudhry, "Why Balwant Singh Rajoana Shouldn't Be Hanged," *Hindu*, March 29, 2012.

8. For new evidence on just how deliberate the hanging was, see "Government behind Parliament Attack, 26/11: Ishrat Probe Officer," *Times of India*, July

14, 2013.

9. Bashaarat Masood, "The Grand (Standing) Mufti of Kasmir," *Indian Express*, February 7, 2013. See also Bashaarat Masood, "J&K Lawyer to Challenge Grand Mufti's Status," *Indian Express*, February 7, 2013, and Aijaz Hussain, "Kashmir Girl Band Breaks up after Threats," *Boston Globe*, February 6, 2013.

10. Aijaz Hussain, "Kashmir Police Publish Nuclear War Survival Tips," *San Diego Union-Tribune*, January 22, 2013.

THE DOCTOR AND THE SAINT: THE AMBEDKAR-GANDHI DEBATE

1. For this account of Khairlanji, I have drawn on Anand Teltumbde, *The Persistence of Caste: The Khairlanji Murders and India's Hidden Apartheid* (New Delhi: Navayana/London: Zed Books, 2010). For one of the first comprehensive news reports on the incident, see Sabrina Buckwalter, "Just Another Rape Story." *Sunday Times of India*, October 29, 2006.

2. For an analysis of the lower court judgment, see S. Anand, "Understanding the Khairlanji Verdict," *The Hindu*, October 5, 2008.

3. On July 11, 1996, the Ranveer Sena, a privileged-caste, feudal militia, murdered twenty-one landless laborers in Bathani Tola village in the state of Bihar. In 2012, the Patna High Court acquitted all the accused. On December 1, 1997, the Ranveer Sena massacred fifty-eight Dalits in Laxmanpur Bathe village, also in Bihar. In April 2010, the trial court convicted all the twenty-six accused. It sentenced ten of them to life imprisonment and sixteen to death. In October 2013, the Patna High Court suspended the conviction of all twenty-six accused, saying the prosecution had not produced any evidence to guarantee any punishment at all.

4. These are some of the major crimes against Dalits and subordinated castes that have taken place in recent times: in 1968, in Keezhvenmani in the state of Tamil Nadu, forty-four Dalits were burnt alive; in 1977, in Belchi village of Bihar, fourteen Dalits were burnt alive; in 1978, in Marichjhapi, an island in the Sundarbans mangrove forest of West Bengal, hundreds of Dalit refugees from Bangladesh were massacred during a left-led government's eviction drive; in 1984, in Karamchedu in the state of Andhra Pradesh, six Dalits were murdered, three Dalit women raped, and many more wounded; in 1991, in Chunduru, also in Andhra Pradesh, nine Dalits were slaughtered and their bodies dumped in a canal; in 1997, in Melavalavu in Tamil Nadu, an elected Dalit panchayat leader and five Dalits were murdered; in 2000, in Kambalapalli in the state of Karnataka, six Dalits were burnt alive; in 2002, in Jhajjar in the state of Haryana, five Dalits were lynched outside a police station. See also the documentation by Human Rights Watch, *Broken People: Caste Violence against India's "Untouchables,"* New York: Author, 1999) and the

Navsarjan report: Navsarjan Trust and Robert F. Kennedy Center for Justice & Human Rights, *Understanding Untouchability: A Comprehensive Study of Practices and Conditions in 1589 Villages*, n.d., http://www.indianet.nl/pdf /UnderstandingUntouchability.pdf.

5. *Babasaheb Ambedkar: Writings and Speeches* (hereinafter BAWS) 9, 296. All references to B. R. Ambedkar's writings, except for *Annihilation of Caste*, are from the BAWS series published by the Education Department, Government of Maharashtra. All references to *Annihilation of Caste* (henceforth AoC) are to the Navayana edition (New Delhi, 2014).

6. Rupa Viswanath writes in "A Textbook Case of Exclusion," *The Indian Express*, July 20, 2012: "Where 'Dalit' refers to all those Indians, past and present, traditionally regarded as outcastes and untouchable, 'SC' is a modern governmental category that explicitly excludes Christian and Muslim Dalits." For the current version of the President's Constitution (Scheduled Castes) Order, which tells us who will count as SC for the purposes of constitutional and legal protections, is entirely unambiguous: "No person who professes a religion different from the Hindu, the Sikh or the Buddhist religion shall be deemed to be a member of a Scheduled Caste." She goes on to say, "It was only under Congress rule, in 1950, that the President's Order explicitly defined SC on the basis of religious criteria, although Christian Dalits were excluded from SC for electoral purposes by the Government of India Act 1935. From that point onwards, Dalits who had converted out of Hinduism lost not only reservations, but also, after 1989, protection under the Prevention of Atrocities Act. Later, SC was expanded to include Sikh and Buddhist Dalits, but official discrimination against Muslim and Christian Dalits remains." If Christians as well as Muslims who face the stigma of caste were to be included in the number of those who can be counted as Dalit, their share in the Indian population would far exceed the official 2011 Census figure of 17 percent. See also Note 2 to the Preface of the 1937 edition of AoC (184).

7. On December 16, 2012, a woman was brutally tortured and gang-raped in a bus in New Delhi. She died on December 29. The atrocity led to mass protests for days. Unusually, a large number of middle-class people participated in them. In the wake of the protests the law against rape was made more stringent. See Jason Burke's reports in the *Guardian*, especially "Delhi Rape: How India's Other Half Lives," September 10, 2013.

8. National Crime Records Bureau, *Crime in India 2011: Statistics* (New Delhi: Author, Ministry of Home Affairs, 2012), 423–24.

9. Privileged castes punish Dalits by forcing them to eat human excreta; this often goes unreported. In Thinniyam village in Tamil Nadu's Tiruchi district, on May 22, 2002, two Dalits, Murugesan and Ramasami, were forced to feed each other human excreta and branded with hot iron rods for publicly declaring that they had been cheated by the village chief. See S. Viswanathan, *Dalits in Dravidian Land: Frontline Reports on Anti-Dalit Violence in Tamil Nadu (1995–2004)*

(Chennai: Navayana, 2005). In fact, "The Statement of Objects and Reasons of the Scheduled Castes and Scheduled Tribes (Prevention of Atrocities) Act, 1989" states this as one of the crimes it seeks to redress: "Of late, there has been an increase in the disturbing trend of commission of certain atrocities like making the Scheduled Caste person eat inedible substances like human excreta and attacks on and mass killings of helpless Scheduled Castes and Scheduled Tribes and rape of women belonging to the Scheduled Castes and Scheduled Tribes."

10. According to the tenets of their faith, Sikhs are not supposed to practise caste. However, those from the Untouchable castes who converted to Sikhism continue to be treated as Untouchable. For an account of how caste affects Sikhism, see Mark Juergensmeyer, *Religious Rebels in the Punjab: The Ad Dharm Challenge to Caste* (New Delhi: Navayana, 1982/2009).

11. BAWS 1, 222.

12. For example, Madhu Kishwar writes: "[T]he much reviled caste system has played a very significant role in making Indian democracy vibrant by making it possible for people to offer a good measure of resistance to centralised, authoritarian power structures that came to be imposed during colonial rule and were preserved even after Independence." Madhu Kishwar, "Caste System: Society's Bold Mould," *Tehelka*, February 11, 2006.

13. See Béteille, "Race and Caste," *The Hindu*, March 10, 2001. Dipankar Gupta, formerly professor of sociology at Jawaharlal Nehru University, was part of the official Indian delegation that in 2007 opposed the Dalit caucus's demand to treat caste discrimination as being akin to racial discrimination. In an essay in 2007, Gupta argued that "the allegation that caste is a form of racial discrimination is not just an academic misjudgement but has unfortunate policy consequences as well." See his articles "Caste, Race and Politics," *Seminar*, December 2001, and "Why Caste Discrimination Is Not Racial Discrimination," *Seminar*, April 2007. For a cross-section of views on the caste–race debate at the United Nations Committee on Elimination of Racial Discrimination, see S. K. Thorat and Umakant, editors of *Caste, Race, and Discrimination: Discourses in International Context* (New Delhi: Rawat, 2004), which features counter-arguments by a range of scholars including Gail Omvedt and Kancha Ilaiah. Also see Balmurli Natarajan and Paul Greenough, eds., *Against Stigma: Studies in Caste, Race, and Justice Since Durban* (Hyderabad: Orient Blackswan, 2009).

14. For a response to Béteille and Gupta, see Gerald D. Berreman in ibid. Berreman says: "What is 'scientifically nonsensical' is Professor Béteille's misunderstanding of 'race'. What is 'mischievous' is his insistence that India's system of ascribed social inequality should be exempted from the provisions of a UN Convention whose sole purpose is the extension of human rights to include freedom from all forms of discrimination and intolerance—and to which India, along with most other nations, has committed itself" (54–55).

15. See www.declarationofempathy.org.

16. Bhagwan Das, *Thus Spoke Ambedkar, Vol. 1: A Stake in the Nation* (New Delhi: Navayana, 2010), 25.

17. Inter-caste and intra-gotra marriages are resisted in the name of "honor"; in extreme cases, the couple, or one of the partners, is killed. For an account of the case of Ilavarasan and Divya from Tamil Nadu, see Meena Kandasamy, "How Real-Life Tamil Love Stories End," *Outlook*, July 22, 2013. For an account of the consequences of violating "gotra laws" in Haryana, see Chander Suta Dogra's recent *Manoj and Babli: A Hate Story* (Penguin Books, 2013). Also see Aniruddha Ghosal, "Day after Their Killing, Village Goes Quiet," *Indian Express*, September 20, 2013; and Prem Chowdhry *Contentious Marriages, Eloping Couples: Gender, Caste and Patriarchy in Northern India* (New Delhi: Oxford University Press, 2007).

18. In 2009, Ahmedabad-based Navsarjan Trust and the Robert F. Kennedy Center for Justice and Human Rights published a joint report, "Understanding Untouchability" (http://www.indianet.nl/pdf/UnderstandingUntouchability .pdf). It listed ninety-nine forms of untouchability in 1,589 villages of Gujarat. It looked at the prevalence of untouchability under eight broad headings: 1. Water for Drinking; 2. Food and Beverage; 3. Religion; 4. Caste-based Occupations; 5. Touch; 6. Access to Public Facilities and Institutions; 7. Prohibitions and Social Sanctions; 8. Private Sector Discrimination. The findings were shocking. In 98.4 percent of villages surveyed, intercaste marriage was prohibited; in 97.6 percent of villages, Dalits were forbidden to touch water pots or utensils that belonged to non-Dalits; in 98.1 percent of villages, a Dalit could not rent a house in a non-Dalit area; in 97.2 percent of villages, Dalit religious leaders were not allowed to celebrate a religious ceremony in a non-Dalit area; in 67 percent of villages, Dalit panchayat members were either not offered tea or were served in separate cups called "Dalit" cups.

19. AoC 17.7.

20. M. K. Gandhi, *The Collected Works of Mahatma Gandhi* (Electronic Book) (New Delhi: Government of India, Publications Division, 1999), vol. 15, 160–61. All references to Gandhi's works, unless otherwise stated, are from this edition (referred to hereinafter as CWMG. Wherever possible, first publication details are also provided since scholars sometimes refer to an earlier edition of the CWMG.

21. Cited in BAWS 9, 276.

22. Cited in CWMG 59, 227.

23. UNI, "India's 100 Richest Are 25 Pc of GDP," November 20, 2009.

24. A Reuters report dated August 10, 2007, and referring to "Report on Conditions of Work and Promotions of Livelihoods in the Unorganised Sector" by the National Commission for Enterprises in the Unorganised Sector included this statement: "Seventy-seven per cent of Indians—about 836 million people—live on less than half a dollar a day in one of the world's hottest

economies." https://ruralindiaonline.org/resources/report-on-conditions
-of-work-and-promotion-of-livelihoods-in-the-unorganised-sector/.

25. S. Gurumurthy, co-convenor of the Hindu right-wing Swadeshi Jagaran
Manch, talks of how caste and capitalism can coexist: "Caste is a very strong
bond. While individuals are related by families, castes link the families. Castes
transcended the local limits and networked the people across [sic]. This has
prevented the disturbance that industrialism caused to neighbourhood societies
in the West, resulting in unbridled individualism and acute atomization." He
goes on to argue that the caste system "has in modern times engaged the market
in economics and democracy in politics to reinvent itself. It has become a
great source of entrepreneurship." See "Is Caste an Economic Development
Vehicle?" *The Hindu*, January 19, 2009.

26. See "Forbes: India's Billionaire Wealth Much above Country's Fiscal
Deficit," *The Indian Express*, March 5, 2013.

27. J. H. Hutton, *Census of India 1931* (Delhi: Government of India, 1935).

28. David Hardiman, *Feeding the Baniya: Peasants and Usurers in Western India*
(New Delhi: Oxford University Press, 1996), 15.

29. See "Brahmins in India," *Outlook*, June 4, 2007. Despite the decline, the
Lok Sabha in 2007 had fifty Brahmin Members of Parliament—9.17 percent
of the total strength of the House. The data given by *Outlook* is based on four
surveys conducted by the Centre for the Study of Developing Societies, Delhi,
between 2004 and 2007.

30. BAWS 9, 207.

31. See Khushwant Singh, "Brahmin Power," *Sunday*, December 29, 1990. Singh's
figures are based on information provided by one of his readers.

32. BAWS 9, 200.

33. Reservation was first introduced in India during the colonial period. For a
history of the policy of reservation, see Bhagwan Das, "Moments in a History
of Reservations," *Economic & Political Weekly*, October 28, 2000, 3381–84.

34. *Selected Educational Statistics 2004–05* (New Delhi: Ministry of Human
Resource Development, 2007), xxii, http://www.educationforallinindia.com
/SES2004-05.pdf.

35. Under the new economic regime, education, health care, essential services and
other public institutions are rapidly being privatized, which has led to a hemorrhage
of government jobs. For a population of 1.2 billion people, the total number of
organized sector jobs is 29 million (as of 2011). Of these, the private sector accounts
for only 11.4 million. See the *Economic Survey 2010–11: Statistical Appendix*, A52,
http://indiabudget.nic.in/budget2011-2012/es2010-11/estat1.pdf.

36. See "Yes Sir," in Ajay Navaria's collection of short stories, *Unclaimed
Terrain*, trans. Laura Brueck (New Delhi: Navayana, 2013).

37. National Commission for Scheduled Castes and Scheduled Tribes, *Fourth
Report* (New Delhi: Author, 1998), 180–81.

38. Prabhu Chawla, "Courting Controversy," *India Today*, January 29, 1999. The lawyers quoted are Anil Divan and Fali S. Nariman. Later, India did get a Dalit Supreme Court Chief Justice in K. G. Balakrishnan (2007–10).

39. S. Santhosh and Joshil K. Abraham, "Caste Injustice in Jawaharlal Nehru University," *Economic & Political Weekly*, June 26, 2010, 27–29.

40. Ibid., 27.

41. The note submitted to the Jawaharlal Nehru University vice-chancellor was signed by Yoginder K. Alagh, T. K. Oommen, and Bipan Chandra (among others). Alagh is an economist and a former Member of Parliament (Rajya Sabha), a former union minister and regular newspaper columnist. Oomen was president of the International Sociological Association (1990–94) and published an edited volume titled *Classes, Citizenship, and Inequality: Emerging Perspectives* (New Delhi: Dorling Kindersley, 2010). Chandra is a Marxist historian, former president of the Indian History Congress, and former chairperson of the Centre for Historical Studies at Jawaharlal Nehru University.

42. Anuradha Raman, "Standard Deviation," *Outlook*, April 26, 2010.

43. The Justice Rajinder Sachar Committee was appointed by prime minister Manmohan Singh on March 9, 2005, to assess the social, economic, and educational status of the Muslim community of India; its 403-page report was tabled in Parliament on November 30, 2006. The report establishes that caste oppression affects India's Muslims too. According to Teltumbde (*The Persistence of Caste*, 16), "working from t,he Sachar Committee data, the [Scheduled Castes] and [Scheduled Tribes] components of India's population can be estimated at 19.7 and 8.5 per cent respectively."

44. According to economist Sukhadeo Thorat, "Nearly 70 per cent of SC households either do not own land or have very small landholdings of less than 0.4 ha [hectare]. A very small proportion (less than 6 per cent) consists of medium and large farmers. The scenario of landownership among SCs is even grimmer in Bihar, Haryana, Kerala and Punjab, where more than 90 per cent of SC households possess negligible or no land." Sukhadeo Thorat, *Dalits in India: Search for a Common Destiny* (New Delhi: Sage, 2009), 56. Citing Planning Commission data, another research paper states that the majority of the Scheduled Castes (77 percent) are landless, without any productive assets and sustainable employment opportunities. According to the Agricultural Census of 1990–91, the essay says, "Around 87 per cent of the landholders of scheduled castes and 65 per cent of scheduled tribes in the country belong to the category of small and marginal farmers." B. B. Mohanty, "Land Distribution among Scheduled Castes and Tribes," *Economic & Political Weekly*, October 6, 2001: 1357–68.

45. National Commission for Scheduled Castes and Scheduled Tribes, *Fourth Report*, 176.

46. Express News Service, "13 Lakh Dalits Still Engaged in Manual Scavenging: Thorat," *The New Indian Express*, October 8, 2013. See also the status papers

on the website of the International Dalit Solidarity Network, http://idsn.org /caste-discrimination/key-issues/manual-scavenging/.

47. Data are from the Indian Railways website and Agrima Bhasin, "The Railways in Denial," Infochange News and Features, February 2013.

48. See the interviews of Milind Kamble and Chandra Bhan Prasad, respectively the chairman and mentor of the Dalit Indian Chamber of Commerce and Industry, in Shekhar Gupta, "Capitalism Is Changing Caste Much Faster than any Human Being. Dalits Should Look at Capitalism as a Crusader against Caste," *The Indian Express*, June 11, 2013. For an analysis of how India's policies of liberalization and globalization since 1990 have actually benefited rural Dalits of Uttar Pradesh's Azamgarh and Bulandshahar districts, see Devesh Kapur, Chandra Bhan Prasad, Lant Pritchett, and D. Shyam Babu, "Rethinking Inequality: Dalits in Uttar Pradesh in the Market Reform Era," *Economic & Political Weekly*, August 28, 2010, 39–49. See also Milind Khandekar's *Dalit Millionaires: 15 Inspiring Stories* (Penguin, 2013). For a critique of the "low-intensity spectacle of Dalit millionaires," see Gopal Guru, "Rise of the 'Dalit Millionaire': A Low Intensity Spectacle," *Economic & Political Weekly*, December 15, 2012, 41–49.

49. Sam Jones, "Anti-caste Discrimination Reforms Blocked, Say Critics," *The Guardian*, July 29, 2013.

50. Ruth Vanita, "Whatever Happened to the Hindu Left?" *Seminar*, April 2002.

51. Sukta 90 in Book X of the *Rig Veda* tells the story of the myth of creation. It describes the sacrifice of the Purusha (primeval man), from whose body the four varnas and the entire universe emerged. When (the gods) divided the Purusha, his mouth became Brahmin, his arms Kshatriya, his thighs Vaishya, and Shudra sprang from his feet. See Wendy Doniger, trans., *The Rig Veda* (New Delhi: Penguin, 2005). Some scholars believe that Sukta is a latter-day interpolation into the *Rig Veda*.

52. Susan Bayly shows how Gandhi's caste politics are completely in keeping with the views of modern, privileged-caste Hindu "reformers." Susan Bayly, "Hindu Modernisers and the 'Public' Arena. Indigenous Critiques of Caste in Colonial India," in *Vivekananda and the Modernisation of Hinduism*, William Radice, ed. (New Delhi: Oxford University Press, 1998), 93–137.

53. In 2012, the newsmagazine *Outlook* published the result of just such a poll conducted on the eve of Independence Day. The question was: "Who, after the Mahatma, is the greatest Indian to have walked our soil?" Ambedkar topped the poll and *Outlook* devoted an entire issue (August 20, 2012) to him.

54. See Ambedkar's *Pakistan or the Partition of India* (1945), first published as *Thoughts on Pakistan* (1940), and featured in BAWS 8.

55. Anthony Parel, *"Hind Swaraj" and Other Writings* (Cambridge: Cambridge University Press, 1997), 188–89.

56. In a 1955 interview with BBC radio, Ambedkar said, "A comparative study of Gandhi's Gujarati and English writings will reveal how Mr. Gandhi was deceiving people."

57. Cited in BAWS 9, 276.

58. AoC 16.2.

59. See Kathryn Tidrick, *Gandhi: A Political and Spiritual Life* (London: I. B. Tauris, 2006), 281, 283–84. On May 2, 1938, after Gandhi had a seminal discharge at the age of sixty-four, in a letter to Amritlal Nanavati he said: "Where is my place, and how can a person subject to passion represent non-violence and truth?" (CWMG 73, 139).

60. BAWS 9, 202

61. Dhananjay Keer, *Dr. Ambedkar: Life and Mission* (Bombay: Popular Prakashan, 1990), 167. First published 1954.

62. For an analysis of the radicalism inherent in the Ambedkar statue, in the context of Uttar Pradesh, see Nicolas Jaoul, "Learning the Use of Symbolic Means: Dalits, Ambedkar Statues, and the State in Uttar Pradesh," *Contributions to Indian Sociology* 40, no. 2 (2006): 175–207: "To Dalit villagers, whose rights and dignity have been regularly violated, setting up the statue of a Dalit statesman wearing a red tie and carrying the Constitution involves dignity, pride in emancipated citizenship and a practical acknowledgement of the extent to which the enforcement of laws could positively change their lives" (204).

63. "The State represents violence in a concentrated and organised form. The individual has a soul, but as the State is a soulless machine, it can never be weaned from violence to which it owes its very existence. Hence I prefer the doctrine of trusteeship." *Hindustan Times*, October 17, 1935; CWMG 65, 318.

64. *Young India*, April 16, 1931, in CWMG 51, 354.

65. Das, *Thus Spoke Ambedkar*, vol. 1, 175.

66. Jefferson says this in his letter of September 6, 1789, to James Madison. In Philip B. Kurland and Ralph Lerner, *The Founders' Constitution* (Chicago: University of Chicago Press, 1986), http://press-pubs.uchicago.edu/founders/documents/v1ch2s23.html.

67. Ambedkar argues in "Castes in India," his 1916 essay, that women are the gateways of the caste system and that control over them through child marriages, enforced widowhood and sati (being burnt on a dead husband's pyre) are methods to keep a check on women's sexuality. For an analysis of Ambedkar's writings on this issue, see Sharmila Rege, *Against the Madness of Manu: B. R. Ambedkar's Writings on Brahmanical Patriarchy* (New Delhi: Navayana, 2013).

68. For a discussion of the Hindu Code Bill, its ramifications, and how it was sabotaged, see ibid., 191–244. Rege shows how from April 11, 1947, when it was introduced in the Constituent Assembly, until September 1951, the bill was never taken seriously. Ambedkar finally resigned on October 10, 1951. The Hindu Marriage Act was finally enacted in 1955, granting divorce rights to

Hindu women. The Special Marriage Act, passed in 1954, allows intercaste and interreligious marriage.

69. Ibid., 200.

70. Ibid., 241. Ambedkar's disillusionment with the new legal regime in India went further. On September 2, 1953, he declared in the Rajya Sabha, "Sir, my friends tell me that I made the Constitution. But I am quite prepared to say that I shall be the first person to burn it out. I do not want it. It does not suit anybody. But whatever that may be, if our people want to carry on, they must remember that there are majorities and there are minorities; and they simply cannot ignore the minorities by saying: 'Oh, no, to recognise you is to harm democracy'" (Keer, *Dr. Ambedkar*, 499).

71. AoC 20.12.

72. Gail Omvedt, *Seeking Begumpura: The Social Vision of Anticaste Intellectuals* (New Delhi: Navayana, 2008), 19.

73. Unpublished translation by Joel Lee, made available through personal communication.

74. Gandhi, *Young India*, March 17, 1927, in CWMG 38, 210.

75. Ambedkar said this during his speech delivered as Chairman of the Constitution Drafting Committee in the Constituent Assembly on November 4, 1948. See Das, *Thus Spoke Ambedkar*, vol. 1, 2010, 176.

76. For an analysis of Gandhi's relationship with Indian capitalists, see Leah Renold, "Gandhi: Patron Saint of the Industrialist," *Sagar: South Asia Graduate Research Journal* 1, no. 1 (1994): 16–38. Gandhi's approach to Big Dams is revealed in a letter dated April 5, 1924, in which he advised villagers who faced displacement by the Mulshi Dam, being built by the Tatas to generate electricity for their Bombay mills, to give up their protest (CWMG 27, 168):

1. I understand that the vast majority of the men affected have accepted compensation and that the few who have not cannot perhaps even be traced.

2. The dam is nearly half-finished and its progress cannot be permanently stopped. There seems to me to be no ideal behind the movement.

3. The leader of the movement is not a believer out and out in non-violence. This defect is fatal to success. Seventy-five years later, in 2000, the Supreme Court of India used very similar logic in its infamous judgement on the World Bank-funded Sardar Sarovar Dam on the Narmada river, when it ruled against tens of thousands of local people protesting their displacement and ordered the construction of the dam to continue.

77. *Young India*, December 20, 1928, in CWMG 43, 412. Also see Gandhi's *Hind Swaraj* (1909) in Parel, *"Hind Swaraj" and Other Writings*.

78. Rege, *Against the Madness of Manu*, 100.

79. BAWS 5, 102.

80. In Das, *Thus Spoke Ambedkar*, Vol. 1, 51.

81. AoC, preface to 1937 edition.

82. Cited in Eleanor Zelliot, *Ambedkar's World: The Making of Babasaheb and*

the *Dalit Movement* (New Delhi: Navayana, 2013), 147.

83. Here, for example, is Ismat Chugtai, a Muslim writer celebrated for her progressive, feminist views, describing an Untouchable sweeper in her short story, "A Pair of Hands": "Gori was her name, the feckless one, and she was dark, dark like a glistening pan on which a roti had been fried but which a careless cook had forgotten to clean. She had a bulbous nose, a wide jaw, and it seemed she came from a family where brushing one's teeth was a habit long forgotten. The squint in her left eye was noticeable despite the fact that her eyes were heavily kohled; it was difficult to imagine how, with a squinted eye, she was able to throw darts that never failed to hit their mark. Her waist was not slim; it had thickened, rapidly increasing in diameter from all those handouts she consumed. There was also nothing delicate about her feet which reminded one of a cow's hoofs, and she left a coarse smell of mustard oil in her wake. Her voice however, was sweet." From *A Chugtai Collection*, trans. Tahira Naqvi and Syeda S. Hameed (New Delhi: Women Unlimited, 2003), 164.

84. In 1981, all the Dalits of the village of Meenakshipuram—renamed Rahmat Nagar—in Tamil Nadu's Tirunelveli district converted to Islam. Worried by this, Hindu supremacist groups such as the Vishwa Hindu Parishad and the Rashtriya Swayamsevak Sangh together with the Sankaracharya of Kanchipuram began to work proactively to "integrate" Dalits into Hinduism. A new "Tamil Hindu" chauvinist group called the Hindu Munnani was formed. Eighteen years later, P. Sainath revisited Meenakshipuram and filed two reports: "One People, Many Identities," the *Hindu*, January 31, 1999; and "After Meenakshipuram: Caste, Not Cash, Led to Conversions," the *Hindu*, February 7, 1999. For a similar case from Koothirambakkam, another village in Tamil Nadu, see S. Anand, "Meenakshipuram Redux," *Outlook*, October 21, 2002.

85. Cited in Omvedt, *Seeking Begumpura*, 177.

86. The figure Ambedkar cites is drawn from the Simon Commission report of 1930. When the Lothian Committee came to India in 1932, Ambedkar said, "The Hindus adopted a challenging mood and refused to accept the figures given by the Simon Commission as a true figure for the Untouchables of India." He then argues that "this is due to the fact that the Hindus had by now realised the danger of admitting the existence of the Untouchables. For it meant that a part of the representation enjoyed by the Hindus will have to be given up by them to the Untouchables" (BAWS 5, 7–8).

87. See note 69 at 9.4 of this AoC edition.

88. He says this in the April 1899 issue of the journal *Prabuddha Bharata*, in an interview to its editor. In the same interview, when asked specifically what would be the caste of those who "re-converted" to Hinduism, Vivekananda says: "Returning converts . . . will gain their own castes, of course. And new people will make theirs. You will remember . . . that this has already been done

in the case of Vaishnavism. Converts from different castes and aliens were all able to combine under that flag and form a caste by themselves—and a very respectable one too. From Ramanuja down to Chaitanya of Bengal, all great Vaishnava Teachers have done the same."

89. The names of these organizations translate as Forum for Dalit Uplift; the All-India Committee for the Uplift of Untouchables; and the Punjab Society for Untouchable Uplift.

90. AoC 6.2.

91. Bayly, "Hindu Modernisers and the 'Public' Arena."

92. The term was coined by V. D. Savarkar (1883–1966), one of the principal proponents of modern, right-wing Hindu nationalism, in his 1923 pamphlet *Essentials of Hindutva* (later retitled *Hindutva: Who Is a Hindu?* [Nagpur: V. V. Kelkar]). The first edition (1923) of this work carried the pseudonymous "A. Maratha" as author. For a critical introduction to Hindutva, see Jyotirmaya Sharma, *Hindutva: Exploring the Idea of Hindu Nationalism* (Delhi: Harper Collins, 2005).

93. Cited in Vijay Prashad, "The Untouchable Question," *Economic & Political Weekly*, March 2, 1996, 554–55.

94. BAWS 9, 195.

95. A few privileged-caste Hindu members of the Ghadar Party later turned toward Hindu nationalism and became Vedic missionaries. On Bhai Parmanand, a founder-member of the Ghadar Party who later became a Hindutva ideologue, see note 11 in the prologue to AoC.

96. For a monograph on the Ad Dharm movement, see Juergensmeyer, *Religious Rebels in the Punjab*.

97. Rupa Viswanath, in *The Pariah Problem: Caste, Religion, and the Social in Modern India* (New York: Columbia University Press, 2014), details the history of the colonial state's alliance with the landed castes against landless Dalits in the context of the Madras Presidency.

98. Davis, *Late Victorian Holocausts*, 7.

99. BAWS 9, 1.

100. Ibid., 3.

101. See Faisal Devji, *The Impossible Indian: Gandhi and the Temptation of Violence* (Boston: First Harvard University Press, 2012), chapter 3, "In Praise of Prejudice," especially 47–48.

102. Cited from *Young India*, March 23, 1921, in ibid., 81.

103. Golwalkar, *We, or Our Nationhood Defined*, 55–56.

104. Stanley Wolpert, *A New History of India* (New York: Oxford University Press, 1993). First published 1973.

105. BAWS 17, part 1, 369–75.

106. Nathuram Godse, *Why I Assassinated Mahatma Gandhi* (New Delhi: Surya Bharti Prakashan, 1998), 43.

107. BAWS 3, 360.

108. Cited in BAWS 9, 68.

109. *Harijan*, September 30, 1939, in CWMG 76, 356.

110. See Ramachandra Guha, *India before Gandhi* (New Delhi: Penguin, 2013).

111. Tidrick, *Gandhi*, 106.

112. For an archive of Gandhi's writings about his years in South Africa (1893–1914), see G. B. Singh, *Gandhi: Behind the Mask of Divinity* (New York: Prometheus Books, 2004).

113. Maureen Swan, *Gandhi: The South African Experience* (Johannesburg: Ravan Press, 1985), 52.

114. Kaffir is an Arabic term that originally meant "one who hides or covers"—a description of farmers burying seeds in the ground. After the advent of Islam, it came to mean "non-believers" or "heretics," those "who covered the truth (Islam)." It was first applied to non-Muslim Black people encountered by Arab traders along the Swahili coast. Portuguese explorers adopted the term and passed it on to the British, French, and Dutch. In South Africa, it became a racial slur the Whites and Afrikaners (and Indians like Gandhi) used to describe native Africans. Today, to call someone a Kaffir in South Africa is an actionable offense.

115. CWMG 1, 192–3.

116. Ibid., 200.

117. For a history of indentured labour in South Africa, see Ashwin Desai and Goolam Vahed, *Inside Indian Indenture: A South African Story, 1860–1914* (Cape Town: HSRC Press, 2010).

118. Between the early 1890s and 1913, the Indian population in South Africa tripled, from 40,000 to 135,000; Guha, *India before Gandhi*, 463.

119. Ibid., 115.

120. CWMG 2, 6.

121. Adam Hochschild, *To End All Wars: A Story of Loyalty and Rebellion, 1914–1918* (London: Houghton Mifflin Harcourt, 2011), 33–34.

122. During World War II, he advised the Jews to "summon to their aid the soul-power that comes only from non-violence" and assured them that Herr Hitler would "bow before their courage" (*Harijan*, December 17, 1938, in CWMG 74, 298). He urged the British to "fight Nazism without arms" (*Harijan*, July 6, 1940, in CWMG 78, 387).

123. CWMG 34, 18.

124. CWMG 2, 339–40.

125. *The Natal Advertiser*, October 16, 1901, in CWMG 2, 421.

126. CWMG 5, 11.

127. Ibid., 179.

128. Jeff Guy, *The Maphumulo Uprising: War, Law, and Ritual in the Zulu Rebellion* (Scotsville, South Africa: University of KwaZulu-Natal Press, 2005), 212.

129. According to a note on the first page of CWMG, vol. 34: "Gandhiji started writing in Gujarati the history of Satyagraha in South Africa on November 26,

1923, when he was in the Yeravada Central Jail; vide Jail Diary, 1923. By the time he was released, on February 5, 1924, he had completed 30 chapters . . . The English translation by Valji G. Desai, which was seen and approved by Gandhiji, was published by S. Ganesan, Madras, in 1928."

130. Ibid., 82–83.

131. Ibid., 84.

132. Of a total population of 135,000 Indians, only 10,000, who were mostly traders, lived in the Transvaal. The rest were based in Natal. Guha, *India before Gandhi*, 463.

133. CWMG 5, 337. This is from Clause 3 from Resolution 2 of the Five Resolutions passed by the British Indian Association in Johannesburg, following the "Mass Meeting" of September 11, 1906.

134. *Indian Opinion*, March 7, 1908, in CWMG 8, 198–99.

135. CWMG 9, 256–7.

136. *Indian Opinion*, January 23, 1909, in CWMG 9, 274.

137. In a letter dated May 18, 1899, to the Colonial Secretary, Gandhi wrote: "An Indian may fancy that he has a wrong to be redressed in that he does not get ghee instead of oil" (CWMG 2, 266). On another occasion: "The regulations here do not provide for any ghee or fat to Indians. A complaint has therefore been made to the physician, and he has promised to look into it. So there is reason to hope that the inclusion of ghee will be ordered" (*Indian Opinion*, October 17, 1908, in CWMG 9, 197).

138. *Indian Opinion*, January 23, 1909, in ibid., 270.

139. *Young India*, April 5, 1928, in CWMG 41, 365.

140. Joseph Lelyveld, *Great Soul: Mahatma Gandhi and His Struggle with India* (New York: Alfred A. Knopf, 2011), 74.

141. Cited in Howard Zinn and Anthony Arnove, *Voices of a People's History of the United States* (New York: Seven Stories Press, 2004), 265.

142. Ibid., 270.

143. Cited in Omvedt, *Seeking Begumpura*, 219.

144. In G. P. Deshpande, ed., *Selected Writings of Jotirao Phule* (New Delhi: LeftWord, 2002), 25.

145. Ibid., 38–40.

146. Cited in Ambedkar, "What Congress and Gandhi Have Done to the Untouchables," in BAWS 9, 276.

147. See Jad Adams, *Gandhi: Naked Ambition* (London: Quercus, 2011), 263–65; and Rita Banerji, *Sex and Power: Defining History, Shaping Societies* (New Delhi: Penguin, 2008), especially 265–81.

148. CWMG 34, 201–2.

149. *Hind Swaraj* in Parel, *"Hind Swaraj" and Other Writings*, 106.

150. Ibid., 97.

151. See Gandhi's preface to the English translation of *Hind Swaraj*, in ibid., 5).

152. Savarkar, the militant Hindutva ideologue, said a true Indian is one whose *pitrabhoomi* (fatherland) as well as *punyabhoomi* (holy land) is India—not some foreign land. See his *Hindutva,* 105.

153. Parel, *"Hind Swaraj" and Other Writings,* 47–51.

154. Ibid., 66.

155. Ibid., 68–69.

156. Ramachandra Guha wrote in *India before Gandhi*: "Gandhi wrote *Hind Swaraj* in 1909 at a time he scarcely knew India at all. By 1888, when he departed for London, at the age of nineteen, he had lived only in towns in his native Kathiawar. There is no evidence that he had travelled in the countryside, and he knew no other part of India" (383).

157. Parel, *"Hind Swaraj" and Other Writings,* 69–70.

158. Gandhi wrote this in 1932, in connection with the debate around separate electorates for Untouchables, in a letter to Sir Samuel Hoare, Secretary of State for India. Cited in BAWS 9, 78.

159. *Indian Opinion,* October 22, 1910, in CWMG 11, 143–4. Cited also in Guha, *India before Gandhi,* 395.

160. Guha, *India before Gandhi,* 463.

161. Ibid., 406.

162. Aiyar quoted in Lelyveld, *Great Soul,* 21.

163. Personal communication, Ashwin Desai, professor of sociology at University of Johannesburg.

164. Lelyveld, *Great Soul,* 130.

165. Tidrick, *Gandhi,* 188.

166. See Renold, "Gandhi." Also see Louis Fischer, *A Week with Gandhi* (New Delhi: Duell, Sloan and Pearce, 1942), quoted by Ambedkar: "'I said I had several questions to ask him about the Congress Party. Very highly placed Britishers, I recalled, had told me that Congress was in the hands of big business and that Gandhi was supported by the Bombay Mill-owners who gave him as much money as he wanted. 'What Truth is there in these assertions,' I asked. 'Unfortunately, they are true,' he declared simply . . . 'What portion of the Congress budget,' I asked, 'is covered by rich Indians?' 'Practically all of it,' he stated. 'In this ashram, for instance, we could live much more poorly than we do and spend less money. But we do not and the money comes from our rich friends'." Cited in BAWS 9, 208.

167. Cited in Shahid Amin, "Gandhi as Mahatma: Gorakhpur District, Eastern UP, 1921–2," in *Selected Subaltern Studies,* ed. Ranajit Guha and Gayatri Spivak (New Delhi: Oxford University Press, 1998), 293.

168. *Young India,* August 18, 1921, in CWMG 23, 158.

169. *Harijan,* August 25, 1940, in CWMG 79, 133–34.

170. Ibid., 135.

171. Ibid.

172. Andrew Carnegie, *The Gospel of Wealth, North American Review*, no. 391 (1889), http://www.swarthmore.edu/SocSci/rbannis1/AIH19th/Carnegie.html.

173. Cited in Amin, *Gandhi as Mahatma*, 290–91.

174. Ibid., 291–2.

175. Tidrick, *Gandhi*, 191.

176. Cited in Singh, *Gandhi*, 124.

177. Tidrick, *Gandhi*, 192.

178. Ibid., 194.

179. Ibid., 195.

180. Zelliot, *Ambedkar's World*, 48.

181. This is from the unpublished preface to Ambedkar's *The Buddha and His Dhamma* (1956). It first appeared as part of a book of Ambedkar's prefaces, edited by Bhagwan Das and entitled *Rare Prefaces* (Jullundur: Bheem Patrika, 1980). Eleanor Zelliot later published it on the Columbia University website dedicated to Ambedkar's life and selected works. http://www.columbia.edu/itc/mealac/pritchett/00ambedkar/ambedkar_buddha/00_pref_unpub.html.

182. BAWS 4, 1986.

183. On May 20, 1857, the Education Department issued a directive that "no boy be refused admission to a government college or school merely on the ground of caste." Geetha Nambissan, "Equality in Education: The Schooling of Dalit Children in India," in *Dalits and the State*, ed. Ghanshyam Shah (New Delhi: Concept, 2002), 81.

184. For an annotated edition of this essay, see Rege, *Against the Madness of Manu*. It also appears in BAWS 1.

185. B. R. Ambedkar, *Ambedkar: Autobiographical Notes*, ed. Ravikumar (Pondicherry: Navayana, 2003), 19.

186. Keer, *Dr. Ambedkar*, 36–37.

187. AoC 17.5.

188. Prashad, "The Untouchable Question," 552. In his speech at the Suppressed Classes Conference in Ahmedabad on April 13, 1921, reported in *Young India* on April 27, 1921, and May 4, 1921 (reproduced in CWMG 23, 41–47), Gandhi discussed Uka at length for the first time (42). Bakha, the main protagonist in Mulk Raj Anand's iconic novel *Untouchable* (1935), is said to be inspired by Uka. According to the researcher Lingaraja Gandhi, Anand showed his manuscript to Gandhi, who suggested changes. Anand says: "I read my novel to Gandhiji, and he suggested that I should cut down more than a hundred pages, especially those passages in which Bakha seemed to be thinking and dreaming and brooding like a Bloomsbury intellectual." Lingaraja Gandhi further says: "Anand had provided long and flowery speeches to Bakha in his draft. Gandhi instructed Anand that untouchables don't speak that way: in fact, they hardly speak. The novel underwent

metamorphosis under the tutelage of Gandhi" (xx). Lingaraja Gandhi, "Mulk Raj Anand: Quest for So Many Freedoms," *Deccan Herald*, October 3, 2004.

189. *Navajivan*, January 18, 1925, in CWMG 30, 71. In the account of Gandhi's secretary, Mahadev Desai, this speech from Gujarati is rendered differently: "The position that I really long for is that of the Bhangi. How sacred is this work of cleanliness! That work can be done only by a Brahmin or by a Bhangi. The Brahmin may do it in his wisdom, the Bhangi in ignorance. I respect, I adore both of them. If either of the two disappears from Hinduism, Hinduism itself would disappear. And it is because seva-dharma (self-service) is dear to my heart that the Bhangi is dear to me. I may even sit at my meals with a Bhangi by my side, but I do not ask you to align yourselves with them by inter-caste dinners and marriages." Cited in Gita Ramaswamy, "Mohandas Gandhi on Manual Scavenging," in *India Stinking: Manual Scavengers in Andhra Pradesh and Their Work* (Chennai: Navayana, 2005), 86.

190. Renold, "Gandhi," 19–20. Highly publicized symbolic visits to Dalit homes has become a Congress Party tradition. In January 2009, in the glare of a media circus, the Congress Party's vice president and prime ministerial candidate, Rahul Gandhi, along with David Miliband, the British foreign secretary, spent a night in the hut of a Dalit family in Simra village of Uttar Pradesh. For an account of this, see Anand Teltumbde, "*Aerocasteics* of Rahul Gandhi," *Economic & Political Weekly*, November 2, 2013, 10–11.

191. Vijay Prashad, *Untouchable Freedom: A Social History of a Dalit Community* (New Delhi: Oxford University Press, 2001), 139.

192. BAWS 1, 256.

193. Keer, *Dr. Ambedkar*, 41.

194. Zelliot, *Ambedkar's World*, 91.

195. See George Gheverghese Joseph, *George Joseph: The Life and Times of a Kerala Christian Nationalist* (Hyderabad: Orient Longman, 2003), 166. Objecting to Sikhs running a langar (free, common kitchen) for the satyagrahis of Vaikom, Gandhi wrote in *Young India* (May 8, 1924), "The Vaikom satyagraha is, I fear, crossing the limits. I do hope that the Sikh free kitchen will be withdrawn and that the movement will be confined to Hindus only" (CWMG 27, 362).

196. Chakravarti Rajagopalachari, a Tamil Brahmin known affectionately as Rajaji, was a close friend and confidant of Gandhi. In 1933, his daughter Leela married Gandhi's son Devdas. Rajagopalachari later served as the acting governor general of India. In 1947, he became the first governor of West Bengal, and in 1955 received the Bharat Ratna, India's highest civilian award.

197. Cited in Joseph, *George Joseph*, 168.

198. *Young India*, August 14, 1924, in CWMG 28, 486.

199. Joseph, *George Joseph*, 169.

200. G. D. Birla *In the Shadow of the Mahatma: A Personal Memoir* (Calcutta:

Orient Longman, 1953), 43.

201. Keer, *Dr. Ambedkar*, 79.

202. Speaking at a Depressed Classes Conference in 1925, Ambedkar said: "When one is spurned by everyone, even the sympathy shown by Mahatma Gandhi is of no little importance." Cited in Christophe Jaffrelot, *Dr. Ambedkar and Untouchability: Analysing and Fighting Caste* (New Delhi: Permanent Black, 2005), 63. Gandhi visited Mahad on March 3, 1927, a fortnight before the first satyagraha, but unlike at Vaikom he did not interfere. For an account of the second Mahad Satyagraha when a copy of the *Manusmriti* was burnt, see K. Jamnadas, *"Manusmriti* Dahan Din," Round Table India, July 14, 2010, roundtableindia.co.in.

203. According to Anand Teltumbde's unpublished manuscript on the two Mahad conferences, Resolution No. 2 seeking a "ceremonial cremation" of the *Manusmriti* was proposed by G. N. Sahasrabuddhe, a Brahmin, who played an important role in the March events as well; it was seconded by P. N. Rajbhoj, a Chambhar leader. According to Teltumbde, "There was a deliberate attempt to get some progressive people from non-untouchable communities to the conference, but eventually only two names materialised. One was Gangadhar Nilkanth Sahasrabuddhe, an activist of the Social Service League and a leader of the cooperative movement belonging to Agarkari Brahman caste, and the other was Vinayak alias Bhai Chitre, a Chandraseniya Kayastha Prabhu." In the 1940s, Sahasrabuddhe became the editor of *Janata*—another of Ambedkar's newspapers.

204. Arjun Dangle, ed., *Poisoned Bread: Translations from Modern Marathi Dalit Literature* (Hyderabad: Orient Longman, 1992), 231–33.

205. Keer, *Dr. Ambedkar*, 170.

206. Cited in Prashad, "The Untouchable Question," 555.

207. Gandhi outlined the difference between satyagraha and duragraha in a speech on November 3, 1917: "There are two methods of attaining one's goal: Satyagraha and Duragraha. In our scriptures, they have been described, respectively, as divine and devilish modes of action." He went on to give an example of duragraha: "the terrible War going on in Europe." Also, "The man who follows the path of Duragraha becomes impatient and wants to kill the so-called enemy. There can be but one result of this. Hatred increases" (CWMG 16, 126–28).

208. BAWS 9, 247.

209. On the fallout with the Girni Kamgar Union, see Anand Teltumbde, "It's Not Red vs. Blue," *Outlook*, August 20, 2012. For how Dange and the Communist Party worked toward ensuring Ambedkar's defeat in the Bombay City North constituency in the 1952 general election, see S. Anand, "Between Red and Blue," *Outlook*, 16 April 16, 2012. Rajnarayan Chandavarkar writes in *History, Culture and the Indian City: Essays* (Cambridge: Cambridge University Press, 2009): "The decision by the socialists and the communists not to forge an electoral pact, let alone join together to combine with Ambedkar's Scheduled Castes Federation, against the Congress lost them the Central Bombay seat.

Dange, for the CPI, Asoka Mehta for the socialists and Ambedkar each stood separately and fell together. Significantly, Dange instructed his supporters to spoil their ballots in the reserved constituency for Central Bombay rather than vote for Ambedkar. Indeed, Ambedkar duly lost and attributed his defeat to the communist campaign. Although the communists could not win the Central Bombay seat, their influence in Girangaon, including its dalit voters, was sufficient to decisively influence the outcome. The election campaign created a lasting bitterness. As Dinoo Ranadive recalls, 'the differences between the dalits and the communists became so sharp that even today it has become difficult for the communists to appeal to the Republicans' or at any rate to some sections of dalit voters" (161). "Republicans" here refers to the Republican Party of India that Ambedkar had conceived of a short while before his death in December 1956. It came to be established only in September 1957 by his followers, but today there are over a dozen splintered factions of the Republican Party of India.

210. D. D. Kosambi, "Marxism and Ancient Indian Culture," *Annals of the Bhandarkar Oriental Research Institute* 26 (1948): 274.

211. For an account of this, see Jan Breman, *The Making and Unmaking of an Industrial Working Class* (Amsterdam: Amsterdam University Press, 2005), especially chapter 2, "The Formalization of Collective Action: Mahatma Gandhi as a Union Leader" (40–68).

212. Ibid., 57.

213. Shankerlal Banker cited in ibid., 47.

214. Annual Report of the Textile Labour Union, 1925, cited in ibid., 51.

215. *Navajivan*, February 8, 1920, cited in BAWS 9, 280.

216. *Harijan*, April 21, 1946, in CWMG 90, 255–56.

217. AoC 3.10 and 3.11.

218. AoC 4.1, emphasis in original.

219. Zelliot, *Ambedkar's World*, 178.

220. E. M. S. Namboodiripad, *History of the Indian Freedom Struggle* (Trivandrum: Social Scientist Press, 1986), 492, emphasis added.

221. The text of the manifesto is reproduced in K. Satyanarayana and Susie Tharu, *The Exercise of Freedom: An Introduction to Dalit Writing* (New Delhi: Navayana, 2013), 62.

222. For a critical piece on the NGO–Dalit movement interface that traces it to the history of colonial and missionary activity in India, see Anand Teltumbde, "Dangerous Sedative," *Himal*, April 2010: "Unsurprisingly, most Dalits in Indian NGOs are active at the field level. Dalit boys and girls appear to be doing social services for their communities, which is what Ambedkar expected educated Dalits to do, and Dalit communities therefore perceive such workers quite favourably—more favourably, certainly, than Dalit politicians, who are often seen as engaged in mere rhetoric. The NGO sector has thus become a significant employer for many Dalits studying for their humanities degree,

typically capped with a postgraduate degree in social work. Further, as the prospects of public-sector jobs have decreased since the government's neoliberal reforms of the mid-1980s and later, the promise of NGOs as employers assumed great importance."

223. For instance, see the list of NGOs that work with the multinational mining corporation Vedanta, under fire for land-grab and several violations against the environment and Adivasi rights, at http://www.vedantaaluminium.com /ngos-govt-bodies.htm.

224. Speech on September 26, 1896, at a public meeting in Bombay where he said he was representing the "100,000 British Indians at present residing in South Africa." See CWMG 1, 407.

225. AoC 8.2–4.

226. BAWS 1, 375.

227. AoC 5.8.

228. There are different aspects of the constitution that govern the Adivasis of the heartland (the Fifth Schedule) and those of the Northeast of India (the Sixth Schedule). As the political scientist Uday Chandra points out, "The Fifth and Sixth Schedules of the Constitution perpetuate the languages and logics of the Partially and Wholly Excluded Areas defined in the Government of India Act (1935) and the Typically and Really Backward Tracts defined by the Government of India (1918) ... In the Schedule V areas, dispersed across eastern, western, and central Indian states, state governors wield special powers to prohibit or modify central or state laws, to prohibit or regulate the transfer of land by or among tribals, to regulate commercial activities, particularly by non-tribals, and to constitute tribal advisory councils to supplement state legislatures. In principle, New Delhi also reserves the right to intervene directly in the administration of these Scheduled Areas by bypassing elected state and local governments. In the Schedule VI areas, dispersed across the seven northeastern states formed out of the colonial province of Assam, state governors preside over District and Regional Councils in Autonomous Districts and Regions to ensure that state and central laws do not impinge on these administrative zones of exception." Utay Chandra, "Liberalism and Its Other: The Politics of Primitivism in Colonial and Postcolonial Indian Law," *Law & Society Review* 47, no. 1 (2013): 155.

229. Cited in BAWS 9, 70.

230. BAWS 9, 42.

231. As prime minister of a non-Congress, Janata Dal–led coalition government from December 1989 to November 1990, Vishwanath Pratap Singh (1931–2008) took the decision to implement the recommendations of the Mandal Commission, which fixed a quota for members of the Backward Classes in jobs in the public sector to redress caste discrimination. The commission, named after B. P. Mandal, a parliamentarian who headed it, had been established in 1979 by another non-Congress (Janata Party) government, headed by Morarji

Desai, but the recommendations of its 1980 report—which extended the scope of reservation in public sector employment beyond Dalits and Adivasis, and allocated 27 percent to Other Backward Classes—had not been implemented for ten years. When it was implemented, the privileged castes took to the streets. They symbolically swept the streets, pretended to shine shoes and performed other "polluting" tasks to suggest that instead of becoming doctors, engineers, lawyers, or economists, the policy of reservation was now going to reduce privileged castes to doing menial tasks. A few people attempted to publicly immolate themselves, the most well-known being a Delhi University student, Rajiv Goswami, in 1990. Similar protests were repeated in 2006 when the Congress-led United Progressive Alliance tried to extend reservation to the Other Backward Classes in institutes of higher education.

232. BAWS 9, 40.

233. See Visalakshi Menon, *From Movement to Government: The Congress in the United Provinces, 1937–42* (New Delhi: Sage, 2003), 52–53.

234. In his 1945 indictment of the Congress and Gandhi, Ambedkar lists the names of these mock candidates in his footnotes: Guru Gosain Agamdas and Babraj Jaiwar were the two cobblers; Chunnu was the milkman; Arjun Lal the barber; Bansi Lal Chaudhari the sweeper (BAWS 9, 210).

235. BAWS 9, 210.

236. Ibid., 68.

237. Ibid., 69.

238. Tidrick, *Gandhi*, 255.

239. Servants of India Society member Kodanda Rao's account cited in Jaffrelot, *Dr Ambedkar and Untouchability*, 66.

240. Pyarelal Nayar, *The Epic Fast* (Ahmedabad: Navajivan, 1932), 188.

241. BAWS 9, 259.

242. As Ambedkar saw it, "The increase in the number of seats for the Untouchables is no increase at all and was no recompense for the loss of separate electorates and the double vote" (BAWS 9, 90). Ambedkar himself lost twice in the polls in post-1947 India. It took more than half a century for Kanshi Ram, the founder of a predominantly Dalit party, the Bahujan Samaj Party, and his protégé Mayawati to succeed in a first-past-the-post parliamentary democracy. This happened *despite* the Poona Pact. Kanshi Ram worked for years, painstakingly making alliances with other subordinated castes to achieve this victory. To succeed in the elections, the Bharatiya Janata Party needed the peculiar demography of Uttar Pradesh and the support of many Other Backward Classes. For a Dalit candidate to win an election from an open seat—even in Uttar Pradesh—continues to be almost impossible.

243. See Michelle Alexander, *The New Jim Crow: Mass Incarceration in the Age of Colorblindness* (New York: New Press, 2010).

244. Louis Fischer, *The Life of Mahatma Gandhi* (New Delhi: HarperCollins,

1997), 400–3. First published 1951.

245. Eleanor Zelliot writes in *Ambedkar's World:* "Ambedkar had written the *manpatra* (welcome address, or literally, letter of honor) for Baloo Babaji Palwankar, known as P. Baloo, upon his return from a cricket tour in England nearly twenty years earlier, and had had some part in P. Balu's selection as a Depressed Class nominee on the Bombay Municipal Corporation in the early 1920s" (254). Baloo supported Gandhi during the Round Table Conferences and supported the Hindu Mahasabha position. Soon after the Poona Pact, in October 1933, Baloo contested as a Hindu Mahasabha candidate for the Bombay Municipality, but lost. In 1937, the Congress, in an effort to split the Untouchable vote, pitted Baloo, a Chambhar, against Ambedkar, a Mahar, who contested on the Independent Labour Party ticket, for a Bombay (East) "reserved" seat in the Bombay Legislative Assembly. Ambedkar won narrowly.

246. For an outline of Rajah's career and how he came around to supporting Ambedkar in 1938 and 1942, see note 5 at 1.5 of "A Vindication of Caste by Mahatma Gandhi" in AoC.

247. The Gujarat Freedom of Religion Act, 2003, makes it mandatory for a person who wants to convert into another religion to seek prior permission from a district magistrate. The text of the act is available at http://www.lawsofindia .org/statelaw/2224/TheGujaratFreedomofReligionAct2003.html. An amendment bill to the Act was sent back to the Legislative Assembly by the then Gujarat governor, Nawal Kishore Sharma, for reconsideration. It was subsequently dropped by the state government. One of the provisions in the amendment bill sought to clarify that Jains and Buddhists were to be construed as denominations of Hinduism. The governor said that the amendment would be in violation of Article 25 of the Indian Constitution. See http://www.indianexpress.com /news/gujarat-withdraws-freedom-of-religion-amendment-bill/282818/1. The Gujarat Animal Preservation (Amendment) Act, 2011, makes "transport of animals for slaughter" a punishable offence, widening the ambit of the original Act, which bans cow slaughter. The Amendment Act has also augmented the punishment to seven years' rigorous imprisonment from the earlier six months. In 2012, Narendra Modi greeted Indians on Janmashtami (observed as Krishna's birthday) with the following words: "Mahatma Gandhi and Acharya Vinoba Bhave worked tirelessly for the protection of mother cow, but this Government abandoned their teachings." Gandhi said, "Anyone who is not ready to give his life to save the cow is not a Hindu". (interview to *Goseva* on September 8, 1933, in CWMG 61, 372). Earlier, in 1924, he said, "When I see a cow, it is not an animal to eat, it is a poem of pity for me and I worship it and I shall defend its worship against the whole world" (reported in *Bombay Chronicle*, December 30, 1924; CWMG 29, 476).

248. For a history of the terms *Harijan*, *Dalit*, and *Scheduled Caste*, see note 8 to the prologue of AoC.

249. BAWS 9, 126.

250. Ibid., 210.

251. Renold, "Gandhi," 25.

252. Tidrick, *Gandhi*, 261.

253. BAWS 9, 125.

254. Ibid., 111.

255. Susie Tharu and K. Lalita, eds., *Women Writing in India, Vol. 1: 600 B.C. to the Early Twentieth Century* (New Delhi: Oxford University Press, 1997), 215.

256. Ambedkar, *Ambedkar: Autobiographical Notes*, 25.

257. *Manusmriti* X: 123. See Wendy Doniger and Brian K. Smith, trans., *The Laws of Manu* (New Delhi: Penguin Books, 1991).

258. *Harijan*, November 28, 1936, in CWMG 70, 126–28.

259. Reported by the columnist Rajiv Shah in his *Times of India* blog of December 1, 2012, http://blogs.timesofindia.indiatimes.com/true-lies/entry /modi-s-spiritual-potion-to-woo-karmayogis. Shah says five thousand copies of *Karmayogi* were printed with funding from the public sector unit, Gujarat State Petroleum Corporation, and that later he was told, by the Gujarat Information Department that it had, on instructions from Modi, withdrawn the book from circulation. Two years later, addressing nine-thousand-odd Safai Karmacharis (sanitation workers), Modi said, "A priest cleans a temple every day before prayers, you also clean the city like a temple. You and the temple priest work alike." See Shah's blog of January 23, 2013, http://blogs.timesofindia.indiatimes.com /true-lies/entry/modi-s-postal-ballot-confusion?sortBy=AGREE&th=1.

260. CWMG 70, 76–77.

261. See "A Note on the Poona Pact" in B. R. Ambedkar, *Annihilation of Caste: The Annotated Critical Edition* (New York: Verso, 2014), 357–76.

262. Dilip Menon, *The Blindness of Insight: Essays on Caste in Modern India* (Pondicherry: Navayana, 2006), 20.

263. This assimilation finds its way into the constitution. Explanation II of Article 25(2)(b) of the constitution was the first time in independent India when the law categorized Buddhists, Sikhs, and Jains as "Hindu," even if "only" for the purpose of "providing social welfare and reform or the throwing open of Hindu religious institutions of a public character to all classes and sections of Hindus." Later, codified Hindu personal law, like the Hindu Marriage Act, 1955, the Hindu Succession Act, 1956, and so on reinforced this position, as these statutes were applied to Buddhists, Sikhs, and Jains. Pertinently, under Indian law an atheist is automatically classified as a Hindu. The judiciary has been sending out mixed signals, sometimes recognising the "independent character" of these religions, and at other times, asserting that the "Sikhs and Jains, in fact, have throughout been treated as part of the wider Hindu community which has different sects, sub-sects, faiths, modes of worship and religious philosophies" (*Bal Patil & Anr* vs *Union Of India & Ors*, August 8,

2005). For Buddhists, Sikhs, and Jains, the struggle for recognition continues. There has been some success; for example, the Anand Marriage (Amendment) Act, 2012, freed Sikhs from the Hindu Marriage Act. On January 20, 2014, the Union Cabinet approved the notification of Jains as a minority community at the national level. Also see note 247 on the Gujarat Freedom of Religion Act.

264. See Ramachandra Guha, "What Hindus Can and Should be Proud Of," *The Hindu*, July 23, 2013.

265. While NGOs and news reports suggest a toll of two thousand persons (see "A Decade of Shame" by Anupama Katakam, *Frontline*, March 9, 2012), then Union Minister of State for Home, Shriprakash Jaiswal (of the Congress Party), told Parliament on May 11, 2005, that 790 Muslims and 254 Hindus were killed in the riots; 2,548 were injured and 223 persons were missing. See "Gujarat Riot Death Toll Revealed," BBC News, May 11, 2005.

266. "Peoples Tribunal Highlights Misuse of POTA", *Hindu*, March 18, 2004. See also "Human Rights Watch asks Centre to Repeal POTA," Press Trust of India, September 8, 2002.

267. See "Blood under Saffron: The Myth of Dalit-Muslim Confrontation," *Round Table India*, July 23, 2013, http://goo.gl/7DU9uH.

268. See Ross Colvin and Sruthi Gottipati, "Interview with BJP Leader Narendra Modi," Reuters, July 12, 2013, http://blogs.reuters.com/india/2013/07/12/interview-with-bjp-leader-narendra-modi/.

269. See "Dalit Leader Buries the Hatchet with RSS," *Times of India*, August 31, 2006.

270. See Zelliot, *Ambedkar's World*, especially chapter 5, "Political Development, 1935–56." For an account of Jogendranath Mandal's life and work, see Dwaipayan Sen, "A Politics Subsumed," *Himal*, April 2010.

271. PTI News Service, March 20, 1955, cited in Zelliot, *Ambedkar's World*, 193.

272. See Gordon Weiss, *The Cage: The Fight for Sri Lanka and the Last Days of the Tamil Tigers* (London: The Bodley Head, 2011).

273. For an account of how Ambedkar's Buddhism is an attempt to reconstruct the world, see Surendra Jondhale and Johannes Beltz, *Reconstructing the World: B. R. Ambedkar and Buddhism in India* (New Delhi: Oxford University Press, 2004). For an alternative history of Buddhism in India, see Gail Omvedt, *Buddhism in India: Challenging Brahmanism and Caste* (New Delhi: Sage, 2003).

274. BAWS 11, 322.

275. BAWS 17, part 2, 444–45. On September 14, 1956, Ambedkar wrote in a letter to Prime Minister Nehru: "The cost of printing is very heavy and will come to about Rs 20,000. This is beyond my capacity, and I am, therefore, canvassing help from all quarters. I wonder if the Government of India could purchase 500 copies for distribution among the various libraries and among the many scholars whom it is inviting during the course of this year for the celebration of Buddha's 2,500 years' anniversary." Nehru did not help him. The book was published

posthumously.

276. Brahminic Hinduism believes in cosmic time that has neither beginning nor end and alternates between cycles of creation and cessation. Each Mahayuga consists of four yuga—Krta or Satya Yuga (the golden age), followed by Treta, Dwapara, and Kali. Each era, shorter than the previous one, is said to be more degenerate and depraved than the preceding one. In Kali Yuga, there is disregard for varnashrama dharma—the Shudras and Untouchables wrest power—and chaos reigns, leading to complete destruction. About Kali Yuga, the Bhagavad Gita says (IX: 32): "Even those who are of evil birth, women, Vaishyas and Shudras, having sought refuge in me will attain supreme liberation." Bibek Debroy, trans., *The Bhagavad Gita* (New Delhi: Penguin, 2005), 137.

MY SEDITIOUS HEART

1. Dr. Gokarakonda Naga Saibaba s/o G. Satayanarayana Murthy v. State of Maharashtra, Criminal Application No. 785 (2015).

2. B. R. Ambedkar, *The Annihilation of Caste*, ed. S. Anand (London: Verso, 2014), 241–42.

3. Mohd Haroon & Ors. v. Union of India & Anr., Writ Petition (Criminal) No. 155 (2013), 2.

4. Sruthisagar Yamunan, "IIT-Madras Derecognises Student Group," *Hindu*, May 28, 2015, http://www.thehindu.com/news/national/tamil-nadu/iitmadras-derecognises-student-group/article7256712.ece.

5. "My Birth Is My Fatal Accident: Full Text of Dalit Student Rohith's Suicide Letter, *Indian Express*, January 19, 2016, http://indianexpress.com/article/india/india-news-india/dalit-student-suicide-full-text-of-suicide-letter-hyderabad/.

6. Dalit Panthers, "Dalit Panthers Manifesto" (Bombay, 1973), quoted in Barbara R. Joshi, ed., *Untouchable!: Voices of the Dalit Liberation Movement* (London: Zed Books, 1986), p. 145. For further discussion, see Roy, "The Doctor and the Saint," 668–787.

7. "The Case against Afza," *Hindu*, February 10, 2013, http://www.thehindu.com/news/national/the-case-against-afzal/article4397845.ece.

8. Mohammad Ali, "BJP MP Sakshi Maharaj Courts Controversy over JNU Unrest," *Hindu*, February 15, 2016, http://www.thehindu.com/news/national/other-states/bjp-mp-sakshi-maharaj-courts-controversy-over-jnu-unrest/article8237932.ece; Abhinav Malhotra, "Sakshi Maharaj Demands Strict Action against Those behind JNU Incident," February 14, 2016, http://timesofindia.indiatimes.com/city/kanpur/Sakshi-Maharaj-demands-strict-action-against-those-behind-JNU-incident/articleshow/50979831.cms.

9. Samreena Mushtaq, Essar Batool, Natasha Rather, Munaza Rashid, and Ifrah Butt, *Do You Remember Kunan Poshpura? The Story of a Mass Rape* (New Delhi: Zubaan Books, 2016).

10. "From the Delhi HC Order Granting Bail to Kanhaiya: 'Those Shouting Anti-National Slogans May Not Be Able to Withstand Siachen for an Hour,'" *Indian Express*, March 3, 2016, http://indianexpress.com/article/india/india-news-india/jnu-row-from-the-high-court-order-granting-bail-to-kanhaiya-those-shouting-anti-national-slogans-may-not-be-able-to-withstand-siachen-for-an-hour/.

INDEX

437
National Crime Records Bureau
(India), 672
National Hydroelectric Power
Corporation (NHPC), 311–12,
316–19, 325–28
National Resettlement and
Rehabilitation Policy (India),
870n16
National Rural Employment
Guarantee Act (NREGA,
India), 478–79, 599, 809
Navajivan, 676
Navsarjan Trust, 932n4, 935n18
Naxalites, 431–32, 492, 513, 524–25,
531, 533–34, 537, 542–43,
548–49, 552–53, 558, 560–62,
565, 588, 593–95, 597, 624,
644, 762–63, 817, 909n4,
927n26; West Bengal uprising
(1969), 491, 505, 555, 585. *See
also* Communist Party of India
(CPI, Maoist); Communist
Party of India (CPI(ML),
Marxist-Leninist)
Nazis, xxiv, 49, 175, 261, 302, 369,
412, 417–19, 424, 426–27, 532,
800, 942n122. *See also* Hitler,
Adolf; Holocaust; neo-Nazis;
Reichstag fire; Third Reich
NDTV, 405–7
Nehru, Jawaharlal, 25, 28, 38, 60,
297, 481, 572, 684, 686, 711,
722, 771, 791, 817, 869n4,
933n13, 936n41, 953n275;

"Dams Are the Temples of
Modern India" speech, 29, 92
neo-Nazis, xxiv. *See also* Nazis
Neruda, Pablo: *Captain's Verses,* 554;
"Standard Oil Company," 623
Netherlands, 79, 103, 716, 942n114
New Economic Policy, 498
New India Foundation, 428
New Mexico (US), xxii;
Albuquerque, 193; Santa Fe,
191
New York City (US), 8, 129, 139,
144, 207–9, 239, 250, 252, 276,
632–34, 739, 744; Manhattan,
129, 277
New York Stock Exchange, 129, 208
New York Times, 199–200, 243, 255,
268, 277, 622, 669
Nicaragua, 135, 140, 193, 213, 256,
258, 330
Nigeria, 203, 270, 417
Nilekani, Nandan, 640, 649
Nilesh, 528–29, 534
Nimad Malwa Kisan Mazdoor
Sangathan (Nimad Malwa
Farmers and Workers'
Organization), 235, 866
Niti, Comrade, 550, 559, 561, 567, 574
"Nitir Judum Pito," 551
Niyamgiri hills, 468, 489, 519, 578,
600, 615
Niyogi, Shankar Guha, 280–82,
297, 866
Nobel Prize, 179, 637, 891n3;
Literature Prize, 732, 740;

ABOUT THE AUTHOR

© MAYANK AUSTEN SOOFI

ARUNDHATI ROY studied architecture in New Delhi, where she now lives. She is the author of the novels *The God of Small Things*, for which she received the 1997 Booker Prize, and *The Ministry of Utmost Happiness*.